# Agriculture and the New Trade Agenda

Negotiating the liberalization of world agricultural trade in the World Trade Organization (WTO) is fraught with difficulty owing to the complexity of the issues and the wide range of interests across countries. In the new round of global trade negotiations under the WTO, different perspectives on trade reform have produced a highly contentious agenda. These issues are addressed from a range of perspectives in this very topical survey of the new trade agenda and its implications for both developing and developed countries. Agricultural trade specialists, including those in universities, in international organizations, and in think tanks, analyze a comprehensive range of topics including interests and options in the new WTO trade negotiations, the new trade agenda from a development patent perspective, new WTO trade rules, trade barriers, tariff negotiations and patent protection for developing countries.

MERLINDA D. INGCO is a Senior Economist at the World Bank. Specializing in empirical and policy analyses, her published books and journal articles cover areas such as non-tariff barriers, agricultural protection, agricultural trade and poverty, commodity markets, food security, and trade. She is the author of *The World Food Outlook* (with Donald Mitchell and Ronald Duncan, Cambridge University Press, 1997).

L. ALAN WINTERS is Professor of Economics at the University of Sussex. He is a Research Fellow of the Centre for Economic Policy Research, London, and a Senior Visiting Fellow of the Centre for Economic Performance, at the London School of Economics. His published books and articles cover areas such as regional trading arrangements, non-tariff barriers, European Integration, East–West trade, global warming, agricultural protection, trade and poverty, and the world trading system. He is the author of a major study funded by the UK Department of International Development: *Trade Liberalization and Poverty: A Handbook* (with Neil McCulloch and Xavier Cirera, 2001).

# Agriculture and the New Trade Agenda

## Creating a Global Trading Environment for Development

Edited by
MERLINDA D. INGCO AND
L. ALAN WINTERS

CAMBRIDGE
UNIVERSITY PRESS

CAMBRIDGE UNIVERSITY PRESS
Cambridge, New York, Melbourne, Madrid, Cape Town, Singapore, São Paulo

Cambridge University Press
The Edinburgh Building, Cambridge CB2 8RU, UK

Published in the United States of America by Cambridge University Press, New York

www.cambridge.org
Information on this title: www.cambridge.org/9780521826853

First published 2004
This digitally printed version 2008

*A catalogue record for this publication is available from the British Library*

*Library of Congress Cataloguing in Publication data*
Agriculture and the new trade agenda : creating a global trading environment for
development/M.D. Ingco and L. Alan Winters, editors.
      p.   cm.
Includes bibliographical references and index.
ISBN 0-521-82685-3
1. World Trade Organization.   2. Produce trade – Government policy – International
cooperation.   3. Tariff on farm produce.   I. Ingco, Merlinda D.   II. Winters, L. Alan.
HF1385.A37   2003
382′.41–dc21   2003053223

ISBN 978-0-521-82685-3 hardback
ISBN 978-0-521-05449-2 paperback

# Contents

# Figures, Tables, and Boxes

**Tables**

**Boxes**

# Contributors

PHILIP ABBOTT, *Purdue University*
KYM ANDERSON, *University of Adelaide*
RICHARD N. BOISVERT, *Cornell University*
BRENT BORRELL, *Centre for International Economics, Australia*
MAURY BREDAHL, *University of Missouri*
DEAN A. DEROSA, *ADR International, Ltd*
DIMITRIS DIAKOSAVVAS, *Organization for Economic Co-Operation and Development*
AZIZ ELBEHRI, *US Department of Agriculture*
JOSEPH F. FRANCOIS, *Erasmus University*
HARRY DE GORTER, *Cornell University*
SPENCER HENSON, *University of Reading*
THOMAS W. HERTEL, *Purdue University*
MERLINDA D. INGCO, *The World Bank*
TIM JOSLING, *Stanford University*
RUPERT LOADER, *University of Reading*
ALEXANDER F. MCCALLA, *University of California, Davis*
WILL MARTIN, *The World Bank*
W. M. MINER, *Center for Trade Policy and Law*
B. ADAIR MORSE, *Purdue University*
CHANTAL POHL NIELSEN, *University of Aarhus, Denmark*
DAVID ORDEN, *Virginia Polytechnic Institute and State University*
DAVID PEARCE, *Centre for International Economics, Australia*
KENNETH PEARSON, *Monash University*
JEFFREY M. PETERSON, *Cornell University*
ALLAN RAE, *Center for Applied Economics and Policy Studies*
DONNA ROBERTS, *Permanent US Mission to the WTO*
SHERMAN ROBINSON, *International Food Policy Research Institute*
GRETCHEN STANTON, *World Trade Organization*
ALAN SWINBANK, *University of Reading*

KAREN THIERFELDER, *US Naval Academy*
JAYASHREE WATAL, *Institute of International Economics*
JOHN WHALLEY, *University of Western Ontario*
L. ALAN WINTERS, *University of Sussex*
ALBERTO VALDÉS, *The World Bank*

# Preface

It is beyond debate that the agricultural negotiations taking place under the WTO's Doha Development Agenda are simultaneously hugely important, complex, and sensitive. Deep interests are at stake in both developing and developed countries and the precise nature of the current instruments of international trade policy rather poorly understood. The factual basis on which to consider any proposed requests or offers in the talks is often lacking, and negotiators are often unsure where their countries' true interests lie on crucial issues. For example, who gains from the current complex system of tariff quotas, what will happen to world prices if agricultural trade is liberalized, how can the activities of state-trading companies (STCs) be assessed, and how large and how warranted a barrier to trade are sanitary and phytosanitary standards (SPS)?

Experience in previous negotiations shows that progress is severely hampered if negotiators do not understand their own interests (or feel that they do not) – and, of course, there is a greater possibility of concluding a harmful or unfair agreement in such circumstances. This is particularly relevant for smaller developing countries which usually do not have the analytical resources or depth of representation in the talks to keep themselves fully informed. Each individual country will have its own specific interests, and there is no alternative to its developing its own view of the outcome. On the other hand, however, many of the issues that developing countries face are common, so that analysis of them is essentially a public good. It is here that international institutions can contribute so greatly by providing factual information and economic analysis to all.

The present volume is part of this contribution. It presents the key findings of a major research and capacity-building program of the World Bank entitled "Developing Countries, Agriculture and the WTO," funded by the United Kingdom's Department for International Development. The chapters were originally presented at a joint World Bank/WTO Conference in Geneva in October 1999. The initial versions have been available on the internet since then, and have already underpinned a great deal of analysis and comment in developing countries and elsewhere. For this volume, they have been revised and partially updated and are being published now to form part of the permanent record and to make them accessible to a wider set of researchers and policy makers. Even when the research has been overtaken by events, as is inevitable with a "live" negotiation, its analytical approach and methods will contribute strongly to the capacities of developing country governments to participate in negotiations and to the chances of achieving a meaningful and fair agreement in this crucial area of world commerce.

A book of this size and complexity requires many hands. Among those whom we should thank explicitly for their input are: the Department for International Development (London) and the Research Advisory Staff of the World Bank for supporting the initial conference; the anonymous referees of all the chapters and of the whole manuscript; John Croome, Bob Thompson, and John Nash for advice, Margaret Amaral, Barbara Docherty, Sandra Lay, and Ingrid Young for editorial and logistical inputs, and the staff of the World Bank Office of the Publisher and Alison Powell of Cambridge University Press for their patience and help in preparing the book.

# Abbreviations

| | |
|---|---|
| ABARE | Australian Bureau of Agricultural and Resource Economics |
| ACP | African, Caribbean, and Pacific |
| ADB | Asian Development Bank |
| AIE | Analysis and Information Exchange |
| AIPO | African Intellectual Property Office |
| AMS | Aggregate Measurement of Support |
| AOSIS | Alliance of Small Island States |
| APEC | Asia Pacific Economic Cooperation |
| ASEAN | Association of Southeast Asian Nations |
| AT | Agricultural Tradability |
| ATC | Agreement on Textiles and Clothing (WTO) |
| BSE | Bovine Spongiform Encephalopathy |
| BULOG | Badan Urusan Logistik (Indonesia) |
| CAP | Common Agricultural Policy |
| CEE | Central and Eastern Europe |
| CES | Constant Elasticity of Substitution |
| CGE | Computable General Equilibrium |
| CGIAR | Consultative Group on International Agriculture Research |
| CIE | Centre for International Economics |
| CIF | Cost, Insurance, and Freight |
| CNPC | Consumer Nominal Protection Coefficient |
| CONASUPO | Compania Nacional de Subsistencias Populares (Mexico) |
| CRS | Constant Returns to Scale |
| CSE | Consumer Support Estimate |
| CTE | Committee of Trade and Environment |
| DNA | Deoxyribonucleic acid |
| DSB | Dispute Settlement Body |
| DSP | Dispute Settlement Procedure |
| DSU | Dispute Settlement Understanding |
| DUS criteria | Distinct, Uniform, Homogeneous (plant varieties) |

| | |
|---|---|
| EAP | East Asia Pacific Group of Companies |
| EC | European Communities |
| ECA | East Central Asia |
| ECJ | European Court of Justice |
| EEPSEA | Economy and Environment Program of South East Asia |
| EIT | Economies in Transition |
| EMS | Equivalent Method of Support |
| EPO | European Patent Office |
| EPZ | Export-Processing Zone |
| EU | European Union |
| EV | Equivalent Variation |
| FAO | Food and Agriculture Organization (UN) |
| FBCI | Food Biotechnology Communications Initiative |
| FDA | Food and Drugs Administration (US) |
| FDDC | Food-Deficit Developing Country |
| FIC | Food Import Capacity |
| FOB | Free on Board |
| FSU | Former Soviet Union |
| GATS | General Agreement on Trade in Services |
| GATT | General Agreement on Tariffs and Trade |
| GDP | Gross Domestic Product |
| GE | General Equilibrium |
| GM | Genetic Modification |
| GM | Genetically Modified |
| GMO | Genetically Modified Organism |
| GSM | Global Sweetener Market |
| GTAP | Global Trade Analysis Project |
| GURTs | Genetic Use Restriction Technologies |
| HAACP | Hazard Analysis and Critical Control Point |
| HIC | High-Income Countries |
| IATRC | International Agricultural Trade Research Consortium |
| IDRC | International Development Research Centre |
| IFPRI | International Food Policy Research Institute |
| IISD | International Institute for Sustainable Development |
| IITSD | International Institute for Trade and Sustainable Development |
| ILO | International Labor Organization |
| IMF | International Monetary Fund |
| IPPC | International Plant Protection Convention |
| IPR(s) | Intellectual Property Right(s) |
| ISAAA | International Service for the Acquisition of Agri-Biotech Applications |

| ISEAS | Institute of Southeast Asian Studies |
|---|---|
| ITC | International Trade Commission |
| JV | Joint Venture |
| LAC | Latin American and Caribbean |
| LDC | Least-Developed Country |
| LIC | Low-Income Countries |
| LIFDC | Low-Income Food-Deficit Countries |
| LMIC | Lower-Middle-Income Countries |
| MENA | Middle East North Africa |
| MFA | Multfiber Agreement |
| MFN | Most Favored Nation (trading status) |
| MMB | Milk Marketing Board (UK) |
| MNC | Multinational Corporation |
| MRL | Maximum Residue Level |
| NAC | Nominal Assistance Coefficient |
| NAFTA | North American Free Trade Agreement |
| NARs | National Agricultural Research Organizations |
| NGO | Non-Governmental Organization |
| NIC | Newly Industrializing Country |
| NIE | Newly Industrializing Economy |
| NPC | Nominal Production Coefficient |
| NPV | Net Present Value |
| NTB | Non-Tariff Barrier |
| NTC | Non-Trade Concerns |
| OECD | Organization for Economic Cooperation and Development |
| OIE | Office International des Epizooties (International Office of Epizootics) |
| PBR | Performance Based Ratemaking |
| PNPC | Producer Nominal Protection Coefficient |
| ppb | parts per billion |
| ppm | parts per million |
| PSE | Producer Subsidy Equivalent |
| PSE | Producer Support Estimate |
| R&D | Research and Development |
| RCA | Revealed Comparative Advantage |
| RER | Real Effective Exchange Rate (Index) |
| ROW | Rest of the World |
| S&D | Special and Differential Treatment |
| SA | South Asia |
| SAP | Structural Adjustment Program |
| SEA | Single European Area |
| SMP | Single Market Program |

| SPS | Sanitary and Phytosanitary Measures |
| SSA | Sub-Saharan Africa |
| SSG | Special Agricultural Safeguard |
| STE | State-Trading Enterprise |
| TBT | Technical Barriers to Trade |
| TFT | Total Factor Productivity |
| TNC | Trade Negotiations Committee (WTO) |
| TRAINS | Trade Analysis and Information System |
| TRI | Trade Restrictiveness Index |
| TRIPS | Trade Related Investment Measures |
| TRIPS | Trade-Related Aspects of Intellectual Property Rights |
| TRQ | Tariff-Rate Quota |
| TSE | Total Support Estimate |
| UMIC | Upper-Middle-Income Countries |
| UNCTAD | UN Conference on Trade and Development |
| UNDP | United Nations Development Programme |
| UNHDR | United Nations Human Development Report |
| UPOV | International Union for the Protection of New Varieties of Plants |
| URAA | Uruguay Round Agreement on Agriculture |
| USDA | United States Department of Agriculture |
| WHO | World Health Organization |
| WIPO | World Intellectual Property Organization |
| WTO | World Trade Organization |
| WTSM | World Trade Simulation Mood |

# 1   Introduction

*Merlinda D. Ingco and L. Alan Winters*

An open trading system has long been recognized as an important element of sound economic policy, and trade liberalization as a necessary step for achieving it. Whereas the multilateral process of trade liberalization under the General Agreement on Tariffs and Trade (GATT) has been successful in opening global trade in manufactures, expanding this process for other sectors, such as agriculture, has proved very difficult to achieve. Difficult questions arise owing to the complexity of the issues and the wide range of interests across countries. In the new round of global trade negotiations under the World Trade Organization (WTO), different perspectives on agriculture have produced a highly contentious agenda. This book analyzes the key issues, diverse interests, challenges, and options for agricultural trade liberalization in the new trade agenda of the WTO, and their implications for both developed and developing countries.

The book is based on the key findings emerging from a major program of research, policy analyses, and capacity-building on agriculture and the new trade agenda in the WTO. The chapters have been prepared by many of the leading specialists in the fields of agriculture and international trade. Major policy questions addressed in this book include: What are the interests and options in the new WTO trade negotiations in agriculture and the new trade agenda from a development perspective? What new WTO trade rules on agriculture and trade policy reform would provide the largest benefits? Who would be the winners and losers under different rules? What are the agricultural trade interests of developing countries? Would market-opening measures be enough to trigger other needed reforms? What aims should developing countries pursue in tariff negotiations? Is there a danger that agricultural liberalization will create a new example of managed trade, like trade in textiles and clothing? How would farm and food trade be affected if both agricultural and non-agricultural trade barriers were slashed? Does patent protection for agricultural products hurt developing countries? These questions are explored from the viewpoint of developed as well as developing and transition economies.

Part I of the book explores the lessons and experience from the actual implementation of the Uruguay Round Agreements on Agriculture (URAA). The research evaluates the experience from actual implementation of selected WTO agreements based on the actual implementation of commitments during 1995–2000, in contrast to previous research based on the negotiated outcome of the Uruguay Round in 1994 (Martin and Winters, 1996). Part I thus sets the stage for the rest the book. Part II explores the diverse interests, options, and objectives in the new trade round. Part III is devoted to the identification and analyses of alternative disciplines and quantitative assessments of future liberalization options. It provides quantitative assessments, not as forecasts, but as analytical views of the options to identify where the biggest gains may occur. Part IV analyzes the new trade agenda and second-generation issues as they affect the agriculture sectors of both developed and developing countries.

**The purpose of this book**

A mercantilist concern only to expand exports and to screen out imports, although prevalent in most public and press discussion of international trade negotiations, reflects too narrow a conception of the gains from trade to permit progress in agricultural trade liberalization. This book is written from the broader perspective that would lead individual countries to take unilateral decisions to liberalize agricultural trade and adopt an enabling domestic policy and institutional environment to promote a competitive agricultural sector. Each chapter of the book is based on the fundamental premise that good economics suggests that an open international trading system is preferable to a closed one, that virtually every nation will benefit from an open international trading system, and that the multilateral approach serves best in maintaining such systems. Good economics are the same for both industrial countries and developing countries, and moving towards a unified trading system requires replacing bad economics with good, not replacing developing country economics with developed, or vice versa. For agriculture, in particular, it is argued that developing countries cannot afford to adopt the costly domestic protection policies used in most industrial countries.

We apply this insight to an examination of the economics underlying the new rules and options on trade and domestic policies that aim to bring agricultural trade more fully under the GATT/WTO disciplines. Getting the underlying economics right will help national governments and private economic interests regain confidence in the relevance of the GATT/WTO by leveraging agricultural trade to achieve national development objectives, including food security. It will also help establish with governments and the public the benefits of an open international trading system in agriculture, and in rekindling the international resolve to extend and defend the global trading system.

During the Uruguay Round the developing countries were, by and large, on the margin of the negotiations, even though analysis showed that the Round would have a relatively greater impact on developing countries than on developed countries. Given the overall importance of agriculture, and the rural economy more generally, in developing countries, developing countries need not only to understand the implications of changes in the global agricultural trading regime, but also actively to participate in them to ensure that their interests are addressed and that the system is more transparent and beneficial to a broader range of participants. Moreover, trade issues are also becoming significantly more complex. As tariffs fall, the trade agenda becomes more heavily weighed towards non-tariff trade measures which are inherently more complex to understand, measure, and analyze. Given the limited resources of many developing countries, there is a clear role for global groups in evaluating their interests and options, and in developing strategies to capture the benefits from the negotiations.

A major theme of the book is that interests, options, objectives, and strategies differ according to countries' size, export orientation, indebtedness, prosperity, trade composition, trade links, and susceptibility to external shocks.[1] For example, net food importers and net food exporters will have different interests on export subsidies. A number of countries benefit from these subsidies, either indirectly by lower world commodity prices, or directly through food aid programs, while others suffer from unfair competition in their export markets. Heterogeneity of interests is also evident in the aftermath of the 1997 Asian financial crisis: the agricultural interests of Thailand and Indonesia were clearly different from those of Korea, for which agricultural exports were not very important. In this latter context, a relevant question is whether agricultural policies have had counter-cyclical effects – for instance, through achieving a better export performance of the agricultural sector than the manufacturing sector, or via its ability to absorb surplus labor.

In commodities that do not compete with industrial country output (such as coffee, tea, etc.) taxes imposed by developing countries on their own agricultural exports have been more detrimental than the global trading regime itself. To be sure, in the very long term, economic development is likely to require a shift towards manufacturing and tertiary activities, since the long-run trend in agricultural commodity prices is downwards. However, in moving in this direction, developing countries must ensure that agricultural policies, be they domestic or international, do not discriminate against agriculture, since it is the surplus savings from agriculture that have traditionally funded the early stages of economic growth.

An important question, increasingly recognized but still unresolved, is how to give poor developing countries a bigger weight in the negotiating process. Beyond the problems associated with insufficient domestic analytical capabilities, most countries simply do not have the resources to be adequately represented in Geneva and in the other venues where the negotiations occur. Most of the developed countries attend negotiations with lawyers, economists, and diplomats, whereas many developing countries must rely on one or two (if any) diplomats in residence in Geneva, with many other tasks to undertake. Clearly groups of developing countries should develop common approaches to the negotiations. Two successful coalitions come to mind: the Cairns Group of agricultural exporters, which includes both developed and developing countries, and the Alliance of Small Island States (AOSIS) formed by the small island nations in an effort to influence the global warming discussions. Even if their overall impact has been limited, they have certainly been more successful in promoting their interests than their members would have been individually.

## Why trade negotiations in agriculture matter

In the seven previous rounds of trade negotiations under the GATT, the agricultural sector largely escaped the multilateral rules and disciplines developed for trade in industrial products. As a result, there were significant distortions in world agricultural markets which, in some cases, degenerated into near-autarky. It must therefore be considered a major achievement of the last multilateral trade round – the Uruguay Round of 1986–94 – to have concluded the Agreement on Agriculture (URAA), which marked a start in bringing more rules-based GATT discipline to agricultural trade and trade-related policies. Path-breaking though that achievement was, however, much remains to be done before international agricultural trade is as fully disciplined or as liberal as trade in manufactures. Further improvements in the rules and in actual implementation are needed if the objectives of real liberalization are to be achieved. After seven years of implementation (1995–2001) of the URAA, import protection against major export products from developing countries remains prohibitively high in the industrial countries and many developing countries. Applied protection in some products has even increased, compared with applied rates before the agreement.

The current agricultural negotiations in the World Trade Organization (WTO) began at a time when protection for agriculture is around the highest ever estimated. World agricultural markets continue to be distorted by high levels of support provided in Europe, North America, and several developing countries. In 2001, total support to agriculture in the OECD countries amounted to US$ 311 billion – back to the levels of domestic support and protection applied before the Uruguay Round. The losers from these arrangements are widespread. Consumers in countries that provide market-distorting support are denied the benefits from competitively produced food and agricultural products, while taxpayers are forced to subsidize high-cost and often environmentally damaging production. Such market-insulating policies depress and destabilize world market prices, disadvantaging producers in economies that either cannot afford, or are unwilling to provide, protection. Efficient farmers are thwarted in their efforts to realize their economic potential because their access to foreign markets is restricted by extensive import barriers that are far higher, on average, for agricultural products than for manufactures.

Developing countries have much to gain from further progress in trade and domestic policy reform and in further opening of global markets for their exports. For a series of reasons, advancing this process during the present WTO negotiations will be important, in order both to realize the gains made possible by previous efforts and to make future progress easier. The benefits stem from the direct effects of successful negotiations on policy and the indirect effects via perceptions of the policy environment in both rich and poor countries. If agricultural policies and expectations about policy move significantly in the direction of economic rationality, adjustments will occur in both rich and poor nations, to the advantage of nearly all. And in the few cases where the direct effects are adverse, the general improvement in efficiency will allow ample resources for supportive complementary policies.

For many countries, agriculture is still an important sector for the economy. Developing countries provide over 50 percent of the world's value added in agriculture (World Development Indicators, on line). In most low- and middle-income developing countries in Sub-Saharan Africa (SSA), East Asia, and Pacific and South Asia, a large proportion (64 percent–70 percent) of the labor force remains dependent on agriculture. Although trade patterns will diversify with development, developing countries will wish to make even more use of agricultural markets, as both exporters and importers. Thus, the future world trading system for agriculture will be a major determinant of the growth and development of many developing countries, and a critical factor in the futures of many in the poorer parts of the world. Moreover, rural growth appears to spill over to the urban economy and thus to poverty alleviation there as well as in agricultural areas themselves. At present, however, world agricultural markets remain significantly distorted by a wide range of domestic policies and border protections which impede the export performance of developing countries and reduce the world market prices of certain commodities.

The depth and complexity of agricultural protection is a major discouragement to investment in food and agro-processing industry in developing countries. Escalating tariff structures in developed countries often render agro-processing activities directly unprofitable in developing ones, but even where they do not, the uncertainty and manipulability of existing regimes makes investment unattractive. A new round that reduced escalation and the uncertainty about the barriers that remained would do much to promote rural industry and development.

Agriculture is the key sector in poverty reduction. Most of the developing world poor are in the rural economy. Most of them draw the bulk of their income directly from agriculture, and those that do not mostly rely on it indirectly by providing goods and services to farmers. The poor necessarily spend a higher proportion of their incomes on food than do the non-poor and so suffer as consumers from inefficiency and their own countries' protectionism. While there are exceptions where traditional crops and risk-sharing are displaced by risky forms of commercial agriculture, increased agricultural exports, higher prices, and stronger income generation provide one of the most effective routes to food security. Moreover, by shifting production to the most efficient locations, freer agricultural trade with fewer subsidies is more likely to promote conservation of the environment, and hence of livelihoods, than the opposite.

The developing countries also have a lot to gain from a multilateral system based on strong rules, both to protect them against pressures from more powerful countries, and to help them improve their own trade and domestic policies. The importance of this system to developing countries has increased greatly as they themselves have become more integrated into the world economy. In recent trade negotiations, developing countries have gained deeper and more secure access to developed markets (through reductions in the restrictions on imports into these markets), in exchange for providing better access to their own expanding markets (through lower tariffs on imports from the developed countries). For many developing countries, food security objectives require access on an assured basis to world market supplies, as well as to agricultural raw materials for encouraging light manufacturing in rural areas. Thus, many developing countries have a stake in building an efficient food system and maintaining market stability. For all these reasons, developing countries will gain by participating fully in WTO agricultural discussions aimed at progressive trade liberalization.

The multilateral trading system can provide a framework to improve developing countries' own trade and domestic policy regimes affecting the rural sector. Agriculture still accounts for a significant share of gross domestic product (GDP) and is, as already noted, a major source of employment in many developing countries. Continuing reform of the global trading system will make it easier for these countries to adopt rural policies that eliminate policy distortions and allocate scarce resources more efficiently, and so provide significant gains in terms of both consumer welfare and incomes. In fact, previous World Bank research (Martin and Winters, 1996) suggested that the gains to developing countries from the Uruguay Round would be much larger, relative to their GDPs, than the gains made by developed countries. And two-thirds of the estimated welfare gains to developing countries resulted from their own trade policy liberalization.

To raise welfare, farmers and households must respond to the new conditions created by a policy reform. The supply response to trade and agricultural policy reform depends heavily upon the credibility of reforms. In fact, establishing the credibility of policy measures is at least as important as choosing the efficient policy solution, for experience in many countries shows that the private sector will not invest if the persistence of reforms is in doubt. Unfortunately, in the past reform programs have frequently been reversed or halted and government policy has frequently been unpredictable. Thus, credibility can be greatly enhanced by a framework of multilateral rules, equipped with instruments that prevent backsliding, through which member governments can lock-in domestic policy reforms. The WTO is the pre-eminent example of such a framework.

Estimates of the potential economic welfare benefits of global agricultural trade reform suggests an increase in the aggregate welfare of the developing world of around US$ 142 billion annually (World Bank, 2001). Most of these gains will come from trade policy reforms within the developing countries themselves – about US$ 114 billion, which is around half of all that developing countries can expect from their own goods market trade liberalizations. But liberalization in OECD countries will deliver about another US$ 31 billion – around a third of what all OECD goods liberalization will generate and more than 50 percent of the official development assistance given to developing countries in 2001. When more dynamic effects of liberalization are considered, including productivity gains, the benefits are potentially much larger.

### Perspectives on the agricultural trade negotiations

The present agricultural negotiations in the WTO started in March 2000, in accordance with the provisions of article 20 of the URAA (see the appendix to this chapter, p. 14). This article provides that, one year before the end of the implementation period for the Uruguay Round commitments for developed countries, negotiations should start on continuing the reform process to achieve the long-term objective of substantial progressive reductions in agricultural support and protection. The negotiations were formally launched in March 2000, with the work carried forward in the WTO's Standing Committee on Agriculture, meeting in special session. During the first phase of the negotiations, which lasted until March 2001, the special sessions received and reviewed more than forty initial proposals put forward by 121 member countries. In a second phase, up to February 2002, these and a smaller number of further proposals were examined in greater depth, in order to assess their implications and political support. However, before this phase had been completed, the context of the agricultural negotiations was greatly altered, and their prospects improved, by the outcome of the fourth Ministerial Conference of the WTO, held in Doha, Qatar in November 2001.

As a result of the Doha Declaration, adopted by WTO member governments at the end of the Ministerial conference, the agriculture negotiations are now taking place in the context of a wider round of multilateral trade negotiations that extends to further trade liberalization for industrial products and services and a wide range of other trade-related issues. The Declaration defines the round as a single undertaking, with a number of important deadlines and a concluding date of "not later than 1 January 2005." It also makes the negotiations as a whole subject to general provisions that stress development aims. For agriculture, the Declaration confirms the commitment of members to the reform program and adds, to a small extent, to what is said in article 20 of the URAA (see the annex to this chapter). In particular, a crucial sentence commits members (though "without prejudging the outcome of the negotiations") to comprehensive negotiations aimed at "substantial improvements in market access; reductions of, with a view to phasing out, all forms of export subsidies; and substantial reductions in trade-distorting domestic support." The new round of negotiations has been placed under the overall supervision of a Trade Negotiations Committee (TNC), established under the authority of the WTO's governing General Council.

The agricultural negotiations have proved highly contentious, with several missed deadlines before the Ministerial Meeting in Cancún, and the prospects for a successful outcome are difficult to predict. The change in their context, as a result of the Doha decisions, will almost certainly be helpful, for several reasons:

- Inclusion in a wider round offers the possibility that countries asked to make painful concessions may obtain compensatory gains in areas outside agriculture
- Goals are now stated somewhat more precisely than in the very general terms of article 20
- The introduction of target dates should keep the negotiations moving along
- The increased political attention given to a broader negotiating round should help to raise the cost of failure.

Nevertheless, the fact must be acknowledged that the changing political context and new developments since the Uruguay Round, combined with the different perspectives and new dimensions on trade reform, have produced a highly contentious agenda. The environment in which the negotiations are taking place is also very different from when the Uruguay Round was launched.

Historically, developing countries have played a passive or reactive role in multilateral trade negotiations. Rich countries – mainly the United States and the European Union (EU) – set the agenda, agreed on the terms, and the other smaller and developing countries went along. As shown during the unsuccessful

WTO Ministerial meeting in Seattle in 1999, and in the successful meeting in Doha in 2001, that is no longer the way the system works: developing countries, now constituting the majority of WTO members, have changed the dynamics of trade negotiations.

Proposals submitted before the Seattle meeting, and since March 2000 in the context of the agriculture negotiations, reflect the differences in approach, policies, and attitudes of the member countries. They include differences in specific objectives for trade in agricultural products, as well as more general issues about the scope and nature of the reform process. While proposals and statements preach liberalization, the reality of policies, in both the industrial and the developing countries, suggests a revival of protectionist influences. The Asian crisis heightened concerns about the adverse impacts of globalization and integration on fragile economies with pervasive poverty. Many developing countries have expressed concerns about whether key areas of the Uruguay Round have been implemented with the intent and the expectations that they had in 1994. The least-developed countries (LDCs), which are still only marginally integrated into the multilateral trading system, have produced proposals clouded with uncertainty and ambiguity as they balance an intellectual climate of liberalization with political pressures for the opposite. Indeed, many governments, responding to domestic pressures, are rethinking their policies and slowing their processes of liberalization. The failure in Seattle showed that neither industrial nor developing countries were politically ready at that time to launch a broader round of negotiations, and while Doha has reversed that, it showed that agriculture remains highly controversial, with widely differing concerns and objectives among both developed and developing countries.

The proposals tabled in the agricultural negotiations show at least two different perspectives:

- One vision reflects the ultimate goal of fully integrating agriculture into the structure of GATT/WTO disciplines that already applies to manufactured goods. This proposal by the Cairns Group of agricultural exporters, comprising both developed and developing countries, wants world agricultural trade to be subject to multilateral rules and disciplines that eliminate restrictions and distortions. This proposal is ostensibly supported by the United States – although the Farm Bill of 2002 suggests substantial reservations – but strongly opposed by the EU and some other WTO members including Japan, Switzerland, the Republic of Korea, and Norway. Some developing countries, such as the net-food importers, also oppose it because they are uncertain about its impact on food prices.
- The alternative vision is one of continued, but marginally more efficient, management of agricultural trade. It promotes the concept of the "multifunctionality" of agriculture, most vigorously by the EU, to oppose moves towards liberalization and total integration.

These developments are taking place against the backdrop of increasing globalization of the world economy – the linking together of countries at different levels of development by technology, information, and knowledge. Globalization of the food and agricultural trading system has brought a new set of issues beyond the so-called "built-in agenda" bequeathed to the WTO by the URAA, and to some extent even beyond the agenda explicitly set out in the Doha Declaration. These new issues include intellectual property associated with food products, food safety, harmonization of standards, and competition policy. At the same time, globalization has engaged a new set of interest groups – the non-governmental organizations (NGOs) – among which many see trade liberalization as inimical to their social and environmental objectives.

## Lessons from the Uruguay Round

This is not the place for a detailed examination of the lessons learned from the experience of the seven-year-long Uruguay Round negotiations and their aftermath. However, some broad conclusions, most of which would be widely supported, can be stated briefly as a background to the new WTO round and to the objectives of this book:
- Negotiations on rules are more complex than market access talks and the gains are less "automatic"
- Effective participation was a challenge for many developing countries and remains in doubt this time around
- Technical and financial assistance for developing countries was insufficient and not always properly targeted: commitments were not binding, so that assistance was often not forthcoming
- A number of agreements emerged that may not be beneficial to some countries, especially least-developed ones
- Implementation issues remain on several Uruguay Round agreements, including the URAA, not least because timetables were unrealistic
- Lax drafting and political compromise mean that significant policy distortions remain
- In the absence of clear monitoring procedures, there are serious information problems about the extent of applied agricultural protection. Information often does not exist, and even when it does, it is opaque.

## An overview of the proposals

An overview of the forty-five formal proposals submitted on behalf of a total of 121 countries during Phase 1 of the work of the special sessions of the Committee on Agriculture – that is, during the period March 2000–March 2001, when WTO members were setting out the goals which they sought to achieve in the agricultural negotiations – shows comprehensive coverage of issues covered by the URAA.[2] More than half the proposals were made by developing countries, with several further proposals supported by groups of both developing and developed countries. A review of the proposals shows substantial divergences in interests among members, but also some common themes.

As regards market access, there is a general call to simplify trade regimes and reduce trade restrictions by cutting tariffs. This involves addressing the remaining problems of tariff peaks, tariff escalation, and the complexities of the tariff regimes implemented after the Uruguay Round, notably the system of tariff-rate quotas (TRQs) and their administration. Specific proposals on the approach to tariff cuts such as "across the board," "zero for zero," and the "Swiss formula" remain matters for negotiation. On the use of the special safeguards mechanism for agriculture, since comparatively few countries reserved the right at the end of the Uruguay Round to use this mechanism, some members have proposed making its use available more widely.

There is a general call to eliminate or substantially reduce export subsidies. These proposals are complemented by proposals aimed at avoiding circumvention of commitments by including disciplines on export credits, food aid, and the operations of state-trading agencies engaged as single exporters. Net-food importers are concerned about the impact that elimination of export subsidies might have on food prices, but some have argued that it could actually benefit them, if the higher prices lead to an increase in prices received by their farmers, thus triggering a supply response, and increased food production. Certainly if they are net importers because of bad policies, they are likely to gain as higher world food prices reduce the impact of those policies.

On domestic support, most liberalization proposals are oriented towards reducing and simplifying the trade-distorting measures. A review of domestic support levels in the industrial countries indicates that total transfers to agriculture in OECD countries have risen since the late 1990s, even though most countries utilized less than half of the support allowed under the commitments on Aggregate Measurement of Support (AMS) agreed under the URAA. This means that these countries have the potential to increase support levels even further. At the same time, developing countries are asking for more flexibility to allocate resources to their agricultural sector, and to expand the "green box" provisions which exempt specified forms of support from reduction commitments.

Two other issues emerge strongly in the proposals: Special and Differential Treatment (S&D) and "Non-Trade Concerns" (NTC). These proposals are linked to domestic support and market access regimes. The ostensible purpose of S&D is to help developing countries to be more integrated into the WTO system, and to participate more fully in it, thus ensuring that they share the benefits from trade. It is dear to the hearts of many developing country negotiators, but mainly, it appears, as a way to avoid, not enhance, integration. NTC is an umbrella which covers a number of issues, including the industrial countries' concept of "multifunctionality," environmental concerns, and food security; it is used mainly by those countries which oppose further agricultural trade liberalization.

Developing countries have repeatedly proposed that the current negotiations should aim at leveling the playing field – i.e. reducing the disparity between themselves and the rich countries in the use of domestic support and protection, and improving market access conditions. As a result, some developing countries have started to focus on how new rules might be introduced to enhance their own internal protection and domestic support. Total domestic support for agriculture in developing countries is a very small proportion of GDP, however, and in certain countries is actually negative as they effectively tax their agricultural sectors. Some proposals, however, have questioned whether developing countries can afford to provide domestic support and subsidies, and have suggested that, in this context, winning concessions at a multilateral level to permit such policies would be meaningless or, at best, a bad bargain for developed countries.

### Key policy issues and messages

On the basis of the work described in this book, we highlight four policy messages about agriculture in the Doha Development Agenda.

### *Reduce high trade barriers and domestic support*

Producer support estimates (PSEs) exceed 60 percent in some countries (Japan, Korea, Norway, and Switzerland) and are about 20 percent in the United States; they are 35 percent in the EU (OECD, 2002). The highest levels of support are directed at temperate products. These are of direct interest to the developing countries that produce temperate products already and also to those which would diversify into them if not discouraged by low prices.

Some agricultural tariffs remain extremely high: on average, they are about six times as high as industrial tariffs, and many exceed 50 percent. Protection also escalates with the level of processing, particularly in markets for processed tropical products, reducing the scope for profitable development of value added activities in developing countries.

High levels of export subsidies in OECD countries remain a major factor in world food markets and have wide effects on world prices and market conditions. Between 1995 and 1998, global export subsidies amounted to over

US\$ 27 billion cumulatively, of which over 90 percent is from the EU (Elbehri and Leetma, 2002).

Agricultural imports into OECD and other major markets face an array of sanitary and phytosanitary measures and other technical requirements. These can be used to restrict trade, and even when they are legitimate, developing countries often have serious difficulties proving that their exports actually meet these standards, owing to the high cost of some testing and certification procedures. Technical capacity constraints seriously hinder developing country compliance with the emerging array of international standards and technical requirements.

*Remove the policy bias against agriculture*

Many developing countries still discriminate against their own agricultural sectors. While the magnitude of this bias has been reduced recently, it still remains significant owing to the operation of inefficient state-owned marketing enterprises and the direct taxation of these exports. In addition, the trade policies of developing countries discourage greater South–South trade in agricultural products, and thus frustrate productive efficiency based on true comparative advantage.

*Make agricultural liberalization pro-poor*

For long-run benefits from trade liberalization developing countries must facilitate adequate supply responses, for example, by investing in complementary infrastructure (e.g. irrigation and rural roads), securing property rights, providing appropriate agricultural extension and technical information, and developing complementary markets for credit, agricultural inputs, and services. In addition, access to assets is critical in determining how the poor respond to trade liberalization. The ability to translate improved market access for agricultural products into significant poverty reduction depends significantly on having a structure of land ownership that encourages labor-intensive use of land, either through smallholder out-grower schemes or large-scale wage employment.

*Price increases are a secondary concern*

Reductions in developed countries' export subsidies and domestic support could raise world prices. This would hit net consumers of tradable food products, and should be met with appropriate safety net mechanisms where these are among the poor. The significance of price increases should not be overplayed, however. Even full trade liberalization will lead to an increase in temperate prices of only around 2 percent–5 percent (Anderson *et al.*, 1999), and these should be viewed against a trend of secular declines in agricultural prices. In many countries the poor are net producers or beneficiaries of the second-round spillovers that arise from agricultural liberalization.

# Appendix   WTO documents on agriculture

## (A) Article 20 of the Uruguay Round Agreement on Agriculture

*Continuation of the reform process*

Recognizing that the long-term objective of substantial progressive reductions in support and protection resulting in fundamental reform is an ongoing process, Members agree that negotiations for continuing the process will be initiated one year before the end of the implementation period, taking into account:
(a) the experience to that date from implementing the reduction commitments;
(b) the effects of the reduction commitments on world trade in agriculture;
(c) non-trade concerns, special and differential treatment to developing country Members, and the objective to establish a fair and market-oriented agricultural trading system, and the other objectives and concerns mentioned in the preamble to this Agreement; and
(d) what further commitments are necessary to achieve the above mentioned long-term objectives.

## (B) Articles 13 and 14 of the Doha Declaration

*Agriculture*

13. We recognize the work already undertaken in the negotiations initiated in early 2000 under Article 20 of the Agreement on Agriculture, including the large number of negotiating proposals submitted on behalf of a total of 121 Members. We recall the long-term objective referred to in the Agreement to establish a fair and market-oriented trading system through a programme of fundamental reform encompassing strengthened rules and specific commitments on support and protection in order to correct and prevent restrictions and distortions in world agricultural markets. We reconfirm our commitment to this programme. Building on the work carried out to date and without prejudging the outcome of the negotiations we commit ourselves to comprehensive negotiations aimed at: substantial improvements in market access; reductions of, with a view to phasing out, all forms of export subsidies; and substantial reductions in trade-distorting domestic support. We agree that special and differential treatment for developing countries shall be an integral part of all elements of the negotiations and shall be embodied in the Schedules of concessions and commitments and as

appropriate in the rules and disciplines to be negotiated, so as to be operationally effective and to enable developing countries to effectively take account of their development needs, including food security and rural development. We take note of the non-trade concerns reflected in the negotiating proposals submitted by Members and confirm that non-trade concerns will be taken into account in the negotiations as provided for in the Agreement on Agriculture.

14. Modalities for the further commitments, including provisions for special and differential treatment, shall be established no later than 31 March 2003. Participants shall submit their comprehensive draft Schedules based on these modalities no later than the date of the Fifth Session of the Ministerial Conference. The negotiations, including with respect to rules and disciplines and related legal texts, shall be concluded as part and at the date of conclusion of the negotiating agenda as a whole.

### Notes

1. Depending on resource endowments and production patterns, interests will also diverge within countries (e.g. the interests of sugar producers in Brazil are unlikely to be the same as those of wheat farmers).
2. In addition, members submitted four technical notes or discussion papers. All can be consulted on, and downloaded from, the WTO website (http://www.WTO.org/english/tratop_e/agric_e/negoti_e.htm). In Phase 2, the special sessions were devoted to in-depth consideration of the proposals made in Phase 1, and most of the additional documentation took the form of informal papers, largely devoted to elaborating or commenting on proposals made in Phase 1.

### References

Anderson, K., B. Hoekman, and A. Strutt, 1999. *Agriculture and the WTO: Next Steps*, CIES Discussion Paper, 99/14, University of Adelaide

Elbehri, A. and S. Leetma, 2002. "How Significant are Export Subsidies to Agricultural Trade? Trade and Welfare Implications of Global Reform," paper presented to the 5th Annual Conference on Global Economic Analysis, Toipei, June

Martin, W. and L. A. Winters, 1996. *The Uruguay Round and the Developing Countries*, Cambridge: Cambridge University Press

OECD, 2002. *Agricultural Policies in OECD Countries: Monitoring and Evaluation*, Paris: OECD

World Bank, 2001. *Global Economic Prospects, 2001*, Washington, DC: World Bank

# 2    Agriculture and the trade negotiations: a synopsis

*Merlinda D. Ingco and L. Alan Winters*

Agricultural trade policy is notorious for its complexity – indeed, many would argue that complexity is a key tool in preserving it from prying eyes and peremptory reform. This book is similarly complex, so in the interests of transparency we offer in this chapter a synopsis of the arguments it covers. The remainder of the book comprises four parts. Part I contains three chapters (chapters 3–5) primarily concerned with the operation of the Uruguay Round Agreement on Agriculture (URAA), which sets the scene for the new round. This is followed by the two chapters in part II (chapters 6 and 7) which identify the commonalities and differences in interest both between developed and developing countries and, more importantly, between developing countries. Part III contains seven studies (chapters 8–14) aimed at quantifying the scope for, and benefits from, agricultural trade policy reform, and analyzing the relative benefits of different reform packages that might emerge from negotiation. The part deals, *inter alia*, with tariff rate quotas, specific commodity markets, broad reform packages and the economy-wide effects of reform. Part IV (chapters 15–21) of the book considers "new" issues: some chapters review the unfinished agenda of the URAA's "new" issues, such as sanitary and phytosanitary standards (SPS) and intellectual property (IP), while others deal with "new new" issues such as the environment and genetically modified foods.[*]

## Part I    Experience with the Uruguay Round Agreement on Agriculture

As we noted in chapter 1, the URAA provides the backdrop and the context for the new round of agricultural trade talks and must inform all analyses of it. The URAA created a new structure of protection, which was intended to make future

---

[*]Although in a few cases there have been significant changes in circumstances since 1999, the basic arguments, analysis and recommendations of the chapters in this book are as relevant now as when they were first written.

liberalization more straightforward and created new rules and agreements that should also open markets up. On the other hand, there is widespread agreement that it did not actually liberalize trade very much itself. Part I contains three chapters.

## How open are OECD markets?

The URAA instituted a major reform of the world agricultural trade system, including the development and implementation of a framework to address trade distortions in three major policy domains: market access, domestic support, and export subsidies. New rules and quantitative guidelines were agreed upon in all three domains and a framework created for moving agricultural support towards less trade distorting forms. In chapter 3, Dimitris Diakosavvas examines the first decade of the URAA and the scene it sets for the new round of trade talks.

Agricultural policy reform under the URAA has not been very significant to date, and the preliminary evidence suggests that its overall effects have been moderate. Without underrating the achievement of the Agreement in bringing agriculture into the mainstream of multilateral trading rules, only limited progress has been made since 1995 in reducing agricultural protection and market insulation.

The new round thus provides an important opportunity for deepening the process of agricultural reform and trade liberalization started by the URAA, and the weaknesses of the URAA define an important starting-point for the next agreement. On market access, negotiations should be more straightforward than in the Uruguay Round because tariffication has already made border protection more transparent. The major question is finding a process to reduce agricultural tariffs, which remain very high in many cases. This requires, *inter alia*, finding ways to reduce the dispersion of tariff rates and devising an appropriate weighting system to be used for calculating overall tariff reductions. Several techniques could be used for the latter, each having its own specific economic features, so these decisions are both contentious and central to the outcome. A second issue concerns tariff-rate quotas (TRQs) which ideally should be eliminated, but if this is not feasible, market access should be expanded by liberalizing all three TRQ parameters: increasing the quotas, reducing the over-quota tariffs and eliminating the in-quota tariffs in combination. In addition, more efficient methods of quota allocation would expand effective market access by increasing the fill rates of tariff quotas.

On domestic support, Diakosavvas argues that a significant reduction of trade distortions would require: addressing the various weaknesses in the Aggregate Measurement of Support (AMS) discipline, including defining and discipling the AMS at a subsectoral level and strengthening the eligibility criteria for exempt policies to ensure that only the least trade-distorting programs are excluded; eliminating the Peace Clause; and reviewing the role of special and differential treatment for developing countries.

The URAA disciplines on export subsidies have been more effective than those on tariffs or domestic support, but further reductions in trade distortions could be achieved by strengthening them. Several specific issues need to be addressed; in particular, Diakosavvas writes, the coverage of the export subsidies disciplines should be broadened to embrace all those policies which have the potential to distort export competition, such as aspects of the parastatal trade agencies, revenue pooling arrangements, international food aid, export credits, export taxes and export restraints. Moreover, the rules concerning "unused" export subsidy allowances, the definition of export subsidies, and the issue of "cross-subsidization" among markets, should be tightened.

*Tariff-rate quotas*

A TRQ, which allows a given quota of imports to enter at a low tariff rate, is ostensibly a guarantee of at least a certain level of market access. TRQs were introduced by the URAA to ensure that the imprecise exercise of increasing MFN tariffs under the heading of tariffication (the conversion of non-tariff protection to tariffs) would not actually reduce market access. The intention was to ensure that in every "tariffied" commodity, at least a minimal level of import penetration was achieved. Chapter 4, by Philip Abbott and Adair Morse, looks at how the fourteen developing countries that use TRQs have applied them in practice.

A TRQ applies a low tariff to imports up to a minimum committed quantity (the quota), generally the larger of either the pre-tariffication level of imports, or 3 (rising to 5) percent of domestic consumption. Imports beyond the quota pay the MFN tariff. Experience with TRQs in developed countries since 1995 has shown that in many cases they introduce new distortions into agricultural trade, handing exceptional benefits (rents) to those lucky enough to obtain quota rights, creating administrative obstacles that may result in imports not even filling the quota, and bunching imports into periods when lower tariffs apply because the quota has not yet been filled.

Abbott and Morse argue, however, that in developing countries these difficulties have not generally emerged. One important reason is that even if developing countries' MFN ceiling tariffs are very high, their applied tariffs are often much lower, and sometimes actually lower than the maximum TRQ tariff rates to which they are committed. Governments do generally seek to give the TRQ rents to domestic agents, but in only a few instances have domestic producer groups with TRQ import rights used them to frustrate imports. Among the many alternative licensing procedures, state trading and licensing-on-demand are the most used for politically sensitive staples (cereals and oilseeds). TRQs established to maintain preferences for preferred suppliers still allow state traders to capture rents (and thus substantially undermine the objectives of the preferences in the first place). They also hinder market development, and encourage the misallocation of resources by diverting trade to high-cost exporters. Finally, TRQs are used only for a relatively small share of developing countries' imports.

Abbott and Morse argue that most import liberalization has resulted from substantial reductions in MFN tariff rates rather than from changes to TRQs. They conclude that in the new round, the reduction of MFN tariffs and the elimination of non-tariff barriers (NTBs) will be far more effective in liberalizing agricultural trade than the expansion of minimum access commitments or the reduction of TRQ tariffs.

### Sanitary and phytosanitary measures

The Uruguay Round Agreement on Sanitary and Phytosanitary Measures (SPS Agreement) has proved highly controversial. An EU ban on imports of US and Canadian beef from cattle raised on growth-promoting hormones led to retaliatory trade action, and other disputes have produced judgments against Australian and Japanese SPS measures affecting imports. The issue of GM food and other crops is further testing the agreement. Developing countries often complain that the SPS agreement gives undue status to international safety and health standards which they play little part in establishing, and which may be unnecessarily stringent. In chapter 5, Gretchen Stanton reviews the operation of the SPS Agreement, and draws essentially optimistic conclusions.

The SPS agreement explicitly recognizes that the protection of health must take priority over international trade. WTO members may restrict imports when necessary to protect human, animal or plant life or health, but unnecessary health and safety regulations should not be used as a means to protect domestic producers from competition. To avoid the latter temptation, SPS measures are to be based on science, used only to the extent necessary, and avoid arbitrarily or unjustifiably discriminating between countries. The agreement encourages governments to base SPS measures on international standards, but does not prevent them from adopting higher standards.

Stanton concludes that the benefits of the agreement are becoming increasingly evident: trade in foods is becoming more predictable, and restrictions less arbitrary, to the benefit of consumers; better transparency of SPS measures allows exporters to identify what conditions their products must meet; advance notification allows governments and traders to seek changes in measures unnecessarily damaging to trade; and consumers benefit from better information about regulations and trade measures.

For developing countries, Stanton suggests, the disciplines of the SPS agreement are particularly valuable because they allow countries with limited resources to challenge unjustified requirements imposed on their exports. Provided exporters meet relevant internationally developed standards, importing countries face the burden of proving that any additional demands are scientifically justified. Developing countries can also rely on international standards to justify their own import regulations, provided they do not discriminate in favour of domestic produce. SPS provisions on the recognition of equivalence of different production methods permits countries to use technologies more appropriate to their development situation.

Chapter 5 reports proposals in the WTO's SPS Committee aimed at increasing developing country participation in standard-setting organizations. On developing country complaints that standards are unnecessarily stringent, however, Stanton comments that "it is difficult to imagine . . . that the level of international standards could be lowered, at a time when consumers around the world are demanding an ever higher quality and safety of food."

## Part II   Interests and options

It is too simple to characterize the trade talks as a battle between developed and developing countries. Within the latter constituency interests vary strongly. The two chapters of part II illustrate this fact, first, via simulation modeling and, second, via an exploration of descriptive *ex post* data. The latter provides an excellent example of how readily available facts and simple analysis will illuminate an important issue.

### Negotiating objectives for developing countries

The interests of different developing countries in agricultural trade are far from identical. However, a unified effort will be required to achieve real gains in reform. Chapter 6 by Kym Anderson attempts to clarify and identify the extent to which interests within developing countries can benefit from agricultural reform. The chapter examines traditional agricultural issues as they affect developing countries, and then focuses upon claims by richer food-importing countries that food safety and agriculture's so-called multifunctional characteristics require stricter barriers to farm trade. If handled badly in negotiations, the latter contention could undermine the interests of developing countries. The chapter concludes by reviewing some of the options facing negotiators from developing countries.

Anderson's estimates suggest that if all merchandise trade distortions were removed globally, almost one-third of the global gains would come from agricultural reform in OECD countries, even though farmers in those countries contribute only 4 percent of global GDP and less than 10 percent of world trade. Within this reform, the most important area is market access. Tariffication appeared to be a great step forward, but the combination of "dirty tariffication" by developed economies, and the high ceiling bindings by developing economies, allowed many countries to increase their actual levels of protection. Reducing bound tariffs from 50–150 percent to the 0–15 percent range of manufactures is one of the most serious and most important challenges. If the past is any guide, the gap will not be closed for several decades. On farm export subsidies nothing less than a ban will bring agriculture into line with non-farm products under the General Agreement on Tariffs and Trade (GATT).

Substantial progress in freeing trade in textiles and agriculture would boost the earnings of the world's poor enormously. In these circumstances, Anderson says, the agenda of the new round should include not only the traditional sectors but also "new trade agenda" items such as investment and competition policies, to allow for linkages and tradeoffs. These new items may cause political and administrative difficulties in some developing countries, but they will also create opportunities for growth. Limited analytical and negotiating resources make some countries hesitant to address these issues, but the drive for market access should push them on.

Non-discriminatory access to OECD markets is more valuable than winning special treatment and tariff preferences. Special treatment delays beneficial reforms, while tariff preferences divide developing countries and weaken their collective bargaining strength.

### Convergent and divergent interests

Where Anderson focuses on the common interests of developing countries in agricultural liberalization, Alberto Valdés and Alex. F. McCalla in chapter 7 focus on the differences. These are considerable, although Valdés and McCalla argue that there is still scope for countries with different but overlapping interests to negotiate collectively.

Valdés and McCalla look at data for 148 developing countries. Each country is classified on the basis of six characteristics: its income level, whether it is a net importer or net exporter of food, and of agricultural products as a whole, its dependence on food trade (measured by the share of food in total trade), its size, its region, and the openness of its agricultural sector. Cross-referencing between these characteristics, the authors challenge a number of conventional myths:

• Not all poor countries are net importers of agricultural products: of the fifty-eight countries classified by the United Nations as Low-Income Food Deficit Countries (LIFDC), twenty-five are net exporters of agricultural products.

• Sixty-three of the total of 148 developing countries reviewed are net agricultural exporters.

- Only one of the World Bank's regions – Middle East and North Africa – consists almost entirely of net importers of agricultural products, although South Asia is not far behind.
- Latin America is not uniformly an "export region": over 40 percent of the thirty-two countries in the region are net agricultural importers.

Two other findings also stand out. First, for developing countries in general, the ratio between the values of food imports and total export earnings is low. However, food import costs are a heavier burden for small countries, especially those in the UN's small island developing country group. Second, the ratio of agricultural trade to total national output varies widely among developing countries, with no close correlation with a country's size or its income level.

Despite all this diversity, several identified groups of developing countries have sufficiently overlapping interests to justify the formation of a collective negotiating position. The potential advantages of a common negotiating position would include not only greater power but also economies of scale in negotiation and the provision of technical analysis and knowledge. Valdes and McCalla suggest that future research should focus on identifying gainers and losers from trade liberalization within each country. This would give governments a much clearer perspective on the welfare importance of trade liberalization.

**Part III    Quantifying the effects of new rules and trade liberalization**

This part of the book attempts to put numbers behind various arguments for agricultural trade reform. Two chapters try to assess the benefits of reforming TRQs – one of the URAA's giant leaps backwards – while most consider the relative merits of different reform packages. One should never take simulation results too literally, but the modeling and other chapters of this part leave an unmistakable message of continuing distortion and economic loss in agriculture. For developed countries, agriculture is a very small sector, whose protection imposes disproportionate costs on the rest of the economy. For developing countries, on the other hand, it is a major source of income and employment which offers absolutely very large returns to reform.

*New rules for agricultural trade policy*

We now have enough experience with the URAA to assess how reforms have been working in each of the three areas of liberalization – market access, export subsidies and domestic support. In chapter 8, Harry de Gorter considers how effective the agreement has been in each area, and makes suggestions for new rules to improve its disciplines.

The introduction of TRQs means that market access is determined by three elements: the size of the TRQ, the duty payable on in-quota imports, and the duty on out-of-quota imports. Liberalization will be guaranteed only if quotas are increased and both duties are reduced. For the biggest trade effects, negotiators should focus on easing the element which in each case is the effective restriction on imports: in developing countries it is predominantly the out-of-quota tariff. But because adjustments could quickly make one of the other elements effective instead, it may be necessary to act on all three. Attention also needs to be paid to how export quotas are allocated, procedures for licensing (which allocate quota rents to exporting and/or importing firms), how the quotas are issued (for instance, first-come, first-served, or on the basis of past shares of trade), and whether quotas and licences can be traded.

Because of high world prices, the binding effect of export subsidy commitments under the URAA has been limited, and it is difficult to tell if the agreement has changed government behavior. Lower observed subsidization probably reflects world market developments rather than liberalization. For further liberalization, de Gorter favors reducing the permitted volume of subsidies exports, although he recognizes that to date it is the value limits, rather than the volume limits, that have begun to bite. He also advocates tighter rules for carrying over unused rights to next year, disaggregating products, limiting input subsidies, export promotion and credit guarantee programs, and disciplining food aid.

Domestic support commitments, de Gorter suggests, have been less meaningful than expected because the starting point for each country (the AMS) was inflated by low prices and high subsidies during the chosen base period, and the inclusion of "blue box" measures (supposedly not trade-distorting) in the AMS, but not in the reduction requirements. The AMS also covers all commodities together, meaning that countries can still increase support to some products by reducing it in others. Because some aspects of the AMS reflect market access rather than domestic support, the chapter proposes a new "flashing amber box" to single out truly trade-distorting policies. The "blue box," which concerns US and EU policies that are ostensibly non-distortionary but do actually affect trade, should be "emptied and locked," not least to re-affirm the multilateral spirit of the WTO. As regards "green box" policies, de Gorter argues that, even if decoupled from production, they can still influence decisions about entering or leaving farming, making investments, and taking other risks.

*Enhancing market access*

The new agricultural negotiations will be the first in which the high level of protection at the border, long hidden by NTBs, is clearly visible. This is because of the Uruguay Round's "tariffication," the conversion of all border measures into tariffs. Chapter 9 by Tim Josling and Allan Rae asks: "What process will lead to the removal of these high trade barriers in a reasonable time period?"

High average tariff rates are not the whole problem with agricultural market access reducing tariff peaks and making tariff levels more comparable across countries, would significantly reduce market distortion. In addition, many agricultural raw materials enter industrial countries with low levels of protection, whereas processed agricultural goods face significant tariffs. This tariff escalation inhibits the development of processing industries in developing countries. Other problems include the continued use of tariffs that depend on world price levels and the system of tariff rate quotas.

Josling and Rae compare the effects of four different approaches to tariff cutting:

- a "sectoral" approach, studied by modeling effects of removal of tariffs on grains and oilseeds
- a cut of 36 percent in all agricultural tariffs
- a formula designed to bring down the highest tariffs fastest and
- a "cocktail" mix of approaches varying with the level of the original tariff, but applied to all tariffs.

All three across-the-board approaches produce gains in welfare for the majority of countries and regions. The greatest gains come from the "cocktail" approach, because it reduces tariffs at both peak and lower levels. Almost half the gains to developing countries come through better market access for processed foods. The sectoral approach on grains and oilseeds delivers welfare gains largely to the most protective importers (Japan and Korea) and a major exporter (the United States), while much of the developing world (except China) suffers welfare losses.

The authors warn that their study assumes no changes in trade policies in the manufacturing and services sectors. If tariff cuts and policy changes took place in these sectors as well, they could well alter the gains to liberalization in agriculture and food markets.

*Tariff-rate quotas and market access*

A key factor in the welfare and trade effects of further liberalization on agriculture will be the treatment of TRQs, which govern market access for many products. In chapter 10, Aziz Elbehri, Merlinda D. Ingco, Thomas Hertel, and Kenneth Pearson approach the issue of market access by testing several alternative scenarios for TRQ liberalization. Their findings suggest that while liberalization generally yields welfare gains for importers, several factors influence the net effects for exporters.

The first part of the chapter studies the effects of liberalizing the US and EU sugar markets. Its aim is to assess the welfare, trade, and production effects on the importing countries, and also the effects on the exporters (mostly developing countries) in terms of the distribution of quota rents, changes in trade patterns, and net social welfare. They conclude that reducing only the US over-quota sugar tariffs would result in a net welfare gain to the United States, but a net loss to exporters as quota rents declined. Both reducing US tariffs

and expanding the TRQs, however, would result in gains on both sides totaling US$ 215 million, and if both the EU and United States liberalized their
sugar markets together, global welfare gains would be substantially higher
(US$ 1,200 million). The welfare gains in exporting regions such as Latin
America and Africa are substantial, particularly when liberalization includes
both quota expansion and tariff cuts, although there are important variations
across liberalization scenarios. For example, the Philippines gains only if the
US market is liberalized, and Africa only if the EU liberalizes, while Latin
America benefits from either liberalization because it exports to both markets.
For sugar at least, therefore, a combination of lower tariffs and higher quotas
seems to be the best approach to liberalization.

The second part of the chapter looks at the consequences of much wider
TRQ liberalization. It assumes action affecting six markets (the United States,
European Union, Canada, Japan, Korea and the Philippines) and covering eight
commodities (rice, wheat, grains, sugar, dairy, oilseeds, fruits and vegetables,
and meat products). Two scenarios are examined: a one-third across-the-board
reduction in tariffs, and a reduction in over-quota tariffs down to the level of
tariffs charged on imports within the TRQs. Importing countries show the traditional gains from trade to be expected from liberalization: a net gain in social
welfare directly related to the size of their import markets and the initial height
of their over-quota tariffs. The trade responses, and the effects on developing
exporting countries, however, depend on the details of the initial regime. For example, cutting over-quota tariffs has no trade effect when it is the in-quota tariff
that actually governs trade. As was also noted in chapter 8, the liberalization of
TRQs is a subtle business and, to be on the safe side, all three components –
the quota and the two tariff rates – need to be liberalized.

*The global and regional effects of trade liberalization*

Chapter 11 by Thomas W. Hertel, Kym Anderson, Joseph F. Francois, and Will
Martin examines what happens to world food trade if both agricultural and non-
agricultural trade are liberalized. The many years of nugatory liberalization in
agriculture have left the sector heavily distorted, and agricultural liberalization
would unwind some of this distortion. But because trade in industrial products and services is also distorted, liberalization effects in these sectors would
interact with the effects of agricultural liberalization.

In the course of post-war multilateral liberalization, high-income countries
have cut their average import duties on industrial products from over 40 percent
to around 1.5 percent, but, if anything, they have actually increased barriers to
imports of agricultural products. By 1995, average protection facing developing country agricultural exports was 16.4 percent, over twice the average rate
affecting their exports of manufactures. For their exports to industrial countries

alone, the disparity was even more striking: barriers against their agricultural exports were on average nearly five times as high as those against their exports of manufactures.

These barriers help explain a large and continuing fall in the share of agriculture in the merchandise exports of developing countries, from nearly 50 percent in 1965 to just over 10 percent in 1995. Nevertheless, agriculture is still much more important to developing than to high-income countries: developing countries are net exporters of agricultural products, developing country consumers spend over 30 percent of their incomes on food, almost three times as much as rich-country consumers; and farm and food activities account for 16 percent of developing country GDP, triple their share in GDP of rich countries.

Between now and 2005, all outstanding Uruguay Round changes in market access will come fully into effect. Industrial tariff cuts are largely in place, but the removal of textile and clothing quotas still lies ahead. Agricultural access is not expected to improve. As a result, the authors expect nearly 45 percent of developing country goods exports in 2005 to go to other developing countries, and 80 percent of total exports to be manufactures.

The chapter analyzes an evenly-spread 40 percent cut in protection affecting agriculture, services, mining, and manufacturing. The agricultural reforms alone – a 40 percent cut in tariffs, export subsidies, and domestic subsidies – produces global gains in welfare of around $70 billion a year. Developed countries gain most, both in dollar terms and as a share of agricultural value added. Relative to GDP, however, gains are largest in regions such as South Asia (apart from India) and Southeast Asia (apart from Indonesia). The impact on trade volumes is mixed, because lower tariffs raise volumes, while subsidy cuts reduce them. If production subsidies are not cut, the global gains fall to $60 billion, but trade volumes grow relatively more, and net food importers in the Middle East, North Africa, South Asia, and China are relatively better off.

Despite its much larger aggregate size, a 40 percent liberalization of manufactures trade yields much the same as a similar liberalization of agriculture. Developing countries get the lion's share of this because both their exports and imports currently face far higher rates of protection then do those of high-income countries.

Inter-sectoral linkages mean that the liberalization of trade in manufactures and services strongly affects agricultural trade. When a country reduces its own protection of manufactures and services, this cuts intermediate input costs in food production, frees up labor and capital available for food production, and encourages consumers to shift from agricultural products to now-cheaper manufactures and services. This outcome, which equates to an increase in the food balance, is likely to be the dominant force in high-income countries. As partners reduce their agricultural protection, the opposite occurs. Better access to other countries' markets for manufactures and services draws resources into those sectors, with food production affected by higher-priced intermediates, more costly labor and capital, and consumers substituting food products for manufactures and services. In this case, the outcome is a deterioration in the food balance, which is characteristic of developing countries in East and Southeast Asia, including China.

Overall, the scenario of across-the-board multilateral liberalization suggests increases in the food trade balances of most developing countries, but not of India, China, and the Middle East/North Africa. It also produces a big deterioration in the food trade balances of heavily protected Western Europe and Japan.

*Economy-wide effects of agricultural trade liberalization*

Since the Krueger, Schiff, and Valdés (1988) (hereafter, KSV) study of the early 1990s, developing countries world-wide have implemented significant trade liberalization and macroeconomic policy reforms. In chapter 12 Dean A. DeRosa asks whether this has eliminated the indirect bias against agriculture that KSV identified. If an appreciable bias against agriculture remains, then WTO negotiations limited to agricultural trade liberalization alone will prove substantially less beneficial than broader multilateral negotiations to liberalize trade in industrial goods and services as well.

Direct protection of agriculture, particularly that enforced through NTBs, declined remarkably in developing countries during the 1990s. This development may have contributed significantly to the higher growth in *per capita* output of agricultural goods in developing countries during the period. Nonetheless, protection remains high in many developing countries. Similarly, although economy-wide discrimination against agriculture is less today than in the KSV study, it remains appreciable and continues to dominate the impacts of sector-specific protection for agriculture in developing countries. Thus a WTO round aiming to liberalize world trade on a multilateral and multisectoral basis offers developing countries the greatest potential for improving domestic price incentives for efficient and internationally competitive agriculture. The economic welfare of consumers is greatest with the liberalization of trade in all goods, not just agriculture alone.

DeRosa finds that agriculture contributes very significantly to output, exports, and employment in developing countries. Thus, the expansion of efficient and internationally competitive agriculture in these countries would enhance rural development, macroeconomic growth, foreign exchange earnings, and economic welfare. He argues that abundant opportunities exist for increases in both North–South and South–South trade. All told, therefore, the returns to reducing both the direct and indirect biases against agriculture are high.

*Liberalizing sugar*

Chapter 13 asks what would happen if the world sugar market were liberalized. Brent Borrell and David Pearce find that developed countries' protection of sugar market comes at great cost, not only to themselves, but also to those developing countries with the potential to expand sugar exports. Although developed country protection lowers world prices for some developing country sugar importers, their gains are small relative to the losses that protection imposes on exporters.

Change will occur only when individual countries unilaterally decide to revamp their policies. Nonetheless, the multilateral process can help to alter the political balance in favour of liberalization in several ways: by bringing publicity and transparency to the arguments for liberalization and informing communities about what they stand to gain; by offering lower adjustment costs than unilateral liberalization because the higher world prices induced by multilateral liberalization help to offset the effects of lower local protection; and because applying an economy-wide framework to trade liberalization highlights broad cross-sectoral gains over narrower concerns.

Borrell and Pearce conclude that multilateral liberalization would raise world sugar prices considerably. Producers in many countries with only light levels of protection would see little negative effect, and might even gain as world price rises offset falls in local protection. In the United States, the price of sugar would fall by only 25 percent under multilateral liberalization. Proponents of liberalizing sugar need to emphasize these facts during the trade talks, the authors argue.

*Bananas: trade as aid?*

The world banana market is dominated by one large and obvious trade distortion: the import restrictions imposed by the European Union. EU banana policy costs consumers about $2 billion per year and delivers only $0.15 billion in aid to the banana growers it is designed to help. The remaining $1.85 billion is collected by others in the supply chain, who fight hard to protect the policy. In chapter 14 Brent Borrell discusses EU banana policy and its several recent revisions. He shows that even in 1990, the then EU policy cost consumers $576 million a year by paying preferred suppliers double the world price for bananas. The cost to consumers of excessive marketing margins in import-restricted markets (compared with the costs to consumers in free-trade Germany) was $917 million a year, and tariff revenue collected on imports cost consumers an extra $112 million a year. The $576 million that consumers paid to preferred suppliers was worth just $302 million a year to those suppliers, because they devoted scarce and expensive resources to growing more bananas in order to qualify for more aid. Finally, the high EU consumer prices lowered EU consumption, yielding a lower world price and lower exports for efficient Latin American exporters. These penalties together cost the Latin exporters $98 million a year.

Borrell then discusses the various reforms proposed for banana policy up to 1999, and finds that none of them satisfactorily addresses the joint problems of economic efficiency and equity. He discusses the important role of the WTO in making challenges to unfair policies feasible and in raising their prominence and transparency.

Banana is only one commodity, of course, and trade is modest compared with that in many other commodities. However, the product is important to many developing country exporters, and it is the most traded fruit. More importantly, the fact that EU trade policy can become so disruptive even after a WTO dispute means that bananas cast an important light on the need for rule making and the reform of the dispute settlement procedure (DSP) in the new round.

## Part IV    "New" issues and the developing countries

Part IV, the final part of the book, considers "new" issues – the so-called "new" issues of the URAA such as SPS, on which we include two further chapters, and issues that are new to the current round such as state-trading and the environment. The focus throughout is on developing countries' positions and interests in these areas.

### Sanitary and phytosanitary barriers

In chapter 15, Donna Roberts, David Orden, and Timothy Josling examine recent evidence that developing countries are accepting and implementing the SPS Agreement by modifying their domestic SPS measures. They also argue that WTO dispute settlement decisions are producing consistent policy leadership, although limited progress has occurred on the equivalence and the harmonization of standards.

Developing countries have reaped benefits as the SPS Agreement has opened new markets. However, new international rules require more public and private investment to meet compliance standards. Agricultural producers have to be innovative and competitive to seize the new opportunities that have been provided, and domestic regulators must provide the public infrastructure to assist in the production of exportable products.

Achieving further benefits from the SPS Agreement for developing countries will also depend on WTO members taking additional steps to discipline their SPS measures, and on whether developing countries can marshal the resources needed to capitalize on the new trade opportunities that these disciplines create. Consumers in developing countries may also benefit from international disciplines on SPS trade barriers if their own regulatory authorities are using such barriers inappropriately.

Chapter 16 presents the results of a detailed survey on the SPS Agreement by Spencer Henson, Rupert Loader, Alan Swinbank, and Maury Bredahl. In contrast to chapter 15, their evidence suggests that developing countries have not, in fact, actively participated in the SPS Agreement. The failure of developing countries to participate even in SPS Committee meetings suggests that the workings of the Agreement will tend to be driven by the priorities of developed countries, and raises serious concerns about the ability of developing countries to benefit at all from the Agreement.

The case studies presented suggest that developing countries face a number of constraints on their ability to respond to key elements of the Agreement, including notifying others of new SPS measures, assessing risks, developing and implementing international standards, demonstrating equivalency, and settling disputes. Their respondents judged that the most significant constraint was insufficient ability to assess the implications of developed countries' SPS notifications. Respondents also cited their inability to participate effectively in dispute settlement procedures and to show that domestic SPS measures are equivalent to developed country requirements. These constraints reflect the relatively poor scientific and technical infrastructure in many developing countries.

While the international community has attempted to overcome the trade-distorting effects of SPS measures by adopting the SPS Agreement, this study suggests that such measures continue to be a major barrier, especially to the EU market. Mostly this reflects poor access to compliance resources, including scientific and technical expertise, information, and funding. The global community clearly needs to finds ways to include developing countries more fully in the workings of the Agreement.

*State-trading in agriculture*

Effective WTO negotiations on agriculture must cover the operations of state-trading enterprises (STEs) as well as the private sector. Improved market access and the elimination of trade-distorting support are the *sine qua non* of WTO negotiations on agriculture. However, William M. Miner argues in chapter 17 that the negotiations must also deal with the potential impact of STEs on agricultural imports, exports, and market competition, just as much as with the policy instruments applied to the private sector.

Many developing countries maintain state entities to handle domestic procurement, imports, and exports. STEs are bound by the rules and commitments of the URAA, and are required to act in a commercial manner; they are also specifically covered by GATT Article XVII on state-trading. However, information on their operations and their impact on agricultural trade is limited.

There are concerns and allegations that they are being used to circumvent the rules on import access, export competition and unfair trade practices. Certainly, they have the potential to do so.

Among the ways of addressing these issues, Miner identifies:

- Prohibiting the use of STEs for trading purposes, although for several reasons, governments are unlikely to accept this.
- The extension of current WTO work on GATT Article XVII, to establish clearer and more effective rules, including a requirement that STEs fully disclose their trading activities. However, this could place them at disadvantage against private traders, particularly multinational enterprises.
- Agreement by governments to force STEs to compete, at least for a portion of trade. This would respond to the greatest concern, the abuse by STEs of monopoly power. However, not all governments have competition and anti-trust laws, and some may not be ready to expose their STEs to direct competition. While these issues could be tackled by developing multilateral rules on competition policies and trade, discussions on trade and competition are at an early stage, and international agreement would take considerable time.

Given the problems inherent in the Article XVII and competition law approaches, Miner argues that the best way of handling the STE problem may be to negotiate specific commitments in an enhanced Agreement on Agriculture. The new disciplines should govern the import and export activities of STEs, their competitive behavior, and their involvement in the administration of the trade regime in areas such as TRQs, minimum access arrangements, domestic marketing, export pricing, export credits, and other competitive practices. To make the disciplines effective and enforceable, greater transparency and monitoring of STE activities, and the actions of their competitors, will be needed.

These policy options would require changes in the operations of the STEs used by many developing countries for much of their trade in food and agricultural products and hence may well be resisted. However, the Agreement on Agriculture provides for the special treatment of developing countries to help them achieve food security objectives, and, Miner argues, similar flexibility may be negotiable for the activities of their STEs where convincing evidence exists that countries face serious constrains.

## The environment

Chapter 18 by John Whalley considers the implications for developing countries of topics such as the multifunctionality of agriculture, and linking subsidies and tariffs to ecological preservation. It begins with a general discussion of the links between agricultural trade and the environment and goes on to argue that a central problem is that such links are unclear. Research provides relatively little quantitative or qualitative information on the externalities associated with agriculture in either developed or developing countries. Whether liberalizing trade intensifies or alleviates such externalities is difficult to conclude in general or even in specific cases. Whalley argues that while developing countries face important environmental dilemmas, WTO negotiations on agriculture are not the best forum in which to seek remedies.

*Intellectual property rights*

Three kinds of intellectual property rights (IPRs) are particularly important for developing country agriculture – patents, plant breeders' rights and geographical indications. For all three, the Agreement on Trade-Related Aspects of Intellectual Property Rights (TRIPS) lays down rights and obligations for WTO member countries' business practices. In chapter 19 Jayashree Watal finds considerable uncertainty about the economic effects of strengthened protection of IPRs in developing countries, not least, she says, because research has provided so little evidence on the costs and benefits of the options still open to these countries under the TRIPS Agreement. Issues of ethics, equity, efficiency, public interest and the environment are all raised by IPRs for agricultural goods. Many of them revolve around the TRIPS provision on patenting biological inventions (Article 27.3(b)). This allows WTO members to exclude plants and animals, and biological processes for their production, from being patentable, provided that new plant varieties can be protected by other means if patenting is not allowed. Developed and developing countries have interpreted these requirements differently in their laws and practice, and the provision is now under review. Developing countries would like its scope to be clearly limited, and to have their concerns on biodiversity and equity expressed in the text.

Meanwhile, agricultural biotechnology is advancing rapidly in developed countries, mostly with patent protection. Among developing countries, Argentina and China are already planting transgenic crops. Biotechnology offers potential benefits through improved agricultural productivity and by reducing malnutrition and disease. However, some fear that with IPRs in the hands of a few multinational companies, these new technologies could be priced beyond the reach of developing countries. The traditional role of government agencies in agricultural research and seed distribution may also be threatened. On the protection of geographical indications, developing country interests diverge. Some Latin American countries want protection eased, while others like Cuba and Venezuela join with Egypt, India, Nigeria, and Turkey in wanting the higher levels of protection given by TRIPS to wines and spirits to be extended to other products.

Amendments to the TRIPS Agreement on these issues seem very unlikely at present. Meanwhile, developing countries will probably adapt to the TRIPS' requirements in different ways. They should set their policies on IPRs affecting agriculture in the light of their levels of technological development, the likely benefits of promoting proprietary products in their domestic and export markets, and public opinion.

## Genetically modified foods

In chapter 20, Chantal Pohl Nielsen, Karen Thierfelder, and Sherman Robinson make a preliminary quantitative assessment of the impact that consumers' changing attitude toward genetic modification (GM) might have on world trade patterns, with emphasis on the developing countries. The analytical framework used is an empirical global general equilibrium model, in which the two primary GM crops, soybeans and maize, are specified as either GM or non-GM. This GM/non-GM split is maintained throughout the entire processing chain: GM livestock and GM food processing industries use only GM intermediate inputs; likewise non-GM livestock and non-GM food processing industries use only non-GM intermediate inputs.

Different perceptions concerning the benefits and risks of GM foods are already leading to the segregation of soybean and maize markets and production systems. The analysis shows that such a segregation of markets may have substantial impacts on trade patterns.

The effects of a factor productivity increase in the GM sectors are then investigated in an environment where there are increasingly strong preferences *against* GM crops in Western Europe and High-Income Asia. An important dilemma for developing countries is whether genetic engineering in agriculture is an opportunity or a misfortune. To the extent that GM crops are profitable, the results suggest that there are gains to be made. Furthermore the antipathy towards GM crops in Western Europe and High-Income Asia does not affect these gains because markets adjust, and trade flows of GM and non-GM products are redirected according to preferences in the different markets.

The underlying assumption of this finding is that production and marketing systems are capable of separating GM and non-GM crops. As consumer attitudes accentuate the differentiation between GM and non-GM products, developing countries face complex questions in determining the right output combinations for national income growth.

## Multifunctionality

The final chapter, chapter 21, develops a general equilibrium (GE) framework to determine the optimal set of policies to address the externalities usually listed under the heading of "multifunctionality," and relates these policies to international trade. Jeffrey M. Peterson, Richard N. Boisvert, and Harry de Gorter analyze the relationship between these jointly optimal environmental policies and free trade. They describe a model economy and derive optimal environmental policies first for a closed economy, then for a small open economy, and, finally, a large open economy. To illustrate the theoretical relationships and explore their potential quantitative impacts, they simulate an empirical version of the model calibrated to the US agricultural sector.

The chapter determines optimal policy rules when agricultural production generates both landscape amenities and pollution from chemical inputs. The optimal subsidy on land and the tax on non-land inputs both depend on the size of both externalities; thus a change in the social value of either land amenities or pollution implies a change in both policies. It is shown that independently determined policies are likely to work at cross-purposes, since a single policy directed at one externality leads to an adverse change in the other. One important implication of this is that an optimal subsidy on agricultural land does not simply equal the net value of land amenities.

In the international arena, small economies operating independently will choose the policies that maximize world welfare, but large economies have an incentive to set policies at non-internalizing levels to exploit terms of trade effects. In particular, large importers will choose policies that increase agricultural factor inputs beyond globally efficient allocations, while large exporters will prefer to restrict factor allocations (and hence agricultural production) in order to raise international prices. For large economies, production policies that are ostensibly justified on environmental grounds can become instruments to distort international prices. Indeed, based on empirical policy simulations, the authors estimate that the United States alone could manipulate its domestic environmental policies to change world prices by about 9 percent.

Even for small countries with environmental concerns, there are additional policy goals such as supporting farm incomes or enhancing food security. Hence, in the WTO negotiations over environmental issues it may be impossible to determine whether so-called "environmental policies" are really vehicles to help achieve some other goal. The key to making domestic policies compatible with free trade lies in the types of policies used. The less that the policy instruments distort trade, the more autonomy nations can have in selecting and executing domestic policy goals.

### Reference

Krueger, A. O., M. Schiff, and A. Valdés, 1988. "Agricultural Incentives in Developing Countries: Measuring the Effect of Sectoral and Economy-Wide Policies," *The World Bank Economic Review*, 2, 255–71

# Part I
# Experience and lessons from the implementation of WTO agreements

# 3 The Uruguay Round Agreement on Agriculture in practice: how open are the OECD markets?

*Dimitris Diakosavvas*

## Introduction

Prior to the WTO the rules that applied to agricultural primary products deviated from the general GATT rules.[1] This resulted in a proliferation of impediments to agricultural trade by means of import bans, quotas setting the maximum level of imports, variable import levies, minimum import prices, and non-tariff measures maintained by state trading enterprises. The URAA has fundamentally changed the way agriculture was treated under the GATT. It imposed specific commitments to reduce support and protection in the areas of domestic support, market access, and export competition. It also strengthened and made more operationally effective rules and disciplines in each of these areas, including export prohibitions and restrictions. It is being implemented over a six-year period (ten years for developing countries) and began in 1995.

The market access provisions established disciplines on trade distorting practices while maintaining historical trade volumes and creating increased access opportunities in highly protected markets.[2] Most importantly, non-tariff barriers (NTBs), such as quantitative import restrictions, variable import levies, and discretionary import licensing, were banned. These barriers were converted to ordinary tariffs (tariffication). Existing and new tariffs were bound and subject to reduction. Developed countries agreed to reduce agricultural tariffs from their base period rates by a total of 36 percent, on a simple average basis, with a minimum cut of 15 percent for each tariff. Current access commitments were put in place to ensure that there was no erosion in market access as a result of the URAA. At the same time, countries also had to provide a minimum level of import opportunities for products previously protected by NTBs. This was accomplished by creating tariff-rate quotas (TRQs), which generally impose a relatively low tariff (in-quota) on imports up to a specified level, with imports above that level subject to a higher tariff (over-quota).

The domestic support provisions are regarded as one of the major breakthroughs of the URAA insofar as they explicitly recognize the direct link between domestic agricultural policies and international trade. A key aspect of the provisions was the distinction between domestic policies which were deemed (i) not to, or to only a minimum extent, distort trade ("green box"); and (ii) all other policies, that is, those that distort trade ("amber box," "blue box" measures and some other exempt measures). The provisions require countries to reduce agricultural support levels arising from those domestic policies, which most unequivocally have the largest effects on production, such as administered prices, input subsidies, and producer payments that are not accompanied by limitations on production. Domestic support reductions are implemented through a commitment to reduce the Total Aggregate Measurement of Support (AMS) for each country. The AMS is an indicator of the support associated with policies considered to have the greatest potential to affect production and trade. It has product-specific and non-product-specific elements, but the commitments themselves are not product-specific but sector-wide applying to the Total AMS. Policies deemed to have no or minimal effect on production and trade, are exempt from reduction commitments ("green box"). As a result of the Blair House Accord (1992), production-linked support related to production-limiting policies is exempt from the disciplines if such payments satisfy certain criteria ("blue box").[3] However, the Due Restraint provision or "peace clause" renders actionable any increase in support, as measured by AMS, or arising from the "production-limiting programs," beyond the levels decided during the 1992 marketing year. Finally, support that is below a certain threshold is not required to be included in the calculation of reduction commitments. This is usually referred to as the *de minimis* provision. A WTO Member shall not provide support in favor of domestic producers in excess of its commitments. Members who do not have a Total AMS commitment shall not provide support to agricultural producers in excess of *de minimis* levels. Binding commitments on the level of support provided through domestic measures are an essential complement to the disciplines on market access and export subsidies.

The export subsidies discipline is considered to be an important accomplishment of the agreement and the one that was expected to have the most immediate trade implications. Not surprisingly, acceptance of a specific discipline on export subsidies was one of the most contentious issues, not only in the agricultural negotiations but in the Uruguay Round as a whole (Josling and Tangermann, 1999). Prior to the URAA, export subsidies were an important policy instrument in agricultural trade, particularly for trade in grains and dairy products. The URAA did not outlaw agricultural export subsidies, but limits were established on the volume of subsidized exports and on budgetary expenditure. Countries that employed export subsidies are committed to reduce the volume of subsidized exports by 21 percent, and the expenditure on subsidized exports by 36 percent. These reductions were to be made from the 1986–90 base period level over a six-year implementation period (a ten-year period for developing countries), on a product-specific basis. Moreover, export subsidies on products not subsidized in the base period are banned.

While it is generally agreed that the URAA provisions represent a significant step in the direction of trade liberalization, it is also recognized that their actual impact on agricultural policies and trade will depend on the limited extent of the reductions and on the way in which they are implemented. The implementation period for the reductions to be made under the URAA is now complete, at least for the developed countries, and a new round of multilateral negotiations on agriculture has already started as mandated by article 20 of the URAA. It is therefore pertinent to examine whether the URAA has been successful in liberalizing agricultural trade and to draw some lessons. An assessment of the implementation experience should provide valuable inputs to the new round of agricultural negotiations.

The next section presents an overall appraisal of trade developments. First, it presents *prima facie* evidence on external openness to agricultural trade by comparing various indicators for periods prior to and following the start of the implementation of the URAA ("the before and after" approach). Then it applies a cross-section and time-series analysis to investigate whether trade liberalization brought about by URAA has an impact on agricultural trade openness. The next section discusses the factors that weaken the effectiveness of the three URAA disciplines in bringing about a reduction in the level of production-related support and protection. The final section presents some concluding remarks.

## Overall appraisal of trade developments

Whether the URAA is successful in liberalizing trade in agricultural products depends on the expectations arising from the Agreement. Some analysts emphasize the new rules and disciplines established in the URAA, and point to their potential effect on future policy-making in world agriculture. Others argue that the quantitative commitments agreed under the URAA were so limited that they did not require major policy changes, and hence that the URAA did not result in an actual liberalization of world agricultural trade.

The trade liberalization impacts resulting from the URAA should be to expand market access and to reduce trade, consumption, and production distortions. The ultimate effects should be an increase in world import demand for agricultural products, and higher and more stable world market prices than otherwise would be the case.

However, identification of the combined effects of the three pillars and the separation of their effects from the influences of other factors are difficult tasks. The complexity of the URAA package, the linkages between the policy instruments that are subject to reform, and the options for their implementation by countries, make quantification difficult, irrespective of the analytical tools used. Statistical evaluation of the trade impacts of the URAA is fraught with difficulties. Three stand out. First what is the counterfactual? Should one just assume a continuation of pre-existing policies and performance in the country concerned? In practical terms, this may be all one can do, although it has an important shortcoming: how does one disentangle the effects of trade reforms from other policy shifts and exogenous shocks, such as technological change and the business cycle? Second, some pre-existing policies were likely to have been unsustainable and would have changed irrespective of the URAA. Third, supply responses and the process of adjustment will differ from economy to economy: how long should one wait before conducting an assessment? The implementation of the URAA is still under way and the effects of the policies implemented are not instantaneous. Growth in agricultural trade will respond to liberalization with a time lag, which in itself will depend on a number of factors, including the way policies are being implemented, the extent of pre-existing distortions, and the flexibility of markets. With these caveats in mind, a preliminary appraisal of the evolution of a number of trade-performance indicators is attempted. Two approaches are used. They are the so-called simple "before and after" approach and a more sophisticated econometric model which takes into account some of the statistical pitfalls of the "before and after" approach.

*The "before and after" approach*

The basic idea is to provide some empirical evidence on external openness to agricultural trade by comparing trade performance indicators for periods prior to and following the start of the implementation of the URAA.[4] This is a difficult task that entails the choice of appropriate benchmarks as well as trade-performance indicators. Both of these choices involve practical problems, and the results should be treated with caution and only tentative conclusions can be drawn. At the outset, it should be emphasized that it is vital not to equate liberalization with openness as trade openness is a function of many factors, such as technological change, reductions in transportation, and communication costs, not just liberalization. Clearly there are no straightforward indicators of liberalization and trade openness and a number of multiple indicators and criteria to identify liberalization are used. Broadly speaking, in the literature, two types of measures of openness (trade barriers) have been used: incidence and outcome-based measures (Baldwin, 1989; Harrison, 1996; Pritchett, 1996).[5] Each of these has its weaknesses and strengths. Incidence-based measures are direct indicators of trade policy, such as the level or dispersion of tariffs. Although these indicators are good proxies for inferring the trade policy of a country, they still have two shortcomings: first, they are imperfect because they cannot capture other types of intervention such as NTBs; second, consistent data on tariffs are not available for many countries and for a sufficient number of years. Outcome-based measures are widely used because they implicitly cover all the sources of distortion and are based on data that are more readily available. Outcome measures can be either price-based, such as rates of protection or PSEs, or trade flows-based. An alternative aggregate measure of tariffs is the Trade Restrictiveness Index (TRI) developed by Anderson and Neary (1996). The TRI measures countries' overall tariff levels using their underlying trade shares in production and consumption and their elasticities of factor substitution and import substitution as weights. This approach is arguably the most theoretically defensible of any single measure as it is the underlying consumer and producer behavior of a country that determines the trade effects of tariffs. However, empirical application of TRI is data-demanding and the results are sensitive to what assumptions are made.[6]

For the purpose of this chapter, the following commonly used indicators were calculated:

• Trade openness calculated as the average share of agricultural imports plus exports in agricultural GDP
• Import penetration ratios defined as the ratio of agricultural imports to consumption
• Export performance calculated as the ratio of agricultural exports to production
• Net trade performance defined as the ratio of exports minus imports to exports plus imports
• Percentage producer support estimate (percentage PSE) and percentage consumer support estimate (percentage CSE) as measures of the cost of agricultural support and implicit tax on consumers due to agricultural policy
• Producer nominal protection coefficients (PNPC) and Consumer Nominal Protection Coefficients (CNPC) as measures of price distortions.

Calculations were initially made either from 1986 to 2000, and in some instances to 2006, but to limit the effects of year-to-year fluctuations more emphasis is given to results based on a six-year-time span: 1989–94 and 1995–2000.

*Trade openness*

The development of world merchandise exports relative to world production could provide some indication as to whether there has been an increase in market openness for world merchandise trade. As portrayed in figure 3.1, the share of trade in the output of world manufactures and agriculture has increased since

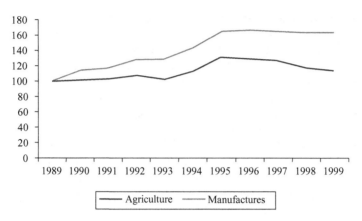

Figure 3.1 World export performance, 1989–1999

the URAA, although agricultural trade expanded less rapidly (almost half). The growth of both manufacture and agricultural exports from OECD countries decelerated during the 1995–9 period as compared to the first half of the 1990s. In the first year of the implementation of the URAA, world agriculture trade growth was strong, but actually declined in 1996 and 1997 as compared to the previous year.

The various indicators of trade openness that were calculated for the OECD area suggest wide variation across countries and commodities. Overall, the import penetration rate was stable or increased for many commodities in the post-URAA era. However, absolute comparisons can be misleading. The significance of the difference between the before-URAA and post-URAA periods was determined through use of parametric tests (i.e. the paired sample $t$-test and the signs test) and non-parametric tests (i.e. the Wilcoxon–Mann–Whitney (WMW) ranked-sums tests, Van der Waerden Scores and the Kolmogorov–Smirnov two-sample test). For clarity of presentation, only the significance levels reported in table 3.1 are based on the WMW procedure. For the URAA implementation period (1995–2000) the difference with the period five years prior to the URAA (1989–94) is statistically significant in only a very few cases. There are more significant results for the 2001–6 period, particularly for livestock products. In a number of cases, the indicators declined in the post-URAA era. The decline was statistically significant for import penetration for refined sugar (2001–6), export performance for wheat (2001–6), and net trade performance for butter and cheese (2001–6). Overall, these results provide support to the argument that for a number of agricultural commodities in the OECD area, market openness in the post-URAA era is not discernibly different from that of the pre-URAA era.

Table 3.1 *Relative comparisons of trade performance indicators OECD countries, 1989–2006*

| | Import penetration | | | | | Export performance | | | | |
| | 1989–94 (1) | 1995–2000 (2) | 2001–6 (3) | Difference (2)–(1) | (3)–(1) | 1989–94 (1) | 1995–2000 (2) | 2001–6 (3) | Difference (2)–(1) | (3)–(1) |
|---|---|---|---|---|---|---|---|---|---|---|
| Wheat | 0.10 | 0.11 | 0.11 | 0.01** | 0.01* | 0.38 | 0.34 | 0.35 | −0.04** | −0.03* |
| Coarse grains | 0.11 | 0.11 | 0.11 | 0.00 | 0.00 | 0.18 | 0.17 | 0.18 | −0.01 | 0.00 |
| Oilseeds | 0.31 | 0.32 | 0.31 | 0.01 | 0.00 | 0.28 | 0.30 | 0.31 | 0.03* | 0.03** |
| Rice | 0.12 | 0.14 | 0.13 | 0.02 | 0.01 | 0.18 | 0.21 | 0.21 | 0.03** | 0.03** |
| Refined sugar | 0.25 | 0.23 | 0.23 | −0.02 | −0.02*** | 0.27 | 0.28 | 0.29 | 0.00 | 0.01 |
| Butter | 0.05 | 0.05 | 0.06 | 0.01 | 0.02*** | 0.19 | 0.18 | 0.20 | −0.01 | 0.01 |
| Cheese | 0.05 | 0.05 | 0.06 | 0.01 | 0.01*** | 0.08 | 0.09 | 0.09 | 0.01 | 0.01*** |
| SMP | 0.12 | 0.13 | 0.13 | 0.01 | 0.01 | 0.31 | 0.35 | 0.34 | 0.04 | 0.03 |
| WMP | 0.10 | 0.08 | 0.06 | −0.02 | −0.04 | 0.56 | 0.60 | 0.60 | 0.04 | 0.04*** |
| Beef | 0.13 | 0.14 | 0.17 | 0.01 | 0.04*** | 0.16 | 0.18 | 0.20 | 0.02 | 0.04*** |
| Pigmeat | 0.04 | 0.05 | 0.06 | 0.01 | 0.02*** | 0.04 | 0.07 | 0.08 | 0.03 | 0.03*** |
| Poultrymeat | 0.03 | 0.04 | 0.04 | 0.01 | 0.01*** | 0.06 | 0.12 | 0.12 | 0.06 | 0.05*** |
| Sheepmeat | 0.18 | 0.18 | 0.20 | 0.01 | 0.02*** | 0.30 | 0.30 | 0.31 | 0.01 | 0.01** |

*(cont.)*

Table 3.1 (*cont.*)

| | Net trade performance | | | | | Trade openness | | | | |
|---|---|---|---|---|---|---|---|---|---|---|
| | 1989–94 (1) | 1995–2000 (2) | 2001–6 (3) | Difference (2)–(1) | (3)–(1) | 1989–94 (1) | 1995–2000 (2) | 2001–6 (3) | Difference (2)–(1) | (3)–(1) |
| Wheat | 0.69 | 0.60 | 0.64 | −0.09** | −0.05 | 0.45 | 0.42 | 0.43 | −0.03** | −0.02* |
| Coarse grains | 0.27 | 0.25 | 0.29 | −0.02 | 0.02 | 0.29 | 0.28 | 0.29 | −0.01 | 0.00 |
| Oilseeds | −0.08 | −0.04 | −0.02 | 0.04 | 0.06*** | 0.60 | 0.63 | 0.62 | 0.04 | 0.02 |
| Rice | 0.20 | 0.12 | 0.08 | −0.08 | −0.12 | 0.31 | 0.38 | 0.39 | 0.07* | 0.08*** |
| Refined sugar | 0.05 | 0.13 | 0.17 | 0.07 | 0.11* | 0.52 | 0.49 | 0.49 | −0.03 | −0.03 |
| Butter | 0.66 | 0.60 | 0.59 | −0.06 | −0.08*** | 0.23 | 0.22 | 0.26 | −0.01 | 0.03** |
| Cheese | 0.28 | 0.26 | 0.23 | −0.02 | −0.05*** | 0.12 | 0.14 | 0.14 | 0.01*** | 0.02*** |
| SMP | 0.53 | 0.57 | 0.55 | 0.04 | 0.02 | 0.41 | 0.45 | 0.44 | 0.04 | 0.03 |
| WMP | 0.84 | 0.90 | 0.92 | 0.06 | 0.08* | 0.61 | 0.63 | 0.63 | 0.02 | 0.02 |
| Beef | 0.12 | 0.13 | 0.12 | 0.01 | 0.00 | 0.29 | 0.32 | 0.36 | 0.03*** | 0.07*** |
| Pigmeat | 0.02 | 0.15 | 0.16 | 0.13*** | 0.14*** | 0.09 | 0.13 | 0.13 | 0.04*** | 0.05*** |
| Poultrymeat | 0.32 | 0.49 | 0.52 | 0.17*** | 0.19*** | 0.10 | 0.16 | 0.16 | 0.06*** | 0.06*** |
| Sheepmeat | 0.34 | 0.33 | 0.30 | −0.01 | −0.04* | 0.45 | 0.46 | 0.48 | 0.01 | 0.03*** |

*Notes:* The null hypothesis is that the median of the variable for the post-URAA period is the same as the median for the pre-URAA (1989–94) period. This hypothesis is tested using a Wilcoxon–Mann–Whitney rank test.

*** Indicates that difference between medians is significant at a 1% two-tail level.

** Indicates that difference between medians is significant at a 5% two-tail level.

* Indicates that difference between medians is significant at a 10% two-tail level.

*Evolution of agricultural support and protection levels*

The average total support estimates for the agricultural sector as a whole (TSE) for the OECD area amounted to US$330.6 billion in 1998–2000, accounting for 1.3 percent of GDP (percent TSE), compared with a nominal US$271.2 billion or 2.2 percent of GDP in 1986–8 (OECD, 2001b). For the same period, support to producers (PSE) was US$250 billion and US$214.8 billion correspondingly. For the OECD as a whole, support to producers as a share of total farm receipts (percent PSE) has exhibited a slow downward trend since 1986–8; it was estimated at 33 percent in 1995–2000, down from 37 percent in 1989–94 and 39 percent in 1986–8 (table 3.2, appendix table 3A.1, p. 64).

Table 3.2 also displays the evolution of producer and consumer nominal protection coefficients (NPCs) by commodity. The producer NPC is an indicator of the nominal rate of protection for producers, measuring the ratio between the average price received by producers, including payments per ton of output and the border price (both measured at farm gate level). The consumer NPC is an indicator of the nominal rate of protection for consumers, measuring the ratio between the average price paid by consumers and the border price (both also measured at farm gate level). The results suggest that although nominal protection has decreased in the OECD area as a whole since the late 1980s, domestic prices are still much higher than world prices. The producer NPC, on average, declined for all commodities, except sugar and pigmeat, between 1995–2000 and 1989–94. For the same period, the consumer NPC did not decline for rice, sugar, beef, and pigmeat. Moreover, the decline in producer NPC for rice and in consumer NPC for eggs is statistically insignificant. Thus, the level of the NPCs remains very high for a number of agricultural products, particularly in the case of rice, sugar, and milk, which over the 1995–2000 implementation period exhibit NPCs higher than 100 percent. Domestic prices are, on average, around 40 percent higher than world prices over the 1995–2000 period across the standard PSE commodities.

These results demonstrate that agricultural protection rates in OECD countries are still high. Moreover, although the composition of support has gradually shifted from measures that support higher farm prices financed by consumers to payments financed by taxpayers, market price support and output-related payments still dominate (appendix table 3A.2, p. 67). In 2000, the last year of the completion the URAA implementation for developed countries, market price support and payments based on output represented 72 percent of overall support to OECD producers. These forms of support continue to insulate farmers from world markets and to impose a burden on consumers. They also have the greatest impact on production and trade, for both OECD and non-OECD countries.

Table 3.2 *Relative comparisons of support indicators, OECD countries, 1986–2000*

| | %PSE | | | | Producer NPC | | | |
|---|---|---|---|---|---|---|---|---|
| | 1986–8 (1) | 1990–4 (2) | 1995–2000 (3) | Difference (3)–(2) | 1986–8 (1) | 1990–4 (2) | 1995–2000 (3) | Difference (3)–(2) |
| Wheat | 47.8 | 39.2 | 34.4 | −4.7 | 1.7 | 1.4 | 1.1 | −0.3*** |
| Maize | 40.0 | 27.4 | 23.8 | −3.6 | 1.3 | 1.2 | 1.1 | −0.1** |
| Other grains | 51.2 | 46.3 | 42.9 | −3.4 | 2.0 | 1.7 | 1.2 | −0.4*** |
| Oilseeds | 26.3 | 22.3 | 16.0 | −6.3 | 1.3 | 1.2 | 1.1 | −0.1 |
| Rice | 80.7 | 79.2 | 77.6 | −1.6 | 4.9 | 4.6 | 4.4 | −0.2 |
| Refined sugar | 54.0 | 47.7 | 46.6 | −1.0 | 2.4 | 1.9 | 2.0 | 0.1 |
| Milk | 57.5 | 55.9 | 49.5 | −6.4** | 2.7 | 2.3 | 1.9 | −0.4** |
| Beef | 32.9 | 32.3 | 34.8 | 2.5 | 1.4 | 1.4 | 1.3 | −0.1 |
| Sheepmeat | 55.0 | 53.8 | 44.7 | −9.1** | 1.9 | 1.6 | 1.2 | −0.4** |
| Pigmeat | 13.9 | 17.8 | 19.7 | 1.9 | 1.2 | 1.2 | 1.2 | 0.0 |
| Poultrymeat | 16.2 | 15.0 | 12.7 | −2.3* | 1.3 | 1.2 | 1.1 | −0.1** |
| Eggs | 15.1 | 14.0 | 11.3 | −2.7 | 1.2 | 1.2 | 1.1 | −0.1** |
| All PSE commodities | 38.7 | 36.6 | 32.7 | −3.9** | 1.6 | 1.5 | 1.4 | −0.1** |

|  | %CSE | | | | Consumer NPC | | | |
| --- | --- | --- | --- | --- | --- | --- | --- | --- |
|  | 1986–88 (1) | 1990–94 (2) | 1995–2000 (3) | Difference (3)–(2) | 1986–88 (1) | 1990–94 (2) | 1995–2000 (3) | Difference (3)–(2) |
| Wheat | −30.0 | −21.4 | −8.6 | 12.8** | 1.8 | 1.5 | 1.2 | −0.3*** |
| Maize | 1.1 | 2.0 | 8.5 | 6.6*** | 1.2 | 1.2 | 1.1 | −0.1*** |
| Other grains | −13.0 | −10.6 | −5.0 | 5.6*** | 1.9 | 1.6 | 1.2 | −0.4*** |
| Oilseeds | −3.3 | −3.1 | −1.4 | 1.7*** | 1.1 | 1.0 | 1.0 | 0.0*** |
| Rice | −77.1 | −74.8 | −77.3 | −2.5 | 4.5 | 4.1 | 4.6 | 0.5 |
| Refined sugar | −58.5 | −48.4 | −50.1 | −1.7 | 2.4 | 2.0 | 2.1 | 0.1 |
| Milk | −56.8 | −52.4 | −44.4 | 8.0** | 2.7 | 2.3 | 1.9 | −0.4** |
| Beef | −27.8 | −25.1 | −22.4 | 2.7 | 1.4 | 1.4 | 1.3 | 0.0 |
| Sheepmeat | −52.7 | −40.9 | −22.6 | 18.3** | 2.1 | 1.8 | 1.3 | −0.4** |
| Pigmeat | −16.0 | −18.0 | −16.5 | 1.5 | 1.2 | 1.3 | 1.3 | 0.0 |
| Poultrymeat | −17.9 | −14.4 | −8.2 | 6.1** | 1.3 | 1.2 | 1.1 | −0.1** |
| Eggs | −15.4 | −13.4 | −8.7 | 4.7*** | 1.2 | 1.2 | 1.1 | −0.1** |
| All PSE commodities | −33.0 | −30.3 | −25.5 | 4.8** | 1.6 | 1.5 | 1.4 | −0.1** |

*Notes:* The null hypothesis is that the median of the variable for the post-URAA period is the same as the median for the pre-URAA (1989–94) period. This hypothesis is tested using a Wilcoxon–Mann–Whitney rank test.
*** Indicates that difference between medians is significant at a 1% two-tail level.
** Indicates that difference between medians is significant at a 5% two-tail level.
* Indicates that difference between medians is significant at a 10% two-tail level.

*A cross-section and time-series analysis*

While easy to employ and seemingly objective, the problem with the "before and after" approach is that it is based on a strict *ceteris paribus* assumption that factors such as technological change, weather conditions, and business cycles do not change between the before-URAA period and the between-URAA or post-URAA periods. This means that before and after estimates of URAA effects will typically be: (i) biased, because this approach incorrectly attributes all of the changes in outcomes between the pre-URAA and URAA periods to URAA factors; (ii) unsystematic over time, because estimated URAA effects for a given year will often be dominated by specific non-URAA influences of that year. Thus, for example, if economic growth rises between the before- and post-URAA periods, one might erroneously conclude that the URAA performed well, and vice versa when economic growth falls. These shortcomings of the "before and after" approach make it a poor estimator of the "counterfactual", defined as the trade performance that would have prevailed in the absence of the URAA. The "before and after" approach is flawed as an estimator of the counterfactual because the situation prevailing before the URAA is not likely to be a good predictor of what would have happened in the absence of the URAA, given that non-URAA determinants can and do change from year to year. This is a non-trivial drawback because the counterfactual is perhaps the most appealing yardstick against which to assess URAA performance and the standard most widely employed in economics to define and measure the impact of government policies. However, the crux of the problem is that the counterfactual is not directly observable and must be estimated.

To deal with some of these deficiencies, a simple trade model was constructed. The modeling strategy adopted follows a pooling of the cross-section and time-series estimation approach where differences in both cross-country and intertemporal dimensions are captured. This approach is broader and incorporates the "before and after" approach as a special case. Following the work of Faini *et al.* (1991), Greenway, Morgan, and Wright (1998), and others, changes in trade performance indicators are postulated to depend on a vector of autonomous policy changes and on changes in the external environment.[7] Further, to capture the impact of URAA liberalization effect we introduce a dummy variable, which takes a value of zero for all pre-URAA years (1989–94) in a given country and a value of unity for all years thereafter (1995–2000). Thus, the optimal or equilibrium value of a trade indicator, $y_{it}^*$, is assumed to be a linear function of $\rho$ exogenous or independent variables, $X_{i,t}$, an intercept, $\alpha_{\iota\tau}$, the dummy variable and an error term:

$$y_{it}^* = \alpha_{\iota\tau} + \sum_{k=1}^{\rho} X_{i,t}' \beta_\iota + \gamma_{\iota\tau}(\text{DUMMY})_{i,t} + \varepsilon_{\iota\tau} t$$
$$= 1, \ldots N; \tau = 1 \ldots, T \tag{1}$$

where $N$ is the number of cross-sectional units and $T$ is the length of the time series for each cross-section.

It is also assumed that the trade-performance indicators follow a partial adjustment process. In particular, the observed adjustment in a trade indicator, $y_{it} - y_{i,t-1}$, is a fraction, $\lambda$, of the optimal or long-term adjustment, $y_{it}^* - y_{i,t-1}$

$$y_{it} - (y)_{i,t-1} = \lambda[(y)_{i,t}^* - (y)_{i,t-1}], \qquad 0 < \lambda < 1 \qquad (2)$$

After substitution, (2) becomes:

$$y_{it} = \lambda \alpha_{i\tau} + (1 - \lambda)(y)_{i,t-1} + \lambda \sum_{\kappa=1}^{\rho} X_{i,t-1} \beta_\kappa$$
$$+ \lambda \gamma (\text{DUMMY})_{i,t} + \lambda \varepsilon_{i,t} \qquad (3)$$

This specification has obvious intuitive appeal in that it models trade performance in a dynamic way and so captures not only the transitional effects of trade reform but also the longer-run impacts. The sample comprises all OECD countries (EU15 as one country). Two trade-performance indicators were employed: import penetration ratio (IP) and export performance ($XP$). The exogenous variables include population ($POP$), real GDP *per capita* ($GDPPC$), real effective exchange rate ($RER$), production ($Q$), world price ($PW$), consumer nominal protection coefficient ($CNPC$) for the case of import penetration specification, and producer nominal protection coefficient ($PNPC$) for the export-performance specification). The $RER$ index is an indicator of competitiveness that takes into account both export and import competitiveness. A fall indicates improvement in competitive position.[8] The $CNPC$ is defined as the ratio between the domestic price paid by consumer and the border price (both at farm gate level) (OECD, 2001b). The data are from the OECD PSE and AGLINK databases.

Estimates of the URAA effects consist of two components. First, in the form of an intercept shift, $\lambda \times \gamma$, which measures average annual change in import penetration ratio following the Agreement. Second, from URAA-induced changes in the $CNPC$ variable as they are captured in the term $\lambda \times \beta \times [CNPC]$.

The fixed effects model was used to estimate (3) as the null hypothesis that the intercepts are the same across countries was rejected in all cases, both for the import penetration and export performance specifications. The fixed effects estimator allows $\alpha_{i\tau}$ to differ across cross-section units ($\alpha_{i\tau} = \alpha_i$) by estimating different constants for each cross-section. In some instances to correct for the fact that the residuals were correlated a mixed variance-component moving average model was estimated using the Da Silva method.

The results of estimating the above equation are reported in table 3.3 and table 3.4. Despite their preliminary nature, a couple of interesting points emerge. First, the coefficients of the lagged dependent variable and of production are significant in most of the cases and with the expected signs. A small estimate

Table 3.3 *Import penetration (IP) model*

| Dependent variable | Wheat | Coarse grains | Oilseeds | Rice | Refined sugar | Butter | Cheese | SMP | WMP | Beef | Pork | Poultry | Sheep |
|---|---|---|---|---|---|---|---|---|---|---|---|---|---|
| Intercept | -0.152 (-0.710) | -0.103 (-0.600) | -0.381 (-1.779)* | 0.741 (1.299) | 0.634 (2.088)** | -0.191 (-1.048) | -0.254 (-1.189) | -4.257 (-1.962)* | 0.145 (0.589) | -0.326 (-1.844)* | -0.279 (-2.635)*** | -0.181 (-2.180)** | 0.524 (1.912)* |
| $IP_{t-1}$ | 0.138 (1.934)** | 0.106 (1.361) | 0.117 (1.555) | 0.553 (8.625)*** | 0.151 (1.725)* | 0.048 (0.684) | 0.729 (14.443)*** | 0.068 (0.899) | 0.168 (2.791)*** | 0.258 (4.435)*** | 0.742 (12.989)*** | 0.710 (11.777)*** | 0.339 (3.139)*** |
| Q | -0.108 (-4.178)*** | -0.060 (-2.886)*** | -0.054 (-5.951)*** | -0.089 (-1.176) | -0.246 (-5.191)*** | -0.088 (-5.597)*** | -0.028 (-5.299)*** | -0.240 (-3.009)*** | -0.053 (-3.768)*** | -0.128 (-6.394)*** | -0.017 (-1.801)* | -0.055 (-3.441)*** | -0.175 (-3.815)*** |
| PW | 0.028 (0.963) | 0.025 (1.258) | 0.049 (1.691)* | -0.008 (-0.092) | 0.086 (1.599) | -0.066 (-1.764)* | -0.021 (-0.456) | 0.556 (1.248) | -0.039 (-0.750) | -0.033 (-1.175) | 0.020 (1.535) | -0.003 (-0.161) | 0.008 (0.221) |
| POP | 0.442 (2.077)** | 0.246 (1.543) | 0.457 (2.281)** | -0.588 (-1.036) | -0.203 (-0.665) | 0.337 (1.858)* | 0.296 (1.452) | 4.360 (2.025)** | -0.055 (-0.230) | 0.657 (3.706)*** | 0.265 (2.534)** | 0.213 (2.411)** | -0.385 (-1.484) |
| GDPPC | -0.027 (-2.651)** | -0.011 (-1.668)* | -0.037 (-3.745)*** | -0.039 (-1.704)* | -0.003 (-0.251) | 0.017 (2.038)** | 0.007 (0.701) | 0.120 (1.253) | 0.055 (4.820)*** | 0.031 (4.356)*** | 0.001 (0.163) | 0.038 (1.289) | 0.003 (0.040) |
| GDPPC² | 0.002 (3.086)*** | 0.001 (1.882)* | 0.001 (2.577)** | 0.002 (1.639) | 0.000 (0.364) | -0.001 (-1.895)* | 0.000 (0.000) | -0.008 (-1.483) | -0.005 (-8.636)*** | -0.001 (-3.750)*** | 0.000 (0.218) | -0.011 (-1.202) | 0.013 (0.798) |
| RER | -0.097 (-2.605)*** | -0.007 (-0.261) | -0.009 (-0.268) | -0.009 (-0.103) | -0.072 (-1.264) | -0.0202 (-0.647) | 0.006 (0.161) | 0.276 (0.799) | -0.004 (-0.092) | -0.100 (-3.694)*** | 0.000 (0.004) | 0.000 (-0.009) | 0.114 (2.786)*** |
| CNPC | -0.004 (-0.177) | -0.004 (-0.325) | -0.004 (-0.399) | -0.001 (-0.043) | 0.025 (1.186) | 0.009 (0.855) | -0.001 (-0.001) | -0.079 (-1.248) | -0.022 (-1.398) | 0.011 (1.132) | 0.024 (2.132)** | 0.003 (0.760) | 0.012 (0.998) |
| DUMMY | -0.008 (-0.607) | -0.012 (-1.149) | -0.005 (-0.378) | 0.049 (1.084) | 0.010 (0.534) | -0.009 (-0.716) | 0.010 (0.678) | -0.400 (-2.539)** | -0.002 (-0.120) | -0.022 (-2.104)** | 0.002 (0.233) | 0.011 (1.924)* | 0.048 (2.958)*** |
| DF | 156 | 123 | 156 | 156 | 112 | 156 | 156 | 170 | 156 | 156 | 156 | 112 | 35 |
| R²-adjusted | 0.968 | 0.987 | 0.982 | 0.895 | 0.887 | 0.922 | 0.938 | 0.101 | 0.925 | 0.947 | 0.925 | 0.983 | 0.987 |
| F-test | 10.349*** | 12.478*** | 10.629*** | 2.837*** | 7.957*** | 11.998*** | 4.666*** | 2.295*** | 11.928*** | 12.357*** | 2.696** | 2.959*** | 12.514*** |

*Notes:* IP = import penetration indicator. The ratio of imports to consumption in volume terms; *DUMMY* = 0 for 1989–94 and 1 for 1995–2000; *t*-values in parenthesis.

*** = Significance at 1% level.

** = Significance at 5% level.

* = significance at 10% level. The *F*-test is for testing the null hypothesis that the intercepts are the same across countries.

Table 3.4 *Export performance (XP) model*

| Dependent variable | Wheat | Coarse grains[a] | Oilseeds | Rice | Refined sugar | Butter | Cheese | SMP | WMP | Beef | Pork | Poultry | Sheep |
|---|---|---|---|---|---|---|---|---|---|---|---|---|---|
| Intercept | 1.093 | 0.460 | 0.282 | 0.516 | 0.154 | 0.583 | −0.212 | −0.709 | 0.361 | −0.197 | 0.183 | −0.017 | 0.614 |
|  | (4.659)*** | (2.978)** | (0.805) | (1.841)* | (0.796) | (2.516)** | (−1.707)* | (−1.642) | (1.081) | (−1.007) | −1.503 | (−0.252) | (1.401) |
| $XP_{t-1}$ | 0.057 | 0.329 | 0.546 | 0.294 | 0.317 | 0.461 | 0.635 | 0.251 | 0.526 | 0.493 | 0.467 | 0.632 | 0.085 |
|  | (0.700) | (4.811)*** | (7.818)*** | (2.489)** | (4.112)*** | (6.847)*** | (14.740)*** | (3.241)*** | (8.382)*** | (7.669)*** | (6.771)*** | (13.411)*** | (0.895) |
| $Q$ | 0.007 | 0.041 | 0.03 | −0.045 | 0.143 | 0.033 | −0.001 | −0.024 | 0.015 | 0.073 | 0.117 | 0.007 | −0.042 |
|  | (0.259) | (2.128)** | (2.013)** | (−1.252) | (4.699)*** | (1.710)* | (−0.472) | (−0.953) | (0.805) | (3.266)*** | (4.407)*** | (0.555) | (−1.762)* |
| $PW$ | −0.049 | −0.063 | −0.084 | 0.054 | −0.020 | −0.113 | −0.03 | 0.076 | −0.001 | 0.020 | 0.021 | 0.012 | 0.076 |
|  | (−1.645) | (−3.335)*** | (−1.765)* | (1.223) | (−0.747) | (−2.378)** | (−1.136) | (−0.85) | (−0.143) | (−0.657) | (1.327) | (1.134) | (−1.019) |
| $POP$ | −0.593 | −0.399 | 0.115 | −0.219 | −0.261 | −0.543 | 0.228 | 0.861 | −0.25 | 0.161 | −0.243 | 0.055 | −0.506 |
|  | (−2.712)** | (−2.699)** | (0.352) | (−0.819) | (−1.325) | (−2.364)** | (1.922)* | (2.034)** | (−0.773) | (0.824) | (−1.795)* | (0.765) | (−0.558) |
| $GDPPC$ | −0.001 | −0.004 | −0.011 | −0.005 | 0.021 | −0.021 | 0.008 | −0.009 | 0.005 | 0.005 | −0.051 | 0.003 | −0.013 |
|  | (−0.108) | (−0.628) | (−0.737) | (−0.041) | (2.380)** | (−1.912)* | (1.418) | (−0.472) | (0.313) | (0.681) | (−1.270) | (0.870) | (−0.713) |
| $GDPPC^2$ | 0.000 | 0.000 | 0.001 | −0.007 | −0.001 | 0.001 | 0.000 | 0.001 | 0.000 | −0.001 | 0.009 | 0.000 | 0.001 |
|  | (−0.520) | (0.087) | (0.775) | (−0.167) | (−2.502)** | (1.580) | (−1.092) | (0.633) | (−0.433) | (−0.418) | (0.698) | (−0.794) | (1.061) |
| $RER$ | −0.022 | 0.0175 | −0.169 | 0.100 | −0.009 | 0.052 | −0.004 | 0.000 | 0.041 | −0.010 | −0.031 | −0.015 | −0.057 |
|  | (−0.563) | (0.692) | (−2.916)*** | (0.442) | (−0.244) | (1.287) | (−0.181) | (−0.001) | (0.688) | (−0.362) | (−1.593) | (−1.394) | (−0.558) |
| $PNPC$ | 0.002 | −0.009 | −0.018 | 0.009 | 0.002 | 0.000 | 0.004 | −0.007 | −0.026 | −0.002 | 0.011 | 0.002 | 0.0164 |
|  | (0.117) | (−1.561) | (−1.551) | (0.873) | (0.338) | (−0.010) | (0.493) | (−0.299) | (−1.337) | (−0.165) | (0.864) | (0.674) | (0.471) |
| $DUMMY$ | 0.034 | 0.018 | 0.013 | 0.006 | 0.002 | 0.029 | 0.0106 | −0.059 | 0.000 | −0.011 | 0.023 | 0.005 | 0.002 |
|  | (2.382)** | (1.811)* | (0.605) | (0.352) | (0.196) | (1.671)* | (1.191) | (−1.946)* | (0.003) | (−0.923) | (3.232)*** | (1.202) | (0.071) |
| $DF$ | 145 | 170 | 134 | 57 | 123 | 156 | 156 | 156 | 156 | 156 | 145 | 156 | 90 |
| $R^2$-adjusted | 0.952 | 0.921 | 0.806 | 0.989 | 0.951 | 0.943 | 0.98 | 0.9 | 0.933 | 0.973 | 0.923 | 0.958 | 0.889 |
| $F$-test | 9.131*** | 12.997*** | 3.040*** | 7.196*** | 9.284*** | 5.096*** | 3.260*** | 5.627*** | 4.284*** | 4.994*** | 4.811*** | 3.720*** | 9.822*** |

*Notes:* $XP$ = export performance indicator. The ratio of exports to production in volume terms; $DUMMY$ = 0 for 1989–94 and 1 for 1995–2000; $t$-values in parenthesis.

*** = Significance at 1% level; ** = Significance at 5 percent level; * = Significance at 10% level.

The $F$-test is for testing the null hypothesis that the intercepts are the same across countries.

[a] The errors component model was used estimated by the Fuller and Battesse method.

of $(1 - \lambda$, the coefficient of the lagged dependent variable, implies a large $\lambda$, which would imply that the trade openness measure would adjust rapidly to changing economic conditions. Our estimates of $(1 - \lambda$ in table 3.3 and table 3.4 suggest that imports adjust to economic conditions more rapidly than exports.

Second, on the import side, the *URAA* dummy variable is statistically significant for skimmed milk powder (*SMP*), beef, poultrymeat, and sheepmeat. The *SMP* and beef dummies have the expected sign (positive). On the export side, the *URAA* dummy variable is statistically significant for wheat, coarse grains, butter, skimmed milk powder, and pigmeat. The wheat, coarse grains, butter, and pigmeat dummies have the expected sign (i.e. positive); the skimmed milk powder dummy does not have the expected sign. Third, in most cases, the coefficients of the policy variables (*CNPC* in the import penetration model and *PNPC* in the export performance model) are not statistically significant. An exception is the equation for import penetration of pigmeat: the *CNPC* coefficient is significant, but of the wrong sign (its sign is expected to be negative). The coefficient of the *PNPC* variable in the export performance model is expected to be positive.

Overall, these results hint that, for several commodities, the URAA did not have a significant impact on either increasing agricultural imports to or exports from OECD countries. One would need, however, to compute the total estimated impact of the *URAAC* – i.e. the impact of the dummies plus the impact through the *CNPC* or *PNPC*. For example, in the cheese import penetration model, both the dummy and the *CNPC* coefficient have the expected signs (they are not statistically significant, though) and one could conclude that the URAA-induced increased imports of cheese (if the cheese *CNPC* declined in the relevant period). In the sheepmeat import penetration model, the dummy has the expected sign (and it is statistically significant), but the *CNPC* coefficient does not have the expected sign; thus, in this case it is not clear whether the URAA induced increased imports of sheepmeat; we need to compute the total impact.

## Weaknesses of URAA

### Market access

Disciplines on market access were significant accomplishments of the URAA, although its shortcomings are also obvious. In many instances, tariff bindings are at very high rates and offered limited market access opportunities.[9] The tariffication process allowed scope for considerable discretion, resulting in agricultural tariff bindings being sometimes far above actual protection rates.[10] Consequently, agricultural tariffs remain high and in addition there is substantial disparity among countries and across commodities. In contrast to manufacturing tariffs, many of which are now of the order of 5–10 percent, agricultural tariffs are, on average, 62 percent, with tariff peaks of over 500 percent (Gibson *et al.*, 2001). Average commodity tariffs range from 50 percent to 91 percent, with the highest tariffs set for tobacco, meats, dairy, sugar, and sweeteners. The high tariffs currently existing in the agricultural sector restrict trade. Another important aspect of tariff profiles that emerged from the URAA is that tariff rates vary over a wide range. Triple-digit tariffs are in place alongside zero tariffs. Increases in tariff dispersion can intensify the distortion effects of tariffs. Empirical evidence suggests that dispersion of tariffs as measured by domestic and international "spikes" increased for most OECD countries in 1996 relative to 1993 (OECD, 2001a). Available evidence also suggests that tariffs tend to increase with the level of processing (tariff escalation[11]), although the extent of escalation differs greatly across countries. Moreover, agricultural bindings are not always transparent. Transparency and comparability of agricultural tariffs is impaired by the use of non-*ad valorem* tariffs such as specific or mixed tariffs. Twenty-five WTO Members, from both developing and developed countries, have non-*ad valorem* bindings on more than 50 percent of their agricultural tariff lines.

In OECD countries, tariff protection is very high in many sectors including dairy (116 percent), grains (78 percent), livestock (82 percent), and sugar and sweeteners (64 percent). OECD tariffs in other sectors are relatively low. Because tariff spikes for sensitive commodities characterize OECD countries' tariff profiles, there is a large dispersion in their tariffs across commodities. Non-OECD countries tend to have higher average tariffs than OECD countries, although less disparity across commodity groups (Gibson *et al.*, 2001). Non-OECD countries use mega-tariffs (over 100 percent) more than OECD countries. However, particularly for developing countries, the tariffs actually applied may be considerably lower than the bound rates. For example, the 1998 applied rate for Latin American countries of 13 percent is less than one-third of their average final bound rate of 45 percent.

The market access provisions have, paradoxically, caused a proliferation of TRQs in agricultural trade, reflecting the high levels of tariffs prevailing in the agricultural sector. TRQs were introduced to establish minimum access opportunities where there had been no significant imports (less than 5 percent of domestic consumption) before the tariffication process or to maintain current access opportunities where the tariffication would otherwise have reduced market access conditions. TRQs are two-tier tariffs that allow some fraction of domestic consumption requirements to be imported at a low tariff (in-quota), while any imports above the minimum access commitments are charged a much higher (over-quota), and often prohibitive, tariff. The distribution of TRQs among countries and product groups reflects the incidence of tariffication. More than 80 percent of all TRQs are concentrated in five of the twelve product groups covered by tariff quotas (WTO, 2000). More than one-quarter of all TRQs apply to fruits and vegetables alone; the four other groups most affected by TRQs are meat, cereals, dairy products, and oilseeds. Although TRQs cover only 6 percent of tariff lines, they are prevalent in the sensitive sectors of meats, dairy, sugar, and cereals. Only thirty-seven of the 142 WTO Members (September 2001) use TRQs. They are concentrated in a small set of countries and commodities. Three countries, Norway (17 percent), Poland (8 percent), and Iceland (7 percent), account for one-third of all TRQs and three commodity groups, fruits and vegetables (26 percent), meat (18 percent), and cereals (16 percent) for 60 percent of all TRQs (appendix table 3A.3, p. 69).[12] All OECD countries, except Turkey, have tariff quota commitments shown in their Schedules with a total of around 700 individual tariff quota commitments. The provision that allowed TRQs to replace the former quantitative restrictions was critical to bringing the Uruguay Round to a successful conclusion.

Although not as economically efficient as tariffs, TRQs are, in general, less trade-distorting than NTBs. It can be argued that TRQs increase market access since, in contrast to import quotas, there is no explicit ceiling on imports under this system. However, TRQs are second-best policy instruments as they retain many of the characteristics of NTBs, which might impede market access. Countries are not obliged to import quantities corresponding to the TRQs and the "fill rate" of many of TRQs has been low. Between 1995 and 2000, on average, TRQs in OECD countries have been only two-thirds filled (figure 3.2). Moreover, the fill rate of tariff quotas has steadily decreased over time. The simple average fill rate for the OECD countries as a whole declined from 67 percent in 1995 to 59 percent in 1999 (appendix table 3A.4, p. 69).[13]

Tariff quotas may not be filled for various reasons. One reason could be that economic conditions, including deficient import demand and changing competitiveness in the importing country, have changed since the reference period. A second reason might be that the method by which TRQs are administered can also influence trade and the likelihood of being filled. Most licensing systems lead to the establishment of vested interests and built-in rigidities. In fact, the degree of TRQ utilization varies among methods of quota allocation (OECD, 2001a). The precise method of administration of TRQs could operate as a second-tier level of protection over and above that provided through the tariffs. Further, TRQs are often allocated totally or partially to specific supplying countries under preferential agreements, thereby limiting market access by other countries.

Another important possibility could be that the levels of the in- and over-quota tariff rates are set too high. The difference between the in-quota and the over-quota tariffs is often so large as to prohibit any trade at the higher rate. If the over-quota tariff is high and the volume of imports within the tariff-quotas remains restricted the tariff quota will exhibit many of the market distorting aspects of a NTB. Over-quota tariff rates for most commodities in many countries are

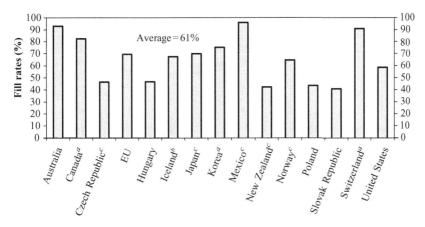

**Frequency distribution of fill rates**

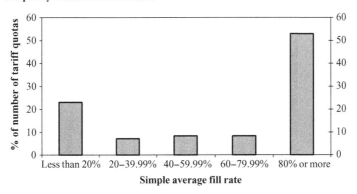

*Note:* [a] Canada, Korea, Switzerland: 1995–8.
[b] Iceland: 1995–7.
[c] Czech Rep., Japan, Mexico, New Zealand, Norway.
*Source:* Author's calculations based on country notifications to WTO.

Figure 3.2  Tariff-quota fill rates OECD countries (simple average), 1995–1999

at triple-digit levels. The average over-quota tariff for twenty-five countries out of forty is higher than 62 percent (Gibson *et al.*, 2001). Seven OECD countries have average over-quota final bound tariffs of more than 130 percent (table 3.5). In general, in-quota tariffs are less than 50 percent, but a few very high tariffs raise the simple average. Thus, the high in-quota and over-quota tariffs significantly impede agricultural trade. These results provide support for the argument that the establishment of tariff quotas could hamper market access and trade flows. Nevertheless, it should be pointed out that the fundamental issue

Table 3.5 *Agricultural tariffs (percent)*

| Country | Tariffs (all lines) | In-quota tariff (TRQ lines) | Over-quota tariff (TRQ lines) | TRQ lines as a share of total |
|---|---|---|---|---|
| *OECD* | | | | |
| Australia | 4 | 10 | 25 | 2 |
| Canada | 23 | 3 | 139 | 22 |
| Czech Republic | 12 | 28 | 48 | 14 |
| EU | 30 | 17 | 78 | 28 |
| Hungary | 29 | 26 | 40 | 50 |
| Iceland | 113 | 49 | 181 | 57 |
| Japan | 58 | 22 | 422 | 21 |
| Korea | 66 | 19 | 314 | 25 |
| Mexico | 43 | 48 | 148 | 13 |
| New Zealand | 7 | 0 | 7 | 1 |
| Norway | 142 | 262 | 203 | 55 |
| Poland | 48 | 31 | 59 | 85 |
| Slovak Republic | 13 | 30 | 42 | 21 |
| Switzerland | 120 | 75 | 210 | 42 |
| USA | 12 | 10 | 52 | 24 |
| *Non-OECD* | | | | |
| Argentina | 35 | | | |
| Brazil | 37 | 7 | 42 | 1 |
| Colombia | 87 | 132 | 137 | 38 |
| Israel | 75 | 79 | 151 | 6 |
| Morocco | 65 | 148 | 115 | 20 |
| Tunisia | 110 | 26 | 109 | 17 |
| Malaysia | 25 | 106 | 248 | 10 |
| India | 114 | | | |
| Indonesia | 48 | 65 | 179 | 1 |
| Pakistan | 101 | | | |
| Thailand | 35 | 27 | 91 | 12 |

*Note:* Tariffs are bound MFN rates based on final URAA implementation.
*Source:* Gibson *et al.* (2001).

is not the existence of TRQs *per se*, but rather the predominance of many very high tariffs (Tangermann, 2001).

*Domestic support*

The discipline on domestic support commitments, although deemed to be a major achievement, proved to be the least binding in most OECD countries. Of the current 142 WTO Members (September 2001), thirty have total AMS reduction commitments. Domestic support is highly concentrated in a few OECD countries, with the EU, Japan, and the United Kingdom accounting for 90 percent of total domestic support (i.e. AMS, blue box, green box, *de minimis*, and S&D) for the OECD area as a whole. Based on information for the period 1995–8, the four years for which sufficient data are available, the evolution of total domestic support shows a downward trend. The value of support subject to reduction commitments in OECD countries declined significantly in the first four years of URAA implementation. The average value of the 1995–8 Current Total AMS for the OECD, US$100 billion, is equal to about 60 percent of the AMS level in the 1986–8 base period for these countries.[14]

Total AMS reduction commitments have generally not been binding, as current total AMS has been kept far below commitment levels (table 3.6). On average, Current Total AMS as a percentage of the AMS commitment level for the OECD was 56 percent in the 1995–8 period. Most countries have fulfilled their support reduction commitments by a large margin. The AMS commitments are close to becoming a binding constraint for only four OECD countries.

Although domestic support from policies with the greatest potential to affect production and trade has decreased since the URAA base period, a number of factors potentially limit the effectiveness of the URAA in trade protection.

First, the base period for support reductions is not representative of average support as it was a period of extremely high support for many commodities and countries. Moreover, many countries have availed themselves of a "credit" by adopting the 1986 level of AMS as the base period level for a commodity in cases where it exceeded the average level for the 1986–8 period. The effect, in many cases, is significantly to exaggerate the final bound level relative to what it would have been had the reduction commitment been applied to the 1986–8 average. In addition, inclusion of support in the base period that was subsequently exempted from reduction as "blue box" support overstates the initial AMS, thereby making it easier for countries that claim "blue box" exemptions to fulfill their commitments. Further, countries are not prevented from introducing new trade-distorting support measures as long as annual bound levels are not exceeded.[15]

Second, a relatively large set of domestic subsidies, covering a broad range of measures, is exempted from the reduction commitments, some of which are not trade and production neutral. In OECD as a whole, almost 60 percent of domestic agricultural support is excluded from the domestic reduction commitments (figure 3.3). During the implementation period, the composition of some OECD countries' domestic support has changed. Reduction of Total Current AMS was simultaneously accompanied by an increase in exempt support, particularly in "green box" support. The largest increases in "green box" expenditures are recorded in the EU, Japan, and the United States. On average, "green box"

Table 3.6 *Ranges of notified current total AMS levels, OECD countries, 1995–1999*

| | Current total AMS as a percentage of total AMS commitment levels | | | | | |
| Year | 0–10 | 11–49 | 50–69 | 70–89 | 90–100 | >100 |
|---|---|---|---|---|---|---|
| 1995 | Czech Republic, Mexico, New Zealand, Poland | Australia, Canada, United States | European Union, Hungary,[a] Slovak Republic | Iceland, Japan, Norway, Switzerland | Korea | |
| 1996 | Mexico New Zealand, Poland | Australia, Canada, Czech Republic, Hungary, United States | European Union, Slovak Republic | Iceland, Japan, Norway, Switzerland | Korea | |
| 1997 | Canada Czech Republic, New Zealand, Poland | Australia, Hungary, Mexico, United States | European Union | Iceland, Japan, Norway, Slovak Republic Switzerland | Korea | |
| 1998 | Czech Republic, New Zealand, Poland | Australia, Canada, Japan Mexico | Hungary,[b] United States | European Union, Korea, Iceland,[b] Norway Slovak Republic Switzerland | | Hungary, Iceland |
| 1999 | New Zealand, Poland | Australia, Canada, Czech Republic, Japan | European Union, Slovak Republic | Iceland,[b] Korea, United States | Iceland, Norway | |

*Notes:* As of June 2003, Mexico and Switzerland have not yet notified for 1999.
[a] De minimis.
[b] With inflation adjustment.
*Source:* OECD (2001a); author's calculations based on country notifications to WTO.

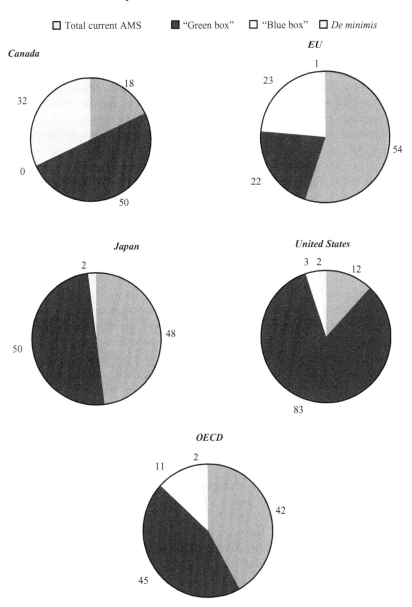

*Source:* WTO notifications and author's calculations.

Figure 3.3  Composition of domestic support, 1995–1998 (percent)

support in OECD countries doubled between 1986–8 and 1995–8. Over the 1995–8 implementation period, "green box" support was higher than AMS support.

It can be argued that, as intended, the constraints on domestic support appear to have contributed towards the "re-instrumentation" of domestic support away from the most trade restrictive measures towards the less trade restrictive ones. However, many exempt support measures, while less trade-distorting than price or output- and input-based supports, still have production and trade effects by reducing risk and keeping resources in agriculture. The total amount of the payment, as well as the detailed design and duration of a program, are critical factors for determining the impact of policies on production and trade. Several "blue box" and "green box" measures in the WTO classification are included in the OECD PSE calculation as payments based on outputs (OECD, 2001a). "Blue box" programs are considered to be less trade-distorting and more transparent than price support measures. Nevertheless, these payments require farmers to produce in order to be eligible for the payment. Payments may be directly dependent on production so long as the volume does not exceed 85 percent of production in the base period or based on fixed area and yields. Moreover, the level of support associated with these measures is very significant. For the EU, for example, payments in the "blue box" were, on average, US$25 billion or 23 percent of total domestic support over the 1995–8 period.[16]

"Green box" policies are assumed to have the smallest effects on production and trade. In fact, the fundamental criterion for "green box" exemptions is that they have "no, or at most, minimal" effects on trade and also "shall not have the effect of providing price support to producers." Thus, changes in the mix of domestic policies away from reliance on AMS policies and toward more "green box" policies might lead to expectations of a reduction in production and trade distortions. However, the question of whether all payments reported in the "green box" have no, or at most minimal, trade and production effects requires further investigation. The eligibility criteria of the URAA for "green box" measures do not always ensure that no or minimal distortions to production and trade result. Although it is virtually impossible to design income support policies that do not have some effects on resource allocation through income, wealth, and risk effects, there is considerable scope for strengthening the disciplines to ensure that the exempt policies are minimally trade-distorting. There is a need for designing more rigorous operational criteria for exemption from reduction commitments. The URAA provisions establishing criteria for "green box" policies focus attention on the way policies are implemented, but do not limit the amount of the subsidy. In addition, the interpretation of what is a "minimal" trade or production effect is not specified.

Third, the application of the *de minimis* provision has led to exclusion of measures that are potentially highly distorting. The *de minimis* provisions are applied on both a product-specific and a sector-wide basis. This creates the potential for the continued support of commodity production at high levels. In OECD countries, the *de minimis* provision includes product-specific support as well as non-product-specific support, particularly input subsidies. In Hungary, Current Total AMS is nil as all product-specific and non-product-specific support is *de minimis*, while in Canada *de minimis support* accounts for 30 percent of total support. In Canada, out of the twenty-two product categories with product-specific non-exempt direct payments, twenty products are exempt under the *de minimis* provision as was the non-product-specific AMS.

Fourth, the AMS, is not in itself an indicator of production and trade distortions: (a) The Current Total AMS reduction commitments are sector-wide, not on product-specific AMS. This allows governments to reduce support for some products, while leaving support for others unchanged or even raised. A cursory look at countries' notifications shows that some of them have increased their support to certain specific products. In Iceland, for example, the Current Total AMS has declined by some 27 percent between the base period and 1997, while support to milk in nominal terms increased by 240 percent. (b) The market price support component of the AMS is based on the domestic administered support price and a fixed external reference price. The domestic administered support price may be a poor proxy for the domestic market price, while the fixed external reference price does not represent the actual border price, which brings into question the measure of price support as defined by the URAA. (c) The exclusion of price support in cases where no administered price exists provides wide flexibility to governments in choosing policy instruments.[17] (d) The AMS includes only support provided through domestic measures and it does not capture distortions arising from trade measures that are excluded from the AMS provisions (e.g. tariffs and export subsidies). Despite the reduction in the Current Total AMS the level of agricultural support as measured by the PSE remains quite high and the gap between the OECD PSE and the AMS is increasing over time (appendix table 3A.5, p. 70).

Finally, the URAA does not provide specific criteria for determining a country's development status.

*Export subsidies*

Export subsidies may take a wide variety of implicit or explicit forms, including direct export subsidies, export credits, state trading, and food aid. The proliferation of export subsidies in the years leading to the Uruguay Round was one of the key issues that were addressed in the agricultural negotiations. Of the WTO's 142 Members (September 2001), twenty-five have scheduled export subsidy reduction commitments (appendix table 3A.6, p. 71). The main

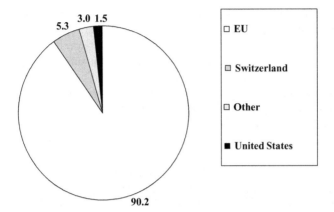

Figure 3.4  Notified subsidized exports, OECD countries, 1995–1998 (percent)

reduction commitments affect OECD countries, particularly the EU, which is the major user, accounting for 90 percent of actual export subsidies notified to the WTO for the 1995–8 period (figure 3.4).[18]

The export subsidy discipline of the URAA proved to be the most binding of the three disciplines. The total amount of subsidized exports has been curtailed and the number of products, which were actually subsidized during the implementation period was much smaller than the number permitted to receive subsidies under the URAA.[19]

However, export subsidies are allowed to continue and a number of policies with the potential to affect export competition such as State-Trading Enterprises (STEs), abuse of international food aid, officially supported export credits on agriculture, export restrictions, and revenue pooling arrangements, were excluded from the discipline. Further, in some cases, the rate of export subsidy remained high and there was a large degree of disparity among commodities. In addition, the provision to carry over unused export subsidies and to cumulate them with their annual commitments in subsequent years weakened the discipline when it did risk becoming binding.[20] Moreover, even if the use of export subsidies has been limited, their potential impacts are still significant since for products such as wheat or some dairy products, existing commitments would still allow a large share of world exports to be affected.

**Concluding remarks**

The URAA marked a historic point in the reform of the agricultural trade system. One of the main achievements of the URAA has been the development and implementation of a framework to address barriers and distortions to trade in three major policy domains (market access, domestic support, and export subsidies). New and operationally effective rules have been established and quantitative constraints have been agreed upon for all three pillars. In addition, the URAA has provided an overall framework for the re-instrumentation of agricultural support towards less trade-distorting policies. Moreover, the URAA has provided the basis for further negotiations.

The experience to date from the URAA implementation period shows that agricultural policy reform has not been significant. Although the immediate trade impacts specific to the implementation of the URAA in OECD countries are difficult to identify and distinguish from the impacts of other events, the preliminary empirical evidence presented suggests that the overall effects have been moderate. Reductions in support and protection were limited largely because of weaknesses of many of the specific features of the URAA. Without underrating the achievement of the URAA in bringing agriculture into the mainstream of multilateral trading rules and securing some reform, limited progress has been made since 1995 in reducing agricultural protection and market insulation.

The new round of negotiations provides an important opportunity for deepening the process of agricultural reform and trade liberalization. The perceived areas of ineffectiveness in the URAA identify areas for progress in the next agreement. On market access, negotiations should be more straightforward than in the past as tariffication has already made the level of border protection more transparent. A major question for the new round is what process could be adopted to reduce agricultural tariffs, which remain in many cases at a very high level. Related questions concern dispersion of tariff rates and the weighting system to be used for further tariff reductions. Several techniques could be used, each having specific economic features. On TRQs, if their elimination is not feasible market access can be expanded by reducing their restrictiveness by increasing import quotas, reducing over-quota tariffs, eliminating in-quota tariffs, or a combination of the three. In this case, more efficient methods of quota allocation could expand market access through increased fill rates of tariff quotas. Nevertheless, a proper assessment of the impact of each of the factors that could potentially affect TRQ fill rates is a project of some magnitude and yet to be commissioned, despite its potential.

On domestic support, significant reduction of trade distortions would require careful scrutiny of the following issues: addressing the various weaknesses of the AMS discipline identified in this chapter, including its sector-wide nature; defining better and strengthening the eligibility criteria for exempt policies to ensure that only the least trade-distorting programs are included; the role of the Peace Clause; and the role of S&D for developing countries.

Disciplines on export subsidies have been more effective than the other two disciplines. Further reduction in trade distortions could be achieved by strengthening the URAA export subsidy provisions. Nevertheless, several issues need to be addressed. In particular, the coverage of export subsidies should be broadened to embrace all those policies which have the potential to distort export competition. These include some aspects of parastatal trade agencies, revenue pooling arrangements, international food aid, export credits, export taxes, and export restraints. Moreover, the rules concerning "unused" export subsidy allowances and the definition of export subsidies, and in particular the issue of "cross-subsidization" among markets, merit re-examination and should be tightened.

There are a number of other potentially important issues for the new round of WTO negotiations, including environmental sustainability, rural development, structural changes in the agro-food sector, food security, food safety, food quality, and animal welfare. In addition to the more traditional issues addressed under the three pillars of market access, domestic support, and export subsidies, these "non-trade" concern issues provide important challenges for the international policy agenda. The challenge is to define the characteristics of appropriate policies to accommodate "non-trade" concerns in ways that are targeted, transparent, and implemented in no more than minimally trade-distorting ways. The Program of Work of the OECD Agriculture Directorate has a number of ongoing projects with the overall objective of defining such policies.

## Appendix tables

Table 3A.1 *OECD: producer support estimates, by commodity, 1986–2000*[a]

|  | 1986–90 | 1990–4 | 1995–2000 | 1997 | 1998 | 1999 | 2000 |
|---|---|---|---|---|---|---|---|
| *Wheat* | | | | | | | |
| USD million | 16,666 | 18,653 | 16,014 | 13,769 | 18,413 | 19,659 | 16,304 |
| Euro million | 14,757 | 15,173 | 14,406 | 12,150 | 16,463 | 18,450 | 17,692 |
| Percentage PSE | 41 | 42 | 34 | 30 | 40 | 45 | 40 |
| Producer NPC | 1.54 | 1.46 | 1.1 | 1.04 | 1.19 | 1.24 | 1.11 |
| Producer NAC | 1.75 | 1.73 | 1.55 | 1.42 | 1.67 | 1.83 | 1.66 |
| *Maize* | | | | | | | |
| USD million | 11,212 | 9,972 | 9,312 | 7,003 | 10,880 | 12,960 | 13,359 |
| Euro million | 10,011 | 8,091 | 8,605 | 6,180 | 9,728 | 12,163 | 14,496 |
| Percentage PSE | 35 | 28 | 24 | 18 | 29 | 34 | 34 |
| Producer NPC | 1.25 | 1.19 | 1.09 | 1.04 | 1.11 | 1.17 | 1.15 |
| Producer NAC | 1.55 | 1.39 | 1.33 | 1.22 | 1.40 | 1.51 | 1.51 |
| *Other grains* | | | | | | | |
| USD million | 10,159 | 10,659 | 9,544 | 8,859 | 11,166 | 10,033 | 7,505 |
| Euro million | 9,004 | 8,681 | 8,442 | 7,817 | 9,983 | 9,416 | 8,144 |
| Percentage PSE | 46 | 49 | 43 | 38 | 53 | 51 | 41 |

(*cont.*)

Table 3A.1 (*cont.*)

| | 1986–90 | 1990–4 | 1995–2000 | 1997 | 1998 | 1999 | 2000 |
|---|---|---|---|---|---|---|---|
| Producer NPC | 1.79 | 1.72 | 1.22 | 1.12 | 1.41 | 1.35 | 1.12 |
| Producer NAC | 1.93 | 1.98 | 1.78 | 1.60 | 2.11 | 2.03 | 1.69 |
| *Rice* | | | | | | | |
| USD million | 27,181 | 29,790 | 29,765 | 27,225 | 22,333 | 27,466 | 29,335 |
| Euro million | 24,039 | 24,265 | 26,272 | 24,023 | 19,968 | 25,777 | 31,831 |
| Percentage PSE | 79 | 80 | 78 | 73 | 74 | 79 | 82 |
| Producer NPC | 4.63 | 4.68 | 4.36 | 3.47 | 3.64 | 4.50 | 5.43 |
| Producer NAC | 4.92 | 4.97 | 4.6 | 3.65 | 3.86 | 4.78 | 5.69 |
| *Oilseeds* | | | | | | | |
| USD million | 5,761 | 4,727 | 4,086 | 2,666 | 4,281 | 5,919 | 6,198 |
| Euro million | 5,063 | 3,806 | 3,782 | 2,352 | 3,828 | 5,555 | 6,725 |
| Percentage PSE | 27 | 21 | 16 | 10 | 17 | 23 | 25 |
| Producer NPC | 1.29 | 1.14 | 1.08 | 1.02 | 1.07 | 1.17 | 1.18 |
| Producer NAC | 1.37 | 1.28 | 1.2 | 1.11 | 1.20 | 1.31 | 1.33 |
| *Sugar (ref. eq.)* | | | | | | | |
| USD million | 5,476 | 6,743 | 5,986 | 5,694 | 6,848 | 7,560 | 5,788 |
| Euro million | 4,852 | 5,483 | 5,385 | 5,024 | 6,123 | 7,095 | 6,280 |
| Percentage PSE | 48 | 50 | 47 | 43 | 51 | 61 | 50 |
| Producer NPC | 2.08 | 1.98 | 1.98 | 1.77 | 2.10 | 2.69 | 2.04 |
| Producer NAC | 1.98 | 2.01 | 1.92 | 1.74 | 2.04 | 2.53 | 1.99 |
| *Milk* | | | | | | | |
| USD million | 47,275 | 53,185 | 44,844 | 42,060 | 50,443 | 45,333 | 39,125 |
| Euro million | 41,693 | 43,214 | 39,787 | 37,114 | 45,101 | 42,545 | 42,454 |
| Percentage PSE | 56 | 57 | 50 | 47 | 56 | 52 | 48 |
| Producer NPC | 2.53 | 2.39 | 1.92 | 1.83 | 2.21 | 2.00 | 1.85 |
| Producer NAC | 2.33 | 2.34 | 1.99 | 1.89 | 2.26 | 2.07 | 1.92 |
| *Beef and veal* | | | | | | | |
| USD million | 24,175 | 28,293 | 28,754 | 30,760 | 28,896 | 29,902 | 25,425 |
| Euro million | 21,354 | 22,957 | 25,555 | 27,143 | 25,836 | 28,063 | 27,589 |
| Percentage PSE | 32 | 33 | 35 | 37 | 37 | 37 | 32 |
| Producer NPC | 1.41 | 1.40 | 1.32 | 1.34 | 1.36 | 1.36 | 1.31 |
| Producer NAC | 1.47 | 1.49 | 1.53 | 1.59 | 1.59 | 1.58 | 1.48 |
| *Sheepmeat* | | | | | | | |
| USD million | 5,113 | 5,728 | 4,821 | 4,079 | 4,443 | 4,733 | 3,489 |
| Euro million | 4,475 | 4,643 | 4,207 | 3,599 | 3,973 | 4,442 | 3,786 |
| Percentage PSE | 56 | 53 | 45 | 37 | 45 | 47 | 40 |
| Producer NPC | 1.86 | 1.56 | 1.25 | 1.15 | 1.26 | 1.26 | 1.13 |
| Producer NAC | 2.28 | 2.15 | 1.83 | 1.60 | 1.83 | 1.89 | 1.67 |
| *Wool* | | | | | | | |
| USD million | 315 | 398 | 173 | 186 | 137 | 138 | 125 |

(*cont.*)

Table 3A.1  (*cont.*)

|  | 1986–90 | 1990–4 | 1995–2000 | 1997 | 1998 | 1999 | 2000 |
|---|---|---|---|---|---|---|---|
| Euro million | 273 | 322 | 151 | 164 | 122 | 130 | 135 |
| Percentage PSE | 7 | 13 | 8 | 7 | 8 | 7 | 6 |
| Producer NPC | 1.01 | 1.04 | 1.02 | 1.02 | 1.03 | 1.02 | 1.02 |
| Producer NAC | 1.08 | 1.15 | 1.08 | 1.08 | 1.08 | 1.08 | 1.07 |
| *Pigmeat* | | | | | | | |
| USD million | 7,556 | 9,735 | 9,885 | 7,250 | 7,058 | 13,284 | 10,251 |
| Euro million | 6,579 | 7,969 | 8,827 | 6,397 | 6,310 | 12,467 | 11,124 |
| Percentage PSE | 15 | 18 | 20 | 12 | 16 | 32 | 22 |
| Producer NPC | 1.22 | 1.25 | 1.22 | 1.08 | 1.16 | 1.46 | 1.25 |
| Producer NAC | 1.18 | 1.22 | 1.25 | 1.14 | 1.18 | 1.46 | 1.29 |
| *Poultry* | | | | | | | |
| USD million | 4,282 | 4,759 | 4,745 | 4,058 | 3,059 | 4,905 | 6,819 |
| Euro million | 3,718 | 3,871 | 4,299 | 3,581 | 2,735 | 4,603 | 7,399 |
| Percentage PSE | 16 | 15 | 13 | 11 | 8 | 13 | 18 |
| Producer NPC | 1.25 | 1.21 | 1.13 | 1.09 | 1.07 | 1.14 | 1.19 |
| Producer NAC | 1.19 | 1.18 | 1.15 | 1.12 | 1.09 | 1.15 | 1.23 |
| *Eggs* | | | | | | | |
| USD million | 2,388 | 2,406 | 2,069 | 1,829 | 1,961 | 1,874 | 1,388 |
| Euro million | 2,115 | 1,956 | 1,798 | 1,614 | 1,753 | 1,759 | 1,506 |
| Percentage PSE | 15 | 13 | 11 | 10 | 12 | 11 | 9 |
| Producer NPC | 1.19 | 1.16 | 1.11 | 1.08 | 1.12 | 1.11 | 1.07 |
| Producer NAC | 1.17 | 1.16 | 1.13 | 1.11 | 1.13 | 1.13 | 1.09 |
| *All commodities – total* | | | | | | | |
| USD million | 240,392 | 279,542 | 253,684 | 227,140 | 253,661 | 273,552 | 245,487 |
| Euro million | 211,903 | 227,315 | 225,937 | 200,428 | 226,798 | 256,729 | 266,378 |
| Percentage PSE | 37 | 37 | 33 | 29 | 34 | 37 | 34 |
| Producer NPC | 1.54 | 1.51 | 1.36 | 1.29 | 1.38 | 1.44 | 1.38 |
| Producer NAC | 1.59 | 1.59 | 1.49 | 1.41 | 1.51 | 1.58 | 1.52 |

*Notes:* [a] provisional.
*Source:* OECD, PSE/CSE database, 2001.

Table 3A.2 *Composition of producer support estimates, 1986–2000*

|  | 1986–8 (%) | 1989–94 (%) | 1995–2000 (%) |
|---|---|---|---|
| *Canada* |  |  |  |
| Market price support and output payments | 66 | 67 | 62 |
| Payments on area/animals, historical entitlements and income | 17 | 17 | 28 |
| Payments on inputs | 16 | 14 | 10 |
| Miscellaneous payments | 2 | 1 | 0 |
| *EU* |  |  |  |
| Market price support and output payments | 91 | 81 | 64 |
| Payments on area/animals, historical entitlements and income | 3 | 10 | 26 |
| Payments on inputs | 6 | 8 | 11 |
| Miscellaneous payments | 0 | 0 | 0 |
| *Japan* |  |  |  |
| Market price support and output payments | 93 | 94 | 94 |
| Payments on area/animals, historical entitlements and income | 0 | 0 | 0 |
| Payments on inputs | 7 | 6 | 6 |
| Miscellaneous payments | 0 | 0 | 0 |
| *Korea* |  |  |  |
| Market price support and output payments | 99 | 96 | 95 |
| Payments on area/animals, historical entitlements and income | 0 | 2 | 1 |
| Payments on inputs | 1 | 2 | 4 |
| Miscellaneous payments | 0 | 0 | 0 |
| *Norway* |  |  |  |
| Market price support and output payments | 70 | 67 | 58 |
| Payments on area/animals, historical entitlements and income | 9 | 12 | 11 |
| Payments on inputs | 21 | 21 | 31 |
| Miscellaneous payments | 0 | 0 | 0 |
| *Poland* |  |  |  |
| Market price support and output payments | 15 | −5 | 78 |
| Payments on area/animals, historical entitlements and income | 25 | 13 | 0 |
| Payments on inputs | 59 | 92 | 21 |
| Miscellaneous payments | 0 | 0 | 0 |

(*cont.*)

Table 3A.2  (*cont.*)

|  | 1986–8 (%) | 1989–94 (%) | 1995–2000 (%) |
|---|---|---|---|
| *Switzerland* | | | |
| Market price support and output payments | 83 | 79 | 65 |
| Payments on area/animals, historical entitlements and income | 6 | 12 | 24 |
| Payments on inputs | 8 | 6 | 8 |
| Miscellaneous payments | 3 | 3 | 3 |
| *Turkey* | | | |
| Market price support and output payments | 65 | 71 | 67 |
| Payments on area/animals, historical entitlements and income | 0 | 0 | 0 |
| Payments on inputs | 35 | 29 | 33 |
| Miscellaneous payments | 0 | 0 | 0 |
| *United States* | | | |
| Market price support and output payments | 53 | 54 | 53 |
| Payments on area/animals, historical entitlements and income | 29 | 22 | 24 |
| Payments on inputs | 18 | 24 | 23 |
| Miscellaneous payments | 0 | 0 | 0 |
| *OECD* | | | |
| Market price support and output payments | 82 | 81 | 72 |
| Payments on area/animals, historical entitlements and income | 8 | 8 | 17 |
| Payments on inputs | 10 | 11 | 12 |
| Miscellaneous payments | 0 | 0 | 0 |

*Source:* OECD, PSE/CSE database 2001.

Table 3A.3 *Who has TRQs?*

| OECD members | No. of tariff quotas | Non-OECD members | No. of tariff quotas | Non-OECD members | No. of tariff quotas |
|---|---|---|---|---|---|
| Australia | 2 | Barbados | 36 | Philippines | 14 |
| Canada | 21 | Brazil | 2 | Romania | 12 |
| Czech Republic | 24 | Bulgaria | 73 | Slovenia | 20 |
| EU | 87 | Colombia | 67 | South Africa | 53 |
| Hungary | 70 | Costa Rica | 27 | Thailand | 23 |
| Iceland | 90 | Ecuador | 14 | Tunisia | 13 |
| Japan | 20 | El Salvador | 11 | Venezuela | 61 |
| Korea | 67 | Guatemala | 22 | | |
| Mexico | 11 | Indonesia | 2 | | |
| New Zealand | 3 | Israel | 12 | | |
| Norway | 232 | Latvia | 4 | | |
| Poland | 109 | Malaysia | 19 | | |
| Slovak Republic | 24 | Morocco | 16 | | |
| Switzerland | 28 | Nicaragua | 9 | | |
| United States | 54 | Panama | 19 | | |
| Total OECD | 842 | Total non-OECD | | | 529 |

*Source:* WTO (2000).

Table 3A.4 *TRQs, by OECD member, 1995–2000*

| | Number of quota lines | | | | | | Fill rates | | | | | |
|---|---|---|---|---|---|---|---|---|---|---|---|---|
| | 1995 | 1996 | 1997 | 1998 | 1999 | 2000 | 1995 | 1996 | 1997 | 1998 | 1999 | 2000 |
| Australia | 2 | 2 | 2 | 2 | 2 | 2 | 99 | 98 | 90 | 91 | 89 | 92 |
| Canada | 21 | 21 | 20 | 20 | | | 78 | 85 | 82 | 85 | | |
| Czech Republic | 24 | 24 | 24 | 24 | 24 | 24 | 44 | 50 | 47 | 45 | 46 | 54 |
| European Union | 53 | 80 | 85 | 42 | 42 | 41 | 76 | 72 | 71 | 66 | 68 | 64 |
| Hungary | 66 | 68 | 67 | 67 | 65 | 59 | 55 | 52 | 45 | 43 | 41 | 45 |
| Iceland | 88 | 87 | 87 | 87 | 87 | | 65 | 67 | 70 | 70 | 71 | |
| Japan | 18 | 18 | 18 | 18 | 18 | 18 | 69 | 72 | 70 | 67 | 71 | 66 |
| Korea | 67 | 67 | 67 | 64 | | | 78 | 76 | 76 | 70 | | |
| Mexico | 11 | 3 | 3 | 3 | 3 | | 80 | 100 | 100 | 100 | 100 | |
| New Zealand | 3 | 3 | 3 | 3 | 3 | 3 | 62 | 40 | 33 | 27 | 50 | 34 |
| Norway | 224 | 222 | 221 | 221 | 221 | 221 | 68 | 64 | 62 | 65 | 64 | 63 |
| Poland | 10 | 13 | 15 | 14 | 19 | 20 | 47 | 52 | 57 | 41 | 31 | 34 |
| Slovak Republic | 24 | 24 | 24 | 24 | 24 | 24 | 37 | 47 | 46 | 43 | 44 | 27 |
| Switzerland | 28 | 27 | 27 | 27 | | | 92 | 92 | 89 | 90 | | |
| United States | 47 | 52 | 53 | 53 | 40 | | 45 | 53 | 55 | 66 | 73 | |
| OECD[a] | 686 | 711 | 716 | 669 | 548 | 412 | 66 | 65 | 64 | 64 | 61 | 57 |

*Note:* [a] Average fill rate has been calculated from the number of notified quota lines.
*Source:* Author's calculations based on country notifications to WTO.

Table 3A.5 Evolution of AMS and producer support estimates, 1986–1998 ($US billion)

| Country | 1986–88 AMS (1) | 1986–88 PSE (2) | 1986–88 (1)/(2) (%) | 1995 AMS (1) | 1995 PSE (2) | 1995 (1)/(2) (%) | 1996 AMS (1) | 1996 PSE (2) | 1996 (1)/(2) (%) | 1997 AMS (1) | 1997 PSE (2) | 1997 (1)/(2) (%) | 1998 AMS (1) | 1998 PSE (2) | 1998 (1)/(2) (%) |
|---|---|---|---|---|---|---|---|---|---|---|---|---|---|---|---|
| Australia | 0.4 | 1.3 | 35 | 0.1 | 1.6 | 7 | 0.1 | 1.6 | 7 | 0.1 | 1.6 | 6 | 0.1 | 1.3 | 6 |
| Canada | 4.1 | 5.6 | 72 | 0.6 | 4.0 | 14 | 0.5 | 3.6 | 12 | 0.4 | 3.1 | 12 | 0.5 | 3.4 | 15 |
| Czech Republic | 1.2 | 4.6 | 26 | 0.0 | 0.6 | 8 | 0.1 | 0.6 | 10 | 0.0 | 0.4 | 9 | 0.0 | 0.8 | 4 |
| European Union | 80.7 | 94.6 | 85 | 65.4 | 123.2 | 53 | 64.7 | 113.9 | 57 | 56.9 | 100.7 | 57 | 52.2 | 110.3 | 47 |
| Hungary | 0.9 | 3.0 | 29 | 0.2 | 0.8 | 21 | 0.1 | 0.6 | 11 | 0.1 | 0.4 | 15 | 0.5 | 1.0 | 48 |
| Iceland | 0.2 | 0.2 | 106 | 0.2 | 0.1 | 131 | 0.2 | 0.1 | 129 | 0.1 | 0.1 | 117 | 0.3 | 0.2 | 212 |
| Japan | 33.8 | 53.4 | 63 | 37.3 | 78.4 | 48 | 30.6 | 62.4 | 49 | 26.2 | 50.5 | 52 | 5.9 | 50.1 | 12 |
| Korea | 2.1 | 12.2 | 17 | 2.7 | 26.7 | 10 | 2.4 | 25.1 | 10 | 2.0 | 20.9 | 10 | 1.1 | 12.5 | 9 |
| Mexico[a] | 9.6 | -0.2 | 570 | 0.5 | 0.8 | 60 | 0.3 | 1.8 | 16 | 1.1 | 5.0 | 21 | 1.3 | 4.0 | 31 |
| New Zealand | 0.2 | 0.4 | 44 | 0.0 | 0.1 | 0 | 0.0 | 0.1 | 0 | 0.0 | 0.1 | 0 | 0.0 | 0.1 | 0 |
| Norway | 2.1 | 2.6 | 80 | 1.5 | 2.9 | 54 | 1.6 | 2.8 | 58 | 1.5 | 2.7 | 56 | 1.4 | 2.6 | 55 |
| Poland | 4.2 | 1.5 | 105 | 0.3 | 3.3 | 8 | 0.2 | 4.4 | 5 | 0.3 | 3.5 | 8 | 0.3 | 3.4 | 9 |
| Switzerland | 3.4 | 5.1 | 67 | 3.6 | 6.3 | 57 | 3.0 | 5.7 | 52 | 2.4 | 4.9 | 48 | 2.3 | 5.0 | 45 |
| United States | 23.9 | 41.9 | 57 | 6.2 | 22.8 | 27 | 5.9 | 29.6 | 20 | 6.2 | 30.5 | 20 | 10.4 | 48.9 | 21 |
| Total | 166.7 | 226.3 | 72 | 118.5 | 271.6 | 42 | 109.7 | 252.5 | 43 | 97.3 | 224.3 | 43 | 76.3 | 243.7 | 31 |

Note: [a] Mexico: 1991 US dollars.
Source: OECD PSE Database; author's calculations.

Table 3A.6 *Who can subsidize exports?*

| OECD members | No. of products | Non-OECD members | No. of products |
|---|---|---|---|
| Australia | 5 | Brazil | 16 |
| Canada | 11 | Bulgaria | 44 |
| Czech Republic | 16 | Colombia | 18 |
| EU | 20 | Cyprus | 9 |
| Hungary | 16 | Indonesia | 1 |
| Iceland | 2 | Israel | 6 |
| Japan | 0 | Panama | 1 |
| Korea | 0 | Romania | 13 |
| Mexico | 5 | South Africa | 62 |
| New Zealand | 1 | Uruguay | 3 |
| Norway | 11 | Venezuela | 72 |
| Poland | 17 | | |
| Slovak Republic | 17 | | |
| Switzerland | 5 | | |
| Turkey | 44 | | |
| United States | 13 | | |
| Total OECD | 183 | Total non-OECD | 245 |

*Source:* WTO (2000).

**Notes**

1. The GATT 1947 allowed countries to use export subsidies on agricultural primary products, whereas the use of export subsidies by developed countries on industrial products was prohibited.
2. Tariffication affected around 14 percent of OECD agricultural trade.
3. In addition to the exemption from disciplines for "green box" and "blue box" policies and *de minimis* exemption, developing countries also received S&D exemptions for certain input and investment subsidies.
4. The "before and after approach" is very popular, particularly in the literature on the effects of IMF and World Bank structural adjustments programs (SAPs).
5. The most common of these measures is the trade openness of a country measured as the ratio of exports plus imports over GDP. Other outcome-based measures are obtained from deviations between actual trade and predicted trade; the predicted values are estimated according to some kind of theoretical framework, such as the Heckscher–Ohlin model or the gravity equations. Therefore, these types of indicators are subject to arbitrariness in the choice of relevant trade theory.
6. Bureau, Fulponi, and Salvatici (2000) use the TRI to measure the welfare effects of URAA tariff reductions for the EU and United States.
7. The impact of post-Uruguay Round liberalization of the trade has also been assessed using computable general equilibrium (CGE) models (see, for example, Hertel, 2000).

8. The RER is a chain-linked index with base period 1995. It is uses a system of weights based on a double-weighting principle which, for each country, takes into account relative market shares held by its competitors on the common markets, including the home market, as well as the importance of these markets for the country in question. A discussion of this methodology is given in Durand, Simon, and Webb (1992).

9. The special agricultural safeguard (SSG) that was put in place to help countries cope with the effect of tariffication has been moderately used in the last six years. Of the thirty-eight WTO Members who have reserved the right to apply the SSG, only eight have used it.

10. Available evidence suggests that the gap between bound and applied tariff rates on agricultural products is important in many developing countries, while in developed countries is not significant.

11. Tariff escalation occurs when the tariff applied on a product "chain" rises as goods undergo further processing, resulting in a higher effective protection for the processing industry than would otherwise be the case.

12. However, 90 percent of TRQs in Norway and Iceland are administered as "applied tariffs" (i.e. unlimited imports are allowed at the in-quota tariff or below). In fact almost one-half of all TRQs notified to the WTO are administered on the basis of "applied tariffs," that is unlimited imports are allowed at or below the in-quota tariff (i.e. the quota is not enforced).

13. Caution should be exercised in interpreting the tariff quota fill rate results as all quotas, irrespective of size, are assigned the same weight. No allowance is made for differences in size between individual tariff quotas. A small tariff quota is given the same weight as a large tariff quota with the same level of fill. Likewise, the simple average does not differentiate between low-value and high-value products.

14. Certain support measures that are included in the base Total AMS were excluded from the Current Total AMS during the implementation period because they met the "blue box" criteria. "Blue box" payments, however, were excluded from the AMS in the implementation period even though they were included in the base year. Including them would result in a smaller decline in domestic support. Combining the 1995, 1996, 1997, and 1998 "blue box" payments with the reported AMS, increases the 1995, 1996, 1997, and 1998 support level to 77 percent of the base.

15. The URAA requires only that countries notify new or modified policies claimed as "green."

16. As of September 2001 the following countries/regions had notified "blue box" programs to the WTO: the EU, Iceland, Norway, the Slovak Republic in 1996 and 1997, the United States in 1995, and Japan in 1998.

17. For example, it opens up the possibility of alleviating the domestic support commitment by eliminating the administered price for those products which had an administered price in the base period, but continuing to provide the same level of support through border measures, providing that the specific commitments on tariff bindings and export subsidy are not breached.

18. The EU is also the largest user of export subsidies of the twenty-five countries that have export subsidy commitments in their WTO schedules.

19. The start of the implementation period coincided with a marked rise in world market prices for cereals that allowed countries to fulfill their reduction commitments easily. In fact, the EU even imposed a tax on cereal exports during that period.
20. Over the first four years of the implementation, six OECD countries availed themselves of the rollover provision (OECD, 2001a).

## References

Anderson, J. and P. Neary, 1996. "A New Approach to Evaluating Trade Policy," *Review of Economic Studies*, 63(1), 107–25

Baldwin, R., 1989. "Measuring Non-Tariff Trade Policies," Working Paper, 2978, National Bureau of Economic Research, Washington, DC

Bureau, J. C., L. Fulponi, and L. Salvatici, 2000. "Comparing EU and US Trade Liberalization Under the Uruguay Round Agreement on Agriculture," *European Review of Agricultural Economics*, 27(3), 259–80

Durand, M., J. Simon, and C. Webb, 1992. "OECD's Indicators of International Trade and Competitiveness," Working Paper, 120, OECD Economics Department, Paris

Faini, R., J. De Melo, A. Senhadji, and J. Stanton, 1991. "Growth-Oriented Adjustment Programs: A Statistical Analysis," *World Development*, 19(8), 957–67

Gibson, P., J. Wainio, D. Whitley, and M. Bohman, 2001. "Profiles of Tariffs in Global Agricultural Markets," Report 796, Economic Research Services, US Department of Agriculture, Washington, DC

Greenway, D., W. Morgan, and P. Wright, 1998. "Trade Reform, Adjustment and Growth: What Does the Evidence Tell Us?," *Economic Journal*, 108, 1547–61

Harrison, A., 1996. "Openness and Growth," *Journal of Development Economics*, 48, 419–47

Hertel, T. W., 2000. "Potential Gains from Reducing Trade Barriers in Manufacturing, Services and Agriculture," Federal Reserve Bank of St. Louis, July–August

Josling, T. and S. Tangermann, 1999. "Implementation of the WTO Agreement on Agriculture and Developments for the Next Round of Negotiations," *European Review of Agricultural Economics*, 26(3), 371–88

Organization for Economic Co-operation and Development (OECD), 2001a. "The Uruguay Round Agreement on Agriculture: an Evaluation of its Implementation in OECD Countries," Paris

    2001b. "Agricultural Policies in OECD Countries: Monitoring and Evaluation 2001," Paris

Pritchett, L., 1996. "Measuring Outward Orientation in LDCs: Can It Be Done?", *Journal of Development Economics*, 49, 307–55

Tangermann, S., 2001. "Has the Uruguay Round Agreement on Agriculture Worked Well?," paper presented at the International Agricultural Trade Research Consortium Meeting, May 18, Washington, DC

World Trade Organization (WTO), 2000. "Tariff and Other Quotas," background paper by the WTO Secretariat, G/AG/NG/S/7 WTO, Geneva

# 4 How developing countries are implementing tariff-rate quotas

*Philip Abbott and B. Adair Morse*

The tariff-rate quota, or TRQ, emerged in the latter part of Uruguay Round negotiations over the Agreement on Agriculture as a sanctioned policy option. Under a TRQ, a country sets a low tariff on imports up to a minimum quantity, and a higher tariff on imports above that quantity. The agreement sets the higher of 3–5 percent of domestic consumption or the level of historical imports as each country's "minimum access commitment," or the quantity subject to the lower tariff. Considerable controversy has emerged over the effectiveness of this trade policy instrument, and how it might be reformed in subsequent WTO negotiations, with particular concerns raised on issues related to administering and implementing TRQs.

This chapter investigates implementation of TRQs by developing countries. We first consider issues that give insight into how and why developing countries have adopted TRQs in a manner different from that found for the United States, the European Union (EU), and other developed countries. We then present data and experience on trade policy reform and on changes in imports, both in- and above-quotas, for the fourteen developing countries reporting on the use of TRQs to the World Trade Organization (WTO). These observations allow us to develop a series of hypotheses and some conclusions on the issues critical to TRQ administration and to future agricultural trade liberalization.

## Issues in TRQ adoption

The TRQ was a compromise between two objectives – tariffication and market access. Economists and negotiators in the Uruguay Round wanted to adhere to the traditional GATT approach of converting non-tariff trade barriers (NTBs) into tariffs and lowering those tariffs, while business interests wanted guaranteed, transparent access to import markets. Negotiators hoped that by combining the two goals, the TRQ approach would help in the process of liberalizing agricultural trade. However, while tariffication was well understood, market access was a rather new and poorly understood concern. Effective market access requires that firms be able to penetrate markets that continue to apply moderate tariffs if NTBs are removed, and if regulations governing trade are applied in a clear and predictable manner. Although TRQs were championed as a tool of market access, negotiators did not have a shared vision of how TRQs might facilitate such access. Nor did negotiators anticipate the results of alternative means of implementing TRQs.[1]

Only now are papers beginning to appear that deal explicitly with TRQs and lay out some of their likely results in controlling trade (Abbott and Paarlberg, 1998; Boughner and de Gorter, 1999; Skully 1999).[2] These critiques and a few case studies have raised concerns that under certain market conditions, TRQs can act much like pure quotas – the very situation the Uruguay Round Agreement on Agriculture (URAA) was supposed to avoid.

Moreover, administrative procedures must arise to allocate the rights to those quotas. The WTO Secretariat has identified several alternatives, including auctioning, bilateral quotas (historical traders), state trading, and producer groups. These are all traditional, well-understood mechanisms for allocating quotas and assigning rents. Other mechanisms include applied tariffs and first-come, first-served; the latter was the approach that negotiators assumed countries would use to implement TRQs. Under these two approaches, the method for allocating quota rights is either non-existent or implicit, so underfill and overfill of TRQs are both likely outcomes. A final approach is license on demand, whose impact depends critically on how a country sets and allocates licenses.

While some WTO members have supported first-come, first-served as the closest alternative to a true tariff regime, critics have noted that this approach creates strong incentives for firms to import early and store their products, undermining the intention of the agreement. More importantly, in a report to the WTO on administration of tariff quotas, Australia noted that firms are unable to contract for services under this mechanism, since it does not assure them of market access. This interference with normal commercial practices is precisely the kind of problem those seeking to improve market access wished to avoid.

None of the mechanisms for allocating TRQs explicitly enhance market access, except to the extent that countries have tariffied NTBs and lowered tariffs. Nevertheless, a country may perceive its minimum access commitment as a lower limit on imports. Then most likely a state trading regime or government procurement operation ensures that the committed level of imports is realized. For market access as envisioned by the business community to occur, countries must commit to more open and transparent trading rules and regimes. Several of the mechanisms for implementing TRQs are clearly not transparent, and could limit trade.

Tariffication came rather late in the Uruguay Round negotiations, and the TRQ as a tariffication mechanism that secures market access arrived even later, as part of a December 1993 US–EU compromise. This compromise caught many developing countries by surprise. By the April 1995 signing of the URAA, only twenty-five developing countries[3] had provided detailed commitments, or offers, similar to those set forth in the US and EU final positions. Most developing countries were allowed simply to bind tariffs rather than submit full commitment schedules. Only a subset of the twenty-five offers by developing countries included market access commitments, and even fewer included reduced tariffs to be applied to those commitments. Only fourteen developing countries currently submit reports to the WTO on TRQs based on those offers.

The way the United States and EU use TRQs illustrates why that approach emerged from the US–EU compromise. By using TRQs to continue bilateral quotas for dairy and sugar imports, the US government maintains a trade regime similar to the one in place before the 1994 Agreement on Agriculture. This approach often gives preferential access to politically favored trading partners. The EU similarly uses TRQs to continue preferential trading arrangements. Those arrangements often act much like pure import quotas.

While developing countries often face bilateral quotas in their export markets, they are far less likely to use such quotas themselves. Developing countries rarely have markets large enough to effectively implement bilateral quotas, nor do they have the same political incentives to establish them, as they are often part of foreign aid programs. Developing countries are likely to consider other policy concerns, including stabilizing the domestic market, as more important than the favoritism inherent in bilateral quotas. Where developing countries may maintain preferential trade, they are more likely to administer such arrangements through state trading rather than bilateral quotas.

To understand what has happened since the 1994 Agreement, it is important to remember that minimum access commitments are not guarantees of minimum import levels (although some developing countries may have perceived them as this). Moreover, the tariff bindings for both TRQs and imports outside those limits are maximums – not necessarily the tariff levels that a country will apply. Many developing and developed countries alike set tariff bindings well above the tariff rates they apply (Ingco, 1995). These commitments were based on 1986 conditions, when world agricultural prices were low and many countries maintained high tariffs. The high tariff bindings have been labeled "dirty tariffication," reflecting the fact that the conversion of trade barriers to bound tariffs would not truly liberalize agricultural markets. However, these commitments have given countries flexibility in establishing applied tariffs and so administering agricultural policy.

Article 4 of the Agreement on Agriculture established TRQs only briefly and vaguely by referring to countries' schedules, which are typically simply tables reporting minimum access commitments. Occasionally, the schedules also contain commitments to lower tariff rates for in-quota imports. Countries' reports to the WTO are often intended to show simply that they are abiding by their minimum access commitment, which is not really a TRQ.

However, although most developing countries have not explicitly implemented TRQs, their applied tariff rates are usually well below both Most Favored Nation (MFN) bindings – those that apply to imports above the quota – and low in-quota tariff rates. Thus, despite dirty tariffication, our results suggest that developing countries have liberalized their agricultural import markets to a substantial degree. Moreover, most countries have continued past trends in agricultural imports or expanded these imports significantly. Imports that are below commitments are simply following prior trends, and expanding imports of these commodities to minimum access levels is probably unrealistic.

We therefore argue that widespread concern over the fact that many TRQs have not been filled is misplaced – at least in the case of developing countries. There is little evidence that TRQ-induced administrative constraints are limiting imports. However, there is also little evidence that TRQs are encouraging freer trade. Instead, substantial cuts in MFN tariffs have encouraged such trade.

We base such findings on a detailed investigation of TRQ implementation in the fourteen developing countries that are submitting tariff-quota reports to the WTO. We have examined these countries' initial URAA offers and documented where they include TRQs. Each country's yearly WTO reports indicate the quantity of in-quota imports for each commodity that the country declares as being under a TRQ regime. We have also used the UNCTAD Trade Analysis and Information System (TRAINS) database to determine the actual tariffs and methods of protection these countries apply to agricultural imports. (The WTO reports only include tariff bindings, or maximum tariffs, whereas TRAINS reports the tariffs countries actually used.) Finally, we have compared actual imports over time with historical trends, both within quotas and in excess of quotas. Time series on agricultural imports taken from the Food and Agriculture Organization's AGROSTAT database allowed us to estimate these trends and compare in-quota imports with total imports.

We use the combined evidence to distinguish between pure tariff regimes, pure quota regimes, two-tiered (true) TRQ regimes, and endogenous quota regimes. An endogenous quota is one that varies from year to year, based on domestic production and other market conditions that determine import requirements. It is a regime often used together with state trading in the past to stabilize domestic markets. That special case, along with explanations of the alternative regimes and conditions under which underfill and overfill of quotas is likely, are presented in the appendix (p. 94).[4]

Our approach allows us to uncover and explain situations that shed light on the debate over TRQ implementation, identify special cases in which underfill and overfill are likely to occur, and highlight cases where high transaction costs could lead to quota underfill. We also use the information – especially the applied tariff rates and the relationship between actual imports and trends – to assess how much countries have actually liberalized trade, and show how those results relate to the trade regimes each country has adopted. Our results reveal the importance of lowering MFN tariffs rather than using TRQs to achieve true liberalization of agricultural markets.

## Results from individual countries

Information across commodities, and special cases from each developing country we investigated, allow us make observations on trade policy and its impact on imports. From this information we are able to pose hypotheses about the effectiveness and problems associated with implementing TRQs.[5]

### Brazil

Brazil notifies the WTO of quota levels and in-quota imports for two commodities, apples and pears. Brazil's submissions report that the country has not implemented a TRQ because applied tariff rates are well below the committed TRQ. This claim is consistent with our data on applied tariffs, both MFN and TRQ rates. The WTO Secretariat has also identified applied tariffs as the implementation mechanism for the two Brazilian commodities. It is likely that these low applied tariff rates represent a substantial liberalization of these two markets in Brazil, and trade data are consistent with this expectation. Since 1995, imports of apples and pears have increased substantially. In particular, relative to the pre-1994 trend, four of the six actual import flows are statistically significantly greater than the trend. Liberalization has thus been achieved, but with low MFN rates, not through a TRQ.

### Costa Rica

Costa Rica notifies the WTO of TRQs on poultry and dairy products. It is one of the few developing countries seeking to implement an auction-like system of allocating quotas. It is interesting to note that although several products see substantial out-of-quota imports, the TRQs seldom fill, and in-quota imports are often at zero. Total imports are significantly above historical trends in some cases.

Poultry and fresh milk are examples of goods that were primarily non-traded prior to the URAA. Significant increases in imports have occurred since 1994, but these imports are well below the country's minimum access commitment. These relatively low import levels nevertheless represent an opening of trade at low (20 percent) MFN tariffs.

Imports of condensed milk following the URAA appear to be largely on trend. Cheese represents a similar situation, with imports falling slightly in 1996 and 1997 after rising in 1995. In these instances, there is little evidence that the trade regime is anything other than a pure tariff case.

Given low tariff levels outside the TRQ, exporters may have little incentive to work through the administrative requirements of the Costa Rican auction system, or to face the risk of competition under that system. The trade barrier established by the MFN tariff is low enough to permit more imports if demand warrants. Reducing the tariff below 20 percent would not be likely to substantially increase imports of these commodities. Hence, this may be a case where administrative requirements keep a quota from filling, but their elimination would probably not bring substantially greater imports.

*Colombia*

In general, Colombia has substantially opened its agricultural markets by lowering its MFN tariffs, not by adhering to a TRQ regime.

Colombia has notified the WTO that it employs TRQs for thirty-three agricultural commodities. These include meat products, dairy products, cereals, oilseeds, vegetable oils, sugar, orange juice, and cotton lint. In nineteen of these cases, applied tariffs are the implementation mechanism, and MFN tariff rates are generally low, ranging from 10 to 20 percent. It is noteworthy that tariff commitments are often well above 100 percent, and that TRQ and MFN tariffs are mostly identical. This is evidence of dirty tariffication, and Colombia could feasibly raise applied tariffs within their WTO commitments. However, this is also evidence that the country has cut tariffs substantially, at least since the mid-1980s. Import levels reflect this liberalization. Where applied tariffs are the implementation mechanism, total imports are often above trend.

For all other products, Colombia's TRQ implementation mechanism is license on demand. In the case of cereals and oilseeds – politically sensitive staples – the country grants import licenses only after domestic production has been sold. Colombia reports low MFN tariffs for these licenses, and imports are often consistent with past trends or slightly above trend. Variations above or below trend may be due to fluctuations in domestic production. This situation may correspond to an applied tariff regime, in that even if the country again lowers MFN rates, imports may remain largely unchanged if low elasticities of demand typify the commodity and the market.

These import markets may also retain characteristics of state trading. If the government is limiting licenses based on projected domestic needs, the licenses may stabilize domestic markets. However, even if Colombia is using licenses as a mechanism for domestic control, the country could be well within its WTO commitments in doing so, as imports are well in excess of quotas, and are on trend or expanding.

The one exceptional commodity in Colombia's license-on-demand regime is poultry. The domestic association INCOMEX, not the Ministry of Agriculture, regulates licenses for poultry imports. However, these imports have also followed the historical trend, after an opening of this market around 1991, and in-quota imports are always well in excess of quotas.

Colombia's only underfilled cases are a few instances of a pure tariff regime, where demand appears insufficient to justify the quota level of imports. If the state intervenes, it ensures that imports are well above minimum access commitments.

*Guatemala*

Guatemala initially submitted TRQ commitments for twelve commodities. For seven of the items, the implementation mechanism is an applied tariff regime, and fill rates are no longer reported. In each of these cases, the MFN tariff is well below the country's bound tariffs. For meat products, only trade in poultry was substantial before the close of the Uruguay Round. However, bovine and swine imports have grown significantly, surpassing minimum access commitments by 1997.

Sorghum is largely a non-traded commodity, and trade has never neared the minimum access commitment. Oil cake imports, on the other hand, have expanded well beyond market access minimums. Apples operate under an applied tariff regime, and imports are now significantly greater than historical trends after expanding rapidly beginning in 1994.

For cereals, Guatemala uses a license-on-demand implementation mechanism. This presents similar difficulties in interpretation as we found for Colombia. Guatemala reports only MFN rates, and they fall well below the country's URAA bindings. Imports appear to be on or slightly above trend, and only in the case of flour is underfill observed. There is substantial overfill in wheat imports. Given the likely low elasticity of demand for cereals, and the fact that Guatemala has historically been a substantial importer of such products, these data are consistent with a trade regime similar to the one that existed before the Uruguay Round. Whether licenses are controlled in the manner of endogenous quotas is open to question. The country applies relatively low tariffs on these commodities, and substantial fluctuation in imports is probably due to variability in domestic production.

The one TRQ offered by Guatemala for which imports are essentially zero is sugar. It is noteworthy that Guatemala exports sugar to the United States under the US TRQ. The high prices available in the US market may well keep

Guatemala active as an exporter, and, not surprisingly, few imports are observed for an export commodity.

## Indonesia

Indonesia reports the use of a TRQ only for rice. Indonesia relies on a parastatal agency (BULOG) to control trade in that commodity, and its implementation mechanism is state trading. The country's rice imports are several orders of magnitude greater than the minimum access commitment, and rice imports were significantly higher than historical trends in two of three post-Uruguay Round years. The fact that the applied MFN tariff rate is zero holds little or no meaning, given that the importing agent is the state trading agency. This trade regime appears to simply continue a pre-existing approach in a country increasingly dependent on imports to meet its food needs.

## Korea

Korea appears to be a country using TRQs to pursue trade regimes quite similar to those that existed prior to the 1994 URAA. The government continues to intervene heavily in agricultural trade and manages its quota levels to accomplish domestic objectives. Rents typically go to domestic interests. However, in many cases, the country's reported quotas exceed its initial minimum access commitments, and trade in a number of sectors has opened since the 1994 agreement.

Korea notifies the WTO of applied tariff rate quotas for twenty-eight agricultural commodities, including meats, dairy products, vegetables, fruits and juices, cereals, oilseeds, oils, and silk.

Korea is one of only two developing countries for which data on applied tariffs from UNCTAD include specific in-quota tariff rates in addition to higher MFN tariff rates. In some cases, Korea's applied MFN tariff rates are relatively low – on the order of 20 to 40 percent – and TRQ rates are comparable. For commodities where applied MFN and in-quota tariff rates are similar, substantial out-of-quota imports can occur. In a number of other cases, applied MFN tariffs are extremely high – over 200 percent – while in-quota tariffs range from 20 to 50 percent. Thus, trading firms can gain great advantage by obtaining the rights to a TRQ.

Korea uses a wide variety of institutional mechanisms to administer its many TRQs. According to the country's WTO submissions, producer groups, processors, cooperatives, and the Ministry of Agriculture typically allocate quotas. The mechanism for allocating quota rights for each commodity group appears to be somewhat flexible. Any rents that might accrue from the lower in-quota rates typically go to the producer association, cooperative, or parastatal administering the quota rather than to the traders. State trading is also a principal mechanism for managing TRQs for many commodities: the implementing agency is an association with ties to the government rather than an official agency of the Ministry of Agriculture.

Underfill is very uncommon in Korea, and imports for most commodities follow historical trends. Nevertheless, imports have increased substantially over the pre-1994 trend in twenty-four of 112 cases. In no case did imports significantly decline; in only three cases did reductions in imports of more than one standard error from trend occur.

### Malaysia

Malaysia notifies the WTO of TRQ use for pork, dairy products, cabbage, coffee, sugar, and tobacco. With the exception of tobacco, the implementation mechanism is license on demand. Because the MFN tariff rate is zero for these commodities, the TRQ rate cannot be lower. Tobacco imports enjoy a relatively low MFN tariff of 8.8 percent, and the WTO Secretariat reports that access is allocated to historical importers. Some degree of state trading is likely in each of these cases.

Historical imports of meat and dairy products were often low, and it was improbable that imports would reach the country's minimum access commitments. Indeed, substantial underfill occurs in several cases. Imports are far below quota for pork and eggs, for example. However, these commodities may be essentially non-tradable.

Total imports into Malaysia also often substantially exceed in-quota imports. Those data show that for all TRQ commodities, Malaysia's total imports are either following historical trends or growing significantly. We observe a statistically significant increase in imports since 1994 for ten of the twenty-four trade flows. In no case are imports even one standard deviation below historical trends. Hence, while Malaysia's TRQs may be substantially underfilled, the country's URAA commitments may have led to substantial opening of trade. However, analysts should consider the unidentified role of the state along with licenses in establishing the method and extent of trade liberalization.

### Mexico

Mexico notifies the WTO that it is implementing a TRQ only for dry milk. For the other commodities for which Mexico included minimum access commitments – wheat, barley, maize, cheese, coffee, meat, animal fats, and potatoes – the country reports that most nations find market access substantially better than quota requirements. Mexico is also implementing TRQs in its trade regime with the United States under the North American Free Trade Agreement (NAFTA). In the case of dry milk, Mexican imports are subject to substantial variation but essentially on historical trend – and always above the minimum access commitment. This is one of the few cases in which a developing country may be applying a bilateral quota, in that the implementation mechanism reported is historical importers. A substantial MFN tariff remains in place (128 percent), but Mexico gives preferential access under NAFTA to its most important dairy trading partners, the United States and Canada.

## Morocco

Morocco reports TRQs for meats, milk, cereals, soybeans, and sugar. Although MFN tariffs for meats are quite high, ranging from 125 to 362 percent, they fall within Morocco's URAA bindings. Tariffs on cereals range from 10 to 125 percent and are substantially lower than the high URAA bindings. While the reported implementation mechanism is first-come, first-served, Morocco offers no specific, lower in-quota tariffs. In its WTO submission, Morocco is required to report the magnitude of the TRQ offer and the in-quota imports. In every case in which total imports exceed – often by substantial amounts – the minimum access commitment, in-quota imports are simply reported as the minimum access commitment.

Moroccan legislation implementing these trade regimes has been made available to us, affording us with insights into the relationship between Morocco's reports to the WTO and its actual trade regime. Prior to the Uruguay Round, Morocco intended to implement a variable levy scheme for cereals, sugar, and oilseeds. Morocco now follows a trade regime for those commodities that is somewhat similar to the EU's treatment of cereals. The country sets a fixed tariff, and when world prices change, it varies that tariff to stabilize the domestic price. The country has adjusted its tariff schedule for cereals five times since the signing of the URAA. No mechanisms exist to implement an institution remotely like the TRQ for cereals, sugar, and soybeans.

Because the tariffs that Morocco employs sometimes reflect cuts in historical rates, and given that meat consumption in Morocco is expanding, we would expect – and do in fact observe – that imports of these commodities are either within historical trends or show significant increases. A prime example is feedstuffs, for which seven out of the nine trade flows in maize, sorghum, and soybeans show a significant rise in imports over trend.

Meats have historically been non-tradable goods in Morocco, and are subject to very high tariffs. The high tariffs and relatively low observed domestic meat prices confirm that these are essentially non-tradable goods. Import levels are also quite low, especially for lamb and poultry. (The substantial 1992 imports of lamb reflected a severe drought in Morocco, biasing the trends.) With the exception of beef imports for 1997, most meat imports in Morocco are substantially above trend. However, we believe that these increases are due to government procurement operations to supply domestic food programs, and thus are due to the Moroccan government's commitment to meet its URAA obligations, not to reduced protection under a TRQ.

Morocco included a footnote in its URAA commitments concerning TRQs. This information is instructive in revealing how the regime operates. The footnote states that Morocco will lower tariffs to TRQ levels where necessary – if imports are not sufficient to fill quotas. Since quotas for cereals, soybeans, and sugar are quite low relative to historical imports, the country meets this obligation in the normal course of importing. For lamb and poultry (but not for beef or milk), meeting minimum access commitments would require increased imports, and government intervention is required to make that happen in the face of prohibitive tariffs.

*Panama*

Since Panama was not a member of the WTO at the signing of the 1994 Agreement, no schedule of commitments is available. However, this country is an example of what may happen with TRQs in the future. Upon joining the WTO, Panama chose to include TRQs as part of its new trade policy regime. (Several Eastern European countries that have also recently joined the WTO have taken similar steps.) Panama began reporting its TRQs only in 1997, and the implementation mechanism is apparently evolving. The notification suggests that the country may sometimes auction its TRQ import lots.

Panama notifies the WTO of TRQs for meats, dairy products, cereals, potatoes, and tomatoes. It does not report its use of in-quota tariffs lower than MNF rates. However, it indicates that its MFN tariffs for these products are relatively low. The country does not specify an implementation mechanism by commodity. An exception is pork, for which the country maintains a bilateral agreement with Costa Rica. Panama is one of the few developing countries to implement a bilateral quota.

Several of these products – meat, dairy, and tomatoes – appear to have been largely non-tradable before Panama joined the WTO, and significant increases above historical trends have occurred. Other imports appear to be largely following historical trends. Moreover, Panama appears to be simply reporting its minimum access commitment as in-quota imports when actual imports are in excess of the required amount. In the two cases where there is underfill (poultry and tomatoes), total imports reported to the FAO are greater than Panama's reported in-quota imports. In the case of poultry, total imports are far in excess of the quota. The mechanisms for operating the auction system for poultry may not yet be in place, and the economic incentives to frequently import tomatoes may not exist.

## Philippines

The Philippines reports the use of TRQs for meats, cereals, potatoes, coffee, and sugar. The country is one of the few using lower in-quota tariff rates in addition to its MFN rates, according to UNCTAD. The Philippines now reports its implementation mechanism as historical importers, although the country previously notified the WTO that it used direct licensing and state trading. The National Food Authority, a state-trading enterprise (STE) handles rice imports, and producer groups handle pork and poultry imports. In general, the Philippines seeks to ensure that rents from TRQs accrue to domestic agents.

For meat products, underfill of TRQs is common, but substantial out-of-quota imports often exist. Imports of all commodities except goat have grown significantly. The Philippines has received a good deal of criticism for using producer groups to implement TRQs for certain commodities, as these groups have not always imported committed quantities. The government has therefore continually updated TRQ procedures, seeking to ensure that those quotas fill. This is an example of why a country may find it difficult to ensure both that quotas fill and that rents accrue to domestic agents. As Filipino MFN tariff rates fall from base to bound levels and approach lower in-quota tariff levels, rents will become less relevant. Growing demand in the Philippines is likely to boost imports of these commodities.

The Philippines invoked special safeguard provisions for rice, using state trading to manage those imports as the TRQ institution allows. In the case of maize, the country historically banned imports to protect producers on outlying islands who have a transportation disadvantage. With the implementation of the TRQ, that ban is no longer effective, and imports now arrive in amounts comparable to those found in the country's earlier history. State trading is also used to manage maize imports. This is another case in which the TRQ instrument permits a country to pursue a post-Uruguay Round regime similar to earlier regimes while also allowing some rise in imports.

The Philippines both imports some sugar and exports sugar under the US TRQ. A substantial increase in Philippines sugar imports has followed the 1994 Agreement. We will address later how this relates to the market incentives stemming from the US TRQ, but reforms under the URAA may have changed the Philippines from a net sugar exporter to a net sugar importer.

*Thailand*

Thailand presents one of the most complex cases for applying TRQs, and one of the cases in which underfill is most common. The fact that Thailand has applied TRQs to essentially non-tradable or export commodities is one clear explanation for this complexity. However, there appear to be several cases in Thailand of license-controlled imports rather than TRQ-influenced quantities, which produce imports well in excess of minimum access commitments. Thailand also appears to maintain substantial government involvement in controlling agricultural trade.

Thailand uses TRQs for a wide variety of agricultural commodities, including dairy products, vegetables, coffee and tea, cereals, oilseeds and oils, tobacco, and silk. Thailand has declared several different implementation mechanisms, and those have been in flux. The country declared license-on-demand as the most common implementation mechanism in 1997, but producer groups manage TRQs for onions, soybeans, and state trading is applied for garlic, coffee, tobacco, and coconut. In general, Thailand ensures that any rents accruing to rights to lower tariffs go to a variety of public and private institutions, including cooperatives, processors, producer associations, and parastatals, although historical importers receive a portion of some quotas.

Thailand does not report specific in-quota tariffs to UNCTAD, and their MFN applied tariffs typically are around 40–60 percent. Those applied rates are often substantially lower than Thailand's URAA bindings, yet somewhat larger than the in-quota tariffs included in its 1994 offer.

Several commodities for which TRQs may be applied were clearly either non-tradables or export goods before 1994. In most of those cases, imports have not occurred or grown since the 1994 Agreement; hence the country reports substantial underfill of these TRQs. For commodities with substantial imports prior to 1994, imports are largely following historical trends, although imports of maize, soybeans, soya cake, and fresh milk are growing significantly.

The implementation mechanism for milk has changed three times since 1994. State trading initially filled the quota and also produced substantial out-of-quota imports. The country gave rights to the quota to producer groups in 1996, and that year saw no in-quota imports but did attract substantial imports well in excess of the quota. In 1997, the country relied on licenses, and again reported no in-quota imports. Total imports fell substantially, to below the quota quantity, but that level was still substantially greater than the historical trend.

Maize and soy imports grew substantially after 1994, well in excess of minimum access commitments. Licenses were used throughout the period for maize, while soybeans have evolved to an applied tariff regime.

Thailand is one of the few developing countries using specific tariffs. An advantage of these tariffs is that they transmit less world price volatility into a domestic market. To the extent that the licensing scheme constitutes state trading or intervention to control imports, this effect would be less relevant.

## Tunisia

This country is one of the few where imports of TRQ-controlled commodities are below historical trends. In fact, it is the only developing country that posted statistically significant declines in import flows.

Tunisia notifies the WTO of TRQs for meats, dairy products, cereals, sugar, almonds, and tomato concentrate, and reports its implementation mechanism as historical importers. While the country's 1994 offer included in-quota tariffs below MFN rates, its applied tariff rates include only MFN rates. In most instances, these MFN rates are below its TRQ tariff commitments. Hence, this is an apparent case of dirty tariffication, with a trade regime applying rates that are in fact quite low.

Tunisia's reported in-quota imports indicate a substantial degree of underfill for all commodities except cereals, sugar, and cheese. Imports of the latter commodities are substantially in excess of quotas, and reported in-quota imports are equal to the quota rather than to actual imports. Imports of those items also appear to be following historical trends, with considerable variability owing to fluctuations in domestic production. The very low tariff rates for cereals, coupled with the report that imports come from historical importers, imply that Tunisia is using a state trading agency or government licensing board to manage trade.

In-quota imports of meat products appear to be substantially below total imports, which in turn are below minimum access commitments and follow historical trends. Almonds and tomato concentrate are largely non-tradable commodities with little to no imports, despite substantial committed quotas. The implementation mechanism used to administer all these quotas appears not to be functioning properly, or – more likely – expectations that Tunisia will import these products are unrealistic.

## Venezuela

Venezuela appears to have substantially reformed its agricultural trade regime. Although its 1994 bindings for many commodities are quite high, indicating dirty tariffication, applied tariffs are generally low. The low tariffs have led to increased imports in some cases, while other imports are following historical trends.

Like several other Latin American countries, Venezuela notifies the WTO of the use of a substantial number of TRQs. Commodities include meats, dairy products, cereals, oilseeds and oils, and feedstuffs from oilseeds. The reported implementation mechanism is applied tariffs for all items except maize and sorghum, for which importers must obtain licenses. In its WTO submission, Venezuela states that it began to administer TRQs for maize and sorghum in 1997, while it is importing all other commodities without quantitative restrictions. MFN tariffs are substantially below both the 1994 bindings and in-quota tariffs contained in the country's URAA offer. The country maintains tariffs on these commodities of 15 or 20 percent, and does not use in-quota tariffs, as reported to UNCTAD.

Imports of these commodities largely follow historical trends, although a few show significant increases and a few others show declines on the order of one standard deviation. Thus, the tariff reductions reflect liberalized trade, but low demand elasticities for many commodities means that imports have increased substantially in only a few cases. The country has recorded some imports of commodities that were largely non-tradable before 1994, but these often remain below minimum access commitments.

One goal of the maize and sorghum licensing scheme is to ensure that domestic production is sold before imports enter the country. Historical data suggest that in 1989 Venezuela curtailed imports of sorghum in favor of maize. Because minimum access included this period, the quota for sorghum has been substantially underfilled, while maize imports are well in excess of minimum access commitments and above historical trends.

### Hypotheses and observations across countries

The results from these fourteen countries suggest a number of conclusions on how developing nations are implementing TRQs and fulfilling their WTO commitments. Although rigorously testing any hypotheses over such diverse trade regimes is impossible, and there are always exceptions, the results do suggest consistent lessons:

- Developing countries have not widely used true TRQs. Commitments by developing countries mostly reflect minimum access guarantees, and include no special provisions such as in-quota tariff schedules for imports under TRQ regimes. In fact, only fourteen developing countries are even notifying the WTO that they are using TRQs. Over half the countries that are doing so are also using applied tariffs. In many other cases, the import regime looks more like state trading than a TRQ.
- TRQs were generally established for two categories of agricultural commodities: non-tradables and politically sensitive staples. Countries frequently report TRQs for meats, dairy products, cereals, oilseeds, and sugar. A few apply TRQs to fruits and vegetables. Trade in meat and dairy products before 1995 represented a very small percentage of domestic consumption, so it was

unlikely that these essentially non-tradable goods would meet the 3–5 percent import objective. While trade in high-value and processed agricultural products is growing rapidly world-wide, that trend remains largely among developed countries. Countries usually used state trading mechanisms to control pre-1995 trade in cereals and oilseeds because of the political sensitivity of those commodities. Hence, they were natural candidates for establishing TRQs – an institutional alternative to state trading that could be used to control imports.

- Quota underfill is a likely and common outcome in cases where countries establish TRQs for non-tradables. Even in developed countries where imports of these products are escalating, fractions of domestic consumption remain relatively low – under 5 percent.

- Quota underfill is also likely to occur for agricultural commodities with relatively low elasticities of demand. In the case of low-income countries with low price elasticities of demand, a reduction in the tariff – and hence a reduction in the domestic price – will at best only marginally increase domestic demand.

- Given the extent of true liberalization in these developing countries, analysts' concern over low fill rates is misplaced. Many developing countries still import low levels of certain commodities. However, trade in these commodities has been liberalized substantially and often expanded, while trade has remained on trend for most other commodities. Imports fall below trend in very few cases – negating the argument that administrative requirements arising from TRQs limit imports. We found little evidence that low fill rates stem from the high transaction costs of fulfilling administrative requirements of TRQs.

- Most agencies administering imports in developing countries have neither a means of establishing binding quotas nor an allocation mechanism to distribute rents from those quotas. If implementation mechanisms do generate rents, however, countries seek to distribute them to domestic agents. Results from individual countries and footnotes attached to their schedules indicate that either a parastatal agency or a domestic producer group usually receives the rights to implement a quota.

- On only a few occasions have domestic producer groups with such control frustrated the intent of TRQs and limited imports. Many implementing institutions are continuing to evolve, owing to governments' efforts to inhibit the private sector from evading the intent of tariff quotas. However, countries are having difficulty establishing mechanisms for implementing TRQs that can both distribute rents to domestic producer groups and maintain incentives for imports. In at least a few cases, low MFN tariffs have ensured increased imports.

- Virtually no developing countries use bilateral quotas. Swine imports in Panama appear to be an exception, along with pork in Costa Rica. This situation differs substantially from that in Eastern Europe, where bilateral quotas are common.
- Particularly for politically sensitive staples such as cereals and oilseeds, countries use either state trading or license-on-demand to control imports. License-on-demand is the least transparent mechanism described in this study. Many countries state that licenses function simply to ensure product quality or safety. If this is the true role of licenses, and they are indeed granted on demand, the TRQ could be operating as a pure tariff regime. In most cases, imports of these commodities were well above committed quotas. However, they could still operate as endogenous quotas under the control of a parastatal agency.
- Where state trading or endogenous quotas are the implementation mechanism, policies to ensure the sale of domestic production are common. Countries may issue licenses only after the domestic crop is sold, or allocate quotas to groups along with a domestic purchase requirement.
- Several countries have sought to implement trade regimes that are consistent with pre-WTO objectives. Countries' WTO reports include many descriptions of trade instruments that are inconsistent with the TRQ framework as originally conceived. For example, state trading agencies often use endogenous quotas to control import flows. Even if the agencies try to raise these quotas to minimum access levels, this mechanism maintains most, if not all, earlier policy objectives. For example, the Philippines commonly uses import bans to control protected sectors, so small quotas are still common. In Morocco, in contrast, the objective of the cereals policy was to enact a variable-levy regime.
- In virtually no case did we find evidence that countries are violating their tariff commitments. While dirty tariffication is common in MFN and in-quota tariff rate bindings, applied tariff rates are generally low, and often fall well below either binding.
- Imports are either on trend or above trend for most developing countries. Roughly half of the 180 commodity/country cases investigated have imports within one standard deviation of the trend forecast. Approximately 20–25 percent of these countries have imports that are significantly greater than trend (at a 5 percent level of significance). There are no statistically significant declines in imports below the trend forecast, and only about 10 percent of the cases declined more than one standard deviation below trend. Thus, either developing countries continued to import at a pace comparable to historical levels or they have significantly opened trade. These countries have virtually never used TRQs to reduce trade.

- The liberalization that has occurred is largely due to substantial reductions in MFN tariff rates applied on these items. Substantial trade liberalization has occurred for agricultural commodities for which countries filed tariff rate quota reports. However, in most cases of real liberalization, the trade regime more closely resembles a pure tariff regime than a TRQ regime. In a few cases government procurement efforts may have been used to fulfill URAA commitments.

The most commonly feared problem with TRQs – high administrative costs that prevent actual liberalization of agricultural markets and continued rent-seeking – is likely to grow in the future. These developing countries, who were caught off-guard by the US–EU compromise, seldom used true TRQs as implemented by developed countries, where administrative problems have been found to be more important. There is already evidence that newer entrants to the WTO, such as those in Eastern Europe, and those negotiating to enter, such as China, are using TRQs far more than existing WTO members to limit or forestall reform. Thus, the new round of trade talks should reform or eliminate this institution. The overall lesson for true trade liberalization is that reducing MFN tariffs and eliminating NTBs will be far more effective in opening trade than higher minimum access commitments or lower in-quota tariffs for a privileged few exporters.

## When developing countries face another nation's TRQ

More serious problems for developing countries may well arise when they face TRQs in their agricultural export markets. The following two cases highlight important problems for developing countries in such a situation. The cases show why tariffication remains an important objective of WTO negotiations, and also why the TRQ fails as an instrument for achieving the benefits of tariffication.

### Morocco

Morocco is a relatively efficient producer of fruits and vegetables, especially tomatoes and oranges. Its production costs fall below those of US and other major producers. Moroccan production costs for these items range from 25 to 30 percent of producer prices found in the EU, its principal export market. However, handling and distribution equipment in Morocco is primitive, and in need of an upgrade to ensure higher-quality tomato exports.

In the past, Morocco has sent virtually all its tomato exports to France, but must consider diversifying its markets with the changes in the European trade regime for these commodities. In the off-season, the French market readily accepted Morocco's tomatoes, but quality seems to constrain Moroccan competitiveness in other destinations, in both the EU and elsewhere.

The EU uses TRQs to implement a minimum entry price scheme, and to give preferential access to certain historical importers into those markets. Many Moroccan fruit and vegetables exports to the EU face stiff TRQs, and thus receive continued preferential treatment. Morocco's quotas into the EU expanded somewhat under the EU–Moroccan Free Trade Agreement, following the 1994 URAA and other changes in European trade regimes. Morocco's export prices can thus be as low as half the minimum EU entry price for quantities up to minimum access commitments. This arrangement can yield substantial rents for the actors in these markets. Both the implementation of these quotas and the institutions in Morocco and the EU are crucial in determining how these rents are shared.

Some analysts consider importing agents in the EU to be oligopolistic, in that they exert monopsonistic buying power. For example, Tangermann (1997) argues that EU distributors can take advantage of their market power and collect all the rents available from the TRQs with Eastern Europe. However, a Moroccan state agency controls exports to the EU, along with a cooperative association of the largest producers, who are generally able to exercise monopoly power. Hence, the market arrangement is a bilateral oligopoly. There is evidence that Moroccan agents and European distributors share rents from lower in-quota tariffs roughly equally. Of course, to maintain these rents Morocco must continue state trading in some form.

The operation of the Moroccan domestic market reflects a situation wherein a state trader has monopoly control and faces an export market with both quantity constraints and higher fixed prices. Domestic prices for tomatoes in Morocco are roughly half of the prices that exporters receive. Producers handle tomatoes for the export market more carefully to ensure higher quality, and dump surplus tomatoes on the domestic market. The state trader uses cooperative arrangements to share rents among producers, and to average producer prices between domestic and export markets.

This trading arrangement creates a disincentive – or at least an excessively high degree of risk – for any producers that invest in improved handling and distribution equipment. Because of the quota and preferential access, Moroccan produce reaches the EU market at a price well below that offered by competitors, so Moroccans have no incentive to upgrade export-related equipment. Without such investments, however, Moroccan tomatoes are not high enough in quality to penetrate other export markets. If it competed on an equal footing with other exporters, Moroccan producers would probably make these investments, and thus expand exports. While the current arrangements may seem to give Morocco a strong comparative advantage, they afford virtually no scope for expanding exports.

This case highlights two serious problems facing a developing country that confronts TRQs in its export markets. Since TRQs generate rents, exporting institutions must exist to capture those rents, slowing or curtailing the privatization process. Such a trading system may also provide a disincentive for investments needed to improve or expand a sector.

*The Philippines*

The Philippines is one of several sugar-producing developing countries that has historically received preferential access to the US sugar market. Before the Uruguay Round agreement, the United States maintained an import quota on sugar. US domestic sugar prices were often two to three times world prices, and any country allocated rights under that quota gained substantial rents. These rents could be viewed as part of the US foreign aid program, as the US allocated them based on political considerations.

Under URAA guidelines, the United States now uses a TRQ for its sugar regime. With a relatively high MFN tariff on sugar and a much lower in-quota tariff, this regime continues to operate much like a pure quota regime. The MFN tariff is essentially prohibitive, and US imports of sugar are close to quota amounts. While countries that are allocated rights to this quota do collect rents, they are somewhat lower than under the previous regime because a portion of the rent as in-quota tariff revenue goes to the US government.

In the Philippines a complex domestic policy regime for sugar arose to share the rents from the US sugar quota between exporting agents, sugar refiners, and cane producers. Abbott observed that the higher prices resulting from this scheme substantially expanded sugar production in the Philippines, to the point where the country would become a sugar importer rather than an exporter if producers were not offered the higher US prices. Thus one result of the quota regime, which continues under the TRQ, is that it enables a country to convert from importing to exporting a commodity for which it does not hold a comparative advantage.

Because the US TRQ now offers lower rents, the benefits to exporting countries are still positive but much lower. Hence, the same domestic institutions must continue to share much smaller rents. In the Philippines, since one result of lower rents is lower prices, incentives to production will decrease. This may be why since 1994 the Philippines has begun to import substantial quantities of sugar.

This case reveals the distortions that can arise from quotas, and hence from a TRQ that operates as a pure quota regime. These distortions prompt countries to export commodities for which they do not have comparative advantage. This is especially likely where the TRQ implementation mechanism is historical importers, or bilateral quotas based on political rather than economic considerations. TRQs can force complex distorting domestic institutions to continue to allocate any rents arising from quotas. Without these institutions, trading agents are likely to capture any rents, and no benefits from the market preference will accrue to producers.

## Appendix  How TRQs operate

Three trade regimes are possible outcomes under a TRQ, as illustrated in figure 4A.1 These include a true TRQ regime, a pure tariff regime, and a quota regime. In figure 4A.1 *MAC* is equal to the minimum access commitment or quota. Imports are denoted by *M* and are determined by a net import demand function that yields imports according to the domestic price in the importing country. *Tiq* is the in-quota tariff and *Tmfn* is the MFN tariff.[6] *Pd* is the domestic price; *Pw* is the world price; and *Pb* represents a border price equal to the sum of the world price plus an applicable tariff. The domestic price (*Pd*) is determined by the world price (*Pw*) plus a tariff (*Tiq* or *Tmfn*) as under a small-country assumption, except when net import demand yields a price falling in a range determined by the low in-quota tariff and the higher MFN tariff. Rents are shown as shaded areas in the cases where they accrue, panels a and b.[7]

As shown in figure 4A.1a, if net import demand at a domestic price equal to the world price plus the MFN tariff exceeds the minimum access commitment, then a true TRQ as envisioned under the initial Agreement on Agriculture would arise. Thus, $Pd = Pw + Tmfn$, and *M* exceeds *MAC*. In that case, the domestic market outcome bears much resemblance to a tariff regime, at the MFN tariff. However, whoever has the rights to import at the lower in-quota tariff (*Tiq*) will collect a rent. Hence, this outcome maintains disadvantages characteristic of a quota. Rent-seeking behavior will occur due to the rents available under this

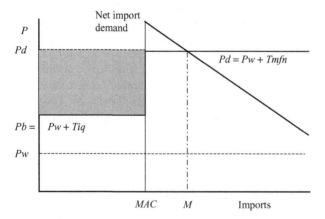

a  TRQ with above-quota imports (true TRQ)

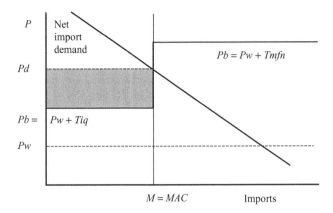

b  TRQ with imports at quota $= MAC$

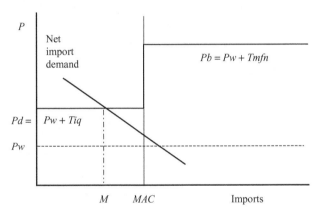

c  TRQ with below-quota imports (pure tariff)

*Notes:* $Tmfn$ = Most Favored Nation (MFN) tariff rate, hence out-of-quota rate
$Tiq$ = In-quota or TRQ tariff rate
$MAC$ = Minimum Access Commitment, hence quota for a TRQ
Net import demand $= M(Pd) =$ Demand$(Pd) -$ Supply$(Pd)$
$Pw$ = World price
$Pd$ = Domestic price
$Pb$ = Border price $= Pw + T$
$M$ = Imports

Figure 4A.1  TRQ regions

regime. An administration mechanism to allocate those rents – and the rights
to the lower tariff on in-quota imports – is necessary even though the market
outcome is much like the pure tariff outcome. The only cases where this is
clearly occurring for the developing countries investigated here are for a few
commodities in the Philippines and Korea.

In figure 4A.1b, net import demand intersects the import supply step function on its vertical portion, at a quantity equal to the minimum access commitment (or quota). Hence, the TRQ policy instrument can behave exactly like a quota. In that case, the domestic price exceeds the sum of the world price plus the in-quota tariff ($Pd > Pw + Tiq$). The MFN tariff is prohibitive, however, in that $Pd$ is less than $Pw + Tmfn$. The difference between $Pd$ and $Pw + Tiq$ is a rent. That rent accrues to whomever holds the rights to the quota under the market institutions that exist. All the issues that arise in the literature on quotas, especially those concerning allocation of rents, are relevant in this situation. This outcome may occur when prohibitively high MFN tariffs have been applied. Our results in fact find very few cases that seem to correspond to this regime.

In figure 4A.1c, net import demand at a domestic price equal to the world price plus the in-quota tariff ($Pd = Pw + Tiq$) is below the minimum access commitment (or quota). In this case the TRQ instrument behaves exactly like a simple tariff. Thus, $M$ is less than $MAC$, and no rent accrues.

### Special cases

Several minor modifications of the three trade regimes help explain quota overfill, quota underfill, and the consequences of higher-than-minimum-access quotas managed by the state, called endogenous quotas. These cases are shown in figure 4A.2.

If countries do not apply or enforce quota-like constraints, imports can exceed the minimum access commitment and the trade regimes may continue to behave like a tariff. This is in fact a very common outcome for the TRQ as applied by developing countries.

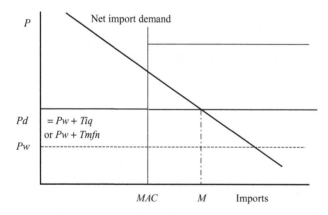

a  TRQ with overfill – quota not binding

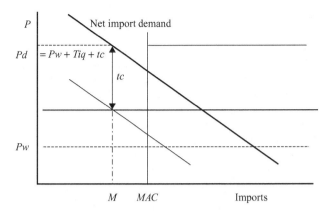

b  TRQ with underfill due to transactions costs (*tc*) of administrative requirements.

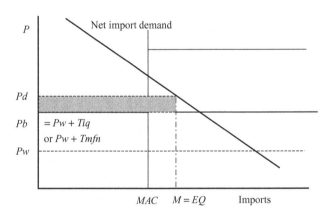

c  TRQ with an endogenous quota (*EQ*)

*Notes:* Tmfn = Most Favored Nation (MFN) tariff rate, hence out-of-quota rate
*Tiq* = In-quota or TRQ tariff rate
*MAC* = Minimum Access Commitment, hence quota for a TRQ
Net import demand = M(Pd) = Demand(Pd) − Supply(Pd)
*tc* = Transactions costs due to TRQ administration
*Pw* = World price
*Pd* = Domestic price
*Pb* = Border price = Pw + T
*M* = Imports
*EQ* = Endogenous quota

Figure 4A.2  Special cases

This special but relevant case is shown in figure 4A.2a. In that case the quota is simply not a binding constraint. Thus, $Pd = Pw + Tiq$, and $M$ exceeds $MAC$.

Another possibility is that there is only an MFN tariff and no lower in-quota tariff. In either situation the administrative procedures do not in fact effectively limit imports or establish a quantity of imports receiving preferential treatment. Hence, this outcome is a pure tariff case. The general outcome, in which the TRQ behaves like a simple tariff with no rents accruing, is the most commonly observed implementation of TRQs by developing countries.

Underfill may also occur, as shown in figure 4A.2b, if administrative requirements add transaction costs that in effect shift demand inward. This is the concern expressed by the WTO Secretariat and others who see low fill rates and this market outcome as problematic. In that case the domestic price includes transaction costs ($tc$) as well as a tariff, or $Pd = Pw + Tiq + tc$. At that domestic price, imports determined by the net import demand function are below the $MAC$; hence the quota is underfilled. This case also operates like a tariff, in that no rents accrue but additional costs to meet administrative requirements do accrue. The administrative costs act like an additional tariff.

The next most common outcome for TRQ implementation and administration in developing countries is a licensing scheme, shown in figure 4A.2c. In this case it is difficult to tell if the license is effectively implementing a quota, or if it simply ensures product quality and the regime is in fact a pure tariff regime. Hence, this administration mechanism is not transparent. Furthermore, the state may be running a variable quota regime rather than a tariff regime, but using a quota higher than the minimum access commitment. Thus, state trading may in fact apply in cases where licenses are identified as the allocation mechanism.[8]

When the quota is above the minimum access commitment and is managed by the state (for example, to stabilize the domestic market), the regime may be called an endogenous quota (Abbott, Patterson, and Young 1998; Boughner and de Gorter, 1999). When this quota regime applies, imports ($M$) will be above $MAC$ and $Pd$ will exceed $Pw + Tiq$, as shown in figure 4A.2c. We identify such cases as endogenous quotas. This case behaves much like a pure quota, except that the effective quota is higher than $MAC$, and rents accrue on all imports. Often this case will be indistinguishable from a tariff regime and will be so designated.

### Notes

1. When this author was working with the Philippines Ministry of Agriculture in preparing its final GATT offer for the Marrakech meeting, we contacted the US trade representative to determine how sugar import quotas would be handled. US negotiators were unaware that they would have to establish an allocation mechanism. The United States has since implemented an allocation mechanism that is based on historical imports and differs very slightly from that which existed before the agreement.

2. Quotas and their consequences have been studied extensively; however, those lessons can be applied to TRQs only when the alternative regimes that may arise under this instrument are understood.

3. We did not include the countries of Eastern Europe because cursory examination suggested results quite different from those for the developing countries reviewed here, especially for late entrants to the WTO. This limitation also kept the research effort manageable. Those countries warrant a specific study to understand their current bilateral and multilateral use of TRQs. When we refer to developing countries, we will be excluding Eastern Europe from that group.

4. In classifying the mechanism that each country used to apply a TRQ to each commodity, we used the WTO Secretariat's assessment but then expanded on this insight. For example, if the WTO classifies a country as using "applied tariffs," if any sources do not contradict this observation, and if the TRQ is either underfilled or overfilled, we suggest there is strong evidence that the TRQ is operating as a pure tariff regime. Country-supplied information on applied tariff rates typically indicates only a MFN tariff rate; this would support the same conclusion. Where imports are very close to or exactly at the quota, and where a mechanism exists to limit imports, we identify the regime as a quota regime. In the few cases where applied tariff rates indicate both an MFN tariff and an in-quota tariff, and where in-quota imports are well below total imports, the country is applying a true TRQ. Where countries require importers to obtain licenses, the extent to which they are applying a quota is not transparent. Because we found that most countries that use licensing overfill their minimum access commitments, these cases may be pure tariff regimes, or situations where the state limits or controls access, though above its commitment. When state trading limits access in a manner varying with market conditions, and not based on a pure tariff outcome, this regime would correspond with an endogenous quota.

5. Further information on data sources, analytical methods, and numerical results are available from the authors on request.

6. This simple illustration of a TRQ assumes specific tariffs. Only minor modification is necessary to incorporate the more commonly used *ad valorem* tariffs.

7. Rent per unit of in-quota imports equals the difference between the domestic price and the world price plus the in-quota tariff. The total value of that rent, which we equate to the concept of rent in the rest of the chapter, is this per unit rent times the volume of in-quota imports.

8. Some definitions of state trading require that the parastatal physically handle a commodity. This definition would exclude licensing. In some developing countries reformed state traders have used licenses after abandoning the idea of physically handling agricultural commodities. Nevertheless, the state can control the essential terms of trade by limiting quantities of imports.

## References

Abbott, P. and P. Paarlberg, 1998. "Tariff Rate Quotas: Structural and Stability Impacts in Growing Markets," *Agricultural Economics*, 19, 257–67

Abbott, P., P. Patterson, and L. Young, 1998. "Plans and Adjustment: A Structural Approach to Modeling Grain Importer Behavior," in T. Yildrim, A. Schmitz and

W. H. Furtan (eds.), *World Agricultural Trade: Implications for Turkey*, Boulder, Colo: Westview Press

Boughner, D. S. and H. de Gorter, 1999. "The Economics of 2-tier Tariff-Rate Import Quotas and the Agreement on Agriculture in the WTO," Department of Agricultural, Resource, and Managerial Economics, Cornell University

General Agreement on Tariffs and Trade (GATT), 1994. *Uruguay Round Agreement on Agriculture*, Geneva

Ingco, M. D., 1995. "Agricultural Liberalization in the Uruguay Round," *Finance and Development*, 32, 43–5

Skully, D. W., 1999. "Tariff-Rate Quota Administration," Economic Research Service, US Department of Agriculture, Washington, DC, January

Tangermann, S., 1997. "Access to European Union Markets for Agricultural Products after the Uruguay Round, and Export Interests of the Mediterranean Countries," UNCTAD INT/93/A34, Geneva, April

United Nations Conference on Trade and Agricultural Development (UNCTAD), 1999. "Trade Analysis and Information Systems," TRAINS Cd-Rom Version 6.0. UNCTAD, Geneva, March

United Nations Food and Agriculture Organization (FAO), 1999. "AGROSTAT Database," Rome

World Trade Organization (WTO), 1995–9. "Committee on Agriculture – Notifications," various countries and submissions – AG/N/cty/# where cty denotes country and # is the submission, MA:1 and MA:2 Submissions, WTO Document Dissemination Facility, Geneva

1996. "Complete Results of the Uruguay Round," Cd-Rom, Geneva

1997a. "Tariff Quotas Administration: First Come-First Served," Australian Paper, WTO Committee on Agriculture AIE/9, October 29, Geneva

1997b. Committee on Agriculture, Administration of Tariff Quotas, Australian Paper, AIE/1, May 13, Geneva

1997c. Committee on Agriculture, Administration of Tariff Quotas, New Zealand Paper, AIE/5, August 12, Geneva

1997d. Committee on Agriculture, Administration of Tariff Quotas, United States Paper, AIE/7, WTO, October 27, Geneva

1998a. "Tariff and Other Quotas," WTO Secretariat, AIE/S1/Rev.1, May 26, Geneva

1998b. "Tariff Quota Administration and Tariff Quota Fill," WTO Secretariat, AIE/S4/Rev.1, June 10, Geneva

1999. Committee on Agriculture, Issues Regarding Market Access Notifications, Canadian Paper, G/AG/W/43, March 12, Geneva

# 5 A review of the operation of the Agreement on Sanitary and Phytosanitary Measures

*Gretchen Stanton*

## Background to the SPS Agreement

The General Agreement on Tariffs and Trade (GATT) established rules for international trade in all goods, including food and agricultural products, in 1948. But the GATT rules also contained an exception which permitted countries to apply measures "necessary to protect human, animal or plant life or health" as long as these did not unjustifiably discriminate between countries nor were a disguised restriction to trade. During the GATT's Tokyo Round of multilateral trade negotiations (1974–9), an Agreement on Technical Barriers to Trade (often referred to as the "Standards Code") was negotiated, which *inter alia* covered technical requirements resulting from food safety and animal and plant health measures.

The focus during the Uruguay Round of multilateral trade negotiations (1986–94) on the liberalization and reform of agricultural trade renewed interest in disciplining the use of non-tariff trade barriers (NTBs), including sanitary and other technical regulations. The Standards Code was rewritten during the Uruguay Round, and at the same time a separate agreement covering sanitary and phytosanitary (SPS) measures was negotiated. The new Technical Barriers to Trade Agreement (TBT Agreement) and the Agreement on the Application of Sanitary and Phytosanitary Measures (SPS Agreement) entered into force along with the Agreement on Agriculture, on January 1, 1995.

## Basic provisions of the SPS Agreement

The SPS Agreement affirms the right of WTO Members to restrict international trade when necessary to protect human, animal or plant life, or health. At the same time, it aims to ensure that unnecessary health and safety regulations are not used as an excuse for protecting domestic producers from trade competition. To avoid SPS measures being used as disguised trade restrictions, the SPS Agreement requires such measures to be based on science. They may be applied only to the extent necessary to protect human, animal or plant life, or health. And they may not arbitrarily or unjustifiably discriminate between countries where identical or similar conditions prevail.

The SPS Agreement covers all measures whose purpose is to protect
• human or animal health from food-borne risks
• human health from animal- or plant-carried diseases
• animals and plants from pests or diseases
• the territory of a country from damage caused by pests.

The SPS Agreement applies to any type of measure, including requirements on final products, processing requirements, inspection or control techniques, and health-related packaging or labeling.

Members are encouraged to base their measures on internationally developed standards, in order to ensure their scientific justification and advance the harmonization of SPS requirements. The SPS Agreement explicitly recognizes the international standards, guidelines, and recommendations established by three intergovernmental organizations: the FAO/WHO Codex Alimentarius Commission, the Office International des Epizooties (OIE), and the FAO International Plant Protection Convention (IPPC). Measures based on international standards developed by these organizations are deemed to be consistent with the SPS Agreement.

Governments may choose to impose measures that result in a level of protection higher than those of an existing international standard. However, in this case, or when no relevant international standard exists, the measures have to be based on a risk assessment. If asked, Members have to explain why the level of protection achieved by an international standard is not sufficient and make their risk assessment available to other Members.

When preparing their risk assessment, Members have to take into account available scientific evidence. In cases where relevant scientific evidence is not sufficient, Members may adopt temporary measures based on the available pertinent information while seeking to obtain the necessary scientific evidence. Although governments have a right to determine the level of health protection which they consider appropriate, arbitrary or unjustifiable differences in levels of protection which result in discrimination or a disguised restriction on trade must be avoided.

Furthermore, in considering what measure to apply to achieve their health objective, a government must choose the least trade restrictive measure that is feasible.

When an exporting Member can demonstrate that its measures achieve the level of protection required by an importing country, then that importing country should accept the exporting country's measures as equivalent. A member cannot refuse to enter into consultations about equivalence if another Member requests them.

The SPS Agreement recognizes that because of differences in climate, existing pests or diseases, or food safety conditions, SPS regulations have to be adapted to local conditions. The SPS Agreement requires Members to recognize pest- or disease-free areas, and to adapt their measures accordingly. These areas can consist of all of a country, part of a country, or all or parts of several countries.

In the interest of transparency, Members have to publish their SPS regulations. In addition, each WTO Member must identify a national notification authority and an enquiry point. They are responsible for submitting notifications, providing the full text of SPS regulations to interested Members, and responding to requests for more information about new or existing measures. In particular, new or changed measures which are not based on international standards and which could affect trade have to be notified to the WTO when they are at the draft stage, except in emergency situations. Members' comments have to be taken into account.

Members are also required to facilitate the provision of technical assistance to help other countries achieve the level of protection desired in their export markets.

## Implementation of the SPS Agreement

A WTO committee has been established to oversee the implementation of the SPS Agreement among Members. All WTO Member governments are automatically members of the SPS Committee, and governments that have observer status in the WTO have observer status in this committee also. The SPS Committee has also granted observer status to the FAO/WHO Codex Alimentarius Commission, the Office International des Epizooties, and the FAO International Plant Protection Convention, as well as to other relevant international governmental bodies, including the World Bank.

The SPS Committee usually meets three times per year. A typical agenda includes discussion on specific trade concerns identified by Members, a wide range of transparency issues, and technical assistance needs and projects carried out by Members, the WTO Secretariat, or observer organizations. In addition, the Committee is monitoring the use of international standards and developing guidelines to assist governments with the objective of achieving consistency in their application of the concept of the appropriate level of SPS protection.

As stipulated by the SPS Agreement, the Committee carried out a three-year review of the operation and implementation of the SPS Agreement, which was finalized in March 1999. In the Three Year Review, Members agreed that the SPS Agreement was a useful set of international trade rules, which had contributed to improving international trading relationships with respect to SPS measures. However, the Committee noted that a number of implementation issues gave concern to some Members, including a number of developing country Members. The Committee welcomed that a substantial number of SPS-related trade matters had been solved through discussions at formal SPS meetings, or through bilateral consultations.

*Transparency*

In the Three Year Review, Members noted that through the establishment of enquiry points and national notification authorities and through notifications, the Agreement had significantly improved transparency in the application of SPS measures. However, transparency could be further improved. Many Members still have not notified any SPS measures, and have not established an enquiry point. Members who notify do not always provide all the information necessary to judge whether the proposed measure in question could affect another Member's exports. To further improve transparency, the Committee made some changes to the recommended notification procedures in the context of the Three Year Review. These included asking countries where possible to indicate which countries would be particularly affected by a proposed regulation.

The Committee also underlined that it is essential that regulations be notified when they are at the draft stage. If sufficient time is then provided for other countries to comment on proposed regulations, potential problems can be identified at a stage where it is still relatively easy to find solutions, for example by modifying the draft measure. Exchanging information electronically, including publishing regulations and unofficial translations on the internet, could significantly facilitate transparency. The Committee therefore encouraged Members to publish their SPS measures on the internet, and to make available even unofficial translations of draft measures.

*Special and Differential Treatment and technical assistance*

The SPS Agreement asks Members to take into account the needs of developing countries in the preparation and application of SPS measures. Where possible, developing country Members should receive longer time frames for compliance with new SPS measures. Developing country Members had been able to postpone the implementation of certain provisions of the Agreement until 1997. Least developed countries could delay the application of the Agreement for a period of five years, which ended at the beginning of the year 2000.

In the Three Year Review, the SPS Committee recognized that the WTO Secretariat and other relevant organizations had provided substantial technical assistance and cooperation over the first three years of the implementation of the Agreement. However, there was a need for enhanced technical assistance and cooperation, especially in the areas of human resource development, national capacity-building, and the transfer of technology and information. Little information was available regarding the implementation of provisions of the SPS Agreement concerning hands-on cooperation, for example between importers and exporters trying to meet their requirements. As a follow-up to the review, the Secretariat has solicited such information from Members through questionnaires on technical assistance.

Countries that need such assistance have been encouraged to make use of Committee meetings to inform Members of their needs. Countries who are willing to provide assistance should use the Committee meetings to make known their projects and willingness. A need for greater coordination of technical assistance activities by Members, and also by the WTO Secretariat and other international organizations was recommended. This need for coordination can partly be addressed through the Integrated Framework for Trade-Related Technical Assistance to Least Developed Countries. Through this framework, the IMF, ITC, UNCTAD, UNDP, World Bank, and WTO are coordinating their assistance efforts in response to country needs' assessments prepared by least developed countries. As of September 2002, further coordination is provided by the Standards and Trade Development Facility through which the FAO, OIE, World Bank, WHO and WTO coordinate their technical assistance activities and jointly administer funding for SPS-related capacity building projects.

*International harmonization*

Harmonization, through the adoption of international standards and guidelines, facilitates trade by reducing the number of different standards exporters have to meet. Harmonization also increases transparency. Moreover, in terms of the SPS Agreement, international standards ensure the scientific justification of the measure. The Committee has welcomed the cooperation of the Codex and of the other international standard-setting organizations recognized by the Agreement, and their continuing work in updating and expanding international standards.

In 1998, the Committee adopted a preliminary procedure to monitor the process of international harmonization and the use of international standards, guidelines, and recommendations. This procedure encourages Members to identify where there are problems with existing international standards, or where an international standard is lacking. Other Members are then asked whether they share the identified concerns, and these are brought to the attention of the relevant standard-setting organizations. In July 2003, the Committee agreed to continue with the monitoring procedure for another three years.

Although there has been increased activity in this area, much remains to be done. Suggestions by Members in the context of the Three Year Review refer not only to a more widespread adoption of international standards, but also to their development. Many developing countries are concerned that their interests are not adequately taken into account in the standard-setting organizations. Some developing countries have indicated that they have difficulties in participating actively in the development of international standards.

Furthermore, while developed countries fear that the standards might become a "lowest common denominator," developing and least developed countries often find the standards unnecessarily stringent. It is difficult to imagine, however, that the level of international standards could be lowered, at a time when consumers around the world are demanding an ever higher quality and safety of food. Although most WTO Members are members of the relevant standard-setting organizations, ways to increase developing countries' participation have been proposed, for example by organizing meetings in developing countries. Once established, standards have to be reviewed regularly to maintain them up to date, especially when scientific information changes. Where problems with existing standards, or the lack of standards have an impact on trade, cooperation and communication between WTO and the standard-setting bodies is especially important.

*Equivalence and adaptation to regional conditions*

Although there has been an increase in the recognition of equivalence and in bilateral negotiations to this end, in the Three Year Review the Committee recognized that further efforts were necessary to implement this provision in view of its importance for trade facilitation, especially for developing country Members. Members acknowledged the need to provide information on their appropriate level of protection and to recognize equivalence in achieving this level of protection, rather than insisting essentially on the sameness of measures. The Committee asked Members to provide more information on bilateral equivalence agreements, and welcomed the work to further the application of equivalence, which is being carried out by Codex and other relevant international organizations.

In 2002, the Committee adopted guidance to further the practical implementation of the provisions on equivalance. These guidelines clarify the information to be provided by an exporting country and the procedures to be followed by the importing country. The Committee also welcomed the fact that an increasing number of Members were applying the concept of adaptation to regional conditions, in particular by recognizing pest- or disease-free areas, or areas of low pest or disease prevalence. There were still some difficulties in the implementation of these concepts, which stemmed from divergences in the interpretation and implementation of international guidelines, excessively lengthy administrative processes in importing countries, and the complexities often involved in risk assessment. The international standard-setting bodies assist Members in the application of pest- or disease-free areas.

## Dispute resolution

Discussions of special trade concerns at SPS meetings draw attention to potential trade conflicts and may help avoid formal disputes. In a few cases, bilateral consultations, sometimes with the participation of the Chairman of the SPS Committee or the WTO Secretariat, help to facilitate the clarification of misunderstandings or otherwise resolve the issues involved. In the Three Year Review, the Committee noted that ad hoc consultations "could be an effective means of satisfactorily solving problems." Over 150 specific trade concerns were raised at SPS Committee meetings between 1995 and 2003.

Independent of the opportunity that the Committee provides in this respect, every WTO Member has the right to take recourse, at any time, to the formal WTO dispute-settlement procedures. Between the establishment of the WTO in 1995 and mid-year 1999, over 175 disputes had been raised under this procedure. Sixteen of these disputes alleged violation of the SPS Agreement. In some cases, a mutually agreed solution was reached; in other cases, the SPS issues are a minor element. Panels and the Appellate Body under the formal WTO procedures have examined four issues involving the SPS Agreement:

- EC Measures Concerning Meat and Meat Products (Hormones), complaints by the United States and by Canada
- Australia – Measures Affecting Importation of Salmon, complaints by Canada and the United States
- Japan – Measures Affecting Agricultural Products (Varietal Testing), complaint by the United States
- Japan – Measures Affecting the Importation of Apples (Fire blight), complaint by the United States.

The Hormones case dealt with food safety; the Salmon case dealt with animal health and the varietal testing and fire blight cases dealt with plant health.

Since these SPS disputes involved scientific or technical issues, the panels sought advice from experts chosen in consultation with the parties. The panel can consult individual experts, establish an advisory technical experts group, or consult the relevant international organizations.

In the Hormones Case, the Panels and the Appellate Body found the EC's import ban on beef from cows treated with certain growth-promoting hormones to be in violation of the SPS Agreement. In particular, because Codex standards existed for five of the six hormones at issue, the Panel judged that the EC was required to justify its ban, and hence its non-application of the international standards, on the basis of an assessment of the risks to human health. The Panel further found that the EC could not justify establishing a higher level of health protection in the case of beef from animals treated with the growth-promoting hormones when compared with other food products containing higher levels of the same hormones, or when compared to the levels of risk apparently accepted from other veterinary drugs. The Appellate Body agreed that the EC's import ban was in violation of the SPS Agreement because it was not based on a risk assessment. However, the Appellate Body did not agree that the different levels of protection from risk established by the EC resulted in discrimination or a disguised restriction of trade. The WTO's Dispute-Settlement Body (DSB) requested the EC to bring its measure into conformity with its obligations, and an arbitrator established that a reasonable period of time for the EC to comply was May 13, 1999. When the EC indicated that it would not be able to comply by that date, both the United States and Canada requested the right to retaliate against EC products to compensate for their lost trade opportunities. The original Panel was convened to determine what would be the appropriate amount of retaliation; its final decision was issued on July 12, 1999. Subsequently, the DSB authorized the United States and Canada to suspend concessions on products of interest to the EC; both countries began to impose 100 percent increased tariffs on certain imports as of late July 1999.

In the Salmon case, Canada alleged that Australia's import prohibition on fresh, chilled, or frozen salmon violated several provisions of the SPS Agreement. The Panel and Appellate Body examined the assessment done by Australia of the risks of introducing fish diseases through salmon imports for human consumption. They found the risk assessment to be lacking in several critical aspects. In addition, the difference in levels of protection sought by Australia from the risk of salmon diseases compared to some other risks accepted by Australia was found to be unjustifiable and a disguised restriction of trade. The DSB requested Australia to bring its measure into conformity with its obligations, and an arbitrator established that a reasonable period of time for Australia to comply was July 6, 1999. When Australia indicated that it would not be able to comply by this date, Canada requested authorization to retaliate against Australian products to compensate for lost trade opportunities. Australia requested that the original Panel be reconvened to determine what would be the appropriate amount of retaliation. Furthermore, on July 19, 1999, Australia announced changes to its import measures on salmon, which it claimed brought it into conformity with its WTO obligations. At Canada's request, the original Panel was asked to examine the compliance of Australia's new measures, which it did prior to examining the question on retaliation. The Panel found that, with one exception, Australia's new measure complied with the SPS Agreement. In June 1999, the DSB agreed to establish a panel to examine the US complaint against Australia's measures applying to salmonids. This complaint, referred to the panel examining the Canadian complaint, was settled bilaterally.

The third SPS issue that has been examined by a WTO dispute settlement panel concerns Japan's approval of quarantine treatment for imported fruit on a variety-by-variety basis. Japan claimed that different varieties of the same type of fruit might respond differently to a quarantine treatment, hence import approval was given only following testing of each variety. The United States complained that Japan's requirement was maintained without sufficient scientific evidence. The Panel and Appellate Body agreed that there was not sufficient scientific evidence to justify Japan's requirement, that Japan had not assessed the risk with respect to all of the products affected by the measure, and furthermore that Japan had failed to publish its import requirements. An interesting issue in the Varietal testing dispute concerns article 5.7 which, in cases where sufficient scientific evidence is not available, allows countries to take provisional measures. Japan invoked this provision, claiming that its requirements were provisional and would be reviewed on the basis of variety-by-variety data supplied by exporters. The Panel and Appellate Body ruled that countries maintaining provisional measures on the basis of article 5.7 have to actively search for scientific evidence that could enable them to undertake a risk assessment to justify their measure. The DSB requested Japan to bring its measure into conformity with its obligations, and the United States and Japan agreed that a reasonable period of time for Japan to comply would be until December 31, 1999.

The fourth complaint examined by a WTO panel also considered Japanese plant protection measures, in this case, regulations setting conditions under which fresh apples could be imported from the United States to guard against the introduction of the plant bacterial disease fire blight. The Panel agreed that there was not sufficient scientific evidence to justify Japan's set of requirements, and that Japan's risk assessment was not sufficiently specific regarding the risk from apples, and had not assessed the risk according to the measures which might be applied. Japan also invoked article 5.7, arguing that if there was not sufficient scientific evidence to justify its requirements, the measure should be considered a provisional one. However, the Panel ruled that this was not a situation in which sufficient scientific evidence did not exist but, rather, there was a wealth of scientific evidence regarding fire blight but it did not support Japan's measures.

### Conclusions

Even after only a few years, the benefits of the SPS Agreement are increasingly evident. International trade in foods is becoming more predictable, and trade restrictions less arbitrary, to the benefit of consumers around the globe. The improved transparency of sanitary requirements and of other technical regulations resulting from the SPS Agreement enables exporters to identify, before shipping, what conditions their products must meet. The advance notification procedures permit governments and traders to seek changes in new requirements that might be unnecessarily damaging to their trade. Consumers also benefit from the requirement that their governments publish all regulations and respond to reasonable enquiries regarding trade measures. More substantively, the SPS Agreement explicitly recognizes that the protection of health must take priority over trade, yet its disciplines ensure that governments do not abuse this right, by using unnecessary health measures as trade barriers.

These disciplines are of particular value to developing countries, whose lack of resources may limit their ability otherwise to challenge unjustified requirements. If developing country exporters can meet the relevant, internationally developed standard for their product, importing countries imposing more stringent requirements face the burden of proving that their additional demands are scientifically justified. This should bring considerable relief to exporters who previously have had to meet the different demands of each of their potential markets. At the same time, developing countries can rely on the internationally developed standards to provide the scientific justification required for their own import regulations, as long as there is no discrimination in favor of domestically produced products.

Other provisions of the SPS Agreement also promise considerable benefits for developing countries, particularly as they seek to expand exports of agricultural products. The recognition of the equivalence of different production methods should in many cases permit countries to use technologies which are more appropriate in their developmental situation. And the increased information regarding sanitary requirements, with the opportunity to seek changes in proposed regulations before they become mandatory, should also ease the burden of developing countries.

The application of the SPS Agreement will continue to evolve as governments gain more experience in its implementation, and as specific trade concerns arise. Developing countries in particular will benefit as they learn to use the SPS Agreement as a tool to maximize their benefits from world food trade.

**Reference**

General Agreement on Tariffs and Trade (GATT), 1994. *The Results of the Uruguay Round of Multilateral Trade Negotiations, The Legal Texts*. Geneva: GATT Secretariat

# Part II
# Interests, options, and objectives in a new trade round

# 6   Agriculture, developing countries, and the Doha Development Agenda

*Kym Anderson*

One of the great achievements of the Uruguay Round of trade negotiations was that it brought agricultural policies under much greater multilateral discipline through the new World Trade Organization (WTO). The Uruguay Round Agreement on Agriculture (URAA) converted non-tariff barriers (NTBs) to agricultural imports into bound tariffs. Those bound tariffs were scheduled for phased reductions, as were farm production and export subsidies, between 1995 and 2000 for industrial countries, with developing countries having an extra four years. The URAA required members to return to the negotiating table by 2000.

What are the interests and options of developing countries in the new round of negotiations? This question is pertinent not only because the vast majority of the world's poor are farmers in developing nations, but also because numerous such nations are less than happy with the URAA outcome. Those concerns must be addressed if the new round is to succeed.

Protection rates on agriculture in OECD countries remain huge. What's more, "dirty" tariffication – the setting of bound rates well above applied rates – and the introduction of tariff-rate quotas (TRQs) in the URAA mean that much bigger commitments will be needed this time significantly to reduce agricultural protection. Reforms in other sectors will also influence agriculture in developing countries, not least because including them in the negotiating agenda can counter farm protectionist lobbies. Adding new issues such as genetically modified organisms (GMOs) to the agriculture agenda could complicate matters by diverting attention from traditional market access issues.

Given the diversity among developing countries, they have more than one set of interests in agricultural trade. Since those interests are not always well understood, this chapter attempts to clarify them and identify the extent to which developing countries would benefit from agricultural reform. The chapter then examines traditional agricultural issues as they affect developing countries, before turning to claims by richer food-importing countries that food safety and agriculture's so-called "multifunctionality" requires stricter barriers to farm

113

trade. If handled badly in the new round, the latter contention could undermine the interests of developing countries. The chapter concludes by reviewing some of the options facing negotiators from developing countries.

## Defining the interests of developing countries

Almost all developing countries have a stake, either direct or indirect, in the agricultural aspects of the new round of multilateral trade negotiations. Consider four groups of such countries. First, exporters of tropical farm products face relatively low tariffs on most of their primary exports, but there are important exceptions such as bananas. Such exporters also face much higher effective tariffs on many processed versions of tropical products, hindering their capacity to export these value added products.

Second, exporters of farm products grown in temperate areas – including grains, livestock products, sugar, and oilseeds – typically face high tariffs and restrictive tariff rate quotas when selling to OECD countries. These countries have a clear interest in seeing those barriers lowered. A subset of countries in this group enjoys preferential access to OECD markets, and, at least in the short term, may lose if OECD countries lower the tariff rates imposed on other importers. However, such producers may gain from sales of farm products with lower tariffs to more than offset the loss of preferences, or they may be able to negotiate compensation in the form of direct aid.

Third, developing countries that are net food importers fear that cuts in agricultural protection by OECD countries will lead to higher international food prices, or less food aid. Yet even those developing countries need not lose if farm supports abroad are cut. If, for example, importers are almost self-sufficient in food, as many net food importers are, and agricultural reforms raise the international price of food, such countries may re-orient themselves to export agricultural products. Some other countries that have a comparative advantage in food maintain policies biased against food production, such that they do not produce enough to export. They, too, would gain if food prices rose, as more resources would move from protected industries back to agriculture (Anderson and Tyers, 1993) The number of poor countries for whom a rise in international food prices might cause some hardship is much smaller than the number that are net importers of agricultural products.

Fourth, developing countries that are rapidly accumulating capital, developing their infrastructure, and industrializing are gradually shifting their comparative advantage from primary products to labor-intensive manufactures. While that would lower their interest in agricultural trade reform, it would heighten their interest in reducing barriers to exports of textiles and clothing. They share that interest with agriculture-exporting developing countries, for if the former could export more manufactures, they would tend to become larger net importers of farm products. Conversely, lowered barriers to farm trade would reduce the need of more land-abundant developing countries to compete with newly industrialized nations in manufacturing. This suggests that the two groups could band together and negotiate as a single voice calling for lowering both sets of trade barriers.

Even if a country's national economic welfare declines following a multilateral trade negotiation, that economy's welfare might have fallen further if it had forgone the economic efficiency gained from reform.[1] Poor economies that lose from further multilateral liberalization under the new round could also secure much more technical and economic assistance than in previous rounds.

What's more, the more sectors a country reforms, the greater its gains will be, because a wider net will reduce the possibility that resources will move to even more inefficient uses, thereby reducing rather than improving national efficiency. Such reforms, politically painful as they may be in the short run, are thus in the longer-run economic interests of developing countries.

Of course, net national economic welfare is not the only criterion that drives governments. Indeed, until recently, it may not have been a major priority at all. However it is steadily becoming more dominant, for at least two reasons. One is the rapid globalization driven by technological and economic changes that penalizes countries with bad economic governance ever more rapidly and severely. The other is the broader mandate of the WTO, which enables developing countries to exchange market access commitments with other countries.

## Traditional issues

### The legacy of the Uruguay Round Agreement on Agriculture

For most farm products, and among OECD countries, actual tariffs provide no less protection today than did the non-tariff import barriers of the late 1980s and early 1990s (Ingco, 1996). This is because most tariffs were bound well above the applied rates – or the tariff equivalents of quantitative restrictions on imports. Indeed, at the end of the Uruguay Round, bound tariffs were set so high that bringing them down to actual applied tariffs will require a very sizable cut (see Hertel, *et al.*, chapter 11 in this volume).

Binding agricultural tariffs at such high levels allows countries to vary the tariffs they actually apply, to stabilize the domestic market. This is similar to the EU's use of its variable import levies and export subsidies. Thus, tariffication under the Uruguay Round has not stabilized international food markets as expected.[2]

Industrial countries agreed to reduce the aggregate level of domestic support (AMS) they provide to farmers by four-fifths of the 1986–8 level by 2000. However, that provision, too, required only modest reform, partly because much of the decline in the AMS in most countries had already occurred by the mid-1990s. What's more, the AMS did not include many forms of support, the most important of which are the direct payments that the United States and European Union (EU) provide to farmers who limit production. The use of such instruments needs to be curtailed, since they may spread to other countries and other commodities as the WTO limits the use of direct domestic price supports.

Because of such limits, the Uruguay Round made only limited progress in reducing protection and insulation in agricultural markets.

### The potential gains from further trade policy reform

According to a study using the global economy-wide model known as the Global Trade Analysis Project (GTAP), the gains from removing remaining tariffs and subsidies from agricultural markets would be huge (Anderson, Hoekman, and Strutt, 2001).[3] This is because protection rates on agricultural products, including processed foods, will still be very high even after the Uruguay Round's provisions are fully implemented at end-2004. At that point, tariffs in the global agricultural sector will be twice as high, on average, as those imposed on textiles and clothing, and nearly four times those on other manufactured products. A regional pattern of distortions will also continue, with OECD countries subsidizing, and developing countries taxing, farm relative to non-farm production and exports.

If all merchandise trade distortions were removed globally, almost one-third of the global gains would stem from agricultural reform in OECD countries, even though farmers in those countries contribute only 4 percent of global GDP and less than 10 percent of world trade. The potential contribution of textile and clothing reforms to global welfare is only one-tenth that of agriculture. This difference reflects the fact that distortions to prices for agriculture are more than twice those for textiles and clothing, and that textiles and clothing contribute only 1.5 percent of the value of world production, and 5 percent of the value of world trade (Anderson, Hoekman, and Strutt, 2001).

Major assumptions are crucial to these results. The results assume the accession of China and Taiwan (referered to as "Chinese Taipei" under the terms of its accession), and that each country would enjoy the same accelerated access to OECD markets under the Uruguay Round Agreement on Textiles and Clothing as other developing countries. Another important postulation is that OECD countries fully implement the textile agreement. The latter is far from certain, particularly if China phases out its "voluntary" export restraints on textiles and clothing by 2005. Dropping this assumption substantially reduces the estimated gains from implementing the Uruguay Round provisions (Anderson *et al.*, 1997), and therefore would raise the potential gains from textile and clothing reform in upcoming trade rounds.

Even so, agricultural protection would remain far more costly to the world economy than barriers to manufactures, even though the latter contribute a much larger share of world production and trade. Moreover, if OECD governments did renege on the spirit of the Agreement on Textiles and Clothing (ATC) of the WTO by using "safeguard" measures to limit their textile imports after abolishing "voluntary" export restraints in 2004, the industrialization of developing countries would slow. Hence their need to depend on farm products to trade their way out of poverty would be greater.

The farm policies of OECD countries contribute about half the cost of global trade distortions to developing economies – nearly as much as trade-distorting policies in developing countries themselves (Anderson, Hoekman, and Strutt 2001). OECD textiles and clothing policies also harm developing countries greatly, but only half as much as OECD farm policies. In so far as a developing country enjoys tariff preferences in OECD markets, it would lose some of that benefit. Whether other gains would offset such losses can be answered only with a great deal more data and modeling.

The Anderson, Hoekman, and Strutt (2001) study found that full liberalization of OECD farm policies would boost global agricultural trade by more than 50 percent, but would cause real international food prices to rise by only 5 percent, on average. Thus any negative effect on food-importing countries from a change in the terms of trade would be small.

*What should be done to further the agricultural reform process?*

Nothing less than a ban on farm export subsidies will bring agriculture into line with non-farm products under the Global Agreement on Tariffs and Trade (GATT). Such subsidies are almost exclusively a Western European phenomenon, apart from sporadic US use. The EU granted five-sixths of all export subsidies in the mid-1990s; the United States, Norway, and Switzerland accounted for all but 2 percentage points of the rest (Josling and Rae, 2004, p. 16).

Gradual reform of domestic subsidies by the United States and the EU – especially further decoupling of farm income support from production, as under the US FAIR Act of 1996 – may allow negotiators to eliminate under the new round the "blue box" category of support programs that are currently not subject to reform. (That category was introduced into Uruguay Round negotiations in 1992 to satisfy just two members, the United States and the EU.) Negotiators could also try to tighten "green box" loopholes, which exempt such things as environmental protection from WTO scrutiny.

The most important area for reform, though, is market access. Tariffication appeared to be a great step forward. However, the combination of "dirty" tariffication by developed economies, and the adoption of very high ceiling bindings by developing economies, allows many countries to vary their protection in response to changes in domestic or international food markets. Reducing bound tariffs from 50–150 percent or more to the 0–15 percent range of manufactures is one of the major challenges. If past rates of reduction are any guide, the gap will not be closed for several decades, and even cutting bound tariffs to applied rates will take time.

At least three options for reducing bound tariffs present themselves. One is a large across-the-board cut. Even if negotiators agreed on a 50 percent cut, however, many high bound tariffs would remain. A second option is the "Swiss formula" used for manufactures in the Tokyo Round, whereby the rate of reduction for each item is higher the greater its tariff level. This helps reduce the variation in rates introduced or exacerbated during the Uruguay Round.

A third option was used successfully in negotiations on information technology – the "zero-for-zero" approach – which eliminates tariffs altogether for selected products. In contrast to the second option, this would increase tariff variation among products, possibly diverting resources from low-cost to higher-cost activities. While that might focus attention on politically difficult items such as dairy and sugar, experience with long-delayed cuts in protection of textiles and cars casts doubt on this option being able to deliver liberalization promptly.

These tariff reductions refer to above-quota imports. There is also a pressing need to reduce in-quota imports – those that meet the minimum access requirements under the Uruguay Round Agreement on Agriculture. Those quotas were introduced ostensibly to guarantee traditional sellers a minimum level of market access, at least equal to that available before tariffication, given that tariffs have been bound greatly above applied rates. As many as thirty-six WTO member countries listed such tariff-rate quotas (TRQs) in their Uruguay Round schedules, of which at least half actively use them. But as the appendix (p. 128) makes clear, this system ensures that agricultural trade policies continue to be very complex. TRQs also reduce the extent to which tariff cuts will encourage imports in the medium term in cases where the out-of-quota tariff is currently prohibitive. Quotas were barely two-thirds filled during 1995 and 1996 on average, according to the WTO Committee on Agriculture (Josling and Rae, 2004).

Agriculture-exporting countries are understandably reluctant to suggest that TRQs be removed when they provide at least some market access at low or zero tariffs. Nor would everyone regard auctioning TRQs as a solution, because that would essentially impose the out-of-quota tariff on quota-restricted trade.

If banning TRQs is not yet possible, the next-best alternative to is to expand them, so as to reduce their importance, increase competition, and lessen the impact of high above-quota tariffs.

One can imagine a positive or negative outcome from expanding TRQs. Optimists might hold that if TRQs were increased by, say, 1 percent of domestic consumption per year, most quotas would quickly become non-binding. Expanding TRQs could therefore be much more liberalizing in the medium term than reducing high above-quota tariffs. Such an approach might require binding within-quota tariffs at a reasonable level, like that for manufactures.

On the other hand, negotiators familiar with the tortuous efforts to remove quotas on textiles and clothing trade might regard agricultural TRQs as a variation on the complex Multifiber Agreement (MFA) (Francois, 1999). Some fifty years from their inception around 1960 may elapse until textile quotas are finally abolished. Is that the expected lifetime of agricultural TRQs?

Those sharing this pessimistic view could advocate a more radical approach to the new round of agricultural negotiations – one that would bring agriculture more into line with non-agricultural goods. Such advocates might call for total elimination of agricultural TRQs, along with export subsidies and export credits, and a major reduction in bound out-of-quota tariffs. To soften the blow, advocates could suggest that the WTO put less emphasis on disciplining domestic farm measures other than direct subsidies. The almost infinite scope for replacing one domestic price-support measure with another makes disciplining them very difficult anyway. And, as Snape (1987) has pointed out, tightening constraints on border measures would ensure that a growing proportion of the cost of support programs would be exposed in a nation's budget, and thereby be subject to domestic political scrutiny.

### Why agriculture needs other sectors in the new WTO round

Agricultural negotiations and analytical efforts have focused primarily on the traditional instruments of agricultural intervention – border measures and producer subsidies. Yet much of the distorted incentives that export-oriented farmers face stem from their own countries' non-agricultural policies (Schiff and Valdés, 1992). Since WTO negotiations focus on reciprocal exchange of market access concessions, export-oriented farmers have an interest not only in better access to food markets abroad, but also in more competition in their own countries' markets for non-farm products. That applies not only to industrial goods but also to services.

There are at least three reasons why WTO's non-agricultural negotiations are relevant to agriculture. One is that a member country that imports farm products and exports non-farm goods and services will be more interested in lowering its impediments to agricultural imports if agricultural-exporting members lower their impediments to non-farm imports. This is because political support from non-food exporters in the first country will compensate for loss of political support from farmers (Grossman and Helpman, 1995; Hillman and Moser, 1995).

Second, farmers use many non-farm goods and services as intermediate inputs, or to transport farm products to consumers. If trade impediments make non-farm products more expensive, net farm incomes decline.[4] Farmers also compete with non-farm sectors for mobile factors of production, most notably investment funds and labor. To the extent that trade impediments support a country's non-farm sectors, its farmers pay higher prices for those factors.

Third, many developing countries cannot engage in WTO market access exchanges that focus only on agricultural goods, because they have relatively little intra-sectoral trade in farm products. For all these reasons, the new WTO round will more likely deliver further agricultural reforms if negotiators also seek cuts in protection in other sectors, including services.

Fortunately, services are already on the new round's agenda. Further liberalization of manufacturing industries is also required, especially in developing countries where industrial tariff rates are still high. Continued textile and clothing reform, which would give a major boost to developing economies, would encourage labor-intensive industrial production in newly industrializing countries. To the extent that farm household labor is attracted to factories, such a change would come at the expense of agricultural production. Hence it would provide new market opportunities for agricultural exporting countries. This effect shows up even in simulations involving across-the-board liberalization of all manufacturing globally (see Hertel, *et al.*, chapter 11 in this volume).

*Agriculture and "new" trade issues*

Some developing countries maintain that including "new" trade issues in the new round would distract attention from more important market access issues. However, inclusion of new issues could convince more OECD non-agricultural groups to support the round, counterbalancing protectionist forces in agricultural and other sectors. Better rules on domestic and technical barriers to trade would also reduce the risk that they will replace tariffs – a risk that has recently grown considerably.

Although competition and investment policies affect agricultural interests in developing countries, the new round may not include them. I thus focus on two emerging issues that directly affect agriculture in developing countries: technical standards – including sanitary and phytosanitary (SPS) measures as well as food safety in the wake of the new biotechnologies – and agriculture's so-called "multifunctionality."

*Sanitary and food safety measures*

The inadequacy of the code created during the Tokyo Round to set SPS standards – plus the desire to limit countries' use of SPS measures to undercut reforms mandated under the URAA – gave birth to the SPS Agreement during the Uruguay Round. The SPS agreement defined new criteria that a country had to meet if it imposed food safety regulations more onerous than those set by international agreement. The SPS agreement, together with the UR's strengthening of the WTO dispute-settlement body, was bound to raise the profile of SPS. That profile has increased even more dramatically, especially in Europe, with the emergence of food safety issues such as "mad-cow" disease, beef hormones, and transgenic food products, also known as genetically modified organisms (GMOs).

Developing countries have a complex set of interests in these developments (Nielsen and Anderson, 2001). One is that the SPS Agreement requires a WTO Member to provide scientific justification for any measure that is more trade-restricting than the appropriate international standard, and to assess the risks involved. The agreement provides at least some technical assistance to help developing countries meet these requirements.

Developing nations also have an interest in maintaining and expanding their access to markets protected by SPS measures. Again, some technical assistance in meeting import standards is helpful. However, numerous importing countries use blunt quarantine instruments excessively to restrict imports well beyond what is needed to protect the health of domestic plants, animals, and citizens. For example, many countries maintain outright bans on certain products. Such levels of protection are equivalent to tariffs over 100 percent. In the absence of requirements that members disclose the degree to which such measures restrict trade, reform is likely to focus on the small number of cases brought before the WTO's dispute settlement body. The complex requirements of such legal proceedings ensure that the pace of reform will be glacial, and skewed toward the concerns of richer WTO Members able to bring such cases.

Who gains and who loses from SPS measures varies. Where a restriction is aimed simply at limiting the cost of disease control for domestic farmers, the latter group gains at the expense of domestic consumers and overseas producers. James and Anderson (1998) provide an example that results in a net national loss, not including the loss to overseas suppliers.

However, domestic consumers are unlikely to fight to liberalize such quarantine barriers, because they are often concerned about possible risks from exotic diseases and imported food. Their demands for higher-quality, safer food and environmental protection rise with *per capita* income.

However, perceptions of the safety of different foods and production and processing methods differ greatly even among countries with similar income levels. The WTO dispute settlement case brought by the United States and Canada against the EU over its ban on beef imports produced with growth hormones shows that such differences are difficult to resolve even with a great deal of scientific advice. The controversy over the banning of intra-EU beef trade stemming from the scare over "mad-cow" disease reveals a similar lesson. How much more likely, then, are trade disputes over issues in which the scientific evidence is far less complete?

The fact that the SPS Agreement does not include consumers' interests has meant that consumers have lacked a voice arguing that they should have better access to lower-priced imported food, and dampened debate over consumers' "right to know" via labeling. (The latter concern is likely to show up in dispute settlement cases under the WTO's Agreement on Technical Barriers to Trade.) However, providing wealthy consumers with more scientific information, and improving the reputation of standards-setting bodies, may be valuable but does little to alter opinions, and in any case such information is scarce (Henson, 1998; Mahe and Ortalo-Magne, 1998).

In the case of policy dialogues surrounding GMOs, attempts to promote science-based assessment of the risks have met with extreme versions of the precautionary principle, manifest in the form of complete bans on their production, importation, and/or sale. Many consumer groups have rejected proposed solutions, such as segregating GMO products and identifying them via labels. Major producing countries in North and Latin America have also rejected such measures, claiming that costly labeling of GMOs is unwarranted because they so closely resemble other foods. The fact that some GMO products are less damaging to the agricultural environment than traditional farm products has done little to dissuade hardened opponents.

How does this issue affect developing countries? Two possibilities are worth mentioning: the impact of new technology in lowering food production costs, and food trade barriers erected in response to consumer concerns, mostly in OECD countries. The former would benefit food-exporting countries and place a premium on sound intellectual property law and enforcement, to ensure that seed companies would sell their products to such countries. If developing countries cannot make productive use of the new biotechnologies, their competitiveness in international markets may erode as food prices fall. Net food-importing countries could benefit from that price fall, and perhaps even more so if OECD countries ban imports of GMO products. The impact is clouded by any premium attached to GMO-free products in international trade (Anderson, Hoekman, and Strutt, 2001). This is clearly an area requiring more empirical research – efforts that ideally would examine the extent to which seed firms, rather than farmers or consumers, could capture the gains from the new technology.

While such issues will increasingly arise under the Uruguay Round's agreements on SPS and technical barriers, they will also affect non-agricultural contexts. As with state trading, subsidies, and competition policies, there is a strong case for developing common disciplines for all types of products. In the case of technical barriers, there is nothing special about food compared with, say, dangerous chemicals or heavy metals involved in producing or disposing of manufactured goods. A common set of rules for risk analysis and management would remove inconsistencies in these areas, and thus prevent disputes.

### *Agriculture's so-called "multifunctionality"*

WTO Members agreed to take "non-trade concerns" into account in continuing the agricultural reform process after 2000. The preamble to the URAA defines those concerns as including maintaining the security of food supplies and protecting the environment. A third concern is sustaining the viability of rural areas. Proponents of these concerns characterize them as positive externalities – in some cases, public goods that are jointly produced along with food and fiber. Proponents thus use the word "multifunctionality" to describe these features of agricultural production.

Does agriculture deserve more price support and import protection than other sectors because it produces non-market externalities and public goods? Do these positive externalities exceed farming's negative externalities by more than the net positive externalities produced by other sectors? If so, to what extent are those farmer-produced externalities undersupplied? And what are the most efficient ways to boost production of the externalities to socially optimal levels? These concerns are not really new but they are being packaged differently.

"Non-trade" concerns are becoming an issue in the WTO in numerous areas, not just with respect to agriculture. They are a direct result of the lowering or outlawing of trade barriers: with declining governmental protection, domestic policies exert more influence on the international competitiveness of certain industries. Despite their "non-trade" adjective, the WTO needs to deal with these concerns because they certainly can affect trade. Ideally they should be handled in the same way for all sectors, such as under an expanded Agreement on Subsidies and Countervailing Measures. However, until that occurs, agricultural negotiations cannot ignore them. A key question is: do they require exceptional treatment, or can existing provisions such as the URAA's "green box" encompass them? The short answer appears to be that existing WTO provisions can address the main cases.

However, both economic theory and practice have taught at least five relevant lessons. First, where several policy objectives exist, an equal number of policy instruments is typically required to deal efficiently with them. Second, the most efficient, lowest-cost measure for achieving a particular objective, such as overcoming a market failure, addresses it directly. Third, trade measures are rarely the most efficient instruments for addressing "non-trade" concerns.

Fourth, trade reform will be welfare-improving as long as domestic interventions deal with the "non-trade" concerns. And fifth, whenever governments intervene to overcome a market failure, there is the risk of government failure that could be more welfare-reducing than the market failure the intervention is trying to offset. The government failure could result simply from insufficient information and analysis for designing an appropriate intervention (bureaucratic failure), or it could result from deliberate political action aimed at rewarding particular groups, even though that action may be costly to the community at large.

Every productive sector generates both marketed and non-marketed products. Some of those non-marketed products are considered desirable and some are considered undesirable. Since tastes and preferences change over time and differ among countries, so too will society's valuation of non-marketed products. And as technologies, institutions, policies, and markets change during development, so will the ability to market previously unmarketable products in each sector.

For farming to receive more assistance than other sectors, agricultural production must not only be a net contributor of externalities and public goods, but also *more* of a net contributor than other sectors, especially sectors that would expand if agricultural supports were to shrink. Demonstrating this contribution is almost impossible, given the difficulties of valuing the externalities and public goods generated by various sectors and the marginal costs of providing them. Hence, the practice of intervening only in the most obvious situations.

Even if a clear case could be made for an intervention, the appropriate measure is unlikely to be import restrictions or output price supports for a broad range of farm commodities. Rather, such a measure should be finely tuned to encourage just the undersupplied public good.

The policy task thus involves several steps. The first two are defining *society's willingness to pay* for the non-marketable by-product, and determining the *most efficient policy instrument* for encouraging farmers or others to supply that by-product. The final step entails determining the *optimal level of encouragement* that equates the marginal social benefit with the marginal social cost of that intervention, bearing in mind the risks associated with one or both forms of government failure.

Specific conclusions from a review of these issues are worth stressing (Anderson, 2000). First, several policy instruments will be necessary to address directly and precisely the policy objectives encompassed in the "non-trade" concerns. General agricultural price-support programs are not among the efficient measures. This is true even of direct domestic supports, let alone indirect supports via import barriers or export subsidies (which also distort consumer prices), because they are far too blunt efficiently to achieve the specific objectives.

The most efficient instruments for boosting food security above the level provided under free markets might be to subsidize the cost of holding stocks of staple foods. Annex 2 of the URAA already permits this. Import restrictions to boost a country's self-sufficiency in certain food items, far from helping, may actually diminish food security for vulnerable groups struggling to pay the high price of protected domestic food. And once bound tariffs decline to applied rates, greater stability in international food markets will boost food security world-wide.

Environmental protection has many facets and so requires a range of policy instruments. Reducing price supports for farm output, as under the URAA, probably provides the single biggest contribution to the rural environment in agricultural-protectionist OECD countries, because it lowers the level and intensity of farm production. While those supports are still in the process of being phased out, additional taxes, charges, or other regulations on farm pollution can offset the extra damage caused by price supports. WTO rules also permit such input taxes.

Since most of the positive externalities and public goods that farming provides can be provided independently of farming, providing payments specifically for those goods is not only possible but also desirable. In fact, non-farmers may be able to provide some of the positive externalities or public goods at lower cost than farmers. Some provision for such payments is made in the URAA and in the WTO's Agreement on Subsidies and Countervailing Measures.

Ensuring the viability of rural areas is a laudable goal, but again the blunt instrument of general farm price supports is far from optimal, especially since agriculture is not the dominant source of income in many rural areas, particularly those near urban areas. Far more appropriate are WTO-consistent targeted adjustment-assistance packages, including retraining, and perhaps subsidies to essential services that would otherwise be withdrawn from remote areas.

In short, WTO rules and URAA reforms are compatible with efficient measures that address "non-trade" concerns. There is plenty of synergy and no need for tradeoffs between domestic policy objectives and agricultural reform. However, measures supposedly designed to deal with "non-trade" concerns inevitably re-introduce farm support, as is already evident as tariffs, export subsidies, and domestic price supports are phased out. Protectionist forces will undoubtedly seek to include such measures on the "green box" list when calculating the Aggregate Measurement of Support (AMS) during the new round of negotiations. Careful scrutiny of the grounds for such inclusion will be a high-payoff activity for negotiators from developing countries.

Both exporting and import-competing countries should welcome the call for closer scrutiny of instruments used to address "non-trade" concerns. This is partly because once superior instruments are adopted at optimal levels, greater food security and environmental protection will result. Equally important, today's blunt instruments used to support farm prices could then be dismantled more rapidly, as there would be even less reason to maintain them. Consumers, taxpayers, and non-farm exporters, together with the world's more-efficient farmers, could join with those anxious to conserve global resources in celebrating this improvement in managing our economy and environment.

## Conclusions and options for developing countries

Several prominent spokespersons have already dubbed the next world trade negotiations as the "development" round. This is partly a response to the disappointment expressed by developing countries regarding the Uruguay Round, and partly a reflection of the fact that their weight in the WTO has grown considerably. Developing countries now comprise five-sixths of the WTO membership of almost 150, and that share will continue to rise as another thirty or so countries gradually complete the accession process.

The new round thus offers the best prospects ever for developing countries in general – and their rural communities in particular – to secure growth-enhancing reforms. In the mercantilist tradition of multilateral trade negotiations, this will inevitably take the form of requests and offers – even though the concessions offered are a win–win game in improving economic welfare in each of the negotiating nations.

Traditional liberalization of access to agricultural markets should be the priority of the next WTO round, given the enormous potential for global gains, particularly among developing countries. Assurances that the EU and United States will honor their commitment gradually to expand market access for textiles and clothing, and not simply to replace quantitative restraints with "safeguard" measures, are also essential.

Substantial progress in freeing up trade in both textiles and agriculture is crucial if the new round is to be a genuine development round. Such reform could boost the earnings of the world's poor enormously, the vast majority of whom live in rural households in developing countries. Rural households would benefit even in newly industrializing economies (NIEs) that take advantage of expanding opportunities to export textile products, if some household members take new jobs in nearby clothing factories.

To aid agricultural development, attention should also focus on reducing protection in other manufacturing and services industries. Such protection still creates a significant anti-agricultural bias in many developing countries, making it more difficult for them to benefit from agricultural trade reform in OECD countries. Reform of manufacturing and service industries can occur unilaterally, but the new WTO round can be a useful instrument through which to lock-in such reforms.

This new round will occur in an environment in which globalization, including ever-faster international transfers of information, ideas, capital, skills, and new technologies, will trigger isolationist reactions. For example, further reductions in traditional farm protection measures will meet significant resistance in OECD countries, as farm groups join with food safety and environmental groups to argue for new forms of agricultural protection.

In these circumstances the agenda of the new WTO round may have to include not only many sectors but also "new trade agenda" items such as investment and competition policies, to allow for linkages and tradeoffs. Such new items may cause political and administrative difficulties in some developing countries, but they will also create opportunities to secure domestic reforms that will boost their economies. Limited analytical and negotiating resources make a number of developing countries hesitant to address such issues. But developing countries may need to discuss at least some of the "new trade agenda" items if they want to ensure that market access to agricultural and textile products remains high on the WTO agenda.

Given the apparent intention to make this new WTO round a development round, and given that many developing countries have embraced major reforms unilaterally since the 1990s, perhaps they should adopt a new approach. They might consider, for example, exchanging more non-discriminatory market access with OECD countries rather than attempting to win special treatment and tariff preferences. Special treatment simply allows developing countries to keep shooting their economies in the foot by delaying beneficial reforms. And tariff preferences tend to divide developing countries into subgroups, weakening their individual and collective bargaining strength.

A striking example of the latter is the prolonged and extremely costly dispute over access to the EU market for bananas. The EU policy entails layers of preferences that have divided developing countries into "we" and "they" groups, and thereby weakening the chances of developing countries to secure a better deal for all. With that in mind, would the EU proposal to provide duty-free access to exports of least-developed countries serve the overall interests of developing countries? If such a deal excluded agricultural and textile products, least-developed countries would gain little of substance, yet OECD countries could use the initiative to avoid opening such areas to other developing countries.

Preferential treatment in the form of food imports has also reduced the resolve of developing countries to fight for market access to protectionist countries. Food export subsidies, export credits, and non-emergency food aid are all by-products of OECD farm support programs. Without those (and textile) protectionist policies, most developing countries would reap expanded trade opportunities, and those that do not could receive direct financial aid, which would transfer resources far more efficiently.

All this suggests a potentially high payoff if developing countries collectively push hard for greater access for farm and textile products, and for technical and economic assistance to aid economic reform, in return for providing more access to their own domestic markets. The political price for making such an offer is now much lower: the forces of globalization reward economies for good economic governance, via inflows of foreign capital – and they also penalize countries that do not correct poor policy choices. Developing countries that agree not to tax or otherwise restrain agricultural exports, and that reduce their high tariffs on imports of food and other products, would not only boost their own economies but also encourage agricultural reforms abroad.

## Appendix    The effects of imposing a TRQ regime on a food-importing economy

Consider what happens when an economy that imports an agricultural product imposes a TRQ regime under the rules of the URAA. Such a regime involves setting a bound tariff (typically more than the tariff actually applied) on out-of-quota sales, and a lower in-quota tariff for a specified volume of imports. As is clear from table 6A.1, the difference between those two tariff rates for various products and among OECD countries is considerable.

Figure 6A.1 depicts the initial impact of imposing such a TRQ regime, where an economy's import demand curve is line $D$. For simplicity, the economy is assumed to be a small enough player that its imports do not affect the international price of this product. Its in-quota tariff is assumed to be zero, in which case the quota volume, $Q$, is imported at the international price $P^*$.

If this were an import quota regime (now illegal under WTO), the domestic price would be $P_q$ and the national economic welfare loss from restricting imports to $Q$, instead of allowing the free-trade volume $Q^*$, would be area $abc$ plus a percentage of the potential quota rent which is area $bcde$. The latter percentage depends on how the import licenses are administered: it is zero only if all licenses go to domestic firms, and those firms are allowed to import from the lowest-cost suppliers abroad. (By contrast, if only $Q_2$ of the $Q$ units were allocated to domestic firms, the national welfare loss would be greater by area $bcrj$.)

It is possible to achieve the same outcome under a TRQ regime as under a traditional import quota. In terms of figure 6A.1, all that is required is to set the out-of-quota applied tariff (and therefore the bound rate) at $P_q - P^*$ per unit or more.

Only if the out-of-quota applied tariff is set at a value of less than $P_q - P^*$ per unit would there be any out-of-quota imports under a TRQ regime. If the applied rate were set at the specific rate of $t_1$ per unit, for example, the domestic price would be $P^* + t_1$ and an additional $Q_1 - Q$ units would be imported.

Table 6A.1 *Tariff quotas and imports, by country and commodity, 1996*

|  | Total imports ($ million)[a] | Tariff quota ($ million)[a] | In-quota imports ($ million)[a] |
|---|---|---|---|
| *OECD countries* | | | |
| United States | | | |
| Sugar | 1,134.96 | 865.15 | 839.36 |
| Dairy | 591.86 | 561.01 | 431.69 |
| Meats | 1,273.92 | 1,299.11 | 864.31 |
| EU | | | |
| Wheat | 4,016.01 | 63.92 | 13.25 |
| Grains | 2,767.24 | 706.67 | 523.07 |
| Sugar | 1,351.44 | 1,169.81 | 1,169.81 |
| Dairy | 342.26 | 272.66 | 270.16 |
| Meats | 5,762.76 | 4,228.49 | 4,228.49 |
| Fruits& Vegetables | 12,366.07 | 2,443.92 | 1,913.41 |
| Japan | | | |
| Wheat | 1,562.11 | 1,484.96 | 1,615.21 |
| Grains | 334.67 | 281.42 | 308.14 |
| Dairy | 818.57 | 745.66 | 693.82 |
| Canada | | | |
| Wheat | 16.22 | 35.33 | 9.55 |
| Grains | 1.34 | 32.15 | 1.51 |
| Dairy | 176.91 | 132.56 | 132.11 |
| Meats | 469.78 | 336.73 | 416.27 |
| *Developing countries* | | | |
| Korea | | | |
| Rice | 50.56 | 26.68 | 26.68 |
| Grain | 1,846.85 | 1,122.23 | 1,663.48 |
| Oilseeds | 550.71 | 343.12 | 537.41 |
| Dairy | 24.39 | 25.93 | 22.06 |
| Meats | 719.79 | 556.02 | 538.21 |
| Fruits & Vegetables | 68.43 | 56.83 | 56.01 |
| Philippines | 0.00 | 0.00 | 0.00 |
| Rice | 50.56 | 26.68 | 26.68 |
| Grain | 463.68 | 32.90 | 32.90 |
| Sugar | 99.70 | 33.19 | 33.19 |
| Meats | 272.27 | 16.69 | 16.69 |

*Notes:* [a] Values represent trade weighted average using WTO country submissions for tariff quota commodities and using average 1995–7 world import unit values from UNCTAD TRAINS.
*Source:* Elbehri *et al.* (chapter 10 in this volume).

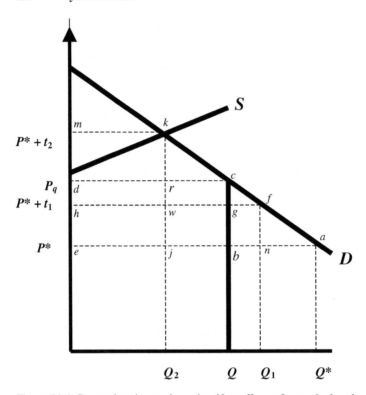

Figure 6A.1 Domestic price, trade, and welfare effects of an agricultural tariff rate quota regime on a small economy

Compared with a prohibitive out-of-quota tariff, this would generate less potential quota rent (lower by area *cdhg*) but would cause domestic consumer surplus net of domestic producer surplus to be higher by area *cdhf*, and the government would collect tariff revenue of area *fgbn*. Hence net economic welfare would be greater by area *fcbn* compared with no out-of-quota imports, again assuming all licenses go to domestic firms and those firms are free to source imports from the lowest-cost suppliers abroad.

If some licenses are valid only for imports from high-cost foreign suppliers (as applies to some products under the EU's Lomé Convention, for example), the welfare of this importing economy would further decline. It could fall by even more than the maximum quota rent for volume $Q$ (area *bcde*). Suppose, for example, the licenses are restricted to imports from a set of countries whose export supply curve measured at CIF prices is line $S$. Even if the out-of-quota applied tariff was more than $t_2$, those foreign suppliers could afford to export only $Q_2$ units to this economy, causing the domestic price to be $P^* + t_2$ rather than $P_q$ because of the quota being underfilled by $Q - Q_2$ units. In this case there would be no quota rents, and the net economic welfare of imposing such a TRQ regime would be much larger than above. Specifically, compared with free trade, the welfare cost of this regime would be area *aemk*, regardless of whether the licenses are allocated to domestic or foreign firms, whereas the cost of the regimes described above are potentially just areas *abc* and *anf*, respectively. To that needs to be added the government's cost of administering the license allocation system, and the lobbying costs of firms seeking a share of those licenses.

### The effect of an international price fall

If the international price of this product were to fall – as it has during implementation of the Uruguay Round – the nominal rate of protection (the percentage by which the domestic producer price exceeds the border price) would remain constant under an *ad valorem* tariff regime, but would rise under a specific tariff regime. However, it would rise even more under a TRQ regime if the out-of-quota tariff had been prohibitive (i.e. above $P_q - P^*$ per unit). Indeed if $P^* + t_2$ was above $P_q$ by more than the fall in the international price, the import volume and domestic price would remain unchanged despite that price fall. It is thus possible that even though supports for agricultural producers were supposed to decline during implementation of the Uruguay Round through cuts in bound tariffs (as well as in producer and export subsidies), plus growth in TRQ volumes, some protection levels may have increased because of a more-than-offsetting fall in international food prices since 1995.

### The effects of a new commitment to lower the bound tariff

Suppose at the end of the URAA implementation period, this economy lowers its bound tariff on this product. If a tariff-only regime were in place, the impacts of that reform would be somewhere between zero and 100 cent of the impacts of an equally large cut in the applied tariff, depending on the extent to which the bound rate exceeds that applied rate. (The proportion starts to rise above zero only after the bound rate reaches the applied rate.) In the presence of a TRQ regime, however, the impacts are even smaller if the out-of-quota tariff is still prohibitive. Indeed, even if licenses were held by domestic firms and imports were sourced from the most efficient suppliers, there would be no impact at all from that reform commitment if the cut in the bound rate were insufficient to bring the applied tariff down to less than $P_q - P^*$ in figure 6A.1. The maximum impacts are possible only if the out-of-quota applied tariff is not prohibitive, *and* the bound rate is not above the applied rate, *and* there are no restrictions on sourcing from lowest-cost suppliers, *and* there is no reduction in the aggregate quota allocation to domestic firms.

## The effects of a new commitment to expand the quota

Even more than a commitment to lower the bound tariff, a commitment to expand the quota could have anything between zero and more than 100 percent of the standard impact described in textbooks. If the quota had not been administered frictionlessly in the past, and had not been fully allocated to domestic firms, and there were changes in favor of domestic importers as part of the new commitment, the economy's actual welfare gain could exceed the maximum gain normally estimated for a quota increase.

## Conclusions

The following conclusions can be drawn from the discussion in the chapter:
- TRQs add considerable complexity to modeling empirically even the domestic impacts of agricultural trade policies and their reform.
- In the presence of TRQs the national welfare cost of agricultural protection can be considerably greater than a given domestic-to-border price wedge would imply if a tariff-only regime prevailed.
- A fall in the border price of the product causes that cost of protection to rise if a TRQ regime with a prohibitive out-of-quota tariff is in place, and by more than if a specific tariff alone is used.
- Modeling an $x$ percent cut in the bound tariff as if it is a cut of that size in the applied rate can overstate the price and quantity effects of reform. That is not only because the bound rate exceeds the applied rate, but also because the applied rate is above the prohibitive tariff in the presence of the quota, such that the actual effects could range (in a non-linear, double-kinked fashion) from zero to 100 percent of the modeled effects.
- The modeled effects of a tariff cut on national welfare, by contrast, could understate or overstate the gains from further reform, depending on how the quota is being administered before and after the next reform.
- An expansion of the market access (quota) commitment need not ease this measurement problem, for it is always possible for the administrator to allocate those quotas to ensure underfill such that no more or even less imports flow in.
- Modeling the effects of the TRQ regime, and changes to it, on bilateral trade flows, and thereby on the welfare of this economy's trading partners, also is more complex than modeling their effects under a tariff-only regime, with in-quota and out-of-quota tariff preferences for some trading partners adding further complications.

Models such as GTAP are in principle capable of handling these complications though careful additional programming. However, generating reliable numbers requires assimilating a much greater volume of policy data than under a tariff-only regime. Until all those data are collected and added appropriately to the model's database, modeling the effects of an *x* percent cut in the bound tariff will generate upper-bound estimates of price and quantity effects, the true impacts being somewhere between those from the model and zero. But it is also possible that modelers may *underestimate* rather than overestimate the welfare effects of reform, depending on the way the quotas are administered before and after the new round of commitments.

A number of the undesirable features of TRQs in OECD food-importing countries are illustrated by Elbehri *et al.* in chapter 10 in this volume. Table 6A.1 summarizes some of the data from that study. The low in-quota and very high out-of-quota tariffs mean potentially huge benefits are going to those allocated quota licenses. In numerous cases quotas are far from being filled, however, one possible reason being that quotas are allocated (inadvertently or deliberately) to high-cost suppliers incapable of making full use of them. And the fact that the quota often represents a high proportion and sometimes 100 percent of actual imports suggests that some out-of-quota tariffs are virtually prohibitive.

### Notes

1. For empirical support for this proposition, see, for example, Ingco (1997) with respect to least-developed countries, and Anderson and Strutt (1999) with respect to Indonesia. Authors in the volume on the Uruguay Round edited by Martin and Winters (1996) also make this point strongly.
2. Francois and Martin (1998) demonstrate, however, that since many agricultural tariffs are specific and farm prices fluctuate from year to year for seasonal reasons, binding those tariffs does lower both the mean and variance of their *ad valorem* equivalents over time.
3. Because that computational exercise removed all trade distortions, many difficulties in the appendix of measuring the effects of partial reform of a tariff rate quota regime are absent.
4. The importance of post-farm gate activities to farm income increases rapidly with urbanization. It is not uncommon for the costs (including normal profits) of getting a farm product from the farm gate to the retail consumer to be several times the farmer's cost of production of the unprocessed product.

### References

Anderson, K., 2000. "Agriculture's 'Multifunctionality' and the WTO," *Australian Journal of Agricultural and Resource Economics*, 44(3), 475–94

Anderson, K., B. Dimaranan, T. W. Hertel, and W. Martin, 1997. "Economic Growth and Policy Reforms in the APEC Region: Trade and Welfare Implications by 2005," *Asia-Pacific Economic Review*, 3(1), 1–18

Anderson, K. and Y. Hayami, 1986. *The Political Economy of Agricultural Protection*, Boston, London and Sydney: Allen & Unwin

Anderson, K., B. Hoekman, and A. Strutt, 2001. "Agriculture and the WTO: Next Steps," *Review of International Economics*, 9(2), 192–214

Anderson, K., C. Nielsen, S. Robinson, and K. Thierfelder, 2001. "Estimating the Global Economic Effects of GMOs," chapter 4 in P. Pardey (ed.), *The Future of Food: Biotechnology Markets and Policies in an International Setting*, Washington, DC: International Food Policy Research Institute

Anderson, K. and A. Strutt, 1999. "Impact of East Asia's Growth Interruption and Policy Responses: The Case of Indonesia," *Asian Economic Journal*, 13(2), 205–18

Anderson, K. and R. Tyers, 1993. "More on Welfare Gains to Developing Countries from Liberalizing World Food Trade,"*Journal of Agricultural Economics*, 44(2), 189–204

Cottier, T. and P. C. Mavroidis (eds.), 1998. *State Trading in the Twenty-First Century*, Ann Arbor: University of Michigan Press

Elbehri, A., M. D. Ingco, T. W. Hertel, and K. Pearson, 2004. "Liberalizing Tariff Rate Quotas: Quantifying the Effects of Enhancing Market Access," chapter 10 in this volume

Francois, J. F., 1999. "Approaches to Agricultural Policy Model Construction," paper presented at the UNCTAD workshop on Agricultural Policy Modeling, 24–25 March, Geneva

   2004. "Market Access Liberalization in the WTO 2000 Negotiations," paper presented at the World Bank Conference on Agriculture and the New Trade Agenda from a Development Perspective, 1–2 October, Geneva

Francois, J. F. and W. Martin, 1998. "Commercial Policy Uncertainty, the Expected Cost of Protection, and Market Access," Discussion Paper, Tinbergen Institute, Erasmus University

Grossman, G. M. and E. Helpman, 1995. "Trade Wars and Trade Talks," *Journal of Political Economy*, 103(4), 675–708

Henson, S., 1998. "Regulating the Trade Effects of National Food Safety Standards," OECD Workshop on Emerging Trade Issues in Agriculture, 25–26 October, Paris, oecd.org/agr/trade/

Hertel, T. W. (ed.), 1997. *Global Trade Analysis: Modeling and Applications*, Cambridge and New York: Cambridge University Press

Hertel, T., K. Anderson, J. Francois, B. Hoekman, and W. Martin, 2004. "The Global and Regional Effects of Liberalizing Agriculture and Other Trade in the New Round," chapter 11 in this volume

Hertel, T. W. and W. Martin, 1999. "Developing Country Interests in Liberalizing Manufactures Trade," paper presented at the World Bank's Conference on Developing Countries and the Millennium Round, 19–20 September, Geneva

Hillman, A. L. and P. Moser, 1995. "Trade Liberalization as Politically Optimal Exchange of Market Access," in M. Canzoneri *et al.* (eds.), *The New Transatlantic Economy*, Cambridge and New York: Cambridge University Press

Hudec, R. E., 1998. "Does the Agreement on Agriculture Work? Agricultural Disputes After the Uruguay Round," IATRC Working Paper, 98-2, Department of Applied Economics, University of Minnesota

Ingco, M. D., 1996. "Tariffication in the Uruguay Round: How Much Liberalization?," *The World Economy*, 19(4), 425–47

1997. "Has Agricultural Trade Liberalization Improved Welfare in the Least-Developed Countries? Yes," Policy Research Working Paper, 1748, World Bank, Washington, DC, April

Ingco, M. D. and F. Ng, 1998. "Distortionary Effects of State Trading in Agriculture: Issues for the Next Round of Multilateral Trade Negotiations," Policy Research Working Paper, 1915, World Bank, Washington, DC

James, S. and K. Anderson, 1998. "On the Need for More Economic Assessment of Quarantine Policies," *Australian Journal of Agricultural and Resource Economics*, 41(4), 525–44

Josling, T. S. and A. Rae, 2004. "Options for Enhancing Market Access in a New Round," chapter 9 in this volume

Josling, T., S. Tangermann, and T. K. Warley, 1996. *Agriculture in the GATT*, London: Macmillan and New York: St Martin's Press

Mahe, L. P. and F. Ortalo-Magne, 1998. "International Co-Operation in the Regulation of Food Quality and Safety Attributes," in *Proceedings of the OECD Workshop on Emerging Trade Issues in Agriculture*, 25–26 October, Paris, oecd.org/agr/trade

Martin, W. and L. A. Winters (eds.), 1996. *The Uruguay Round and the Developing Countries*, Cambridge and New York: Cambridge University Press

Nielsen, C. and K. Anderson, 2001. "GMOs, Trade Policy, and Welfare in Rich and Poor Countries," in K. Maskus and J. Wilson (eds.), *Quantifying Trade Effects of Technical Barriers: Can it be Done?*, Ann Arbor: University of Michigan Press

Roberts, D., 1998. "Implementation of the WTO Agreement on the Application of Sanitary and Phytosanitary Measures: The First Two Years," Working Paper, 98-4, Department of Applied Economics, University of Minnesota, May

Roberts, D. and K. DeRemer, 1997. "Overview of Foreign Technical Barriers to US Agricultural Exports," ERS Staff Paper, 9705, US Department of Agriculture, Washington, DC, March

Schiff, M. and A. Valdés, 1992. *The Political Economy of Agricultural Pricing Policy, 4, A Synthesis of the Economics in Developing Countries*, Baltimore: Johns Hopkins University Press

Skully, D. W., 1999. "The Economics of TRQ Administration," IATRC Working Paper, 99-6, University of Minnesota, May

Snape, R. H., 1987. "The Importance of Frontier Barriers," in H. Kierzkowski (ed.), *Protection and Competition in International Trade*, Oxford: Basil Blackwell

# 7 Where the interests of developing countries converge and diverge

*Alberto Valdés and Alexander F. McCalla*

## Introduction

The environment surrounding trade negotiations has changed since the end of the Uruguay Round. Some of these changes are significant. At least fifty-four new developing countries have joined the WTO since January 1995. In fact, some two-thirds of the WTO Members are now developing nations. Given this substantial representation, the interests of this group will probably have more influence in shaping the agenda of forthcoming negotiations on further liberalizing agricultural trade.

Discussion of these interests often seems premised on the notion that developing countries are a homogeneous group. Such countries do have common interests in liberalizing overall trade, and in creating and maintaining a system that does not discriminate against subsets of countries. These interests also include better-functioning international agricultural markets and access to foreign markets, greater stability of world prices, a better system for resolving trade disputes, clearer guidelines for implementing food safety (also known as sanitary and phytosanitary SPS) measures, and clearer "contingency" provisions such as anti-dumping rules, to reduce the risk that these will be used as thinly disguised protectionism.

Developing countries also have an interest in evaluating the impact of freer trade on world economic growth as well as on growth in individual countries. Accordingly, this chapter also addresses the degree to which developing countries have divergent interests, from a number of perspectives: income level, size, region, net trade position regarding food and other agricultural products, and openness of the agricultural sector. In so doing, the chapter questions several pieces of conventional wisdom: that most developing countries will lose from liberalized trade in agriculture, that all poor countries are dependent on food imports, that all low-income food-deficit countries are small, and that exporters with the most to gain from liberalized trade are few in number, middle-income, and concentrated regionally. The chapter's overall purpose is to lend some realism to the debate over further liberalization of agricultural trade.

The chapter shows that there is no such thing as a typical developing country. As under all trade liberalization, there will be gainers and losers – both among and within countries. If trade negotiators and analysts understand this diversity, they will be better able to debate the implications of specific types of liberalization and devise mitigating measures.

The chapter develops a taxonomy of developing countries and uses it to identify the heterogeneity of interests in specific trade reforms. The analysis then examines specific dimensions of liberalization for subsets of developing countries. These include the implication of changes in agricultural trade rules for countries' domestic policy choices, and the implications of reforms in other countries (especially rich countries) for the markets in which developing countries operate.

## A taxonomy of developing countries

*Economic indicators*

To identify the interests of developing countries as a group as well as those of various subgroups, we used data from the United Nations Food and Agriculture Organization (FAO) and the World Bank to develop a taxonomy of 148 developing nations. This taxonomy classifies these nations according to income level as well as other attributes. Based on a three-year average (1995–7) of FAO data, we also computed two key economic indicators related to agricultural trade for each of these countries:

- Food import capacity (FIC) – defined as the ratio of expenditures on food imports to total export revenue.
- Agricultural Tradability (AT) – defined as the ratio of the value of agricultural trade (the sum of agricultural import expenditures and export revenues) to agricultural GDP.

*Income levels and trade position*

Table 7.1 distributes these 148 developing countries across income categories by cross-referencing World Bank and UN categories. The table reveals that the notion that all poor countries are agricultural importers is simply wrong. Table 7.1 also reveals that:

- Most low-income countries are also food-deficit countries (fifty-eight of sixty-three)
- A significant majority of transition and small island developing countries are in the middle-income category, although more fall into the lower-middle-income classification

Table 7.1 *A taxonomy of developing countries, by income*[a]

|  | 63 low-income countries | 52 low-middle-income countries | 33 upper-middle-income countries |
|---|---|---|---|
| 58 Low-income, food-deficit countries[b] (*LIFDC*) | 58 | 0 | 0 |
| 26 Transition markets (*TRANS*) | 6 | 13 | 7 |
| 29 Small-island developing countries (*SIDC*) | 5 | 15 | 9 |
| 105 Net-food-importing countries (*NFIM*) | 48 | 35 | 22 |
| 43 Net-food-exporting countries (*NFEX*) | 15 | 17 | 11 |
| 85 Net-agricultural-importing countries (*NAIM*) | 30 | 32 | 23 |
| 63 Net-agricultural-exporting countries (*NAEX*) | 33 | 20 | 10 |

*Notes:* [a] The three income categories follow the World Bank definition in the *1999 World Development Report*, namely:

$785 ≤ low-income countries (*LIC*)
$785 < lower-middle-income countries (*LMIC*) ≤ $3,125
$3,125 < upper-middle-income countries (*UMIC*) ≤ $9,655

[b] *LIFDC* from FAO database based on three criteria:

(i) *per capita* income ≤ US$785 in 1996
(ii) Net food trade position averaged over the preceding three years
(iii) Countries that meet the above two criteria may ask to be excluded from this category.

*Source:* FAO data resources.

- While two-thirds (105) of 148 developing countries are net food importers, two-fifths (sixty-three), including thirty-three low-income countries, are net agricultural exporters.

Table 7.2 cross-references various UN categories and reveals the following:

- While only one of forty-six least-developed countries (LDCs) is a net food exporter, a little over one-third (sixteen) are net agricultural exporters
- 80 percent of LDCs are also low-income food-deficit countries
- Twenty-two net food importers and twenty-five low-income food-deficient (LIFDC) countries are net agricultural exporters
- Two-thirds of small island countries are net importers of both food and agricultural products

Table 7.2 *Taxonomy matrix for groups of developing countries*

| LDC | LIFDC | TRANS | SIDC | NFIM | NFEX[b] | NAIM | NAEX | |
|-----|-------|-------|------|------|---------|------|------|------|
| 46  | 38    | 0     | 8    | 45   | 1       | 30   | 16   | LDC[a] |
|     | 58    | 5     | 5    | 47   | 11      | 33   | 25   | LIFDC[b] |
|     |       | 26    | 0    | 18   | 8       | 16   | 10   | TRANS |
|     |       |       | 29   | 20   | 9       | 20   | 9    | SIDC |
|     |       |       |      | 105  | 0       | 83   | 22   | NFIM |
|     |       |       |      |      | 43      | 2    | 41   | NFEX |
|     |       |       |      |      |         | 85   | 0    | NAIM |
|     |       |       |      |      |         |      | 63   | NAEX |

*Notes:* [a] Least-developed countries (*LDC*) following UN classification.
[b] This overlap is puzzling: 11 UN-classified *LIFDC* countries (e.g. India and Sudan) are actually *NFEX* countries.
*Source:* FAO.

- Perhaps most surprising, sixty-three developing countries – about 43 percent – are actually net agricultural exporters.

Overall, many more developing countries are net agricultural exporters than is commonly thought.

**Regional distribution**

Table 7.3 divides groups of developing countries according to their net agricultural and food import/export positions. The table identifies four categories: (1) importers of both food and agricultural products, (2) net importers of food but net exporters of agricultural products, (3) net importers of agriculture but exporters of food, and (4) exporters of both. Table 7.3, which also notes how many countries are members of WTO, reveals that:

- The majority of countries in East Asia and Pacific (eleven of twenty) are net agricultural exporters, while nine are net importers of both food and agricultural products. Of these twenty countries, thirteen countries are members of WTO, with four more having observer status.
- Some 75 percent of developing countries in South Asia are net importers of both food and agricultural products. Only India is a net exporter of both, while Sri Lanka is a net importer of food but a net exporter of agricultural products. Five of eight countries are Members of WTO, with two more being observers.
- In the Latin American and Caribbean region, thirteen out of thirty-two developing countries are net importers of both food and agricultural products, while seventeen are net importers of food. Although closer inspection reveals that ten of the thirteen are small island countries, this dispels the commonly

Table 7.3 *Net food and agricultural imports/exports in developing countries by region*

| | NAIM and NFIM | NAEX and NFIM | NAIM and NFEX | NAEX and NFEX | TOTAL |
|---|---|---|---|---|---|
| East Asia and Pacific[a] | 9 | 3 | 0 | 8 | 20 |
| South Asia[b] | 6 | 1 | 0 | 1 | 8 |
| Latin America and Caribbean[c] | 13 | 4 | 1 | 14 | 32 |
| Europe and Central Asia[d] | 15 | 3 | 1 | 8 | 27 |
| Middle East and North Africa[e] | 13 | 1 | 0 | 0 | 14 |
| Sub-Saharan Africa[f] | 27 | 10 | 0 | 10 | 47 |
| Total | 83 | 22 | 2 | 41 | 148 |

*Notes:* [a] Thirteen are WTO members, four are observer governments, and three are neither.
[b] Five are WTO members, two are observer governments, and one is neither.
[c] All thirty-two countries in this region are WTO members.
[d] Nine are WTO members, fifteen are observer governments, and three are neither.
[e] Four are WTO members, six are observer governments, and four are neither.
[f] Thirty-six are WTO members, four are observer governments, and seven are neither.
*Source:* WTO.

held notion that Latin America is purely an exporting region. All thirty-two countries in this region belong to the WTO.

- In Europe and Central Asia the number of net-importing developing countries roughly equals the number of net-exporting developing countries (Poland – a net agricultural importer but a net exporter of food products – is an exception). A minority of countries in this region (nine) are members of WTO, although fifteen have observer status.

- The Middle East and North African region is clearly the most dependent on agricultural imports. Of fourteen developing countries in this region, thirteen are net importers of both food and agricultural products, with Syria being a net importer of food but a net exporter of agricultural products. Only four countries in this region belong to the WTO, with six more as observers.

- Contrary to prevailing views, while 60 percent of developing countries in Sub-Saharan Africa (SSA) are net importers of agricultural products, some 40 percent are net exporters. Furthermore, thirty-six out of forty-seven countries belong to the WTO, and four more are observers.

These figures reveal that all regions – with the possible exception of the Middle East and North Africa – have mixed interests regarding trade in food and agricultural products, depending on whether they are net importers or exporters. The figures also reveal that participation of developing countries in the WTO is large and growing, with ninety-nine of 148 countries already members and another thirty-one having observer status, often a prelude to membership.

*Food import capacity*

Foreign exchange is critical if a country is to stabilize food consumption through imports. To what extent do food imports burden a country's balance of trade, and by how much can the food-import bill grow in years of unfavorable production and/or world prices? As a crude indicator of these relationships, we computed the food import capacity (FIC) index – the ratio of the value of food imports to total export revenues (merchandise only) averaged for the period 1995–7. The FIC indicates the foreign exchange needed to finance food imports. A low food-importing capacity (FIC) is generally good. It means that the country is not overburdened with food imports.

Table 7.4 presents the FIC for a subset of countries, and includes the lowest and highest observed values for each region. A first noteworthy observation is that the ratio of food-import value to total export value is generally high for small island countries: about 70 percent have a ratio greater than 0.25. Large developing countries such as India, Argentina, and Thailand tend to have much lower ratios. On the whole, the majority of developing countries with a limited food-importing capacity – that is, a high ratio – are typically net food-importing countries, and low-income countries with very small economies, with a few exceptions such as Egypt.

However, some caveats apply, particularly regarding Caribbean nations. Our crude indicator incorporates neither export flows generated from services (such as via tourism), nor remittances generated from overseas workers. Since many Caribbean countries rely heavily on such sources of foreign exchange, our indicator is prone to overestimating actual food import difficulties in this region.

Despite these caveats, the relatively high ratios (above 0.25) for developing countries across all regions clearly suggest that many are potentially vulnerable to foreign exchange constraints. Such ratios can grow significantly in years of domestic harvest shortfalls or higher world prices. Given this reality, some developing nations will probably seek food and financial aid, attempt to protect preferential access to markets in industrial countries, and seek help in implementing an agricultural adjustment and diversification strategy, during new talks on liberalizing agricultural trade.

Table 7.4 *Food import capacity, selected countries*

| Proxy for FIC $= \dfrac{\text{(Value food imports)}}{\text{(Value total exports)}}$ | |
|---|---|
| *East Asia and Pacific* | |
| Thailand | 0.02 |
| Laos | 0.07 |
| Kiribati | 2.12 |
| Samoa | 2.31 |
| South Asia | |
| India | 0.05 |
| Pakistan | 0.19 |
| Sri Lanka | 0.14 |
| Maldives | 0.74 |
| *Latin America and Caribbean* | |
| Argentina | 0.04 |
| Brazil | 0.10 |
| Dominican Republic | 0.50 |
| Grenada | 1.68 |
| Haiti | 2.26 |
| *Europe and Central Asia* | |
| Hungary | 0.03 |
| Latvia | 0.07 |
| Russia | 0.11 |
| Albania | 0.92 |
| Georgia | 0.99 |
| Armenia | 1.08 |
| *Middle East and North Africa* | |
| Saudi Arabia | 0.08 |
| Syria | 0.15 |
| Egypt | 0.80 |
| Lebanon | 1.07 |
| *Sub-Saharan Africa* | |
| Cameroon | 0.05 |
| Burundi | 0.46 |
| Gambia | 1.99 |
| Lesotho | 0.85 |
| Mozambique | 0.94 |
| Sierra Leone | 1.28 |

*Agricultural tradability*

The ratio of trade to GDP is a standard indicator used to rank countries according to the openness of their economies – and thus also their "vulnerability" to trade. The same criteria can be used at a sectoral level to reveal the extent to which fluctuations in world markets can affect agricultural GDP – that is, agricultural income. To capture this scenario, table 7.5 presents countries' ratio of agricultural exports plus imports relative to agricultural GDP during 1995–7.

As expected, very large economies tend to have much lower degrees of openness. For example, in India this indicator measures 0.09, compared with 0.42 in Vietnam and 1.0 in Malaysia. Ecuador, in contrast, has a very high degree of openness, with trade in importables and exportables representing 93 percent of agricultural GDP. The ratio for most Latin American countries has grown significantly since the early 1990s, as they have unilaterally liberalized trade (Quiroz and Opazo, 2000).

Two related measures are important: the extent to which a country's trading partners are highly concentrated, and the extent to which its exported commodities are concentrated in one sector. Even if a country maintains fairly diversified export markets, it could be heavily dependent on one or two major products. In 1995, the United States accounted for some 42 percent of Ecuador's total exports; Ecuador is clearly very susceptible to unilateral measures imposed by the United States. In general, developing countries with otherwise very different characteristics share a common interest in the trade and domestic policies of single large agricultural importing countries such as the United States, or groups of countries in the case of the EU.

**The impact of liberalized trade on different interest groups**

The effect of protection on world prices is perhaps the most visible case of diverging interests between developing countries that are net agricultural importers and those that are net agricultural exporters. For example, the high level of agricultural support in industrial countries results in lower world prices but also contributes to instability in world prices. Lower prices reduce the import bill of food-importing countries (and consumers' food costs) but also reduce export revenues for net exporters.

This situation raises three key questions. What changes in world prices for agricultural products, as well as changes in price stability, can we expect if trade is liberalized further? Second, what effects on domestic welfare will these changes in world prices trigger? Finally, to what extent should countries consider these effects on groups such as rural poor producers and consumers, as opposed to simply overall import demand and export supply?

Table 7.5 *Agricultural tradability, selected countries*

| Proxy for AT = $\dfrac{\text{(Value agri imports)} + \text{(Value agri exports)}}{\text{Agri GDP}}$ | |
|---|---|
| *East Asia and Pacific* | |
| Laos | 0.09 |
| Cambodia | 0.18 |
| Vietnam | 0.42 |
| Malaysia | 1.00 |
| *South Asia* | |
| India | 0.09 |
| Bangladesh | 0.14 |
| Sri Lanka | 0.57 |
| *Latin America and Caribbean* | |
| Brazil | 0.39 |
| Peru | 0.41 |
| Ecuador | 0.93 |
| St. Kitts and Nevis | 3.34 |
| Trinidad and Tobago | 4.99 |
| *Europe and Central Asia* | |
| Albania | 0.20 |
| Georgia | 0.21 |
| Russia | 0.46 |
| Macedonia | 2.56 |
| Estonia | 3.22 |
| *Middle East and North Africa* | |
| Iran | 0.17 |
| Egypt | 0.37 |
| Jordan | 4.16 |
| Bahrain | 7.25 |
| *Sub-Saharan Africa* | |
| Congo, Dem. Republic | 0.10 |
| Nigeria | 0.17 |
| Ethiopia | 0.21 |
| Botswana | 2.68 |
| Djibouti | 5.95 |

Table 7.6 shows how reforms – of both price and non-price trade-related issues such as SPS measures – in industrial countries and developing countries alike would affect different groups of the latter.

Real-world prices for agricultural commodities have been continuously declining for a century, especially for key food staples such as wheat, corn, and rice

Table 7.6 *Perspectives of developing countries on major agricultural trade issues*

| | Reforms in industrial countries | Reforms in domestic trade policies |
|---|---|---|
| 1  Market access | Net Exporters[c] [+] | |
| | Net Importers[a] [−] | Net Importers[c] |
| 2  Export subsidies | Net Exporters[c] [+] | Net Exporters[a] |
| | Net Importers[a] [−] | |
| 3  Domestic support | Net Exporters[c] [+] | Net Exporters[a] |
| | Net Importers[a] [−] | Net Importers[a] |
| 4  Sanitary measures | Net Exporters[a] | Net Exporters[c] |
| | Net Importers[c] | Net Importers[c] |
| 5  Contingency measures | Net Exporters[a] | |
| | Net Importers[c] | Net Importers[c] |
| 6  Dispute settlement | Net Exporters[a] | Net Exporters[c] |
| | Net Importers[c] | Net Importers[b] |
| 7  Preferential access | Net Exporters[a] | |
| | Net Importers[c] | Subset of LDCs[c] |

*Notes*: [a] Very significant.
[b] Fairly significant.
[c] Low significance.
[+] Beneficial.
[−] Adverse.

(Johnson, 1999). Hence, rising prices that accompany freer trade will induce a one-time flattening out of the downward-sloping trend.

Several studies have modeled the impact of trade liberalization on world prices. These studies have found that the effects would be small on grain prices, but somewhat larger for sugar, dairy products, and some meats (Anderson and Tyers, 1990; Tyers and Anderson, 1992; Valdés and Zietz, 1995). However, more recent work appears to suggest that these effects might be substantially larger. Thus, efforts by industrial countries to improve access to their markets, reduce export subsidies, and curb domestic supports would help net-exporting countries – a group, as shown, that is larger than is often supposed. The net impacts on net agricultural importers, in contrast, are likely to be negative. However, to the extent that developing countries transmit increases in world prices to domestic producers, the welfare of farmers, small and large, should rise.

Many less-developed countries (LDCs) have won preferential access to highly protected markets in industrial countries – which not only guarantees some market access but also helps stabilize export prices. Consider the case of such access by low-income exporters of sugar and bananas to the EU. Trade liberalization that lowers tariffs imposed on other producers would erode the value of preferential market access for these low-income exporters – a key issue for countries with narrow trade profiles in products and trading partners. Developing countries that relinquish such preferential market access should push for compensation and define appropriate criteria for phasing out compensation.

Elimination of export subsidies in industrial countries – among the most disruptive existing trade interventions – is clearly a high priority for net agricultural exporters. Few developing countries themselves – just twelve – have registered export subsidies during the WTO notification period established to record Aggregate Measurement of Support, or AMS. Countries with zero AMS levels cannot impose support totaling more than 10 percent of the price of individual products. Thus, most LDCs can maneuver at the negotiating table only below the 10 percent *de minimis* value of agricultural production, or by including such subsidies under "green box" criteria. However, as many have argued, reopening "green box" negotiations would be the metaphoric equivalent of opening Pandora's box, with industrial countries using such negotiations to gain more concessions than they obtained under the Uruguay Round.

Developing countries are likely carefully to scrutinize the domestic trade policy agenda because the interests of domestic agricultural producers may sometimes diverge. These divergences will be particularly prominent between export-oriented and domestic-oriented sectors.

Most developing countries now impose tariffs or use state trading to regulate imports, either to collect revenues or to protect uncompetitive domestic producers. The tariffs many developing countries apply are often actually below the bound tariffs specified in WTO schedules. However, the levels of import tariffs are diverse. Some countries, including Chile, Peru, and Argentina, have already substantially liberalized, and apply relatively low tariff levels on most products (that is, below 15–20 percent). Average tariffs are even lower if one takes into account the tariffs imposed under regional trade agreements, as is the case with several Latin American countries. Thus, further cuts in bound tariffs would not present a major threat to domestic producers in these countries. The most difficult situation would arise for countries that still maintain high protection levels – by definition, the category of net food/agricultural importers. These countries might press for more flexibility in their tariff reduction schedules.

Developing countries have voiced three key concerns regarding non-price-related issues. First, many fear that industrial countries, as well as larger developing countries, might unilaterally apply "contingency" rules that, although allowed under the WTO framework, would protect their domestic industries. For example, when faced with a dumping charge, small low-income countries often cannot muster the financial and technical resources to document their innocence. And while retaliation is the generally prescribed antidote to abuse of anti-dumping rules, this medicine works only when large countries retaliate against small countries and not vice versa (Guash and Rajapatirana, 1998).

Many lower-income developing countries, especially net agricultural importing nations, could face significant difficulties establishing institutions to apply such contingency measures, as well as SPS guidelines, which can be quite costly and require scarce skilled labor. For these countries, financial and technical constraints limit their ability to monitor the markets to which they export, and their own capacity to effectively implement these sections of WTO agreements. A particularly vulnerable group will be developing countries, such as Ecuador, with high concentration in exports and trading partners.

Moreover, many developed countries do not provide clear guidelines regarding "safe" food and agricultural imports, and they often change such guidelines frequently. Clearly, if the frequency of changes is high or if notification of changes is slow, exporting developing countries may not have enough time to adjust their production processes to accommodate the revised standards.

### Next steps

Contrary to what one often hears over the grapevine, a substantial number of developing countries (sixty-three out of 148) are actually net agricultural exporters. Furthermore, although developing countries are often treated as a homogeneous group, they are in fact diverse in many respects. However, several subsets of countries appear to share overlapping interests that are large enough to warrant the formation of a collective negotiating position. In so doing, such countries would improve their chances of placing points of interest on the agenda, exerting more influence during the negotiation process, and sharing technical knowledge and analysis.

The next step in underscoring the interests of different groups of developing countries would be to analyze groups within countries that stand to gain or lose trade liberalization. Examining the specific gainers and losers will give countries a clearer perspective on the welfare importance of trade liberalization.

Many developing countries stand to reap substantial gains from unilateral reform domestic economic policies. There is no *a priori* reason to delay these until after WTO negotiations. However, many countries will need to focus on receiving technical and financial assistance to fully implement WTO agreements and adjust their agricultural sectors to reap the maximum benefits from the trade liberalization process. This last point is actually what trade liberalization is all about: it allows countries to more freely adjust to exploit their individual comparative advantages.

Yet active participation in the WTO and negotiations to further liberalize trade imposes significant costs on developing countries. It is therefore essential that negotiations give special consideration to the most vulnerable countries – particularly least-developed food-importing countries and low-income countries that depend heavily on agricultural exports to fund their development process.

## References

Anderson, K. and R. Tyers, 1990. "The Effects of Tariffication of Food Trade Barriers Following the Uruguay Round," seminar Paper, University of Adelaide, Centre for International Studies

Guash, J. L. and S. Rajapatirana, 1998. "Total Strangers or Soul Mates? Antidumping and Competition Policies in Latin America and the Caribbean," World Bank Policy Research Working Paper, Latin America and the Caribbean Region, Washington, DC, August

Johnson, D. Gale, 1999. Seminar presented at the World Bank

Quiroz, J. and L. Opazo, 2000. "The Krueger–Schiff–Valdés Study 10 Years Later: A Latin American Perspective," *Economic Development and Cultural Change*, 49(1), 181–96

Tyers, R. and K. Anderson, 1992. *Disarray in World Food Markets: A Quantitative Assessment*, Cambridge and New York: Cambridge University Press

Valdés, A. and J. Zietz, 1995. "Distortions in World Food Markets in the Wake of GATT: Evidence and Policy Implications," *World Development*, 23, 913–26

# Part III
# New trade rules and quantitative assessments of future liberalization options

# 8 Market access, export subsidies, and domestic support: developing new rules

*Harry de Gorter*

The Uruguay Round Agreement on Agriculture (URAA) requires countries to reduce agricultural protection in three broad areas: market access, export subsidies, and domestic support. This chapter evaluates the effectiveness of commitments under each of these three pillars, and offers recommendations for strengthening their effectiveness under a new round.

## Re-evaluating market access

### Tariffs and liberalizing trade

Countries have fulfilled their market access commitments through "tariffication" and "quotification." To meet their access commitments, many countries scheduled two tariffs under tariff-rate quotas (TRQs): a lower first-tier for in-quota imports, and a higher second-tier tariff for out-of-quota imports. The URAA imposed no uniformity across countries or commodities regarding these tariffs, so quota rents are also unequal across countries and commodities. Thus the agreement has produced different effects – realized and potential – on trade liberalization in different countries.[1] Many second-tier tariffs have been prohibitively high (aided by the process of "dirty tariffication"), while some countries have used creative methods to minimize access (known as "dirty quotification").[2]

Negotiators did not assume that countries would fill their TRQs: the in-quota tariff may be so high or the quota so large that underfill occurs. What's more, a low quota fill rate does not necessarily imply inefficiency, as supply may be unavailable or demand insufficient.

Nor does a fill rate of 100 percent or more necessarily imply efficiency. Inefficiencies and transaction costs imposed by the schemes for allocating quotas – including country-specific quotas for high-cost importers – can produce quota underfill or partially dissipate rents even if quotas are filled. Meanwhile, out-of-quota importers could be more efficient if they did not incur the same costs and constraints as those importing under the quota.

In-quota fill rates averaged 66 percent across all countries in 1995 but fell to 50 percent in 1999 (WTO, 2000a). Average fill rates can be misleading because some are zero and others are 100 percent, and they are not weighted by trade volume or value.[3] Some countries do not report over-quota imports (extra imports at lower tariff levels), while the European Union (EU) reports import licenses granted and not actual imports.

Analysis shows that reducing just one of the two tariffs or increasing the quota will liberalize trade (see the appendix, p. 167). To maximize liberalization, negotiators need to identify which policy instrument – the tariff or the quota – is most effective in each situation, and focus their efforts on changing that instrument. Under some circumstances, small changes in one policy instrument could change which one is effective.

Identifying which TQR is effective becomes more complicated with unnotified quotas – those that countries have not submitted to the WTO. If these displace in-quota imports, the WTO will underestimate the in-quota fill rate. Imports from high-cost suppliers under preferential in-quota tariff rates may also mean that the in-quota fill rate is undercounted.

Quota underfill, over-quota imports, and imports under preferential tariffs complicate the job of liberalizing trade (de Gorter and Kask, 2000). In deciding which path can further liberalize market access, the quota share of total imports provides critical information. A quota share of 100 percent means that the quota is effective (or that the inefficiencies of the allocation scheme mean that the quota is unfilled yet effective). If the quota share is less than 100 percent, then either the out-of-quota tariff or the preferential tariff is effective.

In these scenarios, part of the out-of-quota imports occurs at the preferential rate and the rest at the out-of-quota rate (for which case the out-of-quota regime is effective). If the preferential tariff is effective, there are no out-of-quota imports. Quota underfill with out-of-quota imports means that quota rents were forgone and are now tariff revenues. But trade inefficiency has been minimized only if high-cost exporters received the quota licenses.

Note that the in-quota fill rate reported by the WTO (2000a) can be more than 100 percent, but an increase in the quota may have no effect on trade because of over-quota imports. Likewise, a quota increase with a fill rate of less than 100 percent may also have no effect on trade, because the inefficiencies that cause underfill may prevent further increases in imports.

*Inefficiencies from the method of administering tariff quotas*

Tariff quotas often require assigning licenses to importing firms, and sometimes allocating quotas to specific countries. The method used to assign these licenses will determine which country receives the rights to quota rents and the bargaining power of importing and exporting firms. Quotas allocated to high-cost importers can dissipate rents.

More than 1,000 of countries' 1,370-plus tariff quotas do not involve granting import licenses.[4] This implies that the rights to rents are not specifically allocated and so may encourage firms to waste resources by seeking a share of rents (WTO, 2000a). Exporting countries can obtain all the rents associated with import quotas if licenses are issued to exporting firms and not to importing firms (or if exporters have market power).

The New Zealand Dairy Board owns a substantial proportion of outstanding quotas in the world market and is estimated to capture $200 million per year in rents (Schluep and de Gorter, 2001). New Zealand also controls import quota rents as an exporter of lamb to the EU, and administers prices and trade on both sides of the Atlantic. For some products, quota specifications are so specific that an importer automatically obtains the rents. An example is the import license for mozzarella that the EU specifies for Pizza Hut products.

The URAA contains no specific provisions instructing countries on allocating import licenses. Countries use tariffs to administer some 50 percent of the quotas, so in fact quotas and licenses have no effect on imports. The remaining methods are license-on-demand, first-come, first-served, historical allocation, auction, and state trading/producer groups (WTO, 2000a). Except for first-come, first-served, all other allocation procedures can involve import licenses.[5] Countries also often impose additional conditions such as domestic purchase requirements and limits on quantities that can arbitrarily increase costs and hence inefficiencies. For example, limits on quota shares do not allow for economies of size and coordination, again dissipating quota rents.

The Agreement on Import Licensing requires that the application process for obtaining a license be as simple as possible and "neutral in application and administered in a fair and equitable manner" (WTO, 1994). No licensing procedures should be trade-distorting or restrictive. However, the importing country decides what is "fair and equitable" and which methods are least "administratively burdensome." Countries allocate most import licenses for a specific year or season.

Of the administration methods, state trading enterprises and historical importers have the highest fill rate, while auctions have the lowest. A competitive auction would ensure that the most efficient, low-cost firms would gain access to the rights to import (Bergsten *et al.*, 1987), but countries do not necessarily award them to such firms. And the granting of a valuable property right creates a constituency that will rent seek and lobby governments to resist trade liberalization, possibly rendering auctions inefficient (Boughner and de Gorter, 1998). Other drawbacks include the possibility that imperfect competition will ensue among domestic or foreign trading firms, or that foreign suppliers will change their price in response to the quota.

The first-come, first-served method has an average fill rate of only 63 percent, as exporters may not risk the cost of shipping a product to a port only to find that the quota has been filled. So the costs of storing goods until the following season, of paying the higher out-of-quota tariff, or of shipping the product elsewhere may be high. Other problems with this method include the tendency to concentrate imports at the beginning of the season (ships may appear early and wait in line), and discrimination against exporters who have different seasons and hence higher costs at the beginning of the quota year (Boughner and de Gorter, 1998; ABARE, 1999; Skully, 1999).

Issuing import licenses based on historical shares can encourage companies to rent seek by importing more than what is optimal. For example, Chiquita is purported to have expanded imports in the EU in 1992 in anticipation of new Common Market Organization efforts to allocate licenses as a proportion of historical imports. Historical import-allocation also enables high-cost firms to operate, at least partly dissipating rents.

Countries usually allocate licenses-on-demand before the season begins, dividing them among firms based on the quota level and the number of licenses requested. This again enables higher-cost importers to obtain the rights to rents, thereby dissipating them somewhat. Producer groups may control imports to protect against lower import prices. Failing to fill the quota is advantageous only if the quota rents are smaller than the producer's loss of surplus stemming from increased imports (ABARE, 1999). There is also the problem of distributing the rents to farmers, which could subsidize domestic production (Schluep and de Gorter, 2001).

Fill rates for quotas administered by State-Trading Enterprises (STEs) are high, perhaps reflecting the ability of importers to overcome transaction and information costs. An STE that controls all imports is visible and perhaps even scrutinized by foreign governments. However, importers can still seek rents. The Japanese Food Agency deliberately allocated import quotas to the United States – a high-cost producer – and excluded Canada (ABARE, 1999), dissipating some of the rents. STEs also have the ability to discriminate on price in their purchases and sell the products at lower prices on the domestic market. STEs can also restrict imports to help domestic farmers. Choi, Sumner and Song (1998) show how the Korean STE imports rice through an open-bidding system, awarding the right to import to the lowest bidder that meets minimum quality standards. This leads to lower-quality imports that are not a close substitute for domestic rice, thus protecting domestic farm incomes.

### Re-evaluating export subsidies

The second pillar of the URAA specifies limits and cuts in export subsidies for twenty-five countries while also prohibiting new subsidies.[6] Several commentators have argued that export subsidies are the most distorting agricultural policy interventions. However, export subsidies raise domestic prices just like import barriers: *both* policy instruments reduce consumption and increase production, thereby distorting trade. Although import controls reduce trade, and export subsidies increase trade, both reduce world prices.

The confusion may stem from the fact that competing export subsidy programs by two or more countries are self-defeating. However, this is true for import restrictions as well. As import restrictions lower world prices, this requires other countries to increase tariffs to maintain the same level of producer support. Indeed, import barriers by some countries increase the need for export subsidies by others, and vice versa. Hence, disciplines on export subsidies should receive the same urgent attention as those affecting market access.[7]

*Expenditures versus quantity limits*

The EU has always accounted for the lion's share of export subsidies – see figure 8.1, which shows a share in the base period of the Uruguay Round of over 70 percent – and it now accounts for about 80 percent of the world total. The United States, meanwhile, spends less on export subsidies than several countries, including Switzerland.

Developed countries agreed to reduce the *volume* of subsidized exports by 21 percent over six years from a 1986–90 base period. Developing countries agreed to 14 percent cuts over a ten-year period. Developed countries also agreed to reduce the *value* of export subsidies by 36 percent, while developing countries agreed to 24 percent cuts over ten years. Other countries have since joined these commitments. The least-developed countries (LDCs) are exempt. Reductions could be made from 1991–2 subsidy levels if they were higher; such "front-loading" allows countries to cut subsidies from higher levels.

The URAA imposes this schedule equally among specific sectors, but does allow countries to distribute the value or volume cuts among different years as they see fit. Countries can also roll over unused subsidies to ensuing years, and aggregate products within a commodity group. These measures have allowed governments to partially circumvent their commitments to reduce export subsidies. Ruiz (2000) shows that front-loading and banking have enabled countries to significantly increase their export subsidies over baseline levels for several commodities.

Countries also circumvent the volume constraint by giving a larger per-unit subsidy to a portion of total exports instead of an average per-unit subsidy. This means that per-unit export subsidies vary significantly across commodities and countries. To ensure trade liberalization, more stringent limits on the value of export subsidies – or a rule that deems total exports of a commodity subsidized if only a portion receive subsidies – are needed.

Overall, countries have used 36 percent of their value allowances and 45 percent of their volume allowances. This suggests that volume limits have been

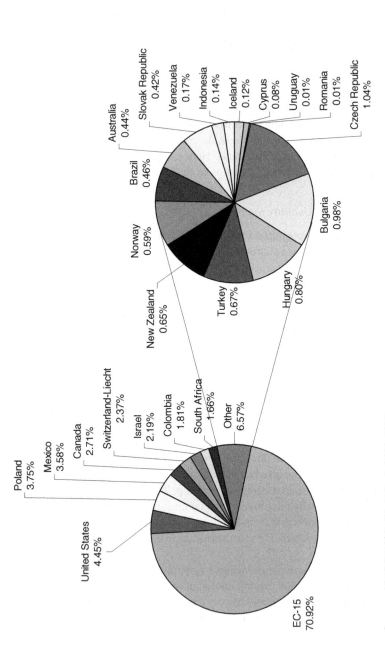

*Sources:* ABARE (1999); World Bank (1990, 1998).

Figure 8.1 Shares in baseline (1986–90) export subsidies from the Uruguay Round

more binding – perhaps because of lower support prices and rising world prices. Volume and value commitments do not usually bind at the same time. A key policy issue is whether any formula for further cuts in export subsidies should focus on volumes or expenditures.

To analyze this, assume that both the volume of subsidized exports and the value of subsidies are limiting in the baseline. In a static framework, a 21 percent cut in the volume of exports with a subsidy may produce a volume equal to the free-trade level. In this case, the volume constraint will be more liberalizing. Unlike with reductions in export expenditures, a less than 100 percent reduction in the volume of subsidized exports can achieve free trade. However, countries may be able to circumvent such a constraint by giving a larger per-unit export subsidy on a smaller volume of exports.

Under equal reductions in volume and value, the volume reduction is always binding (Ruiz and de Gorter, 2000). Cuts in value have to be larger than reductions in volume to be equally effective. Indeed, under URAA reduction commitments of 21 percent in volume and 36 percent in value,[8] the value reduction will not be binding in a static framework. The smaller the initial subsidy, the lower the value reductions needed to be binding. Value commitments become relatively more likely to be binding for larger volumes exported and more elastic trade curves.

This analysis needs to be augmented to allow for shifts in excess supply and demand curves, because there is a time gap between the baseline and the beginning of the implementation period, and during the implementation period. The free trade equilibrium point shifts to the left when the excess supply curve shifts up and/or the excess demand curve shifts down; the reverse occurs when the free trade equilibrium shifts to the right. If both the volume and value reductions are equally binding after the reductions, then volume constraints are always binding in the case of a rightward shift in the free trade equilibrium, and expenditure constraints are always binding in the case of a leftward shift (see Ruiz and de Gorter, 2000). The government's policy goal determines which is more desirable.

Politicians can maximize any of at least four policy targets to fulfill political demands under changing market conditions and subsidy commitments: the per-unit export subsidy, total export subsidy expenditures, the volume of exports subsidized, and domestic price levels. If the free-trade equilibrium shifts right, the volume constraint automatically means that export subsidy expenditures decline, because the per-unit subsidy declines. Indeed, the export subsidy may become ineffective with the volume constraint. However, this will not occur with an expenditure limit.

If only value-reduction commitments are binding after the reductions, then either the volume or the value commitments become binding, depending on market parameters (Ruiz, 2000). If volume-reduction commitments are binding after the reductions, the volume continues to bind for rightward shifts in the free trade equilibrium.

However, if the free-trade equilibrium moves left, then the volume limit becomes less binding and there is "water" in the volume limit. If only value-reduction commitments are binding after the reductions, then value continues to be binding. If volume-reduction commitments are binding after the reductions with a leftward shift in the free-trade equilibrium, then either the volume or the value commitments become binding, again depending on market parameters.

### Consumer-financed export subsidies

Although the URAA limits taxpayer- and producer-financed export subsidies, it does not recognize consumer-financed subsidies. Such a subsidy occurs when price discrimination and pooling revenue for farmers expands output and contracts consumption, causing a gap between domestic and world prices (Sumner, 1996; Schluep, 1999; Schluep and de Gorter, 2001).[9] Consumer-financed support programs for milk in the United States and wheat in Canada require a government policy (i.e. US federal marketing orders) or a sanctioned monopoly producer organization (i.e. the Canadian Wheat Board). The US Northeast Milk Compact results in even higher milk prices in that region, and, with revenue pooling, produces a consumer-financed export subsidy. Taxpayer-financed export subsidies entail consumer transfers as well, because they raise domestic prices. But a consumer-financed export subsidy distorts trade more than a taxpayer-financed export subsidy for a given domestic price (Schluep and de Gorter, 2001).

Any type of export subsidy scheme requires import controls to prevent firms from "recycling" exports. Hence, an export subsidy scheme and reduction commitments may be combined with market access commitments. However, market access commitments often do not cover taxpayer-financed export schemes. In the EU, tariffs for cereals are much higher than per-unit export subsidies, so conflation is minimal. Commitments to reduce both import barriers and export subsidies would be desirable for liberalizing trade.

The URAA implicitly includes many export subsidy commitments in its market access and domestic support components. This means that a decrease in tariffs or domestic support will automatically require a drop in export subsidies and vice versa. For example, the WTO calculates price gaps for the export-enhancement program of the US wheat, rice, poultry, and eggs sectors and includes them in measures of domestic support but not in market access commitments. Excluding consumer-financed export subsidies from discipline may not be so problematic if market access provisions cut tariffs. A major exception is fluid milk for the United States, Canada, and Australia because it is regarded as a non-tradable commodity.

*Producer-financed export subsidies*

The URAA also subjects mandatory or government-regulated producer-financed export subsides to reduction commitments. A producer-financed export subsidy must coexist with a taxpayer- and/or a consumer-financed export subsidy. Adding a producer levy to a taxpayer-financed export subsidy raises the price for both farmers and consumers.

Combining a producer levy with a consumer-financed export subsidy requires two export products. The producer levy is identical to a cut in the price of the second product, whose sales are pooled with those of the first. Hence, introducing a producer levy with a consumer-financed export subsidy has no effect – it is like taking money from one pocket and putting it into another. Farmers receive the same average revenue pooled domestic and export sales, because exports are not pooled at the world price but at some higher price, to justify the use of producer levies (Schluep, 1999; Schluep and de Gorter, 2001).

New Zealand dairy policy under the control of the producer-controlled dairy board maintains price discrimination among multiple world markets for many products. The producer board in New Zealand pools downstream profits, domestic price premiums, and import quota rents, raising farm prices by some 33 percent (Schluep and de Gorter, 2001). Pooling these revenues mimics a production subsidy and is not considered part of domestic support. Price discrimination in world markets leads to higher prices for consumers world-wide, and therefore also to lower consumption and trade.

The finding of the WTO Dispute Settlement Panel (1990) on Canadian dairy policy illustrates the problems with defining export subsidies. The panel deemed exports beyond the production quota at the world price with no revenue pooling an export subsidy. Economists would argue that no distortion exists, because the marginal cost of production equals the world price, as with the EU sugar quota and US peanut quotas. However, the WTO ruled that such a scheme is a producer-financed export subsidy because farmers have to "forgo revenue," milk products sold at the world price were "preferential exports" requiring farmers to "share the cost" of selling milk for less than the pooled price from domestic sales, and the price was "contingent on exports." This legal definition of export subsidies in the URAA, the Agreement on Subsidies and Countervailing Measures, and article XVI of GATT 1994 is clearly inadequate. In a ruling on another Canadian dairy pricing scheme, the WTO deemed a class of milk that involved both domestic and export sales with price pooling not an export subsidy, even though it conformed to the definition of a consumer-financed export subsidy. The panel's decision has implications for other countries' dairy and other commodity policies.

A revised definition of export subsidies should recognize that pooling is important, rely less on criteria such as "contingent on exports," improve the meaning of "preferential exports," and recognize that the effects of producer levies depend on the initial policy. This GATT definition of an export subsidy leaves room for loopholes, circumvention, and misinterpretation, and should be more specific regarding policies that both contract domestic consumption and expand domestic production.

*Other unresolved issues regarding export subsidies*

Public expenditures for promoting exports along with food aid can have market effects like those of an export subsidy. Food aid that displaces commercial imports will depress world prices, while emergency food aid that increases world consumption will increase world prices. Food aid and export promotion programs have complex effects, so determining whether they are export subsidies is difficult.

Government efforts to dispose of excess food stocks are equivalent to standard export subsidies if we include the costs of acquiring these stocks (Peterson, Minten, and de Gorter, 1999). However, Chambers and Paarlberg (1991) and Anania, Bohman, and Carter (1992) focus only on the effects of disposing of public stocks on the world market – showing that export bonuses can lower domestic prices and hence not act like an export subsidy.

The agreement among coffee exporters to withhold 20 percent of their exports and put the excess into stocks (1990) requires a similar analysis – but as an export tax rather than a subsidy. The URAA does not include disciplines on export taxes like that for cereals in the EU in 1998, even though they have effects like those of export subsidies.

Controversy over EU "inward processing relief" for cheese shows how export subsidies for butter and skim milk powder indirectly subsidize cheese exports. These subsidies allow the EU to circumvent limits on export subsidies and could encourage countries to transfer subsidies from one product group to another in the form of input subsidies (Leetmaa and Ackerman, 1998).

Finally, measuring the export subsidy component of export credit guarantees can be very complex. Subsidized risk premiums need to be converted into a present value borne by the taxpayer. It is possible that a government has corrected a market failure by reducing the risk and enhancing the purchasing power of importers, thereby shifting demand for imports and mitigating the effects of the export subsidy. But better criteria for measuring the effects of such subsidies are required.

### Rethinking commitments to cut domestic support

Many analysts considered countries' commitments to reduce baseline *domestic* support the most innovative element of the Uruguay Round. Negotiators established an "amber box" for domestic policies that distorted trade while creating a "green box" for minimally trade-distorting policies, which are exempt from reduction commitments.[10] The Aggregate Measurement of Support (AMS) measures domestic support, which countries agreed to reduce by 20 percent during the 1995–2000 implementation period. This distinction allowed the URAA to focus on trade-distorting policies, negotiate cuts, and provide an incentive for national governments to re-instrument their domestic policies toward non-distorting measures.

The EU, Japan, and the United States account for over 85 percent of the global total of domestic support as measured under the AMS (WTO, 2000b). As of 1998, only Iceland had exceeded its reduction commitments (WTO, 2000b). However, several countries and regions, including Norway, Switzerland, Japan, Korea, and the EU, maintain AMS (excluding the "blue box"), that is over 50 percent of the baseline AMS (which includes the "blue box"). Nevertheless, AMS commitments may have induced governments to re-instrument their policies toward the "green box".[11]

*Major issues related to the "amber box"*

The AMS was designed to measure trade-distorting domestic policies, independent of distortions stemming from import barriers and export subsidies. In reality, however, the AMS is combined with support derived from border policies.[12] For example, the AMS includes price gaps between fixed baseline world prices and administered price supports and other transfers from consumers. The accounting method for price gaps is called the "equivalent method of support," or EMS.[13] This means that the WTO overestimates domestic support in countries that report administered prices, because those include a substantial proportion of support already counted in market access and export subsidies. The AMS also ignores the fact that farm prices often diverge from the "administered price support" defined in the URAA as the intervention price in the EU, or dairy price supports in the United States.

For the world as a whole, the AMS averaged only 38 percent of total domestic support that countries reported in the "amber," "blue," and "green boxes" for 1995–8 (WTO, 2000b). This double counting of border support and the overestimated AMS might mean that the sum of the three boxes exceeded the total Producer Support Estimate (PSE). This is especially possible with countries that are close to the AMS ceiling, such as Korea, Norway, Switzerland, and members of the EU, who rely heavily on administered prices. Indeed, total "domestic support" in the EU alone in 1996 was $121.2 billion (WTO, 2000b), while the total PSE measured by the OECD was $109.3 billion (OECD, 2000). This calls into question the meaning, fairness, and effectiveness of support-reduction commitments.

This problem is particularly acute if it affects one country and not another. For example, EU support for the cereals sector is confined to import tariffs and export subsidies, while US support is in the form of producer subsidies. This means that the EU's AMS is really zero.

One could argue that conflating domestic support with trade protection means that any commitment to reduce support in one category will automatically reduce that in the other. However, it is instructive to analyze US AMS commitments in the sugar, dairy, and peanut sectors to test this assumption.

In the case of sugar, the United States declares an official administered price support for farmers at the beginning of each year. The United States adjusts import quota levels throughout the year to achieve this level. However, the United States is constrained by market access commitments in achieving the price support, and the final price rarely equals the declared price support. Thus the US market access commitment determines the domestic price. If the United States reduces the official price support but does not change import barriers, then the AMS declines but there is no trade liberalizing effect. If the United States does liberalize market access the AMS does not change – but trade is liberalized. In either case, the trade barrier – the import quota – determines domestic support, so the AMS double counts the support afforded by market access commitments.

The AMS calculation for the US dairy sector exemplifies a different anomaly in the relationship between the AMS and the other two pillars of the URAA. The WTO measures the domestic support price by the offer-to-purchase price for each dairy product. In the past several years, the support price has been non-binding and only a fraction of the actual support price that farmers receive. For example, the official support price is approximately $10/hundredweight (cwt), whereas the average milk price that farmers receive from import controls and export subsidies ranges from $12–$15/cwt. The AMS measure is thus irrelevant for dairy products. A cut in the support price will reduce the AMS but have no market effect. A liberalization of market access will have a market impact but will not affect the AMS.

In the US peanut program, the WTO measures the AMS by the price gap between the announced support price for quota peanuts and the world price. A cut in the support price will require an increase in imports through liberalized market access. The peanut program is a non-production-distorting, consumer-financed production subsidy implemented via a quota-allocation scheme. It is therefore truly a "domestic" support program – but the AMS measure is combined with market access commitments. A reduction in one will affect the other, and vice versa.

These three different outcomes in calculating the US AMS for peanuts, dairy, and sugar show how the issue of official and administered prices needs to be revisited. The reason for measuring market price support is that an administered price requires a government decision – members would not commit to reducing something that they did not directly control. However, such reasoning leads to difficulties in comparing the AMS across commodities and countries, because the measure is combined with import barriers and export subsidies, and inaccuracies arise if the actual market price does not equal the support price.

Another example of the latter is the large negative AMS reported by Brazil, where the official support price is below the world price, but market prices are allowed to equal world prices. Although the URAA requires each country to identify market price supports in the form of "administered prices," import barriers that keep domestic prices high with no "official" administered price allow countries to have no AMS. Canada has not been able to identify an administered price for chicken, turkey, or eggs. So there is no "market price support" for Canada's AMS for these products. This shows how arbitrary is the method for calculating the AMS.

A significant problem with cuts in "amber box" policies is that a single AMS aggregates all policies and commodity sectors. This approach allows countries to increase or maintain support in specific sectors if the country reduces support in other sectors because of market conditions or cuts in border support. The "Peace Clause," stating that policies are exempt from WTO policy challenges if support does not exceed levels for that sector in 1992, constrains that possibility somewhat.

Negotiators are best advised to create a *flashing "amber box"* for policies that are truly domestic trade-distorting support policies and that are not conflated with market access or export subsidy commitments. Cuts in domestic support would then exert the maximum effect. Negotiators should also consider basing reduction commitments on a policy type and commodity sector rather than on a single AMS. This will secure a more meaningful drop in trade distortions arising from "amber box" policies.[14]

*Issues related to "blue box" policies*

Major "blue box" policies include EU area payments to farmers for diverting hectarage to cereals, oilseeds, and protein crops; slaughter premiums for beef cattle and calves; and "headage payments" for beef and dairy, with the latter requiring land-density targets to protect the environment. The "blue box" was temporary and was due to be renegotiated by 2003. Negotiators would do well to "empty and lock" the "blue box" by transferring its policies to the appropriate "green box" or "amber box," so the same boxes are used to classify the policies of all countries. This would be consistent with the multilateral character of the WTO, and prevent governments from transferring policies from the "amber box" to the "blue box" to meet AMS reduction commitments.

On their face, area payments appear to increase output, because farmers have to plant a cereal, oilseed, or protein crop to be eligible for the subsidy. However, farmers are required to set aside a proportion of planted hectarage and keep it idle. This decreases output. Hence, the net effect of the subsidy *versus* the set-aside requirement is indeterminate. The outcome depends on the number of hectares set aside and the level of area payments.

The output per hectare or yield upon which area and set-aside payments are based is fixed. This means that area payments do not increase output per hectare. In addition to mandatory set-asides with payments, farmers can volunteer to set aside even more (up to 50 percent of planted hectarage in some regions) and receive the set-aside payments instead of area payments. This further decreases output. Per-hectare set-aside payments now equal area payments under the EU farm policy reforms under Agenda 2000. EU farmers were expected to set aside almost 6 million hectares in 2000. Because of the indeterminate effect of output-reducing price supports, criteria need to be developed to determine the degree to which these supports distort output.[15]

*Issues related to "green box" policies*

All support included in "green box" policies entails taxpayer-funded programs, which are exempt from reduction commitments. A "green box" policy is defined as one where "no production is required in order to receive . . . payments." Future negotiations will have to address the question of whether the programs listed in annex 2 in the URAA are truly non- or minimally trade-distorting.

Two key issues stand out: how to measure the trade-distorting effects of direct payments to farmers (such as the $22 billion distributed to major US field crop farmers in 1999), and how to best deal with the "multifunctionality" of agriculture – its ability to provide both negative and positive externalities.

US "green box" polices such as "production flexibility contracts" and payments for "emergency market loss" compensate farmers for declines in market revenue. According to the US Department of Agriculture, the production value of major US field crops declined by $20.9 billion between 1996–7 and 1999–2000, while direct payments grew by $15.5 billion. This means that subsidies have offset most of farmers' market loss.

Direct payments of this magnitude can offset farmers' fixed costs, which are higher than variable costs for all crops except rice. Countries can cross-subsidize exports by covering farmers' fixed costs and allowing them to remain in business or inducing them to enter production.

Chau and de Gorter (2000) analyzed the distribution of fixed costs across individual US wheat farms by studying the output and export consequences of three scenarios: removal of coupled payments, decoupled payments, and both.[16] Removing coupled payments cuts exports by 56 percent, while removing decoupled payments reduces exports by 41 percent. Hence, removing decoupled payments can have a large impact on the exit decisions of farmers with low-profit farms. However, the overall impact of such payments can remain limited if the output from marginal farms is relatively small. Still, if income payments lead farmers to expect compensation for short-term losses, the distorting effects of decoupled payments can be considerably larger.

Producer payments also have a stabilizing component. Direct government payments produce two types of responses by farmers (de Gorter and Tsur, 1995; Hennessy, 1998). First is the *income effect*, where higher incomes make farmers less risk averse and encourage them to increase production. This creates uncertainty in the marketplace. Second is the *risk effect*, where direct payments reduce the variability of farm revenue and hence farmers' degree of risk.

Farmers receive most "emergency market loss" payments after they have made production decisions. Nevertheless, producers develop expectations of future assistance based on past government actions. As Barry (1999) comments: "It is not hard to plan on government assistance when it comes so easily." Hence, production rises not only through fewer farming exits and more entries, but also because existing farmers expand acreage.

Direct payments can also affect farmers' investment and exit decisions if they face constraints in capital and labor markets. For example, farmers have specialized skills, and so they often have difficulty finding off-farm employment that enables them to leave farming or farm part-time. Government payments allow farmers to stay in agriculture and avoid any costs associated with participating in non-agricultural labor markets (Rude, 1999).

To investigate such effects, Young and Westcott (2000) evaluated the US crop and revenue insurance programs, which reduce variability in farm revenues. They found that subsidies encouraged farmers to participate in insurance programs and increased the acres they planted – especially land that might not otherwise be farmed. In 2001, US crop insurance subsidies rose to $3.5 billion.

Finally, negotiators need to develop criteria for evaluating the effects on trade of policies that aim to enhance the public good, such as subsidies for food aid, research, and the environmental effects of agricultural production. Such policies can be justified if they correct a market failure without distorting production.

## The trade effects of environmental policies

Existing GATT rules place few constraints on a country's right to protect its environment, even though the choice of policy instrument may critically affect comparative advantage. The GATT even allows countries to use trade measures to achieve their environmental goals, as long as the instruments are "necessary" and "least trade-distorting." However, both terms are ill-defined. Because the positive amenities that agricultural production provides are difficult to measure, countries may use environmental policies as a backdoor means to subsidize agriculture.

Because environmental policies can act as trade barriers, analysts need to study the effects of different policies on international trade and define those that are least trade-distorting. A pollution-abatement subsidy can clearly distort comparative advantage more than a user-pay pollution tax. This type of analysis must be extended to include extra-market benefits such as preservation of landscape, wildlife habitat, food security, and rural viability.

Overall, an agricultural sector that fulfills many functions will require policy instruments targeting specific objectives. A single price support or production tax will be more trade-distorting and could make the agricultural sector "dysfunctional."

## Focusing a new round on the most effective policies

The effectiveness of market access disciplines will rest on how tariff quotas are liberalized. The effects of increasing the quota or decreasing the tariffs are complex because they depend on which initial regime is effective – and that regime can change. Over-quota imports, quota underfill, preferential quotas and tariffs, and non-notified quotas complicate this analysis. Hence, negotiators can follow no simple rule in maximizing the liberalizing effects of cuts in barriers to market access.

However, they should implement mechanisms for scrutinizing alternatives for administering quotas, and try to better understand why quota underfill arises. They should also encourage tradability in country-specific export quotas and import/export licenses.

The WTO's definition of an export subsidy is inadequate, because it ignores consumer-financed export subsidies and does not properly identify producer-financed subsidies. Countries can also circumvent their commitments to reduce export subsidies by front-loading and banking unused subsidies.

Because the URAA did not regulate per-unit export subsidies in contrast with import tariffs, governments could raise the per-unit subsidy on a lower proportion of total exports. A new agreement should specify that total exports of any product that receives export subsidies must count in countries' commitments to cut their volume receiving such subsidies.

Meanwhile the AMS – designed to measure trade distortion stemming from domestic support – overestimates this support. The AMS is also problematic because it is combined with border measures, aggregated across all commodity groups, and allows countries to shift support from one sector to another. To maximize cuts in domestic support, negotiators should create a *flashing "amber box"* for policies that are truly domestic and have trade-distorting effects. This box should be measured on a commodity-specific basis, to prevent countries from shifting support among commodities.

Direct payments like those the United States provides to field crop farmers distort production because they cover farmers' fixed costs – keeping them in production when they would otherwise use land for other production or leave it idle. Expectations of future payments can affect farmers' exit, entry, and investment decisions as well. Hence the "green box" definitions of trade distortions need to be tightened, and disciplines developed for direct payments that can distort production. Stricter rules and monitoring are also required for policies designed to internalize the positive and negative externalities of agricultural production.

Overall, because border policies distort trade the most, negotiators should focus primarily on improving market access and reducing export subsidies. Disciplines on domestic support should not impede governments' efforts to re-instrument their trade policies away from market access policies and export subsidies toward domestic support.

# Appendix    The basic economics of tariff-rate quotas

## Policy instruments

Identifying the condition under which either the quota or tariff under tariff-rate quotas (TRQs) becomes effective – that is, which policy instrument determines the level of imports and domestic and world prices – is important.[17] Doing so enables analysts to understand the distribution of quota rents and tariff revenues, their interaction, and the effects on trade and welfare.

Let us formally define the three basic policy instruments in a tariff-quota scheme: the import quota $Q^{quota}$; the first-tier tariff $t_1$ on in-quota imports (including possibly over-quota imports), and the higher second-tier tariff $t_2$ on out-of-quota imports.[18] Only one of the import tariffs or the quota can be *effective* in determining imports and domestic/world prices, rendering the other two policy instruments *redundant*. For a tariff to be effective, therefore, it must change the volume of trade from the bound quota level. Otherwise, each tariff is redundant and the quota becomes effective, in which case the world price plus the second-tier tariff must be greater than (and the world price plus the first-tier tariff must be less than) the domestic price resulting from the import quota alone.

The first-tier tariff can be effective when the world price plus the first-tier tariff is greater than the unobserved or "what if" domestic price that would have occurred if the import quota was the only policy instrument (likewise for the second-tier tariff if the world price including the second-tier tariff is below the hypothetical import determining domestic price).

Figure 8A.1 shows that if the quota level is very high and close to the free trade level (i.e. such as $Q_1^{quota}$ which is close to the intersection of the excess

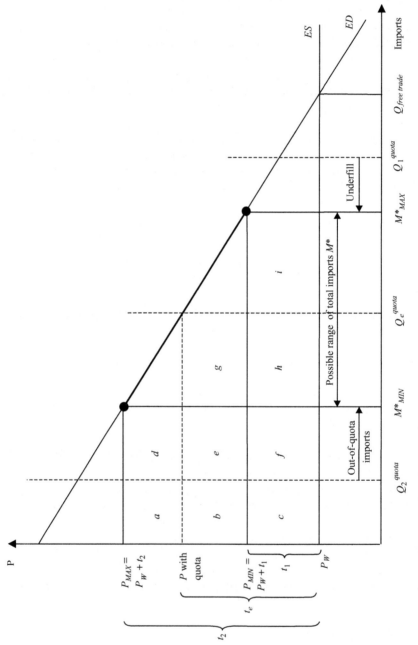

Figure 8A.1  The economics of the three TRQ regimes

demand curve *ED* and the excess supply curve *ES*), then the in-quota tariff $t_1$ is effective and the domestic price $= P_W + t_1$. A tariff causes a wedge between the domestic price and the world price $P_W$. The equilibrium is determined when the wedge between the excess supply (determining $P_W$) and the excess demand (determining the domestic price) curves is equal to the tariff. This equilibrium determines total imports that are lower than free-trade levels. Indeed, when the in-quota tariff $t_1$ is effective, imports would be at the maximum level $M^*_{MAX}$ in figure 8A.1 and would remain so as long as the quota level is to the right of $M^*_{MAX}$. The resulting domestic price would be at the minimum $P_{MIN}$ and quota underfill occurs.

If, on the other hand, the quota is very low and close to the origin like $Q_2^{quota}$ in figure 8A.1, then the out-of-quota tariff $t_2$ is effective. The out-of-quota tariff determines the minimum level of total imports $M^*_{MIN}$ and the maximum possible domestic price $P_{MAX}$ occur under this scenario. Because the quota level is to the left of the minimum level of total imports (the requirement for the $t_2$ tariff to be effective in the first place), out-of-quota imports occur. If the quota falls between the minimum and maximum level of imports, then the quota is effective in determining the domestic price like that depicted by $Q_e^{quota}$ in figure 8A.1.[19] Hence, there are three possible regimes over all levels of the import TRQ $Q^{quota}$:

- The "in-quota tariff regime" where the lower in-quota tariff $t_1$ is operative (for example, $Q_1^{quota}$ in figure 8A.1), where quota rents and out-of-quota revenues are zero, but in-quota tariff revenues are areas $c + f + h + i$.
- The "out-of-quota tariff regime" where the higher out-of-quota tariff $t_2$ is operative (for example, $Q_2^{quota}$ in figure 8A.1), where quota rents equal areas $a + b$, out-of-quota tariff revenues are areas $d + e + f$, and in-quota tariff revenues of area $c$.
- The "quota regime" where the import quota (for example, $Q_e^{quota}$ in figure 8A.1) determines price, where quota rents are areas $b + e + g$, in-quota tariff revenues are areas $c + f + h$, and out-of-quota tariff revenues are zero.

## Flagging a regime switch

Because small changes in one policy instrument can change the regime that is effective, it is important to show how soon the instrument becomes redundant after liberalization. To do this, one can compare out-of-quota imports to the quota and level of quota underfill. This reveals how close one is to a regime switch.

Consider, for example, the case where $t_e$ is close to but less than $t_2$ (i.e. imagine $Q_e^{quota}$ in figure 8A.1 to be close to but to the right of $M^*_{MIN}$). A small reduction in $t_2$ will have no impact on imports. A simultaneous increase in the quota will be required in order for trade liberalization to occur. However, once $t_2$

Table 8A.1 *Policies of key sugar trading nations/regions and ad valorem tariff equivalents*

| Policy Country | Import quotas | Tariff quota | Tariff | Ad valorem bound tariff equivalent (%), 2000 | Surcharge | State trading | Subsidies | Other | Export subsidies |
|---|---|---|---|---|---|---|---|---|---|
| Japan | ✓ | | ✓ | 287 | ✓ | | | 1 Production quotas | ✓ |
| Western Europe | ✓ | ✓ | ✓ | 176 | ✓ | | ✓ | 2 Production quotas | |
| United States | | ✓ | ✓ | 151 | ✓ | | | 3 Compulsory export quotas | |
| Mexico | | | ✓ | 96 | | | | | |
| Indonesia | | | | 95 | | ✓ | | 4 Government-owned mills | |
| Eastern Europe (Poland) | | ✓ | ✓ | 96 | ✓ | | | 5 Government-owned mills production quotas | |
| China | | | ✓ | | ✓ | ✓ | ✓ | 6 Regional government ownership of mills | |
| Philippines | | ✓ | ✓ | 100 | | | | | |
| Ukraine | | | ✓ | | | | | | |
| South Africa | | | ✓ | 105 | | | | | |
| Mauritius | | | | 139 | | | | 1 Export subsidies from EU 2 Import ban 3 Land locked-in | |

falls below $t_e$ (the tariff equivalent when the quota is binding), further decreases in $t_2$ will have maximal effect in liberalizing trade. Hence, for such cases where $t_e$ is close to $t_2$, it may be sufficient to focus on negotiating significant reductions in $t_2$ only, an outcome that is definitely desirable for all cases where $t_e$ is initially greater than $t_2$.

Table 8A.1 summarizes the effects of alternative trade liberalization scenarios. Notice that when the out-of-quota tariff $t_2$ is effective (as with $Q_2^{quota}$ in figure 8A.1), then an increase in the quota has no effect initially until imports under the quota are greater than $M^*_{MIN}$. Conversely, when the quota is initially effective (like $Q_e^{quota}$ in figure 8A.1), then a decrease in $t_2$ has no effect unless $t_2$ goes so low as to generate imports beyond the quota level $Q_e^{quota}$. Hence, because the domestic price with a quota (world price plus some tariff equivalent $t_e$) described earlier is unobserved when the quota is not effective, it is sufficient to observe how large out-of-quota imports are relative to the quota, or the level of quota underfill. This gives information on how close the unobserved $t_e$ plus the world price is to the domestic price. Indeed, to avoid an instrument becoming redundant upon liberalization, it may be necessary to have at least two liberalizing instruments at the same time.

To summarize, to liberalize trade, negotiators should focus on reducing out-of-quota tariffs in cases where out-of-quota imports are relatively small or non-existent. If $t_e$ is far below $t_2$, increasing the quota will have a greater chance of liberalizing trade in the short run. A reduction in $t_1$ will liberalize trade only if $t_2$ is close to $t_1$, in which case both tariffs need to be reduced, and if underfill is significant because $t_1$ is effective – otherwise, quotas will also have to be increased in order to obtain trade-liberalizing effects. This is highlighted in table 8A.1 where one notices that many cells have "0" in them. This analysis shows the importance of understanding the relationship between three tariffs: the in-quota tariff $t_1$, the out-of-quota tariff $t_2$ and the tariff equivalent of the quota when the quota is effective (where the latter can be derived from observed domestic market and world prices).

The share of rents versus tariff revenue depends on the difference between the two tariffs and the size of the import quota. Countries do not administer one uniform tariff-quota policy, which makes it difficult to determine whether an increase in import quotas or a decrease in tariffs will result in more liberalized trade. There is no general rule on how quota rents and tariff revenues will change with trade liberalization.

Out-of-quota tariff revenues exist only if $Q^{quota}$ is to the left of $M^*_{MIN}$, while there are always $t_1$ tariff revenues. Quota rents exist only if $Q^{quota}$ is less than $M^*_{MAX}$. Quota rents can increase with a lower $t_1$ and a higher $t_2$, while $t_2$ revenues decline with an increase in quota levels. The last three columns of table 8A.1 summarize all of the possibilities for changes in rents and tariff revenues. In some cases, the direction of the change in tariff revenues depends on the elasticities of excess supply and excess demand. In other cases, regime switches occur, and so tariff revenues could increase, stay the same, or decrease.

### Notes

1. Countries were more easily able to meet their trade liberalization obligations (a 36 percent cut in the unweighted average of all tariffs) by reducing low-tariff sectors relatively more (in percentage terms).
2. Countries manipulated quantities by choosing different base periods, using net versus gross imports, or calculating consumption at a product aggregation level that suited their purposes.
3. Because the WTO is interested only in committed quota fill rates, the in-quota fill rates reported do not include any over-quota imports.
4. Export quotas may still be allocated in these instances, but export licenses are possible only if export quotas are issued.
5. Note that the importing country may assign import rights to another country, but any firm from a third country may be able to import the product (the import of peanuts from Argentina into the United States by a Canadian firm is one example – over the protest of the Argentine government).
6. Export subsidies were defined as any payments contingent on exports, producer-financed export subsidies, export marketing subsidies, export-specific transportation subsidies, and subsidies on goods incorporated into exports. Food aid and export market promotion and advisory services are exempt. Export credits and credit guarantees are covered by a separate agreement.
7. Commodities with export subsidies are often staple foods imported by food-deficit developing countries (FDDCs). Eliminating export subsidies will increase the import bills of these poor countries. Import barriers by rich countries, on the other hand, hurt exports of poor countries. Fairness argues for eliminating import barriers before export subsidies.
8. For developing countries, the reductions are 14 percent in the volume and 24 percent in the value of export subsidies.
9. Note that the price received is not "contingent on exports," unlike taxpayer- and producer-financed export subsidies.
10. A temporary "blue box" was established for payments related to production-limiting programs or payments based on no more than 85 percent of the base level of production. This box is exempt from reduction requirements. The now-defunct US target price and acreage diversion program, and the EU's area payments with hectarage diversion, are the two predominant policies in this box.
11. For an excellent discussion on all issues related to domestic support in the URAA, see Brink (2000).
12. The AMS is not the same as the Producer Support Estimate (PSE), as measured by the OECD. Only part of border support is included in the AMS for some countries and is excluded in others. In addition, fixed baseline world reference prices are used to measure the current AMS (unlike for the PSE), and the AMS excludes *de minimis* support and that contained in the "blue" and "green" boxes.

13. Because the world reference price is fixed at the 1986–8 base period, the AMS varies only with changes in domestic production and support prices. If the world prices of commodities continue their secular decline, the implied support from administered price supports (with consumer transfers and border protection) will increase, but the AMS measure will not. This may have implications for the effectiveness of the negotiated AMS reduction commitments. However, the baseline time period of 1986–8 had exceptionally low world prices and with "dirty tariffication," the ineffectiveness of AMS reduction commitments may be minimal.

14. A possible loophole in the AMS is the *de minimis* rules that allow for exemption of 5 percent (10 percent for developing countries) of total value of production for each commodity, plus another 5 percent for non-commodity-specific support. In the case of Canada in 1995, *de minimis* support accounted for 28 percent of total AMS.

15. Several factors can have an offsetting effect on the output-reducing aspects of EU area payments. Farmers could take the lowest-quality land out of production, thereby increasing yield per hectare. Furthermore, there are some set-asides that do not occur because small farms with less than 92 tons of production are not required to set aside land. Paying farmers not to produce can also be trade-distorting because farmers may have an incentive to stay in production and even expand production to receive more payments in the future.

16. "Coupled payments" are those disbursed depending on the level of the farmer's output while "decoupled payments" are made independent of output levels.

17. See Moschini (1991), and Boughner and de Gorter (1998), for the basic economics of tariff rate quotas.

18. I ignore in the formal analysis here the possibility of quota underfill (other than that stemming from the in-quota tariff as the effective instrument), over-quota imports with government discretion at in-quota tariffs (where imports can be above the quota), quota and non-quota imports at preferential tariff rates, and "non-notified" import quotas (see de Gorter and Kask, 2000 for more details).

19. A regime switch can also occur with a shift in the free-trade equilibrium, independent of policy changes. For example, large increases in import costs (from an increase in world prices) or insufficient domestic demand (resulting in a leftward shift in excess demand) could make the in-quota tariff regime the effective instrument.

## References

Australian Bureau of Agricultural and Resource Economics (ABARE), 1999. "WTO Agricultural Negotiations: Important Market Access Issues," Research Report, 99.3, Canberra

Anania, G., M. Bohman, and M. A. Carter, 1992. "United States Export Subsidies in Wheat: Strategic Trade Policy or Expensive Beggar-Thy-Neighbor Tactic?," *American Journal of Agricultural Economics*, 74, 534–45

Barry, P., 1999. "Risk Management and Safety Nets for Farmers," *Choices*, 3rd quarter

Bergsten, C. F., K. A. Elliott, J. J. Schott, and W. E. Takacs, 1987. "Auction Quotas and United States Trade Policy," 19, Institute of International Economics, Washington, DC

Boughner, D. and H. de Gorter, 1998. "The Economics of 2-Tier Tariff-Rate Import Quotas: The Agreement on Agriculture in the WTO and US Dairy Policy," paper presented at the IATRC Annual Meeting, December, 13–15, St. Petersburg, Florida, revised April 1999

Brink, L., 2000. "Domestic Support Issues in the Uruguay Round and Beyond," Economic and Policy Analysis Directorate, Agriculture and Agri-Food Canada, agr.ca/policy/epad

Chambers, R. G. and R. L. Paarlberg, 1991. "Are More Exports Always Better? Comparing Cash and In-Kind Export Subsidies," *American Journal of Agricultural Economics*, 73, 142–54

Chau, N. and H. de Gorter, 2000. "Disentangling the Production and Export Consequences of Direct Farm Income Payments," contributed paper, annual meeting of the American Agricultural Economics Association, August 2, Tampa, Florida

Choi, J., D. A. Sumner, and J. Song, 1998. "Importing STEs in Korea and Japan: Evolution, Operation, and Implications," paper presented at the "Role of State and Agricultural Trade" Workshop co-organized by the North American Forum, Stanford University and Agricultural Issues Center, November 20–22, University of California, Davis

de Gorter, H. and U. Kask, 2000. "Analyzing the Economics of Trade Liberalization with Tariff-Quotas in the Uruguay Round Agreement on Agriculture," UNCTAD Working Paper, Trade Analysis Branch, Geneva

de Gorter, H. and Y. Tsur, 1995. "Supply and Welfare Effects of Income Stabilization Programs: NISA versus NTSP," report to Policy Branch, Industry Performance and Analysis Directorate, Agriculture and Agri-Food Canada, Ottawa

Hennessy, D., 1998. "The Production Effects of Agricultural Income Support Policies Under Uncertainty," *American Journal of Agricultural Economics*, 80(1), 46–57

Ingco, M. D., 1996. "Tariffication in the Uruguay Round: How Much Liberalization?," *The World Economy*, 19(4), 425–47

Leetmaa, S. and K. Ackerman, 1998. "Export Subsidy Commitments: Few are Binding, but Some Members Try to Evade Them," Economic Research Service, Agriculture in the WTO/ WRS–98–44, December, Updated in USDA's WTO Briefing Room, 1999

Moschini, G., 1991. "Economic Issues in Tariffication: an Overview," *Agricultural Economics*, 5, 101–20

Organization for Economic Co-operation and Development (OECD), 2000. "A Preliminary Report of Domestic Support Aspects of Uruguay Round Implementation," COM/AGR/APM/TD/WP, February 9, Paris

Peterson, J. M., B. J. Minten, and H. de Gorter, 1999. "Economic Costs of the US Wheat Export Enhancement Program: Manna from Heaven or from Taxpayers?," IATRC Working Paper, 99–2, Washington, DC

Rude, James, 1999. "Green Box Criteria: A Theoretical Assessment," Canadian AgriFood Trade Research Network, CATRN Paper, 1999–02, eru.ulaval.ca/catrn/publications.htm

Ruiz, L., 2000. "The Impacts of Export Subsidy Reduction Commitments in the Agreement on Agriculture: Implications for the Millennium Round," MSc thesis, Cornell University, May

Ruiz, L. and H. de Gorter, 2000. "The Impacts of Export Subsidy Reduction Commitments in the Agreement on Agriculture on International Trade," paper presented at the conference Global Agriculture in the New Millennium, 25–26 May, New Orleans

Schluep, I., 1999. "The Law and Economics of Consumer Only Financed Export Subsidies: A Context for the WTO Panel on Canadian Dairy Pricing Policy," MSc thesis, Cornell University

Schluep, I. and H. de Gorter, 2001. "The Definition of Export Subsidies and the Agreement on Agriculture," in G. Peters and P. Pingalli (eds.), *Tomorrow's Agriculture: Incentives, Institutions, Infrastructure and Innovations*, Aldershot: Ashgate

Skully, D. W., 1999. "Economics of TRQ Administration," International Agricultural Trade Research Consortium Working Paper, 99–6, May

Sumner, D., 1996. "The Role of Domestic Market Price Regulations in International Trade: The Case of Dairy Policy in the United States," paper presented to the AEA, San Francisco, January

World Trade Organization (WTO), 1994. *Agreement on Import Licensing Procedures*, Geneva
  1999. "Final Report on Canada – Measures Affecting the Importation of Milk and the Exportation of Dairy Products," WT/DS103/R, WT/DS113/R,17, March, Geneva
  2000a. "Tariff and Other Quotas," Background Paper G/AG/NG/S/7, 23 May, restricted, Geneva
  2000b. "Member's Usage of Domestic Support Categories, Export Subsidies and Export Credits," Background Paper, G/AG/NG/S/12, 15 June, restricted, Geneva

Young, C. E. and P. C. Westcott, 2000. "How Decoupled are US Agricultural Support for Major Crops?," *American Journal of Agricultural Economics*, 82, 762–7

# 9 Options for enhancing market access in a new round

*Tim Josling and Allan Rae*

## Introduction

Along with textiles and a few other goods, agricultural products represent the last bastion of protected national markets in an era of globalism. The highest tariffs in agricultural markets are several times those for manufactured goods. Table 9.1 shows the unweighted average bound tariff on agricultural commodities for twenty major trading countries. The average agricultural tariff – however it is calculated – is probably about 40 percent. Most industrial tariffs are closer to 5 percent, and some manufactured goods are now traded duty-free.

Because most trade barriers have been tariffied, the new round of negotiations will be the first in which the level of agricultural protection is visible and quantified. The question is: what process would best remove these high trade barriers in a reasonable amount of time? Resistance to open markets for agricultural goods is still strong, but the discrepancy between agricultural and non-agricultural tariffs may persuade trade ministers to urge their colleagues to agree to significant cuts.

How do negotiators cut agricultural tariffs to 5–15 percent, or to zero if tariff-free trade becomes the norm? This goal looks to be a tall order: it implies a lengthy period of significant tariff cuts. But the new round of talks will not succeed unless negotiators take substantial steps to reduce these high tariffs perhaps to an average of 20–25 percent.

The problem extends beyond high tariffs: the distribution of tariff rates is uneven, among both commodities and countries. For example, industrial countries import many agricultural raw materials, including tropical beverages and some tropical fruits, duty-free, or with relatively low levels of protection. Most industrial countries also import agricultural products not grown domestically and the ingredients of animal feed without significant duties. Yet those same countries retain high levels of protection on staple foods and sensitive domestic goods. These different levels of protection among products distort relative prices, just as different levels of protection among sectors distort national and

Table 9.1 *Post-Uruguay Round tariff rates for agricultural goods*

| Product | (%) |
|---|---|
| Grains | 46.7 |
| Oilseeds | 41.7 |
| Fats and oils | 41.6 |
| Meats | 39.3 |
| Milk | 40.7 |
| Dairy products | 47.1 |
| Sugar | 48.7 |
| Fresh fruits and vegetables | 35.5 |
| Processed fruit and vegetables | 35.3 |
| Other agriculture | 24.4 |

*Note:* Data represent average unweighted *ad valorem* bound tariff rates for twenty countries.
*Source:* WTO.

global economies. Different tariff levels across countries also distort the trading system more than if all countries imposed roughly the same tariff levels.

Many countries, especially developing countries, also still channel imports of basic agricultural products through a parastatal import agency (Josling, 1998). Such a situation dilutes the benefits of a tariff-only system considerably. If the state trading agency decides to strictly control imports to support domestic producer prices, replacing a quota with a tariff will not change the agency's behavior. The new round needs to directly address the potential use of state trading to circumvent tariffication.

The Uruguay Round Agreement on Agriculture (URAA) instituted tariff-rate quotas (TRQs) to ensure some market opening, but state trading agencies can still restrict trade below the TRQ level. Moreover, the TRQ system must not become embedded in trade rules: it could easily become a form of managed trade that would lead back to quantity-based commodity agreements and negotiated market shares. TRQs were designed as a temporary palliative where pure tariffication was deemed inadequate or infeasible, and negotiators should eventually consider eliminating the TRQ system.

Considerable preparatory work has occurred in Geneva and in country capitals to prepare for the new round. The WTO Agriculture Committee has established an informal mechanism, the Analysis and Information Exchange (AIE), to aid discussions in advance of formal meetings. The AIE process has focused on issues such as the administration of TRQs and state trading, and many countries have submitted papers to the WTO General Council stating their aspirations for the new round. However, the specific agenda for the new round has not yet been agreed. This leaves the path open to suggestions as to what strategies to ensure further liberalization might succeed.

The new round will encompass three familiar elements: market access, export competition, and domestic support. The initial task will be to devise an approach to each of these items that will produce a balanced package. This chapter will examine the options for enhancing market access.

Four objectives for market access negotiations will bring agricultural markets in line with those of other products. These include substantially reducing average agricultural tariffs, narrowing the dispersion of tariff rates among products, reducing the high protection afforded to value added, which discourages processing, and completing the tariffication process. These objectives require specifics that will provide the talks' real content.

Developing countries have a considerable stake in these negotiations. Many are important exporters of agricultural products. Even those that import agricultural goods could design their development policies in a more predictable environment if world agricultural markets reflected underlying production costs rather than political influence and government intervention. But these countries will also face difficult decisions as liberalization of agricultural trade advances in the WTO. In many cases developing countries' own tariffs on imports of agricultural products are high, and the new round may require such countries to make significant cuts. Moreover, they often gain access to markets of developed countries on concessional terms – preferences that will become less significant as Most Favored Nation (MFN) tariff rates decline.

This chapter identifies the major options for improving market access during the new round of agricultural negotiations and specifies strategies that developing countries could adopt.

## Cuts in agricultural tariffs

The new round of trade talks could pursue further tariff cuts in several ways. The way chosen will have significantly different effects on different countries and commodities.

### Continuation of Uruguay Round cuts

Negotiators could rely on the base established in the Uruguay Round (Tangermann, 1997) and apply the same depth of cut over a similar time frame. A further 36 percent cut in average tariffs from the same base would produce a 72 percent cut over the two reform periods encompassing a dozen years.

This approach emphasizes continuity, and the effect on trade would accelerate over time, as the shrinking base would not dilute the percentage cuts. The use of the same base would also simplify negotiations, as re-opening that issue would cause controversy. But perhaps the strongest reason for supporting this approach is that countries would no longer need to delay unilateral tariff reductions for fear of "paying twice": any unilateral policy changes would count toward reductions after the base period.

However, continuing the same schedule of cuts does pose questions (Tangermann and Josling, 1999). As in the Uruguay Round, should a provision allow countries to lower tariffs on some items by only 15 percent while cutting tariffs on less sensitive (and often less significant) commodities by more than 36 percent – to maintain the (unweighted) average? Perhaps negotiators can limit such averaging by agreeing to a minimum tariff cut for each product for the whole reform period of, say, 50 percent – implying larger reductions for products that escaped the last round. Or perhaps negotiators could insist that countries balance their volume of trade between products with higher- and lower-than-average cuts – that is, use weighted tariff reductions.

Developing countries might argue that they should again be subject to smaller cuts over a longer period: they would certainly object to requirements that they catch up with industrial countries. But if negotiators continue to grant developing countries reduced cuts and longer time horizons, many will fall way behind by the end of the second transition period. This risks splitting the market into a "liberal" and an "illiberal" group of countries, and developing countries risk being left out of expanding trade opportunities.

### Request-and-offer negotiations

At the other extreme from a simple continuation of URAA tariff cuts is a reversion to a time-honored approach known as "request and offer." In this technique, countries ask other nations to cut their tariffs, particularly on commodities for which the former are principal suppliers. The requesting countries, in turn, offer to make cuts in their own tariffs. Once agreed upon, the tariff cut offers are then "multilateralized" to other WTO members. An overall target cut commonly guides such request-and-offer negotiations, but the result is more eclectic.

This technique has severe drawbacks, though its attraction to countries' domestic interests is clear. First, political constraints are likely to severely limit the tariff cuts on offer. It is unlikely that countries will willingly expose their most sensitive sectors unless they are sure of getting significant gains from others. Request-and-offer negotiations are therefore unlikely to reduce tariff disparity. Second, developing countries have so far not been major players in request-and-offer talks: they have had relatively little to give and not sought much in return. A request-and offer-negotiation could well turn into a US–EU–Japan trilateral bargain, with little of interest to developing countries. Some tighter framework for market access negotiations is needed, even if certain aspects of the talks use a modified request-and-offer procedure.

*Across-the-board tariff cuts*

As an alternative to a further round of differentiated tariff reductions based on average cuts, or to a request-and-offer approach, countries could agree on an across-the-board tariff reduction[1] of perhaps 50 percent over seven years. This approach would have the advantage of simplicity and transparency. Such a cut could either rely on the existing base period or bound tariffs as of, say, the year 2000. In the past, such across-the-board cuts have often been riddled with exceptions. A new round would have to keep this tendency under control.

An across-the-board cut would still leave some tariffs at a very high level. Just as problematic, it would give reluctant liberalizers a central role in negotiations. A coalition of countries with domestic reasons to oppose liberalization would strongly object to any bold cut in tariffs, and negotiators could end up with a relatively small cut. Across-the-board cuts would be considerably enhanced if countries would agree to reduce all tariffs – both agricultural and non-agricultural – by 50 percent. Export interests in other sectors would have an incentive to pressure for tariff reductions in agriculture.

*The zero-for-zero approach*

A somewhat different approach is to negotiate "zero-for-zero" agreements that would eliminate tariffs completely on particular goods.[2] This technique has recently seen some success in other areas of trade, such as information technology. It is also consistent with current limits on US negotiating authority – the administration can pursue zero-for-zero deals in certain areas without fast-track authority. This is one reason why Asia Pacific Economic Cooperation (APEC) countries have embraced this approach in their "coordinated unilateral" approach to trade liberalization.

Such a sector approach offers clear advantages. Political constraints on liberalizing products such as dairy and sugar would not hold up a move to more competitive markets in grains, oilseeds, and pigmeat. Trade would expand in the latter markets as protection declined. However, countries could end up with "too much" trade in liberalized commodities, much as regional trade agreements risk encouraging too much trade within regional markets.[3]

Still, the zero-for-zero approach has merit on tactical grounds, if it eventually brings highly protected and thus isolated markets into line. Unfortunately, negotiators will undoubtedly let sensitive commodities off the hook unless the framework for sector-by-sector reductions prohibits long-term exclusions.

The pressure from export interests that usually drives trade liberalization would be more difficult to mobilize if the overall package leaves out sensitive sectors.

*Reducing bound rates to applied rates*

Many countries maintain a considerable gap between the tariffs they bind in their WTO schedules and those they actually apply. This often results from unilateral liberalization and structural adjustment. This outcome, which has been called "policy water," gives a country welcome flexibility to raise tariffs within the bound rate. The problem is that such a system distorts the concept of a bound rate, which is meant to prevent tariff increases that can discourage trade. The system also gives power to local customs officials to discriminate among shipments and raise charges once goods are in transit. Removing such "water" would improve transparency, even if opportunities for market access did not noticeably expand.

Negotiators could also consider a new approach to removing some of this "water." They could, for instance, reduce bindings to no more than the maximum tariff applied in a certain period – say, 1993–8.[4] This approach would lock-in agricultural trade reform more effectively than at present, but it would not eliminate "dirty tariffication," and the tariffs could still contain "water." The approach would also remove only the discretionary element of protection that countries have built into existing bindings. However, the approach would raise the credibility of the liberalization process considerably by, for example, limiting the spread of systems of variable protection that several Latin American countries have adopted to stabilize domestic prices. On the other hand, the approach would appear to reward countries that have kept tariffs as high as possible within their bound levels, and extract further cuts from those that had already pursued unilateral liberalization.[5]

**Reducing tariff peaks**

The striking variability of agricultural tariffs stems from at least three related influences. First, politics have produced strong pressures for trade barriers against imports that compete with staple or basic commodities such as rice, wheat, sugar, and dairy goods. Countries often allow more liberal access for products seen as less essential, such as fruits and vegetables, or for products required for feed or food processing, such as animal feed and oilseeds.[6] Second, government support for basic industries has reflected this political imbalance, with state trading or non-tariff barriers (NTBs) dominating sensitive markets and tariffs protecting other products. Tariffication has finally revealed the magnitude of such protection and led to the problem of tariff peaks.

A third influence has been the method of negotiating cuts in trade barriers, which has allowed certain sectors to escape. Commodity subcommittees within agricultural negotiations have often diverted attention away from the need for a balanced approach (Josling, Tangermann, and Warley, 1996). Request-and-offer techniques have reinforced this tendency to focus on a few sectors. Even when the URAA mandated average cuts in agricultural tariffs of 36 percent, countries obtained some flexibility under the minimum required cut of 15 percent for each product.

Tariff peaks pose a problem to the agricultural trade system for two reasons. The most important is that the economic cost of a tariff is roughly proportional to the square of the tariff.[7] Cutting high tariffs is the surest way to reap gains from trade. Second, high tariffs can generate significant profits for import-competing industries and encourage rent-seeking. Cutting tariff peaks can also be easier than reducing tariffs across the board. Countries may find it easier to "sell" the "water" in their current schedules, in effect making cuts in prohibitive tariffs.

*Formula cuts*

Negotiators could reduce the variability in agricultural tariffs by agreeing on a formula that cuts higher tariffs at a greater rate. The so-called "Swiss formula," a device for reducing high tariffs by more than low tariffs that was used for tariff reductions on industrial goods in the Tokyo Round might be an appropriate model. This approach would certainly achieve liberalization faster than across-the-board cuts. It would also squeeze much of the "water" out of high tariffs while eliminating "dirty tariffication."[8]

Because formula reductions put more of the burden on countries with dispersed tariff rates, they might argue for more uniform cuts. Moreover, the "Swiss formula" appears to be more naturally suited to tariffs in the 5–25 percent range. The coefficient used in the Tokyo Round would drive higher tariffs below 15 percent while exerting little impact on lower tariffs. Countries that swapped quantitative control over imports for mega-tariffs in the Uruguay Round are unlikely to suddenly cut them to such a modest level. However, negotiators can use a much higher coefficient for mega-tariffs.

*Tariff ceilings*

A second approach to reducing tariff dispersion is to place an upper limit on all tariffs on agricultural goods. If negotiators agreed that no agricultural tariff could remain above, say, 100 percent after a transition period, this would cap all mega-tariffs. However, such an approach would imply no tariff cuts for commodities with significant protection under 100 percent. Still, other techniques could complement tariff ceilings. For instance, an across-the-board cut of 36 percent combined with a tariff ceiling of 100 percent could prove palatable to importers as well as attractive to exporters.

## Expanded tariff-rate quotas

A third way to reduce tariff dispersion – and to boost market access – is to continue to expand minimum access as a proportion of consumption. The low tariff that operates within the quota may provide a useful lever. Each country could increase its TRQ, say, of 1 percent of domestic consumption each year over a five-year period.[9] In most markets the quotas would become non-binding before the end of the five-year period. This would effectively tariffy barriers at the reduced tariff that applied to the TRQ.[10]

The main overt political objection could be that importing countries could fix within-quota tariffs at levels that attracted the guaranteed access quantity. However, tariff levels under TRQs were never meant to protect domestic producers. Indeed, making within-quota imports duty-free would make more sense. This implies some form of renegotiation to set tariffs for within-quota trade at a reasonable level. All within-quota tariffs could be bound at, say, 20 percent, and not reduced until they became the operative tariff for the bulk of each country's agricultural trade.

However, expanding TRQs could be politically difficult for a less apparent reason. If goods enter a country beyond the TRQ, then the quota quantity itself will be sold at a price governed by the above-quota imports. In effect, the difference between the within- and above-quota tariff will represent the quota rent, distributed between importing and exporting agents. If those who reap the rent are also influential in setting the agenda for negotiations, they will curtail enthusiasm for expanding TRQs.

## The "cocktail" approach

Each method of expanding market access has merit but might not be adequate alone – suggesting that negotiators pursue a policy "cocktail." We suggest one such mix here. Imagine dividing agricultural tariffs into five categories. Countries could reduce low tariffs – those less than 5 percent – to zero, as neither the level of protection nor the revenue collected are likely to be significant. Such nuisance tariffs could be advantageously removed in agriculture as well as in other areas. Countries could cut moderate tariffs of 5–40 percent by 36 percent, as in the Uruguay Round. Tariffs above 40 percent are probably too high to yield to the same techniques as industrial tariffs: for those categories, negotiators would augment the 36 percent cut by expanding TRQs. Tariffs above 100 percent might require some variant of the "Swiss formula." And for tariffs above 300 percent countries might opt to conduct request-and-offer negotiations.

## Completing the removal of non-tariff barriers

With the partial exception of rice in Japan and Korea, the URAA mandated that countries convert all NTBs into tariffs. However, some vestiges of the old regimes remain, where importers face other obstacles than a known bound duty. The new round should tackle the most egregious of these to complete the transition to transparent trade barriers. The widespread existence of state trading importers is one of the most distorting non-tariff barriers still in effect. State Trading Enterprises (STEs) with special or exclusive rights in import markets contribute to market access impediments.

Under WTO articles, state trading importers are not supposed to grant more protection than that afforded by the bound tariff (article II: 4, GATT 47). This was difficult to enforce when NTBs were permitted, as state trading enterprises could be deemed to administer such barriers. But with tariffication the task of comparing the markup of the state trader with a fixed tariff is relatively straightforward, especially if the WTO Committee on State Trading improves monitoring and reporting.

To address the problem of STEs, negotiators could link them to TRQs – perhaps converting TRQs into an obligation to import rather than an opportunity, thereby reducing the suspicion that STEs might be responsible for quota under-fill. At the other extreme, negotiators could mandate that countries market all (or a share) of TRQs through private channels, thus providing some competition for STEs and facilitating price and markup comparisons.

Any change in the WTO rules on state trading will have a direct impact on many developing countries. However, it is questionable whether it is in their longer-run interest to obtain exemptions or more flexibility in applying stricter rules on STEs. Most economists agree that STEs have often hampered economic development in developing countries and reduced their efficiency of resource use. Many developing countries have therefore found it beneficial to leave trading activities to private enterprises while using tariffs and subsidies to influence market conditions. If developing countries were to receive special treatment regarding STEs, this could send the wrong signal regarding the longer-run need to move away from state-controlled monopolies in agricultural trade.

## The interests of developing countries in market access negotiations

Developing countries have complex interests in the area of market access.[11] Exporters of agricultural products have an incentive to see trade barriers lowered.

On the other hand, many tropical products already enter the main industrial markets duty-free. In these cases expanded market access in industrial markets may have to come from actions other than tariff reduction, such as cuts in domestic taxation.

The other side of the market-access coin – lowering tariffs in developing countries – yields a number of conflicting issues. On the one hand, high tariffs are a regressive tax on imported agricultural goods that place a particularly high burden on low-income consumers while distorting domestic incentives and leading to wasteful resource use. On the other hand, governments need to raise revenue and often feel they have to protect the income streams of local producers for more or less defensible reasons.

Of particular interest to developing countries is the use of variable tariffs in the context of fluctuating world agricultural prices. Again there are two sides of the coin. On the one hand developing countries have a strong interest in stable market conditions. This speaks for limiting the use of variable tariffs because they insulate markets and aggravate instability. Developing countries therefore have an interest in eliminating tariff variability. On the other hand a number of developing countries, in particular in Latin America, use variable tariffs to protect their domestic markets from fluctuations in international prices. One possibility might be to treat this issue as an item under Special and Differential Treatment (S&D), and allow only developing countries to use such variable tariff schemes.

### Re-examining tariff-rate quotas and preferential treatment

Developing countries have a direct interest in the method used to allocate TRQs. Allocating TRQs to the government of an exporting country – as the United States does in the case of its sugar imports – implies a deliberate attempt to influence the pattern of trade. Countries have done so to target development aid or reward political friendship. Such non-market allocation schemes undercut the competitive trade system that is the fundamental goal of the WTO: efficient producers can make no headway against the market shares of the quota holders.[12] Even allocating TRQs based on historical market share does not ensure that the source of supply bears any relationship to the competitiveness of the supplier. Hence, even if developing countries have an interest in receiving specific allocations under TRQs, that system will continue to deny benefits to those with particular comparative advantage.

The sugar market illustrates the range of choices. Cuts in sugar tariffs were generally lower than for many other commodities during the Uruguay Round. If sugar were to escape significant cuts in the new round, countries with preferred access would maintain their market position, but high levels of support in the EU and the United States would continue to constrain the size of the world sugar market. Across-the-board cuts would lead to better market access; formula cuts and tariff ceilings would hit preferences hard. Expanding TRQs would pose the same dilemma. Trade would expand, but the value of current preferences would diminish.

Developing countries also often maintain preferential access to developed country markets for temperate-zone products otherwise significantly restricted by high and sometimes prohibitive tariffs. In this case, cuts in MFN tariffs may not help preferred countries, and could actually reduce their sales and commodity prices. Only when MFN tariffs drop so much that developing country exporters can also gain from better access at MFN rates will the overall outcome be positive for developing countries.

Countries should examine today's preferential systems with a view to deriving lasting benefit from more open access and recognizing that some erosion of preferences is inevitable. Developing countries may find that preserving preference levels is not worth the "negotiating capital" that outcome would require.[13]

*Re-examining Special and Differential Treatment*

A long-standing GATT/WTO obligation entails granting "special and differential treatment" (S&D) to developing countries. Such treatment could modulate efforts to expand market access. What's more, developing countries do not always benefit from such treatment, as those that opt out of or delay certain trade disciplines actually end up with less influence on the negotiating process. It may well be time to identify a few trade policy areas where developing countries have particular difficulties and to forgo broader use of the concept. Developed countries need the emerging markets of developing countries to continue to expand trade in food as in many other goods. Developing countries may find it more advantageous to participate fully in trade liberalization to ensure that the negotiating agenda includes the products and markets of high interest to them.

# Appendix    Quantitative estimates of benefits from market access improvement

We used the Global Trade Analysis Project (GTAP) applied general equilibrium model to illustrate the benefits of four of the tariff-cutting methods we propose in the chapter (Hertel, 1997).[14] The model reveals that simultaneous across-the-board cuts in agricultural tariffs – as opposed to a sectoral approach – produced gains in welfare for the majority of countries and regions.

The most protected importers (such as Japan) and a major exporter (the United States) did capture substantial welfare gains from a *sectoral* approach,

Table 9A.1 *Change in volume of global exports (percent)*

|  | Zero-for-zero (grains/oilseeds) | 36% cut | "Swiss formula" cuts | "Cocktail" |
|---|---|---|---|---|
| Rice | −0.5 | 2.5 | 3.3 | 2.7 |
| Wheat | 6 | 0.6 | 2.7 | 2.9 |
| Other grain | 29.6 | 5 | 8.6 | 9.2 |
| Fruits and vegetables | 0 | 2.7 | 0.6 | 4 |
| Oilseeds | 6.2 | 0.4 | 0.6 | 0.9 |
| Cane and beet | 0.3 | 7.1 | 7.6 | 8.2 |
| Other crops | 0.1 | 2.4 | 0.6 | 3.6 |
| Livestock | −0.5 | −1.3 | −2.7 | −0.6 |
| Milk | 0.1 | 0 | 0 | 0.1 |
| Natural resources | 0.1 | 0 | 0.1 | 0 |
| Meats | −0.2 | 1.7 | 1.2 | 1.6 |
| Processed food | −0.7 | 5.2 | 1.3 | 7 |
| Dairy | 0 | −2.3 | −0.1 | 0.5 |
| White sugar | 0.1 | 4 | 3 | 5.4 |

which in our model eliminated tariffs only on grains and oilseeds. This was due to reduced outputs and lower prices in the protective economies and improved terms of trade for US exporters. The volume of world trade in grains and oilseeds increased, especially in the case of coarse grains (table 9A.1). However, much of the developing world – including South Asia, Central and much of South America, and the Middle East/North Africa – suffered welfare losses when tariff cuts were confined to grains and oilseeds.

Removal of tariffs on grains and oilseeds can also produce impacts on "downstream" livestock sectors, where grains and oilseeds can be significant production inputs. Countries that protect both their grains and livestock sectors could under this scenario experience increased output downstream due to the tariff removal upstream and hence the lower costs of feed inputs. In Japan and ASEAN, for example, such an expansion of the protected livestock sectors offsets to some extent the increase in welfare due to downsizing of the grains sectors. Such effects also impacts negatively on the terms of trade for the traditional exporters of livestock products.

*Across-the-board* agricultural tariff cuts are illustrated by three scenarios – continuation of the 36 percent cut of the Uruguay Round to reduce the average level of tariffs, a "Swiss formula" cut designed to bring down the highest tariffs at a faster rate, and a "cocktail" of a mix of different modalities tied to the level of the original tariff. The latter two in particular should reduce the across-country variance of agricultural tariffs.[15]

Changes in the volume of global trade under these assumptions are shown in table 9A.1. The volume of grains and oilseeds trade increased less under all across-the-board tariff reduction approaches compared with the zero-for-zero approach, since in the latter tariffs on those specific commodities were eliminated. For other commodities, the expansion in trade volumes was generally greatest under the "cocktail" formula, since this not only forced large reductions in the highest tariffs, but also cut moderate tariffs by more than would the "Swiss formula" alone.

In many cases, sectoral output adjustments were substantial. In Japan for example, outputs of wheat, coarse grains, sugar and dairy products fell by much more under the "cocktail" and "Swiss formula," than when a 36 percent tariff reduction was applied. Food import tariffs in the United States are generally considerably less than 85 percent, so the modeled cuts are usually the same in the "cocktail" approach as under the 36 percent formula. Production adjustments under either scenario were therefore similar. The size of the output responses across the tariff reduction experiments was also rather similar in the EU.

The tariff reductions encouraged expansion of the coarse grains, sugar, and livestock sectors in the Central and South American countries. Notable features of the results for Australia and New Zealand were the impacts of the various tariff-reduction approaches on their dairy sectors. Dairy tariffs in some major import markets are very high, and both the Swiss and "cocktail" approaches require such high tariffs to be reduced by more than 36 percent, and consequently milk output expanded the most under these scenarios.

Table 9A.2 compares changes in the total agriculture–food trade balances of each region across the tariff-reduction scenarios. Japan had a food trade deficit in 1995 of over US$ 50 billion, while those of the EU and the Middle East/North Africa exceeded US$ 20 billion. These deficits increased under all scenarios and especially under the "cocktail" formula that gave the greatest tariff reductions. Of the net food exporters, the United States had by far the greatest surplus in 1995, which was estimated to increase from US$ 23 billion to $30 billion under the "cocktail" tariff cuts. Most other regions with a food trade surplus in 1995 increased this surplus under each of the across-the-board approaches to tariff cuts. Also note that of the developing regions, the food trade surplus of Sub-Saharan Africa (SSA) increased by US$ 1.5 billion under the "cocktail" formula. South Asia, however, which was a net-food-exporter in 1995, had its food trade surplus reduced but not eliminated under each scenario.

Table 9A.3 compares changes in global and regional welfare across the four simulated approaches to agricultural and food tariff reductions. It is found that the increases in global welfare under across-the-board tariff reductions are two–three times as high as that from the grains–oilseeds zero-for-zero approach. Further, the global gains from the "cocktail" and "Swiss formula" approaches,

Table 9A.2 *Food trade balance (1995 US$ million)*

| | | Change in total food trade balance | | | |
|---|---|---|---|---|---|
| | Base 1995 | Zero-for-zero | 36% cut | "Swiss formula" | "Cocktail" |
| Australia | 9,246 | 1 | 1,249 | 1,400 | 1,658 |
| New Zealand | 5,099 | −55 | 1,247 | 1,482 | 1,515 |
| Japan | −50,116 | −60 | −2,290 | −1,931 | −4,989 |
| Korea | −7,583 | −316 | −244 | −222 | −88 |
| Asean | 15,079 | −149 | −506 | 98 | 89 |
| China | −11,265 | −1,133 | 53 | 492 | −282 |
| South Asia | 1,506 | −140 | −524 | −554 | −460 |
| Canada | 4,416 | 359 | 132 | 134 | 249 |
| United States | 23,336 | 4,109 | 3,858 | 2,905 | 6,290 |
| Cent. America | 4,635 | −8 | 538 | 340 | 563 |
| South America | 4,393 | −57 | 125 | 266 | 566 |
| Argentina | 9,937 | 199 | 800 | 712 | 1,290 |
| Brazil | 8,706 | −57 | 1,101 | 781 | 1,542 |
| Chile | 2,541 | −74 | 57 | 2 | 125 |
| EU | −22,420 | −2,631 | −5,071 | −5,691 | −9,634 |
| CEE | −2,107 | 153 | 387 | 547 | 381 |
| FSU | −7,899 | −90 | 54 | 270 | 184 |
| ME, North Africa | −21,056 | −341 | −1,086 | −125 | −823 |
| SSA | 6,872 | 12 | 631 | 517 | 1,528 |
| ROW | −3,006 | −275 | −1,788 | −2,225 | −1,623 |

that make the largest cuts to the highest tariffs, exceed the gains from a 36 percent across-the-board cut in tariffs.

The most protective importers and the major exporter captured substantial welfare gains from a sectoral approach, but much of the developing world suffered welfare losses when tariff cuts were confined to grains and oilseeds. In contrast, all but three regions experienced welfare gains in at least two of the three across-the-board tariff reduction scenarios, and most gained under all three. Welfare gains were greatest for Japan, the EU and the Rest of the World (ROW) and both the "Swiss formula" and "cocktail" approaches provided greater gains than did the zero-for-zero option. The fourth-highest gains in welfare under the 36 percent cuts and the "cocktail" liberalization were experienced by the United States, and both gave this country greater gains than did the zero-for-zero cuts in grains and oilseeds.

Looking at the developing regions, South Asia, Central, and much of South America all suffered welfare losses when tariff cuts were confined to grains and oilseeds. In contrast, all these regions gained from a more general reduction in

Table 9A.3 *Welfare changes (1995 US$ million)*

| | Tariff-reduction formula | | | |
|---|---|---|---|---|
| | Zero-for-zero | 36% | "Swiss formula" | "Cocktail" |
| Australia | −10 | 797 | 705 | 1,048 |
| New Zealand | −25 | 702 | 769 | 918 |
| Japan | 6,154 | 3,438 | 8,504 | 6,725 |
| Korea | 896 | 519 | 643 | 776 |
| Asean | 122 | 1,202 | 938 | 1,495 |
| China | 683 | 898 | 888 | 873 |
| South Asia | −90 | 603 | 422 | 561 |
| Canada | −39 | −4 | −49 | −24 |
| United States | 1,256 | 1,956 | 844 | 2,625 |
| Cent. America | −98 | 74 | −61 | 80 |
| South America | −73 | 46 | 35 | 267 |
| Argentina | 159 | 448 | 398 | 722 |
| Brazil | −142 | 1,134 | 437 | 1,716 |
| Chile | −40 | 24 | −15 | 66 |
| EU | 616 | 8,410 | 7,777 | 6,294 |
| CEE | 103 | 216 | 106 | 155 |
| FSU | −96 | −197 | −229 | −226 |
| ME, North Africa | −434 | −1,181 | −1,056 | −1,238 |
| SSA | −19 | 70 | −97 | 470 |
| ROW | 392 | 2,545 | 4,360 | 4,390 |
| Global | 9,316 | 21,698 | 25,319 | 27,693 |

agricultural and food tariffs. China's welfare gains under each of the multicommodity tariff reductions exceeded those from the more restrictive zero-for-zero approach.

Canada, the former Soviet Union (FSU) and Middle East/North Africa experienced welfare losses across all scenarios. Under across-the-board tariff reductions, outputs of grains and some livestock products expanded in Canada while manufacturing and services outputs declined. With output subsidies paid on these agricultural products, these output adjustments caused losses in allocative efficiency that the gains in Canada's terms of trade did not compensate. In contrast, the terms of trade deteriorated in all scenarios for the FSU and Middle East/North Africa, which dominated the allocative effects.

Although our study assumed no changes to trade policies in manufacturing and services, we found that output in those sectors exerted a substantial impact on the welfare changes we observed in several regions. Those two sectors could also sustain tariff cuts and policy reforms as part of the new round of trade negotiations, and such reforms could well alter the gains to liberalization in agricultural and food markets.

## Notes

1. This was the choice made in the Kennedy Round (1964–7) for industrial goods after the previous rounds, based largely on request-and-offer, had not produced the required liberalization.
2. This approach is discussed more fully in Miner *et al.* (1996).
3. The EU knows well the problem of "unbalanced" protection as a result of easy access to oilseeds negotiated in the Dillon Round (1960–1).
4. There would of course be a danger in announcing such a scheme in advance. Countries might choose to raise tariffs to their bound levels to avoid the cut.
5. In many cases the "lower-than-bound-rate" tariffs are a part of regional preferences. In these cases removing the gap between applied and bound rates would reduce any trade distortion arising from the regional agreement.
6. Countries with limited land resources relative to population have sometimes had relatively liberal policies even on staples. But many countries with climatic or other disadvantages to farming have tried to compensate with high levels of protection.
7. The functional form of the import demand curve will determine the relationship between tariff height and welfare gains. "Water" in the tariff will also change this relationship.
8. The "water" in a tariff is the unused protection when no imports can sell at the tariff inclusive price. The "dirty" element in the agricultural tariffs refers to the use of price gaps between domestic and world markets that overstate the existing protection at the time of tariffication, leading to larger than necessary tariffs. Tariff bindings were also often set well above the actual tariff in operation, giving an element of discretion to governments. Thus a reduction in the high rates of tariff removes the "water," cleans up the tariff and removes the discretionary element of ceiling bindings.
9. The issue of TRQ administration is not addressed in detail here.
10. It would also be possible to devise a way to give countries the option of TRQ increases or tariff decreases, as both lead to the same desirable end.
11. This section draws on the ideas contained in Tangermann and Josling (1999).
12. The US sugar import regime, which establishes TRQs for traditional suppliers, was introduced in 1982, and thus pre-dates the Uruguay Round. However, the quotas are now included in the WTO Schedule of the US commitments made in the Uruguay Round. An argument might be made that the quota allocations were in any case likely to be distorting trade, as they did not take into account changes in costs among suppliers. They were also of dubious consistency with GATT article XIII, which endorses the use of market shares for the initial allocation of quotas but argues that they should be revised when changed circumstances render that allocation distorting. The WTO panel report in favor of Ecuador's claim that it should have received a larger share of the EU banana market has confirmed the interpretation of article XIII that quotas should change to reflect cost and competitiveness among suppliers.

13. Settling the issue of the role of preferences in the trade system is also essential to regaining the stability needed for investment and growth.
14. GTAP is a multiregion model built on a complete set of economic accounts and detailed inter-industry links for each economy. We used the latest version 4 GTAP database, which is benchmarked to 1995. The GTAP production system distinguishes sectors by their intensities in five primary production factors: land (agricultural sectors only), natural resources (extractive sectors only), capital, and skilled and unskilled labor. In trade, products are differentiated by country of origin and is solved using GEMPACK (Harrison and Pearson, 1996). We modified the standard GTAP model to allow for substitution between the various feedstuffs in livestock and milk production. The data were aggregated up to the level of twenty regions and seventeen commodities. Nine of the seventeen commodities are farm-produced, and were chosen to represent our interests in liberalizing trade in agricultural products. Trade in certain processed foods is also highly distorted by trade barriers, and we have separate sectors to represent some of these, such as sugar, dairy products, and meats. All remaining production sectors are aggregated into other natural resource-based commodities, textiles and clothing, manufactures and services.
15. Tariff reductions were computed using the Swiss formula:

$$t_1 = a^* t_0 / (a + t_0)$$

where $t_1$ is the new reduced tariff, and $t_0$ is the original tariff. We chose the value $a = 150$ so that tariffs below 85 percent will be reduced by less than 36 percent. This formula approach would result in greater proportionate tariff cuts for the more highly protected products such as rice, sugar, and dairy products.

The "cocktail" approach combined some tariff-reduction options as follows: tariffs less than or equal to 10 percent were eliminated; tariffs between 10 percent and 85 percent were reduced by 36 percent; and tariffs greater than 85 percent were reduced by the above "Swiss formula." Thus the "Swiss formula" would be used to cut the highest tariffs, but lower tariffs (those between 10 percent and 85 percent) would be cut by 36 percent rather than the lower amounts that would apply through use of the "Swiss formula" alone.

### References

Harrison, W. J. and K. R. Pearson, 1996. "Computing Solutions for Large General Equilibrium Models Using GEMPACK," *Computational Economics*, 9, 83–127

Hertel, T. W. (ed.), 1997. *Global Trade Analysis: Modeling and Applications*, Cambridge and New York: Cambridge University Press

Josling, T., S. Tangermann, and T. K. Warley, 1996. *Agriculture in the GATT*, London: Macmillan

Miner, W., T. Josling, D. MacLaren, and S. Tangermann, 1996. "Agriculture and the World Trade Organization: Preparing for the Singapore Ministerial Meeting," paper presented to the International Policy Council on Agriculture, Food and Trade Seminar, October, Calgary

Tangermann, S., 1997. "A Developed Country Perspective of the Agenda for the Next WTO Round of Agricultural Trade Negotiations," paper presented at a seminar in the Institute of Graduate Studies, March 3, Geneva

Tangermann, S. and T. Josling, 1999. "The Interests of Developing Countries in the Next Round of WTO Agricultural Negotiations," paper prepared for the UNCTAD Workshop on Developing a Proactive and Coherent Trade Agenda for African Countries, June 29–July 2, Pretoria

# 10 Liberalizing tariff-rate quotas: quantifying the effects of enhancing market access

*Aziz Elbehri, Merlinda D. Ingco, Thomas W. Hertel, and Kenneth Pearson*

## Introduction

The tariff-rate quota (TRQ) system has become an important instrument of international trade sanctioned by the Uruguay Round Agreement on Agriculture (URAA). The TRQ regime was codified in the URAA as a new policy mechanism to ensure both tariffication and market access. Tariffication required conversion of non-tariff barriers (NTBs) into tariff-equivalents to be lowered over a period of time, while market access ensured that quantities imported before the agreement could continue to be imported.[1] Quotification provided for import opportunities despite the high out-of-quota tariffs. There are nearly 1,400 tariff lines notified under TRQs, about 200 are country-specific rather than global (OECD, 1997). Moreover, many agricultural products covered by TRQ regimes are also subject to domestic protection in OECD countries.

Fourteen developing countries submit market access commitments to the WTO but only two – South Korea and Philippines – seem to have implemented significant TRQ regimes (Abbott and Morse, 1999, see chapter 4 in this volume). (Some developing countries that have recently entered the WTO, such as those in Eastern Europe, or that have sought to enter, such as China, have adopted TRQs to limit liberalization of their agricultural markets.)

Developing countries have adopted TRQs quite differently. The percentage of their TRQs that is actually filled is often low, indicating a lack of quota rents and few significant restrictions on trade (Abbott and Morse, 1999). Moreover, bilateral quotas are uncommon in developing countries – more significant are the TRQs that developed countries impose on the former's exports.

There are basically two problems with the TRQ regime to be addressed in the WTO negotiations: the overall level of access, and the administration of TRQs (IATRC, 2000). Expanded market access will depend on increasing the volume of imports allowed under the current regime of TRQs, either via expanded minimum access commitments (MACs) or via reductions in over-quota tariffs. The other important area of reform is a need for more transparent administration mechanisms and a need to address the significant concerns that have arisen regarding implementation. In many cases, economic inefficiencies and discriminatory practices remain in the administration methods adopted by individual countries in allocating the rights to import and export agricultural products (IATRC, 2000). In some agricultural commodities (i.e. sugar), quota-allocation is often based on diplomatic considerations and historical ties rather than least cost production criteria (Skully, 1999).

Given the importance of market access issues in the WTO round on agriculture, economists have begun focusing attention on the TRQ import regimes (Abbott and Paarlberg, 1998; IATRC, 2000) and the implementation mechanisms (Tsigas and Ingco, 1998; Skully, 1999). What is needed, however, are quantitative models of import regimes that take into account the TRQ mechanism. During the Uruguay Round most quantitative trade policy analyses viewed "policy" in agriculture in terms of tax or subsidy equivalents. In other words, observed price differences are taken as a good approximation of the incidence of price or quantity barriers. Hence the modeling of the Uruguay Round was usually based on tariff equivalents of various policy measures (Martin and Winters, 1995). However, given the prominence of quotas in the current agricultural policy regime (sanctioned via the TRQ mechanism), the modeling of border measures must explicitly come to grips with this unique blend of price and quantity constraints.

In this chapter, we pursue several approaches. First, we use a general equilibrium model that explicitly accounts for TRQ regimes to examine the effects of partial trade liberalization of sugar TRQs in the EU and US markets. This single-sector, multiregion case allows us to sort out the possible interactions between cutting tariffs and expanding quotas. This is particularly critical for developing countries, whose loss of quota rents can offset higher earnings from increased market access.

We then use a set of scenarios to quantify the effects on trade and welfare of comprehensively liberalizing TRQs in eight agricultural sectors in both OECD and developing countries. Our results show that in the case of a single commodity (sugar), when exporters capture large shares of the quota rents, a combination of both tariff reduction and quota expansion improves welfare for both importers and exporters. Multilateral, multicommodity TRQ liberalization also generates substantial welfare gains for importing countries. However, in this case the net impact on exporters depends on the depth of tariff cuts, the distribution of quota rents, and their interaction with changes in trade patterns.

## Setting up the model

To assess the welfare and trade effects of agricultural liberalization, we employ a TRQ model (Elbehri and Pearson, 2000) implemented within an applied general equilibrium model, the Global Trade Analysis Project (GTAP) (Hertel, 1997).[2] The GTAP model is a widely used multiregion multisector applied general equilibrium model. In this section we briefly describe the GTAP model and its TRQ features.[3]

The standard version of the GTAP model is a comparative static, multiregion multisector static model that assumes perfectly competitive markets and constant returns to scale. Unlike similar AGE models, GTAP utilizes a unique representation of consumer demand, represented by a constant difference elasticity, which allows for differences in the income responsiveness of demand in different regions depending upon both the level of development of the region and the particular consumption patterns observed in that region. The model also incorporates estimates of bilateral international transport margins supplied by a global trade and transport sector.

For the TRQ addition to the standard GTAP, the discontinuity inherent in the two-tier tariff system, was modeled as a mixed complementarity problem and the TRQ behavior was handled via a non-differentiable equation which solves for price and quantity equilibrium in either one of the three policy regimes – that is within the quota imports, over-quota imports, or in-quota imports. The TRQ mechanism is implemented at the bilateral level – that is at the level of each trade flow represented by a triple of indices $(i, r, s)$ where $i$ is the commodity, $r$ is the source region, and $s$ is the destination region. The three cases differ in the price-linkage relation between domestic and world prices.

The model also solves for the equilibrium total quota rents $(Q_r)$ associated with each triple $(i, r, s)$ as well as the portions of the total quota rents that accrue to the source (exporter) and destination region (importer) for each commodity $i$. The distribution of quota rents between exporters and importers is performed as part of the model solution based on exogenously specified quota rent shares provided on a bilateral basis. In the case where equilibrium imports are within quota, quota rents reduce to zero.

There are five primary factors in the model: agricultural land, physical capital, skilled labor, unskilled labor, and natural resources. Land and natural resources are fixed factors used by a subset of tradable sectors. While aggregate farm land is a fixed input, it is distributed among crop sectors in response to relative rental rates. Labor and physical capital are used by all sectors. While land is mobile across sectors, capital is set to be sector-specific in the spirit of the Ricardo–Viner trade model. This assumption reflects the short- and medium-term approach where farm structures and some types of capital are relatively immobile (Vasavada and Chambers, 1986). Given the presence of sector-specific factors the supply response of the primary sectors like the sugar crop is restricted.

The GTAP model also includes a welfare decomposition module (Huff and Hertel, 1996) that produces further insight into the sources of regional and global welfare gains and losses from agricultural liberalization.[4]

Table 10.1 *Model commodity and regional aggregation*

| Commodity aggregation | | Regional aggregation | |
|---|---|---|---|
| Rice | Rice | AUS | Australia |
| Wheat | Wheat | JPN | Japan |
| Grain | Grains | KOR | Korea |
| Oilsd | Oilseeds | PHL | Phlippines |
| Sugar | Sugar | THA | Thailand |
| Dairy | Dairy | CHN | China |
| FrVeg | Fruits and vegetables | TWN | Taiwan |
| MeatP | Meats | IND | India |
| Othag | Other agriculture and food | RAS | Rest of Asia |
| Prmsc | Other primary sectors | CAN | Canada |
| Txtcl | Textile and clothing | USA | United States |
| Mnfcs | Other manufacturing | MEX | Mexico |
| Srvcs | Services | BRA | Brazil |
| | | CAC | Caribbean Americas |
| | | RLA | Rest of Latin America |
| | | EU | European Union |
| | | MENA | N. Africa and M. East |
| | | SAF | South Africa |
| | | RAF | Rest of Africa |
| | | ROW | Rest of World |

The underlying database for the GTAP model used in this analysis is the GTAP database version 4 built at the level of fifty sectors and forty-five regions. The production and trade data is benchmarked for year 1995. However, to keep the reporting of results manageable, the database was aggregated to twenty regions and thirteen sectors of which eight sectors are subject to TRQ regimes by selected regions in the model (table 10.1). The regional economies represented include OECD countries as well as a sample of economies from the developing world. The non-OECD countries represent several geographical regions and are both net exporters and importers of agricultural commodities.

## The TRQ data set

To model the TRQ regime, we needed to supplement the GTAP database with additional information. The data reported in table 10.2 are derived from data on annual target quotas, in-quota imports total imports. The agricultural commodities subject to a TRQ regime differ by region. While all OECD countries maintain a TRQ regime for dairy imports, only the EU and United States implement a TRQ for sugar. The United States, EU, and Canada, but not Japan, apply

TRQ regime to meats. Unlike other OECD countries, the United States does not maintain TRQs for grains and wheat. Table 10.2 also shows the commodities that the Philippines and South Korea maintain under TRQ regimes that relate to this analysis.

Table 10.2 also includes benchmark data on quota fill rates as well as tariffs using the schedules that countries submitted under the Uruguay Round.[5] Over-quota tariffs range from 26 percent for meats in the United States to 545 percent for oilseeds in Korea. Japan maintains out-of-quota tariffs ranging up to 491 percent for grains. Both the United States and the EU have highly protective regimes for sugar, with domestic prices far more than 100 percent above world prices.

The final column of table 10.2 shows the quota rent shares assigned to import-ing countries. For the United States, the EU, and Canada, these shares represent a trade-weighted aggregate of individual product indicators. To assign the latter, we used the following rule: a dummy variable takes the value of 1 (meaning that importer gets the entire quota rents) when only an import license is required. We assigned a value of 0 when only an export license is required. A value of 0.5 is assigned in two cases: no import license is required for either importers or exporters or when imports are admitted on a first-come, first-serve basis. We followed the same rule in the case of dairy products for Japan but not for cereals and grains, for which private importers play a minimum role. For Korea and the Philippines, all TRQ commodities were assigned a quota share-allocation factor of 1, following Abbott and Morse (1999). A more refined approach to allocating quota rents would clearly be desirable – an area for further research. However, we believe that our assumptions are reasonable given the state of data availability and the level of aggregation in this analysis.

To make the TRQ data consistent with the underlying structure of the GTAP model, we incorporated the additional TRQ data into the model as ratios rather than flows. For each bilateral flow (defined by commodity, exporter, and im-porter), we used the ratio of quota over imports to determine which of the three policy regimes is initially effective: in-quota, at-quota, and out-of-quota imports. We also introduced the in-quota tariffs and out-of-quota tariffs as a ratio. This approach allowed us to model switches in the TRQ regime while preserving the internal balance of the overall GTAP database.

## Modeling alternative policy scenarios

To assess the economic significance of existing trade distortions and the im-plications of further liberalization, we modeled several policy scenarios. In the first three scenarios, we reduced the EU over-quota tariff by 33 per-cent (scenario *SGEU_T*), expanded the EU quota volume by 50 percent (sce-nario *SGEU_Q*), and then combined those two measures (scenario *SGEU_TQ*) (table 10.3). We focused on the welfare effects for the EU as well as the main

Table 10.2 *TRQ regimes for selected countries and commodities, 1996*

| | Quota/total imports | In-quota imports/quota (quota fill rate) [a] | In-quota *ad valorem* tariff [b] | Out-of quota *ad valorem* tariff [c] | Importer's share of quota rents [d] |
|---|---|---|---|---|---|
| *OECD countries* | | | | | |
| United States | | | | | |
| Sugar | 0.76 | 0.97 | 2.44 | 129.00 | 0.25 |
| Dairy | 0.95 | 0.77 | 10.93 | 70.00 | 0.75 |
| Meats | 1.02 | 0.67 | 5.43 | 26.00 | 0.50 |
| European Union | | | | | |
| Wheat | 0.02 | 0.21 | 0.00 | 87.00 | 0.75 |
| Grains | 0.26 | 0.74 | 34.55 | 162.00 | 0.75 |
| Sugar | 0.87 | 1.00 | 0.00 | 147.00 | 1.00 |
| Dairy | 0.80 | 0.99 | 23.71 | 90.95 | 0.55 |
| Meats | 0.73 | 1.00 | 18.80 | 128.00 | 0.50 |
| Fruits and vegetables | 0.20 | 0.78 | 10.74 | 51.00 | 0.52 |
| Japan | | | | | |
| Wheat | 0.95 | 1.09 | 0.00 | 234.00 | 1.00 |
| Grains | 0.84 | 1.09 | 0.00 | 491.00 | 1.00 |
| Dairy | 0.91 | 0.93 | 29.28 | 344.00 | 0.75 |
| Canada | | | | | |
| Wheat | 2.18 | 0.27 | 0.93 | 49.00 | 0.75 |
| Grains | 23.97 | 0.05 | 0.74 | 58.00 | 0.75 |

(*cont.*)

Table 10.2 (cont.)

| | Quota/total imports | In-quota imports/quota (quota fill rate)[a] | In-quota ad valorem tariff[b] | Out-of quota ad valorem tariff[c] | Importer's share of quota rents[d] |
|---|---|---|---|---|---|
| Dairy | 0.75 | 1.00 | 6.61 | 261.70 | 0.52 |
| Meats | 0.72 | 1.24 | 2.17 | 27.00 | 0.50 |
| *Developing countries* | | | | | |
| Korea | | | | | |
| Rice | 0.53 | 1.00 | 5.00 | 89.00 | 1.00 |
| Grain | 0.61 | 1.48 | 2.89 | 326.44 | 1.00 |
| Oilseeds | 0.62 | 1.57 | 7.93 | 544.65 | 1.00 |
| Dairy | 1.06 | 0.85 | 20.68 | 106.46 | 1.00 |
| Meats | 0.77 | 0.97 | 40.26 | 41.69 | 1.00 |
| Fruits and vegetables | 0.83 | 0.99 | 47.09 | 305.11 | 1.00 |
| Philippines | | | | | |
| Rice | 0.53 | 1.00 | 0.00 | 50.00 | 1.00 |
| Grain | 0.07 | 1.00 | 35.00 | 80.00 | 1.00 |
| Sugar | 0.33 | 1.00 | 50.00 | 80.00 | 1.00 |
| Meats | 0.06 | 1.00 | 28.43 | 36.27 | 1.00 |

*Notes:* [a] Quota fill rate may exceed 1 in case imports subject to in-quota tariffs exceed the declared minimum access commitments.

[b] Uruguay Round tariff schedules reported as in-quota tariff rates. For aggregate commodities, values are trade-weighted *ad valorem* rates.

[c] For OECD countries, these are OECD calculations of *ad valorem* equivalents based on comparing specific tariff rates with world market prices for 1996. These specific tariffs were derived based on import values and volume per-tariff lines. For fruits and vegetables in the EU, the out-of-quota tariff is taken from Swinbank and Ritson (1995). For Korea and the Philippines, these are MFN rates from the TRAINS database.

[d] These quota-allocation shares are based on a simple rule that assigns a share of 1 in the case of a required import license; 0 if an export license required only; 0.5 if both an import license and export line are required; and finally 0.5 if the product is imported on a first-come, first-serve basis.

Table 10.3 *Trade liberalization scenarios for TRQ and non-TRQ commodities*

| Simulation | Description |
|---|---|
| *SGEU_T* | Reduction of over-quota tariff rate for EU sugar TRQ by 33% |
| *SGEU_Q* | Expansion of sugar quota volume for EU by 50% |
| *SGEU_TQ* | Reduction of over-quota tariff rate and expansion of quota volume for EU sugar TRQ by 33% |
| *USEU_T* | USA and EU sugar TRQ liberalization: reduction of the rate of over-quota tariff by 33% |
| *USEU_TQ* | USA and EU sugar TRQ liberalization: reduction of the rate of over-quota tariff by 33% and expansion of 1996 quota by 50% |
| *MULTI_T33* | Multilateral sugar import regime liberalization: global cut in import tariffs or over-quota tariffs by 33% |
| *MULTI_TGAP* | Multilateral trade liberalization: elimination of the gap between over-quota and in-quota tariffs |

sugar exporters – mostly from the developing world. The question is whether expanded market access more than compensates for the loss of quota rents these countries experience following liberalization.

The next two experiments consider over-quota tariff cuts by the EU and the United States (*USEU_T*) and a combination of tariff cuts and quota expansion (*USEU_TQ*). We expect welfare implications for both importers and exporters to be far greater than when either the EU or the United States liberalizes alone. But quota rents may also dissipate, with negative effects on exporters, particularly countries that export to both the United States and the EU.

The final two scenarios evaluate liberalization of all sectors subject to TRQs in the four OECD regions, plus South Korea and the Philippines, which use TRQs. In scenario *MULTI_T33*, a 33 percent cut in above-quota tariffs matches the scenarios for liberalizing sugar. In the final scenario *MULTI_TGAP*, we consider a deeper cut in over-quota tariffs that eliminates the gap between in-quota and out-of quota tariffs. This produces an uneven profile of tariff cuts between commodities and regions, given the initial differences in in-quota and over-quota tariff levels. This scenario allows us to assess the global welfare costs associated with the two-tiered TRQ system, and the consequences of eliminating it.

*Liberalizing TRQs in the sugar market*

Sugar is a highly regulated commodity, particularly within the largest developed economies: the EU, the United States, and Japan. The EU sugar program operates under an intervention price above the world price and is maintained primarily through import restrictions via a TRQ regime and the subsidization of exports to prevent excessive stock increases.[6] In addition to high tariffs on over-quota imports, sugar imports are also tightly controlled through the application of the "special safeguard" provision. Moreover, the EU follows a preferential allocation of sugar import quotas targeted mostly to the African, Caribbean, and Pacific (ACP) group of countries plus India.[7] ACP sugar receives the same support price as internally produced EU sugar and enters the EU duty-free. As a result, economic rents accrue to the ACP exporters under this preferential regime.

For the United States, the sugar TRQs are administered to ensure that the domestic price stays at or above the loan rate (Haley, 1999). The US sugar TRQs are allocated as bilateral quotas to exporting countries on the basis of their average market shares of US sugar imports in the period 1975–81, exclusive of the highest and lowest years (Suarez, 1997). Hence, despite the change in the exporters' relative ability to supply sugar over the years, these quota shares have not changed. The notable exception is Mexico, whose sugar exports to the United States are expected to increase with the implementation of the NAFTA.

Japan is another major sugar importer that intervenes heavily in the sugar market through a mix of producer price supports, levies, and tariffs on imports. Japan's sugar production is only one-third of consumption, and much of the intervention takes place in the form of high import tariffs (Sheales *et al.*, 2000).

Several developments could provide an impetus for further trade liberaliza-tion in sugar, including: EU enlargement, implementation of NAFTA, binding Uruguay Round commitments and the prospects of WTO challenges to export subsidies after the expiry of the "Peace Clause" in 2003–4. However, these must be reconciled with domestic policy goals for the sugar industry. In the US case, the amount of TRQ sugar imports have trended downward closer to the WTO commitments since the late 1990s, making it more difficult to manage the current domestic sugar program (Haley, 1999). Moreover, the prospects of increased sugar imports from Mexico as a result of NAFTA will likely be a fac-tor in any potential changes to current WTO commitments on sugar. The same conflicts in policy goals between market access and domestic support are also found in the EU. The current EU sugar program, initiated in 1995 following the Uruguay Round, was to expire in 2001. While it is expected that the EU sugar program will need to be reformed in the direction of reduced production quotas, lower intervention prices, or both (Swinbank, 1999), the EU Commis-sion decided to postpone any action on the sugar program for at least two years. A proposed Council Regulation, of April 2000, called for an extension of the existing program with some reductions in production quotas but no changes to intervention prices.

Given all these considerations, any new WTO agreement on sugar market access would consist at best of a partial sugar trade liberalization affecting over-quota or MFN tariffs. Depending on the extent of sugar liberalization, such an agreement could have significant consequences for consumers, producers, and processors in the importing countries. For exporters, particularly developing countries, both the welfare and revenue effects will be significant. The revenue effects from a market access agreement would be determined by the offsetting effects of quota rent revenues and trade volume changes. These effects are examined in the present analysis.

*What happens when the EU liberalizes sugar?*

The model shows that a 33 percent cut in EU over-quota sugar tariffs leads to a $555 million increase in the volume of global sugar trade (excluding intra-EU trade). Under this scenario, the EU sees its sugar imports expand by $198.5 million (table 10.5), while its sugar output declines by 4.1 percent (table 10.4). Much of the increased trade is captured by Africa ($US 337.5 million inclusive of South Africa), the Caribbean region ($US 138.4 million), and the Rest of Latin America ($94.9 million) (table 10.5).

Table 10.6 (top half, column (1)) summarizes the changes in quota rents resulting from lower over-quota tariffs. All countries exporting sugar to the EU lose quota rents. The magnitude of these losses mirrors the importance of sugar trade with the EU. The Africa region, exclusive of South Africa experiences the largest loss ($US −138.5 million) followed by the Caribbean group ($US −77.7 million), Latin America ($US −48.1 million) and South Africa ($US −34.6 million). Note that Brazil, which does not benefit from quota rents from sugar exports to the EU, is not affected by these quota losses. The EU shows a net gain in social welfare ($822.5 million), but exporting countries experiences net welfare losses.

When the EU expands its sugar quota by 50 percent rather than cutting over-quota tariffs, world trade volume in sugar increases by only half as much ($187.5 million versus $555 million, table 10.5). Under expanded quotas, the EU increases its imports by $38.9 million and decreases output by 1.2 percent. It also gains $491.3 million in tariffs, compared to a loses of $319.3 million under the first scenario (tariff cut only). This result – combined with the increase in quota rents captured by exporting countries – produces the opposite net effect on social welfare compared with tariff reduction. Under expanded quotas, the EU experiences a net welfare loss ($−168.3 million), while all major sugar exporters experience an overall rise in welfare despite a more moderate expansion of exports than under the tariff-cut scenario.

When the EU combines tariff reduction and quota expansion, the net effects on sugar imports, exports, and output are the same as under the tariff-cut scenario. This is because the binding instrument is the over-quota tariff, which determines equilibrium prices, output, and trade flows.[8]

Table 10.4 *Output effects from partial sugar TRQ liberalization (percentage change)*

| Description Scenario | EU TRQ liberalization | | | EU and US TRQ liberalization | |
|---|---|---|---|---|---|
| | Cut in over-quota tariffs by 33% SGEU_T | Expansion of quota by 50% SGEU_Q | Tariff cut and quota expansion SGEU_TQ | Cut in over-quota tariffs by 33% USEU_T | Tariff cut and quota expansion USEU_TQ |
| Australia | -0.14 | -0.03 | -0.13 | 0.46 | 0.49 |
| Japan | -0.01 | 0.00 | 0.00 | 0.00 | 0.01 |
| Korea | -0.06 | -0.02 | -0.06 | -0.02 | -0.01 |
| Philippines | -0.01 | 0.00 | -0.01 | 2.63 | 2.64 |
| Thailand | -0.15 | -0.03 | -0.13 | 0.06 | 0.09 |
| China | 0.63 | 0.21 | 0.64 | 0.46 | 0.48 |
| Taiwan | 0.01 | 0.01 | 0.02 | -0.64 | -0.61 |
| India | 0.10 | 0.03 | 0.10 | 0.19 | 0.20 |
| Rest of Asia | 0.82 | 0.27 | 0.82 | 0.42 | 0.43 |
| Canada | -0.92 | -0.28 | -0.92 | 7.03 | 7.08 |
| United States | 0.29 | 0.09 | 0.29 | -6.39 | -6.35 |
| Mexico | 1.69 | 0.45 | 1.69 | 1.23 | 1.24 |
| Brazil | 0.06 | 0.02 | 0.07 | 0.46 | 0.47 |
| Caribbean Americas | 7.02 | 2.13 | 6.94 | 6.63 | 6.37 |
| Rest of Latin America | 1.73 | 0.52 | 1.73 | 2.92 | 2.93 |
| EU | -4.08 | -1.19 | -4.07 | -5.16 | -5.13 |
| North Africa and Middle East | 0.11 | 0.04 | 0.11 | 0.06 | 0.07 |
| South Africa | 1.12 | 0.35 | 1.13 | 1.58 | 1.60 |
| Rest of Africa | 6.35 | 1.34 | 6.34 | 4.43 | 4.40 |

*Source:* Model results.

Table 10.5 *Trade effects of sugar market access liberalization*

| | EU TRQ liberalization | | | | | | EU and US TRQ liberalization | | | |
| | Cut in over-quota tariffs by 33% SGEU_T | | Expansion of quota by 50% SGEU_Q | | Tariff cut and quota expansion SGEU_TQ | | Cut in over-quota tariffs by 33% USEU_T | | Tariff cut and quota expansion USEU_TQ | |
| Description Scenario | (%) | ($US Million) | (%) | ($US Million) | (%) | ($US Million) | (%) | ($US Million) | (%) | ($US Million) |
|---|---|---|---|---|---|---|---|---|---|---|
| *Imports* | | | | | | | | | | |
| United States | 0.10 | 0.7 | 0.01 | 0.1 | 0.10 | 0.6 | 19.35 | 135.5 | 19.28 | 135.0 |
| EU | 5.10 | 198.5 | 1.00 | 38.9 | 5.10 | 198.1 | 8.18 | 318.4 | 8.14 | 316.8 |
| *Exports* | | | | | | | | | | |
| Australia | −0.25 | −3.2 | −0.06 | −0.8 | −0.24 | −3.0 | 0.79 | 10.0 | 0.83 | 10.5 |
| Philippines | 0.05 | 0.0 | 0.03 | 0.0 | 0.06 | 0.0 | 15.38 | 0.0 | 15.40 | 0.0 |
| Thailand | −0.25 | −3.1 | −0.05 | −0.6 | −0.23 | −2.8 | 0.10 | 1.2 | 0.14 | 1.7 |
| India | 10.73 | 9.9 | 3.36 | 3.1 | 10.74 | 9.9 | 35.03 | 32.3 | 35.13 | 32.4 |
| Brazil | 0.48 | 8.1 | 0.18 | 3.0 | 0.50 | 8.4 | 2.15 | 36.0 | 2.19 | 36.6 |
| Caribbean region | 10.85 | 138.4 | 3.29 | 42.0 | 10.73 | 136.8 | 8.75 | 111.6 | 8.40 | 107.1 |
| Rest of Latin America | 15.47 | 94.9 | 4.65 | 28.5 | 15.47 | 94.9 | 20.57 | 126.2 | 20.59 | 126.3 |
| EU | −12.09 | −610.9 | −3.70 | −186.9 | −12.06 | −608.9 | −12.60 | −636.6 | −12.51 | −632.0 |
| South Africa | 24.85 | 65.0 | 7.31 | 19.1 | 24.81 | 64.9 | 21.17 | 55.4 | 21.14 | 55.3 |
| Rest of Africa | 46.73 | 272.5 | 9.71 | 56.6 | 46.53 | 271.3 | 40.90 | 238.5 | 40.49 | 236.1 |
| Total World | — | 555.0 | — | 187.5 | — | 555.0 | — | 833.2 | — | 831.3 |

*Source:* Model results.

Table 10.6 Welfare effects of sugar TRQ liberalization, by EU and United States

| | EU TRQ liberalization | | | EU and US TRQ liberalization | |
|---|---|---|---|---|---|
| Description | Cut in over-quota tariffs by 33% | Expansion of quota by 50% | Tariff cut and quota expansion | Cut in over-quota tariffs by 33% | Tariff cut and quota expansion |
| Scenario | SGEU_T | SGEU_Q | SGEU_TQ | USEU_T | USEU_TQ |
| | (1) | (2) | (3) | (4) | (5) |
| | *Changes in tariff revenues ($US million)* | | | | |
| EU | −319.3 | 491.3 | 93.0 | 36.4 | 662.2 |
| United States | −2.1 | −1.3 | −2.5 | −180.0 | 79.4 |
| | *Changes in quota rents ($US million)* | | | | |
| *Importers* | | | | | |
| EU | −124.3 | 90.6 | −17.4 | −157.7 | −22.2 |
| United States | −0.1 | 0.0 | −0.1 | −37.3 | −12.8 |
| Japan | | | | | |
| *Exporters* | | | | | |
| Australia | 0.0 | 0.0 | 0.0 | −15.1 | −2.1 |
| Philippines | 0.0 | 0.0 | 0.0 | −25.3 | −3.0 |
| Thailand | 0.0 | 0.0 | 0.0 | 0.0 | 0.0 |
| India | −6.5 | 4.7 | −0.9 | −6.5 | −0.9 |
| Brazil | 0.0 | 0.0 | 0.0 | −37.5 | −5.1 |

(cont.)

| | | | Changes in welfare ($US million) | | |
|---|---|---|---|---|---|
| Caribbean Americas | −77.7 | 56.3 | −10.8 | −215.6 | −23.9 |
| Rest of Latin America | −48.1 | 35.5 | −6.6 | −143.2 | −18.8 |
| South Africa | −34.6 | 25.6 | −4.8 | −59.0 | −8.1 |
| Rest of Africa | −138.5 | 114.3 | −18.9 | −267.4 | −33.0 |
| *Importers* | | | | | |
| EU | 822.5 | −168.3 | 474.7 | 1165.4 | 577.0 |
| United States | −5.3 | −7.8 | −10.3 | 390.3 | 93.7 |
| Japan | 3.4 | −4.2 | −0.8 | 13.4 | 4.2 |
| *Exporters* | | | | | |
| Australia | 0.2 | 0.6 | 0.6 | −14.9 | 2.0 |
| Philippines | 0.3 | 0.2 | 0.4 | 2.5 | 2.5 |
| Thailand | −1.1 | 0.0 | −0.9 | −0.4 | 0.4 |
| India | −5.7 | 5.8 | 0.6 | −2.2 | 4.0 |
| Brazil | 1.2 | −0.2 | 0.7 | −27.9 | 12.3 |
| Caribbean Americas | −57.7 | 81.8 | 25.2 | −175.4 | 61.7 |
| Rest of Latin America | −46.3 | 45.9 | 3.4 | −137.7 | 11.2 |
| South Africa | −33.1 | 35.2 | 4.2 | −60.1 | 3.8 |
| Rest of Africa | −135.0 | 133.7 | 0.3 | −261.4 | 3.4 |
| *Total* | 723.7 | 261.6 | 708.7 | 890.7 | 870.0 |

*Source:* Model results.

Expanding the EU quota and tariff cuts affects countries' final net welfare via changes in tariff revenue and quota rents. The EU shows a smaller tariff revenue gain ($93 million) compared to the loss ($US −391.3 million) under expanded quotas only (*SGEU_Q*). For exporting countries, the losses in quota rents are much smaller than under the tariff-cut-only scenario. As a result, both the liberalizing importing country (the EU) and the sugar-exporting countries show a positive net social welfare. This reveals that in situations where exporters capture a significant share of quota rents, both tariff reduction and quota expansion are needed to improve the net social welfare of both importers and exporters.

*What happens when the EU and the United States both liberalize sugar?*

Under the scenario *USEU_T*, both the EU and the United States cut over-quota tariff by one-third. In this case, the total volume of EU sugar trade expands 36.4 million, EU output drops by 5.2 percent, quota rents for all participants drop substantially, but net welfare for the EU, including consumers, increases by US$ 1,165.4 million. The larger EU *ad valorem* sugar tariff equivalents (table 10.2), explain the much larger impact on world sugar trade under EU sugar liberalization compared to the United States.

Under the combined cut in over-quota tariffs (by one-third) and expansion of quotas (by 50 percent), extra-EU sugar imports to the EU expand by $316.8 million, while US sugar imports increase by $135.0 million. US sugar output declines by 643 percent, while EU sugar output drops by 5.1 percent. Under this scenario, loss of quota rents are moderate but negative to all participants but gains in welfare are realized for all, too.

Sugar-exporting countries like Australia, Thailand, and the Philippines, showed little production adjustment under EU liberalization, but now show a significant production increase under the combined US and EU partial liberalization of sugar. The Rest of Latin America countries, outside Brazil, which export significant sugar to both the EU and the United States, show a much higher sugar output increase under the *USEU_TQ* scenario (2.9 percent increase in production) compared to the *SGEU_TQ* scenario (1.7 percent). On the other hand, the African region, which exports mostly to the EU, shows an increase in sugar output when the EU liberalizes sugar imports (*SGEU_TQ*) but no additional output response under the combined sugar liberalization scenario by the EU and the United States (*USEU_TQ*).

Export changes under the combined sugar liberalization scenarios differ among exporters. For example, the Latin American exporters, outside Brazil, expand their exports far more under the combined EU–US sugar liberalization by more than under EU liberalization-only scenario (20.6 percent versus 15.5 percent, table 10.5). On the other hand, African exporters show lower increase in exports under the combined sugar liberalization scenario compared to unilateral liberalization by the EU only. The African region, outside South Africa, expand sugar exports by 40.5 percent or $US 236.1 million under the combined EU–US sugar liberalization; but this is slightly smaller than exports increase under the US sugar liberalization-only scenario ($US 271.3 million).

Total net global welfare under combined US and EU sugar liberalization (tariff cut and quota expansion) rises by at lease $870 million under both scenarios (table 10.6). However, the regional distribution of this gain depends on whether the liberalization is restricted to a tariff cut or entails both a tariff cut and a quota expansion. The net welfare gain for the EU is larger under the tariff cut only ($US 1,165 million) than under both tariff cut and quota expansion ($US 577 million). For the United States, net welfare gains are also much larger, at $US 390.3 million, under the tariff cut, compared to $US 93.7 million under the tariff cut plus quota expansion.

Exporting countries experience mixed welfare changes under the US–EU tariff cut only. Exporting countries that benefit from preferential sugar exports and therefore capture quota rents see their overall welfare decline as a result of quota rents' erosion. Under the combined liberalization scenario (*USEU_TQ*), net changes in quota rents are mostly small and negative, and the net welfare effect on most exporting countries is positive. The regions that benefit the most from EU–US sugar liberalization are those exporting to both markets. These include South Africa, the Caribbean region, and Brazil.

These results underscore the importance of the distribution of quota rents in determining the magnitude and direction of welfare changes following market liberalization. The results also show that EU liberalization would exert much greater effects on world trade and welfare than the US sugar liberalization. While many welfare gains accrue to importing countries that liberalize their markets, exporting countries also share in welfare gains if sugar liberalization includes both tariff cuts and expanded quotas.

*Assessing the effects of multilateral liberalization*

To assess the potential impacts of multilateral liberalization of market access, we also modeled a tariff-cut scenario for eight TRQ commodity groups by four OECD entities: the EU, United States, Japan, and Canada, plus South Korea and the Philippines (OECD plus two) (scenario *MULTI_T33*). These commodities include rice, wheat, grains, sugar, dairy, oilseeds, fruits and vegetables, and meat products. For each TRQ commodity-region pair, we cut the over-quota tariff by one-third.[9] This scenario expands global trade by $6,309 million (table 10.7).

Multilateral cuts in over-quota tariffs of TRQ commodities and the resulting expansion of agricultural trade lead to a global welfare gain of $6,915 million (table 10.7). The largest welfare gain is shown by the EU ($3,767 million) and

Table 10.7 Welfare and trade effects of multilateral TRQ liberalization in ($US millions[a])

| | Scenario MULTI_T33, a 33% tariff cut | | | | Scenario MULTI_TGAP, Elimination of in- and out-quota tariff gap | | | |
|---|---|---|---|---|---|---|---|---|
| | Total welfare | Quota rents | Aggregate exports | Aggregate imports | Total welfare | Quota rents | Aggregate exports | Aggregate imports |
| Australia/New Zealand | −15.1 | −232.1 | 468.0 | 342.9 | 562.9 | −585.8 | 2,658.1 | 1,888.5 |
| Japan | 3,715.6 | −5,382.9 | 468.0 | 265.7 | 11,459.1 | −16,237.6 | 4,201.7 | 5,547.6 |
| Korea | 459.4 | −968.4 | 722.1 | 446.0 | 655.1 | −2,350.0 | 1,731.7 | 1,112.5 |
| Philippines | 15.8 | −26.9 | 5.5 | 22.4 | 49.9 | −68.7 | 49.2 | 96.2 |
| China | 70.8 | 0.0 | −67.1 | 26.3 | 313.1 | 0.0 | −242.4 | 108.9 |
| India | −13.0 | −5.7 | −28.5 | −8.3 | −37.5 | −14.4 | −75.7 | −24.7 |
| Rest of Asia | −37.5 | −5.2 | −125.5 | 49.6 | −124.9 | −13.0 | −564.2 | 80.7 |
| Canada | 116.1 | −95.8 | 143.2 | 290.3 | 2.9 | −235.4 | 890.4 | 1,776.7 |
| United States | 632.0 | −363.7 | 666.7 | 1,184.6 | 933.2 | −863.5 | 2,993.5 | 4,345.0 |
| EU | 3,767.0 | −1,886.1 | 1,156.7 | 2,020.9 | 3,495.1 | −4,674.1 | 13,135.5 | 15,217.8 |
| Argentina | 42.2 | −103.4 | 186.1 | 192.5 | 523.4 | −251.3 | 976.8 | 1,022.3 |
| Brazil | −83.2 | −106.4 | 292.5 | 163.0 | −187.7 | −246.4 | 1,169.1 | 626.1 |
| Rest of Latin America | −34.8 | −175.5 | 24.6 | 168.7 | 231.6 | −438.1 | 137.5 | 716.2 |
| Turkey | −1.1 | 0.0 | −20.8 | 8.3 | −0.3 | 0.0 | −89.5 | 34.2 |
| Morocco | −5.3 | 0.0 | −8.0 | −6.2 | −18.3 | 0.0 | −27.4 | −21.7 |
| North Africa/Middle East | 77.8 | −3.2 | 14.8 | 146.7 | 226.4 | −5.0 | 3.8 | 475.8 |
| Sub-Saharan/Southern Africa | 9.5 | −53.3 | 368.2 | 342.4 | 176.5 | −129.7 | 1,757.9 | 1,626.2 |
| Rest of World | −1,801.6 | −354.1 | 2,042.6 | 653.2 | −7,590.0 | −790.6 | 8,379.5 | 2,457.1 |
| Total | 6,914.9 | | 6,309.1 | | 10,670.3 | | 37,085.4 | 37,085.4 |

Notes: [a] Multilateral TRQ liberalization scenarios encompass the following regions and corresponding: United States (sugar, dairy products, meats); EU (grains, sugar, dairy products, fruits and vegetables, meats); Japan (wheat, non-rice grains, dairy products); Canada (grains, dairy products, meats); Korea (rice, grains, sugar, meats, oilseeds, fruits and vegetables, meats); and the Philippines (rice, sugar, meats).
Source: Model results.

Japan ($3,716 million) – two large markets with highly protective agricultural policies. Substantial welfare gains also accrue to the EU because that entity applies TRQs to many of the commodities that this analysis covers. For Japan, the commodities affected by TRQ liberalization (wheat, grains, and dairy products) have very high *ad valorem* tariffs (table 10.2), so even a one-third cut in tariffs translates into a large absolute reduction. Moreover, Japan is a large importer of these commodities.

The United States also shows a significant welfare gain of $632 million, although smaller than the EU or Japan. This is because the volume of US agricultural imports of TRQ commodities (mostly dairy and sugar) is smaller than that of the EU and Japan. In addition, US over-quota tariffs for dairy and sugar are also lower than in the EU and Japan (table 10.2). Korea also registers a substantial welfare gain under multilateral liberalization, at $459 million, resulting from its own tariff cuts on rice, grain, oilseeds, dairy, meats, and fruits and vegetables. Like Japan, Korea's one-third cut in tariffs translates into large absolute cuts; hence the large net welfare gain. Of the four OECD entities, Canada experiences relatively small welfare gains ($116 million) because of its smaller share of expanded imports.

What impacts do multilateral TRQ tariff cuts have on third countries? The answer is mixed. For Australia, the effects on its terms of trade are positive but do not compensate for losses in quota rents. Hence that country experiences a small overall decline in welfare. The small welfare increase for the "rest of Latin America" also reflects a similar situation where efficiency gains from increased imports are largely offset by quota rent losses. For the Africa region, there is also a tradeoff between quota rent losses and welfare effects due to expanded trade (on both the import and the export side).

*Modeling deeper multilateral tariff cuts*

Given the mixed effects on developing countries from a one-third cut in TRQ tariffs, we modeled an alternative scenario with deeper tariff cuts. In this case, we eliminated the gap between out-of-quota and in-quota tariffs. Thus the actual tariff cut differs among commodities, given differing initial in-quota and out-of quota tariffs. For example, the tariff cut for EU dairy products dropped the levy from 91 percent to 23.7 percent, while EU sugar tariffs dropped from 147 percent to 0 percent. The idea was to eliminate the two-tiered tariff structure and then measure the consequences for trade and welfare.

In this scenario, overall global welfare gains reach $10,670 million, with the largest gain captured by Japan (second set of columns in table 10.7). This is not surprising given Japan's high degree of agricultural protection and large market size. Japan's net welfare gain is much larger than under the one-third-cut scenario – the result of much greater efficiency in allocating domestic resources.

The EU's relatively lower but still large welfare gain under this scenario can be explained by much lower tariff revenues. Another contributing factor is a larger deterioration in the terms of trade, despite a significant increase in allocative efficiency.

Canada's loss of welfare under the final scenario compared with the one-third tariff cut results from larger losses of quota rents and tariff revenue. Australia, the Rest of Latin America, Middle East and North Africa (MENA) and the Rest of Africa all experience a significant welfare boost under this scenario owing to strongly favorable terms of trade. Brazil's net drop in welfare stems from its smaller boost in its terms of trade.

**What we can learn**

Several insights emerged from these findings. At least in the sugar market, the model's results seem to settle the issue of whether lower tariffs or higher quotas can best ensure greater market access. The political economy considerations that result from the pattern of quota rents clearly favor a combination of both liberalization measures in the case of sugar.

For example, reducing EU over-quota tariffs produces a net welfare gain for the importing country but a loss for exporting countries because they lose quota rents. However, the combination of tariff reductions and quota expansion produces a win–win situation for both importing and exporting countries. When the United States also liberalizes its sugar market, in addition to the EU, the global welfare gain is substantially higher. In addition to positive welfare gains for the importers (the EU and United States), many exporting regions such as Latin America, the Caribbean region, and Africa also show substantial welfare gains.

These results also show that the effects on exporting countries vary with the liberalization scenario. For example, while the Philippines benefits only when the United States liberalizes its market, Africa benefits mostly when the EU liberalizes its sugar market. The Caribbean region and Latin American countries, which export to both the United States and the EU, are likely to benefit under multilateral liberalization. Non-preferential exporters such as Australia and Thailand also benefit under all scenarios since the tradeoffs between quota rent changes and trade expansion effects are not at issue.

Countries that liberalize their TRQ regimes under a multilateral, multicommodity approach show a net social welfare gain commensurate with their market size and the initial height of over-quota tariffs. This is the traditional gain from the trade effects of liberalization. However, a closer look at trade responses and the effects on developing country exporters reveals some interesting insights.

First, cutting over-quota tariffs produces no trade response when the binding regime for a particular commodity is the in-quota tariff. This was the case for several trade flows given the benchmark data. This implies that the same liberalization instrument may have a drastically different effect depending on which TRQ regime is binding for each market. This adds a new complication not found in traditional tariff liberalization cases outside a TRQ regime.

A second insight is that the net welfare effects of liberalizing the TRQ regimes on exporters, particularly developing countries, depend not only on the expanded export opportunities in specific markets, but equally on the welfare implications of increased efficient use of domestic resources and in the case of preferential exporters, the extent of quota rent changes. The relative importance of these factors for different countries may explain the divergence attitudes of developing countries towards further reforms of TRQ import regimes. Some agricultural-exporting countries will be reluctant to see the TRQs removed because they provide at least some market access at low tariffs. On the other hand, Latin American and Caribbean countries would certainly welcome expanded market access under liberalized TRQs for products such as fruits and vegetables, sugar, dairy products, and meat. In Asia, interest in market access will likely diverge, depending on whether countries are net agricultural exporters or importers.

Overall, since country-specific TRQs by importing industrialized economies are justified as a form of foreign assistance, one policy implication is that tariff cuts negotiated as part of a multilateral agreement could also be complemented with higher quotas, therefore minimizing the welfare losses on those exporting developing countries with preferential treatment. In the long run, however, high-cost producers from developing countries would benefit less from foreign assistance than from shifting their economic activities toward areas in which they enjoy competitive advantage. A move toward a more liberalized trade regime would strongly encourage these adjustments of economic activities, which would benefit developing economies.

# Appendix   The economics of a TRQ regime: a graphical exposition

Figure 10A.1 illustrates three possible regimes under a TRQ. The quota (or minimum access commitment) is represented by $Q$. Under the TRQ, import supplies are represented by a step function with two horizontal lines (assuming perfectly elastic excessive supply function). The lower line represents the in-quota imports and extends from 0 to $Q$. The upper line represents the effective import supply of over-quota imports and extends from $Q$ to infinity.

At the import volume $Q$ there is a discontinuity: a vertical line joins the in-quota and over-quota segments. $M$ represents actual imports, which are

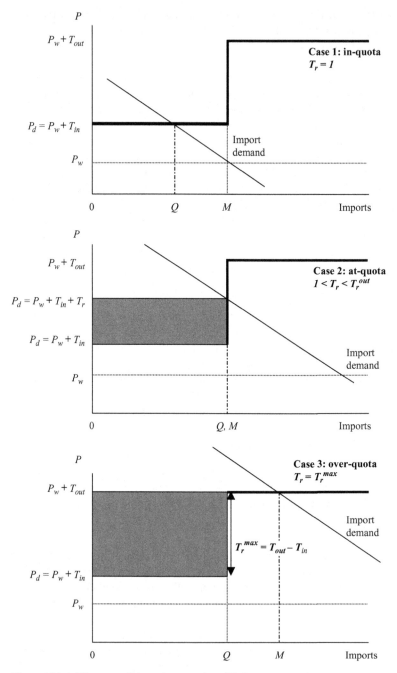

Figure 10A.1  Three possible regimes under a TRQ

determined by a net import demand function, which yields imports according to the domestic price $P_d$ of the importing country. In figure 10A.1, $T_{in}$ represents the in-quota tariff and $T_{out}$ the out-of quota tariff. $P_w$ is the world price. The world price plus an applicable tariff determine the domestic price $P_d$. Under the TRQ regime imports can be below the quota $Q$ when an in-quota tariff is effective (case 1), or equal to $Q$ making the quota effective (case 2) or above $Q$ making the out-of-quota tariff effective (case 3). In cases 2 and 3 we see positive quota rents (shown by the shaded areas), which accrue to either importers or exporters or both, depending on the mechanism by which the TRQ is administered.

In case 1, the domestic price equals the world price plus the in-quota tariff ($P_d = P_w + T_{in}$), net import demand $M$ is below the quota $Q$. The TRQ behaves just like a tariff and no quota rent arises. In case 3, net import demand $M$ exceeds the quota $Q$ and corresponds to the domestic price $P_d$ equal to world price plus the out-of-quota tariff $T_{out}$. In this case, rents are collected by whoever holds the rights to import at the lower in-quota tariff ($T_{in}$). This regime produces both rent-seeking behavior and an administration mechanism to allocate the rents. In case 2, net import demand intersects the import supply step function on its vertical portion at a quantity equal to the quota ($Q$). In this case the domestic price exceeds the world price augmented by the in-quota tariff ($P_d > P_w + T_{in}$). The out-of-quota tariff is prohibitive and the difference between $P_d$ and $P_w + T_{in}$ represents the per-unit rent.

As cases 2 and 3 show, rent per unit of in-quota imports equals the difference between the domestic price and the world price plus the in-quota tariff. The total value of the rent is the per-unit rent times the quota volume. However, this assumes a 100 percent quota fill rate. That is, the quota $Q$ (or minimum access commitment) equals the actual in-quota imports ($INQ$), which countries report separately to the WTO as part of their market access commitments. However, we may observe either quota underfill ($INQ < Q$) or overfill ($M >= INQ > Q$).

Quota underfill may occur if administrative requirements add transaction costs in acquiring rights to in-quota imports (Boughner and de Gorter, 1999). Rights to import via licenses may lead to unfilled quotas, while imports awarded on a first-come, first-serve basis produce uncertainties about quota status, also leading to unfilled quota. In these cases, quota may be unfilled even though total imports may exceed the minimum access commitments ($M > Q$). This is illustrated in figure 10A.2a, where in-quota imports ($INQ$) are below quota volume ($Q$). Quota overfill occurs when in-quota imports exceed minimum access commitments, as is the case when imports are managed by the state for example to stabilize domestic markets (Abbott and Morse, 1999). In this case, either the quota is endogenous or not binding. Under quota underfill, the total value of rents is based on the total volume of in-quota imports ($INQ$) rather than the smaller volume quantity $Q$. This latter case is illustrated in figure 10A.2b.

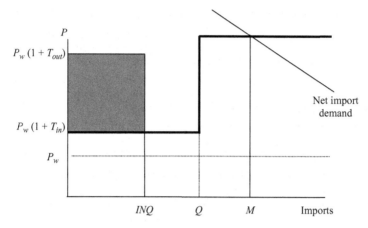

a  Quota underfill

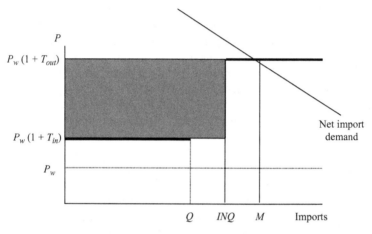

b  Quota overfill

Figure 10A.2  Quota underfill and overfill scenarios

Figure 10A.3 illustrates the implications for trade and revenues of liberalizing the TRQ regime. We consider the case when the over-quota tariff is binding $(M > Q)$. In case 1, the over-quota tariff is reduced (but is still above the in-quota tariff). In this case, imports increase while the total quota rents are reduced. The welfare implications for the importer and exporter will depend on the allocation of quota rents among trading partners, changes in tariff revenues, and the extent of trade expansion. Tariff revenues for the importing country may either increase or decrease depending on the difference between the rectangles $A$ and $B$.

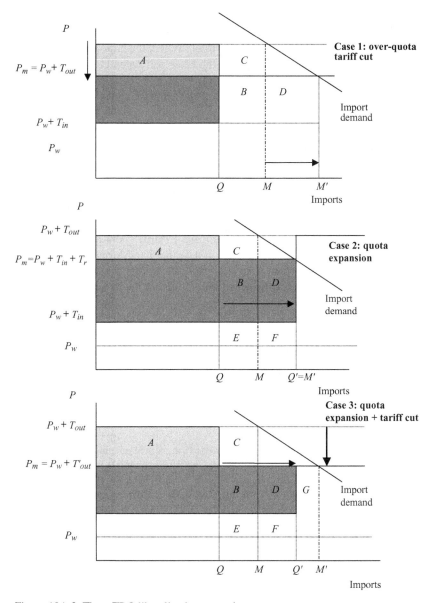

Figure 10A.3  Three TRQ liberalization scenarios

For the exporting country, the net welfare effect will depend on the difference between the loss of quota rents loss and the extra revenue from added exports. In case 2, the quota level expands from $Q$ to $Q'$. Where the importer and exporter share quota rents, the welfare effect on the latter will depend on the sign of the quota rent change. If expanding quotas results in a net increase in quota rents, the exporter will gain in social welfare (from both the added quota rents and from the expanded exports).

For the importer, the welfare effect is also ambiguous and will depend on the net result of the differences between tariff revenues and quota rents. Tariff revenue is likely to drop because in-quota imports (which are charged the lower in-quota tariff, $T_{in}$) replace over-quota imports. The welfare effect may be negative if the size of tariff is greater than any possible increase in quota rents. In case 3, both tariff cut and quota expansion are combined. If we assume the same level of tariff cut and quota expansion as in cases 1 and 2, we would expect the new total quota rents to be between case 1 (tariff quota only) and case 2 (quota increase only). Tariff revenues, on the other hand, would be larger than in case 2 but smaller than in case 1. The net effect of tariff revenue and quota rent changes will determine the net welfare effect for the importer.

### Notes

1. We abstract from special cases such as endogenous quotas (Boughner and de Gorter, 1999) and cases when countries may apply in-quota tariff for over-quota imports.
2. The GTAP model is implemented using the GEMPACK software (Harrison and Pearson, 1996).
3. A full description of the GTAP model is found in Hertel (1997); for a detailed description of how to implement the TRQ regime in GTAP, see Elbehri and Pearson (2000).
4. This decomposition approach may be viewed as a numerical generalization of Baldwin and Venables' analytical decomposition, which accommodates large domestic distortions.
5. These tariffs are on an *ad valorem* equivalent basis and are aggregated to the GTAP commodity level using trade values as weights. For South Korea and the Philippines, the reported values were taken from Abbott and Morse (1999), who extracted these in-quota tariffs from the Trade Analysis and Information System (TRAINS) database. For over-quota tariffs, we took the view that MFN tariff rates would not fully reflect the extent of tariff protection associated with the TRQ regime. For OECD countries we relied on OECD Secretariat estimates of the *ad valorem* equivalents of over-quota tariffs applied to the major agricultural commodities in the four major OECD countries. These *ad valorem* equivalents were calculated based on specific rates derived from import volumes and values per tariff line (OECD, 1997). These specific tariff rates were compared with world market prices for 1996 resulting in over-quota *ad valorem* tariffs. For fruits and vegetables in the EU, because of a lack of readily available estimates for 1996, the reported value of out-of-quota tariff is taken from Swinbank

and Ritson (1995). For Korea and the Philippines, the out-of-quota tariffs represent the applied MFN rates from the TRAINS database.

6. As in all general equilibrium models, prices in the GTAP model are relative to a numéraire. In our implementation, this is taken to be a global primary factor price index as suggested by de Melo and Tarr (1992).

7. Countries that are party to the ACP–EU Partnership Agreement include: Barbados, Belize, Congo, Côte d'Ivoire, Fiji, Guyana, Jamaica, Kenya, Madagascar, Malawi, Mauritius, Saint Kitts and Nevis-Anguila, Surinam, Swaziland, Tanzania, Trinidad and Tobago, Uganda, Zambia, and Zimbabwe.

8. Case 3 of Figure 10A.3a illustrates this equilibrium. The quota expands from $Q$ to $Q'$, while the new equilibrium imports $M'$ is larger than $Q'$. Hence the (lower) over-quota tariff is still the effective policy instrument determining the equilibrium domestic price. This result is dependent on our choice of the level of tariff cut (one-third) and quota expansion (one-half). One can also determine endogenously the rate of quota expansion needed to generate the same welfare increase as those obtained under the one-third tariff-cut scenario.

9. In this chapter, all reported TRQ quotas are on a bilateral basis. Obviously, many TRQs are also implemented on a global basis as well. In that case, modeling TRQs with bilateral quotas may understate the extent of liberalization gains.

### References

Abbott, P. and B. A. Morse, 1999. "How Developing Countries are Implementing Tariff-Rate Quotas," see chapter 4 in this volume

Abbott, P. and P. Paarlberg, 1998. "Tariff Rate Quotas: Structural and Stability Impacts in Growing Markets," *Agricultural Economics*, 19, 257–67

Boughner, D. S. and H. de Gorter, 1999. "The Economics of 2-Tier Tariff Rate Import Quotas and the Agreement on Agriculture in the WTO," Department of Agricultural, Resource, and Managerial Economics, Cornell University

de Melo, J. and D. Tarr, 1992. *A General Equilibrium Analysis of US Foreign Trade Policy*, Cambridge, MA, MIT Press

Elbehri, A. and K. R. Pearson, 2000. "Implementing Bilateral Tariff Rate Quotas in GTAP using GEMPACK," GTAP Technical Paper, 18, Global Trade Analysis Project, Purdue University

Haley, S., 1999. "Stocks-to-Use Ratios and Sugar Pricing Relationship: Implications for US Sugar Policy," in "Sugar and Sweetener," Washington, DC: USDA/ERS, September

Harrison, W. J. and K. R. Pearson, 1996. "Computing Solutions for Large General Equilibrium Models Using GEMPACK," *Computational Economics*, 9, 83–127

Hertel, T. W. (ed.), 1997. *Global Trade Analysis: Modeling and Applications*, Cambridge and New York: Cambridge University Press

Huff, K. and T. W. Hertel, 1996. "Decomposing Welfare Changes in GTAP," GTAP Technical Paper, 5, Global Trade Analysis Project, Purdue University

International Agricultural Trade Research Consortium (IATRC), 2000. "Issues in Reforming Tariff-Rate Quotas in the Agreement on Agriculture in the WTO," IATRC Commissioned Paper, 13, Washington, DC

Martin, W. and A. Winters (eds.), 1995. "The Uruguay Round and the Developing Economies," World Bank Discussion Paper, 307, Washington, DC

Organization for Economic Cooperation and Development (OECD) Secretariat, 1997. Internal document, Paris

Sheales, T., S. Gordon, A. Hafi, and C. Toyne, 2000. "Sugar: International Policies Affecting Market Expansion," ABARE Research Report, 99–14, Canberra

Skully, D. W., 1999. "The Economics of TRQ Administration," Working Paper, 99–6, IATRC, Washington, DC

Suarez, N., 1997. "Origin of the US Sugar Import Tariff-Rate Quota Shares," in "Sugar and Sweetener Situation and Outlook Report. (SSS–221)," US Department of Agriculture, Economic Research Service, Washington, DC September

Swinbank, A., 1999. "EU Agriculture, Agenda 2000 and the WTO Commitments," *The World Economy*, 22(1), 41–54

Swinbank, A., 1997. "Europe's Green Money," in C. Ritson and D. R. Harvey (eds.), *The Common Agricultural Policy*, CAB International, Wallingford, 115–37.

Tsigas, M. and M. D. Ingco, 1999. "Market Access Liberalization in the Next Round of WTO Negotiations: A General Equilibrium Assessment of Tariff-Rate Quotas," selected paper, American Agricultural Economic Association Annual Meeting, August 8–11, Nashville

Vasavada, U. and R. G. Chambers, 1986. "Investment in US Agriculture," *American Journal of Agricultural Economics*, 68(4), 950–60

# 11 The global and regional effects of liberalizing agriculture and other trade in the new round

*Thomas W. Hertel, Kym Anderson, Joseph F. Francois, and Will Martin*

## Introduction

Agriculture is much more important in the economies of developing countries than in high-income countries, as the former remain small net exporters. Consumers in developing countries also spend over 30 percent of their incomes on food – almost three times the share in industrial countries – making them much more vulnerable to price shocks. Agriculture's contribution to GDP in developing countries, at 16 percent, is also around three times as high as its share in industrial countries.

Yet the average rate of protection on bulk agricultural commodities in OECD countries actually rose from 32 to 37 percent between 1997 and 1998. Partly because of these barriers to market access, agricultural exports from developing countries fell from close to a half in 1965 to just over 10 percent in 1995, and are projected to fall further by 2005. Developing countries remain much more reliant on exports of bulk agricultural commodities than industrial countries: the former accounted for 44 percent of global exports of bulk agricultural commodities but only 23 percent of non-bulk agricultural exports in 1995. This locks developing countries into a declining share of world markets for agriculture, as bulk commodities have fallen from 70 percent to around 45 percent of world agricultural exports since 1965.

In developing countries especially, farming is discouraged not only by farm protection policies in high-income countries but also by developing countries' own manufacturing policies and distortions in services markets. Developing countries therefore have an interest in talks on liberalizing non-agricultural as well as agricultural sectors during the next WTO round. This chapter explores the extent to which further multilateral liberalization of not only farm but also non-farm policies will affect markets for farm products, as well as the overall balance of trade and welfare in developing countries.

To perform such an analysis, we first project changes in the world economy from 1995 to 2005, when all liberalization stemming from the Uruguay Round will be complete. We find that the share of manufacturing exports from developing countries will rise during this period as the openness of the agricultural sector declines. We then used the 2005 database to analyze the potential impact of post-Uruguay Round liberalization on changes in farm and food trade, as well as on economy-wide activity and welfare. Specifically, we consider the effects of across-the-board 40 percent cuts in protection for agriculture, mining and manufacturing tariffs, and protection for services. These cuts are slightly deeper than the one-third cuts in protection for agriculture and manufacturing stemming from the Uruguay Round, but they are in line with recent trade talks.

The combined effect of further multilateral liberalization of agriculture and non-agricultural trade increases the food trade balances of most developing regions, with the notable exceptions of India, China, and the Middle East/North Africa region. The heavily protected markets of Western Europe and Japan experience the largest deterioration in their food trade balances.

A 40 percent reduction in agricultural tariffs and export and production subsidies produces global welfare gains of around $70 billion per year. The largest dollar gains – as well as the largest gains as a share of agricultural value added – accrue to developed countries. The gains from a 40 percent liberalization of manufacturing trade are about the same order of magnitude, despite the fact that agriculture is a much smaller percentage of global output. Developing countries again receive the lion's share of the liberalization gains because they face higher rates of protection on manufacturing exports, and because liberalization lowers the efficiency costs imposed by their own protection.

In the next section, we consider the patterns of production, consumption, trade, and protection as well as other structural features of the global economy that are likely to influence the impacts of efforts during a new round to further liberalize agricultural and non-agricultural trade.

### Patterns of consumption, production, and trade

Agriculture is much more important for the developing countries than for the high-income economies of the OECD (table 11.1). The share of food in private consumption in 1995 (at producer's prices[1]) was over 40 percent in South Asia, China, Indonesia, and Sub-Saharan Africa (SSA), while the comparable share for OECD economies was generally less than 15 percent. The sectoral shares of economy-wide value added in food and agriculture in developing countries exceed 30 percent in South Asia and much of Africa, and 20 percent in parts of East Asia. In OECD economies, in contrast, the food sector averages only around 5 percent of GDP.

Yet developing countries' share of global agriculture exports has fallen from nearly half in 1965 to a little more than 10 percent today. Mining and minerals exports have been quite volatile, reaching as high as 50 percent in the early 1980s

Table 11.1 *Structure of the global economy 1995: comparison between agriculture, manufactures, and services*

| Region | Consumption share[a] | | | Value-added share | | | Share in region's exports | | | Exports/Output | | | Imports/Usage | | |
|---|---|---|---|---|---|---|---|---|---|---|---|---|---|---|---|
| | Food | Mnfcs | Svces | Food | Mnfcs | Svces | Food | Mnfcs | Svces | Food | Mnfcs | Svces | Food | Mnfcs | Svces |
| North America | 0.085 | 0.169 | 0.746 | 0.047 | 0.226 | 0.727 | 0.081 | 0.684 | 0.235 | 0.088 | 0.175 | 0.028 | 0.063 | 0.221 | 0.019 |
| Western Europe | 0.128 | 0.213 | 0.658 | 0.055 | 0.233 | 0.711 | 0.086 | 0.696 | 0.218 | 0.172 | 0.340 | 0.051 | 0.190 | 0.346 | 0.041 |
| Aus/NZL | 0.124 | 0.144 | 0.732 | 0.070 | 0.163 | 0.767 | 0.271 | 0.465 | 0.264 | 0.299 | 0.233 | 0.045 | 0.071 | 0.351 | 0.041 |
| Japan | 0.157 | 0.138 | 0.705 | 0.052 | 0.243 | 0.705 | 0.005 | 0.846 | 0.149 | 0.003 | 0.131 | 0.013 | 0.094 | 0.089 | 0.020 |
| China | 0.461 | 0.296 | 0.243 | 0.225 | 0.355 | 0.420 | 0.052 | 0.848 | 0.100 | 0.038 | 0.199 | 0.035 | 0.051 | 0.195 | 0.029 |
| Taiwan | 0.175 | 0.183 | 0.641 | 0.047 | 0.297 | 0.656 | 0.032 | 0.884 | 0.085 | 0.087 | 0.438 | 0.041 | 0.188 | 0.377 | 0.062 |
| OthNICs | 0.259 | 0.250 | 0.491 | 0.093 | 0.266 | 0.640 | 0.021 | 0.669 | 0.310 | 0.047 | 0.389 | 0.142 | 0.166 | 0.466 | 0.083 |
| Indonesia | 0.407 | 0.141 | 0.452 | 0.228 | 0.300 | 0.472 | 0.131 | 0.753 | 0.117 | 0.088 | 0.364 | 0.039 | 0.065 | 0.358 | 0.049 |
| OthSEA | 0.234 | 0.352 | 0.414 | 0.181 | 0.357 | 0.462 | 0.143 | 0.654 | 0.203 | 0.223 | 0.471 | 0.146 | 0.156 | 0.580 | 0.123 |
| India | 0.445 | 0.231 | 0.325 | 0.301 | 0.223 | 0.477 | 0.156 | 0.697 | 0.146 | 0.040 | 0.140 | 0.025 | 0.026 | 0.215 | 0.024 |
| OthSoAsia | 0.439 | 0.264 | 0.297 | 0.312 | 0.209 | 0.479 | 0.121 | 0.711 | 0.169 | 0.049 | 0.233 | 0.049 | 0.124 | 0.414 | 0.060 |
| Brazil | 0.249 | 0.292 | 0.459 | 0.125 | 0.225 | 0.650 | 0.254 | 0.605 | 0.141 | 0.064 | 0.068 | 0.011 | 0.033 | 0.110 | 0.017 |
| OthLatAm | 0.253 | 0.258 | 0.489 | 0.194 | 0.276 | 0.530 | 0.257 | 0.531 | 0.212 | 0.144 | 0.181 | 0.057 | 0.069 | 0.273 | 0.048 |
| Turkey | 0.311 | 0.234 | 0.455 | 0.198 | 0.182 | 0.620 | 0.098 | 0.449 | 0.452 | 0.067 | 0.203 | 0.119 | 0.080 | 0.327 | 0.033 |
| OthMENA | 0.288 | 0.212 | 0.500 | 0.108 | 0.363 | 0.529 | 0.033 | 0.812 | 0.155 | 0.043 | 0.320 | 0.050 | 0.181 | 0.316 | 0.069 |
| EIT | 0.234 | 0.264 | 0.502 | 0.097 | 0.308 | 0.595 | 0.075 | 0.694 | 0.231 | 0.080 | 0.219 | 0.061 | 0.136 | 0.223 | 0.050 |
| SoAfrCU | 0.239 | 0.237 | 0.524 | 0.082 | 0.266 | 0.652 | 0.097 | 0.703 | 0.200 | 0.096 | 0.252 | 0.040 | 0.082 | 0.292 | 0.042 |
| OthSSA | 0.429 | 0.242 | 0.329 | 0.303 | 0.283 | 0.414 | 0.233 | 0.594 | 0.172 | 0.134 | 0.230 | 0.067 | 0.087 | 0.293 | 0.071 |
| ROW | 0.274 | 0.358 | 0.369 | 0.203 | 0.296 | 0.501 | 0.119 | 0.582 | 0.299 | 0.046 | 0.131 | 0.056 | 0.110 | 0.273 | 0.043 |
| World | 0.156 | 0.196 | 0.648 | 0.074 | 0.244 | 0.682 | 0.082 | 0.707 | 0.211 | 0.096 | 0.238 | 0.040 | 0.114 | 0.257 | 0.033 |

*Source:* McDougall, Elbehri and Truong (1998).

*Notes:* [a] "Consumption share" refers to private household consumption at producers' prices. Therefore, wholesale/retail/transport margins are not included.

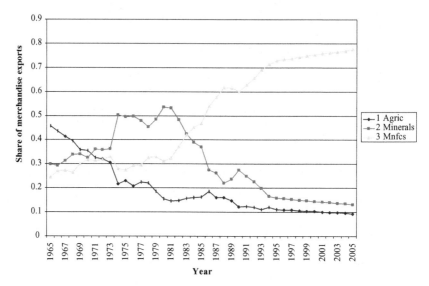

Figure 11.1   Share of merchandise exports from developing countries, 1965–2005

before dropping off with the decline in energy prices. The share of manufactures in the merchandise exports of developing countries has climbed steadily, from about one-quarter in 1965 to three-quarters of merchandise exports today. Of course these averages mask considerable variation across countries. Food products' share of exports is highest – about one-quarter – for Latin America and SSA, while that share averages 5 percent or less in much of East Asia.

Many factors influence the evolution of developing countries' export shares, but one of the most important has been the changing profile of protection in OECD economies, which absorb most of the world's imports. Immediately after the Second World War, OECD manufacturing tariffs averaged about 40 percent, whereas today they are 1.5 percent. This dramatic drop has contributed strongly to the growing share of manufactures in trade for both developed and developing economies (Hertel and Martin, 1999). The OECD's nominal rate of assistance to agriculture, in contrast – which includes domestic support – has risen from 30 percent over the 1965–74 period to nearly 60 percent in 1998 (ABARE, 1990). It is no wonder that the global shares of the two trade sectors have moved in sharply opposing directions.

The falling share of food in global trade masks a significant development in the composition of that trade – namely, the shift from bulk products such as grains to non-bulk products such as meat products, fresh fruits and vegetables, and processed foods (figure 11.1). Developing countries are clearly more reliant on slow-growing bulk food trade. However, their exports are also following the global trend toward non-bulk food exports, which have grown from only 16 percent in 1965 to 42 percent in 1995 (figure 11.2).

Table 11.1 also shows that the agricultural sector in developing countries has limited trade exposure: the ratio of exports to output is three times higher for manufactures than for food products; for countries such as China, this discrepancy is even larger. While the low trade exposure of agriculture is partly due to the perishable nature of many food products, an important contributor is the high level of protection for agricultural trade around the world. Not surprisingly, a similar pattern exists for imports, expressed as a share of total use in each region. Manufactures exhibits the highest exposure to imports, followed by food and services.

To analyze the potential gains from liberalizing both the agricultural and non-agricultural sectors in the new round, we need to look ahead to 2005. The next section details our underlying methodology and key assumptions in doing so (table 11.2, 11.3).

## Projecting to 2005

We begin by using version 4.0 of the Global Trade Analysis Project (GTAP) database, which represents a snapshot of the world economy in 1995 – the first year of implementing the Uruguay Round Agreement (McDougall, Elbehri and Truong, 1998). Table 11.4 reports projected tariff rates for 2005 based on the 1995 GTAP rates, updated to account for anticipated changes stemming from the Uruguay Round and China's accession to the WTO. It is important to note that the 1995 base year represented a period of high world prices and therefore low measured protection – because we estimate OECD border protection using the OECD's Producer Subsidy Equivalent (PSE). This entails observing the difference between world and domestic prices and attributing that to the tariff-equivalent effect of national trade policies. As a result, when world prices are high, measured protection tends to be low in economies using tariff-rate quotas (TRQs), variable tariffs, and other tools for insulating domestic producers from world markets.

Countries based their Uruguay Round agricultural commitments on the late 1980s, when prices were very low and measured protection was at a historic high. In light of this – and the extensive "dirty tariffication" in agriculture (Hathaway and Ingco, 1995; Ingco, 1996), we believe that no further liberalization from 1995 levels is likely under the Uruguay Round Agreement.[2] Accordingly, the tariffs in table 11.4 are based on bilateral tariffs identical to those in the version 4 database for 1995. (Because these tariff averages are trade-weighted, and because intra-EU trade is not taxed, the EU average rate of protection is rather misleading.) In addition to tariffs, we take explicit account of domestic support for agriculture, again based on the OECD's database. We

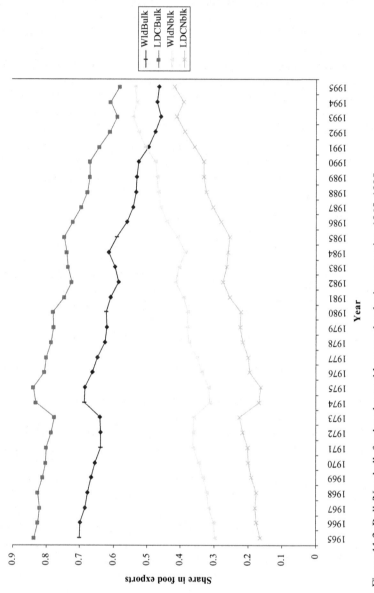

Figure 11.2 Bulk/Non-bulk food trade: world versus developing countries, 1965–1995

Table 11.2 *Elasticities of substitution between domestic and imported goods*

| Commodity (1) | GTAP (2) | This study (3) | Liu, Arndt, and Hertel (2000)[a] (4) |
|---|---|---|---|
| Foodgrains | 2.2 | 4.4 | 3.64 |
| Feedgrains | 2.2 | 4.4 | 3.64 |
| Oilseeds | 2.2 | 4.4 | 3.64 |
| Meatlstk | 2.5 | 5 | 6.6 |
| Dairy | 2.4 | 4.8 | 6.6 |
| Othagr | 2.2 | 4.4 | 3.64 |
| Othfood | 2.2 | 4.4 | 6.6 |
| Bevtobac | 3.1 | 6.2 | 6.6 |
| Extract | 2.8 | 5.6 | 1 |
| Textiles | 2.2 | 4.4 | 4.1 |
| Wearapp | 4.4 | 8.8 | 4.1 |
| Woodpaper | 2.15 | 4.3 | 4.6 |
| Pchemineral | 2.05 | 4.1 | 3.3 |
| Metals | 2.8 | 5.6 | 2.5 |
| Autos | 5.2 | 10.4 | 6.2 |
| Electronics | 2.8 | 5.6 | 4.6 |
| Othmnfcs | 3.25 | 6.5 | 4.6 |
| Houseutils | 2.35 | 4.7 | n/a |
| Tradetrans | 1.9 | 3.8 | n/a |
| Construction | 1.9 | 3.8 | n/a |
| Busfinance | 1.9 | 3.8 | n/a |
| Govservice | 1.9 | 3.8 | n/a |

*Note:* [a] The Liu, Arndt, and Hertel (2000) estimates refer to a nine-year period. These estimates were conducted at a more aggregate level and map somewhat imperfectly to the present aggregation.

treat this as an output subsidy, differentiated by sector. To the extent that these support policies have been decoupled from farmers' decisions, this treatment will overstate the production impact of lowering these subsidies under a future WTO round.

We obtain protection estimates for developing countries from UNCTAD's Trade Analysis and Information System (TRAINS) database. These data include many country/commodity gaps, which we fill using the pre-Uruguay Round estimates of Ingco (1996). Owing to very high WTO bindings in most developing countries, the Uruguay Round is not likely to require further reductions in agricultural protection. Of course, our projected tariffs for 2005 abstract from domestic reforms. For this reason, and because their current bindings are so much in excess of applied tariffs, we view our estimates of further developing country liberalization of agriculture as upper bounds.

Table 11.3 *Cumulative percentage growth rates over the period 1995–2005*
*(percentage annual growth in parentheses)*

| Regions | Pop. | Unskilled labor | Skilled labor | Capital | TFP | GDP This Study | GDP World Bank |
|---|---|---|---|---|---|---|---|
| North America | 11 | 14 | 39 | 39 | low | 31.76 | 31.99 |
| (Namerica) | (1.05) | (1.29) | (3.33) | (3.33) | | (2.8) | (2.8) |
| Western Europe | 1 | 0 | 29 | 9 | high | 25.04 | 27.55 |
| (Weurope) | (0.10) | (0.03) | (2.60) | (0.83) | | (2.3) | (2.5) |
| Australia/ NewZealand | 10 | 11 | 66 | 20 | low | 29.77 | 36.00 |
| (AusNZl) | (0.97) | (1.09) | (5.20) | (1.84) | | (2.6) | (3.1) |
| Japan | 2 | -3 | 32 | 4 | low | 9.45 | 9.91 |
| | (0.20) | (-0.29) | (2.83) | (0.37) | | (0.9) | (0.9) |
| China | 9 | 12 | 43 | 139 | very high | 118.06 | 109.43 |
| | (0.83) | (1.17) | (3.66) | (9.08) | | (8.1) | (7.7) |
| Taiwan | 8 | 13 | 51 | 56 | very high | 68.37 | 70.20 |
| | (0.73) | (1.21) | (4.18) | (4.52) | | (5.3) | (5.5) |
| Other NICs | 9 | 8 | 66 | 23 | high | 41.37 | 44.72 |
| (OthNICs) | (0.84) | (0.73) | (5.18) | (2.09) | | (3.5) | (3.8) |
| Indonesia | 14 | 21 | 126 | 20 | low | 30.21 | 21.38 |
| | (1.31) | (1.96) | (8.47) | (1.82) | | (2.7) | (2.0) |
| Other Southeast Asia | 19 | 26 | 84 | 33 | low | 37.77 | 38.86 |
| (OthSEA) | (1.73) | (2.36) | (6.29) | (2.87) | | (3.3) | (3.3) |
| India | 17 | 23 | 73 | 116 | medium | 76.22 | 71.24 |
| | (1.59) | (2.11) | (5.65) | (8.01) | | (5.8) | (5.5) |
| Other South Asia | 23 | 33 | 77 | 40 | medium | 57.23 | 56.78 |
| (OthSoAsia) | (2.10) | (2.92) | (5.87) | (3.39) | | (4.6) | (4.6) |
| Brazil | 13 | 22 | 70 | -7 | high | 27.05 | 26.56 |
| | (1.26) | (2.04) | (5.46) | (-0.69) | | (2.4) | (2.4) |
| Other Latin Amer. | 18 | 23 | 89 | 27 | medium | 42.18 | 42.82 |
| (OthLatAm) | (1.63) | (2.11) | (6.55) | (2.41) | | (3.6) | (3.6) |
| Turkey | 15 | 22 | 104 | 35 | high | 57.09 | 55.65 |
| | (1.44) | (2.02) | (7.41) | (3.06) | | (4.6) | (4.5) |
| Other Middle East& | 27 | 37 | 109 | 11 | low | 32.96 | 34.18 |
| N.Africa (OthMENA) | (2.43) | (3.17) | (7.64) | (1.07) | | (2.9) | (3.0) |
| Economies in | 3 | 6 | 69 | 36 | low | 30.46 | 20.72 |
| | | | | | | | (*cont.*) |

Table 11.3 (cont.)

| | | Unskilled | Skilled | | | GDP This | World |
| Regions | Pop. | labor | labor | Capital | TFP | Study | Bank |
|---|---|---|---|---|---|---|---|
| Transition (EIT) | (0.27) | (0.06) | (5.37) | (3.09) | | (2.7) | (1.9) |
| South Africa | 23 | 29 | 162 | −1 | low | 39.12 | 32.30 |
| Customs | | | | | | | |
| Union | (2.06) | (2.59) | (10.11) | (−0.10) | | (3.4) | (2.8) |
| (SoAfrCU) | | | | | | | |
| Other | 33 | 37 | 88 | 25 | medium | 46.72 | 48.48 |
| Sub-Saharan | | | | | | | |
| Africa (OthSSA) | (2.87) | (3.19) | (6.50) | (2.23) | | (3.9) | (4.0) |
| Rest of World | 18 | 21 | 83 | 50 | medium | 52.97 | 49.46 |
| (ROW) | (1.65) | (1.90) | (6.22) | (4.15) | | (4.3) | (4.1) |

* The low, medium, high, and very high growth assumptions for total factor productivity (TFP) in manufacturing correspond to annual growth rates of 0.3%, 1%, 2%, and 3%, respectively, TFP growth in other sectors is based on a proportion of this rate. These proportions are: 1.4 (agriculture), 0.5 (services) and 0.0 (mining).

In manufacturing, the most important trade policy developments over the 1995–2005 period are likely to be the completion of manufacturing tariff cuts under the Uruguay Round, implementation of the Agreement on Textiles and Clothing (ATC), and the accession of China and Taiwan to the WTO. We have incorporated these changes by drawing on the work of Francois and Strutt (1999). We obtained China's August 1999 WTO offer from the World Bank and compared it to that country's applied tariffs for 1997. Where the bindings are lower, we took the offer as a change in policy; otherwise, we used the 1997 applied rates. Our treatment of Taiwan's offer is based on their announced target of 4 percent average tariffs for manufactures. We reduce all bilateral tariffs by a proportionate amount to achieve this target in the updated database. The columns (3) and (4) of table 11.4 report the resulting 2005 tariff averages for mining and manufacturing.

We anticipate that the ATC will have a large impact on trade because it accelerates the growth of quotas established under the Multifiber Agreement (MFA), culminating in their abolition at the end of the Uruguay Round implementation period. China and Taiwan, as non-Members of the WTO, remain constrained by the old MFA quotas, so their accession brings important changes in the textiles and apparel trade. While it is unlikely that their accession will allow China and Taiwan to completely eliminate their clothing quotas by the year 2005, we believe that this will follow soon after, and that it will largely be complete before

Table 11.4 *Average rates of protection, by region and sector, 2005*

| Region (1) | Food (%) (2) | Extract (%) (3) | Mnfcs (%) (4) | Constr (%) (5) | BusFin (%) (6) | Trd and Trn (%) (7) | GovSvces (%) (8) |
|---|---|---|---|---|---|---|---|
| North America | 5 | 0 | 3 | 10 | 8 | 69 | 34 |
| Western Europe | 8 | 0 | 1 | 18 | 9 | 84 | 40 |
| Aus/NZL | 4 | 0 | 7 | 24 | 7 | 91 | 31 |
| Japan | 58 | 0 | 2 | 30 | 20 | 71 | 32 |
| China | 18 | 3 | 20 | 41 | 19 | 96 | 42 |
| Taiwan | 41 | 3 | 4 | 5 | 3 | 93 | 36 |
| OthNICs | 21 | 2 | 2 | 10 | 2 | 82 | 37 |
| Indonesia | 5 | 0 | 8 | 10 | 7 | 85 | 43 |
| OthSEA | 25 | 2 | 12 | 18 | 5 | 88 | 40 |
| India | 40 | 3 | 35 | 62 | 13 | 96 | 41 |
| OthSoAsia | 37 | 19 | 20 | 46 | 20 | 92 | 41 |
| Brazil | 4 | 1 | 16 | 57 | 36 | 71 | 44 |
| OthLatAm | 9 | 7 | 10 | 26 | 5 | 79 | 43 |
| Turkey | 31 | 0 | 6 | 46 | 20 | 92 | 40 |
| OthMENA | 15 | 9 | 14 | 10 | 4 | 92 | 40 |
| EIT | 12 | 2 | 9 | 52 | 18 | 71 | 35 |
| SoAfrCU | 8 | 0 | 8 | 42 | 16 | 58 | 26 |
| OthSSA | 13 | 9 | 9 | 11 | 0 | 94 | 43 |
| ROW | 76 | 21 | 33 | 46 | 20 | 97 | 38 |

any cuts under a new round occur. For this reason, we include their abolition in our baseline analysis as well.

Trade in services and investment is growing by leaps and bounds, and international services transactions remain heavily protected in many countries. The columns (5)–(8) in table 11.4 estimate the tariff equivalents of protection for construction services, business and finance, trade and transport, and government services sectors.[3] Note from table 11.4 that business and construction services' trade barriers do not appear to be systematically related to the level of development. While India has the highest tariff equivalent in construction services, trade in business services appears to be more open than in Japan, if we control for income *per capita* and aggregate GDP. Japan's protection of construction services is also quite high, followed closely by Australia and New Zealand.

Unfortunately Francois' estimates omit the trade and transport sectors, which comprise a large share of world services trade. For these sectors, as well as for government services, we draw on the work of Hoekman (1995), developed to analyze the Uruguay Round.[4] In light of the limited specific commitments made under the Uruguay Round's services agreement, we assume that these levels of protection will persist in 2005. As can be seen from table 11.4, protection for transport services (maritime, rail, and air) is particularly high.

When we combine the macroeconomic shocks in table 11.3 with anticipated policy changes, we can simulate the model forward to the year 2005. While the evolution of the economy over this period is not our central focus, this simulation produces a few major structural changes. First, agriculture's share of developing-country exports is even lower in 2005 (figure 11.1), while further tariff cuts, and elimination of quotas on textiles and apparel, further accentuate the relative importance of manufacturing. The differential pattern in tariff cuts makes manufacturing (exports/output) more open, and agriculture slightly less open, in developing countries.

## Analyzing the impact of further cuts in protection

Our analysis of further trade liberalization stemming from a new round hinges on the way we approach that task. In the case of manufacturing, we simply cut *ad valorem* tariffs by 40 percent across-the-board for all sectors and regions. However, the situation is more complicated in agriculture and services. For agriculture, we model a cut in protection that achieves a 40 percent drop in the difference between the market price and the world price for all farm and food products.[5]

A similar set of complications arises in the case of producer subsidies. Here, negotiators seek to distinguish between "coupled" and "decoupled" support. As with TRQs, a proper assessment of reform will require modeling each policy explicitly. Furthermore, some would argue that there is no such thing as a de-coupled farm support policy, as any payments to farmers will tend to keep those workers farming, and thereby bolster production. (Once again, a comprehensive investigation of this issue is beyond the scope of the present study.) We will simply consider the consequences of a 40 percent reduction in the difference between producer prices – which include producer subsidies – and domestic market prices.[6]

The task of modeling cuts in protection is even more difficult for services. Since no physical product is being traded, modeling protection with tariff equiv-alents seems inappropriate. We assume instead that barriers to trade in ser-vices consume real resources on the part of firms attempting to gain access to protected markets, limiting the volume of services that can be delivered at a given cost. Liberalizing services trade can augment the services firms deliver for a given level of export effort, reducing the price of services in the do-mestic market. We capture this phenomenon by introducing a services import-augmenting technical change into the model.[7] We apply this approach to all ser-vices sectors, with the goal of reducing measured protection across-the-board by 40 percent.

Table 11.5 *Average protection (percent* ad valorem*) for food and agriculture, by sector, world-wide, 2005*

|  | Import tariff (%) | Export subsidy (%) | Production subsidy (%) |
|---|---|---|---|
| Foodgrains | 23 | 1 | 6 |
| Feedgrains | 97 | 4 | 11 |
| Oilseeds | 4 | 0 | 9 |
| Meatlstk | 17 | 8 | 2 |
| Dairy | 23 | 27 | 2 |
| Othagr | 11 | 0 | 0 |
| Othfood | 11 | 0 | 0 |
| Bevtobac | 18 | 0 | 0 |

*Liberalizing agriculture*

We turn first to the effects of liberalizing agricultural trade after a new round. Table 11.5 summarizes the global averages for protection and support levels on agricultural commodities after we apply a 40 percent across-the-board cut to 2005 levels. Very high rates of protection on large volumes of feed grain imports into East Asia produce an average global tariff-equivalent of 97 percent. This is followed by dairy, products, foodgrains, beverages and tobacco, and meat products, which have average tariffs around 20 percent. Average protection for other food and agricultural products is much lower.

Table 11.5 shows that dairy products are the most heavily subsidized exports on a global basis, with total subsidy equivalents amounting to 27 percent of world trade (at domestic prices). Meat and livestock products (8 percent), feedgrains (4 percent), and foodgrains (3 percent) follow. The share of global oilseed exports that are effectively subsidized is too small to generate a measurable average subsidy.

Cutting agricultural border prices by 40 percent unleashes a number of counterbalancing forces. First, lower levels of protection in importing regions tend to raise demand for imported food products, stimulating trade. However, cuts in implicit subsidies on exports tend to reduce supply from some of the major exporting regions. Thus the impact on world trade is ambiguous (table 11.6). Indeed, sizable cuts in export subsidies result in a decline in world dairy trade, driven by a drop in subsidized EU dairy exports. The biggest increases in global trade come in beverages and tobacco and other processed food products, where initial protection is very high and export subsidies do not play a role. World trade in other processed food products, other agriculture, and meat and livestock products also grows significantly.

Table 11.6 *Change in world trade volume (percent change)*

| Commodity | Experiment | | | |
|---|---|---|---|---|
| | AgrMkt40 | Agr40 | Emnfc40 | Svces40 |
| Foodgrains | 1.9 | −7.2 | 1.2 | 0.5 |
| Feedgrains | 4.1 | 1 | 0.7 | 0.5 |
| Oilseeds | 0.6 | 5.8 | 0.1 | 0.3 |
| Meatlstk | 5.6 | 4.9 | 1.1 | 0.3 |
| Dairy | −6.7 | −6.9 | 0.1 | 0.7 |
| Othagr | 8.3 | 8.1 | 0.5 | 0.4 |
| Othfood | 12.1 | 11.8 | 0.5 | −0.1 |
| Bevtobac | 27.5 | 27.6 | 0 | 0.8 |
| Extract | 0 | −0.1 | 1.8 | 0.3 |
| Textiles | 0.2 | 0.2 | 16.3 | 0.3 |
| Wearapp | 0.7 | 0.4 | 22.3 | 0.6 |
| Woodpaper | 0 | 0 | 3.6 | 0.4 |
| Pchemineral | 0 | −0.1 | 4.6 | 0.6 |
| Metals | 0 | 0 | 5.5 | 0.4 |
| Autos | 0.3 | 0.5 | 9.4 | 0.9 |
| Electronics | 0.1 | 0.1 | 4.1 | −0.1 |
| Othmnfcs | 0.1 | 0.2 | 5.2 | 0.2 |
| Houseutils | 0 | 0 | 0.1 | 1 |
| Tradetrans | 0.5 | 0.5 | 1.5 | 59.8 |
| Construction | 0.3 | 0.5 | 0.4 | 18.3 |
| Busfinance | 0.1 | 0.1 | 0.5 | 10.8 |
| Govservice | −0.1 | −0.1 | 0.8 | 39.2 |

The 40 percent reduction in market prices changes the regional food trade balances (table 11.7). Western Europe shows an increase of $23 billion in the value of food imports relative to exports, while the net food imports of Japan, China, the Middle East and North Africa, and India also grow. Natural net food exporters, including North and South America and Australia/New Zealand, show the largest increases in their food trade balance. However, Taiwan and other newly industrializing economies (NICs) also see their food exports grow more than imports. Taiwan, China increases its grain and oilseed imports while exporting more livestock products, while the changes for other NICs are driven by greater exports of processed food and beverages and tobacco. The availability of cheaper raw materials makes these exports more competitive.

Table 11.5 shows how simultaneous cuts in producer support might alter these findings. Producer payments are highest for the grains and oilseeds sectors, with producer subsidies for meat and livestock products, including dairy, averaging just 2–3 percent. (We treat these subsidies as output subsidies, ignoring the

Table 11.7 *Change in farm and food trade balance, by region and experiment ($ milion, 2005)*

| | By region and experiment ($ million in 2005) | | | |
|---|---|---|---|---|
| | Experiment | | | |
| Region (1) | AgrMkt40 (2) | Agr40 (3) | Emnfc40 (4) | Svces40 (5) |
| North America | 8883.47 | 10417 | 1820 | −681 |
| Western Europe | −23035.56 | −34895 | 264 | 2453 |
| Aus/NZL | 5912.16 | 6993 | 858 | 345 |
| Japan | −8776.18 | −9321 | −865 | 1404 |
| China | −4702.99 | −3008 | −3008 | −102 |
| Taiwan | 1448.07 | 1779 | −933 | 29 |
| OthNICs | 4849.37 | 5076 | −1632 | −2105 |
| Indonesia | 15.45 | 271 | −282 | −105 |
| OthSEA | 1036.08 | 956 | −371 | −810 |
| India | −1622.36 | −1218 | 220 | −24 |
| OthSoAsia | 97.72 | 323 | −527 | −204 |
| Brazil | 4248.84 | 5714 | 607 | 586 |
| OthLatAm | 6940.44 | 9660 | 1400 | −356 |
| Turkey | 68.66 | 53 | −263 | −692 |
| OthMENA | −2620.39 | −1357 | 834 | 425 |
| EIT | 563.75 | 1166 | 354 | −147 |
| SoAfrCU | 1123.38 | 786 | 104 | −72 |
| OthSSA | 2274.36 | 2791 | 289 | 62 |
| ROW | −1120.31 | −713 | 1010 | 289 |

recent proliferation of decoupled support payments. To the extent that programs are partially decoupled, these estimates overstate the change in output that results from cuts in producer subsidies. Future work will clearly need to refine this approach by modeling domestic programs on a country-by-country basis.)

Table 11.6 and table 11.7 report the changes in global export volume and regional food trade balances stemming from the 40 percent liberalization of both market and producer support in food and agriculture. Apart from Western Europe – where the change in food trade balance drops by an additional 50 percent over cuts in market price support only – the difference between this figure and the earlier one is relatively modest. The results also preserve the same broad ordering as under the more modest liberalization scenario.

Two factors determine the overall welfare gains from multilateral liberalization: a change in the efficiency with which any given economy uses its resources, and changes in countries' terms of trade. Table 11.8 reports the efficiency gain for each region with a 40 percent cut in support for both market price and producers, as a share of value added. Western Europe reaps the largest proportional gains, with the food sector's value added rising by more than 8 percent. But efficiency in the Australia/New Zealand region falls slightly, driven by a large increase in dairy exports for which the domestic price exceeds the world price (an implicit subsidy). However, the decline in efficiency in this region does not mean that real income falls, since we have not yet accounted for changes in the terms of trade.

To determine the effect of liberalization on regions' terms of trade, we can calculate the equivalent variation (EV) – the amount of money that could be taken away from consumers, at initial prices, while leaving them at the same level of utility. If a region's terms of trade improve – that is, export prices rise relative to import prices – then the EV gain will be larger than the efficiency gain. If the terms of trade deteriorate, then the opposite will be the case. Table 11.8 shows that India, with an efficiency/EV ratio of 137 percent, experiences a loss in its terms of trade under liberalization. The ratio for the rest of Southeast Asia is 101 percent, so we conclude that the terms of trade do not change. Despite the small efficiency loss in Australia/New Zealand, that region gains welfare owing to the rise in its export prices relative to the price paid for imports. Latin America, including Brazil, SSA, and North America also gain in terms of trade, which is not surprising given their net exports of food products. South Asia, China, and the Middle East/North Africa region experience the biggest terms of trade losses.

Considering the size of these efficiency and welfare gains relative to the size of the liberalized sector is useful, but comparing these gains with national income – or, better yet, with national expenditure – is best. Recall from table 11.1 that the share of agriculture and food in overall GDP is largest for South Asian economies and SSA (outside of South Africa). Thus, non-India South Asia is one of the biggest winners under liberalized agriculture, since the increase in efficiency per dollar of value added is high, as is the overall importance of this sector to the economy. Western's Europe's high efficiency gain per dollar of value added is diluted by the fact that the food sector represents only about 5 percent of GDP.

The global welfare impact of the 40 percent cut in agricultural protection is roughly $70 billion in 2005 (table 11.8). This contrasts with the somewhat smaller gains ($60 billion) when producer subsidies are left off the table. Most regions – notably Australia/New Zealand, Western Europe, and Latin America – are little changed or slightly better off under the more comprehensive protection cut. However, some regions benefit if producer support is unaltered. The Middle East and North Africa, in particular, suffer less erosion in their terms of trade under cuts in market price supports only.

Table 11.8 Welfare and efficiency gains due to 40 percent liberalization in agriculture, 2005

| Region | Agr40 experiment ratios (percentages) | | | Total EV by experiment ($million) | | | | |
|---|---|---|---|---|---|---|---|---|
| | Eff/$VA | Eff/EV | EV/Exp | Agr40 | AgrMkt40 | Emnfc40 | usFinSvces | T&Tsvces |
| North America | 9% | 11% | 0.035 | 3401 | 1436 | 3310 | 4517 | 52532 |
| Western Europe | 6% | 104% | 0.369 | 36959 | 27810 | 8180 | 8532 | 128593 |
| Aus/NZL | 6% | -12% | 0.377 | 1786 | 1348 | 207 | 209 | 8421 |
| Japan | 6% | 120% | 0.253 | 12552 | 13461 | 6607 | 2564 | 33358 |
| China | 6% | 1067% | 0.012 | 172 | 753 | 22593 | 826 | 8710 |
| Taiwan | 4% | 143% | 0.060 | 265 | 295 | 3288 | 83 | 6072 |
| OthNICs | 3% | 115% | 0.333 | 2672 | 2996 | 5270 | 612 | 23228 |
| Indonesia | 2% | 1183% | 0.002 | 6 | 26 | 792 | 270 | 1474 |
| Oth SEA | 2% | 101% | 0.465 | 1931 | 1247 | 2631 | 393 | 11092 |
| India | 1% | 137% | 0.200 | 1058 | 927 | 3084 | 19 | 3989 |
| OthSoAsia | 1% | 118% | 0.852 | 1176 | 1181 | 1645 | 9 | 2213 |
| Brazil | 1% | 64% | 0.245 | 1988 | 1683 | 4491 | 457 | 3625 |
| OthLatAm | 1% | 48% | 0.360 | 3055 | 2366 | 1449 | 652 | 8611 |
| Turkey | 1% | 123% | 0.142 | 338 | 332 | 619 | 70 | 3524 |
| OthMENA | 0% | -15% | -0.202 | -1506 | -718 | 1074 | 231 | 16667 |
| EIT | 0% | 142% | 0.033 | 301 | 282 | 1391 | 1865 | 10265 |
| SoAfrCU | 0% | 46% | 0.080 | 129 | 54 | 283 | 128 | 1897 |
| OthSSA | 0% | 31% | 0.194 | 436 | 529 | 249 | 30 | 4496 |
| ROW | -1% | 115% | 0.741 | 2601 | 2611 | 2399 | 137 | 3798 |
| World | | | | 69320 | 58619 | 69564 | 21604 | 332565 |

*Liberalizing non-agricultural sectors*

Liberalizing non-agricultural trade is likely to affect trade in food products through four mechanisms. First, manufactures and services provide important inputs to agriculture and food processing, particularly in high-income economies. By lowering the cost of imported, non-food inputs to agriculture, liberalization may have an important impact on food production.

Liberalizing non-agricultural sectors can also affect agriculture through the factor markets. If non-farm liberalization expands manufacturing, the cost of farm labor will rise. This can work in opposition to the first mechanism, or reinforce it where liberalization leads to an exodus of labor and capital from a non-competitive manufacturing sector.

The third mechanism operates through constraints on consumers' budgets. If liberalization lowers the price of manufactures and services, consumers may substitute away from food products. Finally, there is a direct interaction between liberalization of manufacturing and food trade through the trade balance. When a country cuts its manufacturing tariffs and imports rise, exports of other commodities – including agriculture – may also rise.

To understand the latter mechanism, consider what happens when a country unilaterally cuts its non-agricultural protection. Since we hold net capital inflows and outflows constant, increased imports of non-food products must be offset by increased exports of all products. Thus there must be a real depreciation of currency in the region. This translates into lower prices for labor and capital as well as for intermediate inputs, making it easier to export food products. Lower-priced manufactures also encourage consumers to substitute away from food products, so domestic demand falls, adding to export availability. On the other hand, if other regions also liberalize their manufactures or services and thus increase exports, it may become harder for food producers to export. Thus it is useful to consider what actually happens to the balance of trade for food products under alternative liberalization scenarios.

Table 11.7 reports the changes in regional food trade balances when barriers to manufacturing and services are cut by 40 percent. We can compare these results with the changes in food trade balances under agricultural liberalization alone (columns (2) and (3)) to assess the relative importance of policies that directly and indirectly impinge on a region's food trade. As noted earlier, Western Europe and Japan show very strong deterioration in their food trade balance under agricultural liberalization, while the Americas, Australia, and New Zealand offset these changes with growing surpluses. The direct effect of agricultural liberalization on the food trade balance far outweighs the indirect effect of non-agricultural liberalization in these regions.

The improvements in the food trade balance of the Asian NICs that occur under agricultural liberalization are counteracted by a decline in the food trade balance under manufacturing liberalization. The 40 percent cut in manufacturing tariffs stimulates demand for Asian exports of manufactures, drawing resources away from agriculture and food production. However, the direct effects of agricultural liberalization still dominate the non-agricultural effect.

In Indonesia and "other South Asia," the food trade balance declines under a 40 percent liberalization across all sectors, as the impact of manufacturing liberalization on the food trade balance dominates the direct effect of agricultural liberalization. In "other Southeast Asia," liberalized manufactures and services also override the direct effect of agricultural liberalization, and the food trade balance declines.

In the Middle East and North Africa, India, and "the Rest of the World," food trade balances deteriorate under agricultural liberalization. However, in the Middle East and North Africa, the trade balances for manufacturing and services deteriorate under non-agricultural liberalization, and the combined effect increases the food trade balance marginally. In China, as with the other East Asian economies, manufacturing liberalization has a very strong negative effect on the food trade balance, in this case reinforcing the direct effect. Thus China sees a decline of about $6 billion in its annual food trade balance as of 2005 under multisectoral liberalization.

The global gains from a 40 percent cut in mining and manufactures tariffs are similar to those offered by agricultural reforms – roughly $70 billion. However, their distribution across regions is rather different, with relatively more of the gains accruing to developing countries. The case of China is particularly striking. That country's welfare gains under agricultural liberalization are quite small – $172 million – but rise to more than $22 billion under cuts in manufacturing tariffs. In fact, with the sole exception of SSA, all the developing regions gain more under tariff cuts on manufacturing than under agricultural liberalization.

Gains from liberalizing services are much more speculative, given the difficulty of measuring protection in this sector. We have broken the services experiment into two parts. The 40 percent cuts in protection for business services and construction, based on the work of Francois (1999), show relatively modest gains totaling $22 billion in 2005, given the still limited trade in these services. The second part – representing the trade and transport sector – represents a large share of global trade in services. Although the results are quite speculative, the potential global gains are very large indeed: $332 billion in 2005. Accurately modeling restrictions on trade and investment in services sectors should be a high priority for future research.

### The implications for developing countries

These results show that further liberalization of agriculture could yield substantial benefits for the global economy by 2005 – totaling some $70 billion for 40 percent cuts in both market price support and domestic producer subsidies. These gains shrink to $60 billion if domestic subsidies are left unaltered. Overall, these welfare improvements are comparable to the gains that could be obtained from similar cuts in manufacturing tariffs.

However, as Hertel and Martin (1999) have pointed out, the distribution of these gains is quite different. Developing countries make the biggest absolute cuts in manufacturing tariffs because their initial tariffs are higher, but they also enjoy the lion's share of the gains. Because the rates of protection for agriculture are highest in the industrialized economies, in contrast, they are the ones to capture the majority of the gains from liberalized food markets. However, when measured relative to initial income, developing countries, too, include some of the biggest winners from cuts in agricultural protection.

Cuts in agricultural protection as opposed to that of manufacturing and services have the strongest impact on regional food trade balances. However, non-agricultural reforms dominate and reverse the change in the food trade balance for some regions, notably Southeast Asia and parts of South Asia, as well as the Middle East and North Africa. Both sets of multilateral reforms lead to a substantial decline – totaling $6 billion in 2005 – in China's aggregate food trade balance.

All these estimates should be viewed as subject to revision as better information and techniques for estimating protection levels become available. Several areas require immediate attention. Agricultural protection in non-OECD countries is poorly documented. The initiative between Agriculture Canada, the European Commission, the OECD, the USDA/ERS, and UNCTAD will rectify this. More work is needed to represent "decoupled" OECD policies in this type of quantitative framework, although some progress has already been made (Frandsen and Bach, 1998).

Explicit modeling of tariff rate quotas will also be important for future analysis, since the distribution of the associated rents is becoming more significant (see Elbehri *et al.*, 1999, chapter 10 in this volume). Finally, while we have reported on some innovative work aimed at coming to grips with protection in the services sector, much more research will be needed to understand the implications of liberalizing that sector. Such work will have significance not only for trade in services but also for trade in food and agriculture, as the latter depends on services as a production input as well as a mechanism for transporting and adding value to food products.

# Appendix   How we approached the model

To project regional economies to 2005, we employ the widely used GTAP model of global trade, which includes a relatively sophisticated consumer demand system designed to capture price and income responsiveness across countries.

We model trade flows using the Armington approach, which differentiates products by origin.[8] The standard GTAP trade elasticities are reported in column (2) of table 11.2.[9] The column (3) in table 11.2 reports the elasticity of substitution between domestic and imported goods, which have been obtained by doubling the standard GTAP values. This adjustment brings us much closer to the recent estimates by Liu, Arndt, and Hertel (2000) for farm and food products but results in excessively high trade elasticities for fuels and mining products, basic manufactures, and autos compared with the Liu, Arndt, and Hertel (2000) estimates. Thus, the higher trade elasticities would seem to be justified in this study, although non-agricultural trade flows may be excessively responsive to changes in protection.

We employ the simplistic but robust assumption of perfect competition and constant returns to scale in production activities.[10] While this is likely to effectively characterize much of the world's agricultural production, departures from perfect competition are well documented in manufacturing sectors. How is this likely to bias our results? Hertel (1994) explores the general equilibrium implications for agriculture of potential "pro-competitive" effects of trade liberalization on manufacturing markups. He shows that, by ignoring these effects, we are likely to overstate the adjustment in agriculture owing to non-agriculture tariff reductions in a small, open economy. Of course, in a multiregion analysis these interactions become more complex. Nevertheless by ignoring the potential downward adjustment in manufacturing markups in the presence of more intense foreign competition, we may be overstating the impact on agricultural output of liberalizing developing country manufacturing.

Following earlier projections work with the GTAP model (Gehlhar, Hertel, and Martin, 1994; Hertel et al., 1996; Anderson et al., 1997), we assemble external projections for population, skilled and unskilled labor, investment, and capital stock. When combined with assumptions about likely productivity growth rates, this allows us to predict the level and composition of GDP in 2005, as well as trade flows, input use, and a wide range of other variables. This snapshot of the world economy in 2005 provides the starting point for our simulations.

Table 11.3 reports our forecasts for the fundamental drivers of global economic change over the 1995–2005 period. We projected population and unskilled labor by cumulating the average growth rates between 1995 and the 2005. We based the projections of skilled labor in developing countries on forecasts of the growth in tertiary educated labor (Ahuja and Filmer, 1995), and in developed countries on World Bank forecasts. We projected growth rates of physical capital using the Harberger-style perpetual inventory method – that is, by adding investment net of depreciation to update the capital stock in each year. We obtained data for initial physical capital stock for 1995, as well as annual forecasts of gross domestic investment, from the World Bank.

Our projections of productivity growth in total factors vary by sector and region, which we group into four categories according to their assumed rate of annual productivity growth in manufactures. These range from low productivity growth (0.33 percent/year), to medium (1 percent/year), and high (2 percent/year), with a final category of very high (3 percent/year) reserved for China and Taiwan. The latter two countries seem to be growing at rates that cannot be explained with normal rates of productivity growth.[11] By combining these factors of proportion (1.4, 0.5, and 0.0) with growth rates in total factor productivity (TFP), we obtain region- and sector-specific productivity forecasts for the 1995–2005 period.

A difficult aspect of constructing such projections concerns the rate at which natural resources are depleted – or augmented through new discoveries. Rather than attempt to estimate changes in natural resource endowments, we target a particular rate of change in the prices of agricultural and other natural resource-based commodities. Grilli and Yang (1988) report an average rate of price decline for metals in the twentieth century of about 0.8 percent/year, while average grain prices have fallen about 0.3 percent/year. We allow the model to select a rate of augmentation of farmland and natural resources in agriculture and mining that continues these downward trends in prices throughout the 1995–2005 period.

To gauge the reasonableness of our projections, columns (4) and (5) in table 11.3 compare our projected GDP growth rates over this period to those from the World Bank's International Economic Analysis and Prospects Division. By and large, they are quite close. This is hardly surprising, since the two studies share many of the same basic assumptions. However, our projected growth rates for the South Africa Customs Union, economies in transition (EIT), and Indonesia are substantially higher than the World Bank's. The only way the World Bank forecasts for these three regions could be achieved in our framework is to have negative productivity growth rates, or substantial increases in unemployment. We have opted not to do either of these, so our forecasts are higher. Our forecast for China's GDP growth is slightly higher than that of the Bank, but the difference is negligible when viewed in terms of annual growth rates.

### Notes

1. This means that wholesale, retail, and transportation margins are not included. Compared to consumer expenditures at consumer prices, the budget shares for physical products are too low, while the budget share for services is too high.
2. Since China and Taiwan's offers are not linked to the Uruguay Round base year, it would make sense to include their agricultural cuts in our baseline. However, we do not have solid estimates of their current protection rates and, at least in China's case, some of the bindings are clearly well above current protection levels. Therefore, we do not change their agricultural protection rates in the baseline simulation either.

3. These are taken from Francois (1999), who estimates a gravity model of services trade using US data on bilateral services trade. The dependent variable in this model is US exports, and the explanatory variables are the log of *per capita* income and GDP. A dummy variable is used for exports from the United States to Western Hemisphere nations. Francois adopts Singapore and Hong Kong as free-trade benchmarks, and judges predicted imports from the United States relative to these economies. He attributes discrepancies to protectionist policies, and obtains the tariff equivalents of these policies by assuming a constant elasticity of demand function. While this approach is relatively simple, it results in some very reasonable estimates of protection for the construction and business services sectors.

4. These protection measures are much cruder and rely on critical assumptions about the level of prohibitive tariffs, as well as the relationship between observed coverage ratios and the implied tariff equivalent of protection for different sectors. The Hoekman protection estimates for the transport sector are quite high, while the protection estimates for wholesale and retail trade are much lower. While the former sector is the dominant one from a trade in services perspective, we seek to err in the direction of caution by cutting Hoekman's transport estimates in half in order to represent composite protection in the trade and transport sector of our model.

5. In the case of TRQs, we assume that this occurs through an expanded quota or a cut in the out-of-quota tariff, or a combination of the two. Elbehri *et al.* (1999, see chapter 10 in this volume) show that different approaches to reform have different implications for the distribution of quota rents – and hence welfare – between exporters and importers. We simply assume that, like tariff revenues, all quota rents accrue to (and are lost by) importers.

6. This general approach to modeling cuts in agricultural support is also compatible with the way the GTAP database has incorporated protection for farm and food products. GTAP relies on price comparisons to assess the degree of border protection (market price support), and on producer subsidies to construct producer prices. Since these measures of protection are not instrument-specific, it makes sense to think of liberalization in the same summary fashion. In fact, since the version 4 database incorporates the domestic–world price wedges on both the import and export sides, any reduction in support must logically reduce both the import tariff and export subsidy equivalents at the same rate. This is the route that we take.

7. We set the rate at which this technical change occurs according to the tariff-equivalent estimates of Francois (1999) and Hoekman (1995), as discussed above. For example, in the case of India's imports of construction services, Francois has estimated that prices must be 62 percent above their free-trade level if one is to explain the relatively low share of imports in this market. Therefore, in our 40 percent services' trade liberalization experiment, we will consider the impact of import-augmenting technical change that reduces the effective price of construction imports to Indian firms by 40 percent of 62 percent, which equals 24.8 percent.

8. They are assumed to substitute imperfectly for one another to form a composite import aggregate which, in turn, substitutes imperfectly for domestically produced goods. In this way, the model is able to track bilateral trade flows. Validation efforts with the GTAP model (Gehlhar, Hertel, and Martin, 1994; Gehlhar, 1997; Coyle *et al.*, 1998) show that it is able to track, to a reasonable degree, some of the major changes in trade patterns over the past two decades.

9. They are obtained from Jomini *et al.* (1991), who conducted a literature search in addition to performing some of their own estimation work for New Zealand. These elasticities were designed to apply to medium-run analyses. However, work by Liu Arndt, and Hertel (2000) highlights the sensitivity of these trade elasticities to the length of run involved in the simulation. Those authors formally estimate the Armington parameters in the GTAP model for a $10 \times 10$ aggregation of the version 4 database. Their nine-year estimates of the elasticity of substitution between imports and domestic goods are reported in the third column of Table 11.2. (The correspondence with commodity definitions used in the current study is only approximate.) Comparing these estimates to the entries in column (2), we see that in most cases the standard GTAP parameters are too small over the nine-year period. This contrast is particularly striking for processed food products, where the Liu Arndt, and Hertel. (2000) estimate is nearly three times as large as the GTAP value.

10. Alternative versions of the GTAP model feature imperfect competition (Francois, 1998), but these demand additional information and are unstable for projections.

11. Sectoral variation in productivity growth builds on the econometric work of Bernard and Jones (1996). They find that the annual rate of productivity growth over the 1970–87 period in OECD agriculture was about 40 percent faster than that of manufacturing. Similarly, growth in TFP for services was about one-half that for manufacturing, while they did not measure significant productivity growth in mining over this period.

## References

Ahuja, V. and D. Filmer, 1995. "Educational Attainment in Developing Countries: New Estimates and Projections Disaggregated by Gender," World Bank Policy Research Working Paper, 1489, Washington, DC, July

Anderson, K., B. Dimaranan, T. W. Hertel, and W. Martin, 1997. "Asia-Pacific Food Markets and Trade in 2005: A Global, Economy-Wide Perspective," *Australian Journal of Agricultural and Resource Economics*, 41(1), 19–44

Bernard, A. and C. Jones, 1996. "Productivity Growth Across Industries and Countries: Time Series Theory and Evidence," *Review of Economics and Statistics*, 78(1), 135–46

Coyle, W., M. Gehler, T. W. Hertel, Z. Wang, and W. Yu, 1998. "Understanding the Determinants of Structural Change in World Food Markets," *American Journal of Agricultural Economics*, 80(5), 1051–61

Elbehri, A., M. D. Ingco, T. W. Hertel, and K. Pearson, 1999. "Agricultural Liberalization in the New Millennium," paper presented at the World Bank Conference on Agriculture and the New Trade Agenda from a Development Perspective, 1–2 October, Geneva

Francois, J. F., 1998. "Scale Economies and Imperfect Competition in the GTAP Model," GTAP Technical Paper, 14, Center for Global Trade Analysis, Purdue University, www.agecon.purdue.edu/gtap/techpapr

    1999. "A Gravity Approach to Measuring Services Protection," Erasmus University, manuscript

Francois, J. F. and A. Strutt, 1999. "Post Uruguay Round Tariff Vectors for GTAP Version 4," Global Trade Analysis Project, Purdue University, Mimeo

Frandsen, S. and C. Bach, 1998. "European Integration and the Common Agricultural Policy," SJFI (Danish Institute of Agricultural and Fisheries), Economics Working Paper, 1/98

Freeman, F., Melanie, J., Roberts, I., Vanzetti, D., Tielu, A., and Beutre, B., 2000. *The Impact of Agricultural Trade Liberalisation on Developing Countries*, ABARE Research Report 2000.6, Canberra: Australian Bureau of Agricultural and Resource Economics

Gehlhar, M. J., 1997. "Historical Analysis of Growth and Trade Patterns in the Pacific Rim: An Evaluation of the GTAP Framework," in T. W. Hertel (ed.), *Global Trade Analysis: Modeling and Applications*, Cambridge and New York: Cambridge University Press, chapter 14

Gehlhar, M. J., T. W. Hertel, and W. Martin, 1994. "Economic Growth and the Changing Structure of Trade and Production in the Pacific Rim," *American Journal of Agricultural Economics*, 76, 1101–10

Grilli, E. and M. Yang, 1988. "Primary Commodity Prices, Manufactured Goods Prices, and the Terms of Trade of Developing Countries: What the Long Run Shows," *World Bank Economic Review*, 2(1)

Hathaway, D. E. and M. D. Ingco, 1995. "Agricultural Liberalization and the Uruguay Round," in W. Martin and L. A. Winters (eds.), *The Uruguay Round and the Developing Economies*, World Bank Discussion Paper, 307, Washington, DC

Hertel, T. W., 1994. "The Procompetitive Effects of Trade Policy Reform in a Small, Open Economy," *Journal of International Economics*, 36, 391–411

Hertel, T. W. and W. Martin, 1999. "Developing Country Interests in Liberalizing Manufactures Trade," paper presented to the World Bank's Conference on Developing Countries and the Millennium Round, 19–20 September, Geneva

Hertel, T. W., W. Martin, K. Yanagishima, and B. Dimaranan, 1996. "Liberalizing Manufactures Trade in a Changing World Economy," in W. Martin and A. Winters (eds.), *The Uruguay Round and the Developing Countries*, Cambridge and New York: Cambridge University Press

Hoekman, B., 1995. "Assessing the General Agreement on Trade in Services," in W. Martin and L. A. Winters (eds.), *The Uruguay Round and the Developing Economies*, World Bank Discussion Paper 307, Washington, DC

Ingco, M. D., 1996. "Tariffication in the Uruguay Round: How Much Liberalization?" *The World Economy*, 19(4), 425–47

Jomini, P., J. E. Zeitsch, R. McDougall, A. Welsh, S. Brown, J. Hambley, and J. Kelly, 1991. *SALTER: A General Equilibrium Model for the World Economy*, 1, "Model Structure, Database and Parameters," Canberra: Australian Industry Commission

Laird, S., 1999. "Patterns of Protection and Approaches to Liberalization," paper presented to the CEPR Workshop on New Issues in the World Trading System, Centre for Economic Policy Research, London.

Liu, J., T. C. Arndt, and T. W. Hertel, 2000. "Estimating Trade Elasticities for Use in Global, General Equilibrium Analysis," paper submitted to the 2000 Conference on Empirical Investigations in International Economics, University of Colorado, Boulder

McDougall, R. A., A. Elbehri, and T. P. Truong (eds.), 1998. "Global Trade, Assistance, and Protection: The GTAP 4 Data Base," Center for Global Trade Analysis, Purdue University

# 12 Modeling the effects on agriculture of protection in developing countries

*Dean A. DeRosa*

## Introduction

Developing countries have clear but differing interests in greater reform of international trade in agriculture. In low-income countries, agriculture still accounts for a substantial proportion of domestic output, and especially employment (see table 12.1).

In many developing countries, achieving sufficient domestic production plus imports of foodstuffs to sustain a healthy population – popularly termed "food security" – is of considerable concern, often, it is alleged, in the face of highly fluctuating commodity prices and uncertain export earnings.[1] Indeed, food security concerns often give rise to market interventions and trade measures to promote domestic food production and control exports and imports of essential food commodities such as cereal grains.

However, further multilateral liberalization of agricultural trade and domestic economic policies would promote wider global integration of markets for agricultural goods. If such liberalization of trade and economic policies stabilized and even raised world prices for agricultural goods, internationally competitive producers in developing countries would benefit. What's more, both low-income and more advanced developing countries have considerable comparative advantage in a number of non-food agricultural goods and light manufactures. They could export such goods to finance food imports, offsetting periodic or persistent shortfalls in domestic food production.[2]

Direct gains to consumers in developing countries are more problematic, depending upon the extent to which they benefit from artificially low prices for foodstuffs owing to production and export subsidies in industrial countries, and from international food aid. Policy-makers in low-income food-deficit countries (LIFDC) are concerned about the international price-raising effects on agriculture of multilateral trade reforms. However, in other developing countries that maintain high levels of protection (and hence high prices) for domestic farm production, consumers would be expected to gain from agricultural trade

Table 12.1 *Developing countries and agriculture, 1996*

| Developing countries | Population (millions) | Land area Total (000 km²) | Land area Arable % | Education (Index^a) | Per capita income (US $) | Share of agriculture in GDP % | Share of agriculture in Empl.^b % | Share of agriculture in Exports % | Share of agriculture in Imports % |
|---|---|---|---|---|---|---|---|---|---|
| *By income level* | | | | | | | | | |
| Low-income | 3,236 | 39,294 | ... | 38 | 490 | 27 | 69 | 16 | 14 |
| Middle-income | 1,598 | 59,884 | ... | 140 | 2,590 | 11 | 32 | ... | ... |
| Lower-middle | 1,125 | 39,310 | ... | ... | 1,740 | 12 | 36 | ... | ... |
| Upper-middle | 473 | 20,574 | ... | ... | 4,600 | 9 | 22 | 22 | 10 |
| *By region* | | | | | | | | | |
| East Asia & Pacific | 1,732 | 15,869 | 40 | 71 | 890 | 20 | 69 | 12 | 11 |
| Europe, Cen. Asia | 478 | 23,864 | ... | ... | 2,200 | 11 | 23 | ... | ... |
| L. Am., Caribbean | 486 | 20,064 | 43 | 133 | 3,710 | 10 | 26 | 27 | 12 |
| MENA^c | 276 | 10,972 | 31 | 130 | 2,070 | 14 | 35 | ... | ... |
| South Asia | 1,266 | 4,781 | 65 | 62 | 380 | 28 | 64 | 19 | 12 |
| SSA | 596 | 23,628 | 41 | 28 | 490 | 24 | 68 | ... | ... |
| *Memorandum items:* | | | | | | | | | |
| Developing countries | 4,835 | 99,178 | 41 | 124 | 1,190 | 15 | 58 | ... | ... |
| Industrial countries | 919 | 30,951 | 42 | 305 | 25,870 | ... | 6 | 10 | 11 |
| World | 5,754 | 130,129 | 41 | ... | 5,130 | ... | 49 | 11 | 12 |

*Sources:* World Bank (1998); DeRosa (2000).

^a Secondary enrollment rate plus five times the tertiary enrollment rate, both calculated in their respective age cohorts, 1989.

^b 1990.

^c Middle East and North Africa; share of agriculture in GDP refers to 1993.

liberalization, not unlike "protected" consumers of food and other agricultural goods in major industrial countries.

A wider issue for many developing countries – and motivating this chapter – are the implications for agriculture of border measures that protect not only domestic agriculture but also domestic industry. Against the backdrop of import substitution policies, developing countries have widely discriminated against the agriculture sector. Trade policies that promote industrialization divert capital, labor, and other productive resources from agriculture to industry. Tariff walls and NTBs such as import quotas raise the domestic price of capital-intensive manufactures and non-traded goods compared with labor-intensive agricultural goods. These conditions contribute to an overvalued (real) exchange rate.[3]

Inappropriate trade and other macroeconomic policies that produce overvalued exchange rates have undermined the substantial contributions that an efficient agricultural sector can make to economic growth in developing countries. The agricultural sector can contribute to growth directly, through greater production and exports, and indirectly, by raising demand in farm and rural communities for industrial goods and services.[4]

In a seminal study of agricultural pricing policies in developing countries, Krueger, Schiff, and Valdés (1988) (hereafter, KSV) investigated the "bias against agriculture" in a broad sample of developing economies from 1960 to 1985.[5] They found that the impact on agricultural prices of indirect policy interventions – especially protection of domestic industry – greatly outweighed the impact of direct price interventions in the agriculture sector.

Since the KSV study, emerging-market and other developing countries worldwide have pursued significant trade liberalization and other macroeconomic policy reforms, placing in some question the continued significance of the KSV results.[6] However, in the context of a new round of WTO negotiations, the issue of continued macroeconomic policy biases against agriculture is important. If an appreciable bias against agriculture remains in many developing countries, negotiations limited to agricultural trade will prove substantially less beneficial than broader multilateral negotiations to liberalize trade in industrial goods as well.

This chapter considers the bias against agriculture implied by the level and structure of protection in developing countries today. After a brief look at agriculture and trade in developing countries, the chapter reviews changes in protection in developing countries between 1985 and 1996, based on data gathered by the United Nations Conference on Trade and Development (UNCTAD). This information is then used in a partial equilibrium model, similar to that employed by KSV, to determine whether developing countries continue to maintain significant economy-wide policy biases against agriculture. The last section of the chapter summarizes the main findings.

## Developing countries in world agriculture and trade

*Agriculture*

Developing countries account for nearly two-thirds of total agricultural production (table 12.2, lower panel). East Asian and Pacific countries are the largest producing region in the developing world, accounting for 25 percent of world output, followed by Latin American and Caribbean countries (15 percent), and South Asian countries (14 percent). Low-income countries and LIFD countries account for nearly 39 percent and 44 percent of world agricultural production, respectively.[7] By comparison, major industrial countries account for 31 percent of world agricultural production.

Production of primary food commodities and products dominates production of processed foods and agricultural raw materials, in both industrial and developing countries. The most prominent categories of agricultural production are live animals, cereal grains, and vegetables (primary foods), prepared vegetables (processed foods), and natural fibers (agricultural raw materials). In most categories of agricultural commodities and products, developing countries account for between 60 percent and 75 percent of world production.

Wider differences in production of various agricultural goods are apparent by region in table 12.2. For instance, although Latin American and Caribbean countries account for about 15 percent of world agriculture and nearly 30 percent of world output of coffee, tea, and spices, they account for only about 6 percent of world production of cereal grains. Similarly, although Sub-Saharan African countries account for only 5 percent of world agricultural production, they account for over 20 percent of world output of coffee, tea, and spices, and over 15 percent of world output of agricultural raw materials.

Low-income countries and LIFD countries account for shares of cereal grains and other staples, such as vegetables, similar to their shares in total world production of agricultural products – about 40 percent. However, such comparisons may be misleading because they do not consider that low-income countries account for more than 50 percent of the world population, and hence for a large share of world demand for primary foods (table 12.1).

One significant change between the mid-1980s (table 12.2, upper panel) and the mid-1990s (table 12.2, lower panel) is the substantially higher growth of agriculture in developing countries than in industrial countries. During the decade ending in 1996, agriculture in developing countries grew by 36 percent (3.1 percent per annum), compared with 5 percent (0.5 percent per annum) in the major industrial countries. This experience compares favorably to the average rate of population growth in low- and middle-income countries – 1.8 percent per annum. The growth in agricultural production appears to stem mainly from Asia and Sub-Saharan Africa: agricultural output grew by 46 percent in South Asia, 33 percent in East Asia, and 35 percent in Sub-Saharan Africa.[8]

Table 12.2 *World agricultural production, 1985–1986 and 1995–1996*

| Category | World | Industrial countries | Developing countries | East Asian & Pacific countries | European & Central Asian countries | Latin American & Caribbean countries | Middle East & North Africa countries | South Asian countries | SSA countries | Low-income countries | LIFD countries |
|---|---|---|---|---|---|---|---|---|---|---|---|
| | Metric tons (million) | | | Share in world production (%) | | | | | | | |
| | | | | 1985–6 (average values) | | | | | | | |
| Food products[a] | 5,495.1 | 1,897.9 | 3,076.2 | 20.3 | 9.2 | 15.2 | 4.7 | 11.4 | 4.7 | 31.1 | 36.6 |
| Primary foods[a] | 4,131.1 | 1,573.2 | 2,118.5 | 22.8 | 10.4 | 8.6 | 5.3 | 9.8 | 5.1 | 32.8 | 36.7 |
| Live animals[b] | 3,953.6 | 1,011.3 | 2,597.8 | 18.9 | 7.1 | 14.2 | 8.7 | 14.7 | 10.8 | 42.9 | 46.5 |
| Meat products | 156.7 | 77.1 | 60.0 | 17.9 | 12.2 | 11.3 | 3.4 | 3.0 | 3.1 | 21.2 | 23.6 |
| Dairy products | 516.4 | 275.3 | 136.3 | 1.5 | 19.7 | 7.4 | 4.6 | 11.1 | 2.3 | 15.1 | 17.3 |
| Cereal grains | 1,828.7 | 714.1 | 930.8 | 26.3 | 9.8 | 5.9 | 4.1 | 11.8 | 3.0 | 36.0 | 39.1 |
| Vegetables | 974.7 | 266.6 | 604.0 | 32.0 | 10.6 | 6.8 | 6.5 | 7.3 | 9.6 | 42.6 | 47.3 |
| Fruit & nuts | 382.0 | 131.3 | 239.7 | 15.9 | 2.6 | 17.8 | 11.6 | 8.9 | 8.9 | 28.0 | 34.4 |
| Sugar & honey | 101.5 | 34.4 | 58.7 | 13.4 | 7.8 | 27.8 | 4.2 | 8.8 | 4.2 | 19.3 | 32.0 |
| Animal feed stuffs | 106.7 | 53.6 | 48.5 | 15.5 | 4.0 | 18.5 | 2.2 | 7.6 | 1.8 | 21.4 | 23.2 |
| Oil seeds | 64.3 | 20.8 | 40.3 | 31.3 | 4.5 | 12.8 | 2.8 | 9.1 | 7.1 | 31.7 | 40.8 |
| Processed foods | 1,364.0 | 324.7 | 957.8 | 12.9 | 5.6 | 35.1 | 3.0 | 16.1 | 3.5 | 26.1 | 36.1 |
| Fats & oils | 64.6 | 27.4 | 33.8 | 23.3 | 5.0 | 12.0 | 3.1 | 9.7 | 4.5 | 23.3 | 29.4 |
| Cereal preparations | n.a. | n.a. | n.a. | n.a. | n.a. | n.a. | n.a. | n.a. | n.a. | n.a. | n.a. |
| Prepared vegs. | 1,221.9 | 258.8 | 893.6 | 12.4 | 5.3 | 37.6 | 3.0 | 17.1 | 3.4 | 26.6 | 37.3 |
| Cereal preparations | n.a. | n.a. | n.a. | n.a. | n.a. | n.a. | n.a. | n.a. | n.a. | n.a. | n.a. |
| Coffee, tea, spices | 13.7 | 0.9 | 13.1 | 15.8 | 0.0 | 35.0 | 2.8 | 21.0 | 21.1 | 50.0 | 59.7 |
| Beverages | 30.7 | 23.0 | 3.2 | 0.8 | 14.6 | 8.8 | 0.8 | 0.0 | 0.0 | 0.8 | 1.0 |
| Other products | 33.1 | 14.7 | 14.1 | 23.0 | 13.0 | 10.0 | 4.1 | 3.6 | 2.0 | 23.6 | 28.0 |

(cont.)

Table 12.2 (*cont.*)

| Category | World | Industrial countries | Developing countries | East Asian & Pacific countries | European & Central Asian countries | Latin American & Caribbean countries | Middle East & North Africa countries | South Asian countries | SSA countries | Low-income countries | LIFD countries |
|---|---|---|---|---|---|---|---|---|---|---|---|
| *Ag. raw materials*[a] | *38.6* | *7.5* | *27.5* | *34.3* | *8.8* | *8.8* | *5.2* | *19.5* | *4.0* | *46.8* | *58.4* |
| Tobacco & prods. | 6.5 | 1.7 | 4.5 | 40.7 | 5.9 | 10.7 | 3.9 | 9.4 | 3.9 | 47.4 | 49.6 |
| Hides & skins | 0.3 | 0.2 | 0.0 | 0.0 | 5.0 | 6.7 | 3.3 | 5.0 | 0.4 | 5.4 | 6.1 |
| Natural rubber | 4.5 | 0.0 | 4.5 | 85.9 | 0.0 | 1.5 | 0.0 | 7.3 | 5.3 | 19.0 | 45.1 |
| Natural fibers | 27.2 | 5.6 | 18.5 | 24.6 | 11.0 | 9.6 | 6.5 | 24.1 | 3.8 | 51.8 | 63.3 |
| Other raw mats. | 0.0 | 0.0 | 0.0 | 0.8 | 20.7 | 17.6 | 7.4 | 0.0 | 26.8 | 26.8 | 34.7 |
| *All ag. products*[a] | *5,533.7* | *1,905.4* | *3,103.8* | *20.4* | *9.2* | *15.1* | *4.7* | *11.4* | *4.7* | *31.2* | *36.7* |
| | | | | | *1995–96 (average values)* | | | | | | |
| *Food products*[a] | *6,448.1* | *1,981.6* | *4,176.3* | *25.0* | *4.2* | *15.5* | *5.1* | *14.2* | *5.4* | *38.7* | *43.7* |
| *Primary foods*[a] | *4,795.1* | *1,621.9* | *2,908.0* | *27.9* | *5.3* | *9.4* | *5.8* | *11.7* | *6.2* | *40.9* | *44.8* |
| Live animals[b] | 4,310.9 | 956.2 | 3,159.5 | 24.0 | 1.9 | 13.9 | 9.5 | 15.9 | 12.6 | 51.1 | 54.3 |
| Meat products | 203.8 | 91.3 | 102.8 | 28.7 | 4.5 | 12.0 | 3.6 | 3.5 | 3.0 | 31.5 | 34.2 |
| Dairy products | 537.4 | 273.9 | 192.9 | 2.6 | 12.3 | 9.6 | 5.6 | 16.1 | 2.8 | 21.9 | 24.3 |
| Cereal grains | 1,983.6 | 709.7 | 1,166.3 | 30.3 | 5.2 | 6.4 | 4.7 | 14.0 | 3.7 | 42.8 | 46.1 |
| Vegetables | 1,221.7 | 273.0 | 873.5 | 38.9 | 6.1 | 6.3 | 6.6 | 7.6 | 12.1 | 53.4 | 57.6 |
| Fruit & nuts | 481.4 | 139.4 | 346.7 | 23.4 | 0.0 | 19.5 | 11.2 | 9.8 | 8.4 | 35.9 | 42.4 |
| Sugar & honey | 124.1 | 39.5 | 81.5 | 15.2 | 2.1 | 26.6 | 4.0 | 16.9 | 3.4 | 27.0 | 35.3 |
| Animal feed stuffs | 150.8 | 69.4 | 81.0 | 17.5 | 0.1 | 21.2 | 2.0 | 11.4 | 1.9 | 27.0 | 29.4 |
| Oil seeds | 92.3 | 25.6 | 63.3 | 34.7 | 3.2 | 13.2 | 2.8 | 11.5 | 6.9 | 32.8 | 43.6 |

| Processed foods | 1,653.1 | 359.7 | 1,268.4 | 16.5 | 1.2 | 33.0 | 3.0 | 21.4 | 3.1 | 32.6 | 40.5 |
|---|---|---|---|---|---|---|---|---|---|---|---|
| Fats & oils | 93.4 | 35.7 | 56.7 | 29.1 | 0.9 | 12.5 | 3.1 | 11.8 | 4.4 | 25.8 | 35.0 |
| Cereal preparations | n.a. | n.a. | n.a. | n.a. | n.a. | n.a. | n.a. | n.a. | n.a. | n.a. | n.a. |
| Prepared vegs. | 1,468.2 | 287.4 | 1,161.6 | 15.0 | 1.0 | 35.6 | 3.0 | 22.9 | 2.9 | 32.8 | 40.9 |
| Prepared fruits | n.a. | n.a. | n.a. | n.a. | n.a. | n.a. | n.a. | n.a. | n.a. | n.a. | n.a. |
| Coffee, tea, spices | 16.6 | 0.8 | 16.3 | 20.3 | 0.0 | 28.8 | 2.6 | 23.1 | 23.3 | 57.2 | 65.9 |
| Beverages | 26.3 | 19.7 | 2.9 | 1.5 | 13.6 | 8.8 | 0.8 | 0.0 | 0.0 | 3.1 | 3.7 |
| Other products | 48.6 | 16.0 | 30.9 | 44.5 | 3.4 | 8.9 | 4.4 | 4.1 | 1.9 | 44.9 | 48.8 |
| *Ag. raw materials*[a] | 41.5 | 9.2 | 31.1 | 36.6 | 2.6 | 7.0 | 5.7 | 20.9 | 5.2 | 49.8 | 59.2 |
| Tobacco & prods. | 6.8 | 1.5 | 5.4 | 48.1 | 0.0 | 10.6 | 4.3 | 10.1 | 6.5 | 60.1 | 61.0 |
| Hides & skins | 0.4 | 0.2 | 0.1 | 0.0 | 24.7 | 4.5 | 3.2 | 6.2 | 0.4 | 9.9 | 14.1 |
| Natural rubber | 6.5 | 0.0 | 6.5 | 84.6 | 0.0 | 1.7 | 0.0 | 9.2 | 4.5 | 22.9 | 47.8 |
| Natural fibers | 27.6 | 7.4 | 19.0 | 23.0 | 3.9 | 7.3 | 7.3 | 26.7 | 5.0 | 54.2 | 62.0 |
| Other raw mats. | 0.1 | 0.0 | 0.1 | 0.7 | 5.1 | 10.2 | 64.5 | 0.0 | 16.5 | 16.5 | 81.4 |
| *All ag. products*[a] | 6,489.6 | 1,990.8 | 4,207.4 | 25.1 | 4.2 | 15.4 | 5.1 | 14.2 | 5.4 | 38.8 | 43.8 |
| | (17.3) | (4.5) | (35.6) | (44.0) | (−46.4) | (19.6) | (25.2) | (45.6) | (35.0) | (45.8) | (39.9) |

*Notes:* See table 12A.2 for definitions of product categories. Source does not report statistics for all items in categories. For instance, tobacco and related products covers only tobacco leaves. Statistics for European and Central Asian countries are computed as residuals. Values in parentheses are percentage changes during 1985–96.

[a] Excludes live animals.

[b] Unit of measure for live animals is millions of head (billion head for some subcategories, such as poultry and other fowl).

*Source:* FAO (1999).

Moreover, led by remarkable agricultural growth in China[9] and the South Asian countries, total agricultural output grew by 46 percent in low-income countries and 40 percent in LIFD countries during the same period. Of particular analytical interest is whether the robust agricultural growth of these low-income countries can be traced to the sectoral and macroeconomic reforms many of these countries have pursued since the late 1980s.

*Trade and comparative advantage*

World trade in agriculture attained an average annual value of $428 billion in 1995–6 (table 12.3). It accounts for the largest share of world trade in primary products, and for nearly 10 percent of world trade in all goods.

Primary foods ($219 billion) are the largest component of trade in agriculture, followed by processed foods ($141 billion), and agricultural raw materials ($68 billion). Reflecting higher value added and possibly more liberal trade arrangements, trade in manufactures ($3,633 billion) dominates trade in agriculture by a sizable margin. As seen in table 12.3, trade in agriculture compares favorably to trade in chemicals ($468 billion) and trade in iron and steel ($147 billion). However, trade in agriculture is dwarfed by trade in the major categories of manufactures, namely, machinery and equipment ($1,877 billion) and labor-intensive miscellaneous manufactures ("other manufactures," $1,141 billion).

Developing countries are net exporters of primary foods, and net importers of processed foods (table 12.3, third panel). The major industrial countries, which account for the largest proportion of trade in agriculture, exhibit the reverse profile: they are net importers of primary foods and net exporters of processed foods. During 1995–6, both groups of countries conducted nearly balanced trade in agricultural raw materials.

Data on revealed comparative advantage (RCA) in table 12.3 provide an interesting although crude look at the relative advantages (and disadvantages) of developing regions and groups in international trade. These results stem not only from relative endowments of production factors but also from relative demand. The results also reflect countries' trade and other economic policies.[10]

The RCA statistics show that although developing countries as a group have little or no comparative advantage in exporting primary or processed foods, a number of specific regions and income groups *are* competitive exporters (RCA greater than 1.20). These include a number of lower-middle-income countries in Europe and Central Asia, Latin America and the Caribbean, and the Middle East and North Africa (primary foods), and in Europe and Central Asia, South Asia, and Sub-Saharan Africa (processed foods). The RCA statistics also indicate that a number of low- and lower-middle-income countries enjoy substantial comparative advantage in agricultural raw materials, especially in

## Table 12.3 World trade and Revealed Comparative Advantage (RCA), 1995–1996 (average values)

| Category | World | Industrial Countries | Developing Countries | East Asia & Pacific | Eur., Central Asia | Latin Am. & Carib. | Middle East & N. Afr. | South Asia | SSA | Low-income | Lower-middle-income | Upper-middle-income | High-income |
|---|---|---|---|---|---|---|---|---|---|---|---|---|---|
| | US dollars (billion) | | | Developing countries, by region and income group — Share in world trade in category (%) | | | | | | | | | |
| *Exports* | | | | | | | | | | | | | |
| *Primary products* | *1,041.3* | *746.0* | *295.3* | *15.5* | *3.3* | *4.5* | *3.0* | *1.3* | *0.8* | *4.4* | *7.8* | *6.5* | *9.7* |
| Primary foods | 218.7 | 152.0 | 66.8 | 12.9 | 4.2 | 6.1 | 5.4 | 0.9 | 1.1 | 3.7 | 11.4 | 8.4 | 7.1 |
| Processed foods | 141.4 | 105.5 | 35.9 | 9.6 | 4.5 | 5.1 | 3.3 | 1.7 | 1.2 | 4.2 | 7.6 | 6.9 | 6.7 |
| Agr. raw mats. | 67.7 | 42.2 | 25.5 | 24.6 | 3.0 | 4.4 | 3.4 | 1.4 | 0.9 | 6.9 | 9.0 | 6.8 | 15.0 |
| Crude fertilizers | 68.0 | 47.6 | 20.4 | 17.4 | 4.0 | 3.2 | 3.2 | 1.6 | 0.6 | 6.3 | 8.3 | 6.1 | 9.3 |
| Mineral fuels | 313.4 | 226.8 | 86.6 | 15.8 | 3.3 | 4.5 | 1.8 | 1.6 | 0.7 | 3.9 | 6.7 | 6.3 | 10.7 |
| Non-ferrous ores | 99.3 | 69.5 | 29.8 | 21.0 | 1.8 | 3.3 | 2.1 | 1.4 | 0.4 | 4.3 | 5.0 | 6.5 | 14.2 |
| *Manufactures* | *3,632.6* | *2,490.9* | *1,141.6* | *19.8* | *2.3* | *5.0* | *2.6* | *0.8* | *0.9* | *4.0* | *6.3* | *8.3* | *12.9* |
| Chemicals | 468.4 | 311.8 | 156.5 | 18.1 | 2.9 | 6.6 | 3.1 | 1.5 | 1.2 | 5.8 | 8.1 | 9.0 | 10.7 |
| Iron & Steel | 146.9 | 88.5 | 58.5 | 25.7 | 3.2 | 4.3 | 4.4 | 1.4 | 0.8 | 6.6 | 12.2 | 7.7 | 13.4 |
| Machinery & Eq. | 1,876.7 | 1,270.9 | 605.8 | 21.3 | 2.0 | 5.1 | 2.4 | 0.6 | 0.9 | 3.8 | 6.4 | 9.0 | 13.2 |
| Other manufs. | 1,140.8 | 819.8 | 321.0 | 17.2 | 2.5 | 4.3 | 2.7 | 0.7 | 0.8 | 3.4 | 4.6 | 6.9 | 13.2 |
| *All products* | *4,802.4* | *3,325.9* | *1,476.5* | *18.8* | *2.6* | *4.8* | *2.7* | *1.0* | *0.9* | *4.1* | *6.6* | *7.9* | *12.1* |
| *Imports* | | | | | | | | | | | | | |
| *Primary products* | *1,041.3* | *595.7* | *445.6* | *12.1* | *6.3* | *11.3* | *7.6* | *1.0* | *4.4* | *7.6* | *15.5* | *16.6* | *3.2* |
| Primary foods | 218.7 | 158.9 | 59.9 | 6.8 | 2.8 | 12.8 | 1.7 | 1.6 | 1.8 | 6.3 | 7.9 | 11.6 | 1.6 |
| Processed foods | 141.4 | 90.6 | 50.9 | 13.7 | 2.1 | 13.1 | 1.5 | 1.2 | 4.4 | 9.7 | 10.4 | 13.6 | 2.2 |
| Agr. raw mats. | 67.7 | 42.2 | 25.5 | 18.3 | 2.7 | 7.4 | 2.2 | 2.1 | 5.0 | 12.3 | 13.8 | 8.4 | 3.2 |
| Crude fertilizers | 68.0 | 39.6 | 28.4 | 9.6 | 6.8 | 16.3 | 2.6 | 2.1 | 4.3 | 6.9 | 14.9 | 18.0 | 1.9 |
| Mineral fuels | 313.4 | 120.8 | 192.6 | 13.1 | 9.3 | 10.2 | 21.8 | 0.2 | 6.8 | 8.0 | 23.8 | 25.5 | 4.2 |
| Non-ferrous ores | 99.3 | 62.4 | 36.9 | 7.8 | 12.9 | 11.0 | 0.7 | 0.3 | 4.5 | 4.3 | 15.1 | 14.2 | 3.6 |

(cont.)

Table 12.3 (*cont.*)

| | | | | | | | | | | | Developing countries, by region and income group | | |
| Category | World | Industrial Countries | Developing Countries | East Asia & Pacific | Eur., Central Asia | Latin Am. & Carib. | Middle East & N. Afr. | South Asia | SSA | Low-income | Lower-middle-income | Upper-middle-income | High-income |
|---|---|---|---|---|---|---|---|---|---|---|---|---|---|
| *Manufactures* | 3,632.6 | 2,650.1 | 982.5 | 19.0 | 2.0 | 3.3 | 1.3 | 1.0 | 0.4 | 7.3 | 4.0 | 6.1 | 9.7 |
| Chemicals | 468.4 | 389.3 | 79.0 | 8.5 | 2.8 | 2.7 | 1.9 | 0.6 | 0.4 | 3.0 | 3.4 | 4.7 | 5.7 |
| Iron & steel | 146.9 | 101.5 | 45.5 | 10.0 | 10.5 | 6.3 | 1.4 | 0.7 | 2.0 | 6.8 | 8.6 | 9.8 | 5.8 |
| Machinery & eq. | 1,876.7 | 1,447.9 | 428.8 | 18.0 | 1.0 | 3.1 | 0.5 | 0.2 | 0.1 | 3.3 | 2.5 | 6.4 | 10.7 |
| Other manufs. | 1,140.8 | 711.4 | 429.3 | 26.3 | 2.2 | 3.5 | 2.3 | 2.7 | 0.6 | 15.6 | 6.2 | 5.6 | 10.2 |
| *All products* | 4,802.4 | 3,343.5 | 1,458.9 | 17.3 | 3.0 | 5.1 | 2.7 | 1.0 | 1.3 | 7.2 | 6.6 | 8.4 | 8.2 |

US dollars (billions)

Net Exports

| | | | | | | | | | | | | | |
|---|---|---|---|---|---|---|---|---|---|---|---|---|---|
| *Primary products* | 0.0 | 150.3 | −150.3 | 34.7 | −31.3 | −71.4 | −47.8 | 2.9 | −37.3 | −33.3 | −80.0 | −104.5 | 67.5 |
| Primary foods | 0.0 | −6.9 | 6.9 | 13.4 | 3.2 | −14.5 | 8.1 | −1.7 | −1.5 | −5.7 | 7.6 | −7.1 | 12.0 |
| Processed foods | 0.0 | 15.0 | −15.0 | −5.8 | 3.4 | −11.3 | 2.5 | 0.7 | −4.5 | −7.8 | −4.0 | −9.6 | 6.4 |
| Agr. raw mats. | 0.0 | 0.0 | 0.0 | 4.3 | 0.2 | −2.0 | 0.8 | −0.5 | −2.8 | −3.6 | −3.2 | −1.1 | 8.0 |
| Crude fertilizers | 0.0 | 8.0 | −8.0 | 5.3 | −1.9 | −8.9 | 0.4 | −0.4 | −2.5 | −0.4 | −4.5 | −8.1 | 5.0 |
| Mineral fuels | 0.0 | 106.0 | −106.0 | 8.5 | −19.0 | −18.0 | −62.7 | 4.3 | −19.1 | −12.6 | −53.6 | −59.9 | 20.2 |
| Non-ferrous ores | 0.0 | 7.1 | −7.1 | 13.1 | −11.1 | −7.6 | 1.3 | 1.2 | −4.0 | 0.0 | −10.0 | −7.7 | 10.5 |
| *Manufactures* | 0.0 | −159.1 | 159.1 | 27.0 | 12.2 | 61.2 | 48.8 | −8.8 | 18.8 | −117.1 | 82.1 | 179.2 | 114.9 |
| Chemicals | 0.0 | −77.5 | 77.5 | 45.0 | 0.5 | 18.3 | 5.4 | 4.4 | 3.9 | 112.9 | 21.7 | 119.9 | 23.0 |
| Iron & steel | 0.0 | −13.0 | 13.0 | 23.1 | −10.7 | −3.0 | 4.3 | 1.0 | −1.8 | −0.2 | 5.3 | −3.1 | 11.1 |
| Machinery & eq. | 0.0 | −176.9 | 176.9 | 62.4 | 19.0 | 36.8 | 35.4 | 8.8 | 14.5 | 118.7 | 73.5 | 148.1 | 46.6 |
| Other manufs. | 0.0 | 108.3 | −108.3 | −103.6 | 3.4 | 9.0 | 3.6 | −23.0 | 2.2 | −138.4 | −18.4 | 14.4 | 34.2 |
| *All products* | 0.0 | −17.6 | 17.6 | 72.3 | −20.5 | −10.6 | 0.7 | −2.7 | −21.5 | −147.6 | 0.6 | −23.6 | 188.2 |

$RCA^a$

| | | | | | | | | | | | | |
|---|---|---|---|---|---|---|---|---|---|---|---|---|
| *Primary products* | n.a. | 1.03 | 0.92 | 0.82 | 1.28 | 0.92 | 1.12 | 1.35 | 0.92 | 1.06 | 1.18 | 0.83 | 0.80 |
| Primary foods | 1.00 | 0.99 | 0.69 | 1.64 | 1.26 | 2.00 | 0.89 | 1.19 | 0.91 | 1.72 | 1.06 | 0.58 | |
| Processed foods | 1.08 | 0.83 | 0.51 | 1.75 | 1.06 | 1.21 | 1.76 | 1.35 | 1.03 | 1.15 | 0.86 | 0.55 | |
| Agr. raw mats. | 0.90 | 1.23 | 1.31 | 1.18 | 0.91 | 1.27 | 1.43 | 0.98 | 1.69 | 1.37 | 0.85 | 1.24 | |
| Crude fertilizers | 1.01 | 0.98 | 0.92 | 1.54 | 0.67 | 1.18 | 1.65 | 0.70 | 1.53 | 1.25 | 0.77 | 0.77 | |
| Mineral fuels | 1.05 | 0.90 | 0.84 | 1.28 | 0.93 | 0.66 | 1.62 | 0.81 | 0.96 | 1.01 | 0.80 | 0.88 | |
| Non-ferrous ores | 1.01 | 0.98 | 1.12 | 0.70 | 0.67 | 0.77 | 1.49 | 0.50 | 1.06 | 0.76 | 0.82 | 1.17 | |
| *Manufactures* | n.a. | 0.99 | 1.02 | 1.05 | 0.90 | 1.03 | 0.98 | 0.83 | 1.01 | 0.98 | 0.95 | 1.04 | 1.06 |
| Chemicals | 0.96 | 1.09 | 0.96 | 1.14 | 1.36 | 1.14 | 1.58 | 1.38 | 1.40 | 1.22 | 1.13 | 0.88 | |
| Iron & steel | 0.87 | 1.29 | 1.37 | 1.24 | 0.89 | 1.62 | 1.45 | 0.91 | 1.61 | 1.84 | 0.97 | 1.10 | |
| Machinery & eq. | 0.98 | 1.05 | 1.13 | 0.79 | 1.05 | 0.88 | 0.64 | 1.01 | 0.92 | 0.97 | 1.13 | 1.09 | |
| Other manufs. | 1.04 | 0.92 | 0.92 | 0.96 | 0.89 | 0.99 | 0.75 | 0.88 | 0.84 | 0.70 | 0.87 | 1.09 | |
| *All products* | n.a. | 1.00 | 1.00 | 1.00 | 1.00 | 1.00 | 1.00 | 1.00 | 1.00 | 1.00 | 1.00 | 1.00 | 1.00 |

*Notes:* See table 12A.2 for definitions of product categories. Data exclude intra-EU trade.

[a] RCA is computed as share of a category in a region or group's total trade relative to the share of the category in world trade. Values substantially greater (less) than unity indicate comparative advantage (disadvantage) in international trade.

*Source:* United Nations Statistical Office, *Commodity Trade Database* (1999), and author's calculations.

East Asia and the Pacific, the Middle East and North Africa, and South Asia. By comparison, the data suggest that the major industrial countries as a group have no comparative advantage in primary foods (RCA equals 1.00), a modest comparative advantage in processed foods (1.08), and a modest comparative disadvantage in agricultural raw materials (0.90).

Table 12.4 (primary products and manufactures) and table 12.5 (agriculture) also illustrate the significance of North–South trade, with the exception of intra-regional trade in East Asia and the Pacific (as well as trade among major industrial countries). That is, the major industrial countries consistently appear to provide developing countries with the largest markets for their exports and the largest source of supply for their imports. Comparative advantage, especially the relative abundance of low-wage labor, tropical land, and other agricultural resources in many low- and middle-income countries, might well explain this finding. It might also encourage developing countries to focus on exchanging trade concessions with major industrial countries during a "Millennium Round" of WTO negotiations.

However, possibilities for expanded South–South trade should not be entirely discounted. The simple comparative advantage calculations reported in table 12.3 suggest that prominent developing and developed exporting nations might join forces to negotiate reduced barriers to food imports in populous developing countries with comparative disadvantages in agriculture. In other words, although these statistics point to the prominence of North–South trade, the statistics might be biased by economic policies that discourage greater South–South trade. Sectoral or macroeconomic policies may restrict imports directly, or distort trade indirectly through their influence on intermediate variables such as the (real) exchange rate. These restrictions might mask comparative advantage and other economic fundamentals upon which new WTO negotiations might base significant expansion of not only North–South trade but also South–South trade.

### Protection in developing countries

Against the background of new WTO negotiations, this chapter focuses on protection in developing countries and its direct and indirect impacts on agriculture. Data on the recent evolution of protection in developing countries are drawn from the UNCTAD Trade Analysis and Information System (UNCTAD 1994, 1999). This information consists of (unweighted) averages of *ad valorem* tariffs and frequency ratios of quantitative restrictions, licensing requirements, decreed customs valuation measures, and other NTBs, circa 1985 and 1995.[11] The analysis covers a large sample of developing countries grouped by income levels and region. For comparison, the analysis also includes major industrial countries.[12]

Table 12.4 *Directions of world trade in primary products and manufactures, 1995–1996 (average values, billions US dollars)*

Imports by reporting countries in region or group

| Exports by partner countries in region or group | Primary products | | | | | | | | (Agricultural goods) | | | | | | | |
|---|---|---|---|---|---|---|---|---|---|---|---|---|---|---|---|---|
| | EAP | ECA | LAC | MENA | SA | SSA | OECD | WORLD | EAP | ECA | LAC | MENA | SA | SSA | OECD | WORLD |
| East Asia & Pacific (EAP) | 50.8 | 1.2 | 1.1 | 1.8 | 3.4 | 1.0 | 67.1 | 126.3 | 16.0 | 1.0 | 0.7 | 1.5 | 1.9 | 0.7 | 24.7 | 46.6 |
| Europe & Central Asia (ECA) | 4.0 | 15.9 | 0.3 | 2.4 | 0.3 | 0.1 | 42.5 | 65.5 | 0.6 | 4.6 | 0.1 | 0.7 | 0.1 | 0.0 | 4.7 | 10.8 |
| Lat. America, Carib. (LAC) | 10.1 | 2.0 | 18.6 | 2.3 | 0.7 | 0.6 | 83.6 | 117.8 | 3.4 | 1.7 | 8.9 | 1.9 | 0.5 | 0.4 | 34.5 | 51.4 |
| Mid. East & N. Afr. (MENA) | 18.6 | 0.6 | 2.1 | 3.9 | 2.1 | 0.7 | 51.4 | 79.3 | 0.3 | 0.4 | 0.1 | 0.7 | 0.1 | 0.1 | 5.7 | 7.3 |
| South Asia (SA) | 3.0 | 0.6 | 0.2 | 0.7 | 0.7 | 0.3 | 5.4 | 10.8 | 1.8 | 0.5 | 0.2 | 0.6 | 0.6 | 0.2 | 2.8 | 6.7 |
| SSA | 5.1 | 0.7 | 1.1 | 1.1 | 1.8 | 1.9 | 34.1 | 45.8 | 1.2 | 0.5 | 0.2 | 0.5 | 0.3 | 0.7 | 10.0 | 13.5 |
| Industrial countries (OECD) | 69.4 | 13.2 | 23.1 | 19.4 | 4.6 | 4.0 | 461.9 | 595.7 | 35.2 | 8.8 | 13.4 | 12.9 | 1.7 | 2.4 | 217.2 | 291.7 |
| Apparent world (WORLD) | 161.0 | 34.2 | 46.4 | 31.5 | 13.7 | 8.5 | 746.0 | 1,041.3 | 58.5 | 17.6 | 23.6 | 18.7 | 5.2 | 4.6 | 299.7 | 427.9 |
| | LIC | LMIC | UMIC | HIC | … | … | OECD | WORLD | LIC | LMIC | UMIC | HIC | … | … | OECD | WORLD |
| Low-income countries (LIC) | 5.2 | 9.1 | 4.9 | 12.1 | … | … | 47.3 | 78.6 | 2.2 | 6.8 | 2.8 | 5.3 | … | … | 18.7 | 35.9 |
| Lower mid-income (LMIC) | 6.7 | 14.2 | 13.5 | 11.4 | … | … | 115.5 | 161.1 | 4.2 | 5.7 | 7.1 | 3.6 | … | … | 29.7 | 50.3 |
| Upper mid-income (UMIC) | 10.0 | 15.8 | 14.5 | 24.9 | … | … | 107.5 | 172.6 | 4.2 | 5.7 | 7.1 | 3.6 | … | … | 29.7 | 50.3 |
| High income dev. (HIC) | 5.2 | 4.5 | 2.5 | 7.2 | … | … | 13.8 | 33.2 | 0.6 | 0.7 | 0.4 | 1.3 | … | … | 5.8 | 8.7 |
| Industrial countries (OECD) | 18.3 | 37.6 | 32.8 | 45.1 | … | … | 461.9 | 595.7 | 9.5 | 24.2 | 18.6 | 22.1 | … | … | 217.2 | 291.7 |
| Apparent world (WORLD) | 45.3 | 81.1 | 68.2 | 100.7 | … | … | 746.0 | 1,041.3 | 18.8 | 41.7 | 32.6 | 35.1 | … | … | 299.7 | 427.9 |

Table 12.4 (cont.)

**Manufactures**

| | EAP | ECA | LAC | MENA | SA | SSA | OECD | WORLD |
|---|---|---|---|---|---|---|---|---|
| East Asia & Pacific (EAP) | 260.4 | 4.8 | 13.9 | 8.8 | 6.4 | 3.9 | 393.8 | 691.9 |
| Europe & Central Asia (ECA) | 9.6 | 11.8 | 1.1 | 3.0 | 1.0 | 0.2 | 45.6 | 72.2 |
| Lat. America, Carib. (LAC) | 5.7 | 0.2 | 24.9 | 0.7 | 0.7 | 0.4 | 87.2 | 119.9 |
| Mid. East & N. Afr. (MENA) | 5.1 | 0.9 | 0.7 | 2.2 | 1.2 | 0.5 | 36.2 | 46.7 |
| South Asia (SA) | 6.3 | 0.5 | 0.6 | 1.3 | 1.0 | 0.8 | 27.6 | 38.1 |
| SSA | 1.7 | 0.0 | 0.5 | 0.2 | 0.2 | 2.3 | 8.8 | 13.8 |
| Industrial countries (OECD) | 430.0 | 66.2 | 139.4 | 79.4 | 18.8 | 24.5 | 1,891.8 | 2,650.1 |
| Apparent world (WORLD) | 718.9 | 84.4 | 181.1 | 95.5 | 29.2 | 32.6 | 2,490.9 | 3,632.6 |

| | LIC | LMIC | UMIC | HIC | | OECD | WORLD |
|---|---|---|---|---|---|---|---|
| Low-income countries (LIC) | 4.7 | 12.8 | 9.4 | 84.0 | ... | 152.7 | 263.5 |
| Lower-mid-income (LMIC) | 7.9 | 13.8 | 8.6 | 19.7 | ... | 95.6 | 145.7 |
| Upper-mid-income (UMIC) | 6.0 | 13.7 | 18.9 | 29.8 | ... | 152.7 | 221.1 |
| High-income dev. (HIC) | 39.2 | 25.4 | 29.2 | 60.3 | ... | 198.1 | 352.2 |
| Industrial countries (OECD) | 88.6 | 162.2 | 234.2 | 273.3 | ... | 1,891.8 | 2,650.1 |
| Apparent world (WORLD) | 146.4 | 227.8 | 300.3 | 467.0 | ... | 2,490.9 | 3,632.6 |

**All goods**

| | EAP | ECA | LAC | MENA | SA | SSA | OECD | WORLD |
|---|---|---|---|---|---|---|---|---|
| East Asia & Pacific (EAP) | 316.0 | 6.2 | 15.2 | 10.6 | 10.2 | 4.9 | 467.1 | 830.1 |
| Europe & Central Asia (ECA) | 13.9 | 31.0 | 1.4 | 5.4 | 1.4 | 0.3 | 90.4 | 143.8 |
| Lat. America, Carib. (LAC) | 15.9 | 2.2 | 43.6 | 3.1 | 1.4 | 1.0 | 175.6 | 242.7 |
| Mid. East & N. Afr. (MENA) | 23.8 | 1.7 | 2.7 | 6.1 | 3.4 | 1.2 | 90.0 | 128.8 |
| South Asia (SA) | 9.4 | 1.1 | 0.8 | 1.9 | 1.9 | 1.1 | 33.2 | 49.2 |
| SSA | 8.5 | 0.7 | 1.7 | 1.6 | 1.9 | 4.2 | 45.6 | 64.2 |
| Industrial countries (OECD) | 515.0 | 80.5 | 166.7 | 100.8 | 26.5 | 30.0 | 2,424.0 | 3,343.5 |
| Apparent world (WORLD) | 902.4 | 123.3 | 232.1 | 129.5 | 46.6 | 42.6 | 3,325.9 | 4,802.4 |

| | LIC | LMIC | UMIC | HIC | | OECD | WORLD |
|---|---|---|---|---|---|---|---|
| Low-income countries (LIC) | 10.2 | 21.9 | 14.5 | 96.5 | ... | 201.1 | 344.2 |
| Lower-mid-income (LMIC) | 14.8 | 31.1 | 22.4 | 31.3 | ... | 217.1 | 316.7 |
| Upper-mid-income (UMIC) | 16.4 | 29.7 | 33.8 | 56.2 | ... | 268.0 | 404.0 |
| High-income dev. (HIC) | 44.9 | 30.9 | 33.2 | 69.2 | ... | 215.8 | 393.9 |
| Industrial countries (OECD) | 110.4 | 203.7 | 276.5 | 328.8 | ... | 2,424.0 | 3,343.5 |
| Apparent world (WORLD) | 196.7 | 317.3 | 380.4 | 582.1 | ... | 3,325.9 | 4,802.4 |

*Source:* United Nations Statistical Office, *Commodity Trade Database* (1999).
*Notes:* See Table 12A.2 for definitions of product categories; data exclude intra-EU trade.

Table 12.5 *Directions of world trade in agriculture, 1995–1996 (average values, billions US dollars)*

**Imports by reporting countries in region or group**

**Primary foods**

| Exports by partner countries in region or group | EAP | ECA | LAC | MENA | SA | SSA | OECD | WORLD |
|---|---|---|---|---|---|---|---|---|
| East Asia & Pacific (EAP) | 6.0 | 0.5 | 0.1 | 0.4 | 0.2 | 0.3 | 7.4 | 14.9 |
| Europe & Central Asia (ECA) | 0.2 | 2.7 | 0.0 | 0.5 | 0.0 | 0.0 | 2.5 | 6.1 |
| Lat. America, Carib. (LAC) | 1.9 | 1.3 | 4.5 | 1.4 | 0.1 | 0.2 | 18.4 | 27.9 |
| Mid. East & N. Afr. (MENA) | 0.1 | 0.2 | 0.0 | 0.4 | 0.0 | 0.0 | 2.8 | 3.6 |
| South Asia (SA) | 1.3 | 0.2 | 0.0 | 0.4 | 0.4 | 0.2 | 1.1 | 3.6 |
| SSA | 0.2 | 0.1 | 0.1 | 0.2 | 0.1 | 0.3 | 2.9 | 3.9 |
| Industrial countries (OECD) | 18.5 | 4.3 | 8.5 | 8.4 | 1.0 | 1.4 | 116.8 | 158.9 |
| Apparent world (WORLD) | 28.2 | 9.2 | 13.4 | 11.8 | 1.9 | 2.3 | 152.0 | 218.7 |
| | LIC | LMIC | UMIC | HIC | … | … | OECD | WORLD |
| Low-income countries (LIC) | 1.2 | 4.2 | 1.4 | 1.8 | … | … | 5.2 | 13.8 |
| Lower-mid-income (LMIC) | 1.0 | 2.7 | 1.8 | 1.2 | … | … | 10.5 | 17.2 |
| Upper-mid-income (UMIC) | 0.7 | 2.9 | 3.8 | 1.3 | … | … | 16.7 | 25.4 |
| High-income dev. (HIC) | 0.1 | 0.2 | 0.1 | 0.3 | … | … | 2.8 | 3.5 |
| Industrial countries (OECD) | 5.1 | 14.9 | 11.3 | 10.9 | … | … | 116.8 | 158.9 |
| Apparent world (WORLD) | 8.2 | 24.9 | 18.3 | 15.5 | … | … | 152.0 | 218.7 |

**Processed foods**

| Exports by partner countries in region or group | EAP | ECA | LAC | MENA | SA | SSA | OECD | WORLD |
|---|---|---|---|---|---|---|---|---|
| East Asia & Pacific (EAP) | 5.5 | 0.4 | 0.2 | 0.9 | 1.6 | 0.4 | 10.4 | 19.3 |
| Europe & Central Asia (ECA) | 0.0 | 1.6 | 0.0 | 0.1 | 0.0 | 0.0 | 1.3 | 3.0 |
| Lat. America, Carib. (LAC) | 1.0 | 0.3 | 3.4 | 0.4 | 0.4 | 0.2 | 12.8 | 18.5 |
| Mid. East & N. Afr. (MENA) | 0.0 | 0.1 | 0.0 | 0.2 | 0.0 | 0.0 | 1.8 | 2.2 |
| South Asia (SA) | 0.1 | 0.3 | 0.1 | 0.1 | 0.1 | 0.0 | 1.0 | 1.7 |
| SSA | 0.1 | 0.4 | 0.0 | 0.2 | 0.1 | 0.2 | 5.1 | 6.2 |
| Industrial countries (OECD) | 6.8 | 3.2 | 3.5 | 2.8 | 0.3 | 0.8 | 73.1 | 90.6 |
| Apparent world (WORLD) | 13.6 | 6.3 | 7.2 | 4.6 | 2.4 | 1.7 | 105.5 | 141.4 |
| | LIC | LMIC | UMIC | HIC | … | … | OECD | WORLD |
| Low-income countries (LIC) | 0.4 | 1.7 | 0.8 | 1.6 | … | … | 9.2 | 13.8 |
| Lower-mid-income (LMIC) | 0.5 | 1.0 | 0.9 | 0.7 | … | … | 11.6 | 14.8 |
| Upper-mid-income (UMIC) | 3.2 | 2.0 | 2.8 | 1.5 | … | … | 9.8 | 19.2 |
| High-income dev. (HIC) | 0.2 | 0.3 | 0.2 | 0.6 | … | … | 1.8 | 3.1 |
| Industrial countries (OECD) | 1.6 | 5.7 | 5.0 | 5.1 | … | … | 73.1 | 90.6 |
| Apparent world (WORLD) | 6.0 | 10.8 | 9.7 | 9.5 | … | … | 105.5 | 141.4 |

(cont.)

Table 12.5 (*cont.*)

|  | Agricultural raw materials | | | | | | | | Agricultural goods | | | | | | | |
|---|---|---|---|---|---|---|---|---|---|---|---|---|---|---|---|---|
|  | EAP | ECA | LAC | MENA | SA | SSA | OECD | WORLD | EAP | ECA | LAC | MENA | SA | SSA | OECD | WORLD |
| East Asia & Pacific (EAP) | 4.4 | 0.1 | 0.4 | 0.2 | 0.2 | 0.1 | 6.9 | 12.4 | 16.0 | 1.0 | 0.7 | 1.5 | 1.9 | 0.7 | 24.7 | 46.6 |
| Europe & Central Asia (ECA) | 0.5 | 0.3 | 0.0 | 0.1 | 0.0 | 0.0 | 0.9 | 1.8 | 0.6 | 4.6 | 0.1 | 0.7 | 0.1 | 0.0 | 4.7 | 10.8 |
| Lat. America, Carib. (LAC) | 0.5 | 0.1 | 1.0 | 0.1 | 0.1 | 0.0 | 3.3 | 5.0 | 3.4 | 1.7 | 8.9 | 1.9 | 0.5 | 0.4 | 34.5 | 51.4 |
| Mid. East & N. Afr. (MENA) | 0.1 | 0.1 | 0.0 | 0.1 | 0.0 | 0.0 | 1.2 | 1.5 | 0.3 | 0.4 | 0.1 | 0.7 | 0.1 | 0.1 | 5.7 | 7.3 |
| South Asia (SA) | 0.4 | 0.0 | 0.1 | 0.0 | 0.1 | 0.0 | 0.7 | 1.4 | 1.8 | 0.5 | 0.2 | 0.6 | 0.6 | 0.2 | 2.8 | 6.7 |
| SSA | 0.8 | 0.1 | 0.1 | 0.1 | 0.1 | 0.2 | 2.0 | 3.4 | 1.2 | 0.5 | 0.2 | 0.5 | 0.3 | 0.7 | 10.0 | 13.5 |
| Industrial countries (OECD) | 9.9 | 1.3 | 1.3 | 1.7 | 0.5 | 0.2 | 27.3 | 42.2 | 35.2 | 8.8 | 13.4 | 12.9 | 1.7 | 2.4 | 217.2 | 291.7 |
| Apparent world (WORLD) | 16.7 | 2.1 | 3.0 | 2.3 | 0.9 | 0.6 | 42.2 | 67.7 | 58.5 | 17.6 | 23.6 | 18.7 | 5.2 | 4.6 | 299.7 | 427.9 |

|  | Agricultural raw materials | | | | | | | | Agricultural goods | | | | | | | |
|---|---|---|---|---|---|---|---|---|---|---|---|---|---|---|---|---|
|  | LIC | LMIC | UMIC | HIC | | | OECD | WORLD | LIC | LMIC | UMIC | HIC | | | OECD | WORLD |
| Low-income countries (LIC) | 0.6 | 0.9 | 0.6 | 1.9 | … | … | 4.3 | 8.3 | 2.2 | 6.8 | 2.8 | 5.3 | … | … | 18.7 | 35.9 |
| Lower-mid-income (LMIC) | 0.7 | 0.7 | 0.9 | 0.9 | … | … | 6.2 | 9.3 | 4.2 | 5.7 | 7.1 | 3.6 | … | … | 29.7 | 50.3 |
| Upper-mid-income (UMIC) | 0.3 | 0.7 | 0.6 | 0.8 | … | … | 3.3 | 5.7 | 4.2 | 5.7 | 7.1 | 3.6 | … | … | 29.7 | 50.3 |
| High-income dev. (HIC) | 0.2 | 0.2 | 0.2 | 0.4 | … | … | 1.2 | 2.1 | 0.6 | 0.7 | 0.4 | 1.3 | … | … | 5.8 | 8.7 |
| Industrial countries (OECD) | 2.8 | 3.7 | 2.3 | 6.2 | … | … | 27.3 | 42.2 | 9.5 | 24.2 | 18.6 | 22.1 | … | … | 217.2 | 291.7 |
| Apparent world (WORLD) | 4.7 | 6.1 | 4.6 | 10.2 | … | … | 42.2 | 67.7 | 18.8 | 41.7 | 32.6 | 35.1 | … | … | 299.7 | 427.9 |

*Notes:* See table 12A.2 for definitions of product categories, data exclude intra-EU trade.
*Source:* United Nations Statistical Office, *Commodity Trade Database* (1999).

*Agriculture*

Substantial protection surrounds trade in agriculture today, not only in developing countries but also in major industrial countries (table 12.6).[13] Protection is typically higher for foods than for agricultural raw materials. However, within the former category, protection is often greater for higher-value added goods such as processed foods than for primary food commodities and products – a phenomenon known as "tariff escalation."

For example, tariff protection in developing countries for foods averages 25 percent but 15 percent for agricultural raw materials. Similarly, non-tariff protection in developing countries averages 12 percent for foods, compared with 8 percent for agricultural raw materials. Major industrial countries also give greater protection to foods than to agricultural raw materials (table 12.6). Average rates of tariff protection in major industrial countries are lower than in developing countries, but average rates of non-tariff protection are significantly higher.

Low- and middle-income countries in South Asia, the Middle East and North Africa, Sub-Saharan Africa, and East Asia and the Pacific (principally, China, Indonesia, the Philippines, and Thailand) enforce the highest rates of tariff protection for agriculture. In contrast, upper-middle-income and high-income countries, led by those in Latin America and the Caribbean and in East Asia and the Pacific (principally, Korea, Singapore, and Taiwan, China), enforce the highest rates of non-tariff protection.[14]

Overall, table 12.6 reveals the broad decline in protection in developing countries for agriculture during the 1990s. Some upper-middle-income and high-income developing countries did raise their average rates of tariff and non-tariff protection, albeit from initially lower levels than in developing countries generally. (Average tariff rates for foods imposed by high-income developing countries grew from 13 percent to 17 percent, for example.) However, protection for foods and agricultural raw materials declined significantly among all other developing regions and income groups.

*All sectors*

Protection in developing countries for industry and other non-agricultural sectors greatly influences agricultural incentives. Table 12.7 reveals that trade liberalization in developing countries during the last decade – resulting not only from the Uruguay Round but also from unilateral trade reform – has encompassed more than agriculture. Trade reform may be greater in agriculture than in other primary products, but reforms of trade in manufactures have been largest of all and, from an economy-wide perspective, have presumably helped fuel the appreciable expansion of agricultural production during the 1990s. Whereas

Table 12.6 *Agricultural protection in developing countries, 1984–1987 and 1994–1998*

| Developing countries by region, income level | Applied tariff | | | NTB frequency | | |
|---|---|---|---|---|---|---|
| | 1984–7 | 1994–8 | Change[a] | 1984–7[b] | 1994–8[c] | Change[d] |
| | | (%) | | | (%) | |
| *Foods* | | | | | | |
| Developing countries | 30.7 | 25.0 | −18.7 | 47.8 | 12.1 | −74.6 |
| East Asia & Pacific | 22.2 | 25.2 | 13.4 | 33.6 | 19.4 | −42.4 |
| Europe & Central Asia | 8.3 | 13.9 | 67.0 | 42.9 | 2.1 | −95.2 |
| Lat. Am. & Caribbean | 29.5 | 15.2 | −48.7 | 40.2 | 22.1 | −44.9 |
| Mid. East & N. Africa | 27.7 | 26.8 | −3.0 | 60.0 | 14.1 | −76.5 |
| South Asia | 65.5 | 41.8 | −36.2 | 54.4 | 12.0 | −78.0 |
| SSA | 31.2 | 27.0 | −13.6 | 55.4 | 3.0 | −94.5 |
| Low-income | 40.0 | 27.2 | −32.1 | 53.6 | 5.3 | −90.0 |
| Lower-middle-income | 33.9 | 20.3 | −40.0 | 71.3 | 12.6 | −82.4 |
| Upper-middle-income | 20.1 | 17.9 | −11.2 | 13.3 | 21.8 | 63.9 |
| High-income | 12.7 | 17.1 | 34.1 | 23.0 | 17.2 | −25.1 |
| Industrial countries | ⋯ | 6.2 | ⋯ | ⋯ | 28.9 | ⋯ |
| *(Primary foods)* | | | | | | |
| Developing countries | ⋯ | 23.9 | ⋯ | ⋯ | 13.9 | ⋯ |
| East Asia & Pacific | ⋯ | 22.5 | ⋯ | ⋯ | 24.0 | ⋯ |
| Europe & Central Asia | ⋯ | 14.4 | ⋯ | ⋯ | 1.8 | ⋯ |
| Lat. Am. & Caribbean | ⋯ | 14.8 | ⋯ | ⋯ | 24.6 | ⋯ |
| Mid. East & N. Africa | ⋯ | 30.4 | ⋯ | ⋯ | 18.9 | ⋯ |
| South Asia | ⋯ | 36.2 | ⋯ | ⋯ | 11.0 | ⋯ |
| SSA | ⋯ | 24.9 | ⋯ | ⋯ | 3.0 | ⋯ |
| Low-income | ⋯ | 24.7 | ⋯ | ⋯ | 5.5 | ⋯ |
| Lower-middle-income | ⋯ | 21.1 | ⋯ | ⋯ | 13.9 | ⋯ |
| Upper-middle-income | ⋯ | 16.7 | ⋯ | ⋯ | 26.3 | ⋯ |
| High-income | ⋯ | 18.4 | ⋯ | ⋯ | 21.8 | ⋯ |
| Industrial countries | ⋯ | 8.1 | ⋯ | ⋯ | 32.0 | ⋯ |
| *(Processed foods)* | | | | | | |
| Developing countries | ⋯ | 26.4 | ⋯ | ⋯ | 9.8 | ⋯ |
| East Asia & Pacific | ⋯ | 27.1 | ⋯ | ⋯ | 13.5 | ⋯ |
| Europe & Central Asia | ⋯ | 14.4 | ⋯ | ⋯ | 2.3 | ⋯ |
| Lat. Am. & Caribbean | ⋯ | 15.6 | ⋯ | ⋯ | 18.7 | ⋯ |
| Mid. East & N. Africa | ⋯ | 25.5 | ⋯ | ⋯ | 10.4 | ⋯ |
| South Asia | ⋯ | 47.1 | ⋯ | ⋯ | 12.2 | ⋯ |
| SSA | ⋯ | 28.8 | ⋯ | ⋯ | 1.6 | ⋯ |
| Low-income | ⋯ | 29.6 | ⋯ | ⋯ | 4.5 | ⋯ |
| Lower-middle-income | ⋯ | 20.0 | ⋯ | ⋯ | 10.6 | ⋯ |
| Upper-middle-income | ⋯ | 18.8 | ⋯ | ⋯ | 17.4 | ⋯ |
| High-income | ⋯ | 19.4 | ⋯ | ⋯ | 8.2 | ⋯ |
| Industrial countries | ⋯ | 6.2 | ⋯ | ⋯ | 24.8 | ⋯ |

Table 12.6 (*cont.*)

| Developing countries by region, income level | Applied tariff | | | NTB frequency | | |
|---|---|---|---|---|---|---|
| | 1984–7 | 1994–8 | Change[a] | 1984–7[b] | 1994–8[c] | Change[d] |
| | (%) | | | (%) | | |
| *Agr. raw materials* | | | | | | |
| Developing countries | 18.8 | 14.3 | −24.1 | 35.2 | 8.4 | −76.2 |
| East Asia & Pacific | 11.9 | 9.6 | −19.4 | 22.8 | 13.7 | −39.7 |
| Europe & Central Asia | 5.9 | 8.2 | 39.5 | 48.8 | 0.0 | −100.0 |
| Lat. Am. & Caribbean | 23.9 | 8.0 | −66.7 | 20.3 | 20.3 | 0.2 |
| Mid. East & N. Africa | 10.6 | 14.0 | 32.2 | 36.5 | 12.9 | −64.7 |
| South Asia | 39.4 | 30.9 | −21.6 | 43.4 | 2.8 | −93.5 |
| SSA | 21.2 | 15.0 | −29.2 | 39.6 | 0.5 | −98.8 |
| Low-income | 25.5 | 16.1 | −36.7 | 39.2 | 2.6 | −93.4 |
| Lower-middle-income | 17.0 | 10.5 | −38.3 | 45.6 | 8.7 | −80.9 |
| Upper-middle-income | 16.9 | 10.0 | −40.7 | 7.2 | 20.1 | 177.6 |
| High-income | 9.7 | 4.3 | −56.2 | 7.7 | 14.0 | 81.8 |
| Industrial countries | ... | 1.8 | ... | ... | 14.9 | ... |

*Notes:* Protection statistics are simple averages of tariff and NTB measures for countries and product categories; . . . indicates not available.
[a] Change may be biased by differences in data coverage of developing countries between time periods.
[b] "Core" NTBs, including quantitative import restrictions, measures to directly control import prices, and restrictive trade finance measures.
[c] Core NTBs plus automatic licensing of imports, monopolistic measures restricting imports, and technical barriers to imports.
[d] Change may be biased by differences in data coverage of developing countries and NTBs between time periods.
*Sources:* UNCTAD (1994, 1999).

average rates of tariff and non-tariff protection in developing countries for primary products dropped by 18 percent and 79 percent, respectively, and those for agricultural products declined by 21 percent and 75 percent, protection rates for manufactures dropped by 38 percent and 86 percent.

Tables 12.8 and 12.9 provide the most complete picture of tariff and non-tariff protection that developing and industrial countries give to specific products. Beverages and tobacco are the most frequently and highly protected products. Beyond those, protection is most often highest for primary foods such as meat and dairy products, processed foods such as prepared fruits and vegetables, and categories of manufactures: pharmaceuticals, toiletries, and manufactured fertilizers, and textiles and clothing, furniture, and footwear.

Table 12.7 *Protection in developing countries: all goods, 1984–1987 and 1994–1998*

| Developing countries by region, income level | Applied tariff | | | NTB frequency | | |
|---|---|---|---|---|---|---|
| | 1984–7 | 1994–8 | Change[a] | 1984–7[b] | 1994–8[c] | Change[a] |
| | (%) | | | (%) | | |
| *Primary products* | | | | | | |
| Developing countries | 23.3 | 19.0 | −18.4 | 39.5 | 8.5 | −78.6 |
| East Asia & Pacific | 15.2 | 16.3 | 7.0 | 26.5 | 14.1 | −46.8 |
| Europe & Central Asia | 7.1 | 9.8 | 37.8 | 39.3 | 1.3 | −96.7 |
| Lat. Am. & Caribbean | 24.5 | 11.7 | −52.1 | 28.7 | 17.1 | −40.3 |
| Mid. East & N. Africa | 17.8 | 20.1 | 12.7 | 47.8 | 9.5 | −80.1 |
| South Asia | 50.7 | 35.7 | −29.5 | 49.4 | 6.8 | −86.2 |
| SSA | 24.5 | 20.5 | −16.5 | 45.6 | 1.9 | −95.9 |
| Low-income | 31.0 | 21.0 | −32.4 | 44.6 | 3.6 | −92.0 |
| Lower-middle-income | 23.0 | 15.1 | −34.1 | 56.7 | 9.4 | −83.3 |
| Upper-middle-income | 17.2 | 13.2 | −23.1 | 11.1 | 15.9 | 42.8 |
| High-income | 11.0 | 10.2 | −7.1 | 14.2 | 11.8 | −16.8 |
| Industrial countries | ⋯ | 3.7 | ⋯ | ⋯ | 18.1 | ⋯ |
| *(Agricultural products)* | | | | | | |
| Developing countries | 24.8 | 19.6 | −20.8 | 41.5 | 10.2 | −75.3 |
| East Asia & Pacific | 17.1 | 17.4 | 2.0 | 28.2 | 16.5 | −41.3 |
| Europe & Central Asia | 7.1 | 11.0 | 55.6 | 45.9 | 1.0 | −97.7 |
| Lat. Am. & Caribbean | 26.7 | 11.6 | −56.7 | 30.2 | 21.2 | −29.7 |
| Mid. East & N. Africa | 19.1 | 20.4 | 6.8 | 48.2 | 13.5 | −72.0 |
| South Asia | 52.5 | 36.4 | −30.7 | 48.9 | 7.4 | −84.9 |
| SSA | 26.2 | 21.0 | −19.9 | 47.5 | 1.8 | −96.3 |
| Low-income | 32.8 | 21.6 | −33.9 | 46.4 | 4.0 | −91.5 |
| Lower-middle-income | 25.4 | 15.4 | −39.4 | 58.4 | 10.6 | −81.8 |
| Upper-middle-income | 18.5 | 13.9 | −24.6 | 10.3 | 20.9 | 103.9 |
| High-income | 11.2 | 10.7 | −4.9 | 15.3 | 15.6 | 1.8 |
| Industrial countries | ⋯ | 4.0 | ⋯ | ⋯ | 21.9 | ⋯ |
| *Manufactures* | | | | | | |
| Developing countries | 28.7 | 17.9 | −37.5 | 34.3 | 4.7 | −86.4 |
| East Asia & Pacific | 19.0 | 10.7 | −43.5 | 19.1 | 7.3 | −61.9 |
| Europe & Central Asia | 13.6 | 7.7 | −43.2 | 22.9 | 1.4 | −94.0 |
| Lat. Am. & Caribbean | 27.4 | 11.5 | −58.3 | 30.7 | 8.8 | −71.3 |
| Mid. East & N. Africa | 20.5 | 18.1 | −11.6 | 43.1 | 3.4 | −92.2 |
| South Asia | 65.9 | 40.1 | −39.2 | 46.6 | 7.0 | −85.0 |
| SSA | 25.7 | 19.5 | −24.0 | 43.3 | 0.2 | −99.6 |
| Low-income | 35.8 | 20.5 | −42.8 | 41.7 | 1.8 | −95.7 |
| Lower-middle-income | 25.3 | 13.1 | −48.1 | 50.4 | 4.3 | −91.5 |
| Upper-middle-income | 22.9 | 12.8 | −44.1 | 17.3 | 8.5 | −50.9 |
| High-income | 13.6 | 4.9 | −63.7 | 8.9 | 8.0 | −10.1 |
| Industrial countries | ⋯ | 4.1 | ⋯ | ⋯ | 4.6 | ⋯ |

Table 12.7  (*cont.*)

| Developing countries by region, income level | Applied tariff | | | NTB frequency | | |
|---|---|---|---|---|---|---|
| | 1984–7 | 1994–8 | Change[a] | 1984–7[b] | 1994–8[c] | Change[a] |
| *All goods* | | | | | | |
| Developing countries | 27.2 | 18.2 | −33.1 | 35.9 | 5.5 | −84.6 |
| East Asia & Pacific | 17.9 | 11.9 | −33.8 | 21.2 | 8.9 | −57.9 |
| Europe & Central Asia | 11.8 | 8.2 | −30.4 | 27.7 | 1.3 | −95.3 |
| Lat. Am. & Caribbean | 26.6 | 11.5 | −56.6 | 30.2 | 10.7 | −64.7 |
| Mid. East & N. Africa | 19.8 | 18.7 | −5.5 | 44.5 | 4.8 | −89.3 |
| South Asia | 61.7 | 39.1 | −36.6 | 47.6 | 7.0 | −85.3 |
| SSA | 25.4 | 19.7 | −22.2 | 44.0 | 0.6 | −98.7 |
| Low-income | 34.5 | 20.6 | −40.2 | 42.5 | 2.2 | −94.8 |
| Lower-middle-income | 24.7 | 13.7 | −44.6 | 52.3 | 5.4 | −89.6 |
| Upper-middle-income | 21.3 | 12.9 | −39.6 | 15.6 | 10.1 | −35.6 |
| High-income | 12.8 | 6.1 | −52.4 | 10.5 | 9.0 | −14.3 |
| Industrial countries | ⋯ | 4.1 | ⋯ | ⋯ | 7.9 | ⋯ |

*Notes:* Protection statistics are simple averages of tariff and NTB measures for countries and product categories; ... indicates not available.

[a] Change may be biased by changes in composition of developing country groups in sample data between time periods.

[b] "Core" NTBs, including quantitative import restrictions, measures to directly control import prices, and restrictive trade finance measures.

[c] "Core" NTBs plus automatic licensing of imports, monopolistic measures restricting imports, and technical barriers to imports.

*Sources:* UNCTAD (1994, 1999).

Variants of tables 12.8 and 12.9, more disaggregated by product categories and groups of trading countries, might help negotiators identify opportunities to exchange trade concessions in the new WTO round. The tables already reveal wide possibilities for developing and industrial countries to exchange significant trade concessions, not only in agriculture but also in agriculture and manufactures combined.

## Trade liberalization and agriculture: a quantitative analysis

To investigate the implications for agriculture of current levels of protection in developing countries, I used the World Trade Simulation Model (WTSM), a simple computable partial equilibrium model. I patterned the analysis after the seminal approach of KSV (1988) and Schiff and Valdés (1992) – with notable differences. The KSV analysis calculated nominal rates of protection in a large sample of developing countries by comparing domestic and international prices for prominent categories of agricultural imports and exports.

Table 12.8 *Applied tariff rates in developing and industrial countries, 1994-1998 (Percent)*

| | | Product category | EAP | ECA | LAC | MENA | SA | SSA | LIC | LMIC | UMIC | HIC | OECD |
|---|---|---|---|---|---|---|---|---|---|---|---|---|
| Primary Products | Primary foods | Live animals | 8.1 | 10.6 | 8.3 | 27.2 | 27.3 | 16.8 | 16.5 | 13.5 | 12.5 | 4.8 | 47.4 |
| | | Meat products | 22.1 | 21.3 | 18.4 | 54.9 | 45.2 | 30.9 | 30.3 | 31.2 | 22.7 | 13.4 | 7.9 |
| | | Dairy products | 21.1 | 22.5 | 18.5 | 32.4 | 33.4 | 25.8 | 25.8 | 23.1 | 21.8 | 22.2 | 45.5 |
| | | Cereal grains | 37.0 | 8.9 | 11.1 | 12.4 | 14.7 | 13.7 | 14.0 | 11.7 | 10.9 | 54.1 | 2.7 |
| | | Vegetables | 31.9 | 15.6 | 14.7 | 17.9 | 34.3 | 26.4 | 25.5 | 20.4 | 15.3 | 29.4 | 3.5 |
| | | Fruits & nuts | 27.3 | 11.1 | 17.2 | 30.6 | 44.8 | 30.5 | 30.7 | 21.8 | 17.0 | 20.0 | 2.5 |
| | | Sugar & honey | 21.9 | 19.7 | 16.7 | 23.0 | 42.0 | 25.9 | 25.9 | 20.4 | 23.2 | 13.6 | 8.0 |
| | | Animal feed stuffs | 5.8 | 5.6 | 9.3 | 11.6 | 22.7 | 14.4 | 14.3 | 9.8 | 7.4 | 2.7 | 0.7 |
| | | Oil seeds | 20.5 | 3.4 | 7.4 | 13.7 | 32.2 | 18.7 | 18.8 | 9.8 | 8.2 | 23.2 | 1.2 |
| | Processed foods | Fats & oils | 13.1 | 9.5 | 14.5 | 20.8 | 41.2 | 20.4 | 22.8 | 15.4 | 13.5 | 7.3 | 4.4 |
| | | Cereal preparations | 36.6 | 16.9 | 14.8 | 24.5 | 33.7 | 26.5 | 25.8 | 20.2 | 16.9 | 49.3 | 8.5 |
| | | Prepared vegetables | 22.8 | 15.6 | 15.1 | 24.2 | 41.2 | 30.4 | 29.3 | 20.5 | 16.4 | 16.4 | 5.8 |
| | | Prepared fruits | 28.5 | 15.9 | 17.0 | 31.0 | 47.1 | 33.3 | 32.8 | 23.1 | 18.7 | 23.6 | 8.7 |
| | | Coffee, tea & spices | 21.1 | 9.1 | 15.3 | 21.7 | 42.9 | 30.5 | 29.6 | 17.3 | 15.6 | 14.3 | 3.2 |
| | | Beverages | 46.7 | 24.2 | 18.0 | 45.1 | 115.2 | 34.1 | 46.4 | 27.2 | 37.5 | 16.0 | 7.3 |
| | | Oth. processed foods | 20.2 | 17.6 | 16.3 | 24.7 | 46.9 | 30.3 | 30.6 | 20.2 | 19.9 | 12.2 | 13.0 |
| | Agr raw Mat | Tobacco & manufs. | 42.9 | 32.3 | 18.7 | 33.9 | 84.5 | 36.9 | 42.5 | 24.0 | 46.3 | 16.0 | 14.7 |
| | | Hides & skins | 3.9 | 5.2 | 8.0 | 10.1 | 30.6 | 16.4 | 17.3 | 7.8 | 7.0 | 0.6 | 0.1 |
| | | Natural rubber | 5.4 | 1.4 | 7.3 | 8.6 | 21.8 | 9.9 | 10.9 | 6.9 | 6.1 | 0.4 | 0.2 |
| | | Natural fibers | 4.1 | 5.1 | 6.5 | 10.7 | 29.5 | 11.7 | 13.2 | 8.2 | 5.7 | 1.1 | 0.3 |
| | | Oth. agr. raw mats. | 10.1 | 8.4 | 7.1 | 12.2 | 27.7 | 14.4 | 15.0 | 10.5 | 8.3 | 6.3 | 2.0 |
| | Misc. | Mineral ores | 3.4 | 3.4 | 6.2 | 9.4 | 25.0 | 11.4 | 11.9 | 6.8 | 6.1 | 0.7 | 0.2 |
| | | Mineral fuels | 4.2 | 3.0 | 7.0 | 10.6 | 29.3 | 11.4 | 12.8 | 7.2 | 6.3 | 2.2 | 0.9 |
| | | Non-ferrous metals | 5.3 | 5.1 | 8.2 | 12.8 | 31.6 | 14.5 | 14.9 | 9.4 | 8.6 | 2.1 | 2.0 |
| Manufactures | Chem. | Pharmaceuticals | 3.5 | 3.0 | 5.5 | 8.2 | 22.3 | 7.3 | 9.0 | 5.2 | 5.7 | 2.8 | 0.1 |
| | | Toiletry & perfumes | 14.7 | 9.6 | 14.4 | 22.7 | 48.2 | 26.3 | 26.8 | 16.7 | 16.0 | 6.6 | 3.7 |
| | | Manuf. fertilizers | 3.2 | 4.3 | 3.4 | 11.8 | 15.5 | 3.5 | 4.6 | 5.8 | 5.0 | 5.4 | 0.7 |
| | | Iron & steel | 6.2 | 5.9 | 8.8 | 11.1 | 37.1 | 13.2 | 14.7 | 8.7 | 11.2 | 3.4 | 2.9 |
| | Mach. | Non-electric mach. | 5.1 | 4.4 | 7.1 | 10.7 | 30.1 | 10.7 | 12.2 | 6.7 | 9.5 | 3.5 | 2.1 |
| | | Electric machinery | 9.4 | 6.6 | 11.5 | 15.7 | 41.7 | 20.9 | 20.7 | 11.7 | 14.7 | 4.4 | 2.9 |
| | | Transport equipment | 14.4 | 7.9 | 11.0 | 14.3 | 41.3 | 14.7 | 17.3 | 12.8 | 13.3 | 5.1 | 3.1 |
| | Other manufactures | Leather & travel gds. | 11.8 | 9.0 | 14.3 | 21.6 | 39.5 | 26.8 | 26.0 | 16.4 | 14.0 | 3.0 | 5.4 |
| | | Rubber products | 13.0 | 6.2 | 11.6 | 19.4 | 45.7 | 20.8 | 21.3 | 13.5 | 15.5 | 4.9 | 3.9 |
| | | Wood products | 16.5 | 8.5 | 12.8 | 22.7 | 43.3 | 24.6 | 24.2 | 17.6 | 14.4 | 5.1 | 3.4 |
| | | Paper products | 12.4 | 7.1 | 11.7 | 19.8 | 47.1 | 20.6 | 22.0 | 14.3 | 13.5 | 4.5 | 3.3 |
| | | Textiles & clothing | 17.9 | 11.9 | 17.1 | 28.9 | 50.7 | 29.2 | 30.7 | 20.8 | 17.1 | 8.0 | 10.0 |
| | | Non-metallic min prods. | 12.1 | 9.6 | 11.8 | 19.1 | 45.9 | 22.9 | 24.0 | 14.7 | 13.2 | 4.5 | 2.7 |
| | | Furniture | 20.2 | 13.7 | 17.8 | 27.8 | 52.1 | 34.0 | 32.4 | 22.3 | 20.6 | 7.6 | 3.2 |
| | | Footwear | 19.1 | 11.5 | 17.6 | 27.3 | 47.3 | 31.3 | 29.8 | 20.1 | 21.6 | 8.3 | 11.9 |
| | | Professional equip. | 7.6 | 7.5 | 10.8 | 13.0 | 35.3 | 19.7 | 19.8 | 10.8 | 11.8 | 3.4 | 2.3 |

*Notes:* See table 12A.2 for description of product categories; values are simple averages of rates of protection in each country group. EAP refers to East Asia and Pacific, ECA to Europe and Central Asia, LAC to Latin America and Caribbean, MENA to Middle East and North Africa, SA to South Asia, SSA to Sub-Saharan Africa, LIC to low-income countries, LMIC to lower-middle-income countries, UMIC to upper-middle-income countries, HIC to high-income countries, and OECD to major industrial countries. Darkly (lightly) shaded values indicate highest (intermediate) rates of protection in each country group.

*Sources:* UNCTAD (1999), and author's calculations.

## Table 12.9 Frequency of NTBs in developing and industrial countries, 1994–1998 (percent)

| Group | | Product category | EAP | ECA | LAC | MENA | SA | SSA | LIC | LMIC | UMIC | HIC | OECD |
|---|---|---|---|---|---|---|---|---|---|---|---|---|---|
| Primary Products | Primary foods | Live animals | 35.3 | 3.6 | 27.4 | 25.3 | 0.0 | 1.2 | 2.3 | 18.3 | 30.2 | 36.6 | 28.4 |
| | | Meat products | 26.5 | 1.9 | 21.5 | 16.4 | 16.2 | 5.7 | 6.7 | 12.8 | 24.0 | 33.4 | 32.1 |
| | | Dairy products | 28.7 | 3.2 | 23.0 | 30.3 | 16.0 | 0.0 | 2.8 | 19.9 | 23.7 | 28.0 | 62.1 |
| | | Cereal grains | 35.8 | 7.7 | 33.8 | 17.1 | 0.0 | 1.9 | 7.1 | 20.9 | 23.4 | 23.4 | 39.3 |
| | | Vegetables | 28.0 | 0.8 | 29.7 | 21.6 | 12.6 | 4.3 | 8.0 | 14.5 | 32.6 | 22.4 | 30.8 |
| | | Fruits & nuts | 21.3 | 0.0 | 25.7 | 21.6 | 11.0 | 3.6 | 6.6 | 12.8 | 27.3 | 18.2 | 27.9 |
| | | Sugar & honey | 10.3 | 6.5 | 15.5 | 8.5 | 9.2 | 0.1 | 3.5 | 9.0 | 16.4 | 3.6 | 34.3 |
| | | Animal feed stuffs | 11.7 | 0.2 | 20.8 | 14.1 | 4.2 | 0.9 | 2.1 | 9.2 | 25.3 | 1.6 | 21.6 |
| | | Oil seeds | 20.5 | 0.4 | 30.8 | 15.0 | 11.6 | 0.0 | 4.8 | 16.0 | 27.5 | 4.8 | 23.0 |
| | | Fats & oils | 21.5 | 1.5 | 12.0 | 9.8 | 6.4 | 1.3 | 3.3 | 10.3 | 9.7 | 18.8 | 27.6 |
| | Processed foods | Cereal preparations | 14.9 | 1.8 | 21.9 | 11.5 | 16.2 | 0.6 | 4.9 | 10.9 | 20.7 | 10.2 | 27.6 |
| | | Prepared vegetables | 9.9 | 0.0 | 20.0 | 7.0 | 14.2 | 3.1 | 6.2 | 8.0 | 17.1 | 8.0 | 20.8 |
| | | Prepared fruits | 9.9 | 4.3 | 20.7 | 1.6 | 14.2 | 2.9 | 5.2 | 9.7 | 17.6 | 7.8 | 22.8 |
| | | Coffee, tea & spices | 11.8 | 2.2 | 21.6 | 12.1 | 7.4 | 0.1 | 3.2 | 11.5 | 19.9 | 2.8 | 21.5 |
| | | Beverages | 18.6 | 9.2 | 18.3 | 31.6 | 26.4 | 2.9 | 7.3 | 17.7 | 27.4 | 0.2 | 33.3 |
| | | Oth. processed foods | 4.7 | 2.2 | 17.5 | 8.0 | 12.6 | 0.9 | 2.7 | 8.7 | 16.6 | 1.2 | 27.4 |
| | Agr raw Mat | Tobacco & manufs. | 9.5 | 0.0 | 14.8 | 29.1 | 13.2 | 1.4 | 5.2 | 7.8 | 23.6 | 0.0 | 16.9 |
| | | Hides & skins | 7.8 | 0.0 | 18.5 | 6.8 | 0.0 | 0.0 | 1.1 | 3.9 | 21.9 | 10.0 | 25.4 |
| | | Natural rubber | 7.3 | 0.0 | 1.0 | 0.0 | 14.0 | 0.0 | 4.7 | 0.7 | 0.0 | 0.0 | 0.0 |
| | | Natural fibers | 15.0 | 0.0 | 15.7 | 3.6 | 2.0 | 0.0 | 1.2 | 6.5 | 14.5 | 17.8 | 12.1 |
| | | Oth. agr. raw mats. | 16.0 | 0.0 | 26.0 | 19.4 | 2.2 | 0.9 | 3.5 | 12.2 | 24.1 | 16.2 | 14.4 |
| Manufactures | Misc. | Mineral ores | 5.0 | 0.6 | 8.0 | 0.6 | 0.6 | 0.1 | 0.6 | 5.1 | 4.6 | 1.0 | 0.6 |
| | | Mineral fuels | 4.5 | 0.4 | 8.3 | 4.8 | 1.4 | 0.0 | 0.7 | 5.2 | 6.6 | 0.4 | 7.1 |
| | | Non-ferrous metals | 2.2 | 0.9 | 5.4 | 0.6 | 0.4 | 0.3 | 0.8 | 3.6 | 2.4 | 0.0 | 0.3 |
| | Chem. | Pharmaceuticals | 23.0 | 3.3 | 17.2 | 9.6 | 10.8 | 2.6 | 4.5 | 9.1 | 21.6 | 23.1 | 8.8 |
| | | Toiletry & perfumes | 6.8 | 4.8 | 14.5 | 0.5 | 11.4 | 0.2 | 2.6 | 8.0 | 12.0 | 2.4 | 8.1 |
| | | Manuf. fertilizers | 18.4 | 0.0 | 22.0 | 22.8 | 1.2 | 0.0 | 3.3 | 11.4 | 27.5 | 0.0 | 13.8 |
| | Mach. | Iron & steel | 12.5 | 0.0 | 3.6 | 0.1 | 0.2 | 0.0 | 1.8 | 2.3 | 1.0 | 15.2 | 9.6 |
| | | Non-electric mach. | 2.2 | 0.8 | 8.0 | 2.0 | 1.8 | 0.0 | 0.9 | 3.4 | 6.6 | 0.0 | 0.6 |
| | | Electric machinery | 5.3 | 2.6 | 7.5 | 3.5 | 6.8 | 0.0 | 1.9 | 4.0 | 8.2 | 2.6 | 1.5 |
| | | Transport equipment | 10.3 | 3.8 | 11.6 | 6.1 | 11.8 | 0.0 | 2.8 | 8.3 | 10.6 | 5.4 | 4.1 |
| | | Leather & travel gds. | 1.8 | 0.0 | 9.4 | 0.3 | 4.4 | 0.0 | 1.1 | 2.0 | 9.5 | 1.6 | 9.5 |
| | Other manufactures | Rubber products | 1.6 | 0.1 | 3.3 | 4.1 | 1.8 | 0.2 | 0.8 | 2.6 | 2.1 | 0.6 | 0.0 |
| | | Wood products | 3.5 | 0.3 | 10.0 | 0.0 | 2.0 | 1.5 | 2.3 | 1.8 | 11.5 | 0.0 | 1.3 |
| | | Paper products | 2.5 | 0.0 | 3.2 | 0.0 | 5.0 | 0.3 | 1.8 | 1.4 | 1.9 | 0.0 | 0.3 |
| | | Textiles & clothing | 10.5 | 3.0 | 10.9 | 9.6 | 16.8 | 0.1 | 2.9 | 7.1 | 10.4 | 18.4 | 10.8 |
| | | Non-metallic min. prods. | 1.0 | 0.9 | 2.6 | 1.9 | 7.0 | 0.1 | 1.2 | 2.1 | 2.1 | 0.0 | 2.4 |
| | | Furniture | 0.0 | 0.8 | 4.9 | 0.6 | 13.2 | 4.0 | 4.9 | 0.4 | 7.0 | 0.0 | 2.3 |
| | | Footwear | 0.2 | 4.8 | 14.3 | 4.6 | 10.0 | 0.0 | 1.6 | 7.0 | 13.4 | 0.0 | 26.5 |
| | | Professional equip. | 1.4 | 0.9 | 5.8 | 1.6 | 3.8 | 0.0 | 1.1 | 2.2 | 5.5 | 0.3 | 0.3 |

*Notes:* See table 12A.2 for description of product categories; values are simple averages of rates of protection in each country group. EAP refers to East Asia and Pacific, ECA to Europe and Central Asia, LAC to Latin America and Caribbean, MENA to Middle East and North Africa, SA to South Asia, SSA to Sub-Saharan Africa, LIC to low-income countries, LMIC to lower-middle-income countries, UMIC to upper-middle-income countries, HIC to high-income countries, and OECD to major industrial countries. Darkly (lightly) shaded values indicate highest (intermediate) rates of protection in each country group.

*Sources:* UNCTAD (1999), and author's calculations.

By comparison, my analysis relies on tariff and non-tariff measures compiled by UNCTAD to assess nominal rates of protection. It also considers border measures applied only to imports; it does not take into account export taxes, export subsidies, or quantitative controls on exports in developing countries, which would be needed to fully assess the extent of discrimination against agriculture.[15]

Nonetheless, the present analysis is more comprehensive in its coverage of developing countries and traded goods than the KSV analysis. It also improves somewhat on the elasticities' approach to estimating the economy-wide effects of protection employed by KSV. The computable partial equilibrium model of world trade, rather than individual country trade, allows me to investigate not only the bias against agriculture in developing countries, but also the implications of new multilateral negotiations on agricultural trade versus liberalized trade in all goods.[16]

*Simulation Analysis*

*Scenarios*

In this analysis, WTSM is used to estimate the impacts on agricultural prices and trade of liberalizing trade in developing countries, first in agriculture and later in all sectors. The analysis also considers the impacts of successful negotiations to liberalize world trade in agriculture following the WTO built-in agenda, and to liberalize world trade in all goods following an expanded WTO agenda.

In a vein similar to that followed by KSV (1988) and Schiff and Valdés (1992), I assess the economy-wide effects of protection on agricultural incentives. I do so by considering the impacts of eliminating protection – in agriculture as well as other sectors – on domestic producer prices in sectors that compete with agricultural exports and imports. Such trade liberalization gives rise to economy-wide effects operating through adjustment of the real exchange rate. Specifically, it results in an incipient balance of payments deficit that can be brought into equilibrium only if the real exchange rate declines. This increases domestic prices for agricultural exportables, and actual exports. It also serves to moderate declines in domestic prices for agricultural importables, and corresponding increases in agricultural imports, caused by trade liberalization. The analysis views these impacts on domestic prices for agricultural exportables and importables as desirable incentives that encourage agricultural producers in developing countries to become more efficient and internationally competitive.[17]

KSV estimate economy-wide impacts – or, in their terminology, total direct plus indirect impacts – of protection on agricultural incentives in developing countries on a country-by-country basis. The large number of developing countries considered here make such an approach impractical. Instead, the present analysis examines outcomes of simultaneous "unilateral" liberalization by developing countries in the same income group of trade in agriculture (capturing mainly direct effects), and then of trade in all goods (capturing economy-wide effects). This approach inherently involves international feedback effects (the effects of changes in international prices on domestic prices). However, those effects are thought to be mostly small because unilateral trade liberalization is by groups of developing countries that are limited in total economic size, and hence their ability to influence world prices.

The Millennium Round liberalization scenarios involve multilateral liberalization of trade by all developing countries and all major industrial countries simultaneously, first for agriculture and then for trade in all goods. The first such scenario represents the WTO built-in agenda, namely, multilateral negotiations to liberalize world trade in agriculture. The second scenario represents comprehensive multilateral trade negotiations covering world trade in all goods, which promise the greatest economic gains to consumers and producers in all trading countries.

Under all scenarios, countries are assumed to eliminate both tariff and nontariff protection completely in the sectors slated for trade liberalization.[18]

### Results

The results of the unilateral and Millennium Round liberalization scenarios are summarized in table 12.10. The summary presents average changes in exchange rates, agricultural prices, and trade – the latter by primary foods, processed foods, and agricultural raw materials. The summary also presents changes in economic welfare for each group of developing countries and the world.[19]

Under each scenario, the real exchange rate declines to maintain balance of payments equilibrium. Broad-based trade liberalization yields greater depreciation of the exchange rate than liberalization confined solely to agriculture. Millennium Round trade liberalization results in less stringent requirements for exchange rate adjustment than unilateral trade liberalization, because the former stimulates demand for exports and imports simultaneously in each country. These observations are important keys to understanding the WTSM results.

*Unilateral liberalization*   From an economy-wide perspective, unilateral trade liberalization provides the primary guide to the extent and magnitude of discrimination against agriculture in developing countries. The impacts on agricultural prices of unilaterally liberalizing trade in agriculture indicate the direct (sector-specific) effects of protection on incentives to efficient and internationally competitive production. The impacts on agricultural prices of unilaterally liberalizing trade in all goods indicate the total direct and indirect

Table 12.10 *Impacts of trade liberalization on agriculture and economic welfare in developing countries and the world*

| Variable[a] | Unilateral liberalization | | Millennium Round liberalization | |
|---|---|---|---|---|
| | Agriculture | All goods | Agriculture | All goods |
| | | (% change) | | |
| *Low-income countries* | | | | |
| Exchange rate ($/L)[b] | −2.2 | −8.8 | −0.7 | −5.5 |
| Agr. prices: Exportables (L)[b] | 2.8 | 10.2 | 5.6 | 11.1 |
| Primary foods | 2.9 | 10.4 | 5.3 | 10.8 |
| Processed foods | 2.7 | 10.0 | 5.7 | 11.4 |
| Agr. raw materials | 3.0 | 10.0 | 5.9 | 11.3 |
| Agr. prices: Importables (L) | −11.1 | −5.8 | −9.2 | −5.5 |
| Primary foods | −10.5 | −4.7 | −7.9 | −3.8 |
| Processed foods | −13.9 | −9.2 | −11.6 | −8.4 |
| Agr. raw materials | −8.9 | −3.6 | −8.5 | −4.8 |
| Agricultural exports (qty)[b] | 2.1 | 9.0 | 5.4 | 9.6 |
| Primary foods | 2.1 | 9.4 | 5.3 | 9.5 |
| Processed foods | 1.7 | 8.2 | 5.2 | 9.3 |
| Agr. raw materials | 2.6 | 9.8 | 5.8 | 10.4 |
| Agricultural imports (qty) | 35.3 | 16.5 | 26.7 | 16.5 |
| Primary foods | 34.7 | 16.2 | 24.6 | 15.1 |
| Processed foods | 47.6 | 25.2 | 37.7 | 24.1 |
| Agr. raw materials | 20.8 | 5.9 | 16.4 | 9.4 |
| Ec. welfare ($ mill.) | 2,949.3 | 20,385.7 | 2,966.1 | 25,274.4 |
| *Lower-middle-income countries* | | | | |
| Exchange rate ($/L) | −1.6 | −6.4 | −0.9 | −3.6 |
| Agr. prices: Exportables (L) | 2.3 | 6.7 | 5.3 | 7.9 |
| Primary foods | 2.5 | 7.0 | 5.6 | 8.3 |
| Processed foods | 2.2 | 6.9 | 6.3 | 8.9 |
| Agr. raw materials | 1.9 | 6.1 | 3.3 | 5.7 |
| Agr. prices: Importables (L) | −11.1 | −7.3 | −7.8 | −5.6 |
| Primary foods | −10.9 | −7.2 | −8.1 | −5.9 |
| Processed foods | −13.4 | −9.6 | −9.1 | −6.9 |
| Agr. raw materials | −7.7 | −3.7 | −4.2 | −2.1 |
| Agricultural exports (qty) | 1.8 | 6.4 | 4.9 | 7.5 |
| Primary foods | 2.1 | 6.9 | 5.1 | 8.1 |
| Processed foods | 1.8 | 6.2 | 5.8 | 8.1 |
| Agr. raw materials | 1.3 | 6.0 | 2.9 | 5.6 |
| Agricultural imports (qty) | 20.0 | 10.1 | 11.1 | 5.9 |
| Primary foods | 19.1 | 9.4 | 11.6 | 6.4 |
| Processed foods | 22.6 | 12.0 | 10.8 | 5.5 |
| Agr. raw materials | 19.5 | 9.2 | 9.2 | 4.4 |
| Ec. welfare ($ mill.) | 3,278.0 | 17,522.1 | 2,417.3 | 16,964.0 |

Table 12.10 (*cont.*)

| Variable[a] | Unilateral liberalization | | Millennium Round liberalization | |
|---|---|---|---|---|
| | Agriculture | All goods | Agriculture | All goods |
| | | (% change) | | |
| *Upper-middle-income countries* | | | | |
| Exchange rate ($/L) | −0.8 | −5.6 | −0.2 | −2.9 |
| Agr. prices: Exportables (L) | 1.4 | 5.9 | 5.3 | 7.8 |
| Primary foods | 1.4 | 5.9 | 4.3 | 7.0 |
| Processed foods | 1.5 | 6.0 | 6.6 | 8.9 |
| Agr. raw materials | 1.4 | 6.0 | 5.0 | 7.4 |
| Agr. prices: Importables (L) | −11.0 | −7.1 | −7.8 | −5.7 |
| Primary foods | −10.6 | −6.7 | −7.7 | −5.6 |
| Processed foods | −13.1 | −9.3 | −8.6 | −6.5 |
| Agr. raw materials | −8.5 | −4.3 | −6.2 | −4.2 |
| Agricultural exports (qty) | 1.0 | 5.4 | 4.4 | 7.1 |
| Primary foods | 1.0 | 5.5 | 3.3 | 6.4 |
| Processed foods | 1.1 | 5.3 | 5.9 | 8.2 |
| Agr. raw materials | 0.9 | 5.1 | 4.2 | 6.3 |
| Agricultural imports (qty) | 19.3 | 9.0 | 10.5 | 5.3 |
| Primary foods | 17.9 | 7.8 | 10.3 | 5.1 |
| Processed foods | 21.7 | 11.3 | 10.2 | 4.9 |
| Agr. raw materials | 19.8 | 9.3 | 11.7 | 6.9 |
| Ec. welfare ($ mill.) | 2,698.2 | 19,958.5 | 3,095.1 | 19,868.9 |
| *High-income developing countries* | | | | |
| Exchange rate ($/L) | −0.7 | −2.9 | −0.7 | −0.3 |
| Agr. prices: Exportables (L) | 1.2 | 3.4 | 5.6 | 5.1 |
| Primary foods | 1.2 | 3.4 | 5.2 | 4.8 |
| Processed foods | 1.4 | 3.6 | 7.2 | 6.6 |
| Agr. raw materials | 1.1 | 3.1 | 3.9 | 3.2 |
| Agr. prices: Importables (L) | −8.6 | −6.8 | −4.6 | −5.4 |
| Primary foods | −10.5 | −8.9 | −7.5 | −8.4 |
| Processed foods | −10.5 | −8.7 | −5.5 | −6.2 |
| Agr. raw materials | −3.8 | −2.0 | 0.7 | −0.1 |
| Agricultural exports (qty) | 1.3 | 3.6 | 5.7 | 5.2 |
| Primary foods | 1.4 | 4.3 | 5.4 | 5.5 |
| Processed foods | 1.4 | 3.3 | 7.2 | 6.4 |
| Agr. raw materials | 1.1 | 3.1 | 3.9 | 3.2 |
| Agricultural imports (qty) | 22.6 | 17.8 | 12.8 | 14.5 |
| Primary foods | 32.4 | 26.4 | 24.2 | 25.5 |
| Processed foods | 23.2 | 19.1 | 10.6 | 12.8 |
| Agr. raw materials | 7.1 | 3.5 | −2.6 | −0.6 |
| Ec. welfare ($ mill.) | 2,630.6 | 10,332.9 | 1,215.2 | 7,398.0 |

Table 12.10  (*cont.*)

| Variable[a] | Unilateral liberalization | | Millennium Round liberalization | |
|---|---|---|---|---|
| | Agriculture | All goods | Agriculture | All goods |
| | | (% change) | | |
| *World* | | | | |
| Exchange rate ($/L) | ... | ... | ... | ... |
| Agr. prices: Exportables ($) | ... | ... | 5.1 | 4.8 |
| Primary foods | ... | ... | 4.4 | 4.1 |
| Processed foods | ... | ... | 6.1 | 5.9 |
| Agr. raw materials | ... | ... | 5.1 | 4.7 |
| Agr. prices: Importables ($) | ... | ... | ... | ... |
| Primary foods | ... | ... | ... | ... |
| Processed foods | ... | ... | ... | ... |
| Agr. raw materials | ... | ... | ... | ... |
| Agricultural exports (qty) | ... | ... | 5.1 | 5.5 |
| Primary foods | ... | ... | 4.4 | 4.7 |
| Processed foods | ... | ... | 6.2 | 6.6 |
| Agr. raw materials | ... | ... | 5.2 | 5.8 |
| Agricultural imports (qty) | ... | ... | ... | ... |
| Primary foods | ... | ... | ... | ... |
| Processed foods | ... | ... | ... | ... |
| Agr. raw materials | ... | ... | ... | ... |
| Ec. welfare ($ mill.) | ... | ... | 23,260.8 | 130,415.4 |

*Notes:* [a] Changes in variables are relative to base period (average 1995–6) values.
[b] Symbols denote US dollar ($), local currency (L), and quantity (qty). Changes in exchange rates, prices, and trade volumes are simple and weighted averages across countries and traded goods, respectively. The exchange rate represents both the nominal exchange rate and the real exchange rate, where the latter is defined as the relative price of non-traded goods to traded goods. Changes in prices of agricultural importables refer to changes in prices of imports that are assumed market-determined in the base period. Changes in economic welfare are equivalent variations in income computed with respect to expenditures on imports at base-period world prices. Changes in agricultural exports, agricultural imports, and economic welfare are per annum changes.
*Source:* Simulation of WTSM computable partial equilibrium model of world trade, assuming developing countries by income group eliminate all tariffs and NTBs on trade in agriculture or on trade in all goods simultaneously (unilateral liberalization) or in concert with all trading countries (Millennium Round liberalization).

(economy-wide) effects of protection on incentives to efficient and internationally competitive production of agricultural goods.

Broad-based unilateral trade liberalization clearly results in greater stimulus to prices for agricultural exportables and agricultural exports than sector-specific unilateral trade liberalization. In fact, similar to the earlier findings of KSV, the results for broad-based unilateral liberalization indicate that the indirect effects of protection on agriculture in developing countries are substantially greater than the direct effects. The greater incentive to agricultural exportables under broad-based rather than sector-specific unilateral trade liberalization is on the order of 3:1 for lower-middle-income and high-income developing countries, 3.5:1 for low-income countries, and 4:1 for upper-middle-income countries. The greater incentive to agricultural exportables is highest in low-income countries for processed foods (3.7:1), in lower-middle- income countries for agricultural raw materials (3.2:1), and in upper-middle-income countries for agricultural raw materials (4.3:1).[20]

These impacts on domestic prices of agricultural exportables are explained principally by differences in the economy-wide effects of unilateral trade liberalization on the exchange rate. Sector-specific unilateral trade liberalization accomplishes comparatively less in reducing overvaluation of the real exchange rate than broad-based unilateral trade liberalization. The greater magnitude of exchange rate changes under broad-based unilateral trade liberalization – on the order of 5–6 percentage points for most low-income and middle-income countries – summarizes in a single variable the extent of economy-wide bias against agriculture attributable to the indirect effect of protection in developing countries.

This indirect effect on price incentives for agricultural exportables is more modest than found earlier by KSV for developing countries in the 1970s and 1980s.[21] This undoubtedly reflects the substantial liberalization of trade by developing countries during the 1990s. However, the WTSM results indicate that economy-wide discrimination against agricultural exportables in developing countries remains appreciable, and continues to exert greater impact on producers of these exportables than protection in the agricultural sector. Thus, broad-based rather than sector-specific approaches to trade liberalization would provide substantially greater incentives to efficient and internationally competitive agriculture.

The WTSM results for prices of agricultural importables and agricultural imports also support this judgment. Prices of agricultural importables fall to a lesser degree, and agricultural imports see less stimulation, under broad-based rather than sector-specific unilateral trade liberalization.[22] These outcomes again reflect the greater adjustment in the real exchange rate under the former scenario. More fundamentally, they reflect greater incentives to efficient production of agricultural importables, and the less onerous costs of adjustment for producers of import-competing agricultural goods, under broad-based unilateral trade liberalization.

Under broad-based trade liberalization, agricultural imports increase by less than half the amount that they rise under sector-specific unilateral trade liberalization in low-income and upper-middle-income countries – the two groups in which discrimination against agriculture appears to be most pronounced. Moreover, the more modest changes in domestic prices and volumes of agricultural imports under broad-based unilateral trade liberalization better protect consumers.

Overall, the improvement in economic welfare in table 12.10 is generally several times greater under broad-based rather than sector-specific unilateral trade liberalization. For example, the gain in economic welfare for low-income countries is $20.4 billion under unilateral liberalization of trade in all goods, compared with just $2.9 billion under unilateral liberalization of agricultural trade only. Such wide discrepancies are, of course, accounted for by economic gains associated with higher imports of manufactured goods after broad-based trade liberalization – gains that more than offset any shortfalls in economic gains associated with lower imports of agricultural goods.

*Millennium Round liberalization*  The WTSM results suggest that both multilateral liberalization of trade in agriculture and multilateral liberalization of trade in all goods promise significant gains in welfare for the world economy: $23.3 billion and $130.4 billion, respectively. The model also suggests that successful new negotiations would increase both world prices and trade in agriculture by about 5 percent, led by higher prices and greater trade in processed foods.[23] However, the gains in economic welfare that accrue to developing countries in different income groups are often similar to the gains they could achieve through unilateral trade liberalization.

At the same time, some apparent advantages do result from multilateral trade liberalization. The most important is that developing countries capture gains in economic welfare at appreciably less cost in terms of exchange rate depreciation – and, by implication, exchange rate-related adjustments to the domestic economy. Another apparent advantage is that the positive stimulus to domestic prices of agricultural exportables is marginally greater, and the negative stimulus to domestic prices of agricultural importables marginally less, under multilateral trade liberalization. For instance, internationally competitive producers of agricultural exportables in low-income countries face domestic prices that are higher by 5.6 percent under multilateral negotiations to liberalize trade in agriculture, compared with 2.8 percent under sector-specific unilateral liberalization.

To these advantages, of course, must be added the principal advantage of multilateral negotiations from a political economy perspective. Namely, economic policy-makers enlist broader political support for trade liberalization from domestic producers of exportables, to offset the vested interests of domestic producers of import-competing goods in maintaining high levels of protection.

Finally, table 12.10 makes clear that the outcome of multilateral negotiations to eliminate protection for all goods is vastly superior to eliminating protection solely for agriculture, for the world at large and for developing countries. With regard specifically to agriculture in developing countries, the WTSM results are equally unequivocal in favor of multilateral negotiations that liberalize world trade in all goods. Economic gains to agriculture, measured in terms of greater positive stimulus to domestic prices for agricultural exportables and smaller negative stimulus to domestic prices for agricultural importables, are greater under broad-based multilateral trade liberalization for all income groups of developing countries. The greater gains to agriculture in developing countries under broad-based negotiations stem predominantly from greater reduction of economy-wide discrimination against agriculture.

## Conclusions

This chapter has sought to illuminate the importance of agricultural production and trade in developing countries today, against the backdrop of declining protection in the global economy, and a new round of multilateral negotiations to liberalize trade in agriculture and a wider array of traded goods. The chapter has also sought to estimate the economy-wide implications for agriculture of protection in developing countries. The principal findings may be summarized as follows:

- Agriculture continues to contribute significantly to output, exports, and especially employment in lower-income developing countries. Accordingly, expansion of efficient and internationally competitive agriculture would contribute not only to greater rural development but also to improved macroeconomic growth, foreign exchange earnings, and economic welfare. Many opportunities exist in agriculture and other sectors for beneficially expanding trade along not only North–South axes but also South–South axes.
- Protection in developing countries – particularly that enforced through NTBs – declined remarkably during the 1990s. This development may have contributed significantly to higher growth in *per capita* output of agricultural goods in developing countries. Nonetheless, protection in many developing countries – especially low-income countries in regions such as South Asia and Sub-Saharan Africa – remains high by international standards.
- Although economy-wide discrimination against agriculture attributable to protection in other sectors is more modest today, it remains appreciable and continues to outweigh sector-specific protection for agriculture. Broad-based trade liberalization would promote price incentives for efficient and

internationally competitive agriculture in lower-income countries 3–4 times as much as sector-specific liberalization in the case of agricultural exportables, and reduce price incentives by 1–2 times less in the case of agricultural importables.

• Multilateral Millennium Round negotiations offer developing countries the greatest potential for improving domestic price incentives for efficient and internationally competitive agriculture. Under multilateral negotiations to liberalize trade in all goods, not only would economy-wide discrimination against agriculture diminish by the greatest extent, but the economic welfare of consumers in these countries would expand substantially. Such gains would eclipse by several-fold the smaller economic gains from multilateral negotiations to liberalize trade solely in agriculture.

# Appendix    The World Trade Simulation Model (WTSM)

WTSM is an "elasticities-type" model of world trade based on familiar (log-linear) functions for import demand and export supply of merchandise goods in trading countries (table 12A.1).[24] Market-clearing conditions for each category of traded goods determine world prices denominated in US dollars (relative to the price of non-traded goods in the United States), and an equilibrium balance of payments condition determines the nominal (and real) exchange rate for each country.[25] By design, the model focuses on protection as the major element of trade regimes in the world economy. Hence it does not explicitly consider other elements of trade policy, such as export subsidies, export taxes, and quantitative restrictions on exports, which might also loom large in new WTO negotiations on trade in agriculture or other goods.

### Import demand

Import demand ($M_{k(i)}^d$) for traded good $k$ by each country $i$ in WTSM is given by the relationship:

$$M_{k(i)}^d = \left(M_{k(i)}^{da}\right)^{fk(i)} \left(M_{k(i)}^{do}\right)^{[1-fk(i)]} \tag{1}$$

where $M_{k(i)}^{da}$ denotes quantity of imports of good $k$ by country $i$ subject to administered protection measures (NTBs), $M_{k(i)}^{do}$ denotes quantity of imports of good $k$ by country $i$ subject to market prices, and $f_{k(i)}$ is the proportion of imports of good $k$ by country $i$ subject to administered protection.[26]

The demand for market-determined imports is a function of domestic prices for imports:

$$M_{k(i)}^{do} = a_{k(i)}^{do} \left(P_{k(i)}^m\right)^{\eta k(i)} \tag{2}$$

Table 12A.1 *WTSM countries*

| Country | Region | Income level | Protection data 1984–7 | Protection data 1993–8 |
|---|---|---|---|---|
| Albania | ECA | LM | | X |
| Algeria | MENA | LM | X | X |
| Argentina | LAC | UM | X | X |
| Australia | OECD | OECD | | X |
| Bangladesh | SA | LO | X | X |
| Belarus # | ECA | LM | | X |
| Bolivia | LAC | LM | X | X |
| Brazil | LAC | UM | X | X |
| Burkina Faso # | SSA | LO | | X |
| Cameroon | SSA | LO | | X |
| Canada | OECD | OECD | | X |
| Cen. African Rep. | SSA | LO | | X |
| Chad | SSA | LO | | X |
| Chile | LAC | UM | X | X |
| China | EAP | LO | X | X |
| Colombia | LAC | LM | X | X |
| Congo | SSA | LO | | X |
| Costa Rica | LAC | LM | | X |
| Côte d'Ivoire | SSA | LO | X | X |
| Cuba # | LAC | LO | | X |
| Czech Republic | ECA | UM | | X |
| Dominican Rep. # | LAC | LM | | X |
| Ecuador | LAC | LM | X | X |
| Egypt | MENA | LM | X | X |
| El Salvador | LAC | LM | | X |
| Estonia | ECA | LM | | X |
| Ethiopia | SSA | LO | X | X |
| European Union | OECD | OECD | | X |
| Gabon | SSA | UM | | X |
| Ghana # | SSA | LO | X | X |
| Guatemala | LAC | LM | | X |
| Honduras | LAC | LO | | X |
| Hong Kong | EAP | HI | X | X |
| Hungary | ECA | UM | | X |
| India | SA | LO | X | X |
| Indonesia | EAP | LM | X | X |
| Israel | MENA | HI | | X |
| Jamaica | LAC | LM | | X |
| Japan | OECD | OECD | | X |

Table 12A.1  (*cont.*)

| Country | Region | Income level | Protection data 1984–7 | Protection data 1993–8 |
|---|---|---|---|---|
| Kazakhstan # | ECA | LM | | X |
| Kenya | SSA | LO | X | X |
| Korea, Rep. | EAP | HI | X | X |
| Kyrgyzstan | ECA | LO | | X |
| Latvia | ECA | LM | | X |
| Lithuania | ECA | LM | | X |
| Madagascar | SSA | LO | | X |
| Malawi | SSA | LO | X | X |
| Malaysia | EAP | UM | X | X |
| Mali # | SSA | LO | | X |
| Mauritius | SSA | UM | X | X |
| Mexico | LAC | UM | X | X |
| Moldova | ECA | LO | | X |
| Morocco | MENA | LM | X | X |
| Mozambique | SSA | LO | | X |
| Nepal | SA | LO | X | X |
| New Zealand | OECD | OECD | | X |
| Nicaragua | LAC | LO | | X |
| Nigeria # | SSA | LO | X | X |
| Norway | OECD | OECD | | X |
| Oman | MENA | UM | | X |
| Pakistan | SA | LO | X | X |
| Panama | LAC | LM | | X |
| Pap. New Guinea # | EAP | LM | | X |
| Paraguay | LAC | LM | X | X |
| Peru | LAC | LM | | X |
| Philippines | EAP | LM | | X |
| Poland | ECA | UM | | X |
| Russian Federation | ECA | LM | | X |
| Rwanda # | SSA | LO | | X |
| Saudi Arabia | MENA | UM | X | X |
| Singapore | EAP | UM | X | X |
| South Africa | SSA | HI | | X |
| Sri Lanka # | SA | LO | X | X |
| Sudan | SSA | LO | X | X |
| Switzerland | OECD | OECD | | X |
| Taiwan | EAP | HI | | X |
| Tanzania | SSA | LO | X | X |
| Thailand | EAP | LM | X | X |
| Trinidad & Tobago | LAC | UM | | X |

Table 12A.1 (*cont.*)

| Country | Region | Income level | Protection data 1984–7 | Protection data 1993–8 |
|---------|--------|--------------|-------------------------|-------------------------|
| Tunisia | MENA | LM | X | X |
| Turkey | MENA | LM | X | X |
| Uganda # | SSA | LO | | X |
| Ukraine # | ECA | LM | | X |
| United States | OECD | OECD | | X |
| Uruguay | LAC | UM | | X |
| Venezuela | LAC | LM | X | X |
| Viet Nam # | EAP | LO | | X |
| Zambia | SSA | LO | | X |
| Zimbabwe | SSA | LO | X | X |

*Note:* Hatch marks (#) denote countries for which no 1995–6 data are reported in the UN trade database. X denotes availability of protection data in the UNCTAD trade analysis database. Developing country regions are East Asia and Pacific (EAP), Europe and Central Asia (ECA), Latin America and Caribbean (LAC), Middle East and North Africa (MENA), South Asia (SA), and Sub-Saharan Africa (SSA). Developing country income levels are low-income (LO), lower-middle-income (LM), upper-middle-income (UM), and high-income (HI). OECD denotes major industrial countries.
*Sources:* UNCTAD (1999); UN Statistical Office (1999); World Bank (1998).

where

$$P^m_{k(i)} = P^*_k \left(1 + t_{k(i)}\right) / e_{(i)},$$

and where $P^*_k$ is the world price of good $k$ denominated in US dollars, $t_{k(i)}$ is the applied *ad valorem* tariff rate for good $k$ in country $i$, $e_{(i)}$ is the exchange rate of country $i$'s currency in terms of the US dollar, and $\eta_{k(i)}$ is the own-price elasticity of import demand for good $k$ in country $i$.

With the assumption that the volume of administered imports of good $k$ in country $i$ is exogenously determined, total demand for imports of good $k$ in country $i$ is given by the equation:

$$M^d_{k(i)} = a^m_{k(i)} \left(P^m_{k(i)}\right)^{\eta k(i)[1 - f k(i)]} \tag{3}$$

where

$$P^m_{k(i)} = P^*_k \left(1 + t_{k(i)}\right) / e_{(i)}.$$

Equation (3) states that import demand in each country $i$ is a positive function of the exchange rate and the (absolute value of the) price elasticity of import demand, and a negative function of the world price of good $k$, the tariff rate, and the frequency of NTBs.[27]

### Export supply

Export supply $(X^s_{k(i)})$ of good $k$ in each country $i$ is given by the relationship:

$$X^s_{k(i)} = a^x_{k(i)}(P^x_{k(i)})^{\alpha k(i)} \tag{4}$$

where

$$P^x_{k(i)} = P^*_k/e_{(i)},$$

and where $\alpha_{k(i)}$ is the own-price elasticity of export supply of good $k$ in country $i$. Equation (4) states that export supply is a positive function of the world price of good $k$ and the elasticity of export supply, and a negative function of the US dollar exchange rate for the currency of country $i$.

### World market equilibrium

All countries are assumed to be price takers in international markets. Thus, the world price of good $k$ expressed in US dollars, $P^*_k$, is determined largely independently of the behavior of consumers and producers in any single country, or any small group of countries, by the market-clearing condition:

$$\Sigma_i M^d_{k(i)} = \Sigma_i X^s_{k(i)}. \tag{5}$$

That each country $i$ may simultaneously import and export goods in the same traded goods category is assumed to reflect problems of aggregation or the influence of transportation costs for like goods imported and exported from widely separated customs ports in the same country, rather than a departure from the model's underlying assumption of trade in homogeneous (i.e. undifferentiated) goods.[28]

### International payments equilibrium

In WTSM, net earnings from trade in services and long-term international resource flows to finance trade imbalances are exogenously determined. Thus, the condition for balance of payments equilibrium for each country $i$ in the model is given by

$$\Sigma_k(P^*_k X^s_{k(i)} - P^*_k M^d_{k(i)}) + SK^*_{(i)} = 0, \tag{6}$$

where $SK^*_{(i)}$ is the sum of net services exports and net financial inflows from abroad, denominated in US dollars. (If country $i$ is in trade surplus, then $SK^*_{(i)}$

Table 12A.2 *WTSM product categories*

| Product category | Standard International Trade Classification (SITC), Rev. 2 |
|---|---|
| *Primary products* | *(0 to 4) + 68* |
| Primary foods | AGGR |
|   Live animals | 00 |
|   Meat products | 01 |
|   Dairy products | 02–025 |
|   Cereal grains | 041 to 045 |
|   Vegetables | (0541 to 0545) + 05481 |
|   Fruits & nuts | 057 |
|   Sugar & honey | 06 |
|   Animal feed stuffs | 08 – 08142 |
|   Oil seeds | 22 |
| Processed foods | AGGR |
|   Animal & vegetable oils & fats | (091 + 4) – 4111 |
|   Cereal meals, flours, & preparations | 046 to 048 |
|   Prepared vegetables | (0546 to 056) – 05481 |
|   Prepared fruits | 058 |
|   Coffee, tea, & spices | 07 |
|   Beverages | 11 |
|   Other processed agricultural products | 025 + 098 |
| Agricultural raw materials | AGGR |
|   Tobacco & tobacco manufactures | 12 |
|   Hides & skins | 21 |
|   Natural rubber | 232 |
|   Natural fibers | (261 to 265) + 268 |
|   Other agricultural raw materials | 29 |
| Crude fertilizer & mineral ores | 27 + 28 |
| Mineral fuels | 3 |
| Non-ferrous metals | 68 |
| *Manufactured products* | *(5 to 8) – 68* |
| Chemicals | 5 |
|   Pharmaceuticals | 54 |
|   Toiletry & perfumes | 55 |
|   Manufactured fertilizers | 56 |
| Iron & steel | 67 |
| Machinery & equipment | 7 |
|   Non-electric machinery | 71 to 75 |
|   Electric machinery | 76 + 77 |
|   Transport equipment | 78 + 79 |

Table 12A.2 (*cont.*)

| Product category | Standard International Trade Classification (SITC), Rev. 2 |
|---|---|
| Other manufactured products | $(6 + 8) - (67 + 68)$ |
| Leather & travel goods | $61 + 83$ |
| Rubber products | 62 |
| Wood products | 63 |
| Paper products | 64 |
| Textiles & clothing | $65 + 84$ |
| Non-metallic mineral products | 66 |
| Furniture | 82 |
| Footwear | 85 |
| Professional equipment | $87 + 88$ |
| *All product categories* | *0 to 9* |

*Notes:* AGGR denotes sum of SITC numbers in the given product category; negative sign ($-$) denotes "minus."
*Sources:* OECD (1998); UNCTAD (1994).

is the sum of net services imports and net financial outflows to finance trade imbalances in other countries.)

The balance of payments condition in (6) is essential for "closure" of WTSM. However, before other equations in the model, it also serves to determine the real exchange rate of each country,[29] which in economic theory and applied analyses is a key variable for determining the incidence of protection for agriculture in developing countries.

**Baseline data and parameter values**

WTSM employs average annual data on international trade for seventy-five countries from 1995–6 (table 12A.2).[30] The trade data are disaggregated by forty categories of primary commodities and manufactures, and denominated in US dollars. The information on trade in primary commodities includes twenty-one categories of agricultural commodities and products classified by three major groups: primary foods, processed foods, and agricultural raw materials.[31] World prices of traded goods (denominated in US dollars) and US dollar-exchange rates are set equal to unity in the base period, by appropriately scaling trade quantities and national currency units in the model.[32]

Information on tariff rates and NTBs is compiled from the UNCTAD Trade Analysis and Information System, or TRAINS (UNCTAD, 1999). TRAINS information is not available for all low-income and middle-income countries in WTSM. For the developing countries in WTSM not covered by TRAINS information, average protection levels of countries in the same income group (low-income, lower-middle-income, or upper-middle-income) are assumed.

The remaining parameters of WTSM consist of own-price elasticities of demand and supply for traded goods. Following KSV (1988) and Schiff and Valdés (1992), these elasticities are assumed everywhere equal to −2.0 and 1.0, respectively – values that are somewhat higher in absolute magnitude than estimates found by empirical studies.[33]

WTSM is constructed and simulated using VORSIM, a Microsoft Excel-based economic modeling software for solving systems of linear and nonlinear equations (VORSIM 1999).[34]

## Notes

1. For an examination of the growth experiences of Sub-Saharan African countries in relationship to fluctuations in world prices for agricultural and other primary commodities, see Deaton (1999).
2. Many developing countries also have potential if not currently revealed comparative advantage in high-value added horticultural commodities, such as premium fresh fruits and vegetables and cut flowers, as discussed by Islam (1990).
3. A frequent sign of this condition is a wide divergence between shares of agriculture in domestic value added (GDP) on the one hand, and domestic employment on the other. Such divergence arises because industrial protection and inappropriate macroeconomic policies that give rise to an overvalued exchange rate tend to repress domestic prices for labor-using agricultural output. As may be seen in table 12.1, this condition persists in low-income countries today, especially in low-income regions such as South Asia and Sub-Saharan Africa.
4. On the contribution of agriculture to growth and economic development, see, among others, Johnston and Mellor (1961), Mellor (1966, 1995), Johnston and Kilby (1975), Adelman (1984), and Adelman and Robinson (1978). On the issue of "consumption linkage" effects critical to the influence of agricultural growth on the overall growth performance of rural and national economies of developing countries, see, for instance, Mellor and Lele (1973) and Ranis, Stewart, and Reyes (1989).
5. See KSV (1988, 1992), and Schiff and Valdés (1992). See also Bautista and Valdés (1993).
6. Also, more recently, Bautista et al. (1998) argue that policy biases against agriculture are more appropriately analyzed using a general equilibrium framework than a partial equilibrium framework. They argue principally that the partial equilibrium framework employed by KSV misses potentially important interactions between factor markets and goods markets, where the former include markets for intermediate as well as primary factors of production. However, they also contend that other aspects of the KSV analysis are questionable, including the assumption of homogeneous traded

goods, and the representation of exchange rate overvaluation. Unfortunately, Bautista and his associates do not provide empirical results illustrating the importance of their objections to partial equilibrium analysis of policy biases against agriculture for more than a single developing country, namely, Tanzania.

7. In table 12.2, low-income countries and LIFD countries correspond to FAO defi-nitions of both categories. LIFD countries compose a larger group of developing countries than low-income countries because the former include a number of Euro-pean and other economies in transition not traditionally included in low-income or other groups of developing countries.

8. The agricultural growth experience of Sub-Saharan African countries is less favor-able than that of other developing regions, given that the average rate of population growth in the region during the decade ending in 1996 was 2.8 percent per annum. In comparison, total agricultural output during the decade ending in 1996 grew by 25 percent (2.3 percent per annum) in Middle East and North African countries and 20 percent (1.8 percent per annum) in Latin American and Caribbean countries. In European and Central Asian countries, total agricultural output during the same period fell precipitously, by 46 percent (3.9 percent per annum).

9. During the decade ending in 1996, total agriculture output in China grew by 49 percent (4.1 percent per annum), from an average of 753 million metric tons in 1985–6 to an average of 1,121 million metric tons in 1995–6.

10. The RCA index employed here is one frequently specified in applied analyses of international trade relations. It relates the importance of each developing region or income group as a supplier of agricultural or other products to the world market relative to all competing exporting regions or income groups. For further discussion, see Balassa (1979) and Greenaway and Milner (1993).

11. Frequency ratios measure in percentage terms the number of national tariff schedule lines that are affected by a given import control measure within an aggregate trade category. Although tariff-equivalent measures of NTBs might be more desirable for assessing the economic costs of NTBs, frequency ratios are relied upon here because of their greater availability and ease of computation. See Deardorff and Stern (1985), Laird and Yeats (1990), and Laird (1997) for discussion of NTBs, and conceptual and technical problems in computing tariff-equivalent measures of NTBs.

12. See tables 12A.1 and 12A.2 (pp. 277, 281) for countries and product categories included in the analysis.

13. On political economy aspects of protection and agriculture in developing countries versus major industrial countries, see Anderson and Hayami (1986).

14. The prominence of non-tariff protection in table 12.6 is seemingly at odds with the Uruguay Round Agreement on Agriculture (URAA), which mandated tariffication of quantitative measures restricting trade in agriculture. The precise correspondence of the non-tariff barriers covered by the data presented in table 12.6 to those covered by the URAA has not been investigated. The prominence of non-tariff protection in table 12.6 may reflect special treatment for developing countries under the URAA, whereby they were granted a longer time period (ten years, compared with six years for major industrial countries) to convert their non-tariff barriers in agriculture to tariffs (Ingco and Hathaway, 1996).

15. Taxes and quantitative controls on agricultural exports repress agriculture, whereas subsidies to agricultural exports have the opposite effect. From an economy-wide perspective, border measures to restrict or expand exports in other sectors would also affect the performance of agricultural exports, and hence attempts to detect and measure discrimination against agriculture.

16. KSV (1988) also include in their measurement of distortions to agricultural price incentives the impact of overvalued exchange rates in developing countries. For this aspect of their calculations, they assume that an appreciable to substantial portion of financial flows to developing countries during the 1970s and 1980s was unsustainable, and hence call for added exchange rate adjustments to further stimulate agricultural production and exports. Assessing possible misalignment of exchange rates is an uncertain task at best, and arguably it is less called for in the context of balance of payment financing for developing countries today. Thus, the present analysis does not address the issue of overvalued exchange rates in less-developed countries. For further discussion, see Edwards (1988, 1989), Williamson (1994), and, directly with regard to the KSV analysis, Bautista et al. (1998).

17. Whether total agricultural production grows or falls is indeterminate in WTSM. Conceptually, the outcome depends upon the sum of changes in agricultural production not only for export markets but also for domestic markets.

18. In terms of WTSM variables and "simulation mechanics," each scenario involves reducing all relevant $t_{k(i)}$ and $f_{k(i)}$ to zero, solving the model, and comparing outcomes for individual variables to their baseline values (see appendix (p. 276) for definitions of variables). It may be shown that the import demand coefficients, $a_{k(i)}^m$, in (3) of WTSM are implicitly functions of the $f_{k(i)}$-variables. In simulations of the model, however, these import demand coefficients are not adjusted to reflect elimination of NTBs. The direction and magnitude of bias in variables introduced by this shortcoming are uncertain.

19. Changes in economic welfare are computed as equivalent variations in income with respect to expenditures on imports. Owing to conceptual difficulties in appropriately defining and measuring domestic prices of administered imports in each country, WTSM employs based period values of world prices rather domestic prices in the welfare calculations. This methodology undoubtedly introduces a downward bias to the computed changes in economic welfare reported in table 12.10. On measuring changes in economic welfare in applied trade models, see, for instance, Martin (1997).

20. A technical appendix available from the author presents complete results for changes in domestic agricultural prices by the twenty-one categories of agricultural commodities and products in WTSM.

21. Recall that KSV found that agricultural exportables were taxed indirectly by both protection and the exchange rate effects of unsustainable current account imbalances, by a margin of nearly 30 percentage points on average. The corresponding margin of indirect protection for importables was found to be just over 10 percentage points on average. Thus, the overall indirect effect of economy-wide discrimination against agriculture in developing countries in the KSV analysis was on the order of

20 percentage points, compared to 5–6 percentage points on average in present analysis (based on the indirect effects of protection only).

22. Strictly speaking, the impacts on prices of agricultural imports reported in table 12.10 and discussed here refer to impacts on domestic prices of market-determined imports in WTSM. Although domestic prices of administered imports and market-determined imports are assumed equal in each goods category under free trade, base-period domestic prices of administered imports are not explicitly defined in the simulation model.

23. These estimates do not take into account the impacts of eliminating domestic price supports and export subsidies for agriculture in major industrial countries.

24. The theoretical bases for elasticities-type trade models are discussed by Dornbusch (1974, 1975). As noted in the main text, KSV (1988), and Schiff and Valdés (1992) essentially apply an elasticities-type trade model to measure sector-specific (direct) effects versus economy-wide (total direct and indirect) effects of protection on agricultural price incentives in developing countries taken individually, and assuming that world prices for traded goods are exogenous. Previous applications of elasticities-type models of trade in agriculture and manufactures by the author include DeRosa (1992, 1996), and DeRosa and Saber (1999).

25. In each country, the aggregate price of non-traded goods is assumed to be the numéraire. Under this assumption, the nominal exchange rate is equivalent to the real exchange rate, defined as the price of non-tradable goods relative to tradable goods, in each country. See Dervis, de Melo, and Robinson (1982) and Robinson (1989).

26. Import demand in (1) is an ad hoc aggregation of administered imports and price-determined imports. The aggregation avoids the problem of estimating tariff rate equivalents for NTBs. Also, it conveniently introduces frequency ratios of NTBs into the import demand equations of WTSM, allowing the model to incorporate UNCTAD data on both *ad valorem* tariff rates and NTB frequency rates. Notwithstanding these attributes, (1) is not rigorously derived from economic demand theory.

27. That import demand and (further below) export supply are independent of world prices of other traded goods belies the partial equilibrium character of WTSM. That is, the model does not explicitly incorporate the hallmark of general equilibrium models: long-run possibilities for substitution of goods (and resources) in demand and production.

28. The case of US petroleum exported from Alaska to Japan, while Eastern US ports import petroleum from the Middle East, is a prime example. A popular alternative approach to accounting for "two-way trade" in world trade models is to incorporate the assumption of differentiated demands for similar products produced in different countries following Armington (1969). This assumption results in complex systems of bilateral demands for traded goods, and has been subjected to some criticism (for example, Winters, 1984).

29. See n. 25.

30. WTSM is constructed using information for 89 developing countries and industrial countries (see table 12A.1). There is no "rest-of-the-world" bloc. Unfortunately, import data are lacking for some fourteen developing countries, reducing the effective number of countries in the model to seventy-five. Export and import data for all

countries in the model are compiled from the international trade database of the UN Statistical Office (1999).

31. See table 12A.2.

32. By definition, the US dollar exchange rate for the US dollar is always equal to unity. The US real exchange rate can be defined as a weighted average of real exchange rates of the country's major trading partners.

33. See price elasticity estimates for international trade compiled by Stern, Francis and Schumacher (1976), Goldstein and Khan (1985), and DeRosa (1992). As KSV (1988) point out, the assumption of relatively large price elasticity values for import demand and export supply functions in models such as WTSM ensures that magnitudes of simulated price and exchange rate effects under trade liberalization scenarios are not biased upward.

34. A workable version of WTSM that does not require VORSIM is available from the author. However, given the large size of WTSM, stimulating the model does require a premium version of the standard Excel solver, available from Frontline Systems (1999).

## References

Adelman, I., 1984. "Beyond Export-Led Growth," *World Development*, 12, 937–49

Adelman, I., and S. Robinson, 1978. *Income Distribution Policy in Developing Countries: A Case Study of Korea*, Stanford: Stanford University Press

Anderson, K., and Y. Hayami (eds.), 1986. *The Political Economy of Agricultural Protection*, Sydney: Allen & Unwin

Armington, P. A., 1969. "A Theory of Demand for Products Distinguished by Place of Production," *IMF Staff Papers*, 16(1), 159–78

Balassa, B., 1979. "The Changing Pattern of Comparative Advantage in Manufactured Goods," *Review of Economics and Statistics*, 61, 259–66

Bautista, R. M., S. Robinson, F. Tarp, and P. Wobst, 1998. "Policy Bias and Agriculture: Partial and General Equilibrium Measures," TMD Discussion Paper, 25, Trade and Macroeconomics Division, International Food Policy Research Institute, Washington, DC; forthcoming in *Review of Development Economics*

Bautista, R. M. and A. Valdés, 1993. *The Bias against Agriculture: Trade and Macroeconomic Policies in Developing Countries*, San Francisco: ICS Press

Deardorff, A. V. and R. Stern, 1985. "Methods of Measurement of Non-Tariff Barriers," Document UNCTAD/ST/MD/28, United Nations Conference on Trade and Development, Geneva

Deaton, A., 1999. "Commodity Prices and Growth in Africa," *Journal of Economic Perspectives*, 13(3), 23–40

DeRosa, D. A., 1992. "Protection and Export Performance in Sub-Saharan Africa, *Weltwirtschftliches Archiv*, 128(1), 88–124

    1996. "The Uruguay Round Agreement on Agriculture and the International Trade of Sub-Saharan Africa," *Agrekon (South African Journal of Agricultural Economics)*, 35(2), 76–93

    2000. "Agricultural Trade and Rural Development in the Middle East and North Africa: Recent Developments and Prospects," in B. Hoekman and J. Zarrouk (eds.), *Catching up with the Competition: Trade Opportunities and Challenges for Arab Countries*, Ann Arbor, Michigan: University of Michigan Press

DeRosa, D. A. and M. K. Saber, 1999. "Regional Integration Arrangements in the Middle East and North Africa: An Analysis of Egypt's Foreign Trade and Development Interests," Occasional Paper, 13, Center for Economic and Financial Research and Studies, Faculty of Economics and Political Science, Cairo University

Dervis, K., J. de Melo, and S. Robinson, 1982. *General Equilibrium Models for Development Policy*, Washington, DC: World Bank

Dornbusch, R., 1984. "Tariffs and Nontraded Goods," *Journal of International Economics*, 11, 177–85

1985. "Exchange Rates and Fiscal Policy in a Popular Model of International Trade," *American Economic Review*, 65(2), 859–71

Edwards, S., 1988. *"Exchange Rate Misalignment in Developing Countries,"* Occasional Paper, 2 (New Series), Baltimore. Johns Hopkins University Press for the World Bank

1989. *Real Exchange Rates, Devaluation, and Adjustment: Exchange Rate Policy in Developing Countries*, Cambridge, MA: MIT Press

Frontline Systems, 1999. Frontline Systems Inc.: Developers of your Spreadsheet's Solver, http://www.frontsys.com

Goldstein, M. and M. Khan, 1985. "Income and Price Effects in Foreign Trade," in R. W. Jones and P. B. Kenen (eds.), *Handbook of International Economics, II*, Amsterdam: North-Holland

Greenaway, D. and C. Milner, 1993. *Trade and Industrial Policy in Developing Countries*, Ann Arbor, Michigan: University of Michigan Press

Ingco, M. D. and D. E. Hathaway, 1996. "Agricultural Liberalization and the Uruguay Round," in W. Martin and L. A. Winters (eds.), *The Uruguay Round and the Developing Economies*, Cambridge: Cambridge University Press

Islam, N., 1990. *Horticultural Exports of Developing Countries: Past Performance, Future Prospects, and Policy Issues*, Research Report, 80, International Food Policy Research Institute, Washington, DC

Johnston, B. and P. Kilby, 1975. *Agriculture and Structural Transformation*, London: Oxford University Press

Johnston, B. and J. W. Mellor, 1961. "The Role of Agriculture in Economic Development," *American Economic Review*, 51, 566–93

Krueger, A. O., M. Schiff, and A. Valdés, 1988. "Agricultural Incentives in Developing Countries: Measuring the Effect of Sectoral and Economywide Policies," *World Bank Economic Review*, 2(3), 255–72

(eds.), 1992. *The Political Economy of Agricultural Pricing Policy*, Baltimore: Johns Hopkins University Press for the World Bank

Laird, S., 1997. "Quantifying Commercial Policies," in J. F. Francois and K. A. Reinert (eds.), *Applied Methods for Trade Policy Analysis: A Handbook*, Cambridge: Cambridge University Press

Laird, S. and A. Yeats, 1990. *Quantitative Methods for Trade Barrier Analysis*, London: Macmillan

Martin, W. J., 1997. "Measuring Welfare Changes with Distortions," in J. F. Francois and K. A. Reinert (eds.), *Applied Methods for Trade Policy Analysis: A Handbook*, Cambridge: Cambridge University Press

Mellor, J. W., 1966. *The Economics of Agricultural Development*, Ithaca: Cornell University Press

(ed.), 1995. *Agriculture on the Road to Industrialization*, Baltimore: Johns Hopkins University Press for the International Food Policy Research Institute

Mellor, J. W. and U. Lele, 1973. "Growth Linkages of the New Food Grain Technologies," *Indian Journal of Agricultural Economics*, 28, 35–55

Organization for Economic Cooperation and Development (OECD), 1998. "Background Tables/Graphs," OECD Workshop on Emerging Trade Issues in Agriculture, October 26–27, Paris

Ranis, G., F. Stewart, and D. Reyes, 1989. "Linkages in Development: A Philippine Case Study," *Working Paper 89–02*, Manila: Philippine Institute for Development Studies

Robinson, S., 1989. "Multisector Models," in H. Chenery and T. N. Srinivasan (eds.), *Handbook of Development Economics*, Amsterdam: Elsevier

Schiff, M. and A. Valdés, 1992. *The Political Economy of Agricultural Pricing Policy, 4: A Synthesis of the Economics in Developing Countries*, Baltimore: Johns Hopkins University Press for the World Bank

Stern, R. M., J. Francis, and B. Schumacher, 1976. *Price Elasticities in International Trade: An Annotated Bibliography*, London: Macmillan for the Trade Policy Research Centre

United Nations Conference on Trade and Development (UNCTAD), 1994. *Directory of Import Regimes*, Geneva: UNCTAD

1999. *Trade Analysis and Information System (version 6.02, cd-rom)*, Geneva: UNCTAD

United Nations Food and Agriculture Organization (FAO), 1999. *FAOSTAT (cd-rom)*, Rome

UN Statistical Office, 1999. *United Nations Commodity Trade Database*, Geneva: United Nations

VORSIM, 1999. VORSIM Model Building Software for Microsoft Excel in Windows, http://www.vorsim.com

Williamson, J., (ed.), 1994. *Estimating Equilibrium Exchange Rates*, Washington, DC: for International Economics Institute

Winters, L. A., 1984. "Separability and the Specification of Foreign Trade Functions," *Journal of International Economics*, 17, 239–63

World Bank, 1998. *World Development Indicators 1998 (cd-rom)*, Washington, DC: World Bank

# 13 Liberalizing sugar: the taste test of the WTO

*Brent Borrell and David Pearce*

If ever there was a case for multilateral trade liberalization, and if ever there was a liberalization from which the global economy stood to gain, it is sugar. The world sugar market contains some of the largest and most blatant forms of trade protection. Many of these have a 300-year history. The worst are in developed countries, which greatly distort trade and prices in this commodity.

Although the world economy, consumers, and efficient sugar producers stand to gain substantially from liberalization, some producers, especially those in developed countries, stand to lose. And herein lies a political challenge: large vested interests are likely to oppose efforts to liberalize trade in sugar. In the Uruguay Round these vested interests won hands down. Should they win again during the new round, they are likely to further undermine the credibility of developed countries regarding the WTO, and of the WTO itself.

Countries ultimately liberalize trade unilaterally, but multilateral forums can assist that process. The greatest gains in trade liberalization come from reducing the biggest distortions first. Giving prominence to sugar and other highly protected products during the new WTO round makes economic sense. Such prominence will also help counter the vested interests opposed to reform. To aid in that process, this chapter analyzes the costs and benefits of distortions in the sugar market, and of options for reforming that sector.

## A highly protected market

Over 80 percent of world sugar supplies sell at prices above the world price. Producers of over 40 percent of world production receive prices 50 to nearly 400 percent higher than the world price.

In many countries archaic and complex policies raise consumer prices to protect producers from the forces of global competition. European countries initially forced their former sugar-producing colonies to export exclusively to their mother countries, which extracted large import duties. These duties

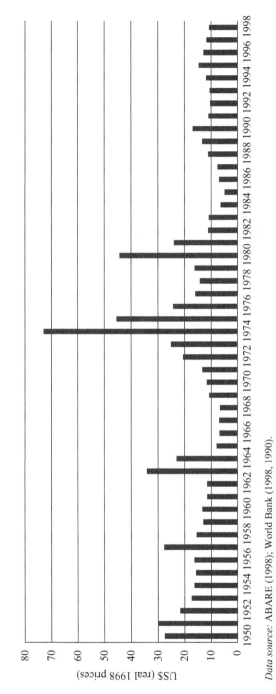

*Data source*: ABARE (1998); World Bank (1998, 1990).

Figure 13.1  World sugar prices (real), 1950–1998

provided indirect incentives for producers in Europe and North America to establish high-cost (mainly temperate-zone beet) sugar production. Countries have added many complex regulations and controls to deal with the unintended and costly consequences, so competitive markets have played only a small role in allocating resources. These industries have a strong interest in maintaining these interventions.

Trade barriers have prevented the world's efficient producing regions from easily competing with and displacing less efficient regions. Trade barriers have also slowed producers' responses to changes in the world market, making the world price highly volatile (see figure 13.1).

Table 13.1 outlines the types of policies that key sugar trading nations and regions operate, as well as their *ad valorem* tariff equivalents bound under the GATT Uruguay Round. These commitments were intended to reduce tariffs and export subsidies and give importing firms minimum access. However, the new measures have done little to reduce sugar protection because countries were already fulfilling many of these commitments.

Given the high levels of protection in the world sugar market and the lack of progress under the Uruguay Round, the potential gains from liberalizing trade through subsequent rounds remain large. Trade liberalization holds the promise of rationalizing the use of global sweetener-producing resources, as more trade would allow low-cost producers to displace high-cost ones. The net result would be lower global production costs and prices and higher consumption and welfare. Expanded output by low-cost producers would increase their income, while high-cost producers could devote their resources to more efficient activities.

### Estimating the gains from liberalizing trade

Estimating the complex changes in production, consumption, trade, prices, consumer benefits, producer benefits, and government revenues that would arise from liberalizing the world sugar market requires a formal and consistent economic model of the industry.

To make such estimates, we used a detailed partial equilibrium model known as the Global Sweetener Market (GSM) model, developed by the Centre for International Economics for the Sugar Division of CSR Australia Ltd.[1] The model represents the economic behavior surrounding production, consumption, and trade for the twenty-four regions and seven classes of sweeteners outlined in table 13.2. The model includes 200 separate sweetener trade flows and trade barriers between regions, and can analyze how consumption, production, trade, prices, and welfare will change as variables affecting the market change. (For a technical overview of the model, see the appendix, p. 308.)

Table 13.1 *Types of policies by country*

| Policy Country | Import quotas | Tariff quota | Tariff | Ad valorem bound tariff equivalent % in 2000 | Surcharge | State trading | Subsidies | Other | Export subsidies |
|---|---|---|---|---|---|---|---|---|---|
| Japan | | | ✓ | 287 | ✓ | | ✓ | 1 Production quotas | ✓ |
| Western Europe | ✓ | ✓ | | 176 | ✓ | | | 2 Production quotas | |
| United States | ✓ | ✓ | ✓ | 151 | | | | 3 Compulsory export quotas | |
| Mexico | | | ✓ | 96 | | | | | |
| Indonesia | | | | 95 | | ✓ | | 4 Government-owned mills | |
| Eastern Europe (Poland) | | ✓ | ✓ | 96 | ✓ | | | 5 Government-owned mills | |
| China | | | ✓ | | ✓ | ✓ | ✓ | 6 Production quotas | |
| | | | | | | | | 7 Regional government ownership of mills | |
| Philippines | ✓ | | ✓ | 100 | | | | | |
| Ukraine | | | ✓ | | | | | | |
| South Africa | | | ✓ | 105 | | | | | |
| Mauritius | | | | 139 | | | | 8 Export subsidies from EU | |

(*cont.*)

Table 13.1 (*cont.*)

| Policy Country | Import quotas | Tariff quota | Tariff | *Ad valorem* bound tariff equivalent % in 2000 | Surcharge | State trading | Subsidies | Other | Export subsidies |
|---|---|---|---|---|---|---|---|---|---|
| India | | | ✓ | 150 | | | | 9 Import ban | |
| Other America | | | ✓ | 35–100 | | | | 10 Land locked-in | ✓ |
| Middle East | | | ✓ | 20–100 | | ✓ | | | |
| Thailand | | | | 99 | | | | 11 Import ban | |
| North Africa | | | ✓ | 20–100 | | | | | |
| FSU | | | ✓ | 20 | ✓ | | | | |
| Canada | | | ✓ | 8 | | | | | |
| Brazil | | | | 35 | | | | 12 Control on ethanol imports | |
| Cuba | | | | | | | | 13 Command economy | |
| Australia | | | | 22 | | ✓ | | | |

*Source:* GSM database; Larson and Borrell (1999).

Table 13.2 *Regions and commodities in the GSM model*

| Regions | | Bilaterally traded commodities | Net traded commodities | Non-traded commodities |
|---|---|---|---|---|
| Australia | Malaysia | Raw sugar | Nutritive sweeteners | Non-centrifugal (rudimentary) sugar |
| Brazil | India | Mill white sugar | Non-nutritive sweeteners | |
| Cuba | Singapore | White sugar (refined from raw) | | |
| Thailand | Mexico | | | |
| Philippines | North Africa | White sugar (from beet) | | |
| Ukraine | Southern Africa | | | |
| United States | Middle East | | | |
| Japan | Other America | | | |
| China | FSU | | | |
| Canada | Eastern Europe | | | |
| Korea | Western Europe | | | |
| Indonesia | Rest of the World | | | |

*Source:* GSM model.

We used the model to compare the world sweetener market in 2008 with and without trade liberalization. The first projection assumes that today's levels of protection remain but that the world market continues to grow because of rising incomes and population. The model also assumes that productivity gains occur in line with rates over the past decade. Little else about the world market changes. This projection provides a baseline scenario.

The second projection assumes that all countries removed all trade protection (tariffs, quotas, and subsidies) in the year 2000, so that by 2008 they had made all adjustments to the new trade environment. This scenario includes the same assumptions about income, population, and productivity growth as the first scenario. This projection provides a free-trade scenario.

As with all model results, those presented here should be treated with some caution. Simulating the removal of long-standing policies may result in activities and trade flows never before observed, and models are always limited in the extent to which they can capture new kinds of activities. However, the model does broadly indicate the results that could be expected if the sugar market were fully liberalized.

*Measuring current levels of protection*

Figure 13.2 shows the relative prices producing regions received and the proportions of the sugar market they supplied for 1997. The figure also indicates the world price – the average real 1998 price for the twelve years to 1998. This price is very close to the average price in 1997. The difference between prices received and the world price measures the amount of protection in a given market.

Only four relatively small importers are trading without protection. Among exporters, Australia, Brazil, and Cuba, which together produce 17 percent of global nutritive sweeteners by volume, are the only free-traders. Among other major exporters, Thai producers receive some subsidies from domestic consumers, while Western European producers receive large subsidies from domestic consumers and large export subsidies from government.

The second panel of figure 13.2 indicates the proportions of production that countries export, their nominal producer subsidies, and their implied export taxes. Nominal producer subsidies amount to over $18 billion a year, or around a third of the total cost of sweeteners to consumers at the wholesale level. Western European producers receive the largest producer subsidies, with a major proportion in the form of export subsidies. Producers in the United States, Mexico, Indonesia, and Eastern Europe also depend heavily on subsidies. Japan produces only a small proportion of global sweeteners, but at extremely high cost.

Producers in Southern Africa, "other America" (Latin America excluding Brazil, Mexico, and Cuba), and the "Rest of the World" also receive substantial export subsidies. Western Europe (the EU) and the United States provide many of these subsidies (figure 13.3), which grant select suppliers quota-restricted access to highly protected markets. Access to the EU market enables suppliers to receive prices that are more than double the world price, on average. Access to the US market enables suppliers to receive prices roughly 80 percent above the world price.

Within Southern Africa, Mauritius, Swaziland, and Zimbabwe are major recipients of EU subsidies – over 70 percent of sugar production in Mauritius receives EU subsidies. A large proportion of exports from the Dominican Republic and the Philippines depend on US export subsidies. Brazil and Australia also receive such subsidies, but they represent less than 1 percent of the value of their exports. Subsidies represent an important proportion of the total value of export sales for most other exporters as well. Developed countries regard many of these subsidies to developing countries as a form of aid.

*The effects of removing all protection*

Model results indicate that the impact of removing trade protection is greatest for the most- and the least-protected producing regions. If countries remove

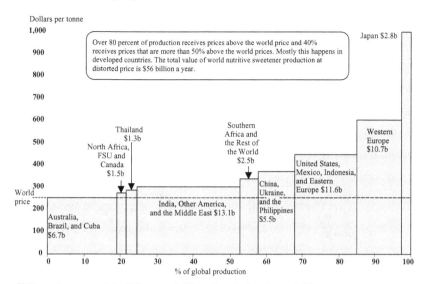

Dollars per tonne

Over 80 percent of production receives prices above the world price and 40% receives prices that are more than 50% above the world prices. Mostly this happens in developed countries. The total value of world nutritive sweetener production at distorted price is $56 billion a year.

Japan $2.8b

Western Europe $10.7b

Thailand $1.3b

North Africa, FSU and Canada $1.5b

Southern Africa and the Rest of the World $2.5b

United States, Mexico, Indonesia, and Eastern Europe $11.6b

World price

India, Other America, and the Middle East $13.1b

China, Ukraine, and the Philippines $5.5b

Australia, Brazil, and Cuba $6.7b

% of global production

$/t Proportions exported, implied export subsidies and nominal producer subsidies

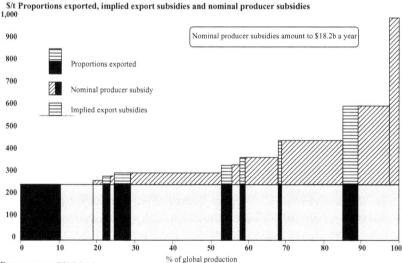

Nominal producer subsidies amount to $18.2b a year

Proportions exported

Nominal producer subsidy

Implied export subsidies

% of global production

*Data source:* GSM database.

Figure 13.2  Relative amount received by producers for sweeteners at the wholesale level, 1997

price protection, prices fall by around 65 percent in Japan, 40 percent in Western Europe, 25 percent in the United States, Mexico, Indonesia, and Eastern Europe, and around 10 percent in China, the Ukraine, and the Philippines. Lower prices in these countries raise consumption and cut sugar production, as high-cost producers use their land, labor, and capital in more profitable activities. In the

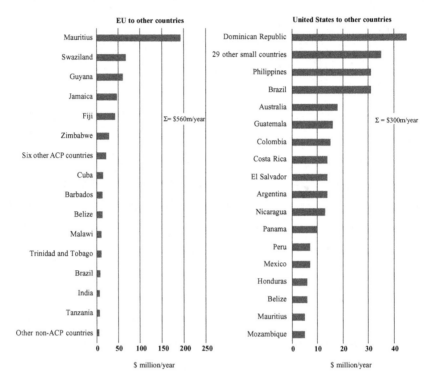

*Data source:* GSM model.

Figure 13.3  Value of export subsidies by the EU and the United States to other countries

United States, for instance, alternative production might include soybeans, corn, or wheat – crops for which US producers have a comparative advantage.

The combination of higher consumption and lower production raises import demand and world prices. Efficient, low-cost producers respond by expanding production. However, price increases in efficient exporting countries cause consumption to fall somewhat in those countries. The combined effects of higher production and lower consumption raise export supplies. Trade rises and net imports and net exports change (figure 13.4 and figure 13.5). In countries where protection and taxation is high – Western Europe, the United States, Japan, Indonesia, and Eastern Europe – net imports increase by over 15 million tons a year. Western Europe and Mexico also cut subsidized exports. Meanwhile unprotected or lightly protected countries – Brazil, "other America," Thailand, Australia, Cuba, and Southern Africa – increase net exports.

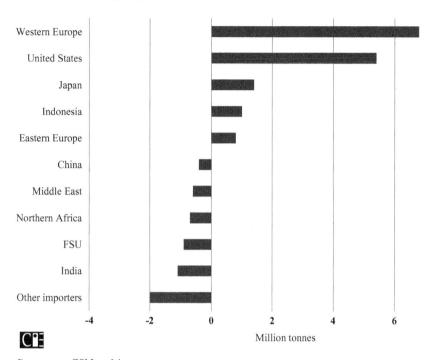

*Data source:* GSM model.

Figure 13.4 Changes in net imports, 2008 (million tonnes)

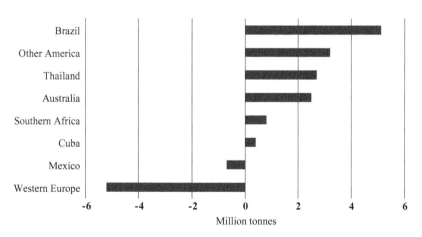

*Data source:* GSM model.

Figure 13.5 Changes in net exports, 2008 (million tonnes)

The interplay of more import demand and more export supplies yields world raw sugar prices 38 percent higher than if no trade liberalization occurs. The prices of mill white and refined sugar also rise, but not as much as the price of raw sugar.

In totally unprotected countries such as Australia, Brazil, and Cuba, prices rise by around 38 percent in line with world price rises. In North Africa, the former Soviet Union, Thailand, India, "other America," and the Middle East, prices rise 15–20 percent. In Southern Africa and the "Rest of the World," they remain largely unchanged. Higher world prices mean higher prices for consumers and lower imports in some lightly protected importing countries (table 13.4).

Figure 13.6 reveals the scale of the shift of production from high-cost to low-cost producers under free trade in 2008. Today's high-cost producers – Japan, Western Europe, the United States, Mexico, Indonesia, Eastern Europe, China, Ukraine, and the Philippines – reduce their share of world production by around 14 percent, and lower-cost producers increase their share correspondingly.

Japan cuts production by 44 percent, the United States by 32 percent, Western Europe by 21 percent, Indonesia by 17 percent, and Eastern Europe by 14 percent. Australia and Thailand expand production by around 25 percent, and "other America," Brazil, and Cuba by around 15 percent.

Global sweetener consumption, meanwhile, increases by only 4 percent overall. Figure 13.7 compares the impact of trade liberalization on consumers and producers.

Among producers, Brazil stands to gain the most – $2.6 billion a year – reflecting its large volume of production and scope as a low-cost producer to respond to higher prices. By 2008 under free trade, Brazil is projected to produce around 16 percent of all nutritive sweeteners. However, as Brazil is also a large consuming nation, Brazilian consumers lose around $1 billion a year because of the rise in price.

India, another large producer, accounts for some 18 percent of world sweetener production by 2008 under free trade. With higher world prices, domestic prices in India rise. This is of some benefit to Indian producers, but not as much as for Brazilian producers, because the price increases are not as great. Despite strong growth in production, India's consumption growth is even more rapid because of rising population and income. As a result, by 2008 India is a net importer of sugar. Extra costs to consumers slightly outweigh gains to producers.

As a large, low-cost producing country exporting around 90 percent of all its sugar output, Australia reaps considerable benefit from higher world prices, although its consumers see some losses. Thailand benefits similarly, but to a lesser degree because it loses protection it now enjoys. Cuban producers benefit more than consumers lose because Cuban producers export so much of their

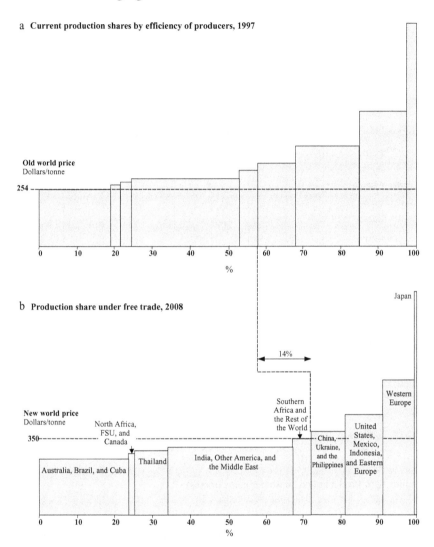

a  **Current production shares by efficiency of producers, 1997**

**Old world price**
Dollars/tonne

254

%

b  **Production share under free trade, 2008**

14%

Japan

Southern
Africa and
the Rest of
the World

Western
Europe

**New world price**
Dollars/tonne

North Africa,
FSU, and
Canada

350

China,
Ukraine,
and the
Philippines

United
States,
Mexico,
Indonesia,
and Eastern
Europe

Thailand

India, Other America, and
the Middle East

Australia, Brazil, and Cuba

%

*Data source:* GSM database and model.

Figure 13.6  How production shares change with free trade, 1997 and 2008

supplies. Producers in "other America" are also significant winners, but with a large proportion of production consumed internally, higher prices also markedly reduce consumer welfare.

For lightly protected importing countries – the Middle East, North Africa, the Former Soviet Union (FSU), Canada, Korea, Malaysia, and Singapore – higher

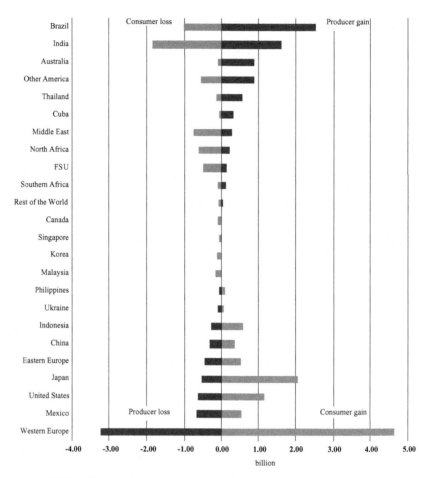

Figure 13.7  Producer and consumer gains (losses)

world prices hurt consumers more than they benefit producers. However, although these countries appear to lose if the sugar sector is liberalized, under
multilateral, multi-sectoral liberalization they may gain overall.

For today's highly protected countries, higher world prices correspond with
sharply lower domestic prices, raising consumer welfare more than they decrease producer welfare. Among highly protected countries, Western European
consumers see large gains of $4.8 billion a year, reflecting the EU's large share
of world nutritive sweetener consumption of 12.5 percent by 2008 and a 40 percent decrease in price. Lower prices also cause EU sugar consumption to expand
somewhat. Western Europe producers lose considerably because of the large

fall in price and some corresponding drop in production. However, producer losses are less than consumer gains because producers now partially subsidize some of their exports through co-responsibility levies, which today amount to 37.5 percent of the domestic price.

Although similar in size to the EU as a sugar consumer, the United States sees lower consumer gains because of smaller price drops, reflecting lower levels of initial protection. US producers also lose less because of smaller price declines, but also because the United States is currently a smaller sugar producer than Western Europe.

In Japan, consumer gains are large because of the 65 percent decline in prices. Producer losses are considerably less than consumer gains because Japan currently produces less than 40 percent of its sugar requirements. Indonesia shows greater consumer gains than producer losses for similar reasons. In Mexico, China, and Eastern Europe, gains and losses roughly match because these regions are relatively self-sufficient.

*Estimating countries' net gains and losses*

Net gains or losses for each country must take into account government tariff revenues and export subsidies. Figure 13.8 presents the net gains and losses for countries most affected by liberalization.

The main net winners are the least-protected efficient exporting countries and large, highly protected importing countries. Except for Australia, the winning exporting countries are developing countries. Except for Indonesia, the winning importing countries are developed countries. Large importing countries with lower levels of protection today – also mainly developing countries – are the main losers, although their losses are small relative to gains. Overall, gains far outweigh losses, with the aggregate gain to the world economy estimated at $4.7 billion a year. If these gains phase in along with liberalization by 2008, the net present value (NPV) of all future annual gains is $80 billion (assuming a 5 percent discount rate).

These results show that developed countries impose protection in the world sugar market at great cost to themselves – but also to developing countries with the economic potential to expand exports. Although developed country protection lowers world prices for some developing country importers, their gains are small relative to the losses this protection imposes on exporters.

Figure 13.3 showed that the EU and the United States awarded a large number of small exporters subsidies of around $0.8 billion a year (based on the twelve-year average world price of $254 per ton). However, under free trade the world price is estimated to rise 38 percent. Moreover, these countries are typically high-cost producers, meaning that they devote expensive resources to producing

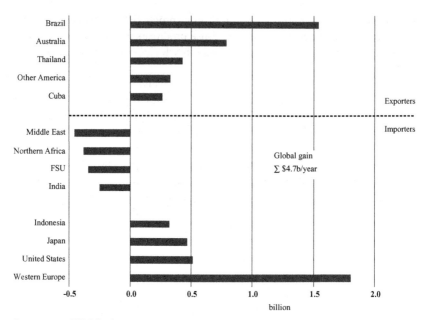

*Data source:* GSM database.

Figure 13.8 Net gains for countries most affected, allowing for government and other transfers

sugar to qualify for the subsidies. Calculating the net loss from removing export subsidies under free trade requires us to take these production costs into account.

Restricted access to protected sugar markets tends to raise production costs in protected countries, as firms lose the incentive to adopt more efficient growing and milling practices. Export subsidies also create a need for government intervention to distribute the subsidies, producing costly side-effects.

In the Philippines, Borrell *et al.* (1994) show that export subsidies have greatly distorted producers' incentives to pursue more efficient growing and milling practices, inflating the costs of production by as much as 30 percent. In Mauritius, export subsidies have been used to sustain special conditions for workers, special land market regulations, and other arrangements that lock resources into the sugar industry and raise costs. Thus, although export subsidies raise domestic prices to over twice the world price, costs also appear to be roughly double the world price. Figures from the Mauritius Chamber of Agriculture show that despite lucrative subsidies to sugar producers, profits totaled only 8 percent of gross revenue in 1991 (CIE, 1994). Although the Chamber of Commerce figures may be somewhat suspect, firms clearly use considerable resources producing sugar to qualify for export subsidies.

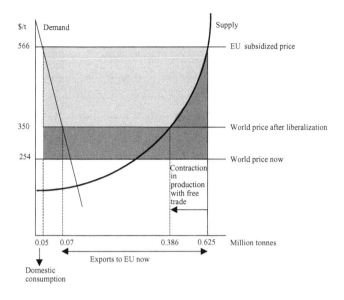

*Data source:* GSM database.

Figure 13.9 The impacts of liberalized trade on Mauritius

Although the model does not separately identify small subsidized producing countries, we can use reasonable assumptions about producer and consumer responses to price changes to estimate the net impact of liberalization on such countries. Figure 13.9 shows that under a shift to free trade, the overall welfare of Mauritius declines by only 56 percent – that is, Mauritius loses $0.109 billion, not the $0.193 billion indicated in figure 13.3. If other small, protected exporters lose export subsidies by the same factor (56 percent), their losses would total $0.448 billion a year, not the $0.8 billion in figure 13.3.

## Half-measures deliver less than half the benefits

Complex market interactions mean that measures aimed at partial liberaliza-tion will be disappointing. Figure 13.10 sets out the impacts on world prices of various trade liberalization scenarios. The first is the free-trade scenario that raises world price by 38 percent. In the second scenario, only the United States and Western Europe liberalize trade. Although those countries account for

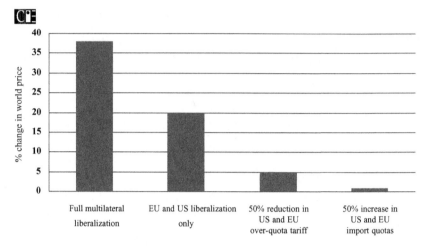

*Data source:* GSM database.

Figure 13.10  Partial reductions in trade barriers have disproportionately small effects

61 percent of distorting producer subsidies, the world price increases by only 52 percent of the free-trade price if those two regions liberalize. The greater the number of countries that liberalize their trade, the greater the increase in import demand, and the larger the increments in world price required to induce increases in export supplies.

The third scenario in figure 13.10 entails 50 percent cuts in over-quota tariffs in the United States and Western Europe. This change produces only a quarter of the price impact of full liberalization by these countries. Current over-quota tariffs are set well above effective levels of protection, so a 50 percent decline in US tariffs does little to reduce domestic producer or consumer prices, or the export subsidies of import quota holders. The effect on EU sugar prices is greater, but protection declines by 20 percent rather than the 50 percent under full EU and US liberalization. Further, for some subsidized producers with marginal exports to the world market, initial reductions in export subsidies may have little effect on prices averaged across all export markets. However, the reductions that do occur will cause cuts in production and exports, with marginal exports to the world market reduced first. As cuts in over-quota tariffs lower export subsidies and production, reductions in export subsidies will become a bigger proportion of the average price reduction. Price and production decreases will become progressively larger, adding to accelerating world price increases.

The final scenario – in which Western Europe and the United States increase their import quotas by 50 percent – produces a minor impact on world prices. Expanding import quotas in these two regions is largely ineffective because such an increase is only about 10 percent of the potential increase that would arise under free trade. Furthermore, small, generally high-cost-exporting nations with quotas have limited ability to respond to higher quotas, and less incentive to respond if higher quotas cause prices and export subsidies to decline. To make expanded quotas effective, the United States and the EU would have to allocate them to efficient exporters such as Brazil and Thailand.

The implication is that half-measures are likely to deliver considerably less than half the benefits of full trade liberalization. This result does not even take into account the political lobbying that would influence the implementation of half-measures. The disappointing outcome of the Uruguay Round bears this out.

## Spotlighting sugar protection in the new round

The United States and Western Europe protect sugar more than most other agricultural products. Subsidies compose nearly 60 percent of the value of EU production and 44 percent of the value of US production. This places sugar protection above or equal to that for milk, the next most-protected product. In Japan, subsidies equal 73 percent of the value of sugar production. In all three regions, protection in tariff-equivalent terms is enormous compared with average tariffs of less than 5 percent across the rest of these economies.

The fact that Australia, Brazil, and Thailand have greatly expanded production and exports with few or no subsidies highlights the extreme competitive disadvantage and high cost of production in Japan, Western Europe, and the United States, especially compared with producers in the tropics. Temperate-zone sugar beet producers operate at a large disadvantage to tropical-zone sugarcane producers.

Cutting the highest levels of protection offers the greatest gains from liberalizing trade. Reducing already low levels of protection may be easier politically but can actually widen the disparities. The easy reductions have been accomplished. Sugar producers in Japan, Western Europe, and the United States will resist change, but the greatest gains from liberalization are found in reducing those tariffs. Circumstances demand a reduction, both economically for success in liberalization, and politically for success in the new round.

With future gains to the global economy from liberalizing sugar estimated at a net present value of $80–$100 billion, the new round could justify expending considerable resources to target those gains. Why countries have not already reaped these gains is well known: the political balance has favored relatively small producer groups in Western Europe, Japan, and the United States over the larger interests of consumers and foreigners. Relatively small numbers of producers have large incentives to form coalitions to lobby to maintain or increase protection, but large numbers of consumers individually have small incentives.

Nonetheless, consumer interests are beginning to coalesce and become better informed. Such groups have the potential to alter the political balance – and political balances do change. The fact that agriculture was included in the Uruguay Round but excluded from previous rounds testifies to this.

Change will occur only when individual countries unilaterally decide to revamp their policies. Nonetheless, multilateral processes can help alter the political balance in favor of liberalization by:
- Bringing publicity and transparency to the arguments for liberalization and informing communities about what they stand to gain
- Reducing adjustment costs of unilateral liberalization to offset higher world prices under multilateral liberalization
- Applying an economy-wide framework to trade liberalization that highlights broad cross-sectoral gains over narrower concerns.

The results presented here confirm that multilateral liberalization has the advantage of raising world sugar prices considerably. Producers in many countries with only light levels of protection will see little negative effect, and may even gain. In the United States, the price of sugar falls only 25 percent under multilateral liberalization. Proponents of liberalizing sugar need to emphasize these facts during the new round.

Targeting sugar's high rates of protection in Japan, Western Europe, and the United States makes economic sense, and giving sugar prominence in the new round would boost the probability of success. By liberalizing sugar and other highly protected agricultural products, Japan, Western Europe, and the United States would also gain considerable credibility in negotiating other major reforms.

## Appendix    Overview of the model

The GSM model used in this analysis is implemented as a set of non-linear, simultaneous, overlapping difference equations. The model encompasses some 40,000 variables and 10,000 equations tracking demand, supply, and trade for seven sweetener types in twenty-four countries or regional groupings (table 13.2).

As a partial equilibrium model, the GSM model contains four basic blocks of equations: demand equations, supply equations, price relationships, and market-clearing equations.

### Demand equations

Demand for the commodities identified in table 13.2 is determined at three levels. At the top level, industrial and household users must choose between all the sweeteners based on tastes and relative prices, with total demand determined by income and population. At the next level, users choose between imported and domestic sources of the sweeteners, again based on preferences and relative prices. At the third level, importers choose between various regional sources for each bilaterally traded sweetener.

These three levels of demand are implemented as nested CES functions in typical fashion. The nest also includes exogenous taste change variables.

## Supply equations

The model contains supply equations for each commodity in each region. In general, we use a constant elasticity formulation, with output in year $t$ a function of producer prices in years $t$ and $t - 1$.

Of course, production of different types of sugar is inter-related. Rudimentary sugars, raw sugar, and mill white are all produced from cane. Their production is modeled as a two-step process, with the total level of cane production determined first and the allocation to different products second. This is modeled as a nested CET function.

White sugar can be produced from beet, in which case we use a simple CES function, or from raw sugar. In the latter case, we explicitly model the refining process, with a production function of the "refining margin" – the difference between raw and refined prices. For artificial sweeteners, we use a constant elasticity formulation.

The supply equations also contain a number of variables used to simulate changes such as in yield, sugar content, and extraction.

## Pricing relationships

A large number of pricing relationships track the value chain for sugar production. For example, they trace the producer price of sugar through to the Freight on Board (FOB) export price then to the Cost, Insurance, and Freight (CIF) import price, and then trace industrial and consumer prices. Pricing relationships are also used to capture various forms of protection, including tariffs and various subsidies.

## Market-clearing

These equations generally ensure that demand equals supply (net of changes in stocks) for each commodity. In the case of bilaterally traded commodities, these equations ensure that production less exports equals consumption plus imports (net of stock changes).

## Closure options

The model contains many more variables than equations. Most variables (such as tariffs and subsidies and various technical change variables) are set exogenously most of the time. The exogenous–endogenous split can be varied, however, to model policies such as quotas or price-support mechanisms.

## Solution technique

The model is solved using the GEMPACK suite of programs, which uses an iterative technique to solve non-linear equations. For information, see http://www.monash.edu.au/policy/gempack.htm.

### Note

1. The model is the property of CSR, and is used here with permission.

### References

Australian Bureau of Agricultural and Resource Economics (ABARE), 1998 "World Sugar Supplies, Consumption, Trade and Prices," *Australian Commodity Statistics*, ABARE, Canberra

Borrell, B., D. Quirke, B. Peña, and L. Noveno, 1994. "Philippine Sugar: An Industry Finding Its Feet," Centre for International Economics, Canberra

Centre for International Economics (CIE), 1994. "Mauritius Looking Beyond the Region," mimeo

Larson, D. and B. Borrell, 1999. "Sugar and Policy Reform," mimeo

World Bank, 1990. "Price Prospects for Major Primary Commodities," Report, 814/90, World Bank

1998. "Commodity Markets and the Developing Countries," World Bank, August

# 14 Bananas: a policy overripe for change

*Brent Borrell*

## Introduction

At the close of the 1990s, the world bananas market was dominated by one large and obvious trade distortion: import restrictions imposed by the European Union (EU). The EU banana policy ostensibly delivered aid to several developing nations by raising the prices these countries received for their bananas in the EU market. However, this policy not only cost EU consumers a whopping $2 billion a year, but only a small portion – about $150 million – reached its target. Banana importers and wholesalers extracted most of the rest.

A wave of articles and editorials lambasted the EU policy on bananas, and over a dozen analytical studies highlighted its enormous costs. The German government and others pursued cases against it in the European Court of Justice (ECJ), and the Hamburg Financial Court attempted to override it. Italy, Sweden, Belgium, Austria, Finland, and Luxembourg, too, publicly opposed the policy. The United States, meanwhile, along with Guatemala, Honduras, Mexico, and Ecuador, filed complaints against the policy through the World Trade Organization (WTO). In every opportunity it had to consider the policy, the GATT or the WTO ruled that EU banana policies were illegal, and eventually awarded the right for the United States to apply punitive tariffs against other EU products in retaliation.

In April 2001, the United States and the EU agreed to phase the EU banana regime into a tariff system by 2006 in exchange for the United States suspending its WTO-authorized punitive tariffs against other EU goods. It remains to be seen what tariff rate the EU will apply but the policy story so far is worth retelling, as it shows:
- The inefficiency and insecurity of aid delivered through trade preferences
- The benefits of tariffs set at reasonable levels compared with quotas
- The benefits of direct compensatory aid
- The prohibitive nature of over-quota tariffs
- The ploys countries use to avoid making even obvious reforms

- The role of the policy transparency process and ensuing publicity
- The fundamental importance of changing the political will and political balance in the country imposing trade barriers
- The preparedness of a major WTO player to ignore international trade rules in favor of domestic political considerations
- The entrenched political powers of those protected by quotas
- The role of dispute-settlement procedures and other WTO disciplines.

The EU could have achieved its aid objective through alternative mechanisms at a fraction of the cost to consumers, and EU policy actually harmed some developing countries attempting to export into the EU market. Still, the policy scheme, with its numerous beneficiaries, persisted for the better part of a decade. The inefficiency of the policy, the difficult path to reform, and the greater efficiency of alternatives suggest that even the most compelling reasons for change can find the resistance from vested interests to be steadfast.

## How EU policies affected the world banana market

As a big, rich trading bloc with little banana production, the EU is an important player on the world market, importing around 40 percent of all internationally traded bananas. The high barriers it imposes on banana imports have been seriously disruptive to trade. The United States – the other major importer of bananas, with around a third of all imports – imposes no barriers.

Some EU countries long restricted banana imports while others imposed fewer barriers. France, the United Kingdom, Spain, Italy, Portugal, and Greece used quota-based import restrictions to provide preferential access and aid to high-cost growers (preferred suppliers) in four territories and seven small African, Caribbean, and Pacific (ACP) countries. The Netherlands, Belgium, Luxembourg, Denmark, and Ireland imposed relatively mild tariff intervention, typically importing their bananas from efficient growers in Latin America (non-preferred suppliers) (table 14.1). Only Germany had a completely free market in bananas.

Consumers in EU import-restricted markets paid much more for bananas, ate fewer of them (8 kilos per person per year in the UK versus 14 kilos in Germany), and ate lower-quality bananas. Although quotas were intended to raise prices for preferred suppliers, they also enabled others in the marketing chain to seek benefits.

Preferential access enabled preferred suppliers to receive prices about double those of non-preferred suppliers (figure 14.1). Quotas also produced marketing margins twice those in the United States, and up to 50 percent higher than in Germany (figure 14.2) (Borrell and Yang, 1990; Borrell and Cuthbertson, 1991).

Table 14.1 *Preferred and non-preferred suppliers of EU banana imports*

| Preferred suppliers ACP countries[a] | Country giving special preference | Non-preferred suppliers Latin America or so-called "dollar"-area countries of Central and South America |
|---|---|---|
| Belize | United Kingdom | Colombia |
| Jamaica | United Kingdom | Costa Rica |
| Surinam | United Kingdom | Guatemala |
| Windward Islands | United Kingdom | Honduras |
| Somalia | Italy | Panama |
| Cameroon | France | Ecuador |
| Ivory Coast | France | Brazil |
| EU overseas territories | | |
| Guadeloupe | France | |
| Martinique | France | |
| Madeira | Portugal | |
| Canary Islands | Spain | |

*Note:* [a] Under the Lomé Convention, all ACP countries have duty-free access to protected EU markets. Germany gives no preference to ACP suppliers.
*Source:* Author's data.

### Measuring the costs of quota-based policies

To estimate the economic costs of the EU's national banana policies, my colleagues and I constructed an economic model of the EU and world banana market (see Borrell and Yang, 1990, 1992). The results, summarized in figure 14.3, show that:

- The cost to consumers of paying preferred suppliers double the world price for bananas was $576 million a year
- The cost to consumers of excessive marketing margins in import-restricted markets (compared with the costs to consumers in Germany) was $917 million a year
- Tariff revenue collected on imports cost consumers an extra $112 million a year
- The value of the $576 million consumers paid to preferred suppliers was worth just $302 million a year to those suppliers, because they devoted scarce resources to grow bananas to qualify for aid
- High EU consumer prices lowered EU consumption, yielding a lower world price and lower exports for efficient Latin American exporters. These penalties together cost these exporters $98 million a year.

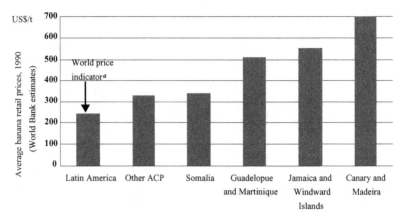

*Note:* [a] Latin American countries receive prices determined by the forces of supply and demand in the world banana market.
*Source:* Borrell and Yang (1992).

Figure 14.1  Most prices of preferred suppliers to EU markets were double the world price

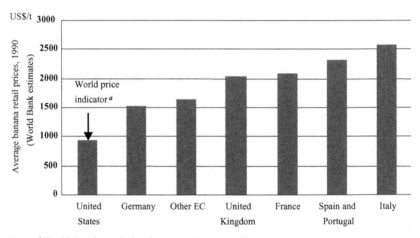

*Note:* [a] The United States had no barriers to the entry of bananas.
*Source:* Borrell and Yang (1992).

Figure 14.2  EU retail banana prices were well above those of the United States

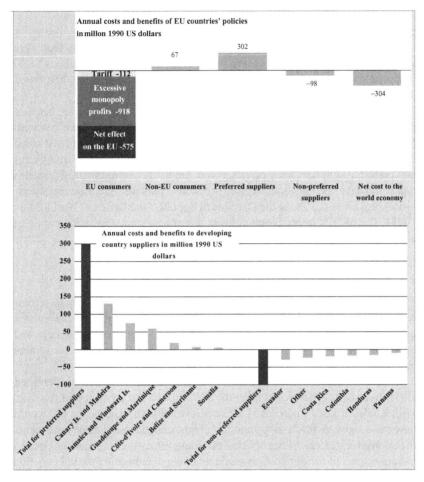

*Source:* Model results.

Figure 14.3 The costly national banana policies of EU countries

Thus, before introduction of the unified policy, consumers in import-restricted EU markets incurred excess costs of $1.6 billion a year but delivered only $300 million a year to the eleven preferred developing economies. The policies meanwhile caused $98 million a year in collateral damage to exporters in other developing countries. The net benefit to developing countries was only $202 million a year.

Put another way, EU consumers paid some $5.30 to deliver $1.00 of net banana aid to eleven developing countries and caused $0.32 in damage to other developing country exporters. Of the $5.30, over $3.00 was siphoned off in excessive marketing margins to EU marketers. About $0.30 was collected as tariff revenue. After allowing for the excessive margins and tariffs that were internal EU transfers, the net cost to the EU was about $2.00, and about $1.00 of this was outright waste for the world economy, while the other $1.00 reached its target as aid.

The outright waste of $1.00 per $5.30 in cost to consumers occurred because preferred suppliers used more resources than necessary to produce bananas. More efficient suppliers in Latin America could have produced at least some of these bananas with fewer and cheaper resources. Moreover, to qualify for aid, preferred suppliers used precious land, labor, and capital to grow bananas that could have been devoted to more productive pursuits, like those in export-processing zones (EPZs) in the Dominican Republic and Jamaica (World Bank, 1993). The old EU quota-based policies were clearly grossly inefficient as an aid mechanism.

### The EU reinforced bad trade policy

The 1992–3 initiative to unify EU markets provided an opportunity to reform the disparate policies of member states. The stated objective of the unified policy was to provide support – that is, aid – to EU territorial producers and banana exporters of the Lomé ACP countries, while ensuring that consumers had access to adequate supplies of good-quality bananas.

Borrell and Yang (1990, 1992) and Borrell and Cuthbertson (1991) identified alternative polices that would meet the EU objectives at a fraction of the cost. With a tariff of just 17 percent as the only restriction to imports, the EU would have raised enough funds to support direct financial aid or deficiency payments to preferred producers. Either option would have virtually eliminated the costs to EU consumers of the old policies while retaining or enhancing the aid benefits. These options would also have virtually eliminated collateral damage to Latin American exporters. The cost to EU consumers of transferring $1.00 of aid would drop from $5.30 to just over $1.00.

A tariff-only plan, like that outlined in the 2001 Bananas Agreement, also offer other advantages:
- It is simpler to administer compared with quota-based schemes
- Transfer of direct aid or deficiency payments reaches their targets, unlike rents from quotas and licenses, which tend to be uncertain and hit-or-miss
- Unlike quotas, the tariff can be set objectively, and therefore be less vulnerable to political interference
- The effects of the tariff are simpler to monitor than those of quotas and licenses
- Open competition eliminates protection for inefficient marketers and encourages greater efficiency, innovation, quality, and consumer-oriented marketing.

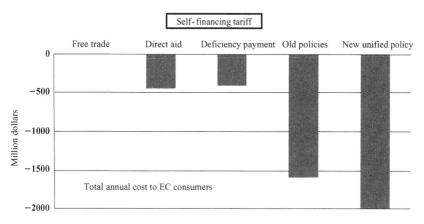

*Source:* Model results.

Figure 14.4 Self-financing tariff options are much less costly than quotas

On July 1, 1993, the EU replaced the disparate import policies of its Member States with a unified policy. However, instead of adopting a more efficient policy, the EU extended the most protectionist and costly of the former national policies to all members. The new policy relied on a prohibitive tariff quota on Latin American imports to boost internal EU prices and raise revenue. This system actually reduced trade in Latin American bananas below the previous level. Meanwhile banana producers in EU territories obtained a duty-free, country-specific quota based on a best-ever reference amount while also receiving a deficiency payment. The system also relied on a system of import licenses to limit competition in the marketing of bananas.

### Costs increased and aid benefits fell

Figure 14.4 and figure 14.5 compare the costs and benefits of self-financing tariff policies, the old disparate policies, and the unified policy. Because the unified policy restricted imports by more than the total national policies it replaced, the EU consumer price rose and the world price fell. This raised the cost to consumers and non-preferred suppliers from $1.6 billion a year to $2.0 billion a year (Borrell, 1996). Yet, aid benefits to preferred suppliers actually declined, because the cumbersome policy forced suppliers to share some of their quota rents with marketers.

Because the policy relied on import quotas to raise consumer prices, the support mechanism was complicated and indirect. Licenses used to allocate the rights to market bananas were also intended to increase demand for fruit from EU territories and ACP countries, bidding their price above the world

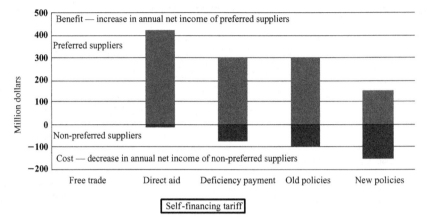

*Source:* Model results.

Figure 14.5  Self-financing tariff options are best for banana-supplying regions

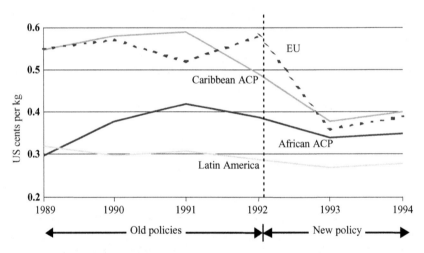

*Source:* FAO (1995).

Figure 14.6  EU and Caribbean ACP prices fell toward African ACP (real) 1994 prices, 1989–1994 (weighted averages)

price. However, instead of providing aid through a cross-subsidy, this policy mainly afforded quota holders windfall gains. Figure 14.6 shows that prices for Caribbean ACP producers and Caribbean EU territorial growers dropped by over 30 percent in the first eighteen months of the unified policy. (As many as 8 percentage points were due to the decline of the Euro against the dollar.) The

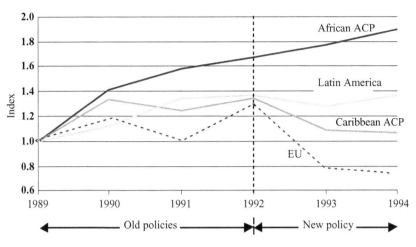

*Source:* FAO (1995).

Figure 14.7 The value of exports fell for most beneficiaries of the new EU banana policy, 1989–1994

support component of the price – the margin by which it is above the world price – dropped by over 60 percent.

The total value of banana exports from ACP and Caribbean EU territorial suppliers also declined by 21 percent – from $473 million in 1992 to $373 million in 1994 (figure 14.7). African ACP exporters experienced a 14 percent increase in export value – a combination of a 22 percent increase in export quantities and a 7 percent drop in prices. Meanwhile, Caribbean ACP and EU territorial exporters experienced a 30 percent drop in export value. This was mainly due to the decline in price, but volume also declined by 13 percent. By 1997, Windward Island exports to the EU had halved.

Data on the Canary Islands, the other main preferred supplier, were not as easily interpreted. However, information from the Commission of the European Communities (1995) suggests that this supplier also faced big declines in export values. Import prices for Canary Island fruit dropped 35 percent and volume dropped 13 percent. Export values could conceivably have dropped by over 40 percent.

The unified policy appears to have failed to achieve its main objective. In its first two years, export values declined by 30 percent or more for about 80 percent of intended beneficiaries. For the other 20 percent – the African suppliers – export values increased owing to increased volume, not price. The increase in African supplies may be due to producers' greater comparative

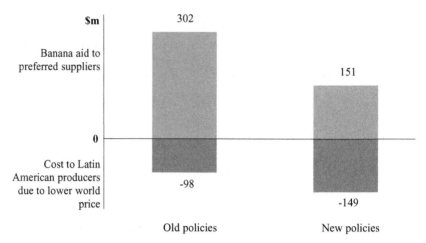

*Source:* Borrell (1996).

Figure 14.8  The net aid effect for developing countries may be zero

advantage: the structure of the African industry is closer to that of efficient Latin American producers.

It appears that the aid component of preferred suppliers' price fell by an average of 50 percent under the unified policy, and potentially slashed the $302 million received under the old policies to around $150 million a year. Worse still, the net cost of further reductions in imports to Latin American suppliers grew from $98 million to $147 million a year (Borrell, 1996). This means that aid to one set of developing countries exactly offset the costs it imposed on another set of developing countries (figure 14.8).

### Further confusion on aid

On January 1, 1999, the EU re-allocated import licenses on the basis of those held during 1994–6. The EU also abolished country-specific quotas for each ACP country while maintaining the total size of the ACP quota. This placed downward pressure on the price received by exporting producers while not impacting the supply available to the consumer market. Elimination of country-specific quotas placed ACP producers in differing regions in direct price competition, as cost structures in African ACP producer firms were appreciably lower than those in Caribbean ACP banana firms.

The unified policy favored marketing companies (mostly EU-owned) that previously benefited under the various national policies awarding them special licenses. These companies were handed a third of the Latin American trade, even though they were not previously competitive enough to win it otherwise. The companies that traditionally marketed Latin American bananas (mostly US-owned) in relatively open EU markets (including Germany, the Netherlands, Belgium, Luxembourg, Denmark, and Ireland, and recent EU entrants Austria, Sweden, and Finland) suffered under this system. These companies saw their markets cut through quotas and licenses that restricted their share to some two-thirds of the total. A 57–28–15 percentage allocation among importers, customs-clearers, and ripeners further restricted this two-thirds market share.

The EU unified policy interfered with the market because it made many decisions on allocating production and marketing resources centrally and bureaucratically. Costly red tape and political uncertainty therefore influenced the marketing of Latin American bananas in the EU.

Some may argue that the higher prices that marketers of Latin American fruit received because of the quota system gave those marketers some compensation. But lower volume reduced economies of scale and scope, and so raised marketers' costs. Compliance with the red tape of complex quota and licensing arrangements also raised costs. Further, the arbitrary nature of the policy – in how it was administered, how licenses were allocated, and its uncertainty in the face of political and bureaucratic interference – introduced investment risk that added greatly to costs. What's more, the arbitrary nature by which the system allocated market share denied competitive companies their comparative advantage – the right to compete through good performance. Thus, whatever the benefits of higher prices, they were offset by higher costs and constrained commercial opportunities.

Under quotas and licenses, winning market share required extensive and expensive lobbying, but even this guaranteed no favor. This is one reason why competitive growth-oriented companies continued to resist quotas.

Overall, if EU consumers pay $2.0 billion to transfer only $151 million a year to preferred suppliers in the form of banana aid, this translates into $13.25 cost to consumers for each $1.00 of benefit to the targeted aid recipient. The unified policy was more than twice as inefficient as the old one, which only cost consumers $5.30 for each $1.00 of banana aid. The increase in cost occurred because the policy deliberately raised windfall gains on the sale of bananas, but banana marketers passed even fewer of the gains back to preferred suppliers in the form of better wholesale prices (figure 14.9).

In moving to a unified policy, the EU missed an opportunity to rationalize its national banana policies. Of all its options, the EU chose the one most discriminatory, most distorting, and most ineffectual. The unified policy failed to provide support to preferred producers or to provide adequate supplies of bananas to consumers. During the years of the unified policy, banana availability to consumers declined 11.5 percent between 1992 and 1994 (figure 14.10),

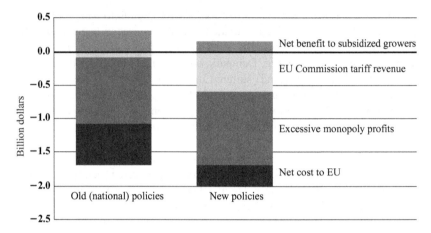

*Source:* Borrell (1996).

Figure 14.9  Total annual benefit to subsidized growers and the cost to EU consumers

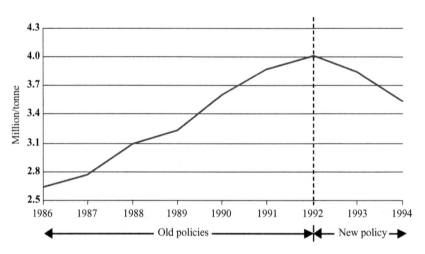

*Source:* Commission of the European Communities (1995).

Figure 14.10  EU banana consumption has dropped 11.5 percent since the new EU policy, 1986–1994

and retail prices rose by at least 42 percent in Germany – the biggest EU market, with 30 percent of trade. Quality may also have dropped (Borrell, 1996).

It is hard to escape the conclusion that the unified policy was pursuing another objective. The most obvious was that it wished to protect and expand the vested interests of EU-based marketing companies. EU consumers, other marketers, and Latin American producers lost substantially under the unified policy, although preferred suppliers, the targeted aid recipient, also appeared to lose. The results made a mockery of a policy that has disrupted the market so much and imposed such high costs on consumers while delivering so little.

## Lessons from the banana story

The banana is only one commodity, and trade is modest compared with that in many other commodities. However, the product is important to many developing country exporters, and it is the most-traded fruit. Growth of trade in fruit and vegetables is more rapid than growth in agricultural trade as a whole, and this trend is expected to continue (Borrell, 1998). But, perhaps more importantly, the fact that EU trade policy could have become so much more disruptive meant that the banana dispute set several precedents and drove home several important lessons for advocates of trade liberalization to consider in the new round.

The combined effect of consistent studies and regular challenges kept the proponents of reform active. Until 1990 little analysis of the costs of EU restrictions on banana trade had occurred. One exception was the work of Noichl (1985). However, while the paper provided a sound theoretical structure for analyzing the EU policy, it did not quantify the costs and benefits nor gain much publicity. Not until Borrell and Yang (1990) built a quantitative model to measure the policy's costs and benefits did the issue gain currency. Numerous studies have since fueled the debate, for example, Jim Fitzpatrick and Associates 1992, McInerney and Peston 1992, Mathews 1992, Read 1994, Kersten 1995, and Messerlin 2001.

The GATT and WTO challenges sparked the debate and made the studies relevant. In addition to instances already cited, a test of the unified bananas policy even succeeded under GATS, an area far removed from agricultural trade. On September 9, 1997, the WTO Banana Panel found that "the EU policy creates less favorable conditions of competition for like services and like service suppliers of the Complainants' origin and is therefore inconsistent with the requirement of Article XVII of GATS."

The case marked the first time the WTO dispute-settlement panel had ruled on GATS, and the ruling holds far-reaching implications. It suggests that any trade impediment that restricts the ability of a foreign company to market its services could be challenged, provided the country imposing the restriction lists the sector under GATS. Perhaps McDonald's in Japan could argue that restrictions on beef and sugar imports constrain its ability to market its food services in competition with providers of services such as fast-food sushi and sashimi.

Table 14.2 *How EU unified banana policy contravened EU competition policy*

| Key features of EU competition law | An economic interpretation of this law as it applied to EU unified bananas policy |
|---|---|
| Article 3(g) of the Treaty of Rome provides that the activities of the EU shall include a system ensuring that competition in the internal market is not distorted | Quotas and licensing guarantee that competition in internal markets is distorted |
| Articles 85 and 86 of the Treaty of Rome further lay out the basis of EU competition policy | The stated object is to deliberately prevent, restrict, and distort competition to orchestrate an indirect monetary transfer to a small group of banana producers |
| The following shall be prohibited as incompatible with the common market: all agreements between undertakings; decisions by associations of undertakings and concerted practices which may affect trade between member states and which have as their object or effect the prevention, restriction or distortion of competition within the common market; and, in particular, those which: | |
| Directly or indirectly fix purchase or selling prices or any other trading conditions; | Quotas and licenses directly fix trading conditions and indirectly fix the selling price |
| Limit or control production, markets, technical development, or investment; | Quotas and licenses limit production, investment, and technical development, and blatantly control markets |
| Share markets or sources of supply; | Licenses mean there is blatant market sharing |
| Apply dissimilar conditions to equivalent transactions with other trading parties, thereby placing them at a competitive disadvantage; and | Conditions applying to licenses produce blatant discrimination against one type of marketing company over another |
| Make the conclusion of contracts subject to acceptance by the other parties of supplementary obligations which, by their nature or according to commercial usage, have no connection with the subject of such contracts (Martin, 1994). | Category A, B, and C licenses include supplementary obligations |
| Exemptions may apply if the action promotes technical or economic progress and consumers share in the benefits. | The policy would appear to cause the exact opposite, so there are no grounds for exemptions |

*Persistence of policy distortions show the power of domestic political considerations*

The unified EU policy is a reminder that countries even as important as those of the EU are prepared to flout international trade rules in favor of domestic political considerations without consequence. In 1992, when the GATT explicitly condemned the EU's restrictive national policies, the EU blocked GATT approval of that ruling and ignored it in structuring the new policy. In 1994, when the GATT again ruled against existing EU banana policies and called for a restructuring of the unified policy, the EU also blocked the ruling. Even supported by strengthened dispute-settlement procedures and new disciplines governing services, licensing, and investments, the WTO rulings against the policy under the GATT and GATS in 1997 did not succeed in provoking sensible reform. In 1999, the WTO ruled that minor changes to the unified policy did not bring it into compliance, and awarded to the United States the right to impose punitive tariffs on EU goods entering the US market. The punitive measures eventually compelled abandonment of the illegal aspects of the unified bananas policy, and the sanctions were suspended in accordance with the Bananas Agreement beginning in July 2001. The EU has agreed to replace quotas with a tariff-only policy after 2005. However, what remains unclear is the tariff level the EU will implement. Early indications from the EU are that it is considering a very high tariff of around €300/t on Latin American imports but a zero tariff (tariff preference) on ACP products. Should this occur, African producer prices could double and their supply expand enormously. This will further displace Latin American fruit. The dispute is far from over yet.

The policy also seemed to flout the EU's own rules on internal competition (table 14.2). Indeed, the bananas policy failed in every category of economic soundness. The unified policy was so blatantly inefficient, and so much effort was expended to change it, that it is a unique example of how quickly bad policy can gain potent political support.

## Conclusions: publicity, transparency, and negotiation remain important

The bananas controversy has raged for nearly a decade and may not be over yet. The effort devoted to mounting GATT and WTO cases indicates that trade rules and dispute-settlement procedures have a place in the policy reform process. If the bananas story provides lasting messages, they are that policy transparency and publicity drive and sustain a wide-ranging debate, that dispute resolution processes provide a way of drawing attention to clearly wrong policy, but that punitive sanctions are dubious allies whose use should be avoided by aggrieved countries when possible. Indeed, no one can deny that if a world backlash of protectionism occurs in the future, the punitive sanction is the one mechanism that will most likely set it into motion, with or without WTO sanctioning. If the European Union puts in place a tariff higher than the current in quota tariff of €75/t after 2009, punitive sanctions may again be placed on the European Union or it will be forced to pay enormous amounts of compensation to Latin American producers.

### References

Borrell, B., 1996. "Beyond EU Bananarama 1993: The Story Gets Worse," Centre for International Economics, Canberra
    1998. "Emerging Issues," in A. Stoeckel (ed.), *World Agricultural Trade: Towards a Strategy for Australia*, Canberra: Rural Industries Development Corporation
Borrell, B. and S. Cuthbertson, 1991. "EC Banana Policy 1992: Picking the Best Option," Centre for International Economics, Canberra
Borrell, B. and M. Yang, 1990. "EC Bananarama 1992," WPS 523, International Economics Department, World Bank
    1992. "EC Bananarama 1992, The Sequel, The EC Commission Proposal," WPS 958, International Economics Department, World Bank
Commission of the European Communities, 1995. *Report on the Operation of the Banana Regime*, Brussels
Jim Fitzpatrick and Associates, Economic Consultants, 1992. "Trade Policy and the EC Banana Market: An Economic Analysis," United Kingdom
Kersten, L., 1995. "Impacts of the EU Banana Market Regulation on International Competition, Trade and Welfare," *European Review of Agricultural Economics*, 22, 321–5
Mathews, A., 1992, "The European Community's Banana Policy after 1992," Discussion Paper, 13, Institut für Agrarpolitck und Marktforsschung, University of Giessen
McInerney, J. and Lord Peston (eds.), 1992. "Fair Trade in Bananas, Report, 239," University of Exeter
Messerlin, P. A., 2001. *Measuring the Costs of Protection in Europe: European Commercial Policy in the 2000s*, Washington, DC, Institute for International Economics, 316–24
Read, R., 1994. "The EC Internal Banana Market: The Issues and the Dilemma," *The World Economy*, 17(2), 219–35
United Nations Food and Agriculture Organization (FAO), 1995. "Banana Information Note," Intergovernmental Group on Bananas, Rome
World Bank, 1993. "The Caribbean: Export Preferences and Performance," chapter 6 in Stanley Lalta and Marie Freckleton (eds.), *Caribbean Economic Development: The First Generation*, Washington, DC: Ian Randle

# Part IV
# New trade issues and developing country agriculture

# 15 Sanitary and phytosanitary barriers to agricultural trade: progress, prospects, and implications for developing countries

*Donna Roberts, David Orden, and Tim Josling*

## Introduction

Access for agricultural products into protected domestic markets remains one of the vexing problems of global economic integration. With the conclusion of the 1986–94 Uruguay Round negotiations, a cohesive multilateral framework emerged to discipline the policies that World Trade Organization (WTO) Member Countries use to protect and support their agricultural sectors. The new multilateral framework includes an Agreement on the Application of Sanitary and Phytosanitary Measures (the SPS Agreement), which provides an international policy regime for trade when there potentially are risks to human, animal, and plant health or life. The hope is that this Agreement will bring SPS regulation affecting international agricultural market access under the governance of multilateral trade rules, with a consequent expansion of trade opportunities.

All nations maintain complex regulatory regimes governing the production, processing, and sales of agricultural commodities and foodstuffs. The SPS Agreement was intended as a bulwark against the widely perceived failure of the General Agreement on Tariffs and Trade (GATT) to prevent the misuse of such measures for protectionist purposes. While reaffirming the right of every nation to protect health and life, the SPS Agreement sought to impose commitments that would minimize adverse trade effects. WTO members agreed to maintain transparent procedures regarding the adoption and application of SPS regulations, and to base their policies on assessment of the associated risks. The Agreement also sought to minimize trade disruptions by requiring countries to recognize the equivalence of other countries' SPS measures, if they could be shown to provide the same level of health or environmental protection. Members were also encouraged to harmonize their measures by adopting standards set by international bodies.

Each of these commitments – transparency, risk-assessment-based decisions, equivalence, and harmonization – was designed to allow countries to define their own standards of protection while facilitating an international market. Supporting these mechanisms have been strengthening WTO dispute-settlement procedures (DSPs) to resolve disagreements over the merits of specific SPS barriers.

Since 1995, when the SPS Agreement went into effect, controversies have continued to arise around the market access conditions it establishes. These controversies stem partly from frustration over the slow resolution of long-standing disputes. SPS controversies also concern which levels of health protection countries should seek, and how best to achieve them. Drafters of the SPS Agreement may not have envisioned the extent to which these factors would bring technical trade barriers into the eye of a political storm.

In this chapter, we examine evidence regarding how the SPS Agreement is being implemented, with an emphasis on the implications for developing countries. We find that institutional innovations under the Agreement have produced specific accomplishments. National regulatory authorities have modified SPS measures to comply with the Agreement and WTO dispute-settlement decisions are defining acceptable regulatory practices. However, only limited progress has occurred under equivalence and harmonization of standards.

Our assessment suggests that developing countries have reaped some benefits as the SPS Agreement has opened new markets. However, once international rules delineate acceptable SPS regulations, private and public investments are required to ensure that exported commodities meet the specified health and safety standards. Agricultural producers have to be innovative and competitive to take advantage of any new opportunities, and domestic regulatory agencies have to provide the public goods – from pest and disease monitoring and eradication programs, to inspection services, to food safety certifications – that enable companies to successfully market their products. Scientific discoveries and new technologies have improved the ability of nations to manage known risks in ways that may threaten some producers seeking market access, but discoveries and new technology can also facilitate trade expansion. Scientific advances also uncover new possibilities and newly discovered risks about which countries must formulate regulations with limited information or imperfect political consensus.

Achieving further benefits from the SPS Agreement for developing countries will depend on whether WTO Members take additional steps to discipline their respective SPS measures, and on whether developing countries can marshal the resources to capitalize on the new trade opportunities these disciplines create. Consumers in developing countries may also benefit from international disciplines on SPS trade barriers if their own regulatory authorities are using such barriers inappropriately.

## Transparency

Governments routinely create or modify SPS regulations to reflect scientific and technological innovations in production, processing, detection, and eradication methods. Regulatory interventions also stem from the sudden emergence of unanticipated health and safety hazards. Annex B of the SPS Agreement (*Transparency of Sanitary and Phytosanitary Regulations*) requires countries to notify trading partners of both routine and emergency changes to their regulatory regimes if they affect trade. The notification requirement constitutes the cornerstone of the Agreement's "transparency provisions," which are intended to facilitate decentralized policing by trading partners to ensure compliance with the SPS Agreement's substantive provisions. Transparency requirements are particularly important because exporters often complained that undocumented SPS measures were a significant impediment to market access prior to the Uruguay Round.

Transparency can't fully stop abuse of SPS measures, but the benefits of this mechanism can be broadly summarized as facilitating "compliance and complaints." The "compliance effect" occurs when advance notice of new or modified measures provides an opportunity for firms to change production methods to meet new import requirements, thereby minimizing the disruptions that such changes can cause to trade flows. The "complaint effect" occurs when prior notification provides an opportunity for trading partners to raise objections about the legitimacy or design of a proposed measure, possibly averting a trade dispute.

There is perhaps more systematic evidence available to gauge fulfillment of the notification obligation than for any other commitment under the SPS Agreement. Just over 1,400 notifications were received over the first five years of the Agreement (figure 15.1). The percentage of countries within each income category that have notified SPS measures range from 86 percent of the high-income countries to 24 percent of least-developed countries (LDCs).[1] More than half of upper-middle-income countries (60 percent) and lower-middle-income countries (52 percent) have also notified SPS regulations. WTO notification is now routine for all major agricultural exporting and importing countries, with the United States alone accounting for more than 200 notifications. This record stands in contrast to reporting before the Agreement came into effect: countries notified only 168 measures to prevent risks to public health and safety between 1980 and 1990 under the Technical Barriers to Trade (TBT) Agreement; fewer than half of those notifications concerned SPS regulations.[2]

One result of this growing transparency has been the institutional innovation of "cross-notification." A cross-notification occurs whenever member countries use the SPS Committee to air a grievance over a specific measure after technical exchanges have reached an impasse. Examination of cross-notifications, in

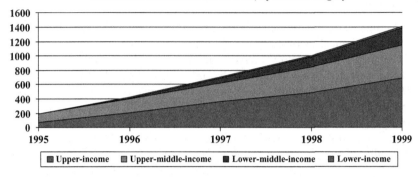

Cumulative total of SPS notifications, by income category[a]

■ Upper-income   ■ Upper-middle-income   ■ Lower-middle-income   ■ Lower-income

*Note:* [a]As defined by the World Bank.
*Source:* WTO SPS notifications and authors' calculations.

Figure 15.1 Notification of SPS measures is increasing the transparency of regulatory regimes, 1995–1999

conjunction with notifications, yields evidence about the compliance and complaint effects of increased transparency. There have been 124 cross-notifications since the Agreement came into force, which implies an upper bound of 9 percent of notified measures that were challenged by trading partners.[3] Thus in nine out of ten instances during this period, exporting countries have indirectly signaled their intent to comply with new or modified regulations, reinforcing the consensus view that the vast majority of SPS measures place legitimate restrictions on trade.

Table 15.1 tallies the 124 separate cross-notifications received by the SPS Committee between 1995 and 1999. Complaints initiated by developed countries account for nearly three-fourths of the cross-notifications. This is a larger percentage than might be anticipated on the basis of the proportion of world agricultural exports originating from such countries, providing circumstantial evidence for the commonly held notion that wealthier countries are better positioned to exercise their rights under the SPS Agreement.[4] But such a conclusion is too facile, as the record also shows that developing countries have frequently joined, if not initiated, complaints. In fact, developing countries have registered objections as co-complainants twice as often as developed countries (eighty-three versus thirty-nine interventions) over this five-year period.

The pattern of cross-notifications and co-complaints indicates that, in numerous instances, developing and developed countries have a mutual interest in the modification of an importer's regulation, and these shared interests facilitate developing countries' efforts to exercise their rights under the Agreement. Developed countries' measures have drawn the most complaints (sixty-seven

Table 15.1 *Complaints (cross-notifications) in the SPS Committee against trade partners*

| | Complaints by developed countries | | | Complaints by developing countries | | | Total complaints |
|---|---|---|---|---|---|---|---|
| Respondents | Issues[a] No. (No. with co-complainants) | Co-complainants (developed) No. of countries | Co-complainants (developing) No. of countries | Issues No. (No. with co-complainants) | Co-complainants (developed) No. of countries | Co-complainants (developing) No. of countries | No. |
| Developed country | 45(13) | 23 | 40 | 22(8) | 9 | 36 | 67 |
| Developing country | 47(6) | 6 | 5 | 10(2) | 1 | 2 | 57 |
| Total | 92(19) | 29 | 45 | 32(10) | 10 | 38 | 124 |

*Note:* [a] Entries exclude fifty "repeat interventions" made by WTO Members who registered complaints against the same measure more than once.

*Source:* WTO Summaries of the Meetings of the Committee on Sanitary and Phytosanitary Measures, G/SPS/R series, 1995–9 and authors' calculations.

compared to fifty-seven for developing countries). About one-third (twenty-one) of the complaints against developed countries have drawn both developed (thirty-two) and developing (seventy-six) co-complainants. Thus, developed and developing countries have shared concerns about SPS barriers to market access in developed countries. Developing countries have been less willing to target the measures of other developing countries in cross-notifications (ten) than developed countries (forty-seven). But the cross-notifications against developing countries have involved mostly unilateral issues, with other developed countries and developing countries lacking interest in, constrained from, or reluctant to support complaints against developing countries.

Responses to these complaints have ranged from silence,[5] to explanations, to modifications of SPS measures. So while it may be too early to make a strong judgment about whether the transparency provisions of the Agreement will significantly curb misuse of SPS measures, it has clearly provided a forum for semi-formal airing of disagreements, thereby promoting symmetry of information among WTO Members. In some instances, Committee discussions have led to correction of information erroneously interpreted by private-industry sources. In other cases, the opportunity to discuss a regulation and its enforcement before other Members has served to pinpoint the source of disagreement between the trading partners involved and inform others about the substance of the dispute. The transparency provisions have also clearly reduced Members' transaction costs in lodging complaints, including those of developing countries dependent upon the import and export of raw and semi-processed agricultural products – sometimes to good effect.

To give one example, developing countries often express fear that increasingly stringent regulation of maximum residue levels (MRLs) of pesticides and natural toxins in agricultural products may impede access to developed country markets.[6] The European Union (EU) notified the SPS Committee in early 1998 of just such a proposed regulation lowering MRLs for aflatoxin in a wide range of foodstuffs. This prompted protests from a large number of WTO Members including Senegal, Gambia, India, Brazil, and the Philippines. These countries argued that the EU's proposed MRLs would significantly raise exporters' costs without improving food safety, because there was no evidence that products that satisfied existing MRLs for aflatoxin posed health risks. The EU later announced that it would revise its proposed aflatoxin MRL for peanuts, adopting the (draft) international standard instead. The EU also announced that it would reconsider its proposed aflatoxin MRLs for other commodities. Without the WTO notification process, developing countries might have had more difficulty learning the details of such a regulation, either to successfully challenge the measure before it was adopted or to prepare for its eventual adoption.

## Risk management based on scientific risk assessment

Multilateral rules for SPS regulations are arguably harder to craft than for any other trade-restricting measure. SPS regulations routinely violate Most Favored Nation (MFN) and national treatment principles because, among other factors, SPS risks can vary according to the source and destination of products. Even when risks vary little across countries, regulations may differ owing to differences in the use of advances in basic science, detection technology, and mitigation methods. Income levels, consumer preferences for food attributes besides safety such as taste and convenience, and the historic incidence of low-probability, high-consequence emergencies can also affect regulatory decisions. This complex mosaic of risks, risk mitigation measures, and other influences has provoked numerous substantive debates among scientists and policy disagreements among regulators. It is in this context that suspicions arise among trading partners that certain SPS measures are of dubious merit, and have been implemented as disguised protection for narrow producer or consumer interests, rather than to protect human health or crops and livestock.

To provide a substantive basis for determining the legitimacy of SPS measures, article 2 (*Basic Rights and Obligations*) obligates Members to ensure that every SPS measure is "based on scientific principles and is not maintained without sufficient scientific evidence." Article 5 (*Assessment of Risk and Determination of the Appropriate Level of Sanitary or Phytosanitary Protection*) is more prescriptive: for example, article 5.1 states that Members must base SPS measures on scientific risk assessment, while article 5.2 and 5.3 list factors, such as disease prevalence or potential production losses, which must be taken into account. The assumption underlying the obligations in these two Articles is that full characterization of the probability and consequences of each hazard will narrow informational gaps between exporters and importers and facilitate common judgments about the need for and design of risk-mitigating measures.

The obligation to reference scientific evidence in defense of a trade-restricting measure clearly reduces the degrees of freedom for disingenuous use of SPS regulatory interventions. In each of the three SPS disputes to reach the WTO Appellate Body since the Agreement came into effect, the measures at issue failed to meet the requirements set out in article 5.1. Similarly, comparing specific risk-related costs across a spectrum of regulatory decisions eases the task of judging the legitimacy of an individual measure. In the Australia–Canada *Salmon* dispute, the Appellate Body judged that the purpose of Australia's ban on fresh salmon imports was regulatory protectionism rather than regulatory protection because the potential disease-related costs associated with other fish imported by Australia exceeded those for salmon.

While hard to quantify, it is apparent that the Agreement has generated broad-based regulatory review by some WTO Members, as major agricultural exporters and importers determine whether they and their trading partners are complying with the obligation to base their risk management decisions on scientific assessments. Evidence suggests that regulatory authorities are either unilaterally modifying regulations, or voluntarily modifying regulations after technical exchanges.

To give just a few examples of accelerated schedules for making long-standing measures consistent with risk-assessment and management obligations, Japan lifted its forty-six-year-old ban on imports of US tomatoes. The United States announced – more than twenty years after the original request from four European countries – that it would allow imports of rhododendron in growing media. Developing country exporters have also benefited from this review: one prominent example is provided by the US decision to lift its controversial eighty-three-year-old ban on imports of Mexican avocados (over the strenuous objections of the domestic industry).[7] More systematic reports, while far from comprehensive, reinforce the anecdotal evidence. WTO Members have collectively reported twenty-four solutions or partial solutions to "specific trade concerns" that have been identified in the SPS Committee between 1995 and 2000, with half of these solutions creating or expanding market access opportunities for developing countries.[8] Far greater is the number of issues that has been resolved before reaching the Committee. One agency alone, the Animal and Plant Health Inspection Service of the US Department of Agriculture, reports resolution of 191 cases in bilateral negotiations over three years.[9]

Other developed and developing countries can undoubtedly offer more examples where the science disciplines of the Agreements were used to prod regulatory inertia. In each case, a finding by scientists that a current measure could be replaced by a less trade-restrictive protocol that still maintained risks at negligible levels was no doubt necessary before any modification could be considered. However enacting these unilateral regulatory changes has become easier now that the SPS Agreement assures policy-makers that their trading partners must conform to the same principles.

However, the science-based disciplines of the SPS Agreement raise a broader normative issue.[10] The Agreement's somewhat myopic focus on the potential risk-related costs of imports faithfully reflects the current risk management decision framework of most WTO Members, which generally ignores the economic benefits of imports.[11] Within this framework, authorities choose measures which reduce risk to negligible levels, rather than measures whose benefits exceed their costs. To cite but one example, one country decided to maintain a ban on imports of bone-in poultry cuts from the United States based on an assessment that shipments posed a risk of three disease introductions in backyard flocks per 100 importation years.[12] Such decisions may be scientifically justifiable, but are not economically justifiable.

The Agreement's omission of rules for factoring the benefits of imports into policy choice is a shortcoming only if this omission is interpreted as a *prohibition* of such considerations. If so, the *status quo* decision framework will remain unperturbed and SPS policy will continue to be biased toward more trade-restrictive measures that exclude welfare-improving imports. But by drawing attention to policies that until recently had largely eluded the scrutiny of economists, an (unintended) effect of the SPS Agreement may be to prompt widespread re-evaluation and – eventually – economic reform of SPS policies.[13] If so, the SPS Agreement may ultimately contribute much more to the liberal trading system than the elimination of those measures that are egregiously protectionist.

## The equivalence obligation

Article 4 of the Agreement (*Equivalence*) requires Members to accept other countries' measures as equivalent to their own – even if they differ – if an exporter shows that its measures achieve the importer's desired level of SPS protection. This provision recognizes that regulatory flexibility allows countries to allocate scarce resources effectively rather than identically. The Agreement also encourages members to create bilateral and multilateral agreements to foster equivalence – a process usually referred to as *mutual recognition*. In this form of regulatory rapprochement, countries typically require assessments of national control *systems* regulating a particular commodity or industry before determining the equivalence of individual *measures*. This is usually a multiyear process that reviews the educational credentials of all regulatory and inspection officials in the sector, as well as a multitude of other factors related to institutional infrastructure. Although labor- and resource-intensive, equivalence assessments allow countries to reduce redundant inspection, control, and testing requirements.

Equivalence usually applies to process standards, since countries can easily compare product standards, which stipulate observable and/or testable attributes of end products. An enormous number – and arguably a growing proportion – of SPS measures are process standards. One of the principal lessons to emerge from two decades of environmental regulation is that process standards are generally an inefficient means of achieving regulatory goals. However, food technologists argue that the unique nature of food hazards – which include pathogens (such as *Salmonella*) that can regenerate and cross-contaminate at several points in the production chain – requires regulating production processes to avoid repeated, expensive tests of conformity with product standards.[14]

Some analysts have challenged this conclusion,[15] but process standards continue to emerge as components of risk management programs, notably in Hazard Analysis and Critical Control Point (HACCP) regulations, which an expanding number of countries mandate for a growing number of food products. The equivalence obligation therefore has the potential to yield significant benefits in international markets for products such as cheeses, meats, fresh produce, and seafood for which process standards are key policy instruments for managing microbial risks.

While the SPS Committee has urged members to submit information on their bilateral equivalence agreements and determinations,[16] none has done so. Consequently, there is no systematic accounting of achievements to date. However, anecdotal evidence suggests such arrangements are still rare.[17] Possibly the most prominent equivalence accord has been a veterinary agreement signed by the United States and the EU in July 1999, after six years of occasionally high-profile negotiations over matters seemingly as trivial as the colors of wall paint in food-processing facilities.[18] The veterinary agreement reduces – but does not eliminate – the need to inspect some $1 billion in EU exports of dairy products, fish, and meat to the United States, and $1 billion in US exports of fish, hides, and pet food to Western Europe. Both the EU and the United States have signed equivalence agreements with other developed countries as well, including Canada, Australia, and New Zealand.[19]

Equivalence agreements may be desirable when achieved, but experience to date suggests that such agreements are difficult to secure. Problems may stem from disorganization and even conflicts of authority within regulatory agencies, but bureaucratic intransigence or organized interest group political economy capture will be factors, as with other regulatory decisions. Perhaps reflecting on its experience with the veterinary equivalence agreement, the United States has stated that the practical use of article 4 may be limited because the actual trade benefits of a determination of equivalence or negotiating an equivalence agreement may not justify the administrative burden.[20]

Numerous regulatory differences remain in contention even between countries generally recognized as having regulatory standards that are rigorously enforced. Most notably, of course, the EU does not recognize genetically modified (GM) commodities as equivalent to traditional varieties, unlike the United States.[21] On the other hand, the United States, Canada, Australia, and New Zealand do not allow imports of some raw-milk cheeses because process standards in the EU and Switzerland are not equivalent to domestic rules requiring the use of pasteurized milk. Another example is the 1997 EU ban on US poultry exports: European authorities do not consider the chlorine decontamination used in US poultry processing plants equivalent to lactic acid decontamination. Globally, the limited access to developed country markets for poultry meat illustrates both the vast potential and the daunting challenge of equivalence. Of the nearly 140 countries that are WTO Members, only fifteen can export fresh, chilled, or frozen poultry meat to the EC, two may export to the United States, one can ship to Canada, and none is allowed to export to Australia.

If equivalence agreements are difficult to negotiate among developed countries, what prospects do developing countries have to benefit from this mechanism? Developing countries have reached few equivalence agreements, and some have expressed concern that such agreements will remain exclusive to the initial negotiating parties, rather than including others that can also meet the equivalence criteria.[22] A number of equivalence arrangements between developing and developed countries do exist, especially for seafood products.[23] However, developing countries – echoing the claims of developed countries – have argued that developed countries often require "compliance" rather than equivalence of measures.[24]

Regulators usually find it awkward to excuse foreign producers from the process requirements that they have imposed on domestic industries. Regulators in developed countries thus concede that complying with domestic process standards might be less costly for foreign exporters than proving that other measures provide equivalent protection. Because many pathogens are relatively rare, statistically reliable test results can require large sample sizes of high-value products. These tests can be prohibitively expensive, particularly for exporters from developing countries lacking laboratory, inspection, and certification infrastructure. Compliance rather than equivalence can therefore be both a pragmatic choice for exporters and expedient outcome for importers.

Yet, compliance can unfairly disadvantage foreign producers if the risks are lower in exporting countries than in the importing country. In the aftermath of the crisis over bovine spongiform encephalopathy (BSE), for example, several countries proposed or adopted new process standards for bovine products that increased costs for exporters in countries where the disease has never been detected. Those countries included Brazil, which protested that the new requirements, which included lengthy chemical treatments for hides and skins, had substantially affected its gelatin exports, even though the International Office of Epizootics (OIE) had reaffirmed in 1998 that hides and skins did not carry BSE.[25] In most circumstances, exporters cannot expect to have recent reports from international standard-setting organizations to bolster their case. More typically, years of data supplied by reputable authorities are necessary to establish (or re-establish) equivalence.

## Harmonizing SPS measures

Article 3 of the SPS Agreement (*Harmonization*) urges the widest possible harmonization of countries' SPS measures based on internationally recognized standards. The Agreement identifies three organizations to promote this objective: the Codex Alimentarius Commission (Codex) for food safety measures, the International Plant Protection Convention (IPPC) for plant health measures, and the OIE for animal health measures.

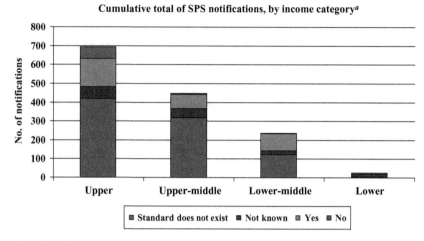

Note: [a]As defined by World Bank
Source: WTO SPS notifications and authors' calculations.

Figure 15.2   Are countries adopting international standards?

The Agreement's endorsement of harmonization stems from repeated complaints by exporters that divergent SPS measures seriously impede trade.[26] The
potential benefits of harmonization for exporters are usually considered large
compared with transparency, because the former eliminates the need to comply
with different regulations. The benefits of harmonization compared with equivalency are also thought to be large, as the former eliminates the need to compare
control systems and measures on a country-by-country basis. Consumers may
also benefit from harmonization if eliminating regulatory heterogeneity among
countries lowers prices and expands product choice.

Despite these potential advantages, harmonization of standards for agricultural products appears to be infrequent. The majority of 1995–9 notifications
from WTO members stated that no international standard existed for the notified measure (figure 15.2). Partial or full acceptance of international standards
as a percentage of total measures notified by income category was highest
for the lower-middle income countries (38 percent) followed by high-income
(22 percent), lower-income (20 percent) and upper-middle-income countries
(17 percent). The high-income countries indicated in 9 percent of their notifications that international standards had not been accepted, compared to
less than 2 percent of the notifications of the countries in the other three income categories. This evidence corroborates the findings of earlier studies on
harmonization.[27]

While voluntary equivalence agreements are designed to increase regulatory
flexibility, harmonization may actually reduce such flexibility in cases where it

is warranted. Differences in actual risks, tastes, and income levels may make harmonization inappropriate. The SPS Agreement and the international standards organization make allowances for these "good" reasons for departures from harmonization.

For example, article 3 of the Agreement does allow a country to maintain measures that are stricter than international standards, in recognition for example that consumers in higher-income countries may be willing and able to pay for a higher level of food safety. And in recognition of the international variation in risks to animal and plant health, much of the activity of the IPPC and the OIE is directed toward development of common *approaches* to risk identification, assessment, and management, rather than toward setting international standards *per se*.

Chance events, information differences, and interest group capture are less positive influences that may preclude harmonization. By disseminating information on analytical techniques and mitigation technologies, standard-setting organizations narrow knowledge gaps and reduce the probability of chance differences from international norms, both "bad" reasons for departures from harmonization. But international standard-setting organizations were never intended to expose or correct interest group capture of national regulatory processes. Standard-setting organizations have typically operated in obscurity, relying on expert committees, consensus-building, and voluntary compliance in pursuit of their respective missions. Codex, for example, was created under the auspices of the UN Food and Agricultural Organization (FAO) and the World Health Organization (WHO) to create standards for developing countries.

Some analysts argue that these organizations themselves have been subject to capture. Critics point to examples where international standards "followed, rather than shaped" national standards – to the advantage of industries from developed countries.[28] Developing countries also report that their minimal participation in key committees gives short shrift to their genuine interests.[29] In 1997, the SPS Committee adopted a provisional procedure for identifying priorities of WTO Members for standard-setting organizations, but developed countries have dominated this exercise as well.[30]

The prevailing judgment is that the SPS Agreement has further politicized decision-making within international standard-setting institutions because it has raised the legal standing of their standards, guidelines, and recommendations. Three specific instances are often cited to support this conclusion: the debate over the *Codex Statements of Principle Concerning the Role of Science in the Codex Decision-Making Process and the Extent to Which other Factors are Taken into Account* ("Statement of Principles"); the 1995 vote on Codex hormone standards; and the 1997 vote on Codex mineral water standards. In the first case, interim compromise language has been negotiated, while in the latter cases the standards for hormone-treated beef (favoring producers in North

America, Japan, Australia, New Zealand, Korea and others) and mineral water (favoring European producers) were approved by slim majorities, rather than by consensus.

In the debate over the Statement of Principles, the United States and the EU sought to propagate decision criteria that favored their domestic agricultural policy regimes.[31] The United States and its allies argued that food safety standards should rest solely on scientific evidence. Europe and its allies sought to introduce a "need" criterion – that productivity-enhancing food technologies threatened the livelihoods of economically marginal farmers and were not "needed" in the face of excess global capacity. A compromise resulted in a statement that Codex standards "shall be based on the principle of sound scientific analysis and evidence," but where appropriate Codex will consider "other legitimate factors" in protecting consumer health and promoting fair trade practices.

Countries have continued to contest the interpretation of "other legitimate factors," but the debate has shifted to the appropriate role – if any – for the precautionary principle in the Statement of Principles. It may be some time before common ground can be found on this issue, as the EU and the United States argued extensively over the issue of whether the principle overrode other WTO legal obligations in the *Hormones* dispute (see p. 345 below). As long as harmonization remains a mechanism for achieving the goals of the SPS Agreement, and standard-setting institutions remain central to harmonization, a high level of political pressure on these institutions is inevitable, despite recent efforts to re-establish neutral credentials by relying as much as possible on consensus decisions.[32]

### Special considerations for developing countries

In addition to the four main mechanisms for achieving its goals, the SPS Agreement contains specific provisions targeted to developing countries. These provisions contain two aspects: that technical assistance be provided to help developing countries promote production and monitoring systems to meet world-wide health and environmental standards (article 9), and that they be accorded special and differential treatment (S&D) (article 10).

The dynamics of the science, technology and consumer preferences that underlie SPS regulation, and the need for private sector investments and public sector institutional activities to keep agriculture competitive in this environment, underscore the value of technical assistance to developing countries. An open world trading system for agriculture requires the undergirding of strong biosecurity systems within each country, and the developing countries face SPS-related challenges as both exporters and importers. They will need international assistance if they are to be a part of the trade system.

Members are encouraged to "take account of the special needs of developing countries" in specifying their regulations. However, it will not often serve the interests of developing countries to seek relaxation of standards that developed countries can defend under the general provisions of the SPS Agreement. Doing so would imply that developing countries cannot meet these legitimate standards, and hurt market receptivity to their products. More compelling is the argument that producers in developing countries are making efforts to meet these standards but are being hampered by structural and institutional weaknesses in their economies. It therefore seems reasonable to argue for international assistance (and many projects with this objective already exist), but not for special treatment on the standards themselves. S&D is often tainted by the suspicion that exempt countries may be doing themselves more harm than good, with little effect elsewhere. In the case of special and differential treatment on legitimate SPS regulations, however, any risk-related burden resulting from S&D is borne within the country that grants the exemption.

## Dispute settlement and the SPS Agreement

The WTO Understanding on Rules and Procedures Governing the Settlement of Disputes – known as the Dispute Settlement Understanding, or DSU – provides the legal infrastructure for enforcing all agreements negotiated during the Uruguay Round, including the SPS Agreement. DSU rules stipulate that when bilateral and multilateral technical exchanges and negotiations reach an impasse, a member can request a ruling by a dispute panel, and subsequently the WTO Appellate Body, if necessary.

Countries brought formal complaints related to fifteen SPS issues over the first six years of the SPS Agreement (table 15.2). In contrast, virtually no SPS trade disputes advanced to dispute settlement during the forty-seven years of the GATT. The increased adjudicatory activity suggests that the post-Uruguay Round legal environment has improved prospects for disciplining the use of questionable SPS measures.

Three of the fifteen complaints only tangentially involved SPS issues. Developed countries have initiated eleven of the remaining twelve disputes – and all but one of these complaints (Switzerland's complaint against Slovakia's restrictions on livestock products) have been directed at other developed countries. One SPS complaint was raised by a developing country (Thailand), and that complaint targeted the measure of another developing country (Egypt). Of the twelve SPS complaints, consultations are pending in seven cases, two were settled by negotiation, and three others have advanced to WTO panels and thence on to the WTO Appellate Body: the EU–United States/Canada *Hormones* dispute, the Australia–Canada *Salmon* dispute, and the Japan–United States *Varietal Testing* dispute.

Table 15.2 *Disputes under the SPS Agreement, 1995–2000*

| Case number(s) | Issue | Complainant(s) | Status |
|---|---|---|---|
| DS 3/41 | Korea – produce inspection | United States | Pending |
| DS 5 | Korea – shelf-life requirements | United States | Settled |
| DS 18/21 | Australia – ban on salmon imports | Canada | Panel and Appellate Body ruled against Australia |
| DS 20 | Korea – bottled-water | Canada | Settled |
| DS 26/49 | EC – ban on use of hormones | United States and Canada | Panel and Appellate Body ruled against EC |
| DS 76 | Japan – varietal testing requirements | United States | Panel and Appellate Body ruled against Japan |
| DS 96 | India – quantitative restrictions | EC | Settled (minor SPS issue) |
| DS 100 | United States – poultry requirements | EC | Pending |
| DS 133 | Slovakia – BSE restrictions | Switzerland | Pending |
| DS 134 | EC – restrictions on rice | India | Pending (minor SPS issue) |
| DS 135 | France – asbestos restrictions | Canada | Panel ruled in favor of France (minor SPS issue) |
| DS 137 | EC – measures on pine wood nematodes | Canada | Pending |
| DS 144 | US – state restrictions on Canadian trucks | Canada | Pending |
| DS 203 | Mexico – measures affecting trade in live swine | United States | Pending |
| DS 205 | Egypt – import prohibition on canned tuna with soyoil | Thailand | Pending |

*Source:* WTO, http:/www.wto.org/wto/dispute/bulletin/htm.

*The* Hormones *case*

The long-running disagreement between the EU and the United States (and later Canada) over the safety of hormonal growth stimulants in beef cattle is regarded as the bellwether test of the new SPS disciplines. The EU has claimed that international standards for the hormones – based on the Codex vote noted above – did not meet its public health goals. The EU also defended its ban on imports of hormone-treated beef as a precautionary approach to managing uncertain risks. The US challenge of the EU ban raised substantive legal questions about the extent to which new multilateral trade rules limit an importer's ability to adopt measures that exceed international standards, and employ the precautionary principle as a legal defense.

The Appellate Body upheld the original panel's decision that the EU ban did not comply with the SPS Agreement (see table 15.3).[33] The judges concurred that the ban was not based on a risk assessment, as there appeared to be no "rational relationship" between the EU's measures and the health risks from consuming hormone-treated beef reported in scientific evaluations. The Appellate Body also ruled that while international standards were not mandatory,[34] the EU had not produced scientific evidence to support the claim that its ban achieved a higher level of health protection. The judges noted that while the EU had broadly argued that the precautionary principle had guided its regulatory decision, it had been unwilling to specifically defend its measure under article 5.7, which permits members to provisionally adopt measures while seeking additional scientific information to complete a risk assessment. The EU did not use this defense because it considered its measure final, not provisional. The Appellate Body ruled that the EU must therefore bring its measure into compliance with the obligations specified in the other Articles of the Agreement.

*The* Salmon *and* Varietal Testing *cases*

Formal consultations also failed to produce negotiated solutions in the Australian–Canadian *Salmon* dispute and in the Japan-United States *Varietal Testing* dispute. These two disagreements centered on measures justified on the basis of protecting, respectively, recreational and commercial fish stocks from a number of diseases, and orchards from coddling moth.

In the *Salmon* dispute, the Appellate Body concurred with Canada that Australia's 1975 ban on imports of fresh, chilled, or frozen (eviscerated) salmon from the Northern Hemisphere was inconsistent with legal obligations in the SPS Agreement. As in the *Hormones* case, the judges concluded that the measures at issue were not based on a risk assessment. The judges concluded that Australia's scientific report was not a risk assessment because it did not evaluate the likelihood that disease would enter or spread, or the potential consequences

Table 15.3 *Jurisprudence in SPS Appellate Body rulings, 1995–2000*

| Dispute | Complainant party | Co-complainants | Appellate Body ruling *(provision violated)* |
|---|---|---|---|
| EC measures concerning meat and meat products *(Hormones)* | United States Canada | Australia, New Zealand, Norway | EC measure was not based on a risk assessment *(article 5.1)* <br> EC did not substantiate the claim that its measure provided a higher level of health protection than the international standard *(article 3.3)* |
| Australia measures affecting the importation of salmon *(Salmon)* | Canada | EC, India, Norway, United States | Australian measures were not based on a risk assessment *(article 5.1)* <br> The ban on salmon imports provided a level of protection that was higher than other measures used by Australia to protect fish stocks, and this variation was a disguised restriction on trade *(article 5.5)* |
| Japan measures affecting agricultural products *(Varietal Testing)* | United States | Brazil, EC, Hungary | Japan's varietal testing requirements were maintained without sufficient scientific evidence *(article 2.2)* and were not based on a risk assessment *(article 5.1)* <br> The testing requirement was not published *(article 7 and Annex B)* <br> Japan did not fulfill its obligation to obtain information for a scientific risk assessment by requiring exporters to submit data *(article 5.7)* |

*Source:* WTO, http:/www.wto.org/wto/dispute/bulletin/htm.

of the diseases.[35] The Appellate Body also concurred with Canada that the salmon import ban provided a level of environmental protection arbitrarily higher than that provided by other Australian sanitary measures, because Australia allows imports of other fish that are potentially vectors for the same or even more virulent diseases.

At issue in the *Varietal Testing* dispute were Japanese requirements that exporters test whether methyl bromide treatments effectively exterminate coddling moths on each new variety of fruit and walnuts. The United States argued that such requirements were unscientific, since Japan could produce no evidence that variety is a causal factor of variation in extermination efficacy, and that the requirements restricted US exports, since the cost of testing discourages exporters from marketing new hybrids in Japan. The Appellate Body concurred with a panel ruling that Japan's phytosanitary measures were not transparent, as they had never been published, and were not based on "sufficient scientific evidence." The judges further ruled that varietal testing measures were not based on a risk assessment, and that the testing requirements could not be justified as a provisional measure under the terms of article 5.7. The judges decided that the fact that the measures had been in effect for forty-eight years belied Japan's claim that its measures were provisional. Moreover, in the judges' view, a government does not fulfill its obligation under article 5.7 to seek additional information to complete a risk assessment by requiring exporters to submit data from costly experiments.

*Implications of the dispute-settlement process*

The decisions in the *Hormones*, *Salmon,* and *Varietal Testing* cases provide important indications of how WTO tribunals would interpret some of the general disciplines of the SPS Agreement. The decisions, which found that the disputed measures in these cases were not based on a risk assessment or that they were maintained without sufficient scientific evidence, held that there must be a rational relationship between the policy choices made by governments and objective scientific assessments that go beyond hypothesis or hazard identification. The requirement that countries reference scientific evidence in dispute proceedings eliminates a strategy of "stonewalling" used to great effect by some governments to defend the most egregiously protectionist SPS measures prior to the Uruguay Round. The "rational relationship" judicial test also suggests that tribunals will be willing to discipline SPS measures based on popular misconceptions of risks, even if the requirements apply equally to domestic and foreign producers, as well as more overtly discriminatory measures.

The Appellate Body's rulings on the Agreement's provisions related to international standards and regulatory decisions based on the precautionary principle should dispel some of the concerns that WTO tribunals would view their mandate as the vigorous promotion of globalization at the expense of national sovereignty on health and environmental issues. The WTO Appellate Body explicitly ruled in the *Hormones* case that the SPS Agreement did not require countries to adopt international standards. This should allay anxieties that the Agreement would promote "downward harmonization" of national standards to facilitate trade. And although the panels and the Appellate Body rulings did not support EU and Japanese arguments that their measures were precautionary, the rulings did highlight the SPS provision that allows countries to adopt measures to temporarily mitigate unfamiliar risks. Countries have adopted a number of precautionary measures since 1995 that exporters have not formally challenged – most prominently in the BSE crisis but also in the wake of the 1999 Belgian dioxin scare.

The outcomes of formal disputes, especially the highly visible *Hormones* case, figure prominently in any judgment about the effectiveness of the SPS Agreement (and the jurisprudence which interprets that Agreement) in helping to improve the world trading system. Together with strengthened DSPs, the SPS Agreement has restored the rule of law to several long-standing disputes.

Establishing the rule of law for SPS measures may be particularly important to developing countries. These countries have not been principal complainants in the formal disputes, and will often lack the resources to pursue such cases. The formal cases between developed countries may nonetheless have desirable spillover effects for developing countries if they can export to the newly liberalized market, or if the legal precedents provide concrete guidance for exercising their rights in future disputes. It is also interesting to note that the three SPS disputes to advance to the Appellate Body have been won by the complainants. This outcome mirrors the historical pattern of other GATT–WTO disputes, but it is notable in the context of SPS regulations because it proves that countries with sophisticated scientific establishments are not immune to successful challenge of their measures.

Unfortunately, not all legally sanctioned results of SPS dispute settlement cases give equally desirable trade outcomes. The EU announced that it would not change its hormones measures by May 1999, as required by a WTO Arbitrator, asserting that it needed to complete additional risk assessments.[36] The United States, Canada, and the EU could not agree on a product labeling regime, nor could the parties agree on a compensation deal that would leave the EU ban in place but include trade concessions on other products. The WTO General Council therefore authorized retaliation by the complainants against $128.1 million of European products. This bellwether SPS case has thus initially resulted in less rather than more international trade, although the parties continue to search for mutually acceptable compensation deals.

Trade sanctions are by far the least preferable outcome of the WTO dispute-settlement process. However, authorized retaliation is superior to unilateral tit-for-tat measures, such as those exchanged by the United States and EU in the 1980s – described as the equivalent of "vigilante justice" in trade.[37] In the *Salmon* case, Canada and Australia have notified a mutually acceptable agreement to the WTO, which allows Canadian salmon to enter Australia markets under certain restrictions. Notification of a mutually acceptable conclusion to the 1997 *Varietal Testing* case by the United States and Japan appears imminent.

## Challenges confronting the SPS Agreement

The SPS Agreement has achieved some success since it came into effect in 1995. The transparency provisions have strengthened countries' obligation to notify others of changes in their SPS policies, made information more available, and provided a forum for informally airing disputes. The Agreement also clearly articulated countries' obligation to base regulatory measures on scientific risk assessment. Strengthened WTO DSPs have provided a new institutional setting in which to test compliance, and the substance of the SPS Agreement has been sustained by panels and the Appellate Body.

For developing countries, more transparency and establishment of the rule of law on SPS barriers may have far-reaching implications. Some developing countries have been active in the WTO's SPS Committee. Specific decisions on SPS barriers can also help countries trading in the affected markets, even if they are not parties to the conflict resolution process. Assessments of whether national measures comply with stated obligations, clarification of obligations through Appellate Body rulings, equivalence agreements, and establishment of international standards can also demonstrate acceptable practices. This demonstration effect can exert a positive impact even where conflicts among trading partners have not erupted.

Future trade among developed countries, between developed and developing countries, and among developing countries will each contribute substantially to the movement of agricultural product in world markets. Despite many common interests among developed and developing countries, a somewhat different nexus of SPS barriers characterizes each of these trade patterns. In developed countries, gridlock often seems to arise because national regulatory systems are responsive to domestic producer and consumer interest groups. Developing country exporters worry that developed countries will exclude their products by adopting regulatory regimes marked by conservative and costly risk management, partly in response to highly publicized incidents of presumed or real food safety or environmental risk. Within developing countries, the scientific infrastructure to evaluate and control pests and diseases that pose risks to human, animal, and plant health may be underfunded. Governments in such countries find international borders a convenient place to intervene, imposing stringent barriers against imported products, including those of other developing countries.

Against this backdrop, and given the fast pace of scientific and technological advance, several challenges confront the SPS Agreement in a new round of international negotiations. The record of accomplishment on transparency and formal dispute settlement related to the SPS Agreement suggest that the negotiating challenge is to "stay the course." Strengthening and extending the notification system to more countries is important, as nuanced interpretations of the Agreement's basic language emanating from dispute-settlement rulings continue to narrow the scope for misuse of SPS barriers. Fostering continued progress under these mechanisms is better than re-opening negotiations and modifying the basic language that obligates risk assessment. The Agreement should retain this firmly stated obligation as its substantive core.

It is more difficult to discern how to continue progress in equivalence and harmonization, where fulfilling international objectives is difficult, the language of the Agreement is less binding, and pressures on the Agreement will intensify. These pressures will come from the dynamics of science, evolving production technologies, and changing consumer preferences for food safety. More insidious pressures stem from domestic producers seeking high levels of agricultural support and protection, particularly in developed countries, and from activist consumer groups that impose their preferences through regulations that reduce broader social welfare. In either case, the WTO to date has provided only limited institutional innovation under the equivalence and harmonization mechanisms to alter domestic regulatory decisions.

Even the risk assessment criterion of the SPS Agreement is not immune to challenge. Within developed countries, the substance and political economy of SPS regulations have become the focus of politicians and lobbying groups who suggest that regulators are compromising protection of human, animal, and plant health to expedite trade. Despite little evidence that growing international trade in agricultural goods and foodstuffs has undermined food safety, international rules are perceived to undercut safety standards by insisting on science-based risk assessment even when scientific evidence may be incomplete.

One key question facing the WTO is whether the SPS Agreement applies to regulations governing the importation of GM foods.[38] The rapid adoption by farmers in the United States, Canada, and Argentina of GM herbicide-resistant soybeans and insect-resistant corn poses a challenge for the global food system, given consumer resistance in other parts of the world, especially Europe.[39] Different regulatory regimes for GM products have proliferated throughout the world, with different countries approving different commodities for release, requiring different tests for detection of trace elements, and adopting different labeling requirements. Most of the recent tensions over restrictions on trade in GM products have been between developed countries in the New and Old World;

it was therefore somewhat surprising that the first formal complaint to reach the WTO over GM foods was lodged by one developing country against another. Egypt banned imports of Thai tuna canned in soybean oil, on the premise that the oil could be the by-product of GM soybeans that had not been approved by Egyptian regulators. Thailand has not questioned the justification of the ban, but has asserted that the oil is not processed from GM soybeans. The parties appear to be headed for a settlement that specifies a mutually agreeable certification scheme. So for the moment, the WTO has not been called to rule in a case over trade in GM products where scientific evidence of risk and public perceptions of risk significantly diverge. This is a safe outcome for the institution, at least temporarily, yet uncertainty surrounding WTO disciplines on GM products may have profound consequences for technology adoption in developing countries, such as Argentina and Thailand, which rely on agricultural exports to generate economic growth.

If these technical and political considerations do not pose enough challenges, the disciplines on human, animal, and plant health and safety measures are only one component of a broader attempt to open the world agricultural trading system through the WTO.[40] Scientific developments, new technologies, and evolving consumer preferences will continue to push SPS measures to the center of the trade policy debate, and more open world markets will continue to confront SPS health- and environment-related conflicts. Yet SPS regulations should not substitute for traditional trade barriers. The SPS Agreement is well on its way to preventing this outcome, and holds promise for achieving much more.

# Appendix

Table 15A.1 *Trade patterns in agricultural, forestry, and fishery products, 1997*

| | Importer | | | |
| | Developed country | | Developing country | |
| Exporter | Value (US$ billion) | Growth rate (1990–7) | Value (US$ billion) | Growth rate (1990–7) |
|---|---|---|---|---|
| *Developed countries* | | | | |
| *Total* | *211.6* | *16* | *92.0* | *21* |
| Bulk commodities[a] | 13.2 | 13 | 10.4 | 14 |
| Processed intermediates | 35.4 | 15 | 18.3 | 23 |

(*cont.*)

Table 15A.1 (*cont.*)

| | Importer | | | |
|---|---|---|---|---|
| | Developed country | | Developing country | |
| Exporter | Value (US$ billion) | Growth rate (1990–7) | Value (US$ billion) | Growth rate (1990–7) |
| Produce and horticultural products | 22.7 | 16 | 3.7 | 27 |
| High-value processed products | 90.1 | 17 | 33.1 | 20 |
| Related agricultural products | 50.2 | 16 | 26.5 | 24 |
| *Developing countries* | | | | |
| *Total* | *159.3* | *19* | *128.0* | *26* |
| Bulk commodities | 37.1 | 17 | 36.4 | 22 |
| Processed intermediates | 27.1 | 17 | 29.1 | 28 |
| Produce and horticultural products | 15.7 | 17 | 12.1 | 25 |
| High-value processed products | 25.8 | 22 | 25.5 | 33 |
| Related agricultural products | 53.5 | 19 | 25.1 | 27 |

*Note:* [a] Bulk commodities include primarily grains and oilseeds; processed intermediates include oilseed meals, vegetable oils, animal feed, pet food, live animals, wool, and hides and skins; horticultural products include fresh fruits and vegetables; high-valued processed products include roasted coffee, cocoa products, beverages, dairy products, eggs, meats and processed fruits and vegetables; related agricultural products include seafood, distilled spirits, leather, fish, wood, yarn, thread, and leather.
*Source:* USDA, Economic Research Service, International Bilateral Agricultural Trade (IBAT) database, developed from UNCTAD bilateral trade data.

**Notes**

The views expressed in this chapter are not to be attributed to any of the institutions with which the authors are affiliated. The authors gratefully acknowledge the research assistance of Mark Gelhar and Gregg Young.

1. Least-developed countries (LDCs) were exempt from the transparency requirements until 2000, and thus only a few have provided official notification of changes in SPS regulations.

2. GATT (1992), p. 32.

3. Because some of the cross-notifications targeted existing rather than newly notified measures, measurement of the compliance effect can only be approximated.

4. World agricultural trade totaled $590.9 billion in 1997, based on UNCTAD data (see appendix, p. 351). Developed countries exports were $303.6 billion, accounting for 51 percent of total world exports of these products.

5. The EU has noted, for example, that as of July 1999, it had had responses to only two of eight follow-up queries it has submitted to trading partners about their notifications over the past two years, "Implementation of the SPS Agreement–Trade Concerns," Submission by the European Communities at the meeting of July 7–8, 1999, G/SPS/GEN/132.

6. Common perceptions of where the problems lie with SPS barriers are not always mirrored in the cross-notifications to the SPS Committee. More than half of the complaints filed by developed countries against other developed countries have concerned measures addressing food safety goals as opposed to commercial production goals. This possibly surprising result may be explained by the idiosyncratic nature of food safety regulations among developed countries, despite the notion that they face similar levels of consumer demand for food safety. The proportions among complaints are reversed for developed country complaints against measures by developing countries: more of these complaints concern commercial production measures – perhaps because developing countries impose stringent border regulations owing to their limited internal monitoring, regulatory, and damage-control capacities. Cross-notification complaints initiated by developing countries also mostly address measures with commercial production goals. Since most of these complaints are against developed countries, this may again seem surprising, given the anecdotal evidence that developing countries are more worried about stringent food safety regulations by developed countries.

7. For a historical account of the avocado dispute, see Orden and Roberts (1997). Before its final ruling, the United States Department of Agriculture (USDA) received more than 2,000 comments, most opposing the proposed rule to allow imports of Mexican avocados under certain seasonal and regional restrictions. This was more comment than the agency had ever received on a phytosanitary regulation. The domestic avocado industry also placed provocative full-page advertisements in several national newspapers. One asserted, against the backdrop of a hangman's noose, "the USDA is about to sign the death warrant for a billion dollar American industry," *The Washington Post*, 11 March, 1996, p. A16.

8. WTO (2000b).

9. USDA/ APHIS (1996, 1997, 1998). Of the 191 plant and animal health issues reported as resolved, 147 cases resulted in increased US exports, while forty-four resulted in increased US imports. Developed and developing countries, respectively, accounted for one-quarter and three-quarters of the cases in each category, roughly equivalent to their respective proportion in the WTO. The APHIS reports are only a partial accounting of SPS issues resolved by the US government because most food safety measures are not included in APHIS' statutory authority (food safety is addressed primarily by the Food and Drug Administration and USDA's Food Safety and Inspection Service).

10. Roberts (2000).
11. The potential benefits of imports appear to be at best intermittently – and at worst opportunistically – factored into risk management decisions. For example, it is not uncommon for regulators to accept imports of live breeding stock (inputs that contribute to a domestic industry's productivity) because of industry "need" while rejecting arguably less-risky meat imports.
12. Biosecurity Authority (2000).
13. A few recent studies of SPS measures raise the prospect that this reexamination has been overdue. See, for example, James and Anderson (1998) and Otsuki, Wilson, and Sewadeh (2000).
14. See MacDonald and Crutchfield (1996). It has also been argued that process standards can serve as a form of technology transfer for developing countries. See Sykes (1995, 137).
15. Antle (1995).
16. WTO (1999c).
17. For example, the chair of the Codex Committee on Food Import and Export Certification and Inspection Systems reports that "the concept of equivalence has not been widely applied" (Gascoine, 1999, 7).
18. "US Poultry Exports to EU Hit as Negotiators Fail to Agree on Equivalence," *World Food Chemical News*, April 2, 1997, 8.
19. "Canada Signs Veterinary Equivalency Agreement with European Union," *World Food Chemical News*, January 6, 1998, 6.
20. WTO (2000a).
21. In the United States, the regulatory approach of the Food and Drug Administration to GM commodities is straightforward. The question asked is whether the modified product is materially different from the non-modified product, in terms of the health risks it might pose to consumers. If the modified product is considered similar to that of the original product, as is often the case, then no separate authorization is needed. Labeling of these products is not mandatory. Voluntary labeling is permitted as long as it is not misleading.
22. See "WTO Agreement on Sanitary and Phytosanitary Measures: Issues for Developing Countries," South Center, July 1999.
23. "Major Exporting Countries Seek Help to Comply with US Seafood HACCP Rule," *World Food Chemical News,* July 11, 1997, 11.
24. See, for example, WTO (1999).
25. WTO (1998b, 5).
26. One study of the international variation in MRLs for fruit illustrates the problem. While the MRL for Malathion on apples is 8.0 parts per billion (ppb) in the United States, it is 0.5 ppb in Germany, France, the Netherlands, and the United Kingdom. The MRL for permethryn on apples is 0.05 ppb in the United States but 1.0 ppb in Europe. An apple exporter must therefore target either the US or European market or meet the highest standard of any of the possible destinations to have flexibility to respond to changing market conditions. See Fischer (1998).
27. For example, one study reports that as of 1993, only 14 percent of developed countries and 12 percent of developing countries had accepted existing Codex commodity standards. (Victor 1999.)

28. Victor (1999).
29. Developing country critics point to the allocation of standard-setting resources to income-sensitive commodities (such as the proposal to set standards for sports drinks) – and to the design of the standards based on capital-intensive solutions to mitigating risks – as showing that their interests are being marginalized. See Permanent Mission of India (1999).
30. As of July 1999, nine proposals had been submitted to the Committee to be forwarded to the relevant scientific organization (WTO, 1999b). Developing countries (Thailand and the Philippines) identified two priorities; the remaining seven were identified by the United States, the EU, and Canada. Several developing countries supported the proposals made by the developed countries; as evident in the cross-notification data, the trade interests of developed and developing countries are not always mutually exclusive.
31. Powell (1997).
32. See, for example, Joint FAO/WHO Food Standard Programme (1999).
33. For discussion of the *Hormones* case, see Roberts (1998).
34. The Appellate Body held that the statement in the SPS Agreement that a measure shall be *based on* an international standard where one exists (except as otherwise provided for in the agreement) does not imply that measures need to *conform to* international standards. If this were so, contended the judges, the SPS Agreement would vest international standards (which are recommendations under the terms of the Codex Commission) with *obligatory* force and effect. To sustain such an assumption, the Appellate Body argued, language far more specific and compelling than that found in article 3 of the SPS Agreement would be necessary.
35. The Appellate Body agreed with the earlier panel finding that the report contained "general and vague statements of mere possibility of adverse effects occurring; statements which constitute neither a quantitative nor a qualitative assessment of probability."
36. The Arbitrator noted "It would not be in keeping with the requirement of *prompt* compliance to include in the reasonable period of time, time to conduct studies or to consult experts to demonstrate the *consistency* of a measure already judged to be inconsistent." WTO (1998c, 15), emphasis in the original.
37. Orden and Romano (1996).
38. Alternatively, the TBT Agreement may be relevant to certain aspects of the regulations for genetically modified commodities. The TBT Agreement covers issues such as labeling (as long as the labels do not suggest a health warning, in which case the disciplines of the SPS Agreement apply). In one important respect the TBT Agreement is arguably not as stringent as the SPS Agreement. Measures do not explicitly have to be based on a risk assessment, although article 2.2 of the TBT Agreement states that "relevant elements of consideration are, *inter alia*: available scientific and technical information." Outside the WTO, the Biosecurity Protocol takes a much more regulated approach to trade in genetically modified living organisms, and products containing genetically modified material.
39. Nelson *et al.* (1999).

40. In general, the extent to which the WTO Agreements embodied substantial new commitments to liberalizing agricultural trade or simply codified existing domestic support policies remains open to question. See Josling (1998). Orden, *et al.* (1999) present an argument along lines of the latter view.

## References

Antle, J., 1995. *Choice and Efficiency in Food Safety Policy*, Washington, DC: American Enterprise Institute Press

Biosecurity Authority, Ministry of Agriculture and Forestry, 2000. "Revised Quantitative Risk Assessment on Chicken Meat Products from the United States," New Zealand Ministry of Agriculture and Forestry, Auckland, April 7

Fischer, R., 1998. "Regulation as a Trade Issue from Chilean Perspective," in "Regulatory Reform in the Global Economy: Asian and Latin American Perspectives," *OECD Proceedings*, Paris

Gascoine, D., 1999. "Harmonization, Mutual Recognition, and Equivalence – How and What is Attainable," paper presented at the Conference on International Food Trade Beyond 2000: Science-Based Decisions, Harmonization, Equivalence and Mutual Recognition, Melbourne

General Agreement on Tariffs and Trade (GATT), 1992. "International Trade, 1990–91," Geneva

James, S. and K. Anderson, 1998. "On the Need for More Economic Assessment of Quarantine/SPS Policies," *Australian Journal of Agricultural Economics*, 1, 525–44

Joint FAO/WHO Food Standard Programme, Codex Committee on General Principles, 1999. "Improvement of Procedures for the Adoption of Codex Standards and Measures to Facilitate Consensus," FAO/WHO CX/GP/99/5, March, Rome

Josling, T., 1998. "Agricultural Trade Policy: Completing the Reform," *Policy Analysis in International Economics*, 53, 86–8

MacDonald, J. and S. Crutchfield, 1996. "Modeling the Costs of Food Safety Regulations," *American Journal of Agricultural Economics*, 78(5), 1285–990

Nelson, G. C., T. Josling, D. Bullock, L. Unnevehr, M. Rosengrant, and L. Hill, 1999. "The Economics and Politics of Genetically Modified Organisms in Agriculture: Implications for WTO 2000," University of Illinois at Urbana-Champaign, College of Agricultural, Consumer, and Environmental Sciences, Bulletin 809, Urbana, Illinois, November

Orden, D. and D. Roberts, 1997. "Determinants of Technical Barriers to Trade: The Case of US Phytosanitary Restrictions on Mexican Avocados, 1972–1995," in D. Orden and D. Roberts (eds.), *Understanding Technical Barriers to Trade*, Washington, DC: International Trade Research Consortium

Orden, D., R. Paarlberg, and T. Roe, 1999. *Policy Reform in American Agriculture: Analysis and Prognosis*, Chicago: University of Chicago Press

Orden, D. and E. Romano, 1996. "The Avocado Dispute and Other Technical Barriers to Agricultural Trade Under NAFTA," paper presented at NAFTA and Agriculture: Is the Experiment Working?, San Antonio, Texas, November

Otsuki, T., J. Wilson, and M. Sewadeh, 2000. "Saving Two in a Billion: A Case Study to Quantify the Trade Effects of European Food Safety Standards on African Exports," paper presented at a Conference on the Economics of Quarantine, Australian Quarantine and Inspection Service, Melbourne, October 24–25

Permanent Mission of India, 1999. "Communication from India: Proposals Regarding the Agreement on Sanitary and Phytosanitary Measures in Terms of Paragraph 9(a)(I) of the Geneva Ministerial Declaration," WT/GC/W/202, Geneva

Powell, M., 1997. "Science in Sanitary and Phytosanitary Dispute Resolution," Discussion Paper 97–50 for Resources for the Future, Washington, DC

Roberts, D., 1998. "Preliminary Assessment of the Effects of the WTO Agreement on Sanitary and Phytosanitary Trade Regulations," *Journal of International Economics Law*, 1(3), 377–405

　2000. "Sanitary and Phytosanitary Risk Management in the Post-Uruguay Round Era: An Economic Perspective," in *Incorporating Science, Economics, and Sociology in Developing Sanitary and Phytosanitary Standards in International Trade*, Washington, DC: National Academy Press

Sykes, A. O., 1995. *Product Standards for Internationally Integrated Goods Markets*, Washington, DC: Brookings Institution Press

USDA/Department of Agriculture Animal and Plant Health Inspection Service (APHIS), 1996. "SPS Accomplishments Report," Washington, DC

　1997. "SPS Accomplishments Report," Washington, DC

　1998. "SPS Accomplishments Report," Washington, DC

Victor, D., 1999. "Risk Management and the World Trading System: Regulating International Trade Distortions Caused by National Sanitary and Phytosanitary Policies," paper presented at the National Research Council Conference on Incorporating Science, Economics, Sociology, and Politics in Sanitary and Phytosanitary Standards in International Trade, Irvine, California, January; published National Academy Press, 2000

World Trade Organization (WTO), 1998a. Committee on Sanitary and Phytosanitary Measures, "Committee on Sanitary and Phytosanitary Measures – Summary of the Meeting Held on September 15–16, 1998 – Note by the Secretariat," G/SPS/R/12, Geneva

　1998b. Committee on Sanitary and Phytosanitary Measures, "Summary of the Meeting Held on September 15–16, 1998," G/SPS/R/12, Geneva

　1998c. Report of the Arbitrator, "EC Measures Concerning Meat and Meat Products (Hormones) – Arbitration under Article 21.3 (c) of the Understanding on Rules and Procedures Governing the Settlement of Dispute – Award of the Arbitrator," WT/DS26/15 and WT/DS48/13, May, Geneva

　1999a. Committee on Sanitary and Phytosanitary Measures, "Committee on Sanitary and Phytosanitary Measures – Specific Trade Concerns – Note by the Secretariat," G/SPS/GEN/204, Geneva

　1999b. Committee on Sanitary and Phytosanitary Measures, "Procedure to Monitor the Process of International Harmonization," G/SPS/13, July, Geneva

　1999c. Committee on Sanitary and Phytosanitary Measures, "Review of the Operation and Implementation of the Agreement on the Application of Sanitary and Phytosanitary Measures," G/SPS/12, Geneva

1999d. Committee on Sanitary and Phytosanitary Measures, "SPS Agreement and Developing Countries: Statement by Egypt at the Meeting of July 7–8, 1999," G/SPS/GEN/128, July, Geneva

1999e. Committee on Sanitary and Phytosanitary Measures, "Submission by European Communities at the SPS Council Meeting of July 7–8, 1999, 'Implementation of the SPS Agreement-Trade Concerns'," G/SPS/132, Geneva

2000a. Committee on Sanitary and Phytosanitary Measures, "Equivalence: Submission from the United States," G/SPS/GEN/212, November, Geneva

2000b. Committee on Sanitary and Phytosanitary Measures, "Specific Trade Concerns," G/SPS/GEN/204, September 27

# 16 How developing countries view the impact of sanitary and phytosanitary measures on agricultural exports

*Spencer Henson, Rupert Loader, Alan Swinbank,*
*and Maury Bredahl*

As the Uruguay Round has liberalized tariff and quantitative barriers to trade, concern has grown about the impact of other measures – many of which are not explicitly trade-related – on agricultural and food exports. In particular, analysts widely acknowledge that technical measures such as food quality and sanitary and phytosanitary (SPS) requirements can impede trade, particularly for developing countries.

The Uruguay Round addressed the impact of these requirements through the SPS and Technical Barriers to Trade (TBT) Agreements. This chapter identifies the specific problems of developing countries in meeting SPS requirements in developed country markets, especially the European Union (EU). We base our findings on the results of case studies and an in-depth survey of developing country officials.

## SPS measures as barriers to trade

Concerns over food safety regulations, labeling requirements, and standards for food quality and composition reflect the global proliferation of such measures, particularly in developed countries (figure 16.1). These measures can damage trade by imposing an import ban or by prohibitively raising production and marketing costs. They can also divert trade from one trading partner to another by discriminating among suppliers. Finally, they can reduce overall trade flows by increasing the costs and barriers for all suppliers.

Attention to the trade impacts of SPS measures has focused largely on developed countries – through, for example, the high-profile dispute between the EU and the United States over the use of hormones to produce beef (*Hormones* case, see also chapter 15 in this volume). Most studies of SPS measures, especially the more rigorous ones, focus on the United States. For example, Thornsbury

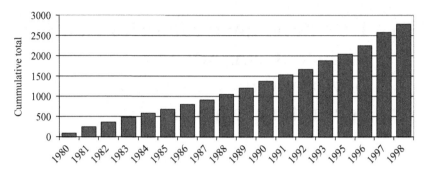

*Source:* OECD (1997); WTO.

Figure 16.1  Notifications of technical measures to GATT/WTO, 1980–1999

*et al.* (1997) put the total impact of technical barriers on US agricultural exports in 1996 at $4,907 million. Of that amount, 90 percent stemmed from measures covered by the SPS Agreement. The impact of food safety standards in particular was estimated at $2,288 million.

However, SPS measures may be even more problematic for developing countries because they predominantly export agricultural and food products. For example, agricultural products accounted for some 25 percent of merchandise exports from Sub-Saharan Africa (SSA) from 1980 to 1997 (World Bank, 1999). Developing countries also find the technical challenges of complying with SPS requirements severe.

Studies have shown that developing countries find it difficult to trade with developed countries owing to differences in food safety and quality standards (Murphy and Shleifer, 1997). However, few have quantified the costs of compliance and the impact on exports of fish, spices, oilseeds, oils and fats, livestock products, and horticultural products (see for example UNCTAD and Commonwealth Secretariat, 1996; Gilmour and Oxley, 1998; Sullivan *et al.*, 1999). One of the more in-depth analyses to date focuses on the Bangladesh frozen shrimp sector.

The EU banned Bangladeshi exports of frozen shrimp from August to December 1997 because of concerns about hygiene standards in processing facilities, and the effectiveness of controls by government inspectors. Cato and Lima dos Santos (1998) estimate that the ban cost shrimp processors $14.6 million. Cato (1998) estimates that the Bangladesh industry spent $17.6 million from 1997–8 to satisfy the EU's hygiene requirements – an average of $239,630 per plant. The total cost required to maintain these plants is estimated at $2.2 million per year. The Bangladesh government also spent some $283,000 and predicts an expenditure of $225,000 per annum to maintain a monitoring program.

Mutasa and Nyamandi (1998) found that 57 percent of responding African countries indicated that border inspectors had rejected food and agricultural exports within the previous two years owing to microbiological contamination, spoilage, and other forms of contamination. Although all of these countries inspected food products before exporting them, financial constraints limited the effectiveness of their testing and inspection facilities and procedures.

Data on US border inspections also indicate the impact of SPS requirements on developing countries (table 16.1).[1] Only the United States systematically collects such data and makes them publicly available. From June 1996 to June 1997, the United States rejected significant imports from Africa, Asia, and Latin America and the Caribbean because of microbiological contamination, filth, and decomposition.[2] This data reveals the considerable problems that developing countries face in meeting basic requirements for food hygiene (FAO, 1999), let alone standards that require more sophisticated and costly monitoring, such as limits on pesticide and heavy metal residues. The costs to exporters of goods rejected at the border can be high, including loss of product value, transport costs, and product re-export or destruction.

### Surveying developing countries' SPS problems

To assess developing countries' problems in complying with SPS requirements in developed countries, we studied the formers' exports to the EU. The study consisted of two stages. First, from October 1998 to March 1999, we pursued ten in-depth case studies (Henson, *et al.*, 2000)[3] by interviewing government personnel responsible for SPS and WTO issues, exporters of agricultural and food products, and non-governmental organizations (NGOs). These case studies enabled us to identify the key issues affecting the ability of developing countries to comply with the EU's SPS requirements. Further details of the study are reported in Henson *et al.* (2000).

To obtain quantitative information on these issues, we then surveyed all low- and middle-income countries (World Bank, 1998) that were members of the WTO and/or Codex Alimentarius in March 1999. We faxed a questionnaire to a named contact at the country's WTO delegation in Geneva or, where a country was not a WTO Member, at the Codex Alimentarius contact point[4] during April 1999. We excluded forty-four countries we could not contact after five attempts. Of ninety-two questionnaires, we received sixty-five fully completed, yielding a response rate of 72 percent.

We asked respondents to indicate the significance of a range of factors that might impede their ability to export agricultural and food products to the EU. (On a five-point Likert scale, 1 denoted "very significant," while 5 indicated "very insignificant.") Respondents considered SPS requirements the most significant impediment to exports to the EU (table 16.2; see box 16.1 for

Table 16.1 *Number of contraventions the US FDA cited for detaining imports, June 1996–June 1997*

| Reason for contravention | Africa No. (%) | Latin America and the Caribbean No. (%) | Europe No. (%) | Asia No. (%) | Total No. (%) |
|---|---|---|---|---|---|
| Food additives | 2 (0.7) | 57 (1.5) | 69 (5.8) | 426 (7.4) | 554 (5.0) |
| Pesticide residues | 0 (0.0) | 821 (21.1) | 20 (1.7) | 23 (0.4) | 864 (7.7) |
| Heavy metals | 1 (0.3) | 426 (10.9) | 26 (2.2) | 84 (1.5) | 537 (94.8) |
| Mould | 19 (6.3) | 475 (12.2) | 27 (2.3) | 49 (0.8) | 570 (5.1) |
| Microbiological contamination | 125 (41.3) | 246 (6.3) | 159 (13.4) | 895 (15.5) | 1,425 (12.8) |
| Decomposition | 9 (3.0) | 206 (5.3) | 7 (0.6) | 668 (11.5) | 890 (8.0) |
| Filth | 54 (17.8) | 1,253 (32.2) | 175 (14.8) | 2,037 (35.2) | 3,519 (31.5) |
| Low-acid canned foods | 4 (1.3) | 142 (3.6) | 425 (35.9) | 829 (14.3) | 1,400 (12.5) |
| Labeling | 38 (12.5) | 201 (5.2) | 237 (20.0) | 622 (10.8) | 1,098 (9.8) |
| Other | 51 (16.8) | 68 (1.7) | 39 (3.3) | 151 (2.6) | 309 (2.8) |
| Total | 303 (100) | 3,895 (100) | 1,184 (100) | 5,784 (100) | 11,166 (100) |

*Source:* FAO (1999).

Table 16.2 *Mean significance scores for factors influencing ability to export agricultural and food products to the EU*

| Factor | Mean score |
| --- | --- |
| SPS requirements | 2.1 |
| Other technical requirements | 2.8[a] |
| Transport and other direct export costs | 2.8[a] |
| Tariffs | 3.3 |
| Quantitative restrictions | 3.8 |

*Note:* [a] Scores denoted *a* are not significantly different at the 5 percent level.

a specific example). Respondents also considered other technical requirements, such as labeling regulations and compositional standards, and transport and other direct export costs, important impediments. Tariffs and quantitative restrictions were considered less important in restricting food and agricultural trade, perhaps reflecting the fact that many benefit from preferential access to EU markets.

---

## Box 16.1  Fresh fish exports from East Africa to the EU

Exports of fish from East Africa, mainly Lake Victoria, to the EU grew considerably throughout the 1990s to become an important element of the region's agricultural and food exports, as well as the livelihood for many predominantly small-scale fishers. For example, Tanzania's exports to the EU of fish and fish products totaled some 48,000 tons in 1997, accounting for 10.2 percent of the country's total exports by value.

In December 1997, the EU imposed restrictions on fish imports from a number of countries bordering Lake Victoria: Tanzania, Kenya, Uganda, and Mozambique. These restrictions reflected concerns about sanitary standards and controls in these countries. The EU introduced these restrictions in two phases. At the end of 1996, EU officials detected *Salmonella* in fish from the region, and undertook inspection visits. Inspectors concluded that controls were inadequate to guarantee that the fish would meet the EU's hygiene requirements (under Directive 91/493/EEC) and, in March 1997, the EU subjected imports to *Salmonella* testing at the port of entry at the suppliers' expense.

EU inspectors conducted other visits to East Africa in late 1997, when the region was reporting elevated levels of Cholera. The inspectors judged that sanitary conditions had not improved, and that the "competent authority" in Tanzania, Kenya, Uganda, and Mozambique did not maintain adequate controls to ensure compliance with the EU's hygiene standards. The EU subsequently required further testing at the EU port of entry for Vibrio *cholera* and Vibrio *parahaemolyticus*. Because of the time these tests took to perform, virtually all East African exports of fresh fish to the EU were effectively prohibited. The EU lifted these restrictions at the end of 1998 after further inspection visits indicated that hygiene standards in the supply chain had improved, and that the "competent authority" had implemented appropriate control system.

In April 1999, further concerns about pesticide residues in fish from Lake Victoria were identified and subsequently exports of fish from Tanzania, Kenya, and Uganda to the EU were prohibited. These restrictions were lifted at the end of 1999 in the case of Tanzania, but remained in place into 2000 for Kenya and Uganda.

The impact of these restrictions on the fish processing sector and fishermen around Lake Victoria has been considerable. In particular, the price realized from fish exports has declined sharply, leading to a reduction in the landed price of fresh fish in these countries, and a consequent impact on the livelihoods of fishing communities around Lake Victoria.

The survey also asked respondents to indicate the significance of SPS requirements as an impediment to agricultural and food exports to developed countries. Respondents named the EU as the market where SPS requirements were the most significant trade impediment, followed by Australia and the US (table 16.3). These results reflect the importance of developed country markets for products subject to extensive SPS controls, such as meat and other animal products, and fresh fruit and vegetables. However, the results also reflect the level and types of SPS controls that different countries apply.

For example, the EU relies on process-based hygiene standards rather than border inspections for imports of many agricultural and food products. Enforcement is charged to a "competent authority" in the exporting country, which is responsible for inspecting suppliers and maintaining hygiene standards. Many developing countries regard these process controls as more onerous than border

Table 16.3 *Mean significance scores for problems stemming from SPS requirements when exporting to developed countries*

| Country | Mean score |
| --- | --- |
| EU | 2.1 |
| Australia | 2.7[a] |
| United States | 2.8[a] |
| Japan | 3.3[b] |
| Canada | 3.4[b] |

*Notes:* [a] Scores denoted *a* or *b* are not significantly different at the 5 percent level.

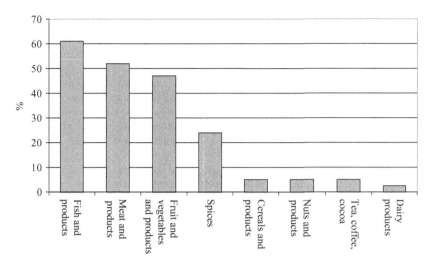

Figure 16.2 Number of developing countries for which SPS requirements have
directly prevented agricultural and food exports to the EU

inspections because of the burden they impose on both suppliers and public authorities. The Bangladeshi frozen shrimp case illustrates this. (Although the
United States is also introducing more process-based hygiene requirements, at
the present time border inspection remains the main form of control for most
of its agricultural and food products.)

Figure 16.2 reports the proportion of countries prevented from exporting agricultural and food products to the EU since 1997 because of SPS requirements.
The products for which SPS requirements posed a particular problem included
meat and meat products, fish and fish products, and fruit and vegetables and
products. The EU applies strict microbiological and animal health requirements
to meat and meat products, and subjects fruit and vegetables to strict controls
against pests and plant diseases. Exports of dairy products from developing
countries to the EU are largely insignificant because other trade measures such
as tariffs exert a greater impact.

The case studies identified a number of problems that could impede developing countries' exports of agricultural and food products. These included lack of
information on SPS requirements, lack of technical and/or scientific expertise,
and financial constraints (see box 16.2). Other issues included lack of awareness
of SPS issues within industry and government and administrative limitations
in developing countries. These constraints sometimes prevented countries from
complying with SPS requirements in the time allowed, or made the cost of
doing so prohibitive.

## Box 16.2  Testing Gambian horticultural exports for pesticide residues

Although horticultural exports to the EU are relatively small, they are of great economic importance to a country the size of Gambia, and an important element of the country's program of export development. Although public authorities, including the Department for Agricultural Services, have implemented procedures to certify SPS exports to the EU, they have experienced a number of problems in meeting those requirements. Indeed, EU officials have rejected some product consignments following border inspection.

The problems facing Gambian authorities are twofold. First, they find it difficult to obtain reliable information on the EU's SPS requirements, particularly regarding pesticide residue levels. The time that information takes to reach Gambia when the EU's requirements change can delay implementation, and the EU can reject products in the meantime. Second, Gambia sometimes lacks the necessary testing equipment. This is a particular problem in detecting maximum residue levels (MRLs) for pesticides, which can exceed the capability of Gambian equipment. Thus, even if Gambian authorities test products and issue certificates, exporters cannot be sure that their products will comply with the EU's requirements.

## Box 16.3  Production of Brazil nuts in Bolivia

Bolivia is the world's largest exporter of Brazil nuts (*castaña*) by far, accounting for about 75 percent of world trade. The product is Bolivia's fourth largest export, most of which it sells to Europe. Brazil nuts grow wild, and indigenous *campesinos* in the far north of the country harvest them by hand from deep in the forest. The *campesinos* pack the nuts into bags ready for transport 600 km to La Paz for air or sea freight to Europe.

EU restrictions on aflatoxins – including limits of 4 parts per billion for aflatoxin B1 – can seriously impede this trade or add significantly to its costs. Although growers could produce the nuts on a plantation scale, such production would not prove economical. Furthermore, the country feels that such an approach would undermine its social objective of offering poor farmers living in remote areas an alternative to producing coca leaf.

The Bolivian government and traders, with assistance from the EU, are considering how to surmount the problem, but investment in better transportation and storage facilities seems inevitable – even though the size of the market may not merit such investment. The country has established some laboratory facilities that are accepted by the EU to allow in-country testing, but such facilities, and inspection in general, also represent major costs.

Box 16.3 shows that SPS requirements – often created based on the structure and *modus operandi* of domestic industry in developed countries – may be incompatible with the production and/or marketing methods in developing countries. Such problems may require the latter to make large-scale, long-term investments, unless developed countries are willing to accept different procedures as "equivalent." These investments, in turn, may make developing country exporters dependent on specific developed country markets.

The survey asked respondents to indicate the significance of each of these problems in exporting agricultural and food products to the EU. Respondents judged the most significant factors "insufficient access to scientific/technical expertise" and "incompatibility of SPS requirements with domestic production/marketing methods" (table 16.4). Problems judged less significant included "poor awareness of SPS requirements within agriculture and the food industry" and "poor access to information on SPS requirements." These results suggest that developing countries are broadly aware of EU SPS requirements, but lack the resources to comply. This situation is exacerbated when SPS requirements conflict with domestic production and marketing methods, or time permitted for compliance is relatively short.

## The SPS Agreement

Although the SPS Agreement should help facilitate trade from developing to developed countries, this result depends on the ability of developing countries

Table 16.4 *Mean significance scores for problems meeting SPS requirements in exporting agricultural and food products to the EU*

| Factor | Mean score |
| --- | --- |
| Insufficient access to scientific/technical expertise | 1.6 |
| Incompatibility of SPS requirements with domestic production/marketing methods | 2.1 |
| Poor access to financial resources | 2.6 |
| Insufficient time permitted for compliance | 3.0[a] |
| Limitations in own country's administrative arrangements for SPS requirements | 3.1[a] |
| Poor awareness of SPS requirements among government officials | 3.1[a] |
| Poor awareness of SPS requirements within agriculture and food industry | 3.5 |
| Poor access to information on SPS requirements | 3.9 |

*Note:* [a] Scores denoted *a* are not significantly different at the 5 percent level.

Table 16.5 *Membership in WTO and international standard-setting organizations, by income group, June 1999[a]*

| Income group | Total countries[b] | WTO | OIE | IPPC | Codex Alimentarius | All |
|---|---|---|---|---|---|---|
| Low | 60 | 40 | 52 | 26 | 51 | 19 |
| Lower-middle | 60 | 34 | 40 | 35 | 49 | 20 |
| Upper-middle | 29 | 24 | 25 | 23 | 31 | 17 |
| High | 38 | 35 | 33 | 25 | 32 | 26 |
| Total | 187 | 133 | 150 | 109 | 163 | 75 |
| *Least-developed* | *29* | *29* | *21* | *11* | *25* | *9* |

*Notes:* [a] Income groups defined by the World Bank.
[b] Excluding the European Communities.
*Source:* World Trade Organization.

to participate in it. The Agreement itself tries to facilitate this by acknowledging the special problems that developing countries may face in complying with SPS measures and instructs members to consider these, especially for least-developed countries (LDCs). For example, members are supposed to give developing countries more time to comply with regulations governing products of special interest to them, where possible. The SPS Committee can also grant developing countries time-limited exemptions that take into account their financial, trade, and development needs. This section aims to assess the degree to which developing countries have actually participated in the SPS Agreement, and discusses their specific concerns about how it has operated.

### The participation of developing countries in the SPS Agreement

Although the majority of low- and lower-middle-income countries were Members of the WTO in June 1999, the rate of membership (62 percent) was significantly lower than among upper-middle or high-income countries (83 and 92 percent, respectively) (table 16.5). Indeed, a number of notable low- and lower-middle-income countries were not WTO Members. Although many were WTO Observers and had indicated their intention to join, they could not participate fully in institutions such as the SPS Agreement.

The SPS Agreement encourages membership in international standard-setting organizations, and indeed active participation in such bodies is critical if developing countries are to ensure attention to their needs and circumstances. Although the majority of low- and lower-middle-income countries were members of the international standard-setting groups, especially the OIE and Codex Alimentarius (table 16.5), the rate of membership was significantly lower

Table 16.6 *Implementation of transparency obligations by WTO Member States, by income group, June 1999*[a]

| Income group | Number of members[a] | Enquiry point | National notification authority | Both |
|---|---|---|---|---|
| Low | 40 | 18 | 15 | 13 |
| Lower-middle | 34 | 30 | 29 | 29 |
| Upper-middle | 24 | 21 | 20 | 20 |
| High | 35 | 33 | 32 | 32 |
| Total | 133 | 102 | 96 | 94 |
| *Least-developed* | *29* | *8* | *6* | *4* |

*Notes:* [a] Income groups defined by the World Bank.
[b] Individual country members, excluding the European Communities.
*Source:* World Trade Organization.

than among upper-middle-income and high-income countries. Furthermore, only 33 percent of low- and lower-middle-income countries were members of all three international standards organizations, compared with 64 percent of upper-middle-income and high-income countries.

The SPS Agreement lays down certain requirements that aim to ensure transparency in their implementation of SPS measures. For example, members must establish two contact points to facilitate communication regarding SPS measures. The first is a single national "enquiry point" that is responsible for responding to queries and providing documents on the application of SPS measures. The second is a single national notification agency that is responsible for notifying the world community of new or amended SPS measures.

Table 16.6 shows that as of June 1999, only 65 percent of low- and lower-middle-income countries had specified an enquiry point, and just 59 percent had specified a national notification agency (these figures include twenty-nine LDCs that were not required to comply until 2000). This indicates a critical weakness in the participation of developing countries.

A further measure of the participation of developing countries is attendance at meetings of the SPS Committee in Geneva. Figure 16.3 details the number of low- and lower-middle-income countries that attended ten of the twelve SPS Committee meetings from November 1995 to September 1998 for which participant lists are available. Almost 50 percent attended no meetings of the SPS Committee, and less than 20 percent attended five or more of these meetings. Many developing countries do not have permanent missions in Geneva, and among those that do, one person is typically responsible for all WTO affairs. Given the importance of other matters within the WTO, it is not surprising

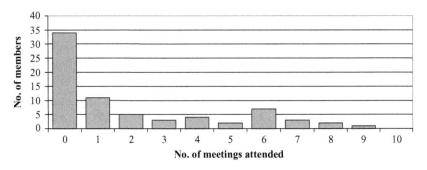

Source: WTO.

Figure 16.3 Participation in SPS committee meetings by developing countries, November 1995–September 1998

that the representation of developing countries within the SPS Committee is so poor.

A number of developing countries have raised concerns about their ability to participate effectively in the SPS Agreement and thus exert real influence. These countries have suggested that the key issue is not whether they are able to attend meetings of the SPS Committee and international standard-setting organizations, but whether they are able to understand and contribute to discussions. The key constraint is the level of technical and scientific know-how of delegates from these countries compared with that of delegates from major developed countries, particularly the EU and United States.

When WTO members implement SPS measures in the absence of an international standard, or where the proposed measure differs from an international standard, they must notify other members through the SPS Committee Secretariat. Table 16.7 details the number of notifications members made as of August 1999. Only 34 percent of low- and low-middle-income countries, including LDCs, had issued any notifications, and notifications by these countries accounted for only 10 percent of the total. While developing countries typically promulgate fewer SPS measures than developed countries, many developing countries have not routinely notified the SPS Committee of new measures that do not conform to international standards (Henson *et al.*, 2000).

These findings suggest that developing countries have not actively participated in the SPS Agreement. While that general conclusion does have exceptions – such as India, Philippines, Egypt, and Indonesia – it raises concerns about the ability of developing countries to benefit from the Agreement. Indeed, the failure of developing countries to participate even in SPS Committee meetings suggests that the workings of the Agreement will tend to be driven by the priorities of developed countries.

Table 16.7 *Notification of SPS measures by WTO Member States, August 1999[a]*

| Income group | Number of members[b] | Number of members notifying standards[c] | Number of measures notified |
|---|---|---|---|
| Low | 40 | 9 | 19 |
| Lower-middle | 34 | 16 | 201 |
| Upper-middle | 24 | 14 | 374 |
| High | 35 | 28 | 1,708 |
| Total | 133 | 67 | 2,302 |
| *Least-developed* | *29* | *4* | *8* |

*Notes:* [a] Income groups defined by the World Bank.
[b] Individual country members, excluding the European Communities.
[c] EU member states are counted as individual notifying members.
*Source:* World Trade Organization.

Table 16.8 *Mean significance scores for factors influencing ability to participate effectively in the SPS Agreement*

| Factor | Mean score |
|---|---|
| Insufficient ability to assess implications of developed country SPS requirements following notification | 1.5 |
| Insufficient ability to participate effectively in DSPs | 2.0 |
| Insufficient ability to demonstrate that domestic SPS measures are equivalent to developed country requirements | 2.6 |
| Insufficient ability to undertake risk assessment of SPS requirements | 3.0[a] |
| Insufficient ability to attend SPS Committee and international standards organization meetings | 3.1[a] |
| Insufficient ability to assess the scientific justification of developed country SPS requirements | 3.7 |

*Note:* [a] Scores denoted *a* are not significantly different at the 5 percent level.

The case studies suggest that developing countries face a number of constraints that limit their ability to respond to key elements of the Agreement, including notifying others of new SPS measures, assessing risks, developing and implementing international standards, demonstrating equivalency, and settling disputes. Table 16.8 reports how survey respondents indicated the significance of these on a five-point Likert scale.

Respondents judged the most significant constraint as insufficient ability to assess the implications of developed countries' SPS notifications. Respondents

Table 16.9 *Mean significance scores for problems associated with operation of the SPS Agreement*

| Factor | Mean score |
|---|---|
| Developed countries take insufficient account of the needs of developing countries in setting SPS requirements | 1.8[a] |
| Insufficient time allowed between notification and implementation of SPS requirements | 2.3[a] |
| Insufficient technical assistance given to developing countries | 2.3[b] |
| Developed countries unwilling to accept developing country SPS measures as equivalent | 2.8[b] |
| Harmonization process takes insufficient account of needs of developing countries | 2.8 |
| Insufficient information given with notifications of SPS requirements | 3.2 |
| Developed countries unwilling to engage in bilateral negotiations with developing countries | 3.7 |

*Note:* [a] Scores denoted *a* or *b* are not significantly different at the 5 percent level.

also cited their inability to participate effectively in dispute-settlement procedures (DSPs), and to show that domestic SPS measures were equivalent to developed country requirements. These constraints reflect the relatively poor scientific and technical infrastructure in many developing countries.

*Developing countries' concerns regarding the SPS Agreement*

Developing countries have a number of concerns about the way the SPS Agreement has been implemented that limit their ability to participate effectively and benefit from it. These largely concern the degree to which developed countries have complied with their commitments, especially in considering the needs and special circumstances of developing countries.

A number of developing countries are critical of the Agreement's transparency mechanisms. While these countries support the notification system, they suggest that it does not take adequate account of their circumstances (WTO, 1998c, 1999a; Henson and Loader, 1999) (table 16.9). In particular, the length of time between Members' notification of new SPS measures and their application date is inadequate for developing countries.

Contrary to the requirements of the SPS Agreement, a number of the latter suggest that developed countries are unwilling to give them additional time to comply or make transitional arrangements. Developing countries also claim that developed countries are reluctant to accept their SPS measures as equivalent (WTO, 1998a, 1998c, 1999a).

Developing countries also express concern about technical assistance that helps them implement the Agreement and members' SPS requirements (WTO, 1998a, 1999a). They claim that technical assistance often fails to address fundamental day-to-day problems reflecting their level of economic development, including developing scientific and technical expertise and modern testing methods.

Finally, developing countries suggest that the form and level of international standards may be inappropriate and/or unachievable for them (WTO, 1998b). Key issues include decision-making processes within the international standard-setting organizations and the ability of developing countries to represent themselves, given their limited financial, scientific, and technical resources.

The SPS Committee discussed a number of these concerns as part of the triennial review of the Agreement in 1999 (WTO, 1999b). The Committee held that many of the transparency concerns could be resolved if Members applied the recommended procedures it had laid down. However, the committee did agree to revise some procedures by making greater use of electronic communication, providing informal translations of documents, and extending the comment period on notifications. The Committee also encouraged Members to give developing countries more time to comply with SPS requirements. However, many developing countries remain concerned about how the Agreement operates and the degree to which developed countries take their special needs into account.

## Toward a more inclusive SPS system

While the international community has attempted to overcome the trade-distorting effects of SPS measures, our study indicates that such measures are a major factor in the ability of developing countries to export agricultural and food products to developed countries. Indeed, such countries consider SPS measures the most important impediment to agricultural and food exports to the EU. To a large extent, this reflects poor access to compliance resources, including scientific and technical expertise, information, and funding. However, the incompatibility of SPS requirements and production and marketing methods in developed countries with those in developing countries is also a major factor. The global community clearly needs to finds ways to include developing countries more fully in the workings of the Agreement.

The WTO and international standard-setting organizations need to modify their procedures to accommodate developing countries and offer more technical assistance. Developed countries also need to be more aware of the needs and special circumstances of developing countries. This should not entail the former lowering standards for protecting human, plant, and animal health, but rather minimizing the incompatibility of SPS measures with the production and marketing systems of developing countries.

Finally, developing countries themselves need to implement the institutional mechanisms that will enable their agricultural producers and food processors to comply with SPS requirements. Toward this end, further research can quantify the costs to developing countries of the existing system and identify solutions to the constraints they face.

## Notes

This work was funded by the UK Department for International Development (DFID). The views expressed are those of the authors and in way represent the policy of DFID.
1. These data are published by the US Food and Drugs Administration (FDA) and cover all food products except meat and poultry.
2. These data must be treated with care when comparing among regions and individual countries. Clearly, the level of rejections will reflect the overall volume of trade. Thus, for example, the total number of violations is greater for Latin America and the Caribbean than for Africa. Further, these data do not account for product that is eventually imported after further testing, or following treatment to bring it into compliance with US SPS requirements.
3. Countries studied were India, Zimbabwe, Egypt, Vietnam, Guatemala, Ghana, Kenya, Ethiopia, Gambia, and Cameroon.
4. A copy of the questionnaire is available on request.

## References

Cato, J. C., 1998. "Economic Issues Associated with Seafood Safety and Implementation of Seafood HACCP Programmes," Rome: FAO

Cato, J. C. and C. A. Lima dos Santos, 1998. "European Union 1997 Seafood-safety Ban: The Economic Impact on Bangladesh Shrimp Processing," *Marine Resource Economics*, 13, 215–27

Gilmour, B. and J. Oxley, 1998. "Trade Facilitation Measures in Processed Food Trade," Economic and Policy Analysis Directorate, Agriculture and Agri-Food Canada, Ottawa

Henson, S. J. and R. J. Loader, 1999. "Impact of Sanitary and Phytosanitary Standards on Developing Countries and the Role of the SPS Agreement," *Agribusiness*, 15(3), 355–69

Henson, S. J., R. J. Loader, A. Swinbank, M. Bredahl, and N. Lux, 2000. "Impact of Sanitary and Phytosanitary Measures on Developing Countries," Centre for Food Economics Research, Department of Agricultural and Food Economics, University of Reading

Murphy, K. M. and A. Shleifer, 1997. "Quality and Trade," *Journal of Development Economics*, 53, 1–15

Mutasa, M. P. and T. Nyamandi, 1998. "Report of the Survey on the Identification of Food Regulations and Standards within the Africa Region Codex Member Countries that Impede Food Trade," paper presented at the Workshop on Codex and Harmonization of Food Regulations, August

Organization for Economic Co-operation and Development (OECD), 1997. "Product Standards, Conformity Assessment, and Regulatory Reform," Paris: OECD

Sullivan, G. H., G. E. Sanchez, S. C. Weller, and C. R. Edwards, 1999. "Sustainable Development in Central America's Non-Traditional Export Crop Sector Through Integrated Pest Management Practices," *Sustainable Development International*, 12, 123–6

Thornsbury, S., D. Roberts, K. DeRemer, and D. Orden, 1997. "A First Step in Understanding Technical Barriers to Agricultural Trade," paper presented at the conference of the International Association of Agricultural Economists, Sacramento, August

United Nations Conference on Trade and Agricultural Development (UNCTAD) and Commonwealth Secretariat, 1996. "The Global Spice Trade and the Uruguay Round Agreements," Geneva, and London

UN Food and Agriculture Organization (FAO), 1999. "Importance of Food Quality and Safety for Developing Countries," Committee on World Food Security, 25th Session, Rome

World Bank, 1998. "World Development Report 1998/99," World Bank

1999. "World Development Indicators 1998/99." World Bank

World Trade Organization (WTO), 1998a. "Special and Differential Treatment and Technical Assistance," Submission by India, Geneva

1998b. "International Harmonization of Standards," Submission by India, Geneva

1998c. "The SPS Agreement and Developing Countries," Geneva

1999a. "SPS Agreement and Developing Countries," Submission by Egypt, Geneva

1999b. "Review of the Operation and Implementation of the Agreement on the Application of Sanitary and Phytosanitary Measures," Geneva

# 17 State trading in agricultural trade: options and prospects for new rules

*W. M. Miner*

## Introduction

Many countries have established specialized state agencies and marketing organizations that intervene – directly and indirectly – in agricultural trade. These
activities are designed to enhance food security, stabilize prices, develop agricultural industries, and protect the domestic market.

Agricultural State-Trading Enterprises (STEs) range from marketing boards
with monopoly control over all supplies, through exclusive import or export
agencies, to parastatal organizations with specific powers to intervene in domestic and foreign markets. These entities exercise complete or partial control
over domestic and international trade in one or more products, and may perform
many other functions. They exist in all types of economies and in both large
and small nations.

The majority of STEs operate in the agricultural sector,[1] most often in grains,
dairy, and sugar products – important components of many national diets. For
example, STE-importing countries accounted for one-third to one-half of wheat
imports from 1994 to 1997, and an even higher proportion of wheat exports
during that period. STEs also manage about half of rice exports and nearly a third
of all rice imports.[2] State trading is also used for meats, fruits and vegetables,
and poultry and eggs, but for these commodities, protecting domestic markets,
managing imports, and promoting exports is likely to be more important than
ensuring food security. State trading in alcohol, spirits, and tobacco primarily
serves to meet countries' fiscal and market-organization goals.

The purposes and operations of STEs differ significantly between developed
and developing countries. In most developed countries, state trading forms
part of a broader policy regime intended to stabilize and support agricultural
markets and producer returns. Exporting state entities may control supplies and
prices, while importing STEs may maintain exclusive authority over imports
and domestic sales, manage stocks, and grade, transport, and process food and
agricultural products.

Developing countries most often use STEs to support macroeconomic policies, including national food security, consumer subsidies, tax revenue, and import and export activities. Their role may also extend to the production level by offering credit, managing risks, controlling production inputs, and providing services to consumers.

Developed countries maintain some of the largest state trading operations.[3] In terms of the value of agricultural *exports*, Canadian, New Zealand, and Australian STEs rank at the top. Turkey and Israel also rely on state entities for substantial agricultural exports.

In terms of the value of agricultural *imports*, Japan and Indonesia operate the largest STEs. Other large STE importers include Egypt, Korea, India, Pakistan, Mexico, Tunisia, Morocco, and Malaysia. A number of Latin American countries also maintained export and import STEs, but eliminated or privatized them as part of broad efforts to open their economies to international investment and competition. Several other developing countries have also curtailed or eliminated the activities of STEs as part of domestic policy reforms. For example, South Africa was among the leading STE exporters until it closed its marketing boards in 1997.

State trading plays a significant role in agricultural trade in many of the countries seeking to accede to the World Trade Organization (WTO). These countries include China, the transition economies of Central and Eastern Europe (CEE), most newly independent states of the Former Soviet Union (FSU), and Algeria, Saudi Arabia, Taiwan, and Vietnam. STEs coexist with private trade in many of these countries, and reforms are under way; STE activities are also under negotiation as part of many of these countries' accession.

As with most forms of agricultural support, the significant role of STEs in countries' agricultural policies and trade emerged during the Depression years and immediately following the Second World War. Early in the Uruguay Round, negotiators generally agreed that internal farm-support policies were largely responsible for the problems with agricultural trade preceding the chaotic conditions of the 1980s. Governments have since greatly reduced their use of STEs, recognizing that they – like other market interventions – have become costly and counter-productive in the age of telecommunications and integrated markets.

WTO rules apply to all trade, including that managed by state entities. However, the limited transparency of these operations, and the difficulty of distinguishing between the roles of government and the private market, have provoked allegations that the STEs that remain are being used to circumvent trade rules. Critics also question whether government trading entities represent "fair" competition. Independent analyses of the impact of STEs have been unable to demonstrate conclusively that STEs do or do not distort markets and trade. However, even though analysts do not agree on the degree to which STEs distort trade, government agencies and parastatal organizations clearly have the potential to avoid or abuse trade rules and commitments.

The importance of an assured and stable food supply to state security and development, as well as the diversity of the roles of STEs, means that countries are unlikely to agree to eliminate them entirely. However, failure to address state trading may jeopardize further significant improvements in access to agricultural markets and cuts in export subsidies. Fortunately, renewed multilateral negotiations provide a unique opportunity to deal with the impact of STEs on agricultural imports, exports, and competitive behavior.

The renewed negotiations will involve an expanded WTO membership, including more countries that use state-controlled enterprises to manage food supplies, and to import and export. With the prospect of participation by China as well as several former centrally planned economies, the issues related to state trading have grown in importance. The renewed multilateral negotiations on agriculture will provide a unique opportunity to deal with all measures that affect the agricultural trade interests of developing countries.

## State trading and trade rules

Article XVII of the initial General Agreement on Tariffs and Trade (GATT) recognized that STEs are legitimate participants in international trade – but also that specific rules are needed to govern their behavior. This article, which the 1994 WTO agreement retains, is intended to ensure that STEs operate in a manner consistent with GATT principles. The article specifies that:

- In purchases and sales, an STE shall act in a manner consistent with the general principles of non-discriminatory treatment prescribed for governmental measures affecting imports or exports by private traders
- An STE shall make any purchases or sales solely in accordance with commercial considerations with respect to price, quality, availability, marketability, transportation, and other conditions of purchase and sale
- An STE shall give foreign enterprises adequate opportunity to compete in such purchases and sales, in accordance with customary business practices
- Members shall limit or reduce obstacles to trade created by STEs, and notify the WTO of the products imported and exported by them
- Importing state traders should not grant protection above that set by bound tariff schedules under article II.[4]

An interpretive note establishes that marketing boards engaged in purchasing or selling are subject to provisions covering private trade or parastal entities. The note also establishes that a state enterprise may charge different prices for its sales in different markets, if it does so to meet supply and demand in commercial export markets. Interpretive notes also clarify that government measures to ensure standards of quality and efficiency in external trade are not considered state trading.

A GATT panel established that article III: 4 – which specifies that imports shall be treated no less favorably than national products – applied to STEs, at least where the state monopoly extended to both imports and domestic distribution.[5] The GATT also extended disciplines relating to import and export restrictions to STEs. Finally, part IV of the GATT provides that developed country Members will make every effort to maintain trade margins at equitable levels where governments directly or indirectly determine the price of products from less-developed countries (LDCs).[6]

Despite these provisions, there is very little evidence that article III: 4 has influenced the behavior of STEs. GATT officials adopted a questionnaire in 1960 to strengthen notification requirements, but this was not followed by stronger enforcement. Although governments are required to notify the WTO of their STEs and provide information on the kinds of activities they engage in, few have fulfilled this requirement, and the Secretariat has not challenged them to do so.

The weakness of the rule is attributed in part to the lack of a clear definition of a state trading entity. Although article III: 4 refers to any enterprise that has been granted "exclusive or special privileges" involving imports and exports, governments have interpreted this phrase for themselves. The requirement that the entity apply "commercial considerations" in its conduct does not identify those considerations. Presumably governments would not accord exclusive or special privileges to an STE if it were designed to act as a normal commercial entity.

A further difficulty is the lack of information on the specific activities of STEs. Since the STEs compete with private concerns, article III: 4 does not require any government "to disclose confidential information which would impede law enforcement or otherwise be contrary to the public interest or would prejudice the commercial interests of particular enterprises." However, this provision means that while governments are obligated to ensure that their STEs respect GATT rules and commitments, the information to determine whether they are doing so is unavailable.

### Recent developments

Negotiators discussed state trading during the Uruguay Round, but they did not alter the substance of article XVII. To make the activities of STEs more transparent, they did clarify the definition of such entities, strengthen their notification requirements, and establish a working group to review them and make recommendations. For example, the Uruguay Round Agreement defines STEs as "governmental and non-governmental enterprises, including marketing boards, which have been granted exclusive or special rights or privileges, in the exercise of which they influence through their purchase or sales the level or direction of imports or exports."[7]

The Agreement on Agriculture, meanwhile, applies to all trade – including STEs – and makes specific references to STEs regarding market access. For example, it specifies that the non-tariff barriers (NTBs) that countries must convert to tariff equivalents include those maintained through STEs. Countries' commitments to cutting export subsidies similarly apply to governments and their agencies. The information that countries supply to the WTO Committee on Agriculture on how they are implementing their market access commitments under the Agreement must include STE activities.

Some members have notified the WTO Secretariat of relatively large importing and exporting agricultural STEs. These include the Canadian Wheat Board, New Zealand Dairy Board, Australian Wheat Board, Queensland Sugar Corporation, Japan Food Agency, Indonesian Badan Urusan Logistik (BULOG), and Mexican Compañía Nacional de Subsistencias Populares (CONASUPO).

The United States has notified the Secretariat of the Commodity Credit Corporation. The EU has notified the WTO of the tobacco monopoly in Italy, and monopolies for tobacco, alcohol, and salt in Austria (the salt monopoly has since been abolished and the operations for tobacco and alcohol have changed, so they no longer operate as STEs).[8] However, the EU has *not* notified the WTO regarding its agencies and committees that intervene in and manage agriculture, contending that these entities are not directly involved in trade.

The WTO Working Party on State Trading has developed a comprehensive questionnaire to determine whether it needs to impose additional disciplines on STEs. The WTO Committee on Agriculture also examined the trade effects of STEs in the analyses and information exchanges used to prepare for new agricultural negotiations. For example, the committee cited concern that STEs use their exclusive marketing powers to compete unfairly in export markets. These allegations have focused on differential pricing, price-pooling arrangements, and the financial backing that governments provide to STEs as potentially trade-distorting. Concern has also focused on export subsidies and pricing practices, dumping, and the terms of competition in national and export markets. On the import side, critics argue that some countries use STEs to circumvent their market access commitments by discriminating in their purchases and operating tariff rate quotas unfairly.

Of course, governments may decide for their own reasons to eliminate state trading, to force these entities to operate openly, or to subject them to competition or anti-trust legislation. The EU did so when it required the United Kingdom to dismantle the monopoly powers of the British Milk Marketing

Board (MMB). Under the North American Free Trade Agreement (NAFTA), each party agreed to proscribe anti-competitive business conduct and cooperate in enforcing competition law. Parties also agreed to establish a Working Group on Trade and Competition to pursue these issues in the free-trade arena. This group might not only lead to further trilateral arrangements but also advance discussions in the WTO Working Group.

## State trading and competition policies

While the limited transparency of STEs prevents competitors from determining whether in fact they are respecting WTO rules and commitments, many similar concerns also apply to the activities of private entities – increasing the complexity of addressing state trading. Many governments are concerned that full disclosure of STE activities could place them at a serious disadvantage in relation to private firms.

Governments are responsible for ensuring that private concerns operating in each country respect WTO rules and commitments – in part by enacting and administering domestic legislation governing business practices and anti-competitive behavior. Draft measures in the Havana Charter to prevent anti-competitive practices such as price-fixing, allocation of markets, and boycotts were not adopted apparently because this was considered a national responsibility.

However, as multinational corporations (MNCs) have grown in size and scope and concern that they operate beyond the reach of national legislation has deepened, international organizations have also tried to develop rules to discipline MNCs. In the early 1980s, for example, the United Nations Conference on Trade and Development (UNCTAD) established a voluntary business practices code, and the OECD also adopted guidelines for multinational enterprises. The WTO Agreements signed in 1994, including the General Agreement on Trade in Services (GATS), the Agreement on Trade Related Investment Measures, and the Agreement on Trade-Related Aspects of Intellectual Property Rights (TRIPS), also include provisions relating to MNCs.

Although concerns over unfair competition by multinationals and STEs are related, at least in agriculture, international talks have focused on each issue separately. The WTO Working Party on State Trading is considering whether to impose further disciplines on STE activity regarding to all goods, while the WTO Working Party on Trade and Competition Policy may develop new disciplines relating to the private sector, particularly MNEs, and their links to WTO rules.

Those who attended the 1996 Singapore Ministerial Meeting of the WTO also agreed to establish a working group on trade and competition policy, as well as one on trade and investment. OECD discussions on international investment led to a draft Multilateral Agreement on Investment that may form the basis of further negotiations among WTO members.

## Options for new negotiations

Various combinations of additional rules and policy options can address concerns over state trading. One option would be to prohibit the use of governmental and parastatal enterprises in trade altogether. However, no proof that they adversely affect trade exists, and in any case, all state trading activities would be unlikely to exert such effects. What's more, attempts to ban STEs would raise sensitive issues regarding national sovereignty. Because these activities are widespread among WTO Members and prevalent in countries seeking accession, few would agree to such a ban. Until developing countries and economies in transition have established adequate domestic markets and an institutional infrastructure, they will be reluctant to forgo all control of sensitive sectors such as food. Pursuing a multilateral ban on STEs and parastatal entities would also be unrealistic because most trade agreements recognize state trading as a legitimate form of business activity.

A second policy option would be to negotiate stronger and more effective rules governing STEs or parastatal entities that obstruct or distort trade, or that have the potential to do so. The WTO Working Party on State Trading is considering just such an option. This option implies the need to clarify and strengthen article XVII to prevent countries from using STEs to avoid other WTO rules and commitments.

More complete rules applying to state trading would require more transparent STE operations, to show that they are respecting all WTO rules and commitments. In fact, if STE activities operated more openly and were subject to international monitoring, new disciplines might be unnecessary, as existing trade rules already apply to STEs. However, article XVII would still require clarification and elaboration to ensure that it effectively disciplines STE activities not explicitly covered by other trade rules.

The need for such clarification implies further negotiations with respect to:
- The definition of what constitutes a state enterprise for the purposes of applying trade law
- Which measures represent the granting of exclusive or special privileges to STEs
- The nature and level of a state transaction that involves imports or exports, and is therefore subject to the article
- The activities of an STE that are inconsistent with the general principles of "non-discriminatory treatment"
- The definition of "commercial considerations," including those related to pricing practices, to which STEs adhere

- The relationship between article XVII and other articles of the GATT
- The requirements that countries provide adequate notification and information regarding the commercial dealings of STEs, or otherwise ensure that they are complying with trade rules.

The Working Group on State Trading, and negotiations during the new round, may strengthen and make enforceable rules on STEs relating to imports and exports of all goods, not just food and agricultural products. For agricultural trade in particular, ensuring competition and transparency might require removing STEs' monopoly on imports, or allocating a share of tariff rate quotas and minimum access to private firms. Ensuring competition might also require that countries apply domestic laws ensuring competition to their STEs.

If countries are unwilling to open their state import operations to competition, they might instead agree to provide enough information to show that they are fulfilling their WTO obligations by converting NTBs into tariff equivalents, maintaining existing access and providing minimum access, and treating imports fairly. For example, they could show that the price markups that STEs impose on imported goods remain within bound tariffs.

However, because the existing article XVII does not require countries to disclose confidential information that would prejudice the commercial interests of an STE, it may be difficult to obtain such information without comparable requirements for private entities. Thus, full resolution of the transparency issue may require complementary progress in competition law.

Similar considerations and policy options apply to exporting STEs. Countries could apply domestic competition legislation and allow private traders to operate in all or part of the export markets. If they face greater competition, STEs could not distort prices between internal and export markets. If countries are unwilling to adjust the monopoly powers of exporting STEs, they might be required to provide enough information to show that they are respecting WTO commitments regarding domestic support and export subsidies. However, again adequate information may not be forthcoming unless private traders face similar requirements.

International rules on competition would help discipline the behavior of both private and state enterprises. Governments might agree to multilateral rules regarding the use and enforcement of national competition legislation similar to anti-dumping rules (article VI), and those applying to countervail.

Although the WTO Working Group on State Trading is considering strengthening and enforcing article XVII to ensure that STEs are not used to circumvent trade rules, these discussions will not necessarily produce new agreements, or proceed in step with new agricultural negotiations. Thus, as a third option, governments could seek additional rules and commitments on state trading that specifically reinforce and extend market access and export subsidy rules under the Agreement on Agriculture. Since government intervention in agricultural trade continues to be widespread despite significant progress in decoupling domestic support from production, consumption, and the market, additional rules and commitments regarding STE activity would further liberalize farm trade. Such rules could rely on experience in implementing the Agreement on Agriculture – as well as preparatory work in the Committee on Agriculture for new negotiations – to negotiate further commitments on market access, domestic support, and export competition.

Some governments may be reluctant to substantially improve access to their markets, such as by removing tariff-rate quotas (TRQs), unless other countries that rely on importing STEs make comparable concessions. Countries may similarly agree to eliminate export subsidies and export credits only if other countries agree to curb the activities of exporting STEs. Indeed, new commitments regarding STEs may prove essential to the success of new negotiations in further liberalizing agriculture. However, since STE organization and activities vary widely, developing rules and commitments appropriate for all sectors and circumstances will be difficult. To address this problem, measures under the second option that ensure STE compliance with WTO rules could include specific commitments for agricultural STEs, possibly in relation to subsectors such as grains, sugar, and dairy.

In sum, work is under way in the WTO to improve the transparency requirements of article XVII and clarify its provisions. However, this could place STEs at a serious disadvantage in relation to multinational enterprises. Since the greatest concern is the potential abuse of their monopoly powers, governments could agree to force STEs to compete, at least for a portion of trade. Domestic competition laws could be used for this purpose, but not all governments have competition and anti-trust laws, and some may not be prepared to open their STEs and parastatals to direct competition. Negotiators could address these issues by developing multilateral rules on competition policies and trade to apply to both private and state trading enterprises.

Discussions of these options are at an early stage, and reaching international agreement in such a complex arena will take time. In any case, revisions to article XVII for all goods and progress in dealing with trade and competition law may not fully address the issues of concern to agriculture. Thus specific commitments in an enhanced Agreement on Agriculture that encompass all the measures that affect agricultural trade may offer the best option.

Since many developing countries rely on STEs to manage a significant portion of their trade in food and agricultural products, these commitments will require them to change their operations. Developing countries may be especially reluctant to accept new trade disciplines if they infringe on their greater flexibility in meeting WTO obligations. For example, developing countries may now obtain special treatment regarding tariffying their NTBs on imports of their predominant staple food (annex 5). The Agreement on Agriculture also exempts developing countries from cutting export subsidies for marketing costs, transport, and freight during the transition period – if they do not circumvent overall commitments to cut trade barriers (article 9.4). Developing countries may also use STEs to hold stocks to ensure food security, and to provide subsidized foodstuffs to the poor under specific conditions. Any new disciplines on state trading may well need to provide developing countries with similar flexibility.

**Notes**

1. GATT notifications.
2. US Department of Agriculture Economic Research Service.
3. US Department of Agriculture Economic Research Service.
4. GATT 1994, article XVII.
5. Analytical Index of the GATT, p. 448.
6. Analytical Index of the GATT, p. 451.
7. Understanding on the Interpretation of article XVII, GATT 1994.
8. WTO documents on EU notifications.

# 18 Environmental considerations in agricultural negotiations in the new WTO round

*John Whalley*

## Introduction

The history of agricultural trade is well known.[1] Articles XI and XVI of the GATT allowed countries to use both export subsidies and quota-based import restrictions to support farm incomes. The 1955 open-ended waiver granted to the United States effectively allowed that country to use any form of trade-restricting measures in agriculture. The terms of Switzerland's 1956 accession, which were similar to the US waiver, and the 1957 European Community Treaty of Rome with its Common Agricultural Policy (CAP) and variable levies, further contributed to undisciplined interventions in agricultural trade.

This lack of discipline allowed trade distortions to grow, as countries moved from net-importer to net-exporter status in key products and competition to provide subsidies to exporters intensified. Attempts to discipline these practices during the Kennedy and Tokyo Rounds for all intents and purposes failed, despite declarations of intent at the launch of each round. The Uruguay Round – driven by agricultural exporters' concerns over their lack of market access, budget concerns over the cost of domestic support programs, and fears of unbridled competition among export subsidizers – injected novel international discipline into the sector. The chosen route was not to unwind all previous departures from GATT/WTO principles but to develop a new structure of restraints that could be progressively tightened to further liberalize trade.

Environmental considerations entered little into these decisions. The main component came in the form of "green box" exceptions, which explicitly exempted countries' payments to farmers for providing environmental benefits from their aggregate measure of support. OECD countries have primarily – and perhaps exclusively – used this provision, and no systematic analysis has examined its size or importance.

With this structure in place, new agricultural negotiations are likely to enhance the disciplines that resulted from the Uruguay Round, further reducing tariffs, countries' aggregate measures of support, and export subsidies (and possibly increase TRQs).[2] This leaves little room for debate over wide-ranging environmental considerations, except perhaps in elaborating the criteria for assessing the risks of sanitary and phytosanitary (SPS) measures.[3] Yet although food security now dominates countries' non-trade concerns, some environmental concerns are likely to emerge during negotiations.

The first is multifunctionality: the claim that agricultural production – and thus trade protection – serves the wider purpose of protecting and promoting rural communities and the rural ecosystem. Norway effectively advanced this position in its submission to the Committee on Trade and Environment (WTO, 1999a).

The second issue is the links between agricultural export subsidies and the environment. A submission by fourteen larger agricultural exporting countries claimed that export subsidies contain no environmental links – presumably to counteract the multifunctionality argument. In a separate submission, Argentina warned that "environmental-champion" countries use such arguments to defend trade-distorting production subsidies to industries such as fisheries.

Other environmental considerations in the new agricultural negotiations could include special credits for tariff cuts yielding environmental benefits, penalties for tariff cuts that harm the environment, and the introduction of environmental considerations into tariff-quota schemes.

This chapter considers the implications of such proposals for developing countries.[4] It begins with a general discussion of the links between agricultural trade and the environment. A central problem is that such links are unclear: research provides relatively little quantitative or qualitative information on the externalities associated with agriculture in either developed or developing countries. Many such externalities are subtle and confined to limited geographical areas, as is the case with water resources. Whether liberalizing trade intensifies or alleviates such externalities is also often unclear, particularly when trade-induced changes involve a national or even the global economy.

However, although estimates range widely and studies are preliminary, the literature does suggest that the social costs associated with rural activities in developing countries substantially outweigh the potential gains to these countries from liberalized agricultural trade. This suggests that developing countries should make environmental considerations a central focus of agricultural negotiations – and even that environmental considerations should dominate trade considerations. However, using agricultural negotiations for such purposes will likely yield only marginal benefits, and alternative and almost certainly superior environmental policy instruments exist.

### Links between liberalized agricultural trade and the environment

The interface between agricultural trade liberalization and environmental issues is complex. From an economist's point of view, the role of environmental goals in trade negotiations rests on the extent to which trade interventions or restrictions on interventions intensify or worsen environmental externalities (Uimonen and Whalley, 1997).

Externalities arise where the actions of one agent affect other agents – and the first agent does not consider these interactions when formulating the best course of action. Thus, a chemical plant emitting particles that affect a nearby laundry provides a classic case of an externality. Pigou (1918) first noted the difference between the marginal private costs and the social costs that such externalities create, and emphasized the need to correct – or internalize – externalities through a (Pigovian) tax.[5] Coase's key contribution (1960) stressed that externalities were reciprocal, and that allocating property rights was required before assigning Pigovian tax liabilities. Coase saw such allocations as essentially affecting income distribution, and suggested that deals between parties could make such an instrument unnecessary – and even counter-productive.

Environmental externalities are a subset of a wider class of externalities[6] with either beneficial or harmful effects. However, the dominant externalities that economists study – including degradation, crowding, waste, and noise – are considered environmental, and most are considered harmful although this is not always the case. The impact of these externalities can be geographically limited (pesticide use that affects neighboring farms), cross-border (acid rain depositions, water use by upstream entities that affects downstream availability), or even global (emissions of carbon and ozone-depleting chemicals). Such externalities can manifest themselves physically or exert cross-border impacts through "existence value" – such as when OECD residents value flora and fauna in tropical rainforests. All these effects have the same underlying structure: one group of agents affects another group, and the economic actions of the first group do not consider these impacts.

From the point of view of agricultural negotiations, the issue is whether trade measures should account for environmental externalities, even though most trade measures are regarded as undesirable. Central is the issue of whether freer trade will intensify harmful environmental externalities, and if so whether this justifies restrictions on moves toward freer trade.

Analysts seem to agree that the best way to internalize an externality is through a Pigovian tax on production, once property rights are assigned, rather than a tax on trade that affects both production and consumption (Anderson, 1992b; Uimonen and Whalley, 1997). However, in the case of a cross-border effect, residents of the source country may well be unwilling to internalize an externality, especially when the damage falls wholly outside their jurisdiction.

This applies to effects with existence value as well as those that take physical form. In such cases, the issue is whether the use of a second-best trade-related instrument is better than using no instrument at all. The literature, perhaps not surprisingly, is ambiguous.[7]

WTO debates on trade and the environment have focused on a range of issues. These include whether countries should be able to use trade-restricting measures for environmental purposes (the tuna–dolphin dispute), and whether countries should use trade sanctions to enforce multilateral environmental agreements in the presence of free-riding (such as with the Montreal Protocol). Other issues include whether countries may impose import duties to counteract lax environmental standards abroad, whether the WTO should allow countries to provide export subsidies for pollution control equipment, whether trade agreements should be allowed to constrain environmental agreements, whether trade negotiations themselves tend to lower environmental standards, and the trade implications of ecolabeling. These are not all externality related as economists usually think of them. Lax standards, for instance, are posed as a competitiveness and unfairness issue comparable to conventional dumping – areas where economists generally have little sympathy for the use of trade restrictions.

## Negotiating the agricultural–environmental linkage

Key to evaluating how environmental considerations could enter trade negotiations is assessing the extent and impact of links between them. Box 18.1 itemizes significant environmental externalities that agricultural negotiators might link to domestic programs.

First are issues related to existence value. According to Norway, in its submission to the WTO Committee on Trade and the Environment (WTO, 1999a):

The agricultural landscape is the most obvious environmental benefit or public good produced jointly with agricultural production. Arable land amounts to only 3 percent of the total land area of Norway; because of this scarcity, extensive measures have been necessary to ensure its protection; including both general policies and specific measures.

Agriculture contributes to the conservation of biological diversity. In Norway, the agricultural landscape is the only habitat of around 10–20 percent of the threatened species. Conserving biodiversity is therefore closely related to protection of the agricultural landscape. Moreover, increased trade in agricultural products increases the risk of alien species being introduced.

Agriculture in Norway contributes to good phytosanitary, zoosanitary, and public health. Under considerably increased trade, control measures may not fully offset the increased risk related to the introduction of contagious substances and diseases.

As this excerpt makes clear, existence value can encompass many considerations – including social identification with the family farm as a key part of
national culture, which Norway did not mention. The claim is that liberalized
agricultural trade reduces protection in high-support countries and thus under-
mines existence value.

Issues of existence value across countries mainly concern deforestation and
loss of biodiversity in developing countries – effects that are widely thought to
occur as the agricultural sector expands and land clearing accelerates. NGOs
in developed countries have cited such considerations as a major theme in the
wider trade and environment debate.[8] However, countries that are custodians
of specific environmental assets fear that trade measures will be used against
them in the name of conservation. This view further inflames conflicts between
developed and developing countries.

---

**Box 18.1  Environmental externalities potentially affected by
agricultural trade negotiations**

1. *Generalized existence value for agricultural–rural activities within countries.*
   Freer agricultural trade induces specialization of production, and in some countries smaller rural communities.
2. *Generalized existence value across countries for country-specific resources.*
   Changing agricultural patterns, including land clearing, affects forests and biodiversity in countries exporting agricultural products or expanding production for
   home markets. This is a major area of concern for OECD-based non-governmental
   organizations (NGOs).
3. *Soil erosion.* Water runoff or windborne erosion deposits soil onto neighboring
   plots and silts up hydro dams in countries with hilly terrain. Such effects are more
   severe in low-income or desertified countries. Erosion in exporting countries may
   worsen or improve with liberalized trade, depending on which crops are exported.
   Erosion can improve in importing countries but worsen in exporting countries.
4. *The use of fertilizers and pesticides.* Heavy use of fertilizers and/or pesticides
   can cause leaching onto neighboring plots. Significant subsidies for fertilizers
   in developing countries exacerbate such effects. Trade liberalization that allows
   more imports and cuts domestic production of crops that need much fertilizer
   may limit such environmental externalities.
5. *Open-access resources.* Ill-defined property rights encourage overexploitation of
   resources such as fisheries, aquifers and water tables, and forests. Higher exports
   from local fisheries can worsen the environment, as can higher catches for the
   home market occurring behind protective trade barriers.
6. *Waste and degradation.* Some environmental practices generate waste and degradation not internalized in the decisions of individual farmers. These include smoke
   and haze from fire-based land clearing (such as in Indonesia) and soil contamination from rearing shrimp in paddies (now banned in Thailand). Liberalization that
   increases production associated with these practices can worsen the environment.

---

7. *Allocation of water resources.* Practices such as common access to water sources (which is lowering water tables in the North China plain), an inability to price and monitor the use of irrigated water, and a lack of adequate metering may intensify or weaken under liberalized agricultural trade.
8. *Global environmental considerations.* Methane emissions from paddy production, the destruction of carbon sinks through forest clearing, and carbon emissions from cattle herds can exacerbate global warming and climate change. Agricultural liberalization that increases global production may intensify these externalities.

Soil erosion arises from a variety of causes, both onsite and offsite. A key cause is population growth, which shrinks plot sizes and creates ever more spillover into neighboring plots, river estuaries, and hydro dams. Windborne soil loss creates such problems in desert countries. Soil erosion reduces agricultural productivity and sometimes the availability of agricultural land *per capita* and the fodder available for cattle.

Fertilizers and pesticides may also contaminate neighboring plots. The 1998 Human Development Report (UN, 1999) estimates that in Burkina Faso and Mali, one person in six has been forced to leave the land as it has turned into desert. The report also estimates that desertification-based soil erosion costs the world $42 billion in lost income every year – $9 billion in Africa alone.

A survey of studies of the cost of soil erosion in developing countries (Barbier, 1996) places annual losses at 1–15 percent of GDP. In a study of Nicaragua, Alfsen *et al.* (1996) estimate annual productivity losses from soil erosion as 1.26 percent for coffee, 2.52 percent for beans, 2.41 percent for maize, and 1.35 percent for sorghum. In a study of soil erosion in Java in 1985, Magrath and Arens (1989) estimated that annual losses represented some 4 percent of the value of harvested crops.

Key agriculture-related externalities arise where property rights are ill defined and resources are overexploited. Such effects can include deforestation associated with land clearing, slash-and-burn cultivation, squatting, and sometimes the collection of firewood. These problems are especially severe in Africa and Central and Latin America. For Ghana, one of the least-severe cases, López (1997) estimated that 25 percent of land is overcultivated at the expense of forests. Shared access to water through common aquifers can similarly lower water tables; such an effect is causing severe problem in the North China plain (see box 18.1). Overexploitation of fisheries is also common.

Some environmentally based externalities extend beyond the immediate area of agricultural activity. The health and safety effects of smoke from fires for forest clearing have become a major issue on Indonesian islands close to Singapore and Malaysia (Glover and Jessup, 1999). Agricultural practices such as shrimp farming in paddy fields in Thailand may also contaminate land, especially where those engaging in such practices rent rather than own the land.

Allocation of water resources is another area with potentially significant agriculture-related externalities. Such effects can arise from the drilling of tube wells where water resources are shared, flooding where irrigated water washes land or where sparse water supplies are dispensed through open irrigation channels, and excess water use where metering is incomplete.

Finally there are the global environmental externalities that liberalized agricultural trade can exacerbate. These include climate change worsened by methane emissions from paddies and deforestation, carbon emissions from cattle, the loss of gene pools through destruction of forests and wildlife, and mangrove losses from shrimp farming and other local fisheries.

Liberalized trade intensifies some of these external effects and mutes others, as it expands agricultural production while also changing its composition and location. Such effects can be subtle: farmers may abandon or embrace more erosive crops. Farming may move away from localities with more intense environmental externalities to areas with less intense effects, or vice versa. Some of these effects will occur across countries, but many will occur within countries but across localities, and entail production methods that differ in their implications. Limited conclusive research makes the net effects unclear.[9]

### The quantitative dimensions of environmental considerations

How important are these core environmental externalities, and how do they compare with gains from trade that accrue through more specialized production?

The presumption is that the specialization of production that accompanies trade that is more liberal will also be more geographically concentrated. The question is whether this is good or bad from a global point of view. If the damage associated with local output is convex to the output axis – assuming that damage remains local – then concentrating production would reduce damage. If damage functions are concave to the output axis, then the opposite would be true. Knowledge of the shape of the damage functions is thus critical.

If population density differs between countries, then damage *per capita* will vary in those countries even though total damage is similar. The general presumption seems to be that moving externality-causing production from high- to low-population countries has merit, but more liberal trade may or may not encourage such a move.

Empirical studies seem to show that gains to developing countries from internalizing key agricultural externalities substantially outweigh gains from removing trade distortions. A review of the environmental regimes in a sample of developing countries by Jha and Whalley (1999) suggests that annual gains from fully internalizing agricultural externalities might reach 10 percent of GDP per year. Degradation-related externalities – including soil erosion, deforestation,

---

**Box 18.2  Estimates by the ADB of environmental costs in Asian countries**

- *China.* Productivity losses from soil erosion, deforestation, and land degradation, water shortages, and destruction of wetlands in 1990: US$ 13.9–26.6 billion annually, or 3.8–7.3 percent of GDP.
- *India.* Total environmental costs: $13.8 billion in 1992, or 6 percent of GDP; urban air pollution costs: $1.3 billion; health costs from water quality: $5.7 billion; soil erosion costs: $2.4 billion; deforestation costs: $214 million. The total excludes traffic-related costs, pollution costs from toxic wastes, and biodiversity losses.
- *Pakistan.* Health impacts of air and water pollution and productivity losses from deforestation and soil erosion: $1.7 billion in the early 1990s, or 3.3 percent of GDP.

*Sources:* Agarwal (1996), ADB (1997), and UN, *Human Development Report 1998* (UN, 1999), cited in Jha and Whalley (1999).

---

general land degradation, and problems related to open access – could account for 70–80 percent of that total.

Jha and Whalley (1999) rely heavily on cross-country comparative studies of Asian countries undertaken for the Asian Development Bank (ADB) (box 18.2). These studies suggest that China's annual productivity losses in the early 1990s from soil erosion, deforestation, and land degradation could have represented 7 percent of GDP. If we include health and productivity losses from urban pollution, which represent 1.7–2.5 percent of GDP, annual costs from environmental damage totaled some 10 percent of GDP. A 1992 study by Smil based on 1988 data (not included in box 18.2, as it was not part of the ADB studies) also puts China's losses from farmland, nutrients, flooding, and timber at around 10 percent of GDP, against losses from pollutants of perhaps 2 percent of GDP.

The ADB studies put the costs of damage from environmental sources in India in 1992 – including urban air pollution, health costs from water quality, soil erosion, and deforestation, and excluding traffic-related costs, toxic wastes, and biodiversity losses – at about 6 percent of GDP. Studies for Pakistan show smaller but sizable effects.

Model-based studies performed during the Uruguay Round generally produced much smaller estimates of gains from liberalizing agricultural trade. These studies were based largely on general equilibrium models that specify production and consumption preferences within countries, with trade by commodity by country given as the difference between the two. Market clearing prevails, and trade interventions change not only the pattern of trade but also consumption and production within regions. Models are benchmarked to a base year.[10]

Table 18.1 *Model-based estimates of the gains from liberalizing agriculture in the Uruguay Round*

|  | HRT[a] (IRTS) (1992 $billion) | FMN[b] (IRTS) (1992 $billion) | GVdM[c] (CRS) (% of income, 2002) |
|---|---|---|---|
| China | −0.8 | 0.27 | −0.2 |
| Indonesia | 0.3 | 0.40 | 0.5 |
|  |  | (East Asia) |  |
| India | 0.2 | −0.21 | 0.0 |
|  | (South Asia) | (South China) |  |
| Argentina | 0.7 | 1.03 | 0.2 |
|  |  | (Latin America) | (other Latin America) |
| Brazil | 0.1 |  | −0.1 |
| EU (12) | 26.4 | 0.47 | 1.9 |
| US | 3.2 | −0.42 | 0.1 |
| Japan | 16.8 | −0.22 | 1.6 |

*Notes:* [a] Harrison, Rutherford, and Tarr (1996, table 8.7).
[b] Francois, McDonald, and Nordström (1996, table 9.11), fixed-capital stock case.
[c] Goldin and van der Mensbrugghe (1996, table 6.5).

These models generally simulate the effects of Uruguay Round cuts in tariffs, domestic support, and export subsidies. Many analysts question the degree of liberalization that has actually occurred – and thus whether the models overstated these effects.[11] While not providing a wholly fair comparison, table 18.1 shows small trade gains compared with the gains from internalizing externalities in box 18.2. China, for instance, would see environmental gains of $13.9–26.6 billion (1990 prices) compared with its estimated gain of $−0.8 to 0.27 billion from liberalized agriculture under the Uruguay Round.

Results from these studies tend to be inconsistent, so they provide only a rough guide to potential impacts. (Compare, for instance, the Harrison, Rutherford, and Tarr, 1996 (HRT) estimates for the EU and Japan to those of Francois, McDonald, and Nordström, 1996 (FMN.) The direction of benefits accruing to developing countries also varies, although the effects are generally small. However, box 18.2 and table 18.1 seem to indicate that developing countries should rank agriculture-related environmental policy higher than agricultural trade policy. In fact, developing countries might conclude that they should make such considerations the centerpiece of new agricultural negotiations.

However, trade policy is a poor – and even ineffective – instrument for pursuing environmental policy. Environmental externalities reflect ill-defined property rights, the cumbersome practices of state-owned entities (including irrigation systems), and weak and ineffective legal systems. And the studies cited above do not capture the losses to developing countries if countries truncate market access on environmental grounds. Although a broad sweep of studies seems to suggest that environmental concerns are important to developing countries, pursuing them through agricultural negotiations seems inefficient and opens the door to new market-closing measures.

## Renewed environmental considerations in agricultural talks

Despite this caution, how might environmental considerations become part of efforts to further tighten tariffs, domestic support, and export subsidies?

Agricultural negotiations will almost certainly be seen largely for what they are – negotiations on agricultural policies, not the environment. Negotiators have already devoted considerable attention to non-trade issues in preparing for new talks, but the key non-trade issue for developing countries seems to be food security.[12] Environmental concerns seem likely to enter the discussion owing to NGO pressure, especially if the agenda for a new round gives such concerns a low profile.

Some negotiators will likely respond that other instruments can deal more effectively with environmental concerns. Developing countries will also likely mute the enthusiasm for adding environmental concerns to the negotiating agenda. These countries have generally viewed the trade and environment debate as threatening to slow their growth and development,[13] and remain wary of justifying access-restricting measures on environmental grounds. Yet some countries will hinge their trade positions on environmental arguments.

Environmental issues will likely shape agricultural negotiations differently than more general trade and environment negotiations. The former could touch on whether new commitments should exempt domestic policies designed to protect the environment, such as integrated pest management programs in Indonesia.[14] New trade agreements could also potentially discipline domestic measures with harmful external effects, such as fertilizer subsidies.

Given the above, the environment could influence the agricultural component of the new WTO trade negotiating round through several scenarios (box 18.3). The first possibility is prolonged general debate on environment links to agricultural trade. The argument by fourteen countries to the CTE that "no environmental benefits can be associated with the provision of export subsidies" seems too strong a claim to go unchallenged. Consider a country exporting two crops: export subsidies for the less erosive crop could reduce overall erosion.

Debate over multifunctionality may also fall into this category. If existence value is accepted as conceptually sound – and environmental economics does rely on it – the argument will not go away. Although agricultural exporters will argue that it is simply a mechanism to legitimize protection – and they might

---

**Box 18.3  Environmental debate in agricultural negotiations**

**General debate on trade links between agriculture
and the environment**

- How does liberalizing agricultural trade affect the environment?
- What are the multiple roles played by the agricultural sector in supporting rural activities and values, including existence value?
- Can some export subsidies be justified on environmental grounds, and should such subsidies be exempt from restraints or treated less severely?
- Should negotiators expand "green box" rules exempting programs that deliver environmental benefits from discipline?
- Should countries gain exemptions from tariff cuts on environmental grounds?
- Should countries win extra credit for tariff cuts that produce environmental benefits?
- Should programs that promote environmental benefits count in calculations of countries' aggregate measure of support?
- Should program expenditures count more harshly if they produce adverse environmental effects?
- Can and should TRQs be designed to incorporate environmental purposes?

**Wider trade and environment debates that agricultural trade
negotiations are unlikely to include**

- The rights of countries to use trade-restricting measures on environmental grounds.
- Multilateral environmental agreements and their use of trade measures.
- Lax environmental standards and subsidies that encourage environmental degradation.
- The use of ecolabeling.

---

be right – we will not know without further study of consumers' willingness to pay, or the development of techniques for setting a price on such values.

Thus such debate will probably prove inconclusive. However, it could legitimize a formal structure for including environmental concerns in agricultural negotiations.

Negotiators seem to think that "green box" provisions from the Uruguay Round will remain in place, but they may delineate more precisely what the environmental benefits of exempt payments to farmers may be. If, as some analysts expect, agricultural negotiations turn on export subsidies, whether environmental benefits justify their use could become a high-profile issue.

Where negotiators deem that particular instruments or programs yield environmental benefits (costs), pressure to treat them preferentially (more harshly) could also emerge. These instruments could include tariffs, TRQs, calculations of countries' aggregate measure of support, and export subsidies. Such provisions would require resolving several difficult issues. How should environmental benefits or damages be defined and measured? Should benefits or damages be calculated globally, such as by taking both importing and exporting countries into account simultaneously, or does harm or benefit in either an importing or an exporting country justify a departure from discipline? How do calculations of environmental benefits or damage account for resource reallocations that occur as an economy responds to external effects?

As box 18.3 reports, most key issues in the trade and environment debate will remain untouched by agricultural negotiations, since nothing in the structure of such negotiations allows such debate. This includes the rights of countries to use trade-restricting measures on environmental grounds, the relationship between multilateral environmental agreements and trade measures, lax environmental agreements and subsidies that encourage environmental destruction and overuse of natural resources, and ecolabeling. Agricultural negotiations will likely prove an unsatisfactory vehicle for resolving such disputes.

Developing countries would seem well advised to pursue their own environmental agenda elsewhere, primarily through domestic policies. The seemingly weak relationship between the environmental content of agricultural negotiations compared with broader trade and environment negotiations may convince developing countries opposed to broader negotiations to take a more relaxed attitude during agricultural talks. As agricultural negotiations would almost certainly be unable to deal with many of the key concerns and issues raised in the wider trade and environment debate, this may be a source of comfort for developing countries.

The bottom line is that developing countries face important environmental dilemmas – perhaps even more significant than trade considerations. However, WTO negotiations on agriculture are not the best forum in which to seek remedies.

### Notes

1. See Hathaway (1987) and Jackson (1989).
2. This echoes Tangermann's (1997) approach to the agricultural content of a new round, although Swinbank (1999) has suggested the focus is likely to be heaviest on export subsidies. Swinbank argues that this is the most binding portion of the Uruguay Round agreements on EU agricultural policies, and that calls are likely to come from elsewhere to eliminate export subsidies on agricultural products rather than merely cut them. APEC trade ministers have made such a call (*Financial Times*, September 11, 1999).
3. See WTO (1998a). A number of other environmental issues could surface during agricultural negotiations, including those involved with the Sanitary and Phytosanitary Agreement, and technical barriers to trade (see Uimonen and Whalley 1997; Uimonen 1998). A major point of conflict in this area has been the dispute between the United States and the EU over the use of hormones in beef (the *Hormones* case, see chapter 15

in this volume). This is a standards issue as much as a trade and environment issue, but it is sometimes included in the latter. Other possible issues include special rules for dispute-settlement cases with environmental content, and whether pre- or post-round environmental impact assessments should be made. I do not touch on these here to keep the chapter focused on what seem to be the key issues linking environmental concerns and agricultural negotiations.

4. The developing countries are, of course, a heterogeneous group with varying interests in both agricultural trade and environmental matters. Such countries include agricultural exporters, net food importers, high-forest-cover countries, and high-population-density countries, to name but four groups.

5. See also Meade's (1952) important classification of externalities as consumption–consumption, consumption–production, and production–production.

6. The fact that my educational attainment raises the probability that misdirected mail sent to me will be appropriately rerouted is an example of a non-environmental externality.

7. See Lipsey and Lancaster (1957).

8. The Norwegian submission to the CTE discusses the implications of a shift in agricultural production away from countries with high domestic supports to those with lower domestic supports as agricultural liberalization proceeds. It emphasizes that low-support countries are generally also high-biodiversity countries, and hence concludes that such a shift of production could be detrimental on environmental grounds.

Both the Uruguay Round decisions of 1994 and the charter of the World Trade Organization (WTO) have been repeatedly characterized by environmental NGOs as lacking environmental content. They point out that the word *environment* hardly appears in approximately 24,000 pages of text and schedules, and that the drafting of the charter of the WTO represented the best chance for a generation to deal, in some fundamental way, with the role that environmental considerations can play in the post-Uruguay Round trading system. Combined with the growing profile of trade and environment conflicts following the 1991 US–Mexico tuna–dolphin GATT Panel report, pressure has been growing for several years from environmental groups to deal centrally with the trade and environment issue in any new trade round. This was reflected in the WTO high-level symposium (HLS) of March 1999, which devoted half of its discussion time to trade and environment issues (see the summary of the proceedings of the HLS by the International Institute for Sustainable Development, IISD, 1999). In the HLS, how a separate agricultural negotiation might deal with the environment was seemingly not a central focus of discussion. Japan did argue that trade rules need to take into account environmental benefits from local production, while New Zealand contested the claim that there were any environmental benefits from domestic subsidies, and Argentina argued that trade-distorting production subsidies in "environmental-champion" countries should be removed.

9. See the analysis of the impacts of tariff cuts for potatoes on soil erosion in Sri Lanka in Weerahewa (1999), where the outcome hinges on whether increased potato production is at the expense of other crops that are more or less erosive.

10. The studies by FMN (1996); HRT (1996); and Goldin and van der Mensbrugghe (GVdM) (1996), cited in table 18.1, are prominent in this literature.

11. See Ingco's (1996) discussion of "dirty tariffication," for instance.
12. The submissions by Norway (WTO, 1999a) and Argentina (WTO, 1998c) seem to be the two instances where environmental issues have been discussed centrally as non-trade issues. Norway has emphasized what it sees as the multifunctional nature of agriculture as a justification for agricultural subsidization; Argentina has warned over the protectionist nature of such subsidies, and the impact on poverty in exporting countries. See the discussion of these positions in IITSD (1999, 7).
13. See Whalley (1996) for a discussion of the trade and environment issue beyond the 1996 Singapore WTO Ministerial.
14. See Resosudarmo (1999).

## References

Agarwal, A., 1996. "Pay-Offs to Progress," *Down to Earth* (Centre for Science and Environment, New Delhi), 5(10), 31–9

Alfsen, K. H., M. A. DeFranco, S. Glomsrod, and T. Johnsen, 1996. "The Cost of Soil Erosion in Nicaragua," *Ecological Economics*, 16, 129–45

Anderson, K., 1992. "Agricultural Trade Liberalization and the Environment: A Global Perspective," *The World Economy*, 15(1), 153–72

Asian Development Bank (ADB), 1997. "Emerging Asia-Changes and Challenges," Manila

Barbier, F., 1996. "The Economics of Soil Erosion: Theory, Methodology and Examples," Special Paper, Economy and Environmental Program of South East Asia, May

Coase, R., 1960. "The Problem of Social Cost," *Journal of Law and Economics*, 3, 1–44

Francois, J. F., H. McDonald, and H. Nordström, 1996. "The Uruguay Round: a Numerically Based Qualitative Assessment," in W. Martin and A. L. Winters (eds.), *The Uruguay Round and The Developing Countries*, Cambridge and New York: Cambridge University Press

Glover, D. and T. Jessup (eds.), 1999. *Indonesia's Fires and Haze: The Cost of Catastrophe*, Singapore and Canada: IDRC/ISEAS

Goldin, I. and D. van der Mensbrugghe, 1996. "Assessing Agricultural Tariffication Under the Uruguay Round," in W. Martin and L. A. Winters (eds.), *The Uruguay Round and the Developing Countries*, Cambridge and New York: Cambridge University Press

Harrison, G. W., T. F. Rutherford, and D. G. Tarr, 1996. "Quantifying the Uruguay Round," in W. Martin and A. L. Winters (eds.), *The Uruguay Round and the Developing Countries*, Cambridge and New York: Cambridge University Press

Hathaway, D. E., 1987. "Agriculture and the GATT: Rewriting the Rules," *Institute for International Economics*, 20

International Institute for Trade and Sustainable Development (IITSD), 1999. "Bridges Between Trade and Sustainable Development"

Ingco, M. D., 1996. "Tariffication in the Uruguay Round: How Much Liberalization?," *The World Economy*, 19(4), 425–47

Ingersent, K. A., A. J. Rayner, and R. C. Hine, 1995. "Expost Evaluation of the Uruguay Round Agricultural Agreement," *The World Economy*, 18(5), 707–28

Jackson, J. H., 1989. *The World Trading System*, Cambridge, MA: MIT Press

Jha, R. and J. Whalley, 1999. "The Environmental Regime in Developing Countries," paper presented at the FEEM/NBER conference, Milan, June

Lipsey, R. G. and K. J. Lancaster, 1957. "The General Theory of the Second Best," *Review of Economic Studies*, 24, 11–32

López, R., 1997. "Evaluating Economywide Policies in the Presence of Agricultural Environmental Externalities: The Case of Ghana," in W. Cruz, M. Munasinghe, and J. J. Warford (eds.), *The Greening of Economic Policy Reform, II: Case Studies*, Washington, DC: World Bank

Magrath, W. and P. Arens, 1989. "The Costs of Soil Erosion on Java: A Natural Resource Accounting Approach," Environment Working Paper, 18, Environment Department, World Bank

Meade, J. E., 1952. "External Economies and Diseconomies in a Competitive Situation," *Economic Journal*, 62, 654–71

Pigou, A. C., 1918. *The Economics of Welfare*, London: Macmillan

Resosudarmo, B., 1999. "The Economy Wide Impacts of Integrated Pest Management in Indonesia," Economy and Environment Program of South East Asia (EEPSEA), Singapore

Smil, V., 1992. "Environmental Changes as a Source of Conflict and Economic Losses in China," paper prepared for a Workshop on Environmental Change, Economic Decline, and Civil Strife, Institute for Strategic and International Studies, Kuala Lumpur, 1991

Swinbank, A., 1999. "EU Agriculture, Agenda 2000 and the WTO Commitments," *The World Economy*, 22(1), 41–54

Tangermann, S., 1997. "A Developed Country Perspective of the Agenda for the Next WTO Round of Agricultural Negotiations," Occasional Paper, WTO Series, 5, Program for the Study of International Organizations, Geneva

Uimonen, P., 1998. "The Environmental Dilemmas of the World Trade Organization," in J. J. Schott (ed.), *Launching New Global Trade Talks: An Action Agenda*, Washington, DC: Institute for International Economics

Uimonen, P. and J. Whalley, 1997. *Environmental Issues in the New World Trading System*, London: Macmillan

United Nations (UN), 1999. *Human Development Report 1998*, New York: United Nations

Weerahewa, J., 1999. "Impact of Trade Liberalization on the Environment: The Case of Tariff Reduction for Potato in Sri Lanka," Economy and Environment Program of South East Asia (EEPSEA), Singapore

Whalley, J., 1996. "Trade and Environment Beyond Singapore," Working Paper, 5768, National Bureau of Economic Research

World Trade Organization (WTO), 1998. "Sanitary and Phytosanitary Measures," WTO Agreement Series, 4, Geneva

    1999. "Environmental Effects of Trade Liberalization in the Agricultural Sector," submission by Norway to the Committee on Trade and Environment, WT/CTE/W/100, Geneva

# 19　Intellectual property rights and agriculture

*Jayashree Watal*

## Introduction

Intellectual property rights (IPRs) can be loosely defined as legal rights governing the use of creations of the human mind.[1] The term covers a bundle of rights, each with different scope and duration as well as varying purpose and effect. Despite their differences, protection against unfair competition is the underlying philosophy of all IPRs. Such rights generally prohibit third persons from commercially exploiting protected subject matter without the explicit authorization of the right holder during a specified duration of time.[2] This enables right holders to use or disclose their creations without fear of losing control over them, thus helping to disseminate them. IPRs are generally believed to encourage inventive activity and aid the orderly marketing of proprietary goods and services. Such rights are limited to a defined territory and have historically been attuned to the circumstances and needs of different jurisdictions, although some specific international intellectual property laws also apply.

The IPRs that raise distinctive issues for the agricultural sector are patents, plant breeders' rights, and geographical indications.[3] Geographical indications are product labels that identify goods from a specified geographical area and are a form of intellectual property that almost exclusively applies to agricultural products.

Patents generally give their holders the legal right to exclude others from making, using, or selling an invention for a limited period – usually twenty years from the application date. In return, patent owners must fully disclose their inventions so that technical knowledge is publicly disseminated. All patent laws allow some exceptions. For instance, almost all countries exclude inventions that are contrary to public order or morality or harmful to life or health. Countries also require holders to allow others to use their inventions in certain circumstances, such as for experimentation, teaching, and research, and may authorize compulsory licenses for specific purposes.

The WTO Agreement on Trade-Related Aspects of Intellectual Property Rights (TRIPS), emanating in 1995 from the Uruguay Round, has strengthened protection of IPRs almost world-wide – a feat never before achieved by a single international intellectual property treaty. In particular, the Agreement brings important standards regarding patents, plant breeders' rights, and geographical indications in developing countries closer to those of developed countries.[4] TRIPS does not harmonize intellectual property laws and procedures, but rather sets minimum standards that different legal systems can implement differently. The agreement also permits widely recognized limits to these intellectual property rights. Generally speaking, developed countries were to comply with TRIPS provisions by January 1996, while economies in transition and developing countries had to implement almost all provisions by January 2000, while least-developed countries (LDCs) must do so by January 2006.

Before the Uruguay Round, some developing countries excluded food products and processes as well as machines, processes, and chemicals useful for agriculture from patenting.[5] Others additionally prohibited patenting of inventions on living organisms such as plants, animals, and microorganisms, or substances obtained by microbiological processes.[6]

To encourage conventional breeding methods used to develop new plant varieties countries developed plant breeders' rights. Such protection generally allows other breeders to use the protected material for producing new plant varieties, and permits farmers to save and use seeds from protected varieties. Plant breeders' rights usually last from fifteen to thirty years, and vary across countries and types of plants.

The criteria used to grant such protection are somewhat weaker than those that apply to patents. New plant varieties have to fulfill three criteria known as "DUS": they have to be distinct (D) from earlier known varieties, uniform (U) or homogeneous – displaying the same essential characteristics in every plant, and stable (S) retaining the same essential characteristics upon reproduction.[7] A fourth criterion, novelty, is also generally added and means that protected plant varieties also must be new to the market, although countries usually grant a grace period of one to four years for sales in domestic and foreign markets, respectively.

With the development of hybrids, plant breeders have also resorted to trade-secret protection to prevent misappropriation of undisclosed parent lines. Seeds produced by hybrid plants typically do not produce the same quality plant, so farmers have to repurchase seed for every crop season to maintain vigorous yield or other characteristics. This approach is also known as biological protection, as distinct from legal protection.[8] Not surprisingly, innovative firms in agricultural biotechnology seek to develop hybrids with built-in biological protection to maximize returns to their research and development (R & D) investments, regardless of local IPR regimes.

Even while TRIPS calls only for "an effective *sui generis* system" for the protection of plant varieties, it has raised fears of increased dependence on imports, price increases, aggressive salesmanship resulting in monoculture, and environmental degradation. Work completed in the pharmaceutical sector shows that prices of patented products are higher than those of off-patent products.[9] Some analysis pertaining to India shows that although price controls and compulsory licenses could moderate prices, they may not achieve no-patent levels.[10] Despite these findings, the fears on patents and prices in the pharmaceutical sector cannot be extended unconditionally to the agricultural sector, for several reasons:

- TRIPS only makes plant breeders' rights – which are generally speaking weaker than patent rights – obligatory for new plant varieties.
- Production of protected plants would usually be local, so fears that a technology would not be used for manufacture in a new location do not apply.
- Local collaboration may be essential for conducting field trials of new crop varieties and adapting them to local conditions.
- Agricultural sales directly target farmers, who are price-sensitive, rather than intermediaries such as doctors.
- The agricultural sector has more competition because no one variety uniquely fulfills consumer demand, unlike pharmaceuticals where unique therapeutic products can exist. Also, because plant breeders' rights exempt other breeders, and public sector research organizations in developing countries have well-developed capabilities in plant-breeding compared with those in the area of industrial research, there is likely to be even more competition for successful varieties.

Nevertheless, IPRs for agricultural goods in developing countries do raise concerns and policy questions quite separate from questions of price and competition. Setting aside the moral, ethical, and environmental dimensions of agricultural biotechnology,[11] we can group these concerns under two separate, though not mutually exclusive, categories:

- *Public domain or public interest*: concerns raised by the patenting of research tools, oligopolistic control of food supply and food security, the role of the public sector, access to new technologies at reasonable terms, and the need to encourage follow-on inventions.
- *Equity*: the need to retain farmers' privilege to save seed, and to remunerate farmers for rural innovations incorporating traditional knowledge as a counter-balance to rewarding modern plant-breeding techniques.

This chapter cannot address all these issues, particularly those relating to the environment. However, since developing countries have raised questions on equity and public interest during preparations for the new WTO round, this chapter will examine them in that context.

## Protecting biotechnological inventions under TRIPS

With a few exceptions, TRIPS obliges countries to make patents available for all inventions that are new, involve an inventive step or, equivalently, are not obvious to persons of ordinary skill in that field, and are industrially applicable or, equivalently, are useful. TRIPS also requires that countries give patent owners the right to exclude others from making, using, selling, or offering for sale the patented invention, including products directly obtained through patented processes. However, the treaty does allow limited exceptions, including the granting of compulsory licenses under certain conditions.

TRIPS also explicitly allows exclusions of patentable inventions that are contrary to public order or morality, including those that are prejudicial to the health or life of humans, animals, or plants, or to the environment in general. However, countries must also prohibit the commercial exploitation of inventions excluded on these grounds. Further, such inventions cannot be excluded from patentability merely because domestic law prohibits their use. In other words, these inventions must be examined against these criteria on a case-by-case basis before they can be excluded from patenting.

The TRIPS provision most relevant to agriculture is article 27.3(b), which allows countries to exclude from patenting plants, animals, and biological processes essential for producing plants and animals. However, the treaty does require countries to allow the patenting of "microorganisms" and of "microbiological" or "non-biological" processes for the production of plants and animals, with extension of patent rights to the products directly obtained through the use of these processes – although the treaty does not define these terms, leaving considerable scope for interpretation. TRIPS also requires countries to institute an "effective" *sui generis* law protecting plant varieties in the event that they are excluded from patenting; countries may also offer both types of protection. Unlike with other IPRs, TRIPS does not oblige countries to comply with the International Union for the Protection of New Varieties of Plants (UPOV)[12] – nor does it detail the scope or duration of protection. However, the treaty does require review of this subsection, and such a review has been under way in the WTO TRIPS Council since 1999.

### *Differing interpretations of article 27.3(b) of TRIPS*

When TRIPS was under negotiation, the United States and EU clearly differed in their approaches to patenting biotechnological inventions. The United States believed that "anything under the sun made by man" except a human being – was patentable, while the EU was grappling with strong domestic resistance to patenting living organisms.

The United States had been granting patents on living materials since its landmark 1980 decision on the patentability of microorganisms.[13] The United States granted its first utility patent on plants in 1986 following *Ex parte Hibberd*, and its first animal patent on the famous Harvard onco-mouse in 1988. However, since the debate had not yet been settled in Europe, negotiators agreed to a minimal level of protection, and to re-visit this provision within four years. Negotiators expected that passage of the European Biotechnology Directive (eventually passed in 1998) – under discussion at the time – would allow them to accept patenting of all eligible biotechnological inventions, including genes, plants, and animals. This expectation has not been fully met, as the EU Directive, while allowing such patents, also permits exceptions such as allowing farmers to reproduce patented plants and animals for use on their own farms.

With the rapid adoption of transgenic plants since the mid-1990s, the small number of successful multinational agricultural biotechnology companies, originating mostly in the United States, are keenly interested in obtaining strong patent protection world-wide. These companies argue that plant breeders' rights – which include breeders' exemption and farmers' privilege – do not allow them to recoup their huge investments in R & D. Indeed, there is evidence that private-sector investment in new plant varieties, in the absence of adequate protection for intellectual property, has occurred mostly in hybrid crops.[14] As an alternative to patents, companies may design transgenic crops to prevent their re-use – leading, paradoxically, to higher levels of protection than are obligatory under TRIPS.

Since the TRIPS text was finalized, some legal scholars have grappled with the intricacies of interpreting its provisions and suggested different ways of implementing them in developing countries.[15] The diversity of these views may stem from the fact that TRIPS was the result of bitter North–South negotiations reflecting strong economic interests on the part of rights owners as well as parties benefiting from weaker levels of protection. The Agreement resolved this conflict of interests through "constructive ambiguity," wherein each side interpreted its provisions differently.

Interpreting ambiguous clauses may be one way for parties to "claw" back much of what they lost during battles over TRIPS. The fact that TRIPS negotiations have no official record enhances this possibility. The dispute-settlement mechanism of the WTO may, if invoked, have to resolve these differing interpretations, although disputes have not yet arisen in many controversial areas partly because developing countries have had extra time to implement them. Meanwhile, the review of the implementation of article 27.3 (b) by the TRIPS Council should throw more light on these issues and a wealth of material is available on the WTO website at IP/C/W/273 and its revision, as well as under document series IP/Q/. . .

The crux of the debate is whether WTO members can exclude from patentability technical processes for creating naturally occurring substances, such as sequences of nucleotides (DNA), if the final product merely reproduces a substance found in nature. Some commentators opine that since TRIPS does not define "invention," countries have some scope for making such exclusions.[16] Almost all jurisdictions exclude biological or genetic materials *as found in nature*, as these are discoveries and not inventions. The disagreement arises over whether they can be excluded from patenting if isolated or reproduced through technical processes.

Does the provision that allows countries to exclude only "essentially biological processes" mean that they must allow all other technical processes, including microbiological processes, and the ensuing products thereof, to be protected under patent rights? Some believe that TRIPS obliges patents on gene sequences and other such products of nature if they are isolated through technical processes, even if the final product merely reproduces nature.[17] The new EU Directive clarifies that inventions that consist of or contain biological material – even if such material has previously occurred in nature – must be patentable if isolated by technical processes and, of course, if new and non-obvious. Thus the EU unambiguously allows the patenting of genes, including human genes, if they can be shown to be non-obvious and industrially applicable.

It is also unclear how "microbiological" processes differ from "essentially biological" ones. The EU Biotechnology Directive sheds some light when it restricts "essentially biological" processes to natural phenomena such as crossing and selection, while defining "microbiological processes as those involving or resulting in microbiological material." Norway in its patent law excludes not only plants and animals but also all processes for their production, and grants patents only to microorganisms and corresponding processes.

Some countries view "microorganism" as any organism that can be seen only through a microscope, while others restrict such organisms to unicellular animals. Yet others restrict the term to organisms such as viruses, algae, and bacteria. Others, such as Canada, add cell lines and hybridomas to unicellular organisms. WTO Members seem to have some freedom to define microorganisms and microbiological processes, as long as they can defend their policies before a WTO Dispute Panel.

TRIPS' exclusion of "plants and animals" from patenting is clearly broader than that given to "plant and animal varieties" under the European Patent Convention, and reiterated in the new EU Directive and many other patent laws of developed and developing countries. In TRIPS negotiations, developing countries were aware of the confusion caused by the European Patent Convention, wherein the exclusion of plant varieties was interpreted as not encompassing plants as such. The broader term used in TRIPS thus excludes both plants and animals, and plant varieties and animal breeds.[18]

However, it is unclear whether the rights of process patentees extend to products directly obtained, including through genetic engineering processes, thereby overriding exclusions of plants and animals.[19] The EU allowed such an extension even before issuing its new Biotechnology Directive. If TRIPS were to be interpreted this way, the protection it gives to biotechnological inventions is stronger than would first appear, at least for patentable processes used to produce plants and animals.

Whether farmers' privilege in the new EU Directive is a significant economic concession to farmers, and should be adopted as a model by developing countries if they award patents for plant and animal inventions, is unclear.[20] Given the high investment entailed in developing new reproductive and genetic technologies applied to crops and livestock, this kind of exception would likely lead to very high initial prices for innovative products in order to include the price of the re-used seed over several further generations, thus benefiting only more well-to-do farmers. Widespread use of this exception could mean that more innovators resort to trade secrets and incorporate protection into their technologies, thus depriving society of the disclosure entailed in patents and plant-breeders' rights.

Some developing countries have taken advantage of the ambiguities of TRIPS to exclude substances found in nature from patenting, even if these are isolated or transformed through technical processes. Both Brazil and Argentina have formulated fairly broad exceptions, and the Andean Group adopted a similar exception in its 1993 Decision 344. Interestingly, Mexico excludes only the patenting of human genes. These countries specify that genes found naturally in plants, humans, and animals cannot be patented, even if produced through novel technical processes.[21] Some countries think that the new EU Directive is incompatible with the requirements of TRIPS.[22]

Other developing countries have gone further than required under TRIPS in protecting biotechnological inventions. In its 1994 Patents Act, Singapore significantly departed from its policy of following the United Kingdom when it removed any specific bar to the patentability of plants and animal varieties. The Singaporean law goes beyond that of Australia, which bars the patentability of human beings. However, Singapore's Patents Act does allow the minister to vary its provisions "for the purposes of maintaining them in conformity with developments in science and technology" – a loophole that could be used to prevent blocks to research.[23]

Korea has long allowed patents on plants except those produced through sexual propagation. The Korean Industrial Property Office has revised its Examination Guidelines for Biotechnology Inventions to allow patents on animals (excluding humans), parts of an animal, processes for creating an animal, and uses thereof, confining exclusions to those that are liable to contravene public order and morality.[24] In its recently adopted patent law, Trinidad and Tobago allows no exclusions for plants and animals and their varieties, granting exceptions only on the grounds of public order or morality – thus going beyond TRIPS requirements and matching the United States.

Table 19.1 shows how selected developed and developing countries are implementing the patent provisions of article 27.3(b) of TRIPS.[25] If on a scale of 1 to 10 the United States could be regarded as having the strongest patent

Table 19.1 *Implementation of TRIPS provisions regarding biotech patents, selected WTO Members*

| Subject | US | JP | EC | SW | AU | CA | NW | KR | SA | TT | AR | BR | CO/CA | CH | SI | MY |
|---|---|---|---|---|---|---|---|---|---|---|---|---|---|---|---|---|
| 1. Product patents on microorganisms, if otherwise patentable | Y | Y | Y | Y | Y | Y | Y | Y | Y | Y | Y | Y | Y | Y | Y | Y |
| 2. Process patents on: | | | | | | | | | | | | | | | | |
| Essentially biological processes | N | Y | N | N | Y | N | N | N | N | N | N | N | N | N | N | N |
| Microbiological processes | Y | Y | Y | Y | Y | Y | N | Y | Y | Y | Y | Y | Y | Y | Y | Y |
| Non-biological processes | Y | Y | Y | Y | Y | Y | N | Y | Y | Y | Y | Y | Y | Y | Y | Y |
| 3. Product patents on biological or genetic material as found in nature, i.e. discoveries | N | N | N | N | N | N | N | N | N | ? | N | N | N | N | N | N |
| 4. Patents on plants and animals *per se*, if otherwise patentable | Y | Y | Y | Y | Y | N | N | Y | Y | Y | N | N | N | N | Y | N |
| 5. Patents on plant and animal varieties | Y | Y | N | N | Y | N | N | Y | N | Y | N | N | N | N | Y | N |
| 6. Exclusion on grounds of morality or public order | N | Y | Y | Y | Y | Y | Y | Y | Y | Y | Y | Y | Y | Y | Y | Y |
| 7. Patents on human body | N | ? | N | N | N | N | N | N | N | ? | N | N | N | N | Y | ? |
| 8. Patents on human genes | Y | Y | Y | Y | Y | Y | Y | Y | Y | N | Y | Y | N | N | Y | Y |
| 9. Breeders' exemption for patents | N | N | Y | N | N | N | N | N | N | N | Y | Y | N | Y | N | N |

*Notes*: Y = Yes; N = No; ? = Unclear.

US = United States; JP = Japan; EC = European Communities; SW = Switzerland; AU = Australia; CA = Canada; NW = Norway; KR = Korea; SA = South Africa; TT = Trinidad and Tobago; AR = Argentina; BR = Brazil; CO/CA = Colombia and other Members of the Cartagena Agreement; CH = Chile; SI = Singapore; MY = Malaysia.

protection for biotechnological inventions, Australia, Japan, Korea, Singapore, Switzerland, and Trinidad and Tobago can be placed at 9. The EC can be placed at 8, provided its members implement the Biotechnology Directive. Austria, Belgium, France, Germany, Italy, Luxembourg, the Netherlands, and Sweden have been referred to the European Court of Justice (ECJ) by the Commission for non-implementation of the Directive in national law, even though this was due to be done by July 2000. Canada[26] and Norway, which exclude plants and animals, can be placed at 5, along with developing countries such as Argentina, Brazil, Colombia, Chile, Malaysia, and South Africa. Strikingly, no clear North–South divide appears in the way WTO Members have so far implemented these provisions.

## Protecting plant varieties under TRIPS

Ambiguity in TRIPS is even greater regarding protection for plant varieties, as the agreement does not specify details such as the scope and duration of such protection. Most developing countries and many developed countries did not maintain any form of protection for plant varieties until very recently. Among developed countries, only the United States, Japan, and Australia allow a choice of patents, plant-breeders' rights, or both on plant varieties; all others allow only plant-breeders' rights.

The WTO has not issued any official guidance as to how to interpret the word "effective" that describes the obligation on the protection of plant varieties. The seed industry would like protection against commercial competition, at least to the extent provided under UPOV (1991).[27] In late 1998, the United States proposed – in the context of the Seattle WTO Ministerial Meeting – incorporating key provisions of UPOV, 1991, into TRIPS. Since then, the EC and Switzerland have also supported the 1991 UPOV standard, although there has been no demand to amend TRIPS to this effect (see IP/C/W/369). Thus at least one major country would like to see UPOV standards in TRIPS.

The United States has had a law protecting some kinds of asexually reproduced plants since 1930, and sexually reproduced plant varieties since 1970, but it has considerably weakened farmers' privilege and breeders' exemptions under this law since 1994. Some European countries, such as Germany, France, and Netherlands, instituted such protection for plant breeders in the 1940s and 1950s.

Although UPOV came into being in 1968, it has had very limited membership until recently. The main thrust toward world-wide protection of plant varieties came only after the TRIPS Agreement, which sparked a rush to join UPOV, although the Agreement itself does not require this; most developing countries have preferred to join the 1978 version. There are crucial differences between

Table 19.2 *Differences between UPOV versions (1978) and (1991)*

| Subject | UPOV (1978) | UPOV (1991) |
|---|---|---|
| 1. Minimum scope of coverage | 5–24 genera or species from time of accession to eight years | 15 to *all* genera and species from the time of accession to 5–10 years, with the lower term applicable to members of UPOV (1978) |
| 2. Breeders' exemption | Breeders free to use protected variety to develop a new one | Exploitation of a subsequent variety that is essentially derived from the protected variety requires right holder's authorization; essential derivation criteria met when essential characteristics of first plant are replicated in the second, e.g. when virtually the whole genetic structure replicated |
| 3. Farmers' privilege to save seed for replanting | Implicitly allowed under the definition of minimum rights, but countries may opt not to do so | Allowed at the option of the member country within reasonable limits and subject to safeguarding the legitimate interests of the right holder |
| 4. Minimum exclusive rights on propagating material | Production for purposes of commercial marketing, offering for sale, marketing, and repeated use for commercial production of another variety and commercial use of ornamental plants or part thereof to produce plants or cut flowers | Production or reproduction; conditioning for the purposes of propagation; offering for sale; selling or other marketing; exporting; importing or stocking for any of these purposes |
| 5. Exclusive rights on harvested material | No such obligation | Same acts as under 4 if harvested material obtained through unauthorized use of propagating material, and if breeder had no reasonable opportunity to exercise his right in relation to the propagating material |

(cont.)

Table 19.2 (*cont.*)

| Subject | UPOV (1978) | UPOV (1991) |
|---|---|---|
| 6. Exception to exclusive rights | Farmers' privilege implicit and breeders' exemption expressly required; see also 3 above | Acts done privately and for non-commercial purposes, for experimental purposes, and for breeding and exploiting other varieties, not essentially derived; see also 3 above |
| 7. Minimum term of protection | 18 years for grapevines and trees and 15 years for all other plants | 25 years for grapevines and trees and 20 years for all other plants |
| 8. National treatment | May limit national treatment and scope of protection to members that also protect the genus and species chosen for protection, or that implement the same scope of protection (although TRIPS makes this obligatory for all WTO Members) | National treatment without exception |

*Source:* Compiled by the author from http://www.upov.int.

the 1978 version of UPOV and the revised one of 1991, as table 19.2 shows. Only UPOV (1991), which entered into force in April 1998, is open to membership now.

Developing countries that are WTO Members do not need to model their legislation on UPOV at all. However, UPOV is the only international model for plant-breeders' rights, and given the uncertainty over how the WTO will interpret the term "effective," adhering to UPOV (1978) seems the preferred option of many. Since UPOV (1978) existed at the time of TRIPS negotiations, this version could be considered a model for legislation in developing countries, provided such legislation is otherwise TRIPS-compatible.[28] Such a law may contain breeders' exemption and farmers' privilege.[29] UPOV (1991), on the other hand, disallows some of this flexibility in that it restricts farmers from exchanging or selling seeds, and requires countries to grant an exclusive right of reproduction for the protected variety. Both versions of UPOV allow countries to restrict exclusive rights for reasons of public interest, subject to equitable remuneration of the right holder.

Today many countries have such laws for protection of new plant varieties, as evidenced by the fifty-three members of UPOV on of July 31, 2003, of which more than a dozen are developing countries, the latter being bound by only the 1978 version of the UPOV.[30] Significantly no Asian developing countries other than China are members of UPOV, although many allowed the patenting of microorganisms and microbiological processes even before this was a TRIPS requirement.[31] Some developed countries became members after 1993: Greece and Luxembourg are the only two EU members yet to join UPOV.

Some developing countries have adopted plant variety protection laws conforming to UPOV (1991). Developing country exporters of cut flowers and ornamental plants, such as Kenya and Chile, see effective protection of plant-breeders' rights as in their long-term interest, because they facilitate access to new and better varieties. Bolivia, Colombia, and Ecuador have plant-breeders' laws that conform substantially to UPOV (1991), as do Morocco, Venezuela, and members of the African Intellectual Property Office (AIPO) in francophone Africa. Argentina, Chile, and Mexico protect all genera and species, even though they follow UPOV (1978).

"All" means, in practice, applications for a few hundred plant varieties, of which the top few ornamental plants constitute the majority. If national treatment under TRIPS applies to plant-breeders' rights, developing countries may want to protect all genera and species, as they cannot apply reciprocity. Developing countries with some capabilities in plant biotechnology that wish to encourage such research – whether in the private or public sector – should seriously consider instituting stronger protection through the UPOV (1991) model, and perhaps through patent protection.

Table 19.3 shows the level of protection that selected developed and developing countries accord to plant varieties. The United States, Japan, EC, Australia, Korea, and South Africa can be placed at 9 on a scale of 0 to 10, as they provide high-level protection but allow compulsory licensing. Colombia and other countries of the Andean group can also be placed at 8, as they allow universal coverage and restrict breeders' exemption but maintain a shorter term of protection. Argentina, Brazil, Canada, Chile, Norway, and Switzerland can be placed at 5, since they follow UPOV (1978) and do not confine breeders' exemption to varieties not essentially derived from the protected one. (Switzerland plans to replace its law with one compatible with UPOV (1991). Strikingly, all countries, including the United States, allow compulsory licenses for plant-breeders' rights, unlike with patents. How many countries actually grant such licenses is unknown.

Clearly, countries see different national interests, and have varied plant-breeders' rights and protection afforded to biotechnological inventions, even while possibly complying with TRIPS.

Table 19.3 *Implementation of TRIPS provisions regarding plant variety protection, selected WTO Members*

| Subject | US | JP | EC | SW | AU | CA | NW | KR | SA | TT | AR | BR | CO/CA | CH | SI | MY |
|---|---|---|---|---|---|---|---|---|---|---|---|---|---|---|---|---|
| 1. Meets standards of UPOV (1991) (* = 1978) | Y | Y | Y | Y* | Y | Y* | Y* | Y | Y | Y* | Y* | Y* | Y | Y* | n | n |
| 2. Following permitted: | | | | | | | | | | | | | | | | |
| Breeders' exemption | Y | Y | Y | Y | Y | Y | Y | Y | Y | Y | Y | Y | Y | Y | n | n |
| Farmers' privilege | Y | Y | Y | Y | Y | Y | Y | Y | Y | Y | Y | Y | Y | Y | n | n |
| Breeders' exemption not for essentially derived variety | Y | Y | Y | N | Y | N | N | Y | Y | N | N | Y | Y | N | n | n |
| 3. Criteria of distinctness, uniformity and stability | Y | Y | Y | Y | Y | Y | Y | Y | Y | Y | Y | Y | Y | Y | n | n |
| 4. Criteria of novelty, i.e. not commercialized | Y | Y | Y | Y | Y | Y | Y | Y | Y | Y | Y | Y | Y | Y | n | n |
| 5. Duration of 15–18 years or below | N | N | N | N | N | Y | N | N | N | N | N | N | N | Y | n | n |
| 6. Duration of 20–25 years or longer | Y | Y | Y | Y | Y | N | Y | Y | Y | Y | Y | N | N | N | n | n |
| 7. Universal coverage | Y | Y | Y | Y | Y | Y | Y | N | N | N | Y | N | Y | Y | n | n |
| 8. Limited coverage | N | N | N | N | N | N | N | Y | Y | Y | N | Y | N | N | n | n |
| 9. Compulsory licensing provided for | Y | Y | Y | Y | Y | Y | Y | Y | Y | Y | Y | Y | Y | Y | n | n |

*Notes:* Y = Yes; N = No; n = not available.

US = United States; JP = Japan; EC = European Communities; SW = Switzerland; AU = Australia; CA = Canada; NW = Norway; KR = Korea; SA = South Africa; TT = Trinidad and Tobago; AR = Argentina; BR = Brazil; CO/CA = Colombia and other Members of the Cartagena Agreement; CH = Chile; SI = Singapore; MY = Malaysia.

*Experience with transgenic crops in developing countries*

Debate over protection of intellectual property regarding plants has to be set in perspective.[32] The global commercial seed market was about US$30 billion in 2000, of which the share of developing countries may be about $7 billion – of which the share of just four countries – China, Brazil, India, and Argentina – constitutes over 80 percent. A huge proportion of farmers in these and other developing countries use farm-saved seed, and hence are not affected by developments in the commercial seed market. International trade in seeds totals only about $3.5 billion – approximately 10 percent of the total commercial seed market. Seeds of horticultural crops account for a third. Thus an overwhelming proportion of the production of commercial seed, particularly of agricultural crops, occurs in the country of sale.[33]

Transgenic or genetically modified (GM) crops are a recent phenomenon. Between 1996 and 1998 the global area used to produce such crops multiplied over fifteen times – from 4.3 million acres to 69.5 million acres. This increase reflects an exceptionally high adoption rate by farmers, at least by agricultural standards. The main breakthrough has come in improving plants' herbicide tolerance and insect resistance. The five principal transgenic crops in 1998, in descending order of importance, were soybean, maize, cotton, canola/rapeseed, and potato. Soybean and corn together comprised 82 percent of the global area under transgenic crops. The United States contained some 74 percent of that global area, with 15 percent in Argentina, 10 percent in Canada, and the remainder in Australia, Mexico, Spain, France, South Africa, and China.

Thus some developing countries have adopted this technology as readily as some developed countries. Indeed, China was the first country to commercialize transgenics, in the early 1990s. By 1996 the global area planted with such crops was split almost equally between developed and developing countries. Argentina's area under transgenic crops increased threefold, from 1.4 million hectares in 1997 to 4.3 million hectares in 1998, mostly because of its use of herbicide-tolerant soybeans, which constituted over 70 percent of the total area planted with that crop. China introduced Bt cotton only in 1998, yet of 63,000 hectares planted with this crop, about 10,000 hectares grew a product developed by the Chinese.

The economic benefits to developing countries of transgenic crops depend on a number of factors, including the need for a particular crop, the infestation of a targeted pest or weed, and the crop's performance under local conditions. Transgenic crops have reduced the use of herbicides and insecticides and boosted average yields. One study indicates that the farmer–company benefit ratio of 2:1 is similar to that of conventional agriculture in the United States.[34]

Developing countries that have adopted these new technologies need to perform similar studies. Studies of the economic benefits of hybrid crops in developing countries reveal benefits to farmers of similar magnitude. For instance, for hybrid sorghum in India, seed companies captured 18.5 percent of the benefits while farmers captured 81.5 percent (Pray and Ramaswami, 1999). These studies also show that seed prices were considerably higher for hybrids developed in the private as opposed to the public sector. However, the value of increases in farmers' yields outweighed increases in the cost of seeds. Indeed, farmers in developing countries are under no more obligation to buy newly developed seeds than are farmers in developed countries. In both cases, farmers make the decision to buy improved varieties after taking into account the economic benefits. However, poorer farmers in developing countries who depend on external financing – usually at usurious interest rates – and who usually lack crop insurance are less capable of sustaining losses and are thus more risk averse. Solutions to these problems must be found, and should not detract from the benefits of the new generation of agricultural biotechnologies.

The potential benefits to developing countries from agricultural biotechnologies go beyond adapting transgenic crops to address local problems with pests or weeds. This technology has the potential to address the malnutrition, disease, and low agricultural productivity that are particular to developing countries and LDCs. For example, genetically modified rice may help reduce iron-deficiency anemia and vitamin A deficiency.[35] Similarly, drought-resistant plants or those that tolerate high levels of soil toxicity could offer better yields and greater food security. This potential must be fully tapped and the technology further developed for the benefit of humanity.

Protection for intellectual property, combined with other appropriate policies, may help realize such potential. The mergers and acquisitions in the seed and "life sciences" sectors exacerbate fears that the resulting products will be unavailable or too expensive. The ten largest global seed firms control about 30 percent of world seed sales, according to the United Nations Development Programme's (UNDP) *Human Development Report 1999* (UNDP, 1999), and these companies increasingly control the IPRs to the new seeds. On the other hand, the public sector has overwhelmingly controlled agricultural research and seed distribution in developing countries, and even in developed countries until the 1990s. In many countries this public sector research is suffering from an acute shortage of funds, and private firms, mostly foreign firms or joint ventures (JVs), are stepping up their research efforts. However, firms are reluctant to introduce new varieties that rival companies can appropriate easily in the absence of strong protection for intellectual property. Until recently in countries such as India that had yet to adopt even plant-breeders' rights, companies confined their research to hybrids. Companies did not market the seed of single-cross hybrids of maize because of the high cost of seed production and the lack of IPR protection (Pray and Basant, 1999).

Changes in intellectual property regimes affect international agricultural research being conducted through the Centres of the Consultative Group on International Agricultural Research (CGIAR) and the National Agricultural Research Organizations (NARs). Developing countries have depended on the CGIAR system for free exchange of germplasm and scientific knowledge. In the year 2000, roughly 15 percent of the research budget of CGIAR centers was devoted to genetic engineering, and these centers have since become key players in agricultural biotechnology. Yet the centers applied for relatively few patents and may even be using proprietary technologies without formal consent. Most analysts agree that these centers should take out at least defensive patents to stake their claims and ensure access to new technologies.[36]

A global trend toward collaboration between private and public sector institutions is now evident. Initiatives such as the Consortium for Genomics Research in the Public Sector of Cornell University have sparked the interest of public sector research organizations in developing countries such as Brazil, China, and India, as well as the CGIAR centers (Herdt, 1999). Developing countries should emulate the intellectual property policies of the CGIAR system, as they evolve, for adoption in their research institutions.

Collaboration appears to be an important way for developing countries to acquire new agricultural technologies, given that the private sector in developed countries controls many of these technologies. Meanwhile in developing countries, the public sector has traditionally maintained a larger research capacity. In agriculture, unlike in industry, products must be adapted to local conditions. Stronger protection for intellectual property may give right holders an incentive to collaborate with local partners to disseminate these technologies. More importantly, for countries with the appropriate education and skill levels, more investment in R & D with strengthened IPR protection may stimulate domestic innovation and create "bargaining chips" for gaining access to other technologies or promoting collaborations.[37] Countries can rely on compulsory licenses on public interest grounds, which TRIPS allows, for essential technologies that are not being licensed widely.

Products that incorporate genetic material and traditional knowledge from developing countries raise equity and biodiversity issues, particularly regarding the need for such countries to share in the benefits of commercialization. These issues apply to industrial biotechnology, especially in the pharmaceutical sector, more than to agriculture, because plants must be adapted to local conditions. For example, the agricultural biotechnology revolution in the United States is based mostly on genetic modification of local plant varieties.[38] However, many analysts contend that farmers should be rewarded for their farm-grown varieties used to create new varieties that are protected by plant breeders' rights. If a future review of TRIPS elaborates the nature and scope of protection for plant varieties, developing countries might want to ensure that right holders disclose the origin of in-bred lines used to produce them. However, negotiators should resolve complex conceptual questions regarding the nature and scope of such farmers' rights, and the way to reward them, in national capitals and specialized forums such as the Food and Agriculture Organization (FAO) and the World Intellectual Property Organization (WIPO).

## Geographical indications under TRIPS

Another important area of IPRs relevant for agriculture is geographical indications. No one enterprise or even group of enterprises owns these distinctive signs. Therefore, unlike trademarks, no entity has the right to authorize or refuse their use. Instead, all undertakings located in a specified geographical area are allowed to use the geographical indication on specified products produced by them. All other entities are prohibited from doing so. Well-known geographical indications can identify agricultural products with special quality or taste characteristics and add considerable value, if protected from unfair competition.

Well-known geographical indications, particularly in agricultural products, mostly identified with the "old world" – synonymous with Europe – but are being used widely in the "new world," including the Americas and Oceania. These factors have made developing an international agreement difficult: even TRIPS has not completely satisfied the *demandeurs* of such protection.

Unlike other IPRs, few countries specifically protect geographical indications in their IPR regimes. As world trade becomes more liberalized, it can be expected that where the desirability of a product with a specific geographic label increases, so too will the opportunity for exploitation by similar or near-exact substitutes which use the geographical indication as a term to describe a unique variety of food product without geographic distinction, or as a process that is no longer associated only with a specific geographic area.

The main *demandeurs* in TRIPS negotiations on geographical indications were the EC and Switzerland. The main opponents were the United States, Australia, Canada, Chile, Argentina, and others who wanted to protect their use of geographical indications of European origin, particularly in the area of wines and spirits. Some countries, including India, attempted to broaden the scope for additional protection from wines and spirits to other beverages such as tea, with little success. Thus developing countries are on both sides of this issue.

TRIPS provides for two levels of protection. First, countries must protect all geographical indications against use that would mislead the public or constitute unfair competition. Most countries meet this obligation if they register geographical indications as collective marks or certification marks, or if they allow parties to institute passing-off actions in civil courts, as is the case in common law countries. Many civil law jurisdictions accord such protection to geographical indications under unfair competition laws. If this had been the only obligation under TRIPS, most developing countries would have been in compliance.

However, article 23 of TRIPS also obliges jurisdictions to protect geographical indications on wines and spirits in absolute terms – without requiring any test of confusion or likelihood of deception. For wines and spirits, article 23.1 prohibits the use of translations of geographical indications or expressions such as "kind," "type," "style," and "imitation" with products originating elsewhere, even when the true origin is clearly indicated. Thus, if Champagne were such a protected geographical indication, the use of a label stating "Champagne-style sparkling wine, Made in the USA" would be prohibited. This higher protection for wines and spirits was available only in the EU prior to TRIPS.[39]

In implementing this provision, several developed and developing countries, including Germany, New Zealand, and Brazil, have opted to provide a higher level of protection to all eligible geographical indications, irrespective of sector, subject to certain registration requirements. Japan provides the higher level of protection through a notification issued under its Law Concerning Liquor Business Associations and Measures for Securing Revenue from Liquor Tax. Other countries have implemented this level of protection for wines and spirits through special laws following bilateral agreements with the EU – such as Australia's Wine and Brandy Corporation Amendment Act of 1993. Yet others, such as the United States and Canada, have declared a large number of geographical indications to be "generic" or "semi-generic."

Reflecting the lack of consensus in this area, article 23.4 calls for negotiating a multilateral system for the notification and registration of geographical indications for wines eligible for protection in participating countries. The article sets no time limit for commencing such negotiations, but it does call for continual review of this section. Under the first such review, in 1996, negotiators decided to begin preparing for talks on the multilateral registration system. This work gained momentum in the TRIPS Council only recently and the EU has made resolving the registration system a top priority in the TRIPS area. On the issue of extension of the higher level of protection for geographical indications to agricultural products, the EU has made linkages to agricultural negotiations, and is seeking absolute protection in all WTO Members for certain products in the run-up to the Cancun Ministerial Meeting.

These efforts have culminated with the EU, Switzerland, and many Central European countries being actively interested in expanding protection to products such as cheese, chocolates, beer, and embroidery in the WTO. Developing countries with an expressed interest in including other products are Morocco, India, Egypt, Mexico, Venezuela, Cuba, Turkey, and Nigeria.[40] The value of agricultural exports from some developing countries of varieties of tea, rice, fruits, vegetables, meat, and other products would be greatly enhanced if a TRIPS Agreement protected specific geographical indications at the same level as wines and spirits.

However, other developed and developing countries will strongly oppose any attempt to expand the scope of protection on geographical indications, and it is not realistic to expect any near-term movement on this matter. Even the major *demandeur* on this issue, the EU, will probably seek to implement existing TRIPS provisions before actively trying to extend them further.

## Immediate prospects for amending TRIPS

Four types of review built into the provisions of the TRIPS Agreement are relevant to the subjects discussed above: the built-in review under article 27.3(b) on biotechnological inventions and plant varieties; the review of implementing legislation of developing countries that commenced in 2000–2002; the general review under article 71 of implementation and possible amendments, which begin in 2000 and is meant to take place every two years thereafter, and the review of article 24.2 relating to the implementation of the provisions on geographical indications. Immediate prospects for any amendments to TRIPS provisions on biotechnological inventions and plant variety or geographical indication protection appear dim.

For years, environmentalists in Europe stalled the EU's proposal for a Directive that would harmonize patent laws for biotechnological inventions among Members. The appellate body of the European Patent Office (EPO)[41] had, until December 1999,[42] virtually blocked patents for plant varieties. Ironically, this issue was also being adjudicated in US courts and it was in January 2000 that the grant of utility patents on plants was definitively upheld.[43] Stiff public opposition to the sale and consumption of GM foods in Europe has further clouded the debate on patents on biotechnological inventions.

The European Directive on patenting biotechnological inventions entered into force in mid-2000, bringing Europe closer to the US level of patent protection, but the Directive allows farmers' privilege for both plant and animal inventions. However, as stated earlier, eight EU members are yet to implement the Directive in their national law. Therefore legal uncertainty on the patenting of biological materials resurfaced, making is difficult for the EU to take a common position on the amendment to TRIPS in this regard.

Non-governmental organizations (NGOs) in developed and developing countries have been actively campaigning against patents for biological materials, voicing concerns regarding morality and ethics as well as biodiversity. Developing countries have actively sought to have the biodiversity set of issues included in any review of TRIPS. The potential for an emerging coalition between powerful lobbies in developed countries and governments in developing countries may explain the caution in the international business community and developed countries over changing these TRIPS provisions, despite the built-in review.[44] This inertia seems paradoxical as *demandeurs* of higher levels of protection for biotechnology would undoubtedly like to fix many ambiguities as soon as possible. These include patents for plants and animals and parts thereof, clarification on whether countries should adhere to UPOV (1991), and possibly tightening exceptions to patent rights. However, some participants may expect to discuss these issues during new agricultural negotiations.

Other *demandeurs* want to see whether the dispute-settlement process will draw on the European biotechnology directive to interpret TRIPS[45] – a shorter and more effective process than the less certain negotiating route. Moreover, Genetic Use Restriction Technologies (GURTs) could prevent proprietary characteristics from showing up in later generations of plants. Lastly, it may be premature to review provisions that most developing countries implemented only in 2000.

Many countries in Latin America, Africa, and South Asia proposed substantive revisions incorporating their concerns regarding biodiversity, equity, and technology transfer. India submitted an amendment to the Committee of Trade and Environment (CTE) as early as 1996 that would oblige patent applicants to disclose the source of origin of genetic resources and any traditional knowledge underlying biotech inventions. Brazil, India and several other developing countries, including those in the Africa Group, have since elaborated on this proposal, adding the concepts of "prior informed consent" and "fair and equitable sharing of benefits." These countries have suggested that TRIPS be made supportive of the provisions of the Convention on Biological Diversity, including those that protect the traditional knowledge, innovations, and practices of indigenous peoples and local communities.

The Doha Development Agenda, adopted in November 2001, explicitly includes a work programme on the relationship between the TRIPS Agreement and the CBD as well as on the protection of traditional knowledge and folklore. Some developed country Members, such as the EU, Norway, and Switzerland, have shown willingness to engage in substantive discussions on the "disclosure proposal." Some developing countries simply want to clarify whether only GM microorganisms should be patentable but there is reluctance on the part of most Members to re-open this and other related definitial issues.

Preliminary US proposals[46] called for limiting the negotiations to certain issues already due to be re-opened in TRIPS. These issues include the elimination of the exclusion for plants and animals and the incorporation of key UPOV provisions protecting plant varieties. The United States has not since pressed for any immediate modification of TRIPS regarding biotechnological inventions.

On the other hand, Japan and the EU have found it necessary to explicitly state in their formal submissions that there should be no attempts to lower standards or reduce protection levels under TRIPS. The dynamics in the WTO TRIPS council have changed somewhat after developing countries successfully negotiated a declaration on the TRIPS Agreement and public health at the Doha Ministerial Meeting in November 2001 which reaffirmed many existing flexibilities in that Agreement and extended the transition period with respect to pharmaceutical products for LDC Members by another ten years, up to 2016.

India has been among the first to join a coalition of countries demanding the extension of protection on geographical indications to other products.[47] This proposal is now part of the implementation agenda in the WTO and has wide support from a range of developed and developing countries.

On the definition relating to biotechnological inventions, the most satisfactory short-run solution for all concerned would leave article 27.3 (b) of TRIPS untouched. In the view of developing countries, TRIPS already allows some flexibility, and national laws and other international forums should protect farmers' rights and traditional knowledge before the WTO negotiates them. This outcome should also be satisfactory for developed countries who, given the ambiguities of the TRIPS text, would like to see how developing countries implement the Agreement. However, proposals to further strengthen TRIPS may reappear during the future biennial TRIPS reviews, undertaken "in the light of any relevant new developments which might warrant modification or amendment."[48]

## Areas for further research

IPRs for agricultural biotech inventions in developing countries pose complex problems relating to development, equity, and biodiversity. In these countries, the debate centers upon unfair exploitation of genetic resources and inequitable sharing of the benefits. However, biotechnology is indisputably one science that can contribute to the solutions of humanity's most difficult problems relating to food, health, and the environment. Developing countries should not lose out on rapid and reasonable access to these technologies in their zeal to preserve biodiversity from real or imagined damage and to control their genetic resources, however laudable these goals.

Some developing countries have already seen the wisdom of moving to the next stage in granting patents for genes, plants, and animals. Many other developing countries may do so once domestic research capability in biotechnology improves. Any collaborative arrangements among publicly funded research bodies, and with the private sector in lead countries, could benefit from joint ownership of intellectual property. Granting IPRs does not necessarily prevent institutions from disseminating these technologies or products to certain groups or to certain areas free of cost or at reasonable prices.

Multilateral developmental institutions can help developing countries develop their research capability by awarding financial and technical assistance for R & D projects, mapping genetic resources, documenting traditional knowledge and local innovations, and providing related training, including legal training. Development institutions could even establish "technology rights banks" to purchase privately developed technologies pertaining to important food crops, to ensure their wide dissemination and adaptation to local conditions at reasonable cost. Such an effort could help resolve the conflict between rewarding private innovations by granting property rights and ensuring their widest possible use in poorer countries. For the private holder of IPRs, the tradeoff between volume and value should make such open licensing attractive.[49]

Much more research is required to fully explore options for reconciling intellectual property rights in biotechnology with the needs of developing countries. In the end, however, private and public sector institutions in the more advanced developing countries should see themselves as generators of intellectual property and competitors to biotech firms in developed countries, rather than as perpetual users. The time frame for achieving this vision will certainly differ from country to country, but the direction should be clear.

More research is also needed to understand the effects of IPRs on developing economies as a whole, and particularly on their agricultural sectors. Country studies can provide a deeper understanding of problems and solutions regarding:

- The proportion of farm-saved seed to purchased seed, and the quantity and price of new varieties, commercialized by the public sector compared with the local and multinational private sector.
- The R & D expenditures of local and multinational private sector seed companies and public sector agricultural research organizations, and their responses to legal and technological protection.
- Cost-benefit analysis for improved/transgenic animal breeds, including the effects of patents and other protections on availability, cost, productivity, returns to farmers, exports, imports, and foreign direct investment in agriculture.
- Plant-breeders' rights and patents filed by and granted to local and multinational firms and public sector organizations in domestic markets and other countries.
- The effects of plant-breeders' rights and patents on the price of protected products, and on national welfare.
- The implications for future research by national and international agricultural research organizations, including the costs of establishing technology rights' banks.

- Evidence of abuse of IPRs and the effect of corrective measures such as compulsory licenses and competition law.
- Evidence of broad patent claims and effects on further innovation.
- The number and nature of public–private collaborations and JVs, and the terms they negotiate regarding technology transfer and the quality of technology transferred.
- Estimates of the costs and benefits and their distribution from improved global protection of geographical indications for agricultural products of interest to developing countries.
- The economic importance of protecting land races and traditional knowledge.

Information is already available on some issues for some developing countries, while data will have to be generated for many others after they establish intellectual property laws. The need to establish a mechanism for financing and generating such data is urgent, so analysis of these questions can rest on firmer ground.

### Notes

This chapter has drawn heavily from chapter 5 of Watal (2001), and has benefited greatly from comments by John Barton, Andre Heitz, and Henry Shands. Views, interpretations, conclusions, and errors are solely attributable to the author and not to any organization or institution with which the author's or has been associated. Comments may be sent to the author at jayashreewatal@hotmail.com.

1. See the WTO definition at http://www.wto.org. The term *ideas* is not used because copyright protects the specific expression of ideas and not ideas themselves.
2. In the case of trademarks, geographical indications, and trade secrets, this may mean an unlimited time, under certain circumstances.
3. Other IPRs such as trademarks and trade secrets are also relevant but do not raise distinctive issues when applied to the agricultural sector.
4. Throughout this chapter, the terms "developed" and "developing" countries are loosely used to define the crucial difference between countries that demanded strengthened IPR protection in the global trading system and those who opposed them. The picture is complicated as national interests differ within particular sectors and IPRs. These complications influenced the positions of different countries during these negotiations.
5. See "Existence, Scope and Form of Generally Internationally Accepted and Applied Standards/Norms for the Protection of Intellectual Property," MTN. GNG/NG11/W/24/Rev 1, dated September 15, 1988, which cites food products excluded by thirty-five countries, food processes excluded by nine, chemical products excluded by twenty-two, fertilizers by two, agricultural machines by one, and methods of agriculture or horticulture by one.
6. See "Existence, Scope and Form of Generally Internationally Accepted and Applied Standards/Norms for the Protection of Intellectual Property," MTN. GNG/NG11/W/24/Rev 1.

7. Traditional land races, developed by farmers in their fields, usually do not meet the criteria of uniformity or stability. This has raised the issue of protecting farmers' rights over such land races, an issue under discussion in the FAO and UN Environment Program. Others suggest substituting "identifiability," which would include land races, for the "distinctness" now required for PBRs. However, this could dilute the certainty that improved varieties will result.

8. A newly patented genetic technology to prevent unauthorized reproduction of seed or the desired characteristic, dubbed Terminator, caused widespread fears that such biological protection could be applied to any plant variety and could eliminate the need for IPR protection altogether. In the wake of debate on this issue, Monsanto, the multinational company that was to buy the company that owns this technology, decided not to do so (*Financial Times*, October 5, 1999, 1). See CBD SBSTTA Report (1999) for more information on this and related technologies.

9. See, for instance, Comanor (1986), CBO (1998).

10. See Watal (1999).

11. Quite often demand for excluding patents of life forms and particularly of genetically modified organisms (GMOs) centers around moral, ethical, or biosafety concerns. This overlooks the fact that patents are not the only signal to R & D in an area, and that patents award only the negative right to exclude and not the positive right to use an invention. Clearly, such concerns have to be addressed outside patent law.

12. *Union Internationale pour la Protection des Obtentions Végétales,* or the International Union for the Protection of New Varieties of Plants.

13. *Diamond, Commissioner of Patents and Trademarks* v. *Chakrabarty*, 447 US 303, 206 U.S.P.Q. 193, excerpted in Adelman *et al.* (1998), 153–6. However, US patents on substances containing living organisms, such as those used in brewing or making cheese, date back to the nineteenth century.

14. See, for example, the results of a detailed survey of agricultural research by private seed companies in India in Pray and Basant (1999).

15. One of the first comprehensive works in this genre is the Max Planck Institute's study by Beier and Schricker (1996). This represents a step forward from past work, which merely reproduced the provisions of TRIPS. Two further analytical monographs are now available: Gervais (1998) and Correa and Yusuf (1998). In addition, there are numerous papers published in law journals on different aspects of the TRIPS Agreement.

16. See UNCTAD (1997, 34), wherein the exclusion is specifically stated to include cells and subcellular components such as genes.

17. See Straus (1998, 109–10). Ossorio (1999) presents legal and ethical arguments on both sides on patenting DNA sequences in the US context.

18. See Straus, (1998, 184–5); and Correa and Yusuf (1998, 195).

19. Correa suggests, in Correa and Yusuf (1998, 205), that such an extension need not be made, as this would nullify the exclusion provided under TRIPS. However, the extension covers only the product as obtained through the patented process not through every process, as in the case of product patents, and it is

unclear whether exceptions to such extension can be defended before a dispute panel.

20. There is a question regarding whether the European provision is compatible with TRIPS. While this is an acceptable exception under plant variety protection law, it is unlikely to be an exception allowed under TRIPS if a WTO Member grants patents for plants, since this exception harms the legitimate interests of right holders and thus violates article 30 of TRIPS.

21. Sigrid Sterckx asks the question: "Why would the mere fact of isolating a substance from its natural environment, or purifying it, by means of technical processes, turn the substance from a 'discovery' to an 'invention'?" See Sterckx (1997, 25). This de-emphasizes the application of the inventive step as a criterion for deciding patent eligibility.

22. See Straus (1998).

23. See Long (1996, 26–40).

24. See "KIPO Revamps Guideline for Biotech Inventions," *World Intellectual Property Reporter*, 12(2), February 1998, 15.

25. This table has been prepared from a reading of the current patent law, supplemented by commentaries in some cases. An attempt has been made to cover major developed country and developing country jurisdictions where TRIPS has been implemented either wholly or partly.

26. However, the issue of patents for multi-cellular organisms is presently before the Federal Court of Appeals in Canada.

27. See position papers on IPRs, available at www.worldseed.org.

28. Reciprocity built into UPOV would have to be replaced by national treatment required under TRIPS, if the definition of IPRs given in TRIPS is determined to cover plant variety protection. This is not clear at this point. Indeed, at least one country (Canada) has, in the WTO's review of legislation, interpreted TRIPS as excluding plant-breeders' rights in its definition of IPRs.

29. See Otten (1994), who argues that it would not be reasonable to interpret the international community as required to adhere to the standards of UPOV (1991) under TRIPS.

30. All developing countries adhere to the (1978) version of UPOV.

31. For instance, this was the case in the patent laws of Malaysia, Singapore, the Philippines, and the Republic of Korea. Others such as China, Indonesia, and Thailand have also allowed such patenting as a part of their TRIPS-implementing legislation.

32. The statistics cited on transgenics in this section are drawn largely from James (1998).

33. See statistics at www.worldseed.org.

34. Falck-Zepeda *et al.* (1998), cited in James (1998).

35. See press release of August 3, 1999, cited at www.rockfound.org/news/072699_rice.html.

36. See Briefing Paper No. 39 at http://www.cgiar.org/isnar/publications/briefing/BP39.htm.

37. This idea finds a place in Barton, Lesser, and Watal (1999).

38. See Watal (2000, ch. 5).
39. See Knaak (1996, 125, 132), where he says that even EU Regulation 1576/89 on geographical indications for spirits, based on a list system, does not extend absolute protection to all spirits in general.
40. See reports on TRIPS Council meetings, available at http://www.wto.org.
41. The EPO has a wider jurisdiction than the EU, as the former includes Switzerland, Norway, and Liechtenstein.
42. The decision upholding plant patents in the EPO is given in case 90001/98, available at www.european-patent-office.org.
43. *Pioneer Hi-Bred International* v. *J.E.M. AG Supply, Inc*, reported in *World Intellectual Property Report*, 14(3), March 15, 2000.
44. See the policy statement of the International Chamber of Commerce on the review of TRIPS article 27.3 at www.iccwbo.org, and also the position paper on the same subject at www.worldseed.org.
45. The impasse in the WTO during the first half of 1999 on the selection of the Director General points to a possible departure from earlier days, when consensus could be built more easily. The Appellate Body of the WTO is widely seen as accommodating to domestic political concerns, particularly of the more powerful members.
46. See WT/GC/W/115 (1998).
47. See "India's Proposals on IPR Issues: Preparations for the 1999 Ministerial Conference," made public in *India and the WTO*, March 1999, available at www.nic.in/commin/wtomar/htm.
48. The United States interprets this to mean a review of implementation in 2000, and a review leading to possible recommendations or modifications of the agreement in 2002. See *Inside US Trade*, August 6, 1999, 12–13.
49. There are parallels in the industrial sector, where right holders voluntarily submit their IPRs to open licensing at reasonable terms, to benefit from seeing their proprietary technologies incorporated into industry-wide standards set by industry associations, governments, or international bodies. Jeffrey Sachs and Michael Kremer suggest that rich governments pledge to purchase at a realistic price unprofitable vaccines, such as for malaria, for mass distribution to encourage the pharmaceutical industry to invest in R & D for such products. This is again an attempt to reconcile incentives for R & D with the public interest. See "A Cure for Indifference," *Financial Times*, May 5, 1999, 14.

### References

Adelman, M. J., R. R. Rader, J. R. Thomas, and H. C. Wegner, 1998. *Cases and Materials on Patent Law, American Case Book Series*, St. Paul, Minnesota: West

Barton, J. H., W. Lesser, and J. Watal, 1999. "Intellectual Property Rights in the Developing World: Implications for Agriculture," paper presented at the World Bank Workshop on Biotechnology, World Bank, June 3–4, Washington, DC

Beier, F.-K. and G. Schricker (eds.), 1996. *From GATT to TRIPs – The Agreement on Trade-Related Aspects of Intellectual Property Rights, IIC Studies*, 18, Max Planck

Institute for Foreign and International Patent, Copyright and Competition Law, Munich: Weinheim

CBD SBSTTA Report, 1999. Convention on Biological Diversity: UNEP/CBD/ SBSTTA/4/9/rev.1, May 17

Comanor, W. S., 1986. "The Political Economy of the Pharmaceutical Industry," *Journal of Economic Literature*, 24, 1178–1217

Congressional Budget Office (CBO), 1998. "How Increased Competetion from Generic Drugs has Affected Prices and Returns in the Pharmaceutical Industry," July

Correa, C. M. and A. A. Yusuf (eds.), 1998. *Intellectual Property and International Trade: The TRIPS Agreement*, Boston: *Kluwer Law International*

Gervais, D., 1998. *The TRIPS Agreement: Drafting History and Analysis*, London: Sweet & Maxwell

Herdt, R. W., 1999. "Enclosing the Global Plant Genetic Commons," lecture at the China Center for Economic Research, May 24, Peking University, mimeo

James, C., 1998, "Global Review of Commercialized Transgenic Crops: 1998," ISAAA Briefs, 8, International Service for the Acquisition of Agri-Biotech Applications, Ithaca

Knaak, R., 1996. "The Protection of Geographical Indications According to the TRIPs Agreement," in F. K. Beier and G. Schricker (eds.), *From GATT to TRIPs – The Agreement on Trade-Related Aspects of Intellectual Property Rights, IIC Studies*, 18, Munich: Weinheim

Long, S., 1996. "Salient Features of the Patents Act 1994 of Singapore," *International Review of Industrial Property and Copyright Law*, 27(1), 26–40

Ossorio, P. N., 2002. "Legal and Ethical Issues in Patenting Human DNA," in J. C. Burley and J. Harris (eds.), *A Companion to Genethics: Philosophy and the Genetic Revolution*, Oxford: Oxford University Press

Otten, A., 1994. "The Uruguay Round TRIPS Agreement: Implications for the Protection of Plant Varieties," presentation at the Workshop on Intellectual Property Rights in Relation to Agricultural and Microbial Biotechnology, March 7, Madras

Pray, C. E. and R. Basant, 1999. "Agricultural Research and Technology Transfer by the Private Sector in India," mimeo

Pray, C. E. and B. Ramaswami, 1999. "Technology, IPRs and Reform Options: Case Study of the Seed Industry with Implications for Other Input Industries," mimeo

Sterckx, S. (ed.), 1997. *Biotechnology, Patents, and Morality*, Aldershot: Ashgate

Straus, J., 1998. "Implications of the TRIPs Agreement in the Field of Patent Law," in F. K. Beier and G. Schricker (eds.), *From GATT to TRIPs – The Agreement on Trade-Related Aspects of Intellectual Property Rights, IIC Studies*, 18, Munich: Weinheim

1998. "Biodiversity and Intellectual Property," in *Yearbook of the International Association for the Protection of Industrial Property*, 37th Congress, Workshops 1–7, May 24–29, Rio de Janeiro

United Nations Conference on Trade and Agricultural Development (UNCTAD), 1997. "The TRIPs Agreement and Developing Countries," UNCTAD/ITE/1, Geneva

United Nations Development Programme (UNDP), 1999, *Human Development Report 1999*, New York: Oxford University Press

Watal, J., 1999. "India," in G. Horstkotte-Wesseler, U. Lele, and W. H. Lesser (eds.), *Intellectual Property Rights in Agriculture: The World Bank's Role in Assisting Borrower and Member Countries*, Washington, DC: World Bank

2001. *Intellectual Property Rights in the World Trade Organization and Developing Countries*, Boston: Kluwer Law International and New Delhi: Oxford University Press

# 20 Genetically modified foods, trade, and developing countries

*Chantal Pohl Nielsen, Karen Thierfelder, and Sherman Robinson*

## Introduction

The current debate about the use of genetic engineering in agricultural production reveals substantial differences in perception of the risks and benefits associated with this new biotechnology. Farmers in North America and a few large developing countries such as Argentina, Mexico, and China are rapidly adopting the new genetically modified (GM) crop varieties as they become available, and citizens in these countries are generally accepting this development. Growing GM crop varieties provides farmers with a range of agronomic benefits, mainly in terms of lower input requirements and hence lower costs to consumers. However, in other parts of the world, especially Western Europe, people are concerned about the environmental impact of widespread cultivation of GM crops and the safety of foods containing genetically modified organisms (GMOs). In response to the strong consumer reaction against GM foods in Western Europe, and to a certain extent also in Japan, separate production systems for GM and non-GM crops are emerging in the maize and soybean sectors.[1] To the extent that GM-critical consumers are willing to pay a price premium for non-GM varieties there may be a viable market for these products alongside the new GM varieties.

Developing countries – regardless of whether they are exporters or importers of agricultural crops – will be affected by changing consumer attitudes toward genetic modification in the developed world. Some developing countries are highly dependent on exporting particular primary agricultural products to GM-critical regions. Depending on the strength of opposition toward GM products in such regions and the costs of segregating production, the developing countries may benefit from segregated agricultural markets, which will have different prices. In principle these countries may choose to grow GM crops for the domestic market and for exports to countries that are indifferent as to GM content, and to grow GM-free products for exports to countries where consumers are willing to pay a premium for this characteristic. Such a market development would be analogous to the niche markets for organic foods. Other developing countries are net importers and can benefit from the widespread adoption of GM technology. Assuming that consumers in those countries are not opposed to GM products, they will benefit from lower world market prices. If changing consumer preferences have an effect on world agricultural markets, this latter outcome may also be affected.

This chapter offers a preliminary quantitative assessment of the impact that consumers' changing attitude toward genetic modification might have on world trade patterns, with emphasis on the developing countries. It extends earlier work described in Nielsen, Robinson, and Thierfelder (2001) and Nielsen, Thierfelder, and Robinson (2001). The analytical framework used is an empirical global general equilibrium model, in which the two primary GM crops, soybeans and maize, are specified as either GM or non-GM. This GM and non-GM split is maintained throughout the entire processing chain: GM livestock and GM food-processing industries use only GM intermediate inputs; likewise non-GM livestock and non-GM food-processing industries use only non-GM intermediate inputs.

The following section provides a concise overview of the current status of GM crops in food production and briefly discusses selected issues related to the segregation of GM and non-GM marketing systems. The following section presents the main features of the multi-regional CGE model and describes the scenarios. The empirical results are then examined, and a final section identifies areas for future research and concludes.

## Genetic engineering in agriculture

### Background

The most recent research and development advances in modern biotechnology have introduced an ever-widening range of genetically engineered products to agriculture.[2] While traditional biotechnology improves the quality and yields of plants and animals through, for example, selective breeding, genetic engineering is a new biotechnology that enables direct manipulation of genetic material (inserting, removing or altering genes).[3] In this way the new technology speeds up the development process, shaving years off R & D programs. Protagonists argue that genetic engineering entails a more controlled transfer of genes because the transfer is limited to a single gene, or just a few selected genes, whereas traditional breeding risks transferring unwanted genes together with the desired ones. Against that advantage, antagonists argue that the side-effects in terms of potentially adverse impacts on the environment and human health are unknown.

Genetic engineering techniques and their applications have developed rapidly since the introduction of the first GM plants in the 1980s. In 1999, GM crops occupied 40 million hectares of land – making up 3.4 percent of the world's total agricultural area and representing a considerable expansion from less than 3 million hectares in 1996.[4] Cultivation of transgenic crops has so far been most widespread in the production of soybeans and maize, accounting for 54 percent and 28 percent of total commercial transgenic crop production in 1999, respectively. Cotton and rapeseed each made up 9 percent of transgenic crop production in 1999, with the remaining GM crops being tobacco, tomato, and potato (James, 1997, 1998, 1999).

To date, genetic engineering in agriculture has mainly been used to modify crops so that they have improved *agronomic* traits such as tolerance to specific chemical herbicides and resistance to pests and diseases. Development of plants with enhanced agronomic traits aims at increasing farmer profitability, typically by reducing input requirements and hence costs. Genetic modification can also be used to improve the final *quality* characteristics of a product for the benefit of the consumer, food-processing industry, or livestock producer. Such traits may include enhanced nutritional content, improved durability, and better processing characteristics.

The United States holds almost three-fourths of the total crop area devoted to GM crops. Other major GM producers are Argentina, Canada, and China. At the national level, the largest shares of genetically engineered crops in 1999 were found in Argentina (approximately 90 percent of the soybean crop), Canada (62 percent of the rapeseed crop), and the United States (55 percent of cotton, 50 percent of soybean, and 33 percent of maize) (James, 1999). The USDA figures for the United States (USDA, 2000b) are similar in magnitude: it is estimated that 40 percent of maize and 60 percent of soybean areas harvested in 1999 were genetically modified.

Continued expansion in the use of transgenic crops will depend in part on the benefits obtained by farmers cultivating transgenic instead of conventional crops relative to the higher cost for transgenic seeds.[5] So far the improvements have been not so much in increased yields per hectare of the crops, but rather by reducing costs of production (OECD, 1999). Empirical data on the economic benefits of transgenic crops are still very limited, however. The effects vary from year to year and depend on a range of factors such as crop type, location, magnitude of pest attacks, disease occurrence, and weed intensity.

In developing countries one of the main reasons for low crop yields is the prevalence of biotic stresses caused by weeds, pests, and diseases. The first generation of improved transgenic crops, into which a single trait such as herbicide tolerance or pesticide resistance has been introduced, can provide protection against several of these. The development of more complex traits such as drought resistance, which is a trait controlled by several genes, is under way and highly relevant for tropical crops that are often growing under harsh weather conditions and on poor-quality soils. There are not many estimates of the potential productivity impact that widespread cultivation of transgenic crops may have in developing countries, but according to James and Krattiger (1999, 1) "[a] World Bank panel has estimated that transgenic technology can increase rice production in Asia by 10 to 25 percent in the next decade."

*GM-potential crops in world production and trade*

The data used in the empirical analysis described below are from version 4 of the Global Trade Analysis Project (GTAP) database, which is estimated for 1995 (McDougall, Elbehri, and Truong, 1998). As discussed above, the main crops that have been genetically modified to date are soybeans and maize. The sectoral aggregation of this database therefore comprises a cereal grains sector (which includes maize but not wheat and rice) and an oilseeds sector (which includes soybeans) to reflect these two GM-potential crops. The livestock, meat and dairy, vegetable oils and fats, and other processed food sectors are also singled out, since they are important demanders of oilseeds and cereal grains as intermediate inputs to production.

The importance of trade in GM-potential crops varies across the regions. Table 20.1 shows that the value of oilseed exports relative to value of total production is significant for the Cairns Group, the United States, and the Rest of South America. Cereal grain exports are also moderately large in value terms for the first two regions, but otherwise most of the production value of these two crops is captured on the domestic markets. For the Cairns Group, the Rest of South America, the United States, and Sub-Saharan Africa (SSA), the impact of genetic engineering would be much larger if these techniques were applicable to the crops contained in the much larger aggregate "other crops" sector. On the import side, the value of oilseed imports into Western Europe amounts to almost 40 percent of the total value of oilseed absorption. High-income Asia is also heavily dependent on imports of oilseeds and to a lesser extent cereal grains.

In general, the trade dependencies for livestock and processed food products are lower than for the agricultural sectors described above. However, trade in these products is still important for developing regions. For example, SSA exports 16 percent of its processed food products and 11 percent of its meat and dairy products. Low-income Asia exports 10 percent of its processed food products and 13 percent of its meat and dairy products. South America exports 11 percent of its processed food products.

Table 20.2 shows data on export market shares. The United States is by far the dominant exporter of both cereal grains and oilseeds and High-income Asia is the main importer of cereal grains and the second largest importer of oilseeds. In terms of processed food trade, countries in the Cairns Group and Western Europe are large exporters of meat and dairy products and other processed

Table 20.1 *Trade dependence: agricultural and food products, 1995*

| | Cairns Group | High-income Asia | Low-income Asia | United States | Rest of South America | Western Europe | SSA | Rest of the World |
|---|---|---|---|---|---|---|---|---|
| *Value of exports in percent of total production value* | | | | | | | | |
| Cereal grains | 9.7 | 0.2 | 0.7 | 16.0 | 0.7 | 3.7 | 4.3 | 0.7 |
| Oilseeds | 15.7 | 4.1 | 2.7 | 28.7 | 32.4 | 1.8 | 5.8 | 11.2 |
| Wheat | 28.5 | 0.0 | 0.3 | 39.2 | 6.6 | 6.8 | 0.1 | 1.5 |
| Other crops | 15.4 | 0.7 | 3.5 | 18.9 | 29.2 | 4.7 | 20.0 | 6.6 |
| Livestock | 7.3 | 0.2 | 1.5 | 2.4 | 2.9 | 1.2 | 2.4 | 1.7 |
| Veg. oils fats | 32.8 | 4.8 | 3.2 | 7.2 | 4.0 | 4.3 | 10.3 | 6.7 |
| Meat and dairy | 10.2 | 0.4 | 12.6 | 4.9 | 1.5 | 3.1 | 11.3 | 1.7 |
| Oth pr. foods | 12.6 | 0.7 | 10.3 | 5.2 | 10.9 | 6.2 | 15.7 | 4.1 |
| *Value of imports in percent of total absorption value* | | | | | | | | |
| Cereal grains | 7.2 | 18.3 | 5.5 | 0.9 | 14.8 | 5.0 | 7.2 | 10.3 |
| Oilseeds | 6.5 | 71.1 | 0.9 | 2.4 | 55.2 | 38.2 | 0.4 | 10.6 |
| Wheat | 11.9 | 17.1 | 10.4 | 3.4 | 51.4 | 3.7 | 15.5 | 17.7 |
| Other crops | 5.5 | 6.5 | 2.3 | 17.8 | 5.7 | 18.3 | 1.4 | 8.0 |
| Livestock | 0.9 | 5.4 | 1.5 | 2.1 | 1.6 | 2.3 | 0.4 | 2.4 |
| Veg. oils fats | 3.1 | 19.0 | 17.2 | 5.0 | 15.3 | 4.1 | 14.5 | 23.1 |
| Meat and dairy | 2.0 | 9.9 | 6.4 | 1.8 | 8.9 | 1.5 | 35.1 | 10.4 |
| Oth pr. foods | 4.6 | 4.2 | 3.5 | 4.6 | 5.9 | 3.6 | 15.8 | 10.3 |

*Source:* Multiregion GMO model database derived from GTAP version 4 data.

food products. High-income Asia is a major importer of other processed food products. Developing countries account for a small share of global trade in GM-potential crops and processed products.

Bilateral export patterns indicate that Low-income Asia and South America depend on both Western Europe and High-income Asia as markets for their exports (see table 20.3 and table 20.4). Sub-Saharan Africa depends primarily on Western Europe, sending 68 percent of its other crops, and 93 percent of its vegetable oils and fats to that region (see table 20.5).

## The global CGE model and scenarios

### The global CGE model with segregated food markets

The modeling framework used in this analysis is a multiregion computable general equilibrium (CGE) model consisting of eight regions, which are

Table 20.2  *Composition of world trade, 1995*

|  | Cairns Group | High-income Asia | Low-income Asia | United States | Rest of South America | Western Europe | SSA | Rest of the World | Total |
|---|---|---|---|---|---|---|---|---|---|
| *Value of exports in percent of value of world trade* | | | | | | | | | |
| Cereal grains | 11.29 | 0.10 | 1.06 | 75.88 | 0.55 | 9.29 | 0.71 | 1.13 | 100 |
| Oilseeds | 26.48 | 0.48 | 6.89 | 49.83 | 4.18 | 2.43 | 2.52 | 7.20 | 100 |
| Wheat | 31.88 | 0.01 | 0.64 | 48.20 | 0.86 | 15.68 | 0.03 | 2.69 | 100 |
| Other crops | 28.05 | 1.83 | 8.78 | 16.29 | 15.01 | 7.47 | 12.44 | 10.13 | 100 |
| Livestock | 40.41 | 1.27 | 8.95 | 17.73 | 4.06 | 15.57 | 1.59 | 10.41 | 100 |
| Veg. oils fats | 55.86 | 2.16 | 3.50 | 11.37 | 1.30 | 18.22 | 1.67 | 5.91 | 100 |
| Meat and dairy | 34.65 | 1.05 | 4.68 | 24.33 | 1.01 | 29.84 | 0.45 | 3.98 | 100 |
| Oth pr. foods | 27.44 | 3.70 | 8.90 | 16.39 | 6.54 | 27.83 | 2.30 | 6.89 | 100 |
| *Value of imports in percent of world trade* | | | | | | | | | |
| Cereal grains | 8.50 | 40.82 | 8.97 | 3.42 | 11.42 | 8.14 | 1.27 | 17.46 | 100 |
| Oilseeds | 9.65 | 29.88 | 2.20 | 2.85 | 9.54 | 38.99 | 0.19 | 6.71 | 100 |
| Wheat | 8.45 | 13.99 | 21.40 | 2.00 | 9.49 | 5.10 | 4.74 | 34.82 | 100 |
| Other crops | 9.48 | 17.94 | 5.88 | 15.43 | 2.20 | 35.47 | 0.75 | 12.86 | 100 |
| Livestock | 4.79 | 28.59 | 9.62 | 14.66 | 2.12 | 25.43 | 0.26 | 14.53 | 100 |
| Veg. oils fats | 4.10 | 10.50 | 25.26 | 7.81 | 5.69 | 17.04 | 2.71 | 26.90 | 100 |
| Meat and dairy | 6.74 | 32.60 | 2.36 | 8.75 | 6.51 | 14.10 | 2.40 | 26.53 | 100 |
| Oth pr. foods | 10.63 | 26.08 | 3.30 | 15.31 | 3.65 | 17.60 | 2.73 | 20.69 | 100 |

*Source for tables 20.2–20.5:* Multiregion GMO model database derived from GTAP version 4 data.

Table 20.3  *Pattern of exports from Low-income Asia, 1995*

|  | Cairns Group | High-income Asia | Low-income Asia | United States | South America | Western Europe | SSA | Rest of the World | Total |
|---|---|---|---|---|---|---|---|---|---|
| Cereal grains | 19.5 | 33.1 | 0.0 | 0.0 | 0.0 | 7.6 | 1.7 | 38.1 | 100 |
| Oilseeds | 31.5 | 34.5 | 0.0 | 1.8 | 0.0 | 17.8 | 0.4 | 13.9 | 100 |
| Wheat | 13.3 | 2.7 | 0.0 | 0.0 | 0.0 | 1.3 | 24.0 | 58.7 | 100 |
| Other crops | 11.2 | 28.4 | 0.0 | 10.7 | 1.2 | 21.5 | 1.4 | 25.7 | 100 |
| Livestock | 4.8 | 53.2 | 0.0 | 6.9 | 0.1 | 30.7 | 0.0 | 4.2 | 100 |
| Veg. oils fats | 17.1 | 44.3 | 0.0 | 6.6 | 0.0 | 22.1 | 0.0 | 9.9 | 100 |
| Meat and dairy | 5.9 | 56.0 | 0.0 | 0.4 | 0.1 | 9.0 | 0.5 | 28.0 | 100 |
| Oth pr. foods | 13.8 | 46.9 | 0.0 | 7.6 | 0.3 | 11.6 | 3.6 | 16.0 | 100 |

Table 20.4 *Pattern of exports from South America, 1995*

|  | Cairns Group | High-income Asia | Low-income Asia | United States | South America | Western Europe | SSA | Rest of the World | Total |
|---|---|---|---|---|---|---|---|---|---|
| Cereal grains | 91.8 | 1.6 | 0.0 | 1.6 | 0.0 | 4.9 | 0.0 | 0.0 | 100 |
| Oilseeds | 49.6 | 10.6 | 0.0 | 13.1 | 0.0 | 25.2 | 0.5 | 1.0 | 100 |
| Wheat | 4.0 | 0.0 | 0.0 | 0.0 | 0.0 | 46.5 | 0.0 | 49.5 | 100 |
| Other crops | 7.3 | 5.7 | 2.9 | 44.3 | 0.0 | 33.4 | 0.1 | 6.4 | 100 |
| Livestock | 4.7 | 1.4 | 0.0 | 89.6 | 0.0 | 4.2 | 0.0 | 0.2 | 100 |
| Veg. oils fats | 43.1 | 1.1 | 0.6 | 26.0 | 0.0 | 24.3 | 0.0 | 5.0 | 100 |
| Meat and dairy | 17.1 | 19.1 | 0.3 | 37.4 | 0.0 | 23.3 | 0.3 | 2.5 | 100 |
| Oth pr. foods | 11.9 | 9.6 | 7.6 | 39.6 | 0.0 | 25.9 | 0.1 | 5.4 | 100 |

Table 20.5 *Pattern of exports from Sub-Saharan Africa, 1995*

|  | Cairns Group | High-income Asia | Low-income Asia | United States | South America | Western Europe | SSA | Rest of the World | Total |
|---|---|---|---|---|---|---|---|---|---|
| Cereal grains | 39.0 | 14.3 | 2.6 | 0.0 | 1.3 | 27.3 | 0.0 | 15.6 | 100 |
| Oilseeds | 8.2 | 29.1 | 0.0 | 4.5 | 0.0 | 31.1 | 0.0 | 27.0 | 100 |
| Wheat | 100.0 | 0.0 | 0.0 | 0.0 | 0.0 | 0.0 | 0.0 | 0.0 | 100 |
| Other crops | 7.7 | 4.0 | 5.9 | 5.5 | 0.2 | 68.0 | 0.0 | 8.7 | 100 |
| Livestock | 3.8 | 9.9 | 6.5 | 2.3 | 0.0 | 25.6 | 0.0 | 51.9 | 100 |
| Veg. oils fats | 3.4 | 0.4 | 0.0 | 0.4 | 0.0 | 92.7 | 0.0 | 3.0 | 100 |
| Meat and dairy | 8.9 | 0.6 | 0.6 | 0.6 | 0.0 | 76.4 | 0.0 | 12.7 | 100 |
| Oth pr. foods | 4.9 | 13.6 | 0.4 | 3.6 | 0.0 | 74.0 | 0.0 | 3.4 | 100 |

interconnected through bilateral trade flows: the Cairns Group, High-income Asia, Low-income Asia, the United States, the Rest of South America, Western Europe, SSA and the Rest of the World. We begin from a standard global model and segment the GM-potential sectors – cereal grains and oilseeds. We also segregate intermediate users of GM and non-GM crops.[6]

In order to operate with segregated GM and non-GM sectors in the extended model, the base data must also reflect this segregation. First of all, the base data are adjusted by splitting the cereal grain and oilseed sectors into GM and non-GM varieties.[7] It is assumed that all regions in the model initially produce some of both GM and non-GM varieties of cereal grains and oilseeds. The assumed shares are adapted from estimates provided in James (1999) and

USDA (2000a).[8] The Cairns Group, Low-income Asia, the United States, and the Rest of South America regions in the model are the extensive GM-adopters.

The structures of production in terms of the composition of intermediate input and factor use in the GM and non-GM varieties are initially assumed to be identical. The destination structures of exports are also initially assumed to be the same, and this determines the resulting import composition by ensuring bilateral trade flow consistency.

The next step is to identify the sectors that use cereal grains and oilseeds as intermediate inputs as GM and non-GM sectors to reflect the concept of identity preservation. The GM/non-GM split is applied to the following sectors: livestock, vegetable oils and fats, meat and dairy, and other processed foods. In the base data the GM/non-GM split for these four sectors is determined residually, based on the share of GM inputs of cereal grains and oilseeds in total (GM plus non-GM) inputs of cereal grains and oilseeds for each sector. These shares are then used to split the data into GM and non-GM varieties of the four processing sectors. At this stage, the described procedure leaves all agricultural and food sectors using some of both GM and non-GM inputs. The input–output table is then adjusted so that GM sectors use only GM inputs and non-GM sectors use only non-GM inputs.[9]

In the model the decision of consumers to place GM versus non-GM varieties in their consumption bundle is endogenized. Final demand for each composite good (i.e. GM plus non-GM) is held fixed as a share of total demand, while introducing an endogenous choice between GM and non-GM varieties. In this way, all the initial expenditure shares remain fixed, but for six of the food product categories (oilseeds, cereal grains, livestock, vegetable oils and fats, meat and dairy, and other processed foods), a choice has been introduced between GM and non-GM varieties. All other expenditure shares remain fixed, as illustrated by figure 20.1.[10]

### GM and non-GM production technologies

As mentioned above, the distinguishing characteristic between the GM and non-GM maize and soybean sectors is the level of productivity. The GM cereal grain and oilseed sectors are assumed to benefit from increased productivity in terms of primary factor use as well as a reduction in chemical use.[11] The available estimates of agronomic and hence economic benefits to producers from cultivating GM crops are very scattered and highly diverse (see, e.g., OECD, 1999 for an overview of available estimates). Nelson *et al.* (1999), for example, suggest that glyphosate-resistant soybeans may generate a total production cost reduction of 5 percent, and their scenarios have GM corn increasing yields by between 1.8 percent and 8.1 percent. For present purposes, the GM-adopting cereal grains and oilseed sectors are assumed to make more productive use of the primary

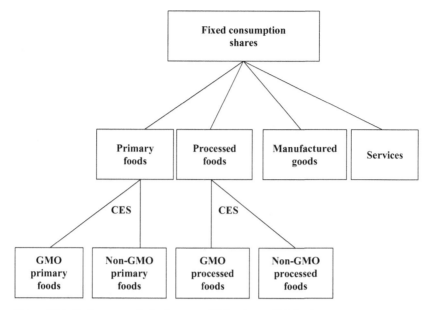

Figure 20.1 Endogenous choice between GM and non-GM foods

factors of production as compared with the non-GM sectors. In other words, the same level of output can be obtained using fewer primary factors of production, or a higher level of output can be obtained using the same level of production factors. In our scenarios, the GM oilseed and GM cereal grain sectors in all regions are assumed to have a 10 percent higher level of factor productivity as compared with their non-GM (conventional) counterparts. Furthermore, there seems to be evidence that cultivating GM varieties substantially reduces the use of chemical pesticides and herbicides (see, e.g., Pray *et al.*, 2000). Hence the use of chemicals in the GM oilseed and GM cereal grain production is reduced by 30 percent to illustrate this cost-saving effect.

## Consumer preferences

There are many ways to formally model changes in consumer preferences. This chapter illustrates how two such ways can be implemented in a CGE model. This is done by shifting and altering the curvature of the indifference curve between GM and non-GM commodities. Each alternative has a different interpretation of what consumers might mean when they say they disapprove of GM foods.

The starting point for the consumer preference experiments is that food products come in two varieties, distinguished by their method of production: GM and non-GM. The model has the representative consumer who views these two

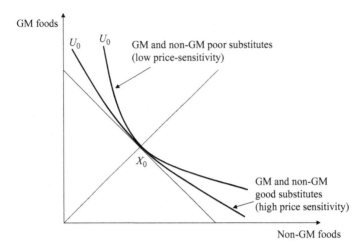

Figure 20.2  Consumer preferences modeled as different degrees of price-sensitivity

varieties as imperfect substitutes. Three different consumer-response scenarios are examined. In the base case consumers in all countries are relatively indifferent with respect to the introduction of GM techniques in food production, and so they find GM and non-GM food varieties highly substitutable.

The next two experiments then attempt to reflect the fact that citizens in Western Europe and High-income Asia dislike the idea of GM foods. In the second experiment this is illustrated by lowering the elasticities of substitution between the GM and non-GM varieties for consumers in these two regions. Consumers in these regions are assumed to be less sensitive to a given change in the ratio of prices between GM and non-GM varieties. They are seen as poor substitutes in consumption in these particular regions. Citizens in all other regions are basically indifferent, and hence the two varieties remain highly substitutable in consumption in those regions.

The change in consumer preferences described in experiments 1 and 2 corresponds to altering the curvature of the indifference curves of consumers in Western Europe and High-income Asia as illustrated in figure 20.2. The two curves in the figure correspond to the same level of utility, $U_0$. When the relative prices of GM and non-GM foods change, consumers in Western Europe and High-income Asia are in the second experiment assumed to be less inclined to shift consumption toward GM varieties as they were in the base case, where substitutability was high. The representative consumer is on the same budget line (same expenditure on the composite food product, i.e. GM plus non-GM, and hence same level of utility).

It is not clear, however, whether reduced price sensitivity is an appropriate interpretation of consumers' critical approach to GM foods. In some rich

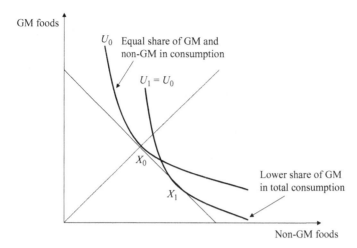

Figure 20.3  Consumer preferences modeled as a structural change

countries, where consumers can indeed afford to be critical of these new techniques in food production, irrespective of how cheap these products may become (relative to non-GM foods), some consumers may simply not want to consume them. In this case, we are changing the ratio of GM to non-GM foods demanded at a given (constant) price ratio, holding utility constant. This is illustrated in figure 20.3, where the representative consumer in Western Europe and High-income Asia is as well off as before but now with a lower share of GM foods in her consumption bundle. The total value of expenditure on each composite food item remains the same. In other words, consumers still spend the same amount on their consumption of food, but the composition is changed in favor of non-GM varieties. In the experiment we reduce the GM share of foods in consumption in Western Europe and High-income Asia to 2 percent.

*Empirical analysis: price and trade*

*Base case experiment*   The increase in factor productivity and the reduced need for chemicals in the GM cereal grain and oilseed sectors causes the cost-driven prices of these crops to decline. The magnitude of this price decline in the different sectors and regions will differ, depending on the shares of primary production factors and chemicals in total production costs. In sectors and regions where these costs make up a large share of total costs, the impact of the productivity shock in terms of lower supply prices will be greater than in sectors and regions where the share is smaller. Intermediate users of GM inputs (the GM livestock and GM processed-food producers) will benefit from lower input prices.

The non-GM product markets will be affected by the productivity gain in the GM sectors in three ways. First, there will be increased competition for primary factors of production and intermediate inputs because GM production will increase. Second, consumers domestically might change their consumption patterns in response to the new relative prices, depending on their initial consumption pattern and substitution possibilities. Third, importers will change their import pattern depending on the relative world prices, their initial absorption structures and the substitution possibilities between suppliers. In all three cases, the initial cost, consumption and import structures on the one hand, and the substitution possibilities between products for input use, final consumption, and imports on the other, will determine the net impact of the productivity experiment. The net effects are theoretically ambiguous and hence must be determined empirically.

Figure 20.4a and figure 20.4b depict, for developing and developed countries, the price wedges that arise between the non-GM and GM varieties in the base case experiment, where GM and non-GM foods are considered to be good substitutes in consumption in all regions. Generally, the relative price of non-GM to GM commodities rises, and the percentage point differences between the prices of non-GM and GM varieties of cereal grains and oilseeds are between 6.3 and 9.4. As described above, the price wedges vary across the regions in part because they have different shares of primary factor and chemical costs in total production costs. Hence the extent to which the individual regions benefit from the productivity increase differs.

The lower GM crop prices in turn result in lower production costs for users of GM inputs, thereby reducing those product prices relative to the non-GM varieties as well. As can be seen in figure 20.4a and figure 20.4b, the price wedges that arise between the GM and non-GM livestock and processed food products are much smaller than the price wedges between GM and non-GM primary crops because the cost reduction concerns only a part of total production costs. Relatively speaking, oilseeds constitute a large share of production costs in vegetable oils and fats production (compared with oilseed and cereal grain use in other food production), and hence the spillover effect is largest.

The lower GM crop prices mean improved international competitiveness for exporters of these crops. Hence, as table 20.6 shows, the United States, a large exporter of cereal grains and oilseeds, increases its exports of GM crops in this base case by 9.0 percent. There are also large percentage increases in exports from the developing countries that are GM-adopters, but the improvement is from a lower base. Owing to the reduced relative competitiveness of non-GM crops, exports of this variety decline somewhat. The large importers of these crops, High-income Asia and Western Europe, increase their imports of the cheaper GM varieties. This is particularly so in the case of oilseeds because

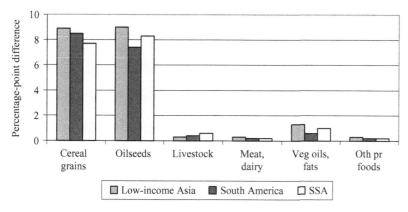

a  Developing countries

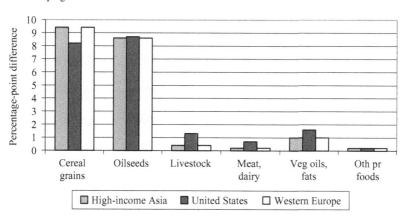

b  Developed countries

Figure 20.4  Base-case experiment: price wedges between non-GM and GM products

these two regions are highly dependent on imported oilseeds from countries that are enthusiastic GM-adopters. Imports of the non-GM varieties decline slightly due to the reduced relative price competitiveness of non-GM products in an environment where consumers find GM and non-GM food varieties to be good substitutes.

*Price-sensitivity experiment*  As can be seen by figure 20.5a and 20.5b, the price wedges resulting from the price-sensitivity experiment are not markedly different from the ones reported in the base case experiment. It may be mentioned, however, that the prices for GM cereal grains and especially oilseeds are slightly lower on the Western European and High-income Asian markets

Table 20.6 *Selected trade results of base experiment, percentage changes*

|  | Low-income Asia | South America | Sub-Saharan Africa | High-income Asia | United States | Western Europe |
|---|---|---|---|---|---|---|
| *Exports* | | | | | | |
| NG cereal grains | −8.0 | −7.2 | −4.1 | −3.4 | −2.4 | −3.0 |
| GM cereal grains | 22.6 | 15.4 | 23.0 | 17.4 | 9.0 | 16.5 |
| NG oilseeds | −9.1 | −5.4 | −3.0 | −3.0 | −2.1 | −2.9 |
| GM oilseeds | 16.7 | 12.8 | 20.7 | 13.5 | 8.6 | 17.6 |
| NG livestock | −0.4 | −0.8 | −0.3 | −0.4 | −0.4 | −0.2 |
| GM livestock | 0.9 | 1.0 | 2.0 | 0.7 | 2.1 | 1.1 |
| NG meat and dairy | −0.4 | −0.5 | −0.1 | −0.3 | −0.5 | −0.2 |
| GM meat and dairy | 0.8 | 1.0 | 1.2 | 0.8 | 1.6 | 1.0 |
| NG veg. oils and fats | −2.2 | −1.4 | −0.6 | −1.9 | −1.3 | −1.0 |
| GM veg. oils and fats | 3.7 | 2.1 | 3.6 | 6.4 | 3.4 | 3.9 |
| NG other pr. food | −0.4 | −0.3 | −0.1 | −0.2 | −0.3 | −0.2 |
| GM other pr. food | 0.9 | 0.8 | 1.1 | 0.8 | 0.7 | 0.8 |
| *Imports* | | | | | | |
| NG cereal grains | −12.3 | −8.7 | −4.8 | −0.2 | −1.8 | −0.3 |
| GM cereal grains | 19.7 | 14.4 | 32.8 | 1.7 | 2.7 | 0.8 |
| NG oilseeds | −14.8 | −8.4 | −5.5 | −3.0 | −4.3 | −1.7 |
| GM oilseeds | 16.4 | 9.0 | 27.4 | 10.7 | 5.1 | 9.2 |
| NG livestock | −0.5 | −0.6 | −0.4 | −0.2 | −0.9 | −0.1 |
| GM livestock | 0.9 | 1.6 | 2.6 | 1.2 | 0.8 | 1.1 |
| NG meat and dairy | −0.4 | −0.5 | −0.2 | −0.3 | −0.9 | −0.1 |
| GM meat and dairy | 0.5 | 1.2 | 1.1 | 1.0 | 1.3 | 0.9 |
| NG veg. oils and fats | −2.6 | −1.4 | −0.8 | −1.7 | −1.3 | −0.9 |
| GM veg. oils and fats | 3.6 | 2.4 | 4.7 | 4.7 | 1.9 | 3.9 |
| NG other pr. food | −0.5 | −0.3 | −0.2 | −0.2 | −0.3 | −0.1 |
| GM other pr. food | 0.7 | 0.7 | 1.1 | 0.8 | 0.6 | 0.8 |

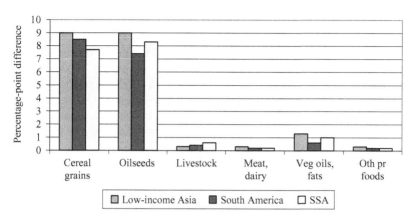

a  Developing countries

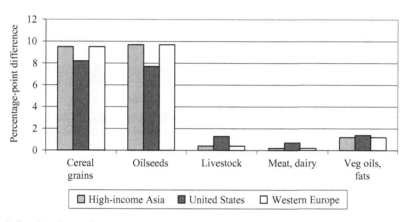

b  Developed countries

Figure 20.5  Price-sensitivity case: price wedges between non-GM and GM products

when consumers are critical (less price-sensitive): larger price reductions are required in order to sell GM-varieties in GMO-critical markets. Conversely, demand for non-GM crops is relatively stronger, and hence the prices of non-GM oilseeds, for example, are higher. Hence we find that the price wedges for especially oilseeds, but also cereal grains, are larger in High-income Asia and Western Europe in the price-sensitivity experiment. In large oilseed-producing markets such as the United States, the price of the non-GM variety falls slightly more and the price of the GM variety falls less as compared with the base case – the price wedges are smaller.

Compared with the base case, the increase in GM oilseed and cereal grain exports from the United States is smaller when consumers in their important export markets are less responsive to the GM/non-GM price difference (table 20.7). Consequently, on the import side, the results show that the declines in imports of the more expensive non-GM oilseeds into High-income Asia and Western Europe are smaller. The decreases in non-GM cereal grain imports have even turned into minor increases. High-income Asia and Western Europe still increase their GM oilseed imports in this price-sensitivity experiment (although at lower rates) because of their high dependence on importing from GM-enthusiastic regions. This result is due to the fact that there is a symmetry in the trade dependence concerning oilseeds: US oilseeds make up a large share of oilseed imports into High-income Asia and Western Europe, and exports for High-income Asia and Western Europe make up a large share of US exports. For this reason changes in consumer preferences in these countries will have an impact on the trading conditions for US producers.

A similar pattern holds for the developing countries that are GM-adopters. Exports of GM varieties do not expand as much, and exports of the non-GM varieties do not decline as much, in the price-sensitivity experiment compared to the base case. In absolute terms, the changes in the United States are larger because that country is a larger exporter on world markets. Also, Low-income Asia and the Rest of South America are less dependent than is the United States on Western Europe and High-income Asia for sales of cereal grains and oilseeds. These developing countries are also dependent on the Cairns Group as a market for exports.

*Structural change experiment*    In this final experiment consumers in Western Europe and High-income Asia simply turn against GM foods. Compared with the previous experiment, final demand in these regions is very insensitive to relative price differences between GM and non-GM food varieties. Consumers in Western Europe and High-income Asia are assumed simply to shift their consumption patterns away from GM varieties in favor of non-GM varieties, regardless of the relative price decline of GM foods. This shift is measured relative to the experiment in which price-sensitivity in these regions is low to begin with. Hence the effects of this structural shock are an addition to the second experiment.

The results show that this rejection is clearly a much more dramatic change compared with reduced price-sensitivity. Critical consumers simply do not want GM-products. The price of GM varieties in the GMO-critical countries declines further because of the almost complete rejection of these products, whereas the price of non-GM foods increases. This leads to substantially larger price wedges in the GM-critical regions as compared with the previous experiments, as is evident from figure 20.6a and figure 20.6b. The larger price wedges between

Table 20.7 *Selected trade results of price-sensitivity experiment,*
*percentage changes*

| | Low-income Asia | South America | Sub-Saharan Africa | High-income Asia | United States | Western Europe |
|---|---|---|---|---|---|---|
| *Exports* | | | | | | |
| NG cereal grains | −7.9 | −7.2 | −4.0 | −3.3 | −2.2 | −2.8 |
| GM cereal grains | 22.3 | 15.2 | 22.2 | 16.5 | 8.5 | 15.0 |
| NG oilseeds | −8.2 | −4.6 | −2.3 | −1.5 | −0.7 | −2.4 |
| GM oilseeds | 14.7 | 10.7 | 18.9 | 8.7 | 4.9 | 13.8 |
| NG livestock | −0.3 | −0.8 | −0.3 | −0.3 | −0.3 | −0.2 |
| GM livestock | 0.6 | 1.0 | 1.8 | 0.4 | 1.9 | 0.8 |
| NG meat and dairy | −0.3 | −0.4 | −0.1 | −0.2 | −0.4 | −0.1 |
| GM meat and dairy | 0.6 | 0.8 | 0.8 | 0.6 | 1.4 | 0.7 |
| NG veg. oils and fats | −1.8 | −1.4 | −0.4 | −1.2 | −1 | −0.7 |
| GM veg. oils and fats | 2.3 | 1.6 | 2.2 | 5.4 | 2.9 | 3.0 |
| NG other pr. food | −0.3 | −0.3 | −0.1 | −0.1 | −0.2 | −0.1 |
| GM other pr. food | 0.7 | 0.7 | 0.7 | 0.6 | 0.5 | 0.6 |
| *Imports* | | | | | | |
| NG cereal grains | −12.3 | −8.7 | −4.8 | 0.1 | −1.8 | 0.1 |
| GM cereal grains | 19.7 | 14.5 | 32.8 | 0.3 | 2.8 | −1.7 |
| NG oilseeds | −14.8 | −8.5 | −5.5 | −0.7 | −4.7 | −0.8 |
| GM oilseeds | 17.3 | 9.5 | 28.4 | 5.1 | 6.6 | 2.8 |
| NG livestock | −0.5 | −0.6 | −0.4 | −0.1 | −0.9 | 0.0 |
| GM livestock | 1.0 | 1.6 | 2.6 | 0.9 | 0.8 | 0.5 |
| NG meat and dairy | −0.4 | −0.5 | −0.1 | −0.1 | −0.8 | 0.0 |
| GM meat and dairy | 0.5 | 1.2 | 0.9 | 0.6 | 1.2 | 0.4 |
| NG veg. oils and fats | −2.4 | −1.3 | −0.6 | −0.4 | −1.2 | −0.5 |
| GM veg. oils and fats | 3.5 | 2.4 | 4.3 | 1.4 | 1.8 | 2.1 |
| NG other pr. food | −0.4 | −0.3 | −0.2 | −0.1 | −0.3 | −0.1 |
| GM other pr. food | 0.7 | 0.7 | 1.0 | 0.4 | 0.6 | 0.4 |

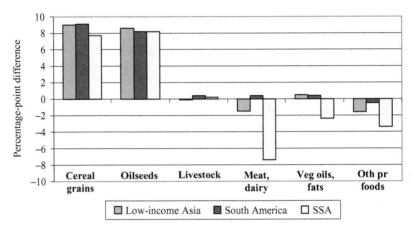

a  Developing countries

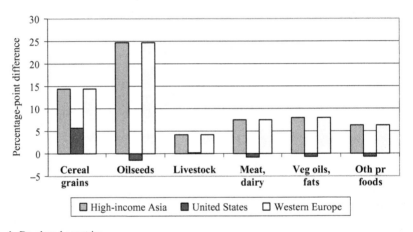

b  Developed countries

Figure 20.6  Structural change case: price wedges between non-GM and GM products

GM and non-GM primary crops follow through the entire food processing chain. The price increase for non-GM foods is, however, moderated by the fact that there are markets for non-GM products in all regions in the model. All countries can produce both varieties and hence supply both GMO-indifferent and GMO-critical consumers.

Total US GM cereal grain and oilseed exports fall by 17 percent and 33 percent, respectively (table 20.8), while exports of the non-GM varieties increase by 8 percent and 15 percent, respectively. These changes are a direct reaction to the relative prices obtainable on their key export markets, namely High-income

Table 20.8 *Selected trade results of structural shift experiment, percentage changes*

| | Low-income Asia | South America | SSA | High-income Asia | United States | Western Europe |
|---|---|---|---|---|---|---|
| *Exports* | | | | | | |
| NG cereal grains | −1.7 | −5.4 | 0.8 | 4.0 | 8.1 | 3.8 |
| GM cereal grains | 4.1 | 7.9 | −2.0 | −42.5 | −17.4 | −30.7 |
| NG oilseeds | 1.6 | 4.3 | 5.1 | 12.9 | 14.5 | 2.2 |
| GM oilseeds | −9.6 | −12.1 | −5.9 | −45.8 | −33.3 | −33.7 |
| NG livestock | 10.6 | 1.4 | 3.4 | 10.6 | 10.5 | 8.1 |
| GM livestock | −43.0 | −5.3 | −19.1 | −36.6 | −36.1 | −40.2 |
| NG meat and dairy | 11.3 | 4.1 | 6.9 | 17.1 | 9.1 | 8.9 |
| GM meat and dairy | −39.5 | −23.6 | −48.4 | −39.3 | −32.7 | −38.4 |
| NG veg. oils and fats | 6.5 | 1.6 | 6.4 | 11.3 | 3.7 | 6.5 |
| GM veg. oils and fats | −35.6 | −14.8 | −50.2 | −29.7 | −10.6 | −29.2 |
| NG other pr. food | 7.5 | 3.6 | 6.9 | 11.1 | 5.4 | 8.0 |
| GM other pr. food | −35.3 | −19.8 | −50.6 | −39.6 | −30.3 | −37.4 |
| *Imports* | | | | | | |
| NG cereal grains | −12.6 | −10.0 | −4.0 | 18.9 | −0.1 | 9.8 |
| GM cereal grains | 21.2 | 19.4 | 34.8 | −70.7 | 0.7 | −59.1 |
| NG oilseeds | −14.1 | −9.9 | −4.2 | 23.5 | −6.0 | 10.3 |
| GM oilseeds | 28.8 | 17.4 | 40.3 | −56.8 | 22.7 | −60.4 |
| NG livestock | −0.1 | −1.9 | 1.8 | 19.5 | 1.4 | 9.4 |
| GM livestock | 5.6 | 10.5 | −1.7 | −56.0 | 1.4 | −58.3 |
| NG meat and dairy | 2.2 | −0.8 | 6.2 | 23.3 | 1.0 | 8.6 |
| GM meat and dairy | 2.3 | 5.0 | −28.7 | −68.6 | 2.8 | −62.8 |
| NG veg. oils and fats | 0.8 | 0.4 | 5.4 | 24.8 | 2.6 | 9.5 |
| GM veg. oils and fats | 1.5 | 2.3 | −11.2 | −72.4 | −1.7 | −59.5 |
| NG other pr. food | 3.4 | 0.9 | 3.9 | 15.4 | 2.6 | 8.5 |
| GM other pr. food | −1.0 | 4.2 | −10.5 | −66.8 | 0.2 | −60.2 |

Asia and Western Europe. The prices of GM cereal grains and oilseeds on these markets plummet and the prices of non-GM varieties increase slightly.

For Low-income Asia and South America, exports of GM oilseeds decline, similar to the export response in the United States. However, exports of GM cereal grains still expand. These countries are less dependent on GM-critical regions for cereal grains than is the United States. For example, South America sends 92 percent of its cereal grain exports to the Cairns Group.

Changing consumer attitudes in Western Europe and High-income Asia also affect SSA's trade patterns. While that region is not a GM-adopter, it does have strong trade ties to Western Europe. Its imports of GM-processed products declines, despite the fact that it is not a GM-critical region. Instead, its major import source changes its production patterns and therefore the structure of its exports.

Table 20.8 shows that imports of GM cereal grain and oilseeds into Western Europe and High-income Asia decline substantially (between –57 percent and –71 percent). Conversely, imports of non-GM crops increase substantially, at slightly higher prices. The sourcing of these non-GM crop imports is spread across all regions, because in the model all regions are assumed to be able to produce both varieties and to be able to credibly verify this characteristic to importers. Clearly, this is a simplification of reality, and one can easily imagine that for some regions, living up to the principles of identity-preservation and verification would be very costly, thereby putting them at a cost disadvantage. Such effects are not captured in this model. The increases in non-GM cereal grain and oilseed imports are supplemented by increases in own-production in both High-income Asia and Western Europe.[12]

*Empirical analysis: production*

Being a major exporter of both crops, the increased demand for GM cereal grains and oilseeds in the base case experiment filters through to an increase in production of these crops in the United States. The effect is dampened, however, by the fact that its major destination regions (High-income Asia and Western Europe) have much larger non-GM sectors (relative to their GM sectors), which are required to use only non-GM inputs.[13] This also means, for example, that the production of non-GM crops does not fall as markedly in the United States as it does in, e.g., Low-income Asia, a region that is not very heavily engaged in international trade in these particular crops. Figure 20.7 compares the impact on production in the United States of the different and changing assumptions made about consumer preferences in Western Europe and High-income Asia. Since exports make up a relatively large share of the total value of production in these sectors, particularly for oilseeds, we see that there is a marked effect on the composition of production. Production of GM crop varieties increases

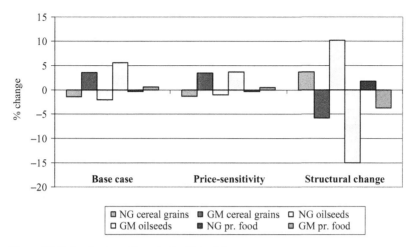

Figure 20.7  Production effects in the United States

in the first two experiments, while production of non-GM varieties declines somewhat. The impact is slightly less when consumers in High-income Asia and Western Europe are less sensitive to the GM/non-GM price difference.

In the structural shift experiment, however, the production of GM oilseeds in the United States declines by 15 percent in spite of the factor productivity gain and the reduced chemical requirements. This is because the United States is so highly dependent on exporting especially oilseeds to the GM-critical markets and because a structural consumer preference change has much more of an impact on this region's trading opportunities compared with the reduced price-sensitivity experiment. The production of non-GM oilseeds, on the other hand, increases by 10 percent – another direct reflection of the fact that the importance of the GMO-critical export markets is relatively less dependent on exports of these particular crops.

An interesting question is whether these changing preferences in Western Europe and High-income Asia can open opportunities for developing countries to export non-GM varieties of cereal grains and oilseeds to these regions. SSA has some production of oilseeds, for example, and although exports of these crops do not account for a significant share of total production value at present, they might if niche markets for non-GM crops develop in Western Europe. Similarly, Low-income Asian countries might look into expanding their production of, e.g., non-GM oilseeds if nearby niche markets in High-income Asian countries developed (figure 20.8).

Although the differences are very small, comparing the trade and production results of the three experiments indicates that this might be a path to follow if the price premia obtainable for non-GM varieties are large enough to outweigh

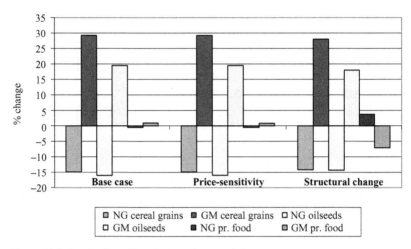

Figure 20.8 Production effects in Low-income Asia

the relative decline in productivity and any identity-preservation and labeling costs. But even more significant in value terms for these countries are exports of processed foods, i.e. vegetable oils and fats, meat and dairy products, and other processed foods. Factors such as existing trade patterns, proximity of markets, historical ties, etc. will determine whether or not producers will choose to forgo productivity increases and lower costs in GM production in order to retain access to their traditional export markets by selling non-GM products. For a region like SSA, with strong ties to Western Europe, changing consumer attitudes toward GM foods are expected to be an important determinant of future decisions regarding genetic engineering in food production. As seen in figure 20.9, production of GM processed-food products expands in the first two experiments but declines in the structural shift case. There, Western Europe's increase in demand for non-GM processed foods changes the pattern of production. Results for South America are shown in figure 20.10.

*Empirical analysis: absorption*

In this modeling framework, where we are operating with a representative consumer, we are implicitly aggregating over two consumer types – those who are indifferent about GM products and those who are concerned about potential hazards of consuming GM products. We have considered two changes in preferences concerning GM-inclusive foods. First, attitudes harden. The size of the two groups does not change, but those who are concerned about GM products become more price-sensitive. As described above, this changes the curvature of the indifference curve, as shown in figure 20.2 (p. 438). Second, we have considered the effects of a structural preference shift – more people

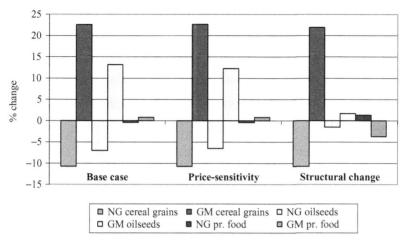

Figure 20.9  Production effects in South America

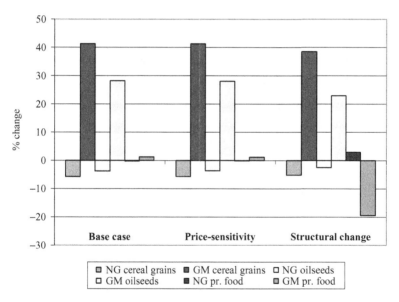

Figure 20.10  Production effects in Sub-Saharan Africa

believe that there are health hazards from consuming GM foods and choose to consume less, and the share of consumption of GM foods drops, regardless of relative price changes. In essence, the group of GM-sensitive consumers expands, which causes the indifference curve to shift, as depicted in figure 20.3 (p. 439).

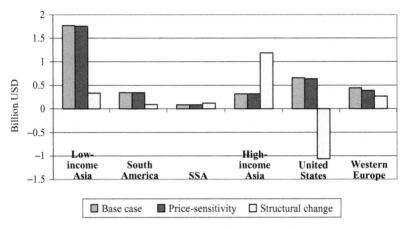

Figure 20.11  Changes in total absorption

As discussed above, the level of utility is assumed to stay the same when the indifference curve shifts. The representative consumer is on the same budget line with a different combination of GM and non-GM foods, and we do not assume that the consumer obtains additional utility from her decision to increase the share of non-GM products she consumes. With this assumption, real absorption is an appropriate welfare measure. It indicates the change in the total amount of goods and services consumed following a change in preferences. The results of the experiments show that global absorption increases by $7.4 billion in the base case, where consumers are assumed to find GM and non-GM foods to be good substitutes. Increasing the price-sensitivity of GM-critical consumers in High-income Asia and Western Europe lowers this gain in total absorption marginally to $7.2 billion. As the previous results have shown, the structural shift experiment represents a much more dramatic change in preferences, and hence we find that the global absorption gain is only $0.02 billion in that experiment.

The absorption results are reported for selected regions in figure 20.11 for the three experiments. The changes are reported in billion dollars and it should be noted that the percentage changes are very small. It is clear from this figure that Cairns Group, Low-income Asia, and the United States are the main beneficiaries of the productivity increase given that these are the regions assumed to be intense adopters of the GM crop varieties. All other regions also experience an increase in total absorption, albeit at a lower absolute level. Reducing the price-sensitivity of consumers in High-income Asia and Western Europe reduces the increase in global absorption only marginally and does not change the distribution of the gains across regions. Most importantly, all regions still gain in terms of aggregate absorption from the productivity increase and hence lower product prices in spite of the increased aversion towards GM foods in High-income Asia and Western Europe.

Interpreting consumer preference changes as a structural shift, however, alters the absorption results dramatically. Because our model has completely segregated GM and non-GM production systems, restricting input use to either GM or non-GM varieties, the structural preference shift has a strong effect on the demand for non-GM intermediates, and not all regions experience increases in total absorption in this experiment. Despite the productivity gain in the large GM crop sectors in the United States, these results reveal that aggregate absorption declines in these regions when consumers in important export markets turn against their main product and there is little diversion to other markets. Total absorption declines by $0.9 billion in the United States. Although this decline amounts to a percentage change of only 0.007 percent, it illustrates how different types of preference changes will have very different impacts on total absorption results.

It is particularly interesting that the increases in total absorption in *all* the developing country regions are *not* affected when GM-critical regions become more price-sensitive (comparing the base case to the price-sensitivity experiment). Low-income Asia is the major beneficiary in absolute terms, being both a net importer of the two crops and basically indifferent as to GM content. Hence the region benefits from substantially lower import prices on GM crops. Despite the high dependence on the GM-critical regions for its exports of oilseeds, the increase in total absorption in South America is unaffected by the preference changes there because bilateral trade flows adjust well – trade diversion offsets the effects of demand shifts in the GM-critical regions. In SSA the gains are small in absolute terms, mainly due to the small share of these particular crops in production and trade, but they are also unaffected by preference changes in GM-critical regions.

When consumers in Western Europe and High-income Asia reject GM varieties, the developing countries that are GM-adopters (Low-income Asia and South America) have less of an absorption gain. Interestingly, SSA has the biggest absorption gain in the structural shift scenario. In this case, the effective improvement in its international terms of trade leads to increased imports and a gain in absorption (and an appreciation of its real exchange rate).

## Conclusions

The very different perceptions – particularly in North America and Western Europe – concerning the benefits and risks associated with the cultivation and consumption of GM foods are already leading to the segregation of soybean and maize markets and production systems into GM and non-GM lines. By using a global CGE model, this analysis has shown that such a segregation of markets may have substantial impacts on current trade patterns. The model distinguishes between GM and non-GM varieties in the oilseed and cereal grains sectors, as well as in the processing sectors that use these crops as inputs. GM crop production is assumed to have higher factor productivity as compared with conventional production methods. It is also assumed that the non-GM processing sectors can verify that they use only non-GM intermediate inputs.

The effects of a factor productivity increase in the GM sectors are then investigated in an environment where there are increasingly strong preferences *against* GM crops in Western Europe and High-income Asia. The change in preferences is modeled two ways. First, as a change in substitution elasticity – consumers perceive GM and non-GM crops to be poor substitutes in these regions. Alternatively, as a reduction in the share of the GM variety consumed – consumers reject GM varieties, regardless of the price differential.

The empirical results indicate that trade patterns adjust to changes in consumer attitudes when markets are segregated. Non-GM exports are diverted to the GM-critical regions, while GM exports are diverted to the indifferent regions. Historical trade patterns matter as well. We find that when consumers in Western Europe reject GM varieties, they produce and export more non-GM varieties. This affects the non-GM composition of SSA's imports because that region depends strongly on Western Europe.

An important question for developing countries is whether genetic engineering in agriculture is an opportunity or a dilemma. The results of this empirical analysis offer some insights into the trade and welfare effects of adopting the new technology in a market with GM-critical regions. All of these results, it should be noted, are based on the heroic (and controversial) assumption that any environmental risks and hence externality costs associated with GM crops are manageable. To the extent that adopting GM crops provides farmers with productivity benefits that outweigh the additional costs of GM seeds, the results seem to suggest that there are large welfare gains to be made for developing countries that adopt such a technology. Furthermore, changing GM preferences in Western Europe and High-income Asia do not affect these gains because markets adjust, and trade flows of GM and non-GM products are re-directed according to preferences in the different markets.

The underlying assumption of this finding is, however, that production and marketing systems are indeed capable of dealing with the separation of GM and non-GM crop-handling systems – certainly a challenge for countries in the developing world. The difficulties and costs involved in separating GM and non-GM marketing and handling systems present the developing countries with a dilemma: they must decide whether or not to use their limited resources on developing such a capacity. For SSA, for example, current exports of GM-potential crops do not constitute a large share of total production, and so there may well be benefits to adopting GM crop varieties since consumers in the domestic market are indifferent, and this is the major market to be served.

On the other hand, in order to ensure future export markets, it may well make sense to establish identity preservation systems so that guaranteed non-GM products can serve GM-critical consumers in Western Europe – Africa's major export market for agricultural products. Indeed, a market for non-GM processed foods for exports can coexist with the production of GM processed foods for domestic consumption, allowing producers to exploit a niche market in GM-critical regions. Furthermore, GM technology may expand to other crops that are a large share of total production. The technology is evolving rapidly, and agricultural producers and policy-makers in SSA and other developing countries must closely follow the development of the international GM debate.

### Notes

1. Another response to the growing concerns about GM products has been the agreement on the Cartagena Biosafety Protocol, which was concluded in January 2000, but is yet to be ratified. See Nielsen and Anderson (2000) for a discussion of the relationship between this Protocol and the WTO rules, and an empirical analysis of the world trade and welfare effects of a Western European ban on GM imports.
2. The first part of this section draws on Nielsen and Anderson (2000).
3. Definitions of genetic engineering vary across countries and regulatory agencies. For the purpose of this chapter a broad definition is used, in which a GMO is one that has been modified through the use of modern biotechnology, such as recombinant DNA techniques. In the following, the terms "genetically engineered," "genetically modified," and "transgenic" will be used as synonyms.
4. Calculations are based on the FAOSTAT statistical database, accessible at www.fao.org.
5. As long as private companies uphold patents on their transgenic seeds they will be able to extract monopoly rents through price premiums or technology fees.
6. The basic model is described in Lewis, Robinson, and Thierfelder (1999) and Nielsen, Thierfelder, and Robinson (2001).
7. As will be discussed below, the distinguishing characteristic between these two varieties is the level of productivity. Furthermore, there may be environmental risks and hence externality costs associated with GM crops, they are impossible to estimate at this time and this chapter makes no attempt to incorporate such effects in the empirical analysis.
8. See Nielsen, Thierfelder, and Robinson (2001) for the breakdown of GM shares by country and commodity.
9. Intermediate use in the GM sectors is restricted to only GM inputs and intermediate use in the non-GM sectors is restricted to only non-GM inputs. This is an important difference compared to the authors' earlier work (Nielsen, Robinson, and Thierfelder, 2001) where intermediate users of oilseeds and cereal grains had a choice between GM and non-GM varieties.

10. See Nielsen, Thierfelder, and Robinson (2001) for details on how to calibrate the constant elasticity of substitution (CES) aggregate of the GM and non-GM varieties.

11. Note that this is an asymmetric shock and that it will therefore have different effects in different regions because of different cost structures: the shares of primary factor costs and chemical costs in total production costs are different.

12. Note that Western Europe might be restricted by the Blair House agreement in terms of increasing acreage for oilseed production and so the reported production increase may not be allowed.

13. Comparing these production effects with the results of our previous analysis, which did not have the identity-preservation requirement in place (Nielsen, Robinson and Thierfelder, 2000), we see that the effects reported here are substantially smaller. This is precisely because the identity-preservation requirement introduces much stronger restrictions on intermediate input choice for livestock producers and food processors. In our previous analysis intermediate users had a free choice between GM and non-GM varieties and could therefore benefit fully from the lower GM prices. In this model, however, intermediate users are required to use only GM or non-GM inputs.

## References

James, C., 1997. "Global Status of Transgenic Crops in 1997," ISAAA Briefs, 5, International Service for the Acquisition of Agri-Biotech Applications, Ithaca

    1998. "Global Review of Commercialized Transgenic Crops: 1998," ISAAA Briefs, 8, International Service for the Acquisition of Agri-Biotech Applications, Ithaca

    1999. "Global Status of Commercialized Transgenic Crops: 1999," ISAAA Briefs, 12: Preview, International Service for the Acquisition of Agri-Biotech Applications, Ithaca

James, C. and A. Krattiger, 1999. "The Role of the Private Sector," Brief 4 of 10 in *A 2020 Vision for Food, Agriculture and the Environment. Biotechnology for Developing/Country Agriculture: Problems and Opportunities*, ed. G. J. Persley, Washington, DC: International Food Policy Research Institute

Lewis, J. D., S. Robinson, and K. Thierfelder, 1999. "After the Negotiations: Assessing the Impact of Free Trade Agreements in Southern Africa," TMD Discussion Paper, 46, International Food Policy Research Institute, Washington, DC, September

McDougall, R. A., A. Elbehri, and T. P. Truong (eds.), 1998. "Global Trade, Assistance, and Protection: The GTAP 4 Data Base," Center for Global Trade Analysis, Purdue University

Nelson, G. C., T. Josling, D. Bullock, L. Unnevehr, M. Rosegrant, and L. Hill, 1999, "The Economics and Politics of Genetically Modified Organisms: Implications for WTO 2000," Bulletin 809, College of Agricultural, Consumer and Environmental Sciences, University of Illinois at Urbana-Champaign, November

Nielsen, C. P. and K. Anderson, 2000. "GMOs, Trade Policy, and Welfare in Rich and Poor Countries," paper prepared for a World Bank Workshop on Standards, Regulation and Trade, April 27, Washington, DC, adelaide.edu.au

Nielsen, C. P., S. Robinson, and K. Thierfelder, 2001. "Genetic Engineering and Trade: Panacea or Dilemma for Developing Countries," *World Development*, 29(8), 1307–24

Nielsen, C. P., K. Thierfelder, and S. Robinson, 2001. "Consumer Attitudes Towards Genetically Modified Foods, The Modeling of Preference Changes," SJFI Working Paper, 1/2001, Danish Institute of Agricultural and Fisheries Economics, Copengagen

Organization for Economic Co-Operation and Development (OECD), 1999. "Modern Biotechnology and Agricultural Markets: A Discussion of Selected Issues and the Impact on Supply and Markets," Directorate for Food, Agriculture and Fisheries. Committee for Agriculture, AGR/CA/APM/CFS/MD(2000)2, Paris

Pray, C. E., D. Ma, J. Huang, and F. Qiao, 2000. "Impact of Bt Cotton in China," paper presented at a seminar at the IFPRI (International Food Policy Research Institute), May

US Department of Agriculture (USDA), 2000a. "Biotech Corn and Soybeans: Changing Markets and the Government's Role," 12 April, ers.usda.gov

    2000b. "Biotechnology: US Grain Handlers Look Ahead," *Agricultural Outlook*, April, Economic Research Service/USDA, Washington, DC

# 21 Multifunctionality and optimal environmental policies for agriculture in an open economy

*Jeffrey M. Peterson, Richard N. Boisvert, and Harry de Gorter*

## Introduction

Though agriculture has long been recognized as a polluter, it has also more recently been noted as a provider of non-market benefits. Examples of these public goods that are by-products of agriculture include landscape amenities, a habitat for wildlife, and the preservation of agrarian cultural heritage (OECD 1997a; 1997b; Bohman *et al.*, 1999). Though many of these benefits are difficult to define and measure, non-market valuation studies have found substantial non-market values for farmland in different regions around the world (Beasley, Workman, and Williams, 1986; Hackl and Pruckner, 1997; López, Shah and Altobello, 1994). The notion of agriculture providing a set of non-market goods and bads as joint products with market goods has given rise to the term "multifunctionality" (Lindland, 1998; Nersten and Prestegard, 1998; Runge, 1998). Conceptually, a "multifunctional" agriculture means that the agricultural production process is a multioutput technology, where some outputs are privately traded commodities and others are public goods. This case differs from standard environmental models where some activity in the economy generates a single externality.

The realization that agriculture is multifunctional has important implications for policy-making at both the domestic and international levels. In the domestic sphere, policies aimed at the various externalities from agriculture are typically legislated and administered independently. Likewise, the economics literature almost always examines externalities in isolation, either implicitly or explicitly assuming that other (potentially related) externalities are fixed or unimportant. If agriculture is multifunctional, the interrelationships among its externalities imply that "compartmentalized" government programs may work at cross-purposes (Poe, 1997). For example, many governments use price supports in combination with acreage subsidies in an effort to internalize the positive externalities from agricultural production, but it has been

458

shown that the level of these policies must affect the amount of agricultural pollution generated and vice versa (Ollikainen, 1999). Jointness among externalities implies that policies to correct them must also be selected jointly, but the proper design of such a set of agro-environmental policies remains largely unexplored.

In the international arena, as evidenced by the controversy surrounding the agenda for the new round of WTO negotiations, the complexity of agricultural externalities will also make new trade agreements difficult to achieve (Anderson and Hoekman, 1999; Runge, 1999; Blandford and Fulponi, 1999). Many countries have made known their fear that, without adequate safeguards, free trade will jeopardize the public good functions of agriculture. Trading partners who seek access to those markets, on the other hand, question whether so-called "environmental safeguards" may be trade-distorting protectionism in disguise (ABARE, 1999; Bohman et al., 1999).

High-cost agricultural-producing countries with high levels of support, notably the EU, Japan, Norway, South Korea, and Switzerland, insist that subsidies on farm commodities are the most efficient way to secure public goods that are by-products of farm output. National food security and an authentic agricultural landscape, for example, cannot be produced separately from farm commodities (WTO, 1999a, 1999b, 1999c; Norwegian Royal Ministry of Agriculture, 1998). Further, reduced subsidies and freer trade would generate additional production in low-income and low-support countries; high-support countries have argued that such an expansion in those countries could damage the environment (because of deforestation and the lack of environmental regulations).

Lower-cost producers would stand to gain considerably from reduced support in protected countries. These governments have argued that price supports as a way of obtaining agricultural public goods are neither optimal nor desirable. Such policies distort market incentives toward the intense use of polluting inputs, and there exist less-distorting policy instruments to achieve the same goal (WTO, 1998; Bohman et al., 1999). Moreover, they argue, the weight of empirical evidence suggests that freer trade would improve environmental quality in both developed and developing nations, although even more could be gained if free trade were combined with environmental protection policies (e.g. Anderson, 1992a; Whalley, 1999). Yet the most fundamental concern is that, however high-minded the purpose of public good-providing policies may be, those policies may be manipulated to distort terms of trade.

For the case of a single externality, the relationship between environmental policy and trade has been a subject of much study (Krutilla, 1991; Anderson, 1992b; Beghin et al., 1994; Copeland, 1994; Schamel and de Gorter, 1997). This literature has revealed the potential for using an environmental policy as a tool to distort trade: A large importer, for example, may select lax environmental regulations to encourage domestic production, reduce the demand for imports, and lower prices to domestic consumers. However, the relationship between trade and a set of joint policies aimed at multiple externalities (i.e. the multifunctional case) has not yet been studied.

This chapter develops a general equilibrium framework to determine the optimal set of internalizing policies under multifunctionality and relates these policies to trade. The model is based on an aggregate multioutput technology, where two basic factors (land and non-land inputs) produce two private commodities (agricultural and industrial goods) and two public goods (the positive and negative externalities from agriculture). Because the focus is on the agricultural sector, the model abstracts from marginal changes in industrial externalities. Production in the economy is cast in a modified Hecksher–Ohlin framework where agriculture generates two externalities.

The analysis identifies the interdependence among optimal environmental policies. In principle, a welfare maximum can be achieved through a combination of a subsidy on agricultural land and a tax on agricultural non-land inputs, but the levels of these policies must be selected jointly. In particular, if the pollution function for each acre is convex, a marginal acre of land reduces total pollution, and the optimal subsidy on an acre of farmland therefore exceeds the amenity value of that acre. Based on a set of stylized policy simulations of the aggregate US agricultural sector, this interaction between policies appears to be empirically important; the estimated optimal subsidy for farmland is about 50 percent larger than its amenity value.

The relationship between these joint environmental policies and trade is also characterized. Small economies have no incentive to distort environmental policies away from their internalizing levels, but large economies will manipulate domestic policies in order to exploit terms of trade. Consistent with observation, large importers such as Japan can improve domestic welfare by oversubsidizing public goods, while large exporters such as the United States prefer strict regulations to limit pollution. Empirical simulations of US agriculture suggest that environmental policies can be effective at distorting trade. If these policies were used to exploit terms of trade, the United States alone could increase world agricultural prices by an estimated 9 percent over a base case of no environmental policy.

The remainder of the chapter is organized as follows. A theoretical section first describes the model economy and then derives optimal environmental policies for a closed economy, a small open economy, and a large open economy. To illustrate the theoretical relationships and explore their potential quantitative impacts, the next section simulates an empirical version of the model for the US agricultural sector. The conclusions drawn from our findings and their implications for policy are examined in the final section.

## The model economy

Let $x$ and $y$ represent agricultural and non-agricultural goods, respectively. These two commodities can be produced from two basic factors, land $L$ and non-land inputs $Z$. In addition, the agricultural production process generates non-market amenities $a$ and emissions of pollution $e$. The technology set for aggregate production in this economy is:

$$T = \{(x, y, a, e, L, Z) \in \Re^6_+ : (L, Z) \text{ can produce } (x, y, a, e)\}$$

If there are no direct links between the agricultural and non-agricultural production processes, then a tradeoff between the output of the two commodities occurs only because inputs must be diverted away from one industry in order to increase production in the other. Assume the two technologies can be represented by the production functions:

$$F_x(L_x, Z_x) \quad \text{and} \quad F_y(L_y, Z_y)$$

where $L_i$ and $Z_i$ are the amount of land and other inputs allocated to the production of good $i$, respectively.

Let $L$ and $Z$ represent the endowment of land and non-land inputs, respectively, and assume the entire endowment of each factor is homogeneous in quality. Presuming non-wasteful allocations, production is subject to the feasibility conditions:

$$L_x + L_y = L$$
$$Z_x + Z_y = Z$$

Each $F_i(\cdot)$ is strictly increasing, strictly concave, and exhibits constant returns to scale. By homogeneity, $F_i(L_i, Z_i) = L_i F_i(1, Z_i/L_i) \equiv L_i f_i(z_i)$, where $z_i$ represents the $Z_i/L_i$ ratio (per-acre input) and $f_i(\cdot)$ is the per-acre production function.

Without loss of generality, aggregate emissions of agricultural pollution can be expressed as a function of the agricultural inputs $L_x$ and $Z_x$: $e = G(L_x, Z_x)$.[1] If $L_x$ and $Z_x$ both double (thus keeping $z_x$ constant), total emissions must also double when land is of undifferentiated quality. Hence, $G(\cdot)$ is homogeneous of degree one. By the same argument as above, emissions may be equivalently expressed as $e = L_x g(z_x)$, where $g(\cdot)$ represents the amount of pollution generated per acre. Assume that $g$ is strictly increasing, strictly convex, and that $g(0) = 0$. Under these conditions, pollution falls with marginal increases in the agricultural land base, i.e., $\partial e/\partial L_x < 0$.[2]

The non-market amenities from agriculture, such as open space and a habitat for wildlife, depend only on the quantity of agricultural land. The extent to which pollution detracts from any of these amenities can be captured in consumers' preferences with respect to $e$. As above, homogeneous land implies that the amenity function is homogeneous of degree one, or that each acre of land provides a fixed amount of amenity services. If we choose to measure these services so that each acre of farmland provides one unit of amenities, then $a = L_x$.[3]

Consumers' preferences are represented by the aggregate utility function $u(x, y, a, e)$, where $u(\cdot)$ is strictly quasi-concave, strictly increasing in $x$, $y$, and $a$, and strictly decreasing in $e$. National income $I$ is the total payments received on the factors used in the two industries. Consumers use income to purchase $x$ and $y$, but cannot influence the levels of $a$ and $e$. Taking $y$ to be the numéraire and letting $p$ be the price of $x$, indirect utility is:

$$v(p, I, a, e) = \max \quad u(x, y, a, e)$$
$$\text{s.t.} \quad px + y \le I, \quad (x, y) \in \Re_+^2$$

The function $v(\cdot)$ can be interpreted as social welfare for a given combination of price, income, and externalities. The solutions to the maximization problem $x(p, I, \cdot)$ and $y(p, I, \cdot)$ are the demands for agricultural and manufactured goods, respectively.

## Optimal policies in a closed economy

Because $a$ and $e$ are public goods, the market price system cannot internalize the marginal amenity benefits of agricultural land and the marginal cost of pollution, and producers will not choose the socially optimal factor allocation unless there is some policy intervention. Below, the optimal policies are determined using the following procedure: first, social welfare is derived as a function of the factors $L_x$ and $z_x$, and the welfare maximization problem is solved to determine the optimal allocation of the two factors. Second, the free-market allocations of $L_x$ and $z_x$ are derived under an arbitrary policy scheme, and the optimal scheme is then chosen so that the free-market and welfare-maximizing allocations coincide.

Social welfare in this economy $v(\cdot)$ can be written as a function of $L_x$ and $z_x$, provided the utility function is properly restricted so that $x(\cdot)$ is monotonic in $p$. To verify this, note that monotonicity of demand implies a unique market clearing price $p$ for any amount of agricultural production. Further, profits are always zero due to constant returns to scale, and factor payments to households (national income $I$) must therefore equal total revenue from the two industries. Thus, $p$ and $I$ can be regarded as functions of $L_x$ and $z_x$ that are implicitly defined by the equations:

$$x(p(L_x, z_x), I(L_x, z_x), \cdot) = L_x f_x(z_x) \tag{1}$$
$$I(L_x, z_x) = p(L_x, z_x) L_x f_x(z_x) + (L - L_x) f_y(z_y) \tag{2}$$

where $z_y \equiv Z_y/L_y = (Z - z_x L_x)/(L - L_x)$. The problem of maximizing social welfare in a closed economy can therefore be written:

$$\max \quad v(p(L_x, z_x), I(L_x, z_x), L_x, L_x g(z_x)) \tag{3}$$

$$L_x \in [0, L], \quad z_x \in [0, Z/L_x]$$

Under appropriate assumptions on $u(\cdot)$ and $F_i(\cdot)$, a solution to this problem
cannot occur on the boundary of the constraint set.[4] If a solution exists, it must
satisfy the first-order conditions for an interior maximum:

$$v_p p_L + v_I I_L + v_a + v_e g(z_x) = 0 \tag{4}$$

$$v_p p_z + v_I I_z + v_e L_x g'(z_x) = 0 \tag{5}$$

where subscripts denote derivatives. The Envelope Theorem applied to the
consumer's utility maximization problem implies that $v_I = u_y$, $v_a = u_a$, and
$v_e = u_e$; $v_p = -x(p, I)v_I$ by Roy's Identity; and the first-order conditions for
utility maximization require that $p = u_x/u_y$. Substituting these conditions, the
derivatives of $I$ from (2), and the market-clearing condition (1) into (4) and (5),
one obtains the following equivalent conditions expressed in terms of the utility
and production functions (see the demonstration in the appendix, p. 477):

$$\frac{u_x}{u_y} f_x(z_x) - [f_y(z_y) - f_y'(z_y)(z_y - z_x)] + \frac{u_a}{u_y} + \frac{u_e}{u_y} g(z_x) = 0 \tag{6}$$

$$\frac{u_x}{u_y} f_x'(z_x) - f_y'(z_y) + \frac{u_e}{u_y} g'(z_x) = 0 \tag{7}$$

Each of these conditions requires the net marginal benefits of each factor to be
zero. Equation (6) defines the optimal allocation of $L_x$. The first term is the
marginal benefit of using land to produce $x$, the term in brackets is the marginal
opportunity value of using land to produce $y$, $u_a/u_y$ is the marginal amenity
benefit of land in agriculture, and the last term (note that $u_e < 0$) is the marginal
cost of pollution. Because each term has been divided by $u_y$, the benefits and
costs are compared in terms of the numéraire. In (7), the optimal choice of $z_x$
is determined by setting to zero the sum of the marginal benefits of producing
$x$, the marginal opportunity value in terms of $y$ production forgone, and the
marginal environmental cost.

Although each of the preceding equations describes the optimal allocation of
one factor, they are collectively a simultaneous system in both variables ($L_x$ appears in both equations through the expression for $z_x$). Letting ($L_x^o$ $z_x^o$) represent
the socially optimal allocation, simultaneity implies any shift in preferences that
changes either $u_a$ or $u_e$ will induce a change in both $L_x^o$ and $z_x^o$.

Several types of policies have been proposed to internalize the environmental
effects of agriculture. Consider four policy instruments that may be imposed
jointly: a subsidy on agricultural output ($s_x$), a subsidy on agricultural land ($s_L$),

a tax on agricultural input ($t_z$), and a direct tax on pollution ($t_e$).[5] The policy problem is therefore to determine a policy scheme $s = (s_x, s_L, t_z, t_e)$ that allows the socially optimal outcome to be decentralized through free markets. Given a set of policies $s$, a price $p$, and factor endowments ($L, Z$), the "invisible hand" of competition will solve the revenue maximization problem (Dixit and Norman, 1980):

$$\max \quad (p + s_x)L_x f_x(z_x) + s_L L_x - t_z L_x z_x - t_e L_x g(z_x)$$
$$+ (L - L_x)f_y(z_y)$$
$$L_x \in [0, L], \quad z_x \in [0, Z/L_x]$$

Because the maximand is strictly concave, the unique solution must satisfy the first-order conditions:

$$(p + s_x)f_x(z_x) + s_L - t_z z_x - t_e g(z_x)$$
$$- [f_y(z_y) + f_y'(z_y)(z_y - z_x)] = 0 \tag{8}$$
$$(p + s_x)f_x'(z_x) - t_z - t_e g'(z_x) - f_y'(z_y) = 0 \tag{9}$$

Using the fact that $u_x/u_y = p$ and comparing (6) and (7) to (8) and (9), the welfare-maximizing policies $s_x$, $s_L$, $t_z$, and $t_e$ must satisfy:

$$s_x f_x\left(z_x^o\right) + s_L - t_z z_x^o - t_e g\left(z_x^o\right) = \frac{u_a}{u_y} + \frac{u_e}{u_y} g\left(z_x^o\right) \tag{10}$$

$$s_x f_x'\left(z_x^o\right) - t_z + t_e g'\left(z_x^o\right) = -\frac{u_e}{u_y} g'\left(z_x^o\right) \tag{11}$$

where the derivatives of $u(\cdot)$ are evaluated at the socially optimal levels $L_x^o$ and $Z_x^o$. If pollution can be observed and measured, the simplest choice of policies is to set $(s_x, s_L, t_z, t_e) = (0, u_a/u_y, 0, -u_e/u_y)$. This policy scheme is the Pigovian outcome where each externality is rewarded by its marginal social value. Thus, if the effluent can be taxed directly, neither an output subsidy nor an input tax is necessary.

A major difficulty in regulating agricultural pollution is that damages cannot be observed and policies must instead regulate outputs and inputs directly.[6] If the effluent tax $t_e$ is eliminated, (10) and (11) comprise a system of two equations in the three unknowns $s_x$, $s_L$, and $t_z$. This arrangement allows a degree of freedom in selecting policies, and suggests that a social optimum can be obtained by combining commodity policy with input taxes and subsidies. However, this result depends on the simplification of only two factors, and does not hold in general. Indeed, the possibility of using *any* commodity policy disappears if there exist other factors of production that are unregulated and do not affect the externalities $a$ and $e$.[7]

Among the four policies in $s$, only $s_L$ and $t_z$ are both feasible (because they act on observable transactions) and remain valid in more general cases (because they do not act on other factors of production). If the policy set is limited to these two instruments, (10) and (11) imply they must satisfy:

$$t_z = -\frac{u_e}{u_y} g'\left(z_x^o\right) \tag{12}$$

$$s_L = \frac{u_a}{u_y} + t_z z_x^o + \frac{u_e}{u_y} g\left(z_x^o\right) \tag{13}$$

In words, the optimal tax is the marginal social cost of applying agricultural inputs at $z_x^o$. The optimal subsidy in (13) is made up of two components. First, farmers are rewarded for the amenity benefit per acre of farmland $u_a/u_y$. Substituting the expression for the tax into (13), the second and third terms of the subsidy are equal to $(u_e/u_y)[g(z_x^o) - g'(z_x^o)z_x^o] = (u_e/u_y)(\partial e/\partial L_x)$ (see n. 2, p. 480). Thus, the subsidy rewards farmers by the combined social value of amenity benefits and the marginal change in pollution. This is a generalization of Holtermann's (1976) result for a single externality; a welfare maximum can be achieved through taxes/subsidies on inputs that penalize or reward each input by its marginal contribution to the externality. Here, the social value of pollution $u_e/u_y$ and the change in pollution with respect to $L_x$ are both negative, and the optimal subsidy therefore exceeds the amenity value of farmland.

Therefore, even if agricultural land provides no landscape amenities (i.e. $u_a \equiv 0$), it should still be subsidized in conjunction with the input tax $t_z$. Further, subsidizing land by the "net" value of amenities per acre will not achieve an efficient allocation of resources. Landscape amenity value net of pollution cost is $[u_a/u_y + (u_e/u_y)g(z_x^o)]$, but a subsidy of this amount falls short of the optimal subsidy in (13) by the amount $t_z z_x^o$. Thus, an empirical study of the willingness-to-pay for farmland amenities will not estimate the appropriate land subsidy, even if it accounts for the cost of agricultural pollution. Determining whether this difference is likely to be empirically significant is an important goal of the empirical analysis below.

The optimal levels of $s_L$ and $t_z$ are based on the welfare-maximizing allocations $L_x^o$ and $z_x^o$, which are in turn determined in a simultaneous system ((6) and (7)). Consequently, any change in the value of either externality (i.e. a shift in $u_a/u_y$ or $u_e/u_y$) would induce an adjustment in both the optimal allocation $(L_x^o, z_x^o)$ and policy choice $(s_L, t_z)$. For example, suppose the value of agricultural land amenities increases by \$$b$ per acre. In general, this change would lead to some (non-zero) adjustment in the optimal input tax even if $u_e/u_y$ remains fixed, while the optimal land subsidy would change by some amount other than \$$b$.

## Open economies

Suppose the economy described above is opened to international trade. For simplicity, assume that: (a) foreign and domestic production technologies are identical, (b) foreign agriculture does not generate any externalities, and (c) foreign utility does not depend on domestic allocations. Under these assumptions, the allocations that maximize global welfare are the solution to the following combined Pareto problem:

$$\max \quad u(x, y, L_x, L_x g(z_x)) + \alpha u^*(x^*, y^*)$$

$$\text{subject to:} \quad x + x^* = L_x f_x(z_x) + L_x^* f_x(z_x^*)$$
$$y + y^* = (L - L_x) f_y(z_y) + (L^* - L_x^*) f_y(z_y^*)$$
$$L_x \in [0, L], \quad z_x \in [0, Z/L_x],$$
$$L_x^* \in [0, L^*], \quad z_x^* \in [0, Z^*/L_x^*]$$

where $\alpha$ is the relative welfare weight of foreign consumers, and asterisks denote foreign variables. The first-order necessary conditions for allocations of land and other inputs (assuming an interior solution) simplify to:

$$u_x f_x(z_x) - u_y[f_y(z_y) - f_y'(z_y)(z_y - z_x)] + u_a + u_e g(z_x) = 0 \quad (14a)$$
$$u_x f_x'(z_x) - u_y f_y'(z_y) + u_e g'(z_x) = 0 \quad (14b)$$
$$u_x^* f_x(z_x^*) - u_y^*[f_y(z_y^*) - f_y'(z_y^*)(z_y^* - z_x^*)] = 0 \quad (14c)$$
$$u_x^* f_x'(z_x^*) - u_y^* f_y'(z_y^*) = 0 \quad (14d)$$

Equations (14a) and (14b) describe the optimal levels of $L_x$ and $z_x$, respectively, while (14c) and (14d) correspond to the optimal allocations in the foreign economy. In the foreign country, each factor is employed in agriculture until the marginal benefits of agricultural production equal the opportunity value of manufactured production. The domestic allocation equations include terms for the externalities, and are equivalent to the closed economy conditions in (6) and (7).

Though a global perspective is of theoretical interest, it is reasonable to assume that the home government wishes only to maximize domestic welfare. The remainder of this section determines the allocations that are optimal from this domestic viewpoint, and compares each outcome with those that maximize global welfare. The small-country and large-country cases are analyzed in turn.

A small open economy views the world price of agricultural goods as an exogenous variable. Now regarding $p$ as a parameter, national income is:

$$I(L_x, z_x) = pL_x f_x(z_x) + (L - L_x) f_y(z_y)$$

The social welfare-maximization problem becomes:

$$\max \quad v(p, I(L_x, z_x), L_x, L_x g(z_x))$$
$$L_x \in [0, L], \quad z_x \in [0, Z/L_x]$$

with first-order conditions:

$$v_I I_L + v_a + v_e g(z_x) = 0 \quad \text{and} \quad v_I I_z + v_e L_x g'(z_x) = 0$$

Substituting the derivatives of $I$ from the definition above and the envelope conditions $v_I = u_y$, $v_a = u_a$, and $v_e = u_e$, these conditions reduce to (see the appendix, p. 477):

$$pf_x(z_x) - [f_y(z_y) - f'_y(z_y)(z_y - z_x)] + \frac{u_a}{u_y} + \frac{u_e}{u_y}g(z_x) = 0$$

$$pf'_x(z_x) - f'_y(z_y) + \frac{u_e}{u_y}g'(z_x) = 0$$

Because $p = u_x/u_y$, these conditions imply exactly the same factor allocation that maximizes world welfare in conditions (14a) and (14b). Therefore, the optimal domestic policy for a small open economy is also optimal from a global point of view.

If the home economy is large enough so that changes in domestic production and consumption affect the world price, the price must be regarded as endogenous. The policy problem becomes:

$$\max \quad v(\tilde{p}L_x, z_x)\tilde{I}(L_x, z_x), L_x, L_x g(z_x)$$
$$L_x \in [0, L], z_x \in [0, Z/L_x]$$

The price and income relations $\tilde{p}$ and $\tilde{I}$ satisfy:

$$x(\tilde{p}, \tilde{I}, \cdot) + x^*(\tilde{p}) = L_x f_x(z_x) \tag{15}$$
$$\tilde{I} = \tilde{p}L_x f_x(z_x) + (L - L_x)f_y(z_y) \tag{16}$$

where the arguments of $\tilde{p}$ and $\tilde{I}$ have been suppressed to simplify notation, and $x^*(\cdot)$ is the demand for exports. The first-order conditions are:

$$v_p\tilde{p}_l + v_I\tilde{I}_L + v_a + v_e g(z_x) = 0 \quad \text{and}$$
$$v_p\tilde{p}_z + v_I\tilde{I}_z + v_e L_x g'(z_x) = 0$$

Substituting the derivatives of $v(v_I = u_y, v_a = u_a, v_e = u_e)$ and $\tilde{I}$, the condition $\tilde{p} = u_x/u_y$, Roy's Identity $v_p = -xv_I$, and market clearing, these conditions become (see the demonstration in the appendix, p. 477):

$$\frac{u_x}{u_y}f_x(z_x) + x^*(\tilde{p})\tilde{p}_L[f_y(z_y) - f'_y(z_y)(z_y - z_x)]$$

$$+ \frac{u_a}{u_y} + \frac{u_e}{u_y}g(z_x) = 0 \tag{17}$$

$$\frac{u_x}{u_y}f'_x(z_x) + x^*(\tilde{p})\tilde{p}_z - f'_y(z_y) + \frac{u_e}{u_y}g'(z_x) = 0 \tag{18}$$

Compared to those that maximize world welfare ((14a) and (14b)), each of these conditions contains the extra term $x^*(\cdot)\tilde{p}_j$, or the product of exports and the change in price with respect to factor $j$. Assuming that $x_p < 0$ and $x_p^* < 0$, the derivatives of the market-clearing condition (15) with respect to $L_x$ and $z_x$ imply that $\tilde{p}_L < 0$ and $\tilde{p}_z < 0$. Thus, a domestic planner could decrease the world price by increasing either of the factor allocations to agriculture. If the domestic economy is an agricultural importer, then $x^* < 0$ and the extra terms in each condition are positive. This implies that the marginal benefits of $L_x$ and $z_x$ are higher *vis-à-vis* the small economy case, and the optimal allocations are therefore higher as well. If the home economy is an exporter ($x^* > 0$), the extra terms are negative, implying a smaller allocation of factors to agriculture.

These results are intuitively consistent with the use of subsidies and taxes to regulate a single externality (Krutilla, 1991); importers gain from policies that increase production and decrease the world price, while the reverse is true for exporters. If policy interventions must be justified on the basis external benefits and costs, the model predicts that importers' policies will emphasize the benefits of agricultural land and undervalue the environmental costs of agricultural inputs, while exporters are likely to do the opposite.

These predictions generally coincide with observed differences policies and negotiating tactics across nations. Importers, such as Japan, Norway, and Switzerland, all have significant policy schemes aimed at protecting farmland, and argue for the importance of the extra-market benefits from agriculture in trade negotiations. If these countries retain domestic farmland against free market pressures, and succeed in convincing their trading partners to do the same, the resulting high level of agricultural production will lower world prices and benefit consumers in importing nations. Large exporters like the United States, on the other hand, have sought to protect the environment from agricultural pollution by "harmonizing up" environmental regulations across all trading partners. If this strategy is successful, world supply will contract owing to the extra cost of environmental regulations, and producers in exporting countries will receive a higher price.

## A stylized empirical application to US agriculture

To illustrate the relationships between policies and their quantitative significance, this section simulates the model developed above for agricultural environmental policies in the United States. In the international trade arena, the United States is a net agricultural exporter, and has a significant market share of several major commodities. Thus, it is generally believed the US is a "large" country because its trade volume is significant enough to have a measurable effect on world prices. Conversely, agriculture comprises only a small part of the US economy. In 1994, the aggregate value added from agricultural production was $104 billion or 1.5 percent of the $6.9 trillion economy, and the cost of food items (which includes processing costs and the value of food retail services) make up only about 10 percent of household expenditure.

US agriculture has been cited as the source of numerous forms of pollution such as soil erosion, nutrient runoff into streams and lakes, offensive odors, and contamination of water supplies. Here, the focus is on the harmful effects of agricultural chemicals on human health. This form of pollution was selected because its link to agriculture is well documented, the problem is widespread, and to date a limited (though growing) set of regulations have been imposed to control chemical use at the farm level. On the positive side, the agricultural landscape has been found to provide a significant amenity value to residents on the suburban fringes of major cities (Beasley, Workman, and Williams, 1986; Halstead, 1984; Krieger, 1999) These values have led to a significant policy interest in the preservation of open space, even at the national level of government (e.g. Office of Management and Budget, 2000).

*Simulation model*

Based on the observations made above, several simplifying assumptions can be made in modeling the US agricultural sector. First, the small share of agriculture in gross domestic product (GDP) implies that changes in the farm sector have almost no effect on prices or production in the rest of the economy. Second, the income effect on the demand for food items is likely to be negligible because it is a necessity item that makes up a small share of consumption expenditures. Third, although pollution and landscape amenities enter the utility function and therefore influence food demand, their effects are not thought to be empirically important.

Given these simplifications, the agricultural sector can be described by the following model:

$$x = B_x P^{-\eta_x} \tag{19}$$

$$x^* = B_x^* P^{-\eta_x^*} \tag{20}$$

$$x + x^* = F_x(L_x, Z_x) \tag{21}$$

$$p\frac{\partial F_x}{\partial L_x} = p_L - s_L \tag{22}$$

$$p\frac{\partial F_x}{\partial Z_x} = p_z + t_z \tag{23}$$

$$L_x = B_L p_L^{\eta_L} \tag{24}$$

$$Z_x = B_Z p_Z^{\eta_Z} \tag{25}$$

$$a = L_x \tag{26}$$

$$e = L_x g(Z_x/L_x) \tag{27}$$

where $\eta_x$ and $\eta_x^*$ are the elasticities of domestic and export demand, respectively; $\eta_L$ and $\eta_Z$ are the supply elasticities of the land and non-land inputs facing agriculture; $p_L$ and $p_Z$ are the equilibrium prices of land and non-land inputs;

and the $B_i$'s are demand and supply constants. This system of nine equations uniquely determines the nine unknowns: $x$, $x^*$, $L_x$, $Z_x$, $p$, $p_L$, $p_Z$, $a$, and $e$, which must be solved simultaneously with the land subsidy $s_L$ and input tax $t_z$.

Equations (19) and (20) specify the domestic and export demands to be of the constant elasticity form. Equation (21) is the market-clearing condition for agricultural goods. The profit-maximizing conditions for land and non-land inputs are represented in (22) and (23), which state that the marginal value product of each factor must equal its (post-policy) market price. Equations (24) and (25) are the market-clearing conditions for land and non-land inputs, respectively, where the supplies of both factors are assumed to follow constant elasticity functions. Equations (26) and (27) are re-statements from the conceptual model, relating the externalities $a$ and $e$ to the production factors $L_x$ and $Z_x$.

This model is based on a framework that has been widely used to simulate the aggregate effects of several different policies in agriculture (Floyd, 1965; Gardner, 1987). Though it describes the agricultural sector in isolation, the model preserves the relevant general equilibrium effects of non-fixed factor prices through the supply functions for $L_x$ and $Z_x$. In order to implement the model empirically, it is necessary to specify several functional relationships and parameter values. First, an aggregate utility function must be specified to calculate the welfare-maximizing levels of $s_L$ and $t_z$. In addition, functional forms for $F_x$ and $g$ must be selected and parameterized, and parameter values for the supply and demand equations must also be chosen. These elements of the empirical model are discussed in turn below.

Aggregate utility is assumed to follow the money metric, quasi-linear form (Mas-Collel, Whinston, and Green, 1995):

$$u(x, y, a, e) = \phi(x) + y + \gamma a - \delta e \qquad (28)$$

where $\phi(\cdot)$ is the utility of food, $y$ is the dollar value of non-food consumption, $\gamma$ is the marginal value of landscape amenities, and $\delta$ is the marginal health cost of chemical pollution. $\phi(\cdot)$ represents the function that produces constant elasticity demands. Thus, maximizing (28) subject to the budget constraint $px + y \leq I$ results in the demand function (19), which is independent of income and the environmental measures $a$ and $e$. To parameterize utility, values must be selected for the elasticity of demand $\eta_x$ (which appears in $\phi$), and the environmental parameters $\gamma$ and $\delta$. Based on a substantial body of empirical evidence that supports a highly inelastic demand for food, the parameter $\eta_x$ is varied over the range 0.2 to 0.5.

Poe (1999) summarizes several non-market valuation studies that have attempted to estimate the external benefits of farmland. Halstead (1984), Bergstrom, Dillman, and Stoll (1985), and Krieger (1999) have converted estimates of household willingness to pay to amenity values per acre by aggregating over households to obtain social willingness to pay, and dividing by the number of acres in the study region. Applying the estimates from these studies to a similar conversion procedure for aggregate data, estimated amenity values of farmland range from less than $1 per acre to $11 per acre. Since the base values are from study regions where farmland is considered scarce, these per-acre values may be overestimated. The parameter $\gamma$ is thus varied from $0 to $10.

Because there is no standardized measure of agricultural pollution, $\delta$ is normalized to unity and $e$ is measured in dollars of health costs that are attributable to agricultural chemicals. The two primary categories of chemicals that pose health risks to humans are pesticides and nitrates that occur in drinking water from the use of nitrogen fertilizer. Because the health costs of these pollutants cannot be directly observed, we must rely on estimates from the environmental literature.

Poe (1998) has estimated a damage function that relates household willingness-to-pay for improved water quality to observed contamination levels. Households whose water supply exceeds the European health standard of 4.4 parts per million (ppm) are willing to pay about $170 per year for safer drinking water, while households that exceed the EPA standard of 10ppm are willing to pay an average of $380. Based on population data compiled by the Environmental Working Group, these estimates imply aggregate nitrate damages of approximately $2.3 billion. Other studies have estimated household willingness-to-pay for general improvements in water quality, including the removal of all agricultural and industrial contaminants (Powell, 1990; Schultz and Lindsay, 1990). These estimates imply aggregate damages from all water pollutants in the range of $3.8–$6.2 billion per year.

Pimentel *et al.* (1992) estimate that the direct health cost of pesticides (including treatment of poisonings and pesticide-induced cancers as well as accidental fatalities) totals $780 million per year, and that the indirect costs through drinking water contamination total $1.8 billion per year. Combining the direct and indirect health costs of all agricultural chemicals, the body of evidence suggests aggregate damages in the range of $3–$7 billion, although these may be overestimates because they potentially account for non-agricultural contaminants. The base value of $e$ is thus varied from $2 billion to $5 billion.

The functional relationship between chemical application rates and damage to human health is not yet completely understood. Because yield is a concave function of polluting inputs, physical properties imply the pollution function must be convex (Siebert *et al.*, 1980). Thus, convexity is a natural property to impose on the health costs of pollutants as well, but there is little scientific justification for any particular functional form. Here, health costs are assumed to follow a quadratic form: $e = B_e Z_x^2 / L_x = L_x B_e z_x^2$. This function has linear derivatives in $Z_x$ and $z_x$, and therefore imposes constant marginal health costs. Thus, the specification is a linear approximation to the underlying marginal health cost function; this simplification seemed reasonable given the stylized focus of the application and the approximate nature of the data.

Data on aggregate agricultural production are available from the USDA-Economic Research Service (Ahearn *et al.*, 1998; Ball *et al.*, 1997). This data series includes indices of aggregate output as well as inputs in several categories for the years 1948–94. For our purposes, agricultural technology was assumed to be separable so that input categories can be further grouped into a "land aggregate" $(L_x)$, which is made up of land and other factors that are combined with it, and a "non-land aggregate" $(Z_x)$. In particular, the land aggregate includes indexes of land itself, capital equipment, and labor; the non-land aggregate is made up of chemicals, fuel and electricity, and other purchased inputs. When technology is separable the production decision can be divided into two stages, where inputs are combined in a least-cost way within each aggregate in the first stage, and the profit-maximizing levels of the aggregates are chosen in the second stage (Chambers, 1998).

To be able to compute quantity and price series for $L_x$ and $Z_x$, it is necessary to employ an indexing procedure that combines the inputs within each aggregate factor. Because the underlying functional form of the technology is unknown, any index must be regarded as an approximation that reflects the productive capacity of the various inputs. Here, it is assumed that the inputs within each aggregate are combined in Leontief fixed proportions. Though this procedure abstracts from substitution of the inputs within the aggregates, it greatly simplifies the analysis because the implicit price of each aggregate becomes a linear expression of the category prices. Consequently, a subsidy on land alone is equivalent to a subsidy on the entire land aggregate $L_x$, and a tax on chemicals is equivalent to a tax on the non-land aggregate $Z_x$.[8]

To solve the second-stage problem, it is necessary to specify a functional form that relates $L_x$ and $Z_x$ to agricultural output. Here, a Cobb–Douglas form is assumed: $F_x(L_x, Z_x) = B_x L_x^{\beta_L} Z_x^{\beta_z}$, where $\beta_L + \beta_Z = 1$ by constant returns to scale. Under profit maximization, $\beta_L$ and $\beta_Z$ are the cost shares of the land and non-land aggregates, respectively. Calculating the average shares over the years 1948–94 resulted in point estimates of $\beta_L = 0.71$ and $\beta_Z = 0.29$; the parameters are varied over the ranges [0.5, 0.9] for $\beta_L$ and [0.1, 0.5] for $\beta_Z$.

The remaining parameters to be chosen are the elasticity of export demand and the supply elasticities for the aggregate factors $L_x$ and $Z_x$. Export demand is probably quite elastic, but may not be perfectly elastic because the United States is a large country. To explore the consequences of market power in international trade, the export demand elasticity was varied between 2 and $\infty$. The extreme values represent the polar cases of a very large economy with substantial market power, and a small economy with no market power. Because land makes up a

Table 21.1 *Parameter values*

| Parameter (1) | Symbol (2) | Range (3) | Primary value (4) |
|---|---|---|---|
| Elasticity of domestic demand | $\eta_x$ | 0.2–0.5 | 0.3 |
| Elasticity of export demand | $\eta_x^*$ | 2–∞ | 5.0 |
| Supply elasticity of $L_x$ | $\eta_L$ | 0.1–0.3 | 0.2 |
| Supply elasticity of $Z_x$ | $\eta_Z$ | 5–15 | 10.0 |
| Production elasticity of $L_x$ | $\beta_L$ | 0.5–0.9 | 0.71 |
| Production elasticity of $Z_x$ | $\beta_Z$ | 0.1–0.5 | 0.29 |
| Marginal value of amenities ($/a) | $\gamma$ | 0–10 | 5.0 |
| Aggregate external health costs ($ billion) | $e$ | 2–5 | 3.5 |

significant part of the aggregate $L_x$, we would expect its supply elasticity to be quite small. On the other hand, the inputs in $Z_x$ can be produced at very nearly constant cost, implying a relatively high supply elasticity. Thus, the parameters $\eta_L$ and $\eta_Z$ are varied over the ranges [0.1, 0.3] and [5, 15], respectively. Table 21.1 summarizes the range of parameter values, along with a set of "primary" values that are used in the simulations reported below. The constants $B_i$ are determined by calibrating the model relationships to base data for 1994; these base values are reported in the second column of table 21.2.

## Results

To explore the relationships among domestic environmental policies, the model is initially solved under three policy experiments for the small-economy case. The assumption of a small economy precludes the possibility of distorting trade, and ensures that the simulated policies include only externality correcting components. In the first policy scenario, chemicals are taxed at their marginal external cost with no land policy, while the second scenario subsidizes land at its amenity value but does not tax non-land inputs. These two experiments thus correspond to policy schemes that target each externality independently. The third experiment is based on the relationships derived in the theoretical section and includes both a land subsidy and a chemical tax that simultaneously correct both externalities.

The results of these experiments are reported in table 21.2. When the tax is imposed in isolation (scenario 1), farmers pay a $0.13 tax per lb of chemicals.[9] Even though estimated chemical use and health costs fall in this scenario (by about 14 percent and 27 percent, respectively), the increased cost of farming drives land out of agriculture and reduces total production. Thus, in an independent effort to improve water quality, the tax policy has damaged the public good function of agriculture and has reduced the aggregate value of

Table 21.2 *Base data and simulation results*

| | | Small economy | | | |
|---|---|---|---|---|---|
| Variable (1) | Base data (1994) (2) | Tax only (Scenario 1) (3) | Subs. only (Scenario 2) (4) | Joint policy (Scenario 3) (5) | Large economy[a] (6) |
| Land subsidy ($/acre) | 0.00 | 0.00 | 5.00 | 7.67 | −7.38 |
| Chemical tax ($/lb) | 0.00 | 0.13 | 0.00 | 0.13 | 0.29 |
| Food price[b] | 1.00 | 1.00 | 1.00 | 1.00 | 1.09 *8.7[c]* |
| Production ($ billion) | 166.61 | 158.32 *−5.0* | 167.91 *0.8* | 160.29 *−3.8* | 170.04 *2.1* |
| Net exports ($ billion) | 19.17 | 10.88 *−43.2* | 20.46 *6.7* | 12.85 *−33.0* | 13.73 *−28.4* |
| Consumption ($ billion) | 147.44 | 147.44 | 147.44 | 147.44 | 156.31 *6.0* |
| Agricultural land (million acres) | 975 | 967 *−0.8* | 983 *0.8* | 979 *0.4* | 968 *−0.7* |
| Rent on land ($/acre) | 121.35 | 116.30 *−4.2* | 126.32 *4.1* | 123.93 *2.1* | 117.31 *−3.3* |
| Chemical use (billion lb) | 44.8 | 38.3 *−14.4* | 45.1 *0.7* | 38.8 *−13.4* | 36.6 *−18.2* |
| Price of chemicals ($/lb) | 1.08 | 1.06 *−1.5* | 1.08 *0.1* | 1.06 *−1.4* | 1.06 *−2.0* |
| Input intensity (lb/acre) | 46.0 | 39.7 *−13.6* | 45.9 *−0.1* | 39.6 *−13.7* | 37.8 *−17.6* |
| Health costs ($ billion) | 3.50 | 2.56 *−27.0* | 3.52 *0.6* | 2.61 *−25.3* | 2.36 *−33.4* |
| Land amenity Value ($ billion)[d] | 4.87 | 4.83 *−0.8* | 4.91 *0.8* | 4.89 *0.4* | 4.84 *−0.7* |

*Notes:* [a] Assumes an export demand elasticity of 5.

[b] Index of all agricultural prices, 1994 = 1.

[c] Numbers in italics are percentage changes from base values.

[d] Assumes an amenity value of $5 per acre.

farm production. If instead a subsidy is introduced to protect farmland without any regulations on chemical use (scenario 2), the stock of farmland and the value of production increase from their base values, but so do aggregate chemical use and estimated health costs. In sum, a policy to independently improve one externality leads to an adverse change in the other.

Only if the subsidy and tax are imposed jointly can there be an improvement in both externalities (scenario 3). The tax on chemicals of $0.13 per lb, if imposed jointly with the land subsidy of $7.67 per acre, will achieve an efficient allocation of both factors. Farmland rises from its base value by 4 million acres, and external health costs fall by an estimated $900 million (25 percent). The optimal subsidy on an acre of farmland includes the $5 it contributes to amenity value as well as its marginal effect on pollution; an extra acre of agricultural land, *ceteris paribus*, reduces external health costs by $2.67. Thus, the optimal subsidy differs from the amenity value of farmland by more than 50 percent.

In the joint policy case, the fall in non-land inputs outweighs the effect of the increase in farmland, and domestic production decreases by $6.6 billion. Net exports contract by a matching amount, but the international price is not affected because of the small-economy assumption. If the economy is large enough so that export quantities influence the world price, optimal environmental policies include components that improve domestic welfare through trade distortion. Thus, the resulting tax and subsidy may differ substantially from the external cost of chemicals and amenity benefits of farmland.

Column 6 in table 21.2 corresponds to this large-economy case, where the tax and subsidy are imposed jointly and the elasticity of export demand is set at 5. Since the United States is an exporter, it will have an incentive to select policies that restrict production and in turn raise the international price. Therefore, the chemical tax of $0.29 is more than twice as high as the small-economy case, while the subsidy becomes negative (−$7.38) so that land is taxed as well. These policies do result in some environmental improvements because external health costs are reduced by over 30 percent, but these gains are partially offset by a 0.7 percent decrease in the stock of farmland.

The "environmental" policies provide additional welfare benefits through trade distortion. They have succeeded in raising international prices by 9 percent and expanding US production by 2 percent. Net exports decrease compared to base values where environmental consequences are ignored completely, but are about $900 million larger than the small-economy case where trade-distorting effects are precluded.

Though the cases of alternative parameter values are not reported, the results in table 21.2 are generally quite robust as market and production parameters are varied. With environmental parameters set at their primary values and the other domestic parameters ($\eta_x$, $\eta_L$, $\eta_Z$, $\beta_L$, and $\beta_Z$) individually varied across their ranges, the small-economy tax ranges from $0.12 to $0.14 per lb while the subsidy is between $7.04 and $7.81 per acre. These parameters have a somewhat greater impact on the policies for a large economy; with the export elasticity set at 5, the tax and subsidy range from $0.18 to $0.39 per lb and from −$12.79 to −$2.40 per acre, respectively. The environmental and trade parameters naturally have a more direct effect on the environmental policies.

The different environmental values would imply small-economy input taxes from $0.08 to $0.18 per lb and small-economy land subsidies between $2.68 and $12.67 per acre. With environmental parameters at their primary values, the extreme case of an export demand elasticity of 2 implies an optimal tax and subsidy of $0.37 per lb and −$14.28 per acre, respectively.

## Policy implications

This chapter has determined the optimal policy rules when agricultural production generates both landscape amenities and pollution from chemical inputs. The optimal subsidy on land and tax on non-land inputs depends on the size of both externalities, and a change in the social value of either land amenities or pollution therefore implies a change in both policies. It has been shown empirically that independent policies are likely to work at cross-purposes; a single policy directed at one externality leads to an adverse change in the other.

One important implication of empirical research is that an optimal subsidy on agricultural land does not equal the net value of land amenities. Numerous studies have estimated the social amenity benefits from land in agriculture using non-market valuation techniques, but these estimates cannot be interpreted as the appropriate farmland subsidy, even if the values are "corrected" to account for the value of pollution generated per acre. A simulation of US agriculture suggests the interaction between policies is empirically important; if the incentive to use environmental policy as a trade-distorting tool is ignored, the estimated optimal land subsidy is about 50 percent larger than the amenity value of farmland. In the large-economy case, the policies include components that improve domestic welfare through terms of trade, and the optimal tax and subsidy differ even more from the social values of the two external effects.

The model here abstracts from the site-specific factors that cause environmental values to be spatially heterogeneous. As a practical matter, proposed policies differ by location, and tend to focus on areas that are known to be environmentally sensitive or farming regions in close proximity to large population centers. Yet our findings are even more important for policy-making in these areas, because the interaction among joint policies is more pronounced if the social values placed on the external effects from agricultural production are large.

In the international arena, small economies will choose the same policies that maximize world welfare, but large economies have an incentive to set policies at non-internalizing levels to exploit terms of trade effects. In particular, large importers will choose policies that increase agricultural factors beyond globally efficient allocations, while large exporters prefer to restrict factor allocations (and hence agricultural production) to raise the international price. For large economies, production policies that are ostensibly justified on environmental grounds can become instruments to distort international prices. Indeed, based on empirical policy simulations, we estimate that the United States alone could manipulate its domestic environmental policies to change the world price by about 9 percent.

Even for small countries with environmental concerns, there are additional policy goals such as supporting farm incomes or enhancing food security. In the WTO negotiations over environmental issues, therefore, it may be impossible to determine whether so-called "environmental policies" are really vehicles to help achieve some other goal. The key to making domestic policies compatible with free trade lies in the types of policies used. The less the policy instruments distort trade, the more autonomy nations can have in selecting and executing domestic policy goals.

# Appendix

### Derivation of optimal factor allocation conditions: closed economy

From (2) in the text (p. 462) the derivatives of national income $I$ are:

$$I_L = p_L L_x f_x(z_x) + p(\cdot) f_x(z_x) - [f_y(z_y) - f'_y(z_y)(z_y - z_x)]$$
$$I_z = p_z L_x f_x(z_x) + p(\cdot) L_x f'_x(z_x) - L_x f'_y(z_y)$$

Substituting these derivatives and Roy's Identity ($v_p = -x(p, I)v_I$) into (4) and (5) gives:

$$-x(p, I)v_I p_L + v_I p_L L_x f_x(z_x) + v_I p(\cdot) f_x(z_x)$$
$$- v_I[f_y(z_y) - f'_y(z_y)(z_y - z_x)] + v_a + v_e g(z_x) = 0$$
$$-x(p, I)v_I p_z + v_I p_z L_x f_x(z_x) + v_I p(\cdot) L_x f'_x(z_x)$$
$$- v_I L_x f'_y(z_y) + v_e L_x g'(z_x) = 0$$

The market-clearing condition (2)) implies that the sum of the first and second terms in each of the above equations is zero. The Envelope Theorem implies that $v_I = u_y$, $v_a = u_a$, and $v_e = u_e$; and $p(\cdot) = u_x/u_y$ by the first-order conditions of utility maximization. Substituting these relationships into the remaining non-zero terms and dividing the second equation by $L_x$ gives:

$$u_x f_x(z_x) - u_y[f_y(z_y) - f'_y(z_y)(z_y - z_x)] + u_a + u_e g(z_x) = 0$$
$$u_y f x'(z_x) - u_y f'_y(z_y) + u_e g'(z_x) = 0$$

Dividing each of these equations by $u_y$ reveals (6) and (7) in the text.

## Derivation of optimal factor allocation conditions: small open economy

Because the price $p$ is a parameter for small economies, the derivatives of national income $I$ are:

$$I_L = pf_x(z_x) - [f_y(z_y) - f_y'(z_y)(z_y - z_x)]$$
$$I_z = pL_x f_x'(z_x) - L_x f_y'(z_y)$$

Substituting these derivatives and the envelope conditions ($v_I = u_y$, $v_a = u_a$, and $v_e = u_e$) into the welfare-maximizing conditions gives:

$$u_y pf_x(z_x) - u_y[f_y(z_y) - f_y'(z_y)(z_y - z_x)] + u_a + u_e g(z_x) = 0$$
$$u_y pL_x f_x'(z_x) - u_y L_x f_y'(z_y)_z + u_e L_x g'(z_x) = 0$$

The small-economy conditions on page 467 are obtained by dividing the first of these equations by $u_y$ and the second by $u_y L_x$.

## Derivation of optimal factor allocation conditions: large open economy

From (16) in the text the derivatives of the large-economy national income function $\tilde{I}$ are:

$$\tilde{I}_L = \tilde{p}_L L_x f_x(z_x) + \tilde{p}(\cdot)f_x(z_x) - [f_y(z_y) - f_y'(z_y)(z_y - z_x)]$$
$$\tilde{I}_z = \tilde{p}_z L_x f_x(z_x) + \tilde{p}(\cdot)L_n f_x'(z_x) - L_x f_y'(z_y)$$

Substituting these derivatives and Roy's Identity ($v_p = /xv_I$) into the conditions for a welfare maximum gives:

$$-x(\tilde{p}, \tilde{I})v_I \tilde{p}_L + v_I \tilde{p}_L L_x f_x(z_x) + v_I \tilde{p}(\cdot)f_x(z_x)$$
$$- v_I[f_y(z_y) - f_y'(z_y)(z_y - z_x)] + v_a + v_e g(z_x) = 0$$
$$-x(\tilde{p}, \tilde{I})v_I \tilde{p}_z + v_I \tilde{p}_z L_x f_x(z_x) + v_I \tilde{p}(\cdot)L_x f_x'(z_x)$$
$$- v_I L_x f_y'(z_y) + v_e L_x g'(z_x) = 0$$

By the market-clearing condition ((15) in the text), the sum of the first and second terms in the first of the foregoing equations is $x^*(\tilde{p})\tilde{p}_L v_i$. Similarly, the first and second terms in the second equation sum to $x^*(\tilde{p})\tilde{p}_z v_I$. Proceeding as above, substitute these relationships along with the envelope and utility-maximization conditions ($v_I = u_y$, $v_a = u_a$, and $v_e = u_e$; and $\tilde{p} = u_x/u_y$) into the preceding conditions and divide the second condition by $L_x$:

$$x^*(\tilde{p})\tilde{p}_L u_x + u_x f_x(z_x) - u_y[f_y(z_y) - f_y'(z_y)(z_y - z_x)]$$
$$+ u_a + u_e g(z_x) = 0$$
$$\frac{x^*(\tilde{p})\tilde{p}_L u_x}{L_x} + u_y f_x'(z_x) - u_y f_y'(z_y) + u_e g'(z_x) = 0$$

Dividing each of these equations by $u_y$ reveals (17) and (18) in the text.

For exporters (importers), the term $x^*(\tilde{p})\tilde{p}_j$ ($j = L, z$) in (17) and (18) will be negative (positive) as claimed in the text, provided that the derivatives of $\tilde{p}(\cdot)$ are negative. To determine the signs of $\tilde{p}_L$ and $\tilde{p}_z$, differentiate the market-clearing condition (15) to obtain:

$$x_p \tilde{p}_L + x_I \tilde{I}_L + x_p^* \tilde{p}_L = f_x(z_z) \tag{15a}$$

$$x_p \tilde{p}_z + x_I \tilde{I}_z + x_p^* \tilde{p}_z = L_x f_x'(z_z) \tag{15b}$$

Solving condition (17) for $(u_x/u_y)f_x(z_x) = \tilde{p}(\cdot)f_x(z_x)$ and substituting the resulting expression into $\tilde{p}_L$ above gives:

$$\tilde{I}_L = \tilde{p}_L L_x f_x(z_x) - x^*(\tilde{p})\tilde{p}_L - \frac{u_a}{u_y} - \frac{u_e}{u_y}g(z_x)$$

$$= x(\cdot)\tilde{p}_L - \frac{u_a}{u_y} - \frac{u_e}{u_y}g(z_x)$$

where the second equality follows from market clearing. Similarly, (18) and the expression for $\tilde{I}_z$ above imply:

$$\tilde{I}_z = x(\cdot)\tilde{p}_z - L_x\frac{u_e}{u_y}g'(z_x)$$

Substituting the foregoing expressions for $\tilde{I}_L$ and $\tilde{I}_z$ into (15a) and (15b) and rearranging gives:

$$\tilde{p}_L = \frac{f_x(\cdot) + x_I\frac{u_e}{u_y} + x_I\frac{u_e}{u_y}g(z_z)}{x_p + x_I x(\cdot) + x_p^*}$$

$$\tilde{p}_z = \frac{L_x\left[f_x'(\cdot) + x_I\frac{u_e}{u_y}g'(z_z)\right]}{x_p + x_I x(\cdot) + x_p^*}$$

The Slutsky equation and the assumption that $x_p^* < 0$ ensure that the denominator of both of these expressions is negative. Assuming that food is a normal good, the numerator of $\tilde{p}_L$ is always positive when $(u_a/u_y) + (u_e/u_y)g(z_x) > 0$ (i.e. when net externalities are positive). A sufficient set of conditions for both numerators to be positive is:

$$\tilde{p}f_x(\cdot) + \frac{u_a}{u_y} + \frac{u_e}{u_y}g(z_x) > 0$$

$$\tilde{p}f_x'(\cdot) + \frac{u_e}{u_y}g'(z_x) > 0$$

Thus, as long as the net marginal benefit of each factor in agriculture is positive (i.e. the sum of marginal private and external benefits outweigh marginal costs), the price function must be decreasing in both arguments. Alternative cases (for example, when the cost of pollution on each acre is larger than the combined value of farm production and amenity benefits) are ruled out by assumption.

**Notes**

1. If emissions are some function of agricultural output, i.e. $e = h(x)$, pollution can also be expressed as $e = h(F_x(L_x, Z_x)) = G(L_x, Z_x)$.

2. To verify, $\partial e/\partial L_x = g(z_x) + L_x g'(z_x)(-Z_x/L_x^2) = g(z_x) - g'(z_x)z_x$. The last expression has the same sign as $g(z_x)/z_x - g'(z_x) < 0$, where the inequality follows from the Mean Value Theorem. Intuitively, an acre increase in $L_x$ produces two effects on $e$: the extra pollution on the acre added, and the decrease in pollution on the acres previously in production that follows from a change in the input ratio $Z_x/L_x$. If pollution satisfies CRS, the change in the input ratio decreases pollution by $g'(\cdot)z_x$; the net effect is always negative because "average pollution" $g/z_x$ must be less than "marginal pollution" $g'$ if $g$ is convex (the opposite of the analogous relationships for a concave production function). More generally, if pollution is not necessarily CRS, the effect on total pollution from an increase in farmland depends on the heterogeneity of land; bringing an environmentally sensitive acre of land into production may increase total pollution. However, provided that the pollution function on every parcel of land is convex, the extra pollution from an extra acre is likely to be outweighed by the combined decrease in pollution on the acres already in production.

3. Conceptually, a more general amenity function relates the quantity of agricultural land to the amount of amenity services produced. Because of the obvious difficulties in measuring and observing amenity services *per se*, the valuation literature assumes that amenities are produced in proportion to the agricultural land base and attempts to estimate the value of amenities per acre (Poe, 1999).

4. More precisely, if marginal utilities and marginal products become infinite as their respective arguments approach zero, then there must be a positive allocation of both factors to both industries.

5. Because amenities are proportional to $L_x$, the subsidy on agricultural land is equivalent to a direct subsidy on amenities. All these policies that operate on prices are meant to represent a broader class of policy tools. Because there is an equivalent restriction on factor quantities for every tax, the input tax can also represent regulations that limit input use. Similarly, when land is initially taxed (as it is in most countries), the land subsidy is equivalent to policies that reduce property tax burdens or place controls on land use conversion.

6. In principle, pollution could be inferred from observations on inputs if the pollution function is known or estimable. In this case, farmers would be charged from predicted levels of pollution based on their input use. Administratively, such a scheme would be inferior to one with an equivalent outcome that acts on inputs directly.

7. To see this, suppose there were a third factor, $W$, that is neither taxed nor subsidized and does not influence $a$ or $e$. The socially optimal allocation of $W$ must satisfy $(u_x/u_y)(\partial F_x/\partial W) - \partial F_y/\partial W = 0$, while the free-market allocation can be described by $(p + s_x)(\partial F_x/\partial W) - \partial F_y/\partial W = 0$. Because $p = u_x/u_y$, social optimality requires that $s_x = 0$.

8. In particular, the aggregate factor index functions are:

$$L_x(l, K, N) = \min\{l, K/b_K, N/b_N\} \quad \text{and}$$
$$Z_x(C, E, M) = \min\{C, E/b_E, M/b_M\}$$

where $l$ represents land, $K$ is capital, $N$ is labor, $C$ is chemicals, $E$ is fuel and electricity, and $M$ is purchased materials. The coefficients $b_K$ and $b_N$ are the quantities of capital and labor that must be combined with each acre of land, respectively, and $b_E$ and $b_M$ are the amounts of energy and materials used with each unit of chemicals. The implicit price of the land aggregate is the cost function of $L_x$, or: $p_L = \{\min \ p_l l + p_K K + p_N N : L_x(l, K, N) = 1\} = p_l + b_K p_K + b_N p_N$. By a parallel argument, the price of the non-land aggregate is: $p_Z = p_C + b_E p_E = b_M p_M$. Thus, an addition or subtraction to $p_l$ or $p_C$ implies the same change in $p_L$ and $p_Z$. If there are substitution possibilities within the aggregate factors, the linear price relation is a first-order approximation to a concave function. Since this concave function rises more slowly for price increases and falls more quickly for price decreases, the linear approximation will estimate a lower bound on the subsidy and an upper bound on the tax.

9. Note that chemicals include all nutrients and the active ingredients of pesticides.

## References

Ahearn, M., J. Yee, V. E. Ball, R. Nehring, A. Somwaru, and R. Evans, 1998. "Agricultural Productivity in the United States," Bulletin 740, Economic Research Service, US Department of Agriculture, Washington, DC

Anderson, K., 1992a. "Agricultural Trade Liberalization and the Environment: A Global Perspective," *The World Economy*, 15, 153–72

  1992b. "The Standard Welfare Economics of Policies Affecting Trade and the Environment," in K. Anderson and R. Black (eds.), *The Greening of World Trade Issues*, Ann Arbor: University of Michigan Press

Anderson, K. and B. Hoekman, 1999. "Agriculture and the New Trade Agenda," paper presented at the American Economic Association Annual Meeting, January 3–5, New York

Australian Bureau of Agricultural and Resource Economics (ABARE), 1999. "'Multifunctionality': A Pretext for Protection?," ABARE Current Issues, 99.3, Canberra

Ball, V. E., J. Bureau, R. Nehring, and A. Somwaru, 1997. "Agricultural Productivity Revisited," *American Journal of Agricultural Economics*, 79, 1045–63

Beasley, S. D., W. C. Workman, and N. A. Williams, 1986. "Estimating Amenity Values on Urban Fringe Farmland: A Contingent Valuation Approach," *Growth and Change*, 17, 70–8

Beghin, J., S. Dessus, D. Roland-Holst, and D. van der Mensbrugghe, 1994. "The Trade and Environment Nexus in Mexican Agriculture. A General Equilibrium Analysis," *Agricultural Economics*, 17(2–3), 115–32

Bergstrom, J. C., B. L. Dillman, and J. R. Stoll, 1985. "Public Environmental Amenity Benefits of Private Land: The Case of Prime Agricultural Land," *Southern Journal of Agricultural Economics*, 17, 139–49

Blandford, D. and L. Fulponi, 1999. "Emerging Public Concerns in Agriculture: Domestic Policies and International Trade Commitments," *European Review of Agricultural Economics*, 26, 409–24

Bohman, M., J. Cooper, D. Mullarkey, M. A. Normile, D. Skully, S. Vogel, and E. Young, 1999. "The Use and Abuse of Multifunctionality," Economic Research Service, US Department of Agriculture, Washington, DC, November, econ.ag.gov/briefing/wto

Chambers, R. G., 1988. *Applied Production Analysis: A Dual Approach*, Cambridge and New York: Cambridge University Press

Copeland, B. R., 1994. "International Trade and the Environment: Policy Reform in a Polluted Small Open Economy," *Journal of Environmental Economics and Management*, 26, 44–65

Dixit, A. and V. Norman, 1980. *Theory of International Trade: A Dual, General Equilibrium Approach*, London: Cambridge University Press

Floyd, J. E., 1965. "The Effects of Farm Price Supports on the Return to Land and Labor in Agriculture," *Journal of Political Economy*, 73, 148–58

Gardner, B. L., 1987. *The Economics of Agricultural Policies*, New York: Macmillan

Hackl, F. and G. J. Pruckner, 1997. "Towards More Efficient Compensation Programmes for Tourists' Benefits from Agriculture in Europe," *Environmental and Resource Economics*, 10, 189–205

Halstead, J. M., 1984. "Measuring the Nonmarket Value of Massachusetts Agricultural Land: A Case Study," *Journal of the Northeastern Agricultural Economics Council*, 13, 12–19

Holtermann, S., 1976. "Alternative Tax Systems to Correct for Externalities and the Efficiency of Paying Compensation," *Economica*, 43, 1–16

Krieger, D. J., 1999. "Saving Open Spaces: Public Support for Farmland Protection," American Farmland Trust Center for Agriculture in the Environment Working Paper, CAE/WP99–1

Krutilla, K., 1991. "Environmental Regulation in an Open Economy," *Journal of Environmental Economics and Management*, 20, 127–42

Lindland, J., 1998. "Non-Trade Concerns in a Multifunctional Agriculture," paper presented to OECD Workshop on Emerging Trade Issues in Agriculture, October 26–27, oecd.org/agr/trade/Paris

López, R. A., F. A. Shah, and M. A. Altobello, 1994. "Amenity Benefits and the Optimal Allocation of Land," *Land Economics*, 70, 53–62

Mas-Collel, A., M. D. Whinston, and J. R. Green, 1995. *Microeconomic Theory*. New York: Oxford University Press

Nersten, N. K. and S. S. Prestegard, 1998. "Non-Trade Concerns in the WTO Negotiations," paper presented at the International Agricultural Trade Research Consortium Annual Meeting, Florida

Norwegian Royal Ministry of Agriculture, 1998. "Non-Trade Concerns in a Multifunctional Agriculture: Implications for Agricultural Policy and the Multilateral Trading System," June

Office of Management and Budget, Executive Office of the President of the United States, 1999. Budget of the United States Government, Fiscal Year 2000, Washington, DC

Ollikainen, M., 1999. "On Optimal Agri-Environmental Policy: A Public Finance View," paper presented at the IXth European Association of Agricultural Economists Congress, Warsaw

Organization for Economic Co-operation and Development (OECD), 1997a. "Environmental Benefits from Agriculture: Issues and Policies," The Helsinki Seminar, Paris

  1997b. Helsinki Seminar on Environmental Benefits from Agriculture: Country Case Studies, GD(97)110, Paris

Pimentel, D., H. Acquay, M. Biltonen, P. Rice, M. Silva, J. Nelson, J. Lipner, S. Giordano, A. Horowitz, and M. D'Amore, 1992. "Environmental and Economic Costs of Pesticide Use," *BioScience*, 42, 750–60

Poe, G. L., 1997. "Extra-Market Values and Conflicting Agricultural Environmental Policies," *Choices*, 3, 4–8

1998. "Valuation of Groundwater Quality Using a Contingent Valuation Damage Function Approach," *Water Resources Research*, 34, 3627–33

1999. "'Maximizing the Environmental Benefits Per Dollar Expended': An Economic Interpretation and Review of Agricultural Environmental Benefits and Costs," *Society & Natural Resources*, 12, 571–98

Powell, J. R., 1990. "The Value of Groundwater Protection: Measurement of Willingness-to-Pay Information and its Utilization by Local Government Decision-Makers," Dissertation, Department of Agricultural Economics, Cornell University

Runge, C. F., 1998. "Emerging Issues in Agricultural Trade and the Environment," OECD Workshop on Emerging Trade Issues in Agriculture, October 26–27, Paris, oecd.org/agr/trade/

Schamel, G. and H. de Gorter, 1997. "Trade and the Environment: Domestic versus Global Perspectives," Humboldt-Universität zu Berlin, Wirtschafts- und Sozialwissenschaften an der Landwirtschaftlich-Gärtnerischen Fakultät, Working Paper, 34/97

Schultz, S. D. and B. E. Lindsay, 1990. "The Willingness to Pay for Groundwater Protection," *Water Resources Research*, 26, 1869–75

Siebert, H., J. Eichberger, R. Gronych, and R. Pethig, 1980. *Trade and Environment: A Theoretical Enquiry*, Amsterdam: Elsevier

Whalley, J., 1999. "Environmental Considerations in a New Multilateral Agricultural Negotiations, and Associated Developing Country Concerns," paper presented at the Conference on Agriculture and the New Trade Agenda in the WTO 2000 Negotiations, 1– 2 October, Geneva

World Trade Organization (WTO), 1998. "Non Trade Concerns in the Next Agricultural Negotiations," submission by Argentina to the Committee on Trade and Environment, WT/CTE/W/97, Geneva, August, wto.org/wto/ddf/ep/public.html

1999a. "Environmental Effects of Trade Liberalization in the Agricultural Sector," submission by Norway to the Committee on Trade and the Environment, WT/CTE/W/100, Geneva, January, wto.org/wto/ddf/ep/public.html

1999b. "Preparations for the 1999 Ministerial Conference: Negotiations on Agriculture," Communication from Japan to the General Council, WT/GC/W/220, Geneva, June, wto.org/wto/ddf/ep/public.html

1999c. "Preparations for the 1999 Ministerial Conference: Negotiations on Agriculture," Communication from Switzerland to the General Council, WT/GC/W/261, Geneva, July, wto.org/wto/ddf/ep/public.html

# Author index

# Subject index